Preface

This book began as a series of class notes and PowerPoints during my tenure at Silicon Valley College. The material was expanded and grew for my classes at DeAnza Community College. When Schroff Development Corporation approached me to write this textbook, I was initially reluctant. After all, there are a plethora of textbooks on the market for AutoCAD and I didn't feel that I had anything additional I could add.

I was convinced to go forward with this text because the class notes I prepared for my classes would often go through double and even triple printings at the DeAnza College Bookstore. This meant that people who were not even enrolled in my class were coming into the bookstore to purchase my notes. Obviously, my material was filling in gaps.

The major gap was applying the knowledge of AutoCAD to mechanical drafting. Knowing how to draw a line in AutoCAD is not the same as understanding which line type is required when creating technical drawings. This text provides the necessary information on how to use AutoCAD as a tool to work as a mechanical drafter or designer.

This text should be used in combination with a basic AutoCAD reference manual or with an instructor who can provide guidance on basic AutoCAD.

Files used in this text can be downloaded from
www.SDCpublications.com/downloads/978-1-63057-017-0

Acknowledgements

Feel free to email me if you have any questions, comments, or problems with any of the exercises in this text. I get email from all over the world and usually respond within twenty-four hours. My email address is elise_moss@mossdesigns.com.

I have been teaching for more than a decade. I started using AutoCAD in 1982 while I was still attending college. Even then, there was no doubt in my mind that Computer Aided Drafting, as it was called then, was the future of design. AutoCAD continues to evolve and it remains one of the most popular drafting software products in the world. My students amaze and inspire me every day. When I write my textbooks, I imagine one of my students sitting in front of me struggling, trying to figure out how to use a mouse, how to locate the right icon, and feeling frustrated with the effort, but not giving up. This text is intended for classroom use and for beginner learners.

Infinite thanks to Ari for his encouragement and his faith.

Elise Moss
Los Gatos, CA

Autodesk AutoCAD 2017: Fundamentals

Elise Moss

SDC Publications

SDC Publications
P.O. Box 1334
Mission, KS 66222
913-262-2664
www.SDCpublications.com
Publisher: Stephen Schroff

ISBN-13: 978-1-63057-017-0
ISBN-10: 1-63057-017-6

Printed and bound in the United States of America.

Classroom Setup

Each student should be equipped with an AutoCAD workstation using either Windows 10. Windows XP is no longer supported by Autodesk or Microsoft. AutoCAD 2017 is certified by Autodesk to work in Windows 10. AutoCAD 2017 is the first release operating under the new licensing model. This means users can pay for a monthly or annual subscription to use the software.

The student exercises should be copied to each student workstation in a directory called c:\class. A backup of each exercise should be kept in a safe place either on each computer or on a network server to refresh the drawing files after each class. Auto Tracking should be turned off before the class starts and not turned on until it is covered in class.

In order to demonstrate commands and exercise solutions, the instructor workstation should be equipped with an overhead projector, large screen television/monitor or a VGA splitter that feeds multiple VGA monitors on each student desk.

If students are working off a network and are not assigned a specific workstation, they should be aware that any modifications they make to their toolbars or display will change when they move to a different workstation. For this reason, the use of profiles and workspaces is covered early in the text. I recommend to my students to use a flash or "jump" drive to save their work. This protects them from other students messing with their work, either on purpose or by accident, as well as any hardware or server failures. The exercises demonstrate how to plot to dwf files because each classroom may have a different printer type available and there is no way to cover all the different printer type setups. However, students can certainly submit any assignment to the instructor using dwf files, thus cutting down on paper and toner usage. 2017 includes a PDF driver so students can also print to PDF if they desire. The 2017 release includes some additional PDF capabilities. Autodesk has eliminated the STUDENT VERSION watermark from student software starting in the 2015 release. If you have an earlier version and your students want to avoid the STUDENT VERSION watermark when they plot as they want to use their classwork to show a prospective employer, I recommend a screen capture software, such as Snipping Tool (which is included with Windows), Greenshot (which is free), SnagIt or HyperSnap. Simply do a Plot Preview and then screen capture the previewed plot minus the water mark and print that. You can also use the free snapshot tool that comes with Windows called Snipping Tool.

Autodesk offers free software to all students in an accredited course. I urge students to take advantage of this opportunity. For more information, visit http://students.autodesk.com/ or ask your instructor.

Autodesk provides a Cloud interface where users can save their files as well as their desktop settings to an Autodesk server. If your classroom has internet access, students can create Cloud accounts and use them to store their work. An exercise on how to create a Cloud account is included in the first chapter of this text. I also suggest to students to use Dropbox, GrabCAD's Workbench, Chapoo, or some other free cloud-based site as resources where they can store their files. If you save your files to one of these websites, then you can access your work from any computer with an internet connection.

Table of Contents

Lesson 3.0 – Drawing Lines

Lesson 4.0 – Draw Commands

Lesson 5.0 – Modify Commands

Lesson 9.0 – Dimensions

Lesson 10.0 – Text Tools

Lesson 11.0 – Blocks and Templates

Lesson 12.0 – Viewports and Layouts

About the Author

Lesson 1.0 – The AutoCAD Environment

Estimated Class Time: 1.5 Hours

Objectives

This section introduces the interface available within AutoCAD starting with the Pointing Device. The AutoCAD window includes the Pull-Down (POP) menus, Toolbars, the Drawing Window, Command Prompt, Work Spaces, Ribbon, and Status Bar. In addition, you will learn special Keyboard options and Shortcut (Cursor) menus, how to use the Dialog Boxes, and how to access AutoCAD's on-line Help.

- **Work Space**
  Customize which menus and toolbars are available; modify the appearance of the work environment.
- **Pointing Device**
  Use the mouse for selecting options in the AutoCAD window.
- **Shortcut Menus**
  Right-click your pointing device to display context sensitive Shortcut (Cursor) menus.
- **AutoCAD Window**
  The AutoCAD window consists of the following areas:
- **Title Bar**
  Minimize and maximize the AutoCAD window from the title bar.
- **Pull-Down Menu**
  Select commands from the Pull-Down (POP) menu headings.
- **Toolbars**
  Use AutoCAD toolbars as another method for selecting commands.
- **Drawing Window**
  Create your drawing and drawing layouts in this area.
- **Command Prompt**
  The Command Prompt will prompt you for the next step.
- **Status Bar**
  This area contains handy toggle switches and displays the x,y,z coordinates.
- **Dialog Boxes**
  Create your drawing and drawing layouts in this area.
- **Keyboard Options**
  Use the keyboard to type command options, text, or press Escape to cancel commands.
- **Help Menu**
  Use the AutoCAD Help menu to learn more about the program.

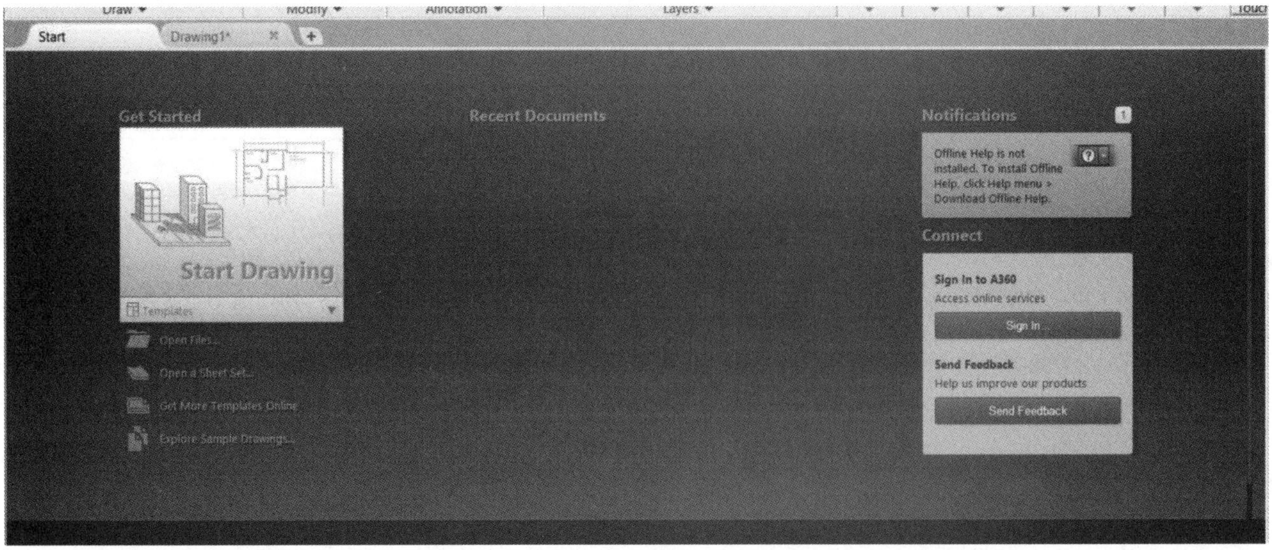

The Start tab acts as a launch pad for users. You can see a list of Recent Documents, open files, get on-line templates, get Help, and see Tool tips.

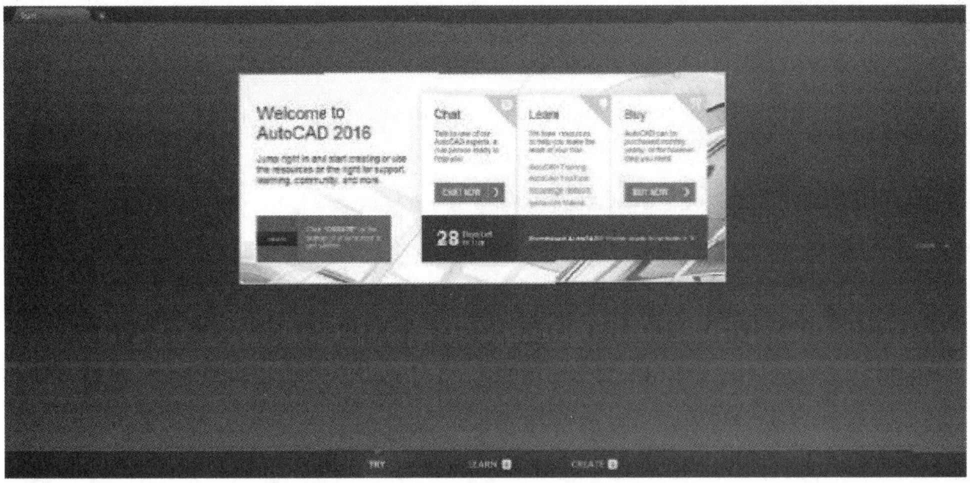

If you are using a 30 day trial version of AutoCAD, the Start tab includes a TRY page. From the Try page, you can access a live chat with an AutoCAD expert. The expert can answer your questions and help you get started with using AutoCAD. You can also go directly to the Autodesk store from the Try page to purchase a software license and look at pricing options. Starting in 2017, users will no longer be able to purchase perpetual licenses. Instead, you will have to pay a monthly or annual subscription to use the software.

Work Space

Command Overview

The Workspace tool allows you to customize the appearance of your work environment.
By default, AutoCAD comes with three defined workspaces:
3D Modeling, Drafting & Annotation, and 3D Basics.

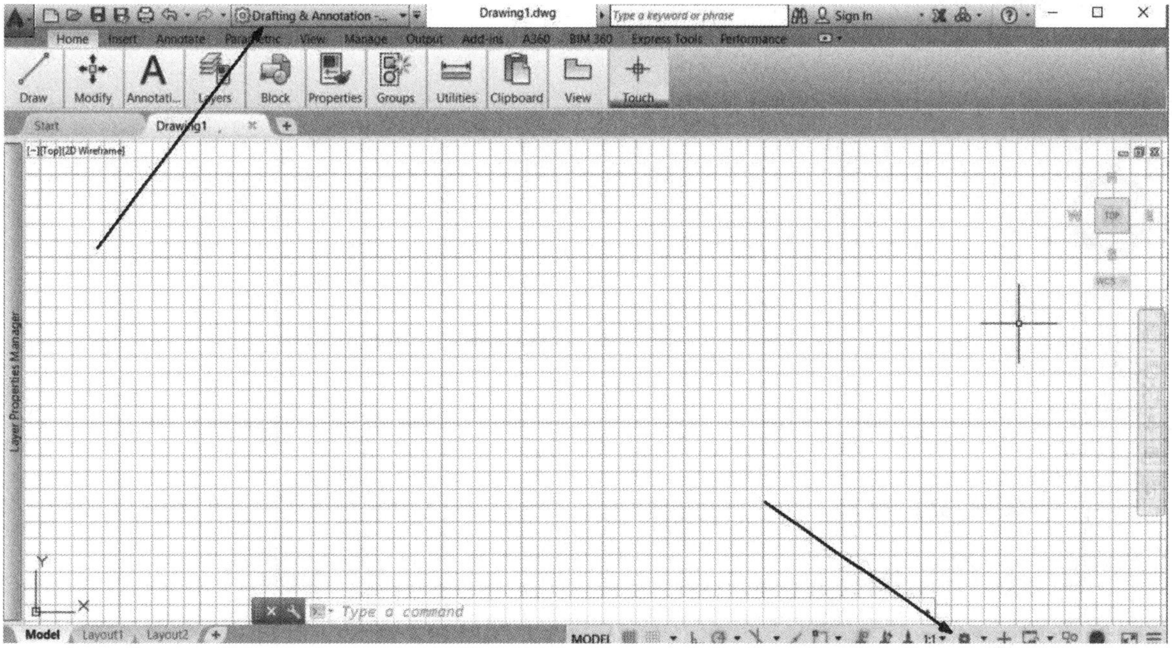

Workspaces can be accessed in different locations on your screen: the Quick Access Toolbar and in the Status Bar.

If you want to save your current work environment (system settings, active toolbars, and menus) simply select 'Save Current As' to apply the active settings to a new or existing workspace.

Tips & Tricks

Select the down arrow on the Quick Access Toolbar to add or remove tools from the toolbar.

Place a check by left clicking on the item to add it to the toolbar.

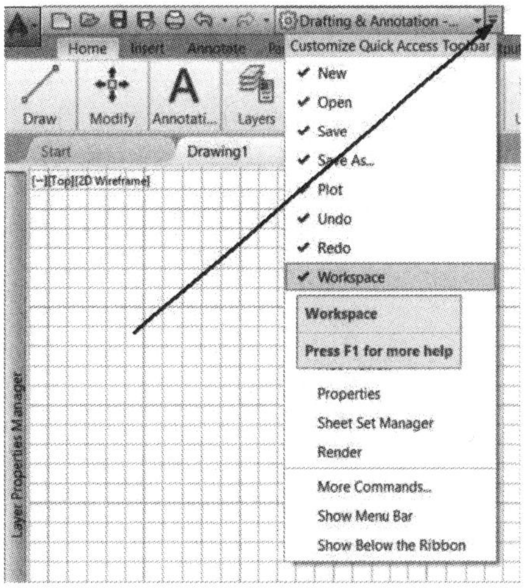

Command Exercise

Exercise 1-1 – Workspace

Drawing Name: **(none, start from scratch)**
Estimated Time to Completion: 5 Minutes

Scope

1. *Create a workspace called AutoCAD Classic.*
2. *Close the Tool Palettes.*
3. *Locate the AutoCAD Classic workspace on the toolbar.*
4. *Set the AutoCAD Classic workspace as Current.*

Solution

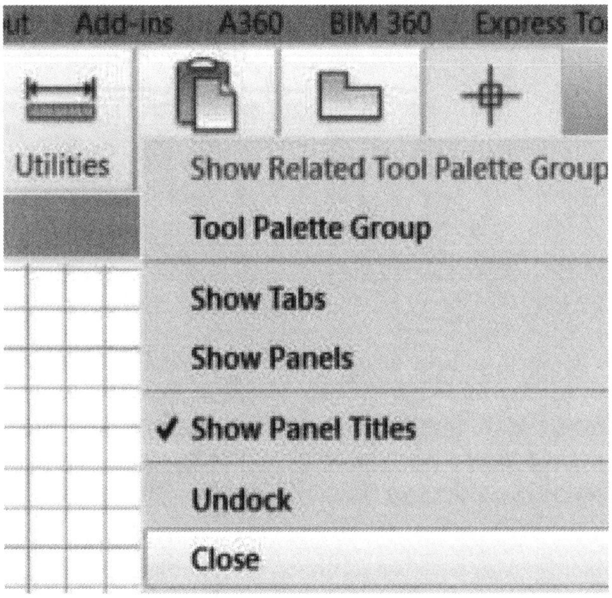

1. Right click on the ribbon and select **Close** from the drop-down menu.
2. Type **CUI** on the command line.

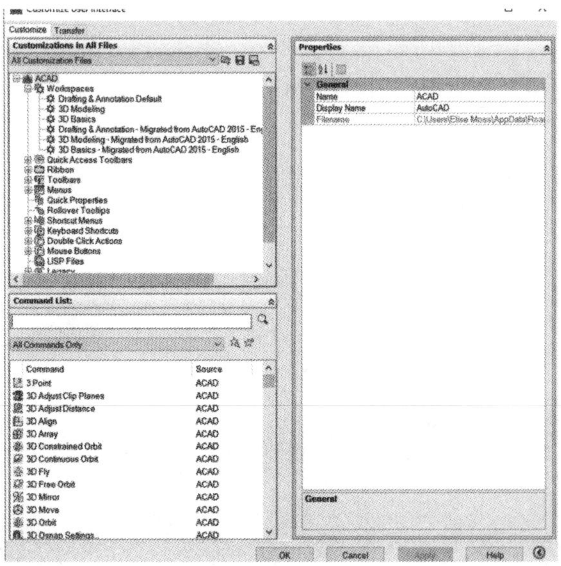

The Customize User Interface dialog appears.

This dialog allows you to customize your work environment.

For users who are most comfortable with the "classic" toolbar interface, we will create a workspace similar to AutoCAD Release 14.

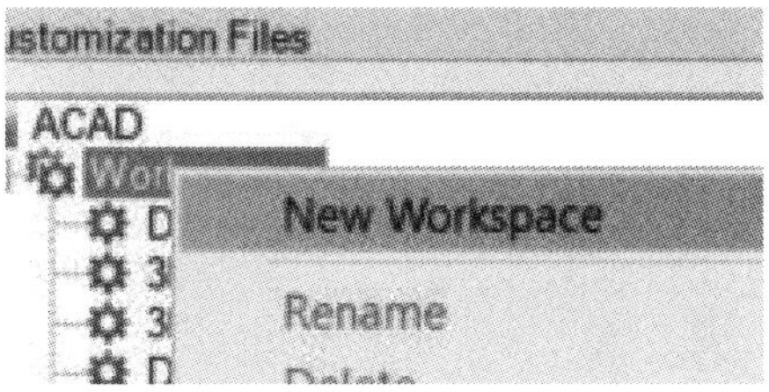

3. Highlight **Workspaces**. Right click and select **New Workspace.**

4. Rename the new workspace **AutoCAD Classic**.

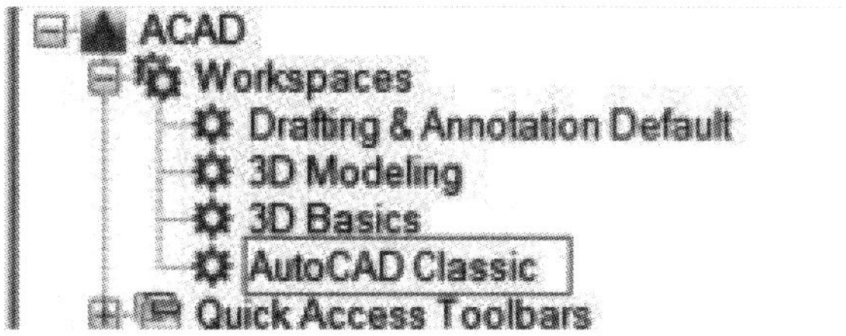

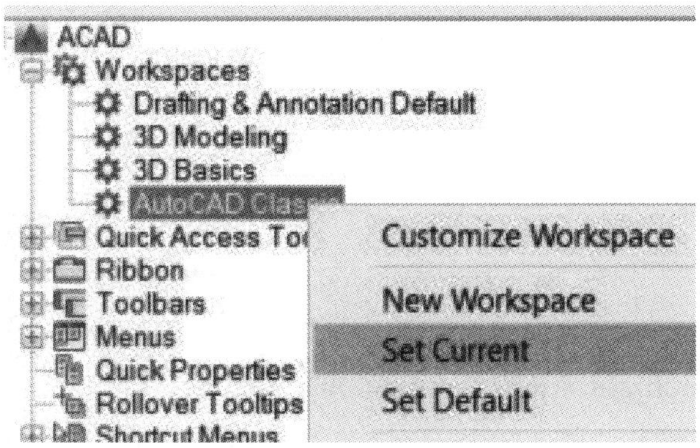

5. Right click on the new workspace and select **Set Current.**

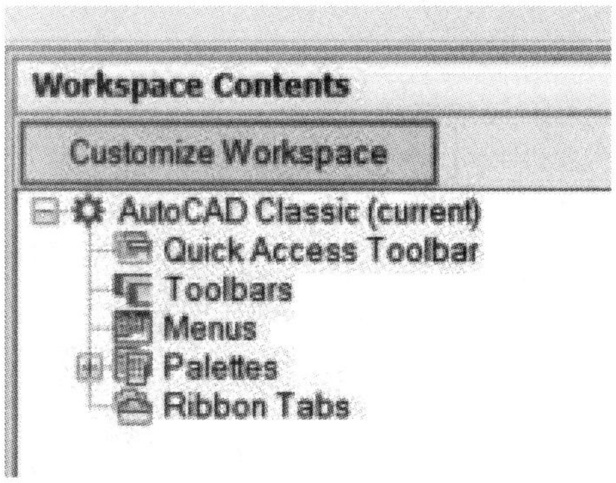

6. Click on the **Customize Workspace** button in the top right panel.

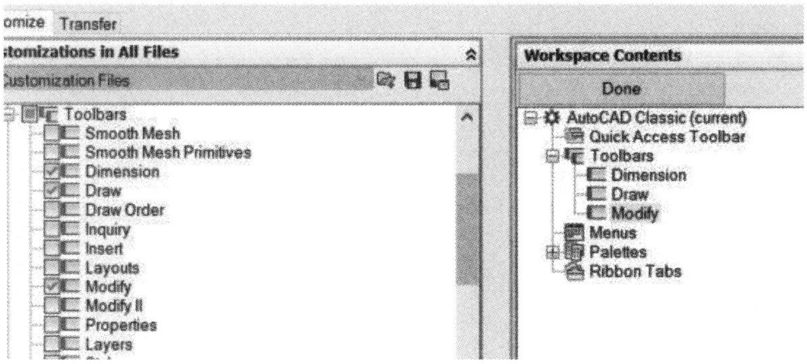

7. Place a check next to **Dimension**, **Draw** and **Modify** under Toolbars in the left panel.

Notice how the toolbars are added in the right panel as they are checked.

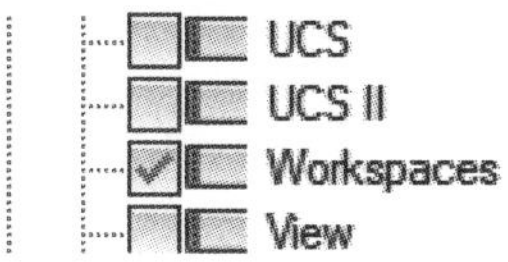

8. Place a check next to **Workspaces** under Toolbars.

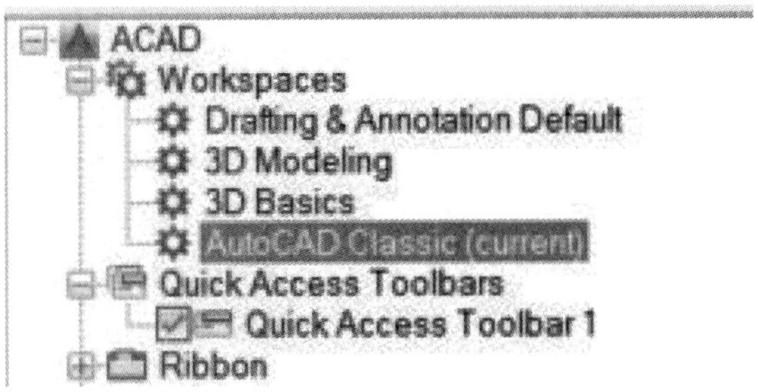

9. Enable Quick Access Toolbar 1 in the left panel.

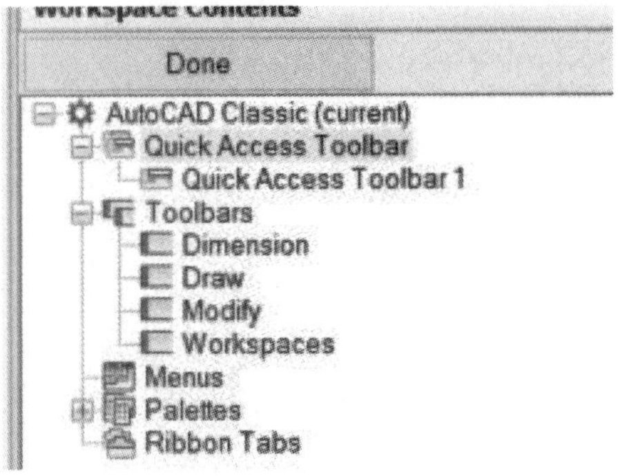

Note that the selected toolbars are now listed in the Workspace Contents.

10. Press **Done**.

11. Press **OK** to close the CUI dialog box.

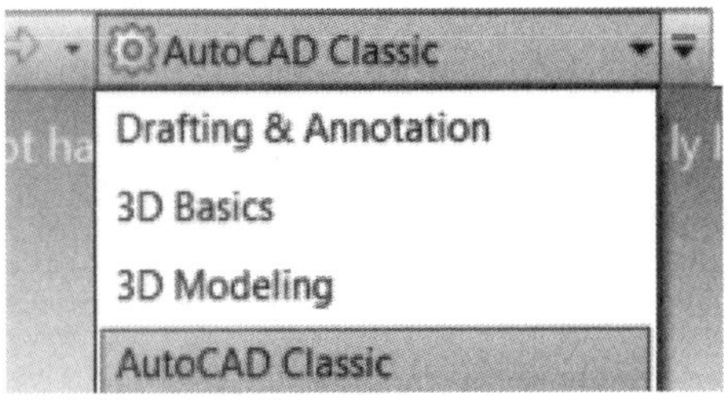

12. The workspace drop-down list now includes AutoCAD Classic.

Select the **AutoCAD Classic** workspace.

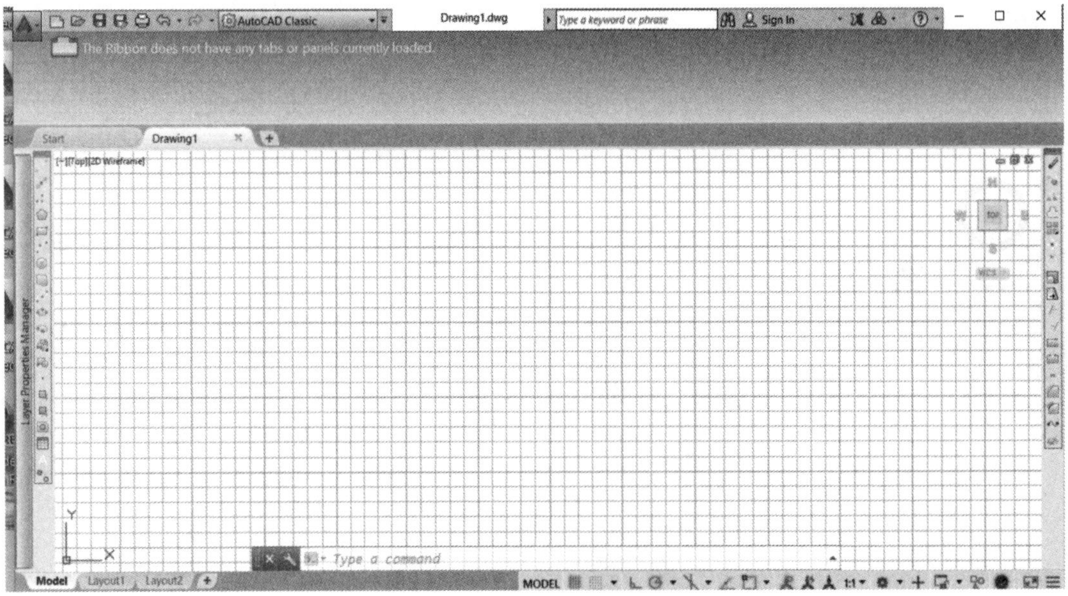

The workspace now just shows toolbars without the ribbon.

Pointing Device—Mouse

Command Overview

Use the pointing device to select objects and options. This tutorial reviews the functions of a two or three-button mouse, though there are other pointing devices available. The pointing device is configured in the *Systems Tab* in the *Options* dialog box. The default setting is automatically set to the "current system pointing" device; this will typically be a two button mouse, the three button mouse, or the Microsoft IntelliMouse®. The left button (LMB) is typically the Pick button and the right button (RMB) is the <ENTER> button. Pressing the <ENTER> button when the cursor is in the Drawing Window activates a Shortcut Menu with the option to repeat the last command. This feature can be disabled in the *User Preferences* Tab of the *Options* dialog box, by removing the checkmark from "Shortcut menus in drawing area." If this option is selected, pressing the right button on the mouse (RMB) will either execute a command, proceed with the command (by accepting the default option), or if the Command Prompt is blank, repeat the last command. Using shift + the <ENTER> button activates the Object Snap shortcut menu. These shortcut menus will be covered later in this Tutorial in the topics that follow.

Two Button Mouse:

Button	**Action**
Left (LMB)	Use to pick or select objects or options
Right (RMB)	Use to <ENTER> to complete the command, repeat the last command, or access a context sensitive cursor menu
Shift + Right (RMB)	Brings up the Object Snap cursor menu

Three Button Mouse:

Button	**Action**
Left (LMB)	Use to pick or select objects or options
Right (RMB)	Use to <ENTER> to complete the command, repeat the last command, or access a context sensitive cursor menu
Middle Button	Brings up the Object Snap cursor menu

Button	**Action**
Left (LMB)	Use to pick or select objects or options
Right (RMB)	Use to <ENTER> to complete the command, repeat the last command, or access a context sensitive cursor menu
Shift + Right (RMB)	Brings up the Object Snap cursor menu
Middle Button (press + drag)	Use to pan the drawing
Middle Button (roll)	Use to zoom the drawing

Microsoft IntelliMouse:

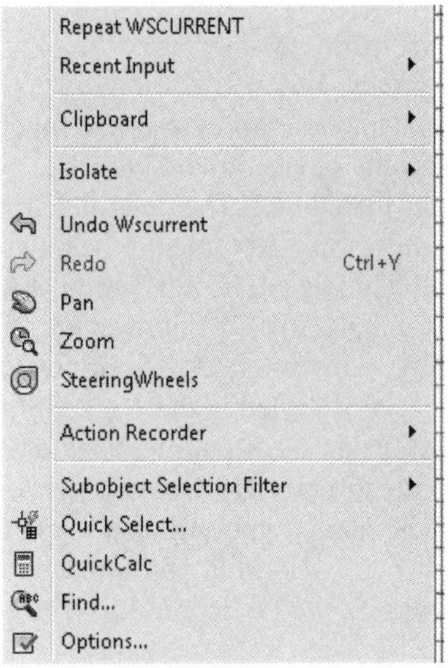

The RMB Shortcut Menu

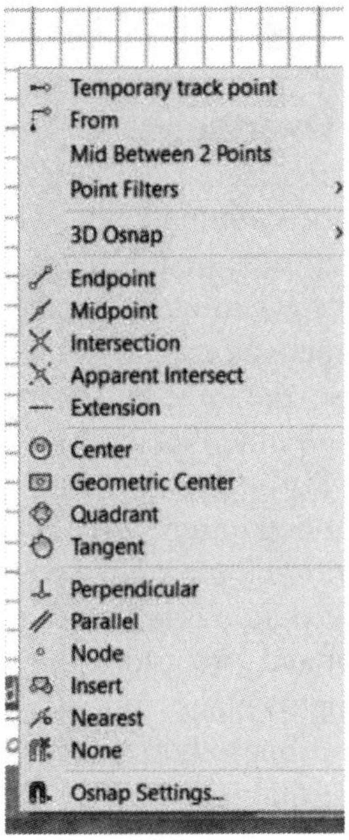

The Shift + RMB Shortcut Menu

General Procedures

1. Pick a command from the toolbar using the left button on the mouse.
2. Follow the Command Prompt prompts.
3. Press <ENTER> to complete the command or continue to the next step. Press <ENTER> again to repeat the command, or select a choice from the Shortcut menu.

Tips & Tricks

- Picking in a blank area of the drawing window will create a selection window. Press escape to cancel this selection window, or simply make the other corner.
- Making a selection window from right to left will select all objects the window crosses. Making a selection window from left to right will only select the objects completely within the selection window.
- Picking objects in the drawing window when the Command Prompt is blank will highlight the objects and display the *grips*. Press Escape (**Esc** on the keyboard) two times to cancel the grips and the selection.
- The left and right button functions can be reversed from the Windows Settings menu (from the Start bar). Select "Control Panel" then select "Mouse."

Command Exercise

Exercise 1-2 – Using the Mouse

Drawing Name: **(none, start from scratch)**
Estimated Time to Completion: 5 Minutes

Scope

Practice the Left and Right button mouse functions:

1. *Draw line segments.*
2. *Press the right button on the mouse to repeat the line command.*
3. *Practice selecting a single object.*
4. *Practice making a selection window.*
5. *Activate the object snap shortcut (cursor) menu.*
6. *Activate the toolbar shortcut menu.*
7. *Activate the Command Prompt short cut menu.*

Solution

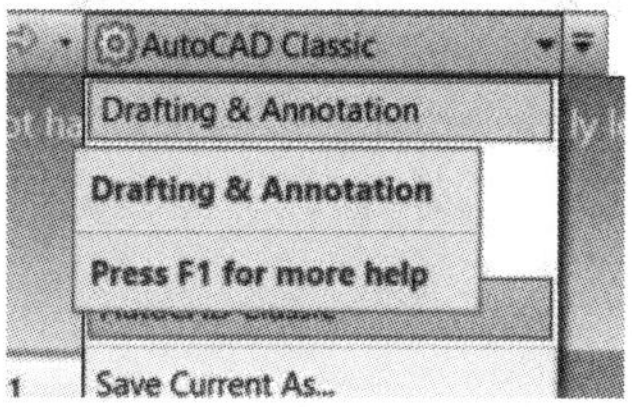

Set the Workspace to **Drafting & Annotation**.

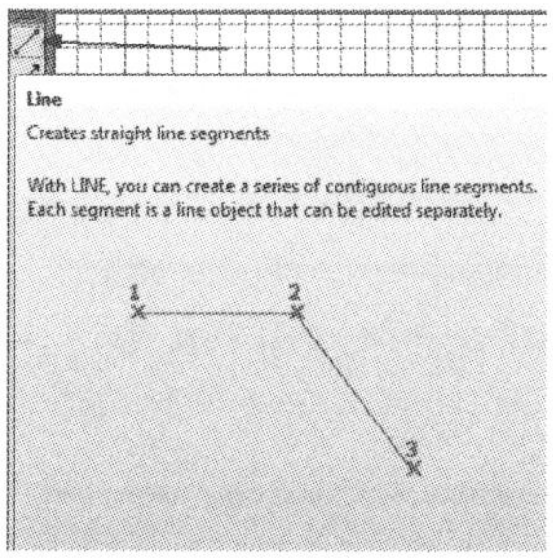

1. Locate the line command from the Draw Toolbar or the Home ribbon and draw some line segments. Press the right button on the mouse. This will bring up a context sensitive cursor menu. Select 'Enter' to complete the line command, so that the Command Prompt is blank.

➢*To turn off the rollover help tips, type ROLLOVERTIPS on the Command Prompt and enter 0.*

2. Press the right button on the mouse again. This will bring up a context sensitive cursor menu. Select 'Repeat Line' to repeat the line command. Complete the line command, so that the Command Prompt is blank.

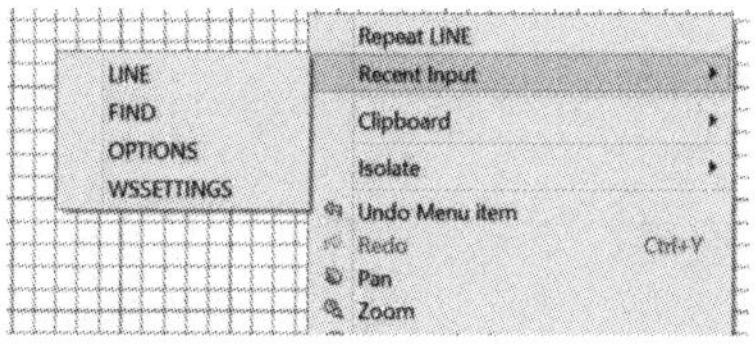

Note that if you expand Recent Input, you can select any of your most recent commands.

3. Pick one of the line segments. *Notice that it is highlighted and notice the grips (these are the blue boxes on the line).*
4. Press <ESC> once to cancel and clear the grips.

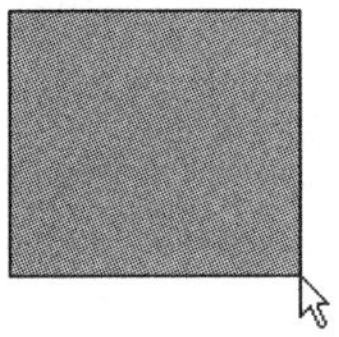

5. Pick in the blank area of the drawing. Notice this will create a rectangular selection window. You will be prompted to select the other corner. Make the selection window from Left to Right and notice that only the objects completely within the window will be selected. Press <ESC> to cancel the selection. Now make the window from right to left and notice that the lines that are crossed by the selection box are now highlighted. Press <ESC> again to exit.

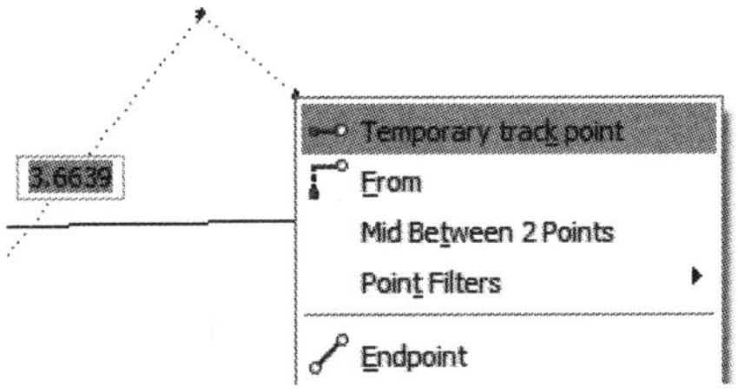

6. Activate the object snap shortcut (cursor) menu using the mouse button according to the pointing device you are using or by holding down the SHIFT button and right clicking the mouse.
7. Press <ESC> to cancel this menu.

8. Press the RMB in the Command Prompt area to view the menu shown. Press <ESC> to cancel.

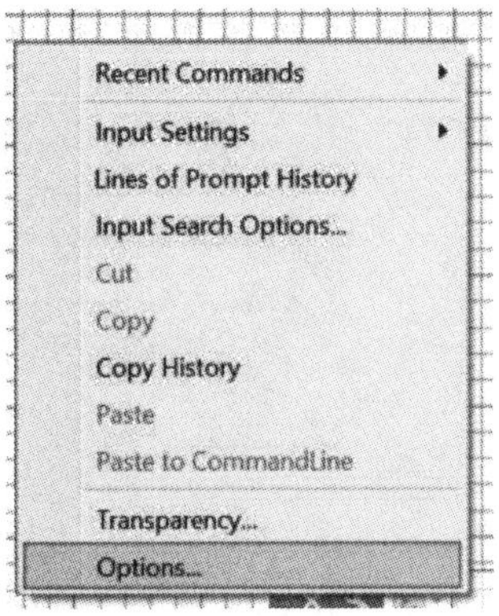

Extra: *If you have the Microsoft Intellimouse, roll the middle button to zoom the drawing in and out in the drawing. Press the middle button and drag to pan.*

Tips & Tricks

- *The shortcut menus are context sensitive and are determined by the location of the cursor when the right button on the mouse is selected.*
- *To turn on the old menus, type MENUBAR and then 1.*

AutoCAD Window

Overview

The AutoCAD window consists of a Title Bar, Pull-Down Menus, Toolbars, a Drawing Window, the Ribbon, the Command Prompt, and the Status Bar.

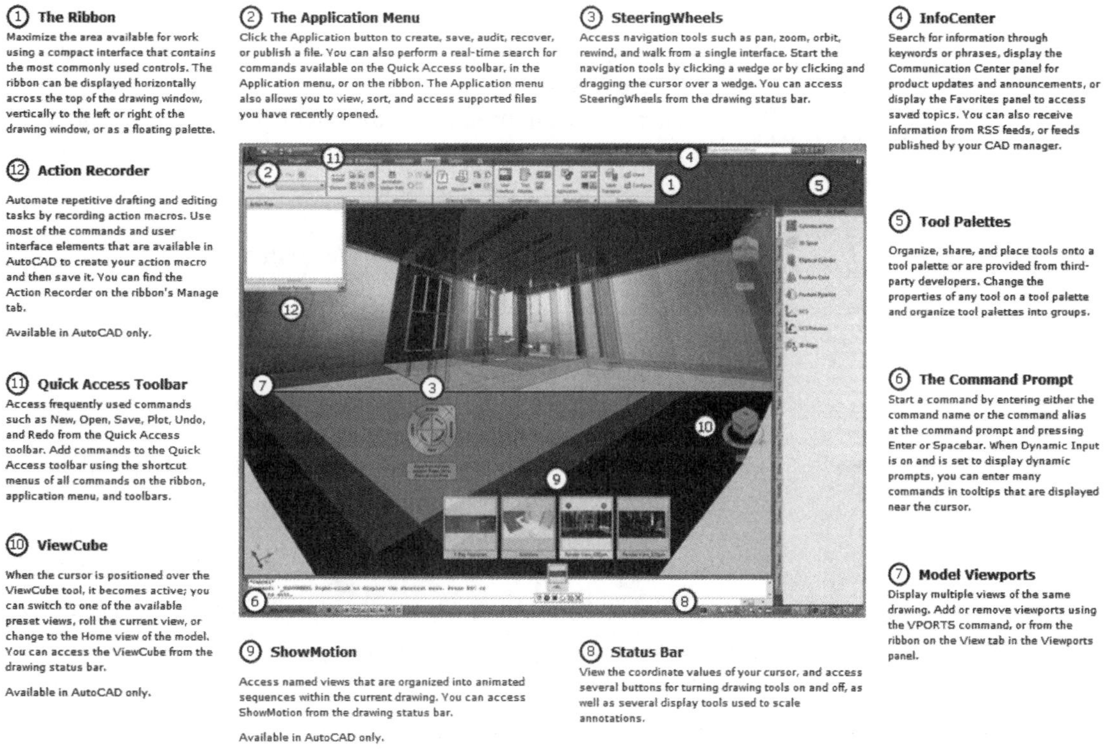
1 The Ribbon
Maximize the area available for work using a compact interface that contains the most commonly used controls. The ribbon can be displayed horizontally across the top of the drawing window, vertically to the left or right of the drawing window, or as a floating palette.
2 The Application Menu
Click the Application button to create, save, audit, recover, or publish a file. You can also perform a real-time search for commands available on the Quick Access toolbar, in the Application menu, or on the ribbon. The Application menu also allows you to view, sort, and access supported files you have recently opened.
3 SteeringWheels
Access navigation tools such as pan, zoom, orbit, rewind, and walk from a single interface. Start the navigation tools by clicking a wedge or by clicking and dragging the cursor over a wedge. You can access SteeringWheels from the drawing status bar.
4 InfoCenter
Search for information through keywords or phrases, display the Communication Center panel for product updates and announcements, or display the Favorites panel to access saved topics. You can also receive information from RSS feeds, or feeds published by your CAD manager.
12 Action Recorder
Automate repetitive drafting and editing tasks by recording action macros. Use most of the commands and user interface elements that are available in AutoCAD to create your action macro and then save it. You can find the Action Recorder on the ribbon's Manage tab.
Available in AutoCAD only.
5 Tool Palettes
Organize, share, and place tools onto a tool palette or are provided from third-party developers. Change the properties of any tool on a tool palette and organize tool palettes into groups.
11 Quick Access Toolbar
Access frequently used commands such as New, Open, Save, Plot, Undo, and Redo from the Quick Access toolbar. Add commands to the Quick Access toolbar using the shortcut menus of all commands on the ribbon, application menu, and toolbars.
6 The Command Prompt
Start a command by entering either the command name or the command alias at the command prompt and pressing Enter or Spacebar. When Dynamic Input is on and is set to display dynamic prompts, you can enter many commands in tooltips that are displayed near the cursor.
10 ViewCube
When the cursor is positioned over the ViewCube tool, it becomes active; you can switch to one of the available preset views, roll the current view, or change to the Home view of the model. You can access the ViewCube from the drawing status bar.
Available in AutoCAD only.
7 Model Viewports
Display multiple views of the same drawing. Add or remove viewports using the VPORTS command, or from the ribbon on the View tab in the Viewports panel.
9 ShowMotion
Access named views that are organized into animated sequences within the current drawing. You can access ShowMotion from the drawing status bar.
Available in AutoCAD only.
8 Status Bar
View the coordinate values of your cursor, and access several buttons for turning drawing tools on and off, as well as several display tools used to scale annotations.

The AutoCAD Window

AutoCAD Window Detail	Location	Function Overview
Title Bar	Top	•Lists the name of the current drawing. •Contains buttons to minimize, maximize or exit AutoCAD. •Contains buttons to minimize, maximize or close the current drawing.
Pull-Down Menu	Beneath the Title Bar	•Lists AutoCAD commands by category. •Also referred to as "POP." •Words followed by a black arrow will display an additional list of related options. •Words followed by an *ellipsis* (...) will open a *dialog box*.
Toolbars	Docked at sides or floating in the drawing window	•Displays commands as icons (buttons) in related toolbar categories. •The toolbar pictured in the top row is the *Standard Toolbar*. •The toolbar beneath it is the *Object Properties Toolbar*. •Accessing a command from a toolbar is usually a faster, more direct approach. •The toolbars contain most of the commands, but not all of them.
Tool Palettes	Floating or Docked	•Displays commands, blocks, or hatches as icons (buttons) in related categories. •The Tool Palette can be set to be transparent, so you can see drawing objects underneath. •You can set the properties of the tools on the Tool Palette. For example, you can set a line tool to always place on a specific layer and/or line type. •You can create a Tool Palette for all your blocks. •You can hide or display Tool Palettes easily.
Drawing Window	Middle area	•Area where the drawing is created. •The Model tab is for creating the drawing or 3-dimensional model. •The Layout tabs are for creating the finished layout for plotting or printing.
Command Prompt	Bottom	•Area where AutoCAD prompts the user for the next step. •The user must press <ENTER> after typing the Command or Command Prompt options. •The escape key (ESC) will cancel any command leaving the Command Prompt blank and ready for the next command. •Ctl+9 displays or hides the Command Prompt window.
Status Bar	Beneath the Command Prompt	•Displays the coordinates of the cursor location. •Displays the ON/OFF status of special toggle switches. •Single-click to toggle these options ON or OFF.
Dynamic Input	At the end of the cursor	•When DYN is enabled, you can close the Command Prompt window and enter prompts at a smaller window located at the end of the cursor.

Title Bar

Locator

Overview

The Title Bar will display the name of the drawing. Buttons are displayed in the upper right-hand corner to minimize, maximize, re-size, or close the AutoCAD window or an individual drawing file. Remember that when any program is minimized, it will remain listed in the Start Bar.

General Procedures

To maximize the AutoCAD Window, select the following icon:	
To maximize the Drawing Window, select the following icon:	
To minimize the AutoCAD or Drawing Windows, select the Minimize button.	
To bring the AutoCAD Window to the foreground, select AutoCAD from the Start bar.	
AutoCAD has tabs to allow for easy switching between drawing files.	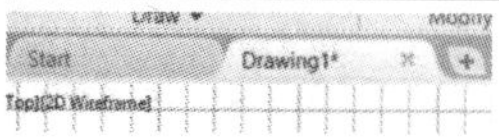

Tips & Tricks

- Keep the AutoCAD and Drawing windows maximized for optimum drawing space.
- Use the Alt+Tab keys to alternate between programs, or select the program from the Start bar.
- Practice Minimizing and Maximizing the AutoCAD and Drawing Windows.

Drawing Window

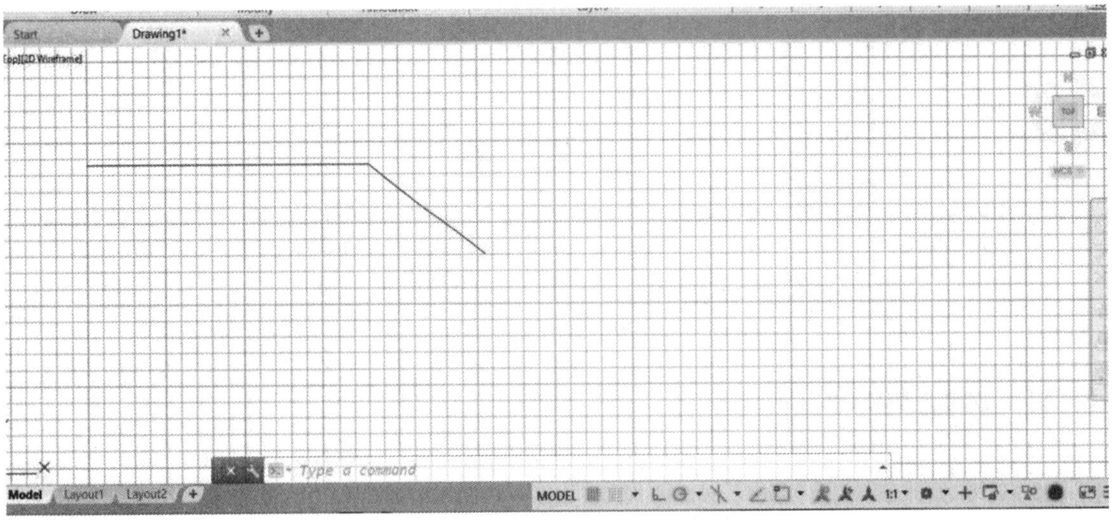

AutoCAD Drawing Window

Overview

When working in the Drawing Window, be sure that the Model Tab is selected. Later this text will cover how to create a drawing Layout. The cursor must be in the Drawing window in order to pick points for drawing objects, or select objects to modify. Right-click in the drawing window to execute a command, proceed with the next step of the command, or if the Command Prompt is blank, repeat the last command. Picking (LMB) in a blank area of the drawing window will initiate a selection window or box. You must pick the opposite corner whether you want to select an object or not, or press Escape to cancel the selection window. Multiple drawings may be opened in one AutoCAD session. Minimize a drawing window, or use the options from the **Window** Pull-Down menu to select the current drawing. Close the drawings that are not being used.

Tips & Tricks

- The Model Tab should be selected when creating a drawing.
- The cursor must be in the Drawing window in order to pick points for drawing objects, or select objects to modify.
- Right-click in the drawing window to execute a command, proceed with the next step of the command, or if the Command Prompt is blank, repeat the last command.
- Picking (LMB) in a blank area of the drawing window will initiate a selection window or box. You must pick the opposite corner whether you want to select an object or not, or press Escape to cancel the selection window.
- Close drawings that are not being used.

Command Prompt

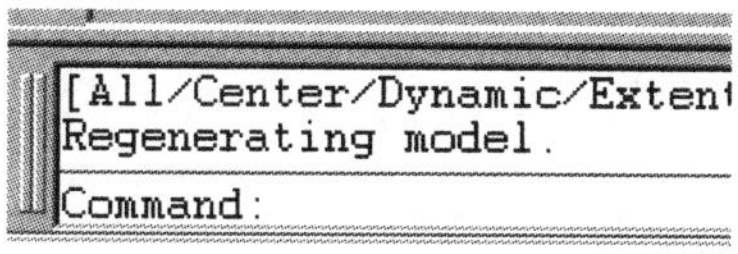
[All/Center/Dynamic/Exten
Regenerating model.
Command:

AutoCAD Command Prompt Window

Command Overview

The Command Prompt at the bottom of the AutoCAD window will prompt the user for the next step. It is important to read the Command Prompt. A blank Command Prompt means that AutoCAD is waiting for the user to begin a command. Remember to press <ENTER>, after typing a command, a command alias, a Command Prompt option, or after selecting objects. Generally it is best to view three lines of text at the Command Prompt. The scroll bar to the right of the Command Prompt window can be used to view previous Command Prompts. The **F2** function key will display the entire Text Window. The up and down arrows on the keyboard will carry the last option typed to the bottom Command Prompt. A Command Prompt option that is in parentheses or < > is known as the *default.* It is unnecessary to type the default option over again; simply press <ENTER> to accept the default. Pressing the <ENTER> button on the mouse (RMB) when the cursor is in the Command Prompt area will bring up a Shortcut Menu.

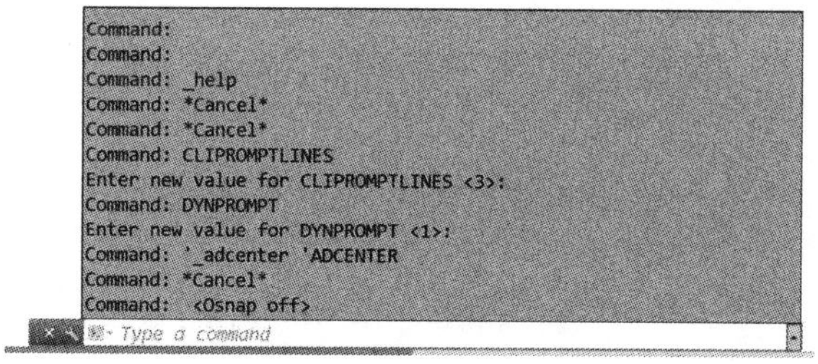
Command:
Command:
Command: _help
Command: *Cancel*
Command: *Cancel*
Command: CLIPROMPTLINES
Enter new value for CLIPROMPTLINES <3>:
Command: DYNPROMPT
Enter new value for DYNPROMPT <1>:
Command: '_adcenter 'ADCENTER
Command: *Cancel*
Command: <Osnap off>
Type a command

AutoCAD Text Window

The F2 function key will open the AutoCAD Text Window, which will display all previous Command Prompts. These lines can be viewed and copied, but they cannot be changed. Left click in the drawing window to close the AutoCAD Text Window.

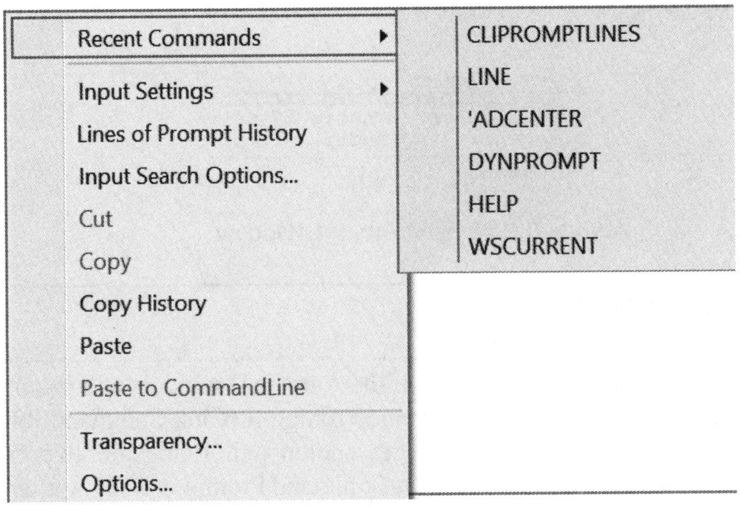

Command Prompt Shortcut Menu

Right-click (RMB) in the Command Prompt area to bring up the Command Prompt shortcut menu. This can be used to copy highlighted text, or access the Options dialog box.

Command Prompt	**Overview**
Recent Commands	Lists recently used commands.
Input Settings 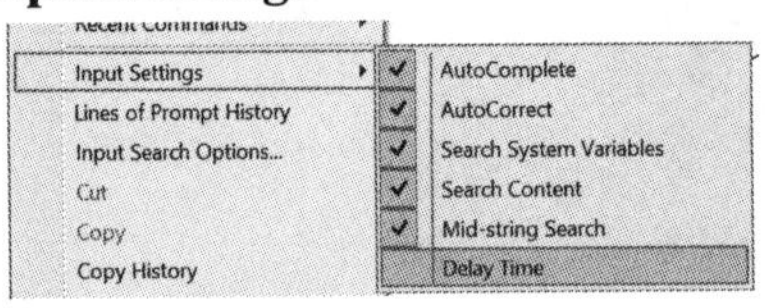	User can set how the command prompt responds to typed entries.
Lines of Prompt History	Sets the number of lines displayed in the command window.
Input Search Options	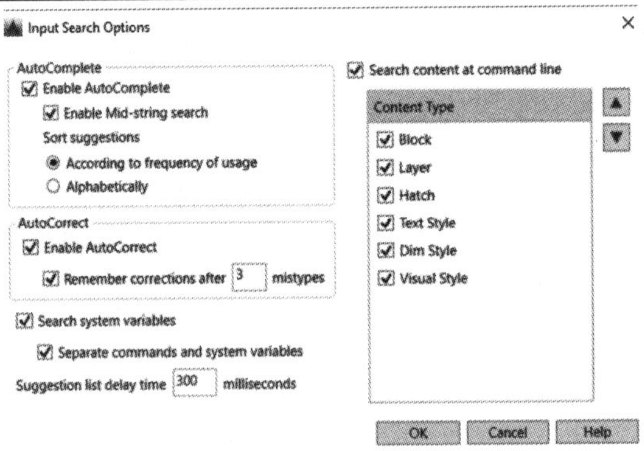
Cut	Cut selected text to the clipboard.
Copy	Copies highlighted words from the text window to a clipboard.
Copy History	Copies everything from the text window to the Clipboard.
Paste	Pastes copied text to the Command Prompt.
Paste to CmdLine	Pastes highlighted words from the text window to the Command Prompt.
Transparency...	Sets the transparency of the command window.
Options...	Opens the Options dialog box to set user preferences.

General Procedures

How to follow the Command Prompt prompts:

1. Type the command, the command alias or the Command Prompt option and Press <ENTER>.
2. Follow the Command Prompt prompts:
   - When prompted to select objects, pick the objects then press <ENTER> to continue.
   - When presented with Command Prompt options, type the capitalized letter of the option and press <ENTER> to continue.
   - When presented with a default choice in parentheses or < > press <ENTER> to accept the default, or type the preferred option and press <ENTER>.

Tips & Tricks

- It is important to remember to read the Command Prompt, as this is your line of communication with AutoCAD.
- Use the keyboard <ENTER> button or the right button (RMB) on the mouse.
- When using the RMB, be sure that the cursor is in the drawing window.
- To disable the command options cursor menu, select Options, the User Preferences tab, "Right Click Customization" and "Repeat Last Command." Apply & Close.

Status Bar

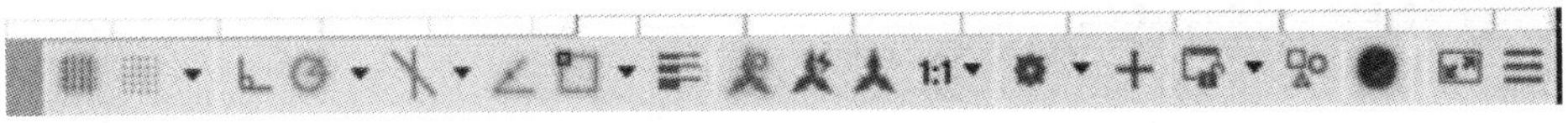

Status Bar

Overview

The Application Status Bar is at the bottom of the AutoCAD window. Select (LMB) the buttons to turn the options ON or OFF, or use the corresponding function keys. Right-click (RMB) to access the Settings dialog box for the corresponding Status Bar options or other options that apply. The Status Bar shown has all options enabled. You can elect to turn off/disable options you don't use.

Status Bar Option	Overview	Function Key
COORDINATES	Displays the Cartesian coordinate for the cursor.	**CTL+I**
MODEL SPACE	Displays the active space—whether you are in model or layout mode.	
GRID	This switch turns the Grid ON and OFF. The Grid is a visual tool, and does not restrict cursor selection. Grid spacing may or may not be equal to the Snap spacing. However, if the Grid spacing is set to 0, it will be equal to the Snap spacing.	**F7**
SNAP MODE	Snap ON will restrict the cursor to select points at designated X and Y increments. Snap spacing may or may not be equal to the Grid spacing. However, if the Grid spacing is set to 0, it will be equal to the Snap spacing.	**F9**
INFER CONSTRAINTS	Adds sketch constraints as you draw. For example, when you draw a horizontal line, a horizontal constraint will be added.	
DYNAMIC INPUT	Displays prompts in a tooltip near the cursor as you move through different commands	
ORTHO MODE	Use Ortho (for orthogonal) ON when dragging the mouse to: Draw straight lines Move, Copy, or Mirror objects along a linear plane Rotate objects in 90-degree increments. ORTHO is either ON or OFF and does not have a Settings option.	**F8**
POLAR TRACKING	Turns Polar Snap ON/OFF. When Polar Snap is ON, the angular direction and the distance from the last point selected will be tracked and displayed according to the Polar Tracking settings.	**F10**
ISOMETRIC DRAFTING	Use to create an isometric view.	
OBJECT SNAP TRACKING	Object Snap Tracking (AUTOSNAP or OTRACK), when ON, will combine with OSNAP (which must also be ON) to allow the cursor to track along alignment paths based on other object snap points in the drawing. To use object snap tracking, you must turn on one or more object snaps.	**F11**

Status Bar Option	Overview	Function Key
2D OBJECT SNAP	When Object Snap (OSNAP) is ON, the cursor will always gravitate to specified points on objects in the drawing. Unlike SNAP, which follows a grid pattern, OSNAP refers to objects in the drawing and will display object snap markers. When Object Snap (OSNAP) is ON, the cursor will always gravitate to specified points on objects in the drawing. Unlike SNAP, which follows a grid pattern, OSNAP refers to objects in the drawing and will display object snap markers.	**F3**
LINEWEIGHT	Line weights can be specified according to the LWT settings and applied to the lines being drawn when LWT is on. When LWT is off, objects will be drawn using the line weights as designated by the layer (ByLayer). Visibility of lineweight is controlled from the lineweight settings dialog box (choose it from the Format POP, or type *lineweight*). Select "Display Lineweight." Line weights can be specified according to the LWT settings and applied to the lines being drawn when LWT is on. When LWT is off, objects will be drawn using the line weights as designated by the layer (ByLayer). Visibility of lineweight is controlled from the lineweight settings dialog box (choose it from the Format POP, or type *lineweight*). Select "Display Lineweight."	
TRANSPARENCY	This sets the value for the system variable TRANSPARENCYDISPLAY to ON or OFF (1 for ON or) for OFF. Object transparency is controlled by layer. If TRANSPARENCYDISPLAY is set to OFF, the object transparency is overridden.	
SELECTION CYCLING	This tool allows you to tab through a selection set when there are elements overlapping or lying on top of each other.	
3D OBJECT SNAP	Snaps to grips on 3D solids	**F4**
DYNAMIC UCS	This controls the appearance of the UCS icon when modeling in 3D.	**F6**
SELECTION FILTERING	Use to select edge, face, or vertex when editing 3D objects.	
GIZMO	Controls the visibility of gizmos used for editing 3D objects.	
ANNOTATION VISIBILITY	Display dimensions, notes, and other types of text used in the drawing.	
AUTO SCALE	Changes the size of text and dimensions depending on view scale.	
ANNOTATION SCALE	Displays the annotation scale of the current or active view. Model space should always show 1:1.	

Status Bar Option	Overview	Function Key
WORKSPACE SWITCHING	Allows you to quickly switch between workspaces or create a new workspace environment.	
ANNOTATION MONITOR	Turns the annotation monitor on or off. When the annotation monitor is on, it flags all non-associative annotations by placing a badge on them. A non-associative annotation is not enabled as annotative and has no annotation scales.	
UNITS	Displays the current drawing units.	
QUICK PROPERTIES	Displays the Quick Properties dialog when an element is selected.	
LOCK UI	Locks the location and sizes of toolbars, panels, and dockable windows. 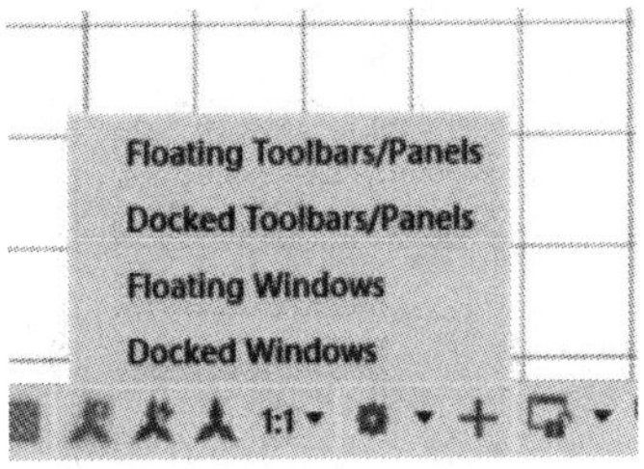 	
ISOLATE OBJECTS	Allows you to create a selection set of elements and hide all other elements.	
GRAPHICS PERFORMANCE	Sets hardware acceleration on or off and provides access to display performance options. Improves the use of your hardware resources, but it is only available if you have an approved graphics card. Visit Autodesk's website and search for recommended hardware.	
CLEANSCREEN	Toggles just the drawing window visible.	**CTL+O**

- Select either the Status Bar button, or select the corresponding function key from the keyboard.
- A Status Bar option can be turned ON or OFF while using a draw or modify command. Therefore, beginning the Line command, and deciding to turn ORTHO on or off while in the middle of the command is acceptable.
- To enable or disable the display of different status bar options, left click on the Customize icon and toggle the desired icon ON/OFF.

General Procedures

1. Select the Status Bar button to toggle it ON or OFF.
2. Right-click the Status Bar button to access the corresponding Settings dialog box.

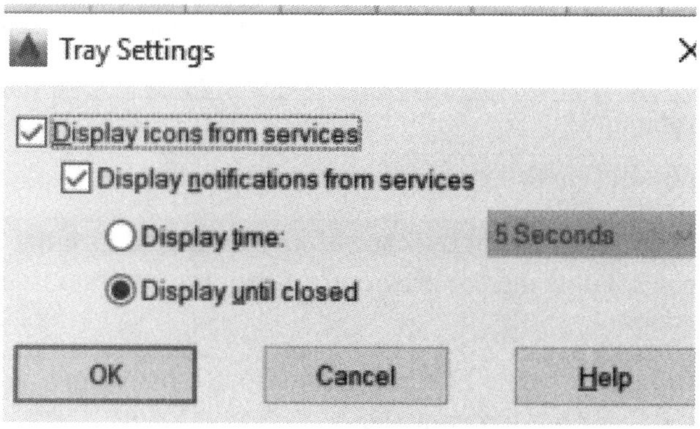

Type **TRAYSETTINGS** at the command prompt to control the balloon notifications. Balloons will display when you plot, when updates are available, etc. To turn off the balloon notifications, you can simply disable the boxes and press 'OK'.

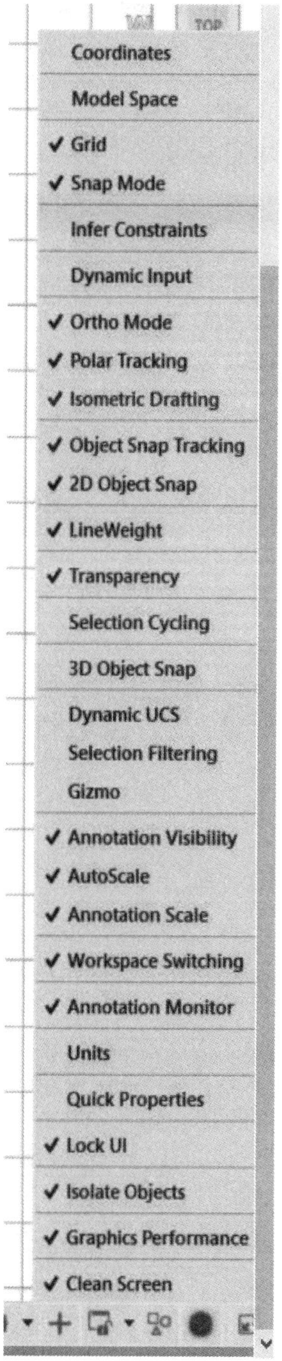

Left click on the menu icon on the Status Bar and a list of available buttons appears. A check mark next to the name indicates that the button is active and visible. To hide a button, simply left click on the name.

Note that the Status buttons have their own submenu.

Keyboard Options

Overview

Commands, command aliases, or *system variables* can be typed at the keyboard. It is important to remember to press <ENTER> to execute the command, and follow the Command Prompt prompts. When choosing a Command Prompt option, type the capitalized letter(s) of the desired option. Pressing <ENTER> or the spacebar will execute the command. When typing Text, however, the <ENTER> key is the same as a carriage return on a typewriter, and the spacebar will type a space. Function Keys are used to toggle some options ON or OFF.

Keyboard Option	Overview
ESC	Escape. Cancels all commands.
Enter	Executes a command.
Spacebar	Works like the <ENTER> key except when typing text.
Arrows	Moves the cursor position. In the case of the Command Prompt, the up and down arrows will bring the previously typed information to the last Command Prompt.
Ctrl	Use the Control key + single keys to begin selected commands as indicated in the Pull-Down menus (i.e. Ctrl+S will Save).

Left Side Status Bar

Model space is the default drawing space. All elements should be drawn 1:1. The Layout tabs are used to lay out sheets where views are placed.

Command Alias	**Command Aliases are shortcut keys that can be typed to access a command when the Command Prompt is blank. Some of the command aliases include:**
A	Arc
B	Block Definition dialog box
C	Circle
CO	Copy
D	Dimension Style Manager dialog box
E	Erase
ED	Edit Text
F	Fillet
H	Boundary Hatch dialog box
I	Insert Block dialog box
L	Line
LA	Layers Properties Manager dialog box
M	Move
O	Offset
P	Real-Time Pan
PE	Edit Polyline
PL	Draw Polyline
PU	Purge
R	Redraw
Re	Regenerate Drawing

Function Keys	Function Keys, located at the top or side of the keyboard, activate the following options:
S	Stretch
T	Multiline Text
U	Undo (last command)
V	View dialog box
W	Write Block dialog box
X	Explode
Z	Zoom

F1	Activates the AutoCAD Help Menu
F2	Opens the AutoCAD Text Window
F3	Turns OSNAP (object snap) ON or OFF
F4	Toggles 3D Object Snap
F5	Toggles through the three Isoplanes: Top, Right, and Left.
F6	Toggles through the three coordinate options: ON, OFF or display Polar Coordinates.
F7	Turns the GRID ON or OFF
F8	Turns ORTHO ON or OFF
F9	Turns SNAP ON or OFF
F10	Turns POLAR Tracking ON or OFF
F11	Turns OTRACK (object snap tracking) ON or OFF
F12	Toggles Dynamic Input

General Procedures

1. Type the command, command alias, or system variable at the Command Prompt.
2. Press <ENTER> to execute the command, or follow the Command Prompt prompts.

Tips & Tricks

- Remember to press the <ENTER> key after typing a command, a command alias, or a system variable.
- Commands, aliases, or system variables are not case sensitive.
- A *default* is the most common or last option selected and will be shown in parentheses. Press <ENTER> to accept the default. It is not necessary to type the default over again.
- When in doubt about a command location, type it (and remember to press <ENTER>). This will usually begin the desired command.
- System variable settings will be covered in this tutorial at the appropriate topic.

Command Exercise

Exercise 1-3 – Start Page

Drawing Name: **(none, start from scratch)**
Estimated Time to Completion: 5 Minutes

Scope

Explore the New Start tab

1. *Draw line segments.*
2. *Press the right button on the mouse to repeat the line command.*
3. *Practice selecting a single object.*
4. *Practice making a selection window.*
5. *Activate the object snap shortcut (cursor) menu.*
6. *Activate the toolbar shortcut menu.*
7. *Activate the Command Prompt short cut menu.*

Solution

1. Click on the Start tab.

Notice that the Start tab is divided into four sections or panels. The first panel is a link to the Learning tools. You can also connect to your free A360 account.

The second panel allows you to create a new drawing, open files, open a sheet set, get on-line templates, or explore sample drawings.

The third panel lists recent documents and you have the option of controlling how the documents are viewed.

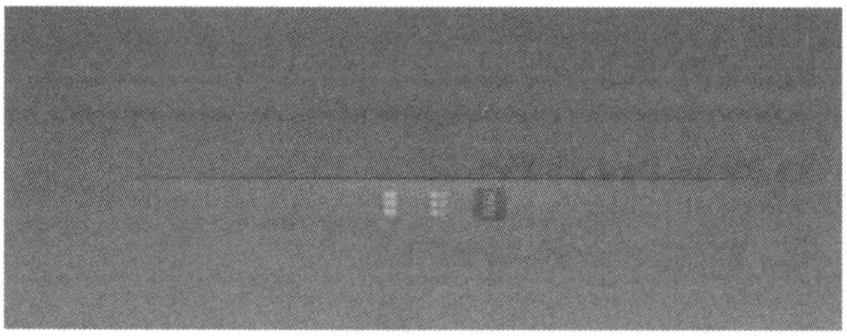

There are three small icons located at the bottom of the screen.

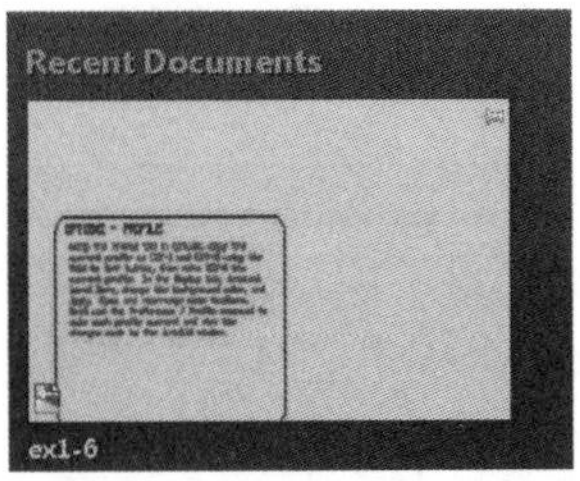

If the first icon is selected, the recent drawings will be displayed in preview mode with the file name only.

If the second icon is selected, the recent drawings will be displayed in preview mode with the file name along with the date last modified.

If the third icon is selected, the file name is displayed with no preview along with the date last modified.

Notice the pin icon on the right of the drawing file name. If you don't want a file to drop off the list, you can pin it in place so it will always be available.

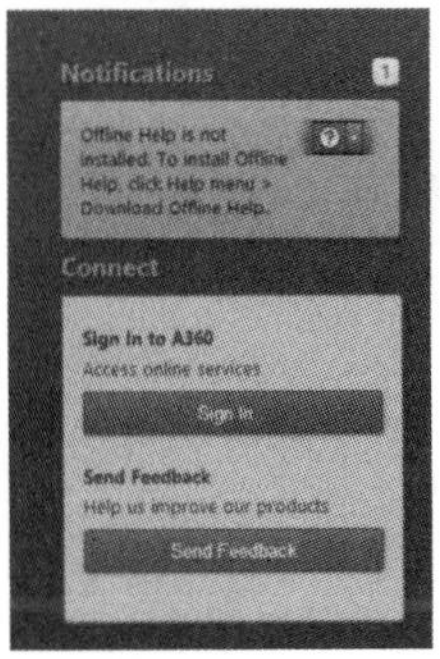

The fourth panel is a community resource area. You can read notifications about service packs and other Autodesk news.

You can also log into your Autodesk 360 account. *There will be an exercise later on how that works.*

Tips & Tricks

- You can turn off the Start Page by typing STARTMODE on the command line and then 0.
- If you press Ctl+Home, you will automatically switch from the active drawing back to the Start tab.
- If you have a drawing where you store blocks, linetypes, dimension styles, etc. you can pin it to the Start tab so it is always front and center.

Help Menu

Command Locator

Command Overview

AutoCAD Help can be invoked at any time. If the Command Prompt is blank, the Help menu will open at one of the tabs, depending on which tab was selected the last time Help was used. If help is invoked while in the middle of a command, the Help menu will open to the page covering that command.

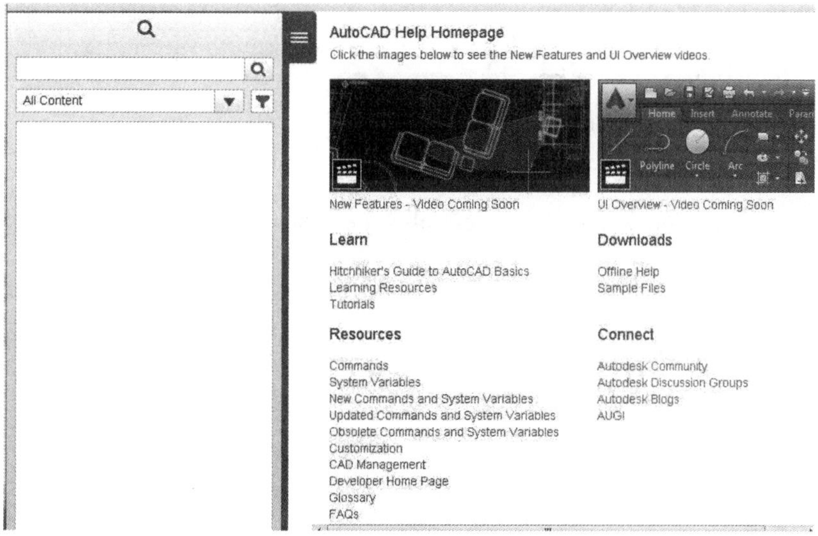

AutoCAD Help

General Procedures

To access help when in the middle of a command:

1. Select the question mark in the toolbar.

To use the Help Contents tab:

1. Select Help Topics / Contents Tab.
2. Open a topic by double clicking on it, or single-click and select Open.

To use the Help menu Index tab:

1. Select Help Topics / Index Tab.
2. Begin to type the word.
3. Double-click the index entry, or single-click and select Display.

To use the Help menu Find tab:

1. Select Help Topics / Find Tab.
2. If the setup Wizard appears, select Next.
3. Begin to type the word.
4. Double-click the index entry, or single-click and select Display.

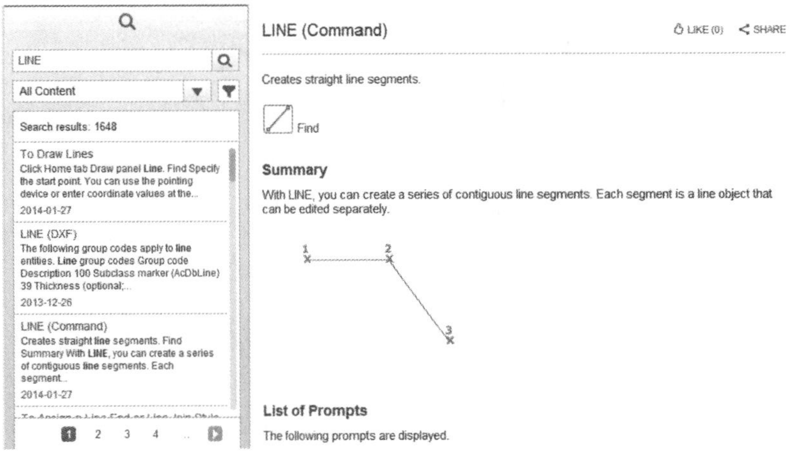

If you press F1 in the middle of the Line command, you will see this dialog.

Command Exercise

Exercise 1-4 – Dynamic Input

Drawing Name: **(none, start from scratch)**
Estimated Time to Completion: 5 Minutes

Scope

Control the appearance of Dynamic Input

Solution

1. Verify that ORTHO is enabled.

Toggle it on using the icon on the status bar or press F8.

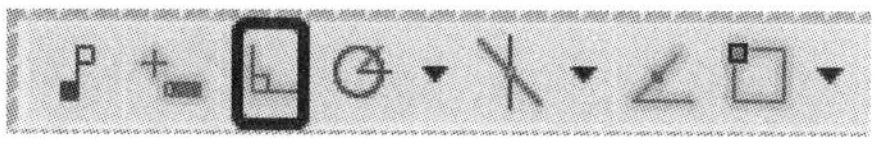

2. Start the LINE command.
3. Left click in the window to place the line starting point.
4. Move the cursor around the drawing window.
5. RMB and select ENTER to exit the LINE command.

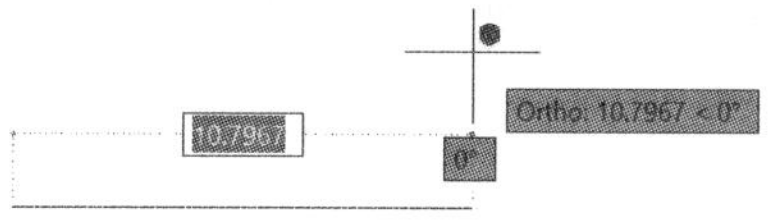

Note how the coordinates in the input bar change depending on the cursor location.

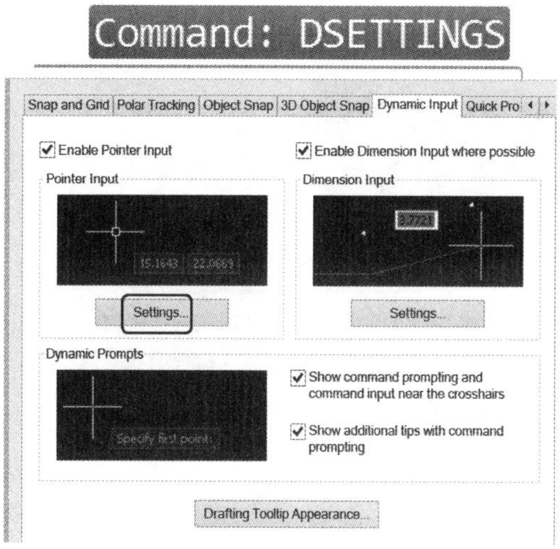

6. Type **DSETTINGS** on the command prompt.
7. Activate the **Dynamic Input** tab.
8. Select the **Settings** button under Pointer Input.

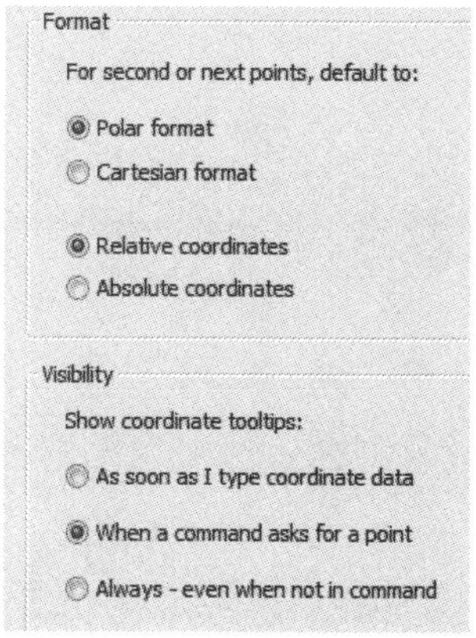

9. Press **OK**.

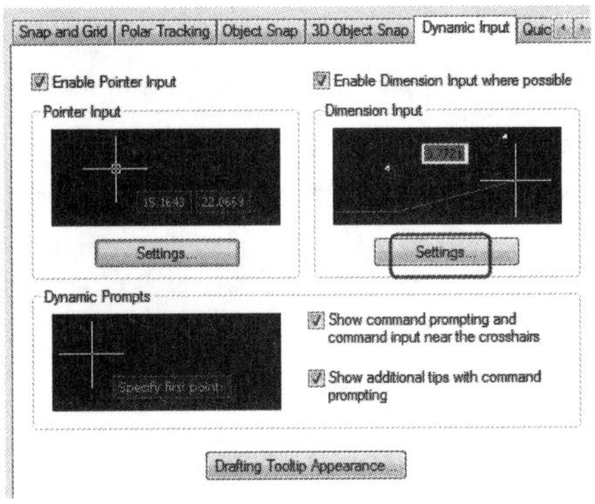

10. Select the **Settings** button under Dimension Input.

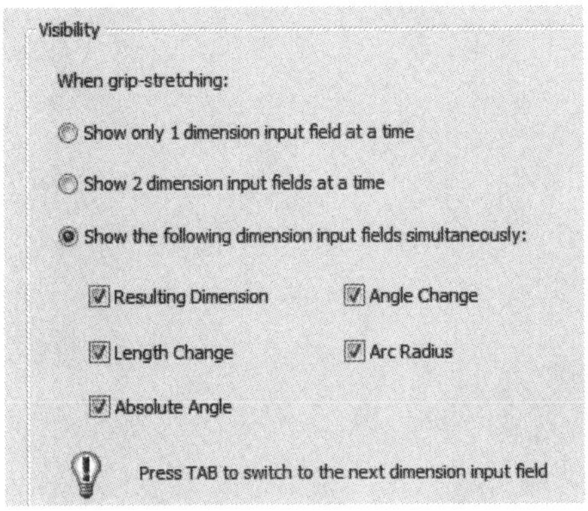

11. Enable **Show the following dimension input fields simultaneously**.
12. Enable all the options.
13. Press **OK**.

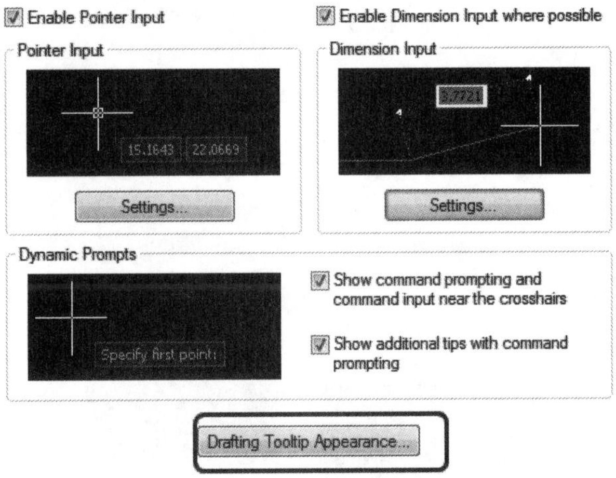

14. Select **Drafting Tooltip Appearance** under Dynamic Prompts.

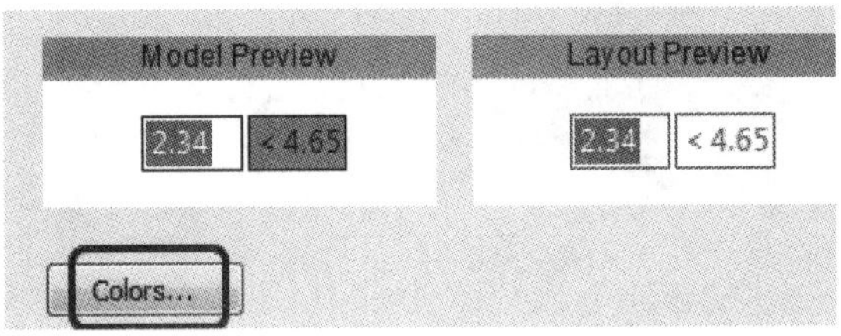

15. Select the **Colors** button.

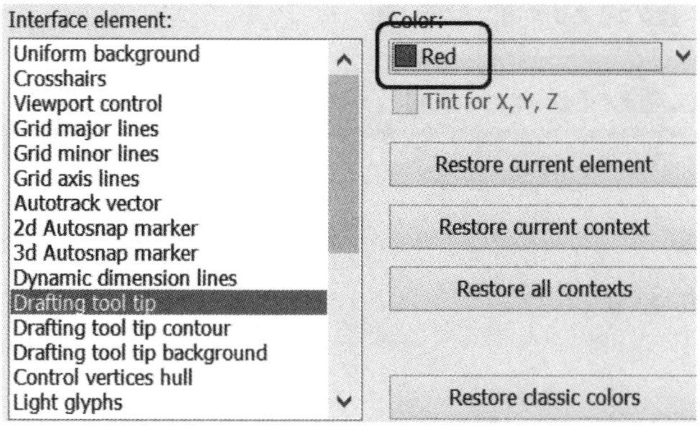

16. Highlight the **Drafting tool tip** in the Interface element box.
17. Set the color to **RED**.
18. Press **Apply & Close**.

Note you can adjust the size of dimensions as they appear. This is especially helpful if you have vision problems.

19. Press **OK** twice to close the dialog.

Note how the display has changed.

20. Start a LINE.
21. Pick a point to start the line.

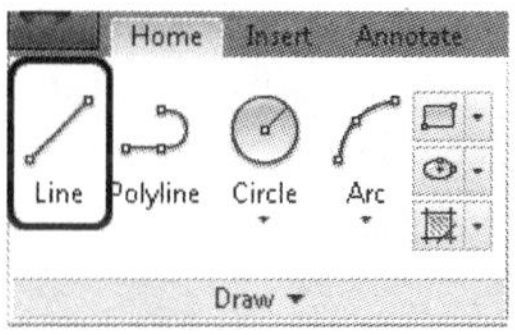

22. Press the up and down arrows on your keyboard.

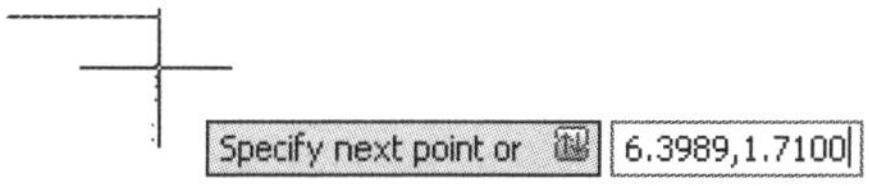

Note that AutoCAD is keeping track of the coordinates selected.

Autodesk allows users to automatically save their files to a free cloud account. The Cloud is a server that is available as long as the user has a live internet connection. Users can store files on the account and access them from anywhere. The storage limitation is 3GB. Autodesk calls their cloud server Autodesk 360.

Students may want to download and install the Autodesk 360 Mobile App to their mobile device (smartphone, iPhone, iPad, tablet, etc.). This free software allows them to view, mark up and modify files they have uploaded to their Cloud account.

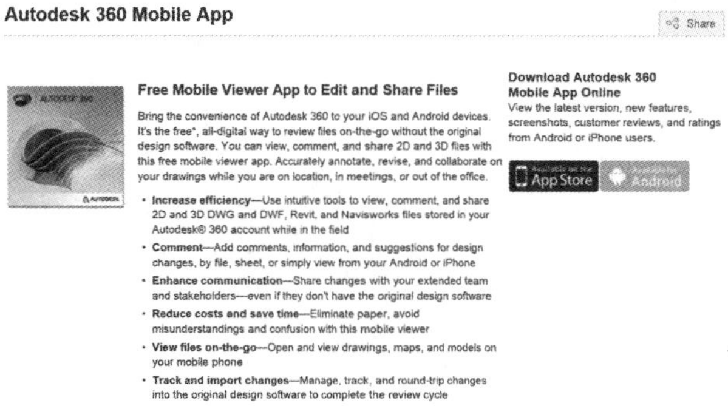

Command Exercise

Exercise 1-5 – Create an Autodesk 360 Account

Drawing Name: **(none, start from scratch)**
Estimated Time to Completion: 5 Minutes

Scope

Create an account on Autodesk 360.

You must have an internet connection to access the Autodesk server.

Solution

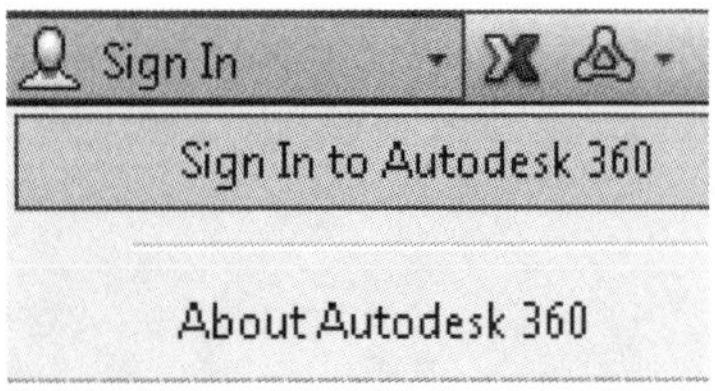

Next to the Help icon at the top of the screen:

1. Select **Sign In to Autodesk 360**

If you have an existing Autodesk ID, you can use it.

If not, select the link that says **Need an Autodesk ID**.

You may have an existing Autodesk ID if you have registered Autodesk software in the past.

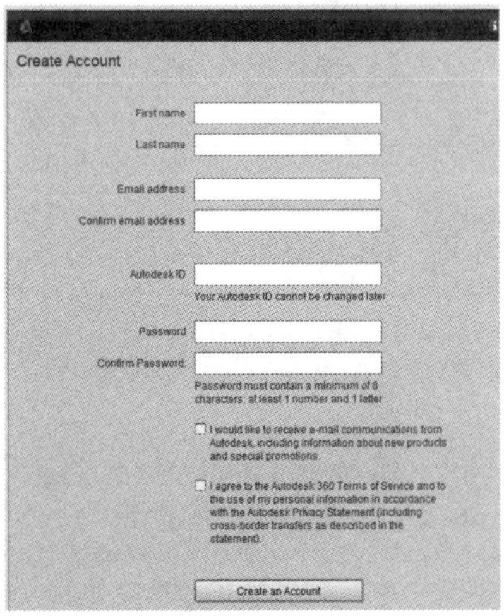

2. Fill in the form to create an Autodesk ID account.

Be sure to write down the ID you select and the password.

3. Once the account is created, you will be asked to log in to your account.

There will be a slight pause while the server validates the log in.

You will then be asked to check your settings.

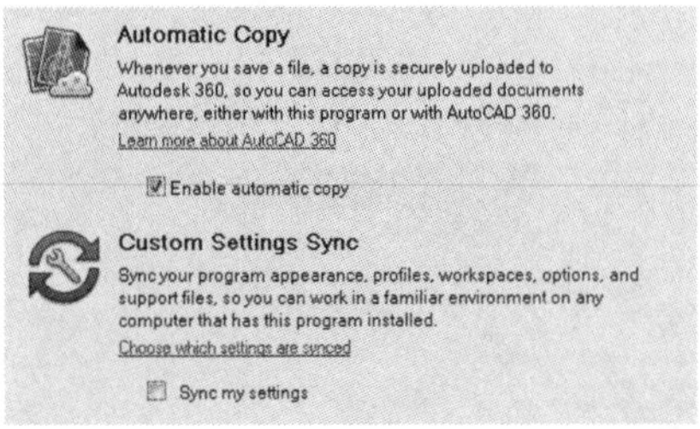

You can automatically save your work to the Cloud.
If you do this, you will be able to access your files anywhere you have internet access.

You will see the name you selected as your Autodesk ID in the Cloud sign-in area.

Profiles

Command Locator

Options Dialog—Profiles Tab

Command Overview

The Profiles Tab of the Options dialog box allows you to copy your Preferences settings to a personalized profile (.ARG file). This can be exported to the network or a floppy disk. When you use AutoCAD on another computer workstation, simply import your own .arg profile file.

Available Profiles – List all available profiles for the system.

Set Current – Makes the selected profile the current profile.

Add to List – Displays the Add Profile dialog box to save the selected profile under a different name.

Rename – Selecting this button will open the Change Profile dialog box allowing you to rename and change the description of the selected profile.

Delete – Deletes the selected profile (unless it is the current profile).

Export – Exports a selected profile as an .ARG file.

Import – Imports a selected profile that was created by using the Export option.

Reset – Resets the values in the selected profile to the system default settings.

Tips & Tricks

- Most users set up their tool palettes and change the user environment to the way they like to work. If you are spending time on more than one work station—for example, working in a classroom or office and then also working at home—you can save your profile and import to any work station, so you don't have to set-up your work station each time.

Command Exercise

Exercise 1-6 – Create a Profile

Drawing Name: **pref4.dwg**
Estimated Time to Completion: 10 Minutes

Scope

Using the Profile tab in Options, copy the current profile as CAD–1 and CAD–2, then make CAD–1 the current profile. In the Display tab, deselect Scroll Bars, change the background color, and Apply. Open and rearrange some toolbars. Next use the Options / Profile command to make each profile current and view the changes made to the AutoCAD window.

Solution

1. Invoke the Options command by right-clicking in the display area of the screen and selecting **Options...**

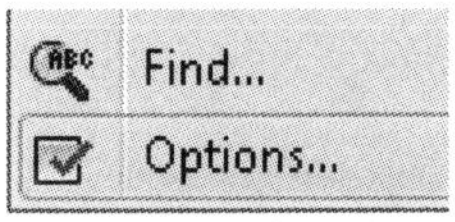

2. Select the *Profiles* tab and copy the current profile by using the **Add to List...** button.

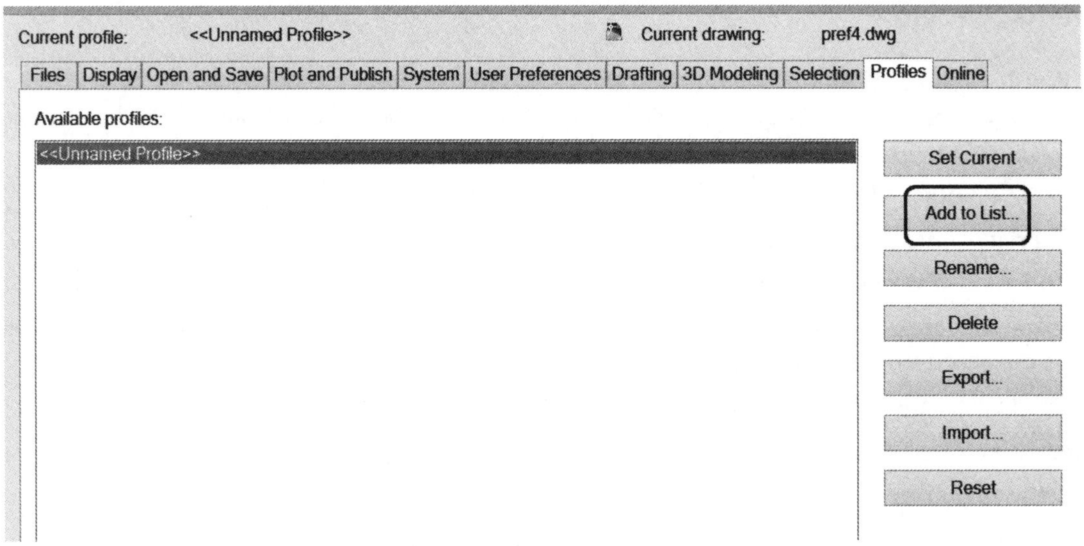

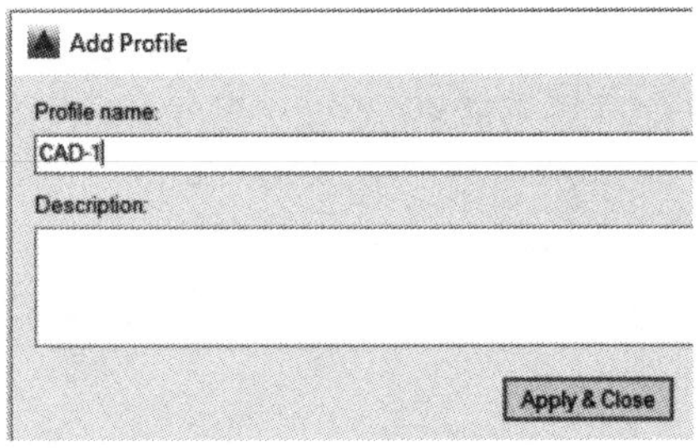

3. Name the profile *CAD–1* and press **Apply & Close**.

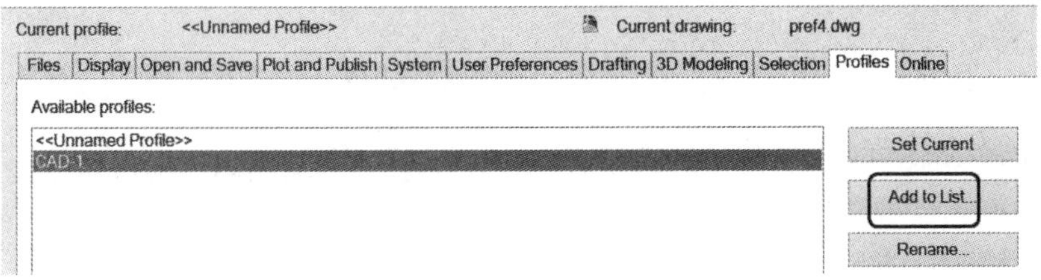

4. Highlight the *CAD-1* Profile and select **Add to List** to create another profile.

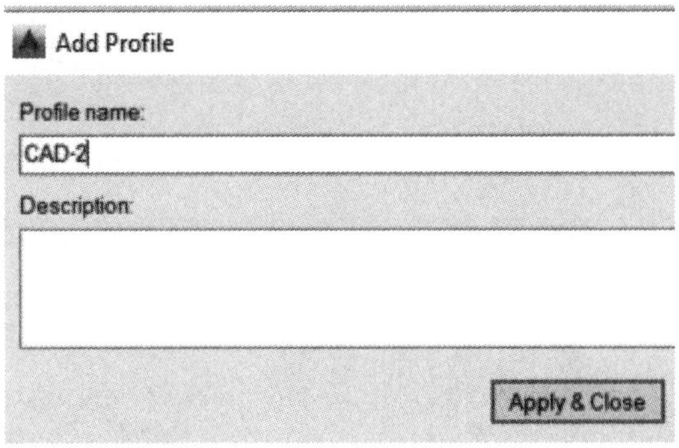

5. Name this profile *CAD-2* and press **Apply & Close**.

6. Highlight the *CAD-1* profile and select **Set Current**.

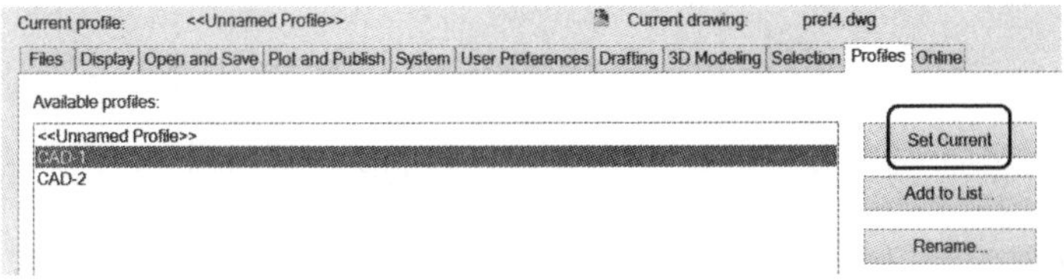

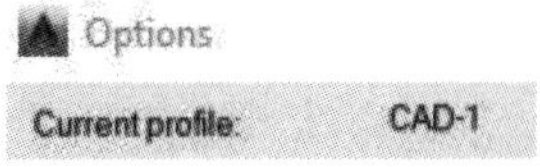

You will see the CAD-1 Profile listed as the current profile.

7. In the Display tab of the dialog box, enable **Display Scroll Bars**.

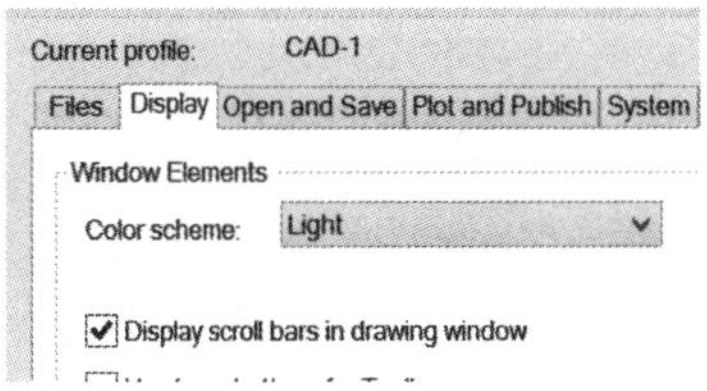

8. Select the **Colors** button.

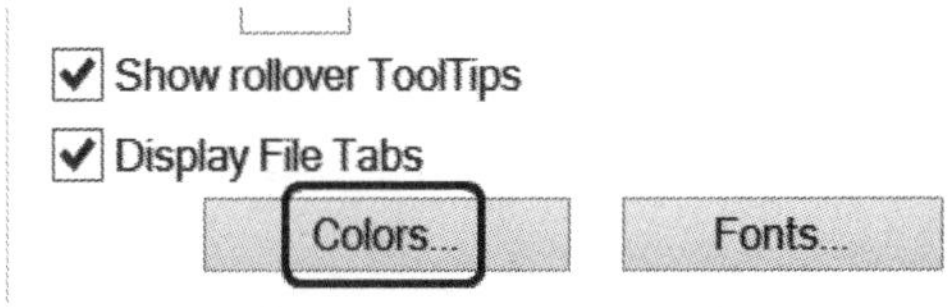

9. Change the Display Window background color.

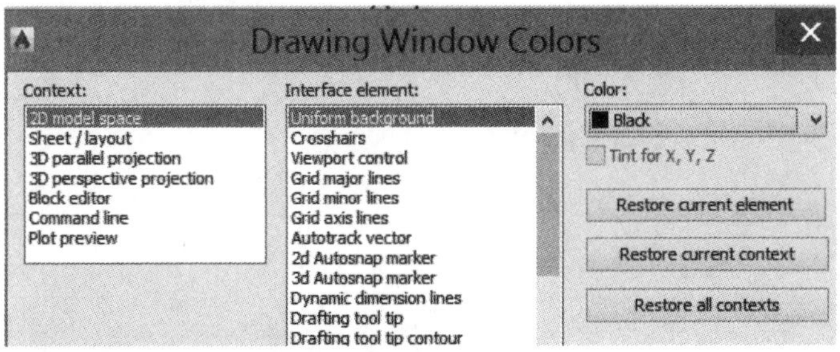

10. Press **OK** to apply the changes and exit the dialog box.

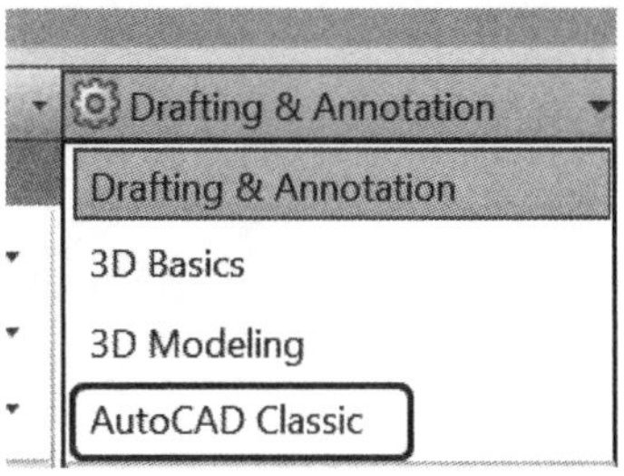

11. Change the workspace to **AutoCAD Classic**.

12. Place your cursor in the Command window.
13. RMB and select **Options**.

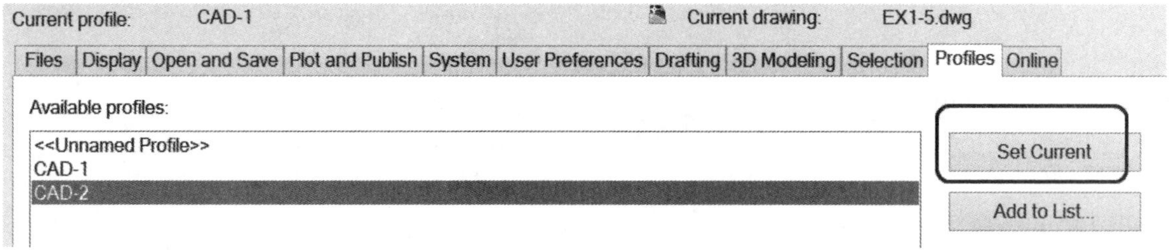

14. Select the **Profiles** tab.
15. Highlight the **CAD-2** profile and **Set Current**.
16. Press **OK** to close the OPTIONs dialog.

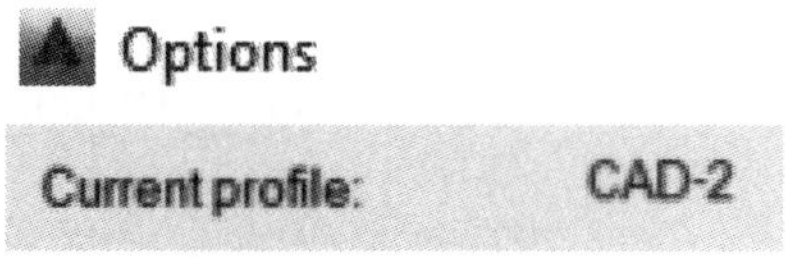

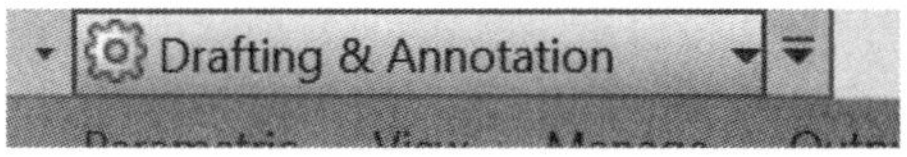

Note that the workspace is set to Drafting & Annotation.

The ribbon should be visible and the window color should be back to the default color.

17. Place your cursor in the Command window.
18. RMB and select **Options**.
19. Set the **CAD-1** profile current.

Close the Options dialog box.

20. Type **RIBBONCLOSE** to close the ribbon.

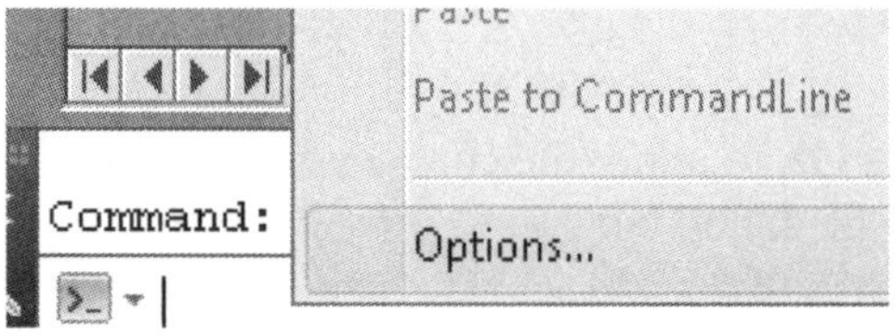

21. Place your cursor in the Command window.
22. RMB and select **Options**.
23. Set the **CAD-2** profile current.

Notice that the ribbon is not controlled by the profile.

*To restore the ribbon, type **RIBBON**.*

Command Exercise

Exercise 1-7 – Export a Profile

Drawing Name: **exportprofile.dwg**
Estimated Time to Completion: 5 Minutes

Scope

Export a profile for use at a different workstation.

Solution

1. Place your cursor in the Command window.
2. RMB and select **Options**.

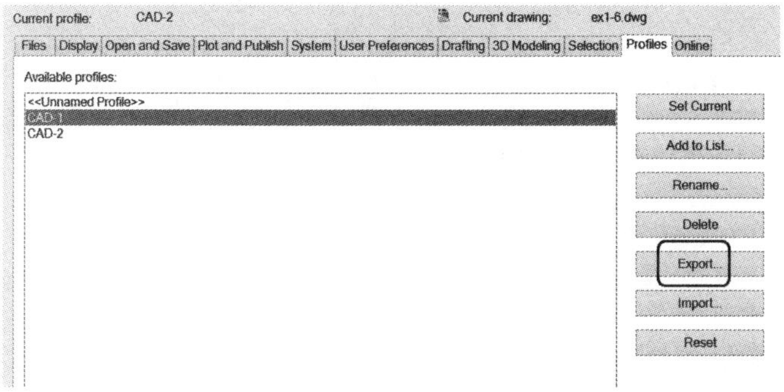

3. Go to the **Profiles** tab.
4. Highlight the **CAD-1** profile.
5. Select **Export**.

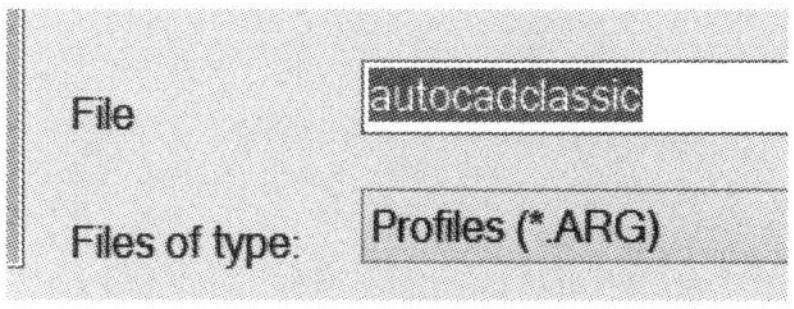

6. Browse to a folder to save the profile file.
7. Rename the file *autocadclassic.arg*.
8. Press **Save**.
9. Press **OK** to exit the dialog.
10. Close the file.

Start a new drawing.

11. Place your cursor in the Command window.
12. RMB and select **Options**.

13. Select the Profiles tab.

Note that the profiles you created are stored on your workstation, so any drawing you open or create will now have the profiles available.

14. Press **OK** to close the dialog.

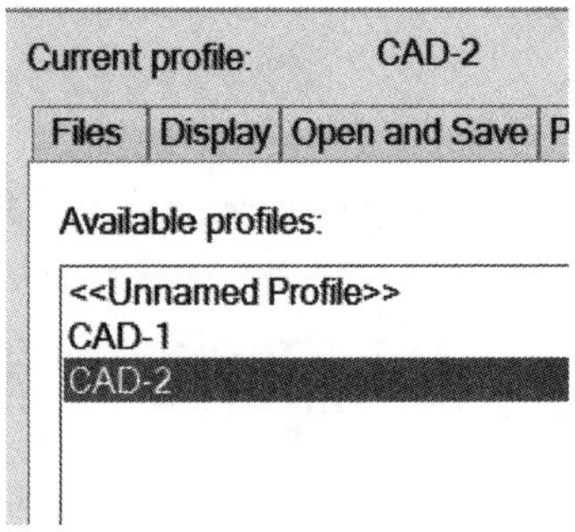

➢Store your profile files on Autodesk 360 so they will be available at any workstation.

➢To import a profile, go to the Options/Profiles dialog and select Import. Then select the profile file you want to use.

15. Press Ctl+Home on your keyboard. This should switch you to the Start tab.

The Home button is located in the middle of the keyboard above the arrow keys.

Click on the A360 link on the far right panel.

You need to have an internet connection in order to use Autodesk 360.

16. Select **Upload.**

17. Select **Select File.**

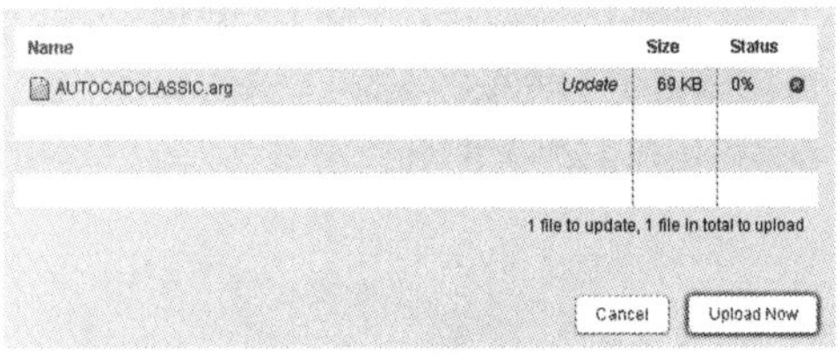

18. Browse to locate the *autocadclassic.arg* profile file. Select it and press **Open.**

19. Press **Upload Now**.

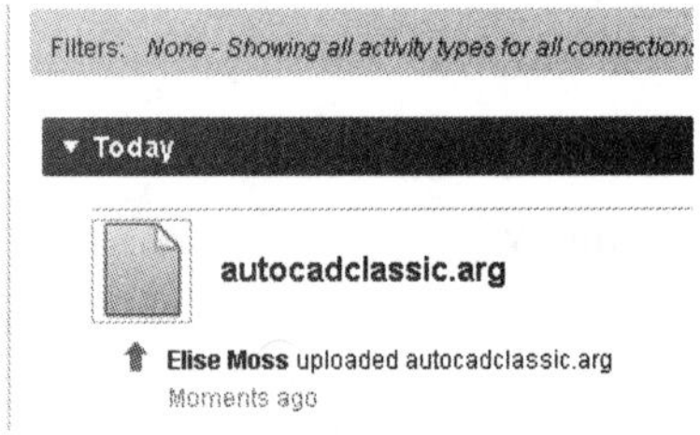

20. Click Refresh to see the file as uploaded.

The profile is now available for you from any internet connection.

Review Questions

1. Which is the Pick button and which is the <ENTER> button on the mouse?

2. Name the areas of the AutoCAD Screen:

3. How do you close the ribbon?

4. How do you open the ribbon?

5. What is the hotkey for Help?

6. How do you switch from one open drawing to another open drawing?

7. What happens if you press the enter button on the mouse when the cursor is:
   - ❑ In the drawing window?
   - ❑ Over the Command Prompt?

8. What does the Escape key do?

9. How can a dialog box be closed?

10. At a blank command prompt, what commands are initiated by typing the following letters?

E	**C**	**M**
A	**L**	**P**
R	**Z**	**U**

11. Where is the Quick Access toolbar?

12. What panel of the ribbon holds the LINE tool?

Review Answers

1. Which is the Pick button and which is the <ENTER> button on the mouse?

   Left Button (LMB) : Pick
   Right Button (RMB): <ENTER>

2. Name the areas of the AutoCAD Screen:

   Title Bar, Quick Access Toolbars Drawing Window, Command Prompt, Status Bar, Ribbon

3. How do you close the ribbon?

   RIBBONCLOSE.

4. How do you open the ribbon?

   RIBBON

5. What is the hotkey for Help?

   F1

6. How do you switch from one open drawing to another open drawing?

   Select the tabs at the top of the drawing window.

7. What happens if you press the enter button on the mouse when the cursor is:
   In the drawing window?

   A Shortcut Menu appears related to the last or current command.

   Over the Command Prompt?

   The Command Prompt Shortcut Menu appears.

8. What does the Escape key do?

   Cancels a command.

9. How can a dialog box be closed?

   Select OK, Close, the X in the upper right hand corner, or the Escape key

10. At a blank command prompt, what commands are initiated by typing the following letters?

E *Erase*	**C** *Circle*	**M** *Move*
A *Arc*	**L** *Line*	**P** *Pan*
R *Redraw*	**Z** *Zoom*	**U** *Undo*

11. Where is the Quick Access Toolbar?

    The docked toolbar at the top.

12. What panel of the ribbon holds the LINE tool?

    The DRAW panel.

Lesson 2.0 – View Commands

Estimated Class Time: 1 Hour

Objectives

This Lesson will cover the different ways to view drawings. Learn to Pan and Zoom in *real time*, and use the other Zoom options. Views can be Named and Saved, then Restored. The drawing window can be divided into Multiple Viewports.

- **Pan Realtime**
  Pan the drawing with the motion of the cursor in *real time*.
- **Zoom Realtime**
  Zoom the drawing with the up and down motion of the cursor in *real time*.
- **Zoom Window**
  Make a zoom window around an area to view close up.
- **Zoom Previous**
- **Zoom Options**
  Additional zoom options are located in the fly-out on the Standard Toolbar.
- **Regen**
  Regenerate the drawing to smooth out circles and arcs.
- **Named Views**
  Name and Save drawing Views and make them current when needed.
- **Multiple Viewports**
  Display different views of the drawing in multiple viewports.

Pan Realtime

Command Locator

Navigation Bar	**Pan**
Command	**Pan**
Alias	**P**
RMB Shortcut Menu	**Drawing Window**
Navigation Bar	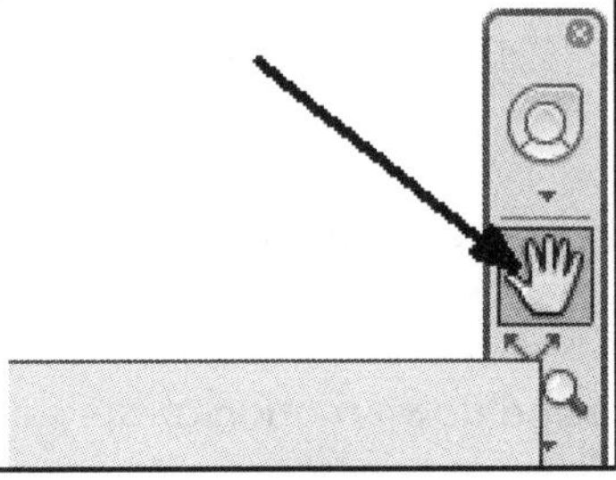

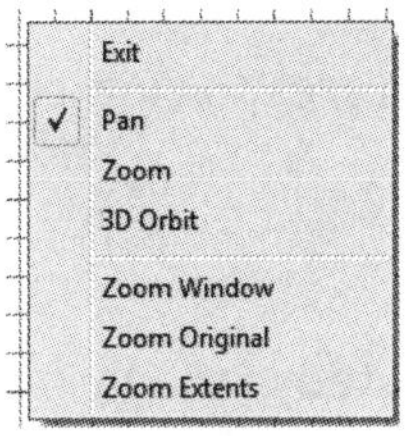
Exit
Pan
Zoom
3D Orbit
Zoom Window
Zoom Original
Zoom Extents

Pan Realtime Shortcut Menu

Real Time Pan / Zoom Shortcut Menu Options:	Overview
Exit	Exits the Realtime Pan or Zoom commands
Pan	Invokes the Realtime Pan command
Zoom	Invokes the Realtime Zoom command
3D Orbit	Rotates the drawing three-dimensionally
Zoom Window	Zooms to a window made by pressing the pick button and dragging it around the area to view
Zoom Original	Displays the drawing in the original zoom setting
Zoom Extents	Zooms to the extents of the drawing objects

Command Overview

With the Pan Realtime command, pick a point in the drawing window. Press the LMB and drag the drawing view in real time. Right click (RMB) to access the shortcut menu and select Exit, or one of the other options. The Escape key will also exit the Pan Realtime command.

General Procedures

1. Invoke the Pan Realtime command.
2. Pick a point in the drawing window (LMB), press and drag to pan the view.
3. Right-click (RMB) to access the shortcut menu and pick Exit.

Tips & Tricks

- The shortcut menus for Pan Realtime and Zoom Realtime are identical.
- When dragging the cursor in Pan Realtime, the mouse can be picked up and relocated in the drawing window if the cursor reaches the edge of the drawing window.

Zoom Realtime

Command Locator

Navigation Bar	**Navigation / Zoom**	
Command	**Zoom**	
Alias	**Z**	
RMB Shortcut Menu	**Drawing Window**	
	Navigation Bar	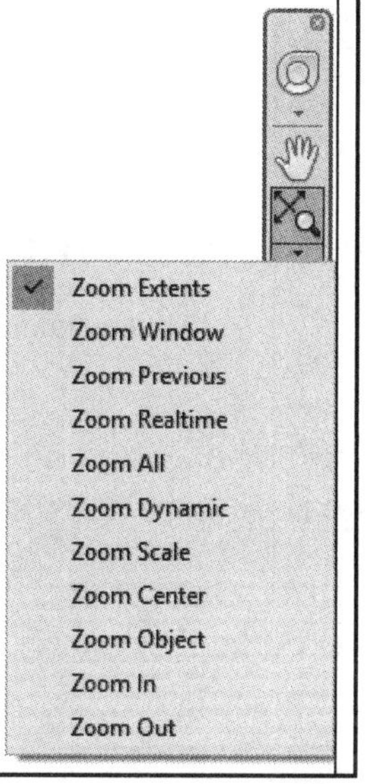

Zoom Extents
Zoom Window
Zoom Previous
Zoom Realtime
Zoom All
Zoom Dynamic
Zoom Scale
Zoom Center
Zoom Object
Zoom In
Zoom Out

Command Overview

With the Zoom command, pick a point in the drawing window. Drag the mouse up or down to zoom in or out. Right click (RMB) to access the shortcut menu and select Exit, or one of the other options. The Escape Key will also exit the Zoom command.

General Procedures

1. Invoke the Zoom command.
2. Pick a point in the drawing window (LMB), press and drag up to zoom in and down to zoom out.
3. Right-click (RMB) to access the shortcut menu and select Exit or one of the other options.

Tips & Tricks

- Remember to drag up to zoom in and down to zoom out.
- When dragging the cursor in Zoom, the mouse can be picked up and relocated in the drawing window if the cursor reaches the top or bottom of the drawing window.

Zoom Window

Command Locator

Toolbar Menu	**Navigation / Zoom Flyout**
Command	**Zoom, Window**
Alias	**Z**

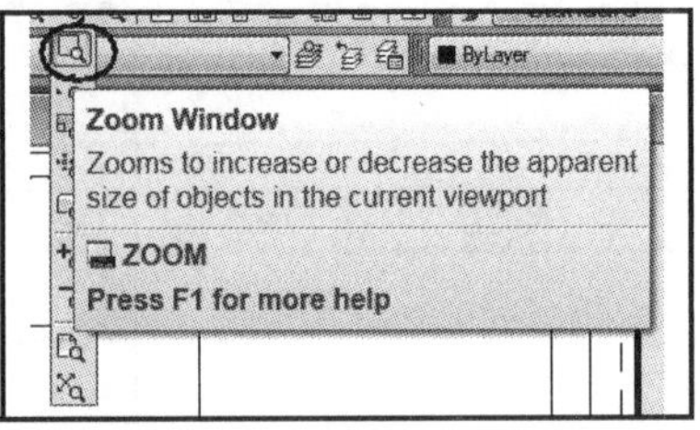
ByLayer
Zoom Window
Zooms to increase or decrease the apparent size of objects in the current viewport
ZOOM
Press F1 for more help

Command Overview

Use the Zoom window command to view a selected area of the drawing.

General Procedures

1. Invoke the Zoom Window command.
2. Pick the first corner of the view window, then drag the mouse and pick the opposite corner.

- When the Zoom Window command is invoked, the opposite corner of the window must be made or press Escape to cancel the Zoom command.
- When invoking the Zoom command, the Window option is a default. Just begin the first corner of the zoom window.
- Zoom commands can be used while in the middle of other commands.

Zoom Previous

Command Locator

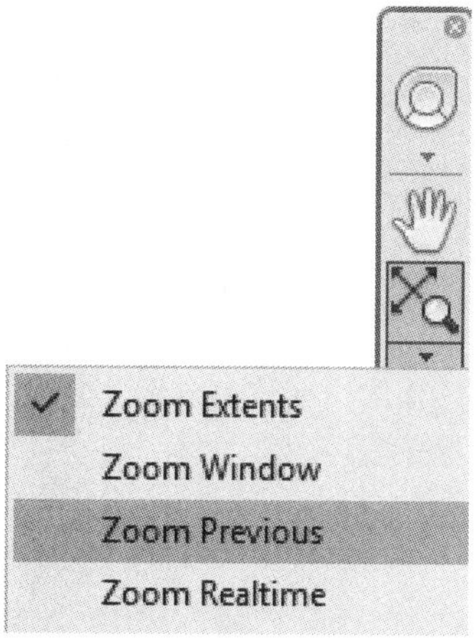

Toolbar Menu	**Navigation / Zoom Previous**
Command	**Zoom / P**
Alias	**Z / P**

Command Overview

The Zoom Previous command displays the previous view.

General Procedures

1. Invoke the Zoom Previous command using the button in the Standard toolbar. If typing the alias Z, press <ENTER>, then type P (and <ENTER> for the Previous option).

Tips & Tricks

- Zoom previous can be accessed from the Zoom command by typing 'P' and pressing <ENTER>.
- Zoom Previous can go back until no previous views are found.

Zoom Options

Command Locator

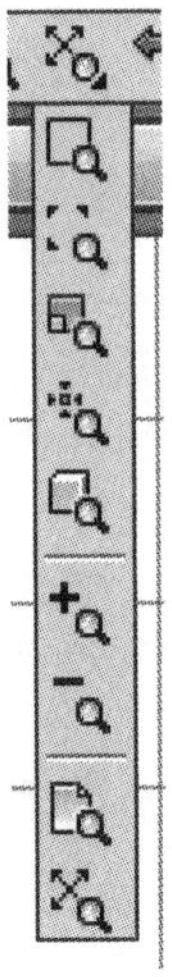

Toolbar Menu	**Navigation / Zoom Fly-out**
Command	**Zoom (type capitalized letter of the desired option)**
Alias	**Z (type capitalized letter of the desired option)**

Command Overview

Other zoom options are available within the Zoom command. These can be accessed from the fly-out button on the Standard Toolbar under the Zoom Window command. These options are also available by typing the capitalized letter of the desired option after invoking the Zoom command.

Zoom Option	Button	Overview
Zoom		Zoom Realtime – zoom in and out.
Zoom Previous		Zoom back through previous views.
Zoom Window		Zooms to a selected window.
Zoom Dynamic		Displays the zoom window. LMB to scale or pan the view window. RMB to display the Shortcut menu.
Zoom Scale		Zoom to a specific scale relevant to the last zoom or to actual scale in paper space (x/xp).
Zoom Center		Makes a selected point in the drawing the Center of the drawing.
Zoom Object		Select an entity in your drawing and the view will adjust to center on the selected object.
Zoom In		This will zoom at a scale of .5x.
Zoom Out		This will zoom at a scale of 2x.
Zoom All		This will zoom to view all of the geometry in the drawing as well as the area designated by the Drawing Limits.
Zoom Extents		This will zoom to view only the geometry in the drawing.

General Procedures

1. Invoke the Zoom command option from the fly-out in the Standard Toolbar.
2. If typing the alias Z, press <ENTER>, then type the capitalized letter of the desired option and press <ENTER>.

Tips & Tricks

- The most important Zoom options are Window, All and Extents.
- Zoom All or Extents occasionally to be sure bits of the drawing have not gotten thrown out into space.
- If the desired fly-out option is the visible button on the Standard Toolbar, simply select it. It is not necessary to display the fly-out list to select that option.

Command Exercise

Exercise 2-1 – Real Time Zoom

Drawing Name: **pan1.dwg**
Estimated Time to Completion: 10 Minutes

Scope

Zoom and Pan the drawing in real time. Use the RMB to switch between some basic zoom modes.

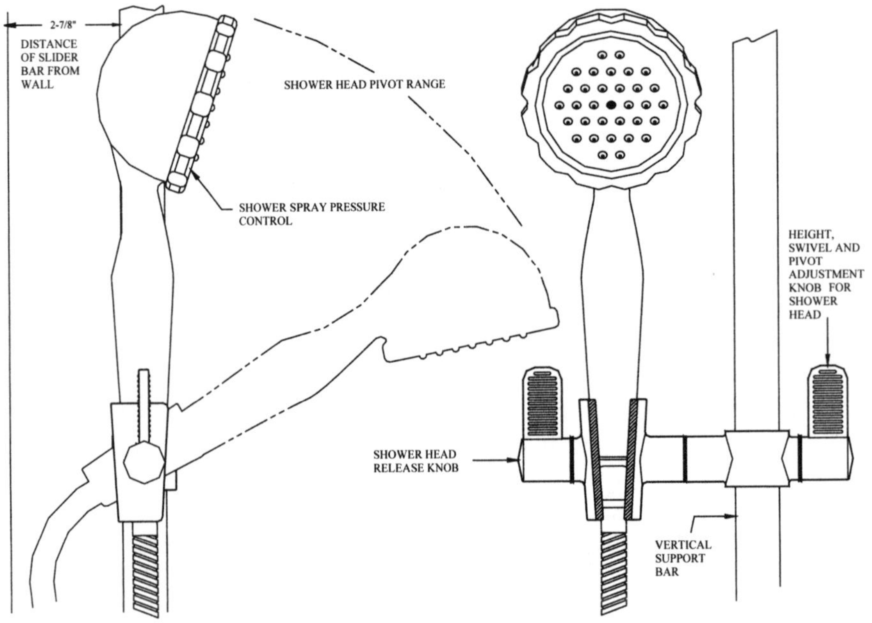

Figure 1 – Zoom and Pan Exercise

Solution

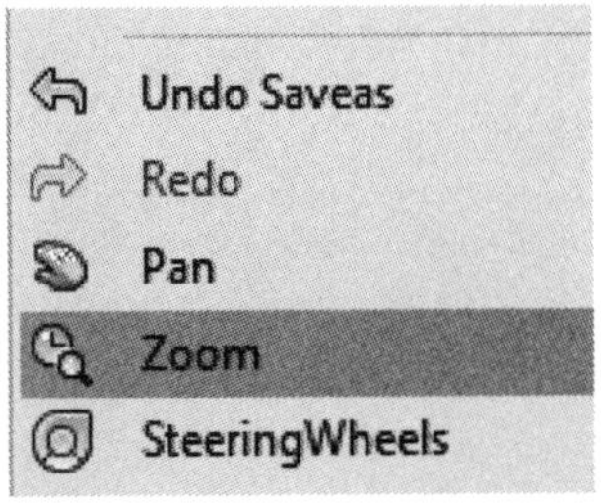

1. Invoke the Zoom command (z or zoom) or Right click in the screen and select Zoom.

2. *Press ESC or ENTER to exit, or right-click to display shortcut menu.*
Pick a point in the middle of the drawing window. Hold the LMB down and drag the mouse up and down. Notice how you zoom in as you move the mouse up and zoom out as you move the mouse down.

3. *Press ESC or ENTER to exit, or right-click to display shortcut menu:*
Hold the mouse down and drag the mouse to the top of the screen. Let go of the LMB and move the mouse to the center of the screen. Hold the LMB down and drag the mouse to the top of the screen. This allows you to continue to zoom in. Repeat the process but zoom out by dragging the mouse down instead of up.

4. *Press ESC or ENTER to exit, or right-click to display shortcut menu:*
   Press the <ENTER> or <ESC> key to end the command.

5. Invoke the Pan command (p or pan) or Right click in the screen and select Pan.

6. *Press ESC or ENTER to exit, or right-click to display shortcut menu:*
   Select a location in the middle of the screen and hold your LMB down and drag your mouse up, down, right and left. Notice how the drawing pans as you move your mouse. Let go of the LMB, reposition the mouse and repeat the steps above to continue panning in one direction.

7. *Press ESC or ENTER to exit, or right-click to display shortcut menu:*
   Press the RMB and select zoom from the view shortcut menu. Zoom in or out by holding the LMB down and dragging the mouse up and down.

8. *Press ESC or ENTER to exit, or right-click to display shortcut menu:*

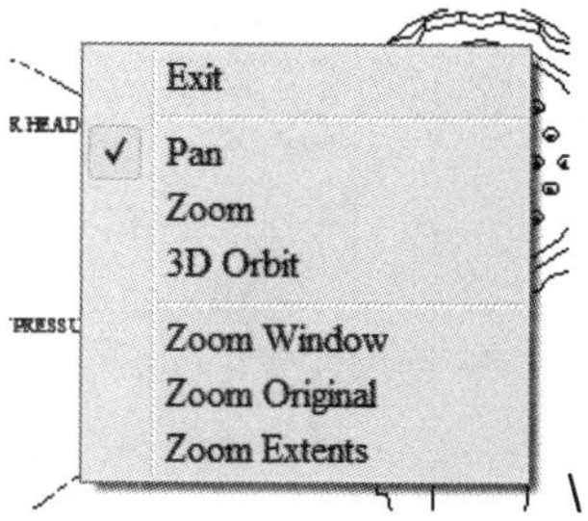

   Press the RMB and switch back to Pan. Pan through the drawing.

9. *Press ESC or ENTER to exit, or right-click to display shortcut menu:*
   Press the RMB and switch to Zoom Window in the shortcut menu. You will create a window with your mouse that will represent the area to zoom in on. Position your mouse to create a rectangular window. Hold your LMB down and drag the mouse diagonally to create a window. Release the left mouse button to finish the command and zoom in on the drawing. Notice that this method is a *drag and release* and works slightly differently then the regular Zoom Window command.

10. *Press ESC or ENTER to exit, or right-click to display shortcut menu:*
    Press the RMB and select Zoom Extents. Notice how AutoCAD zooms to the extents of the drawing. Press the RMB and select the Zoom Original option in the shortcut menu. Notice how the drawing zooms to the original settings that existed when the ZOOM / PAN command was first invoked.

The Microsoft IntelliMouse offers many user friendly viewing options that are automatically invoked by using the Wheel on the IntelliMouse. AutoDesk recommends using the Microsoft IntelliMouse with AutoCAD.

Command Exercise

Exercise 2-2 – Zoom

Drawing Name: **zoom1.dwg**
Estimated Time to Completion: 10 Minutes

Scope

Zoom this drawing out several times then use the Zoom Window option and pick just inside the corners of the red rectangle.

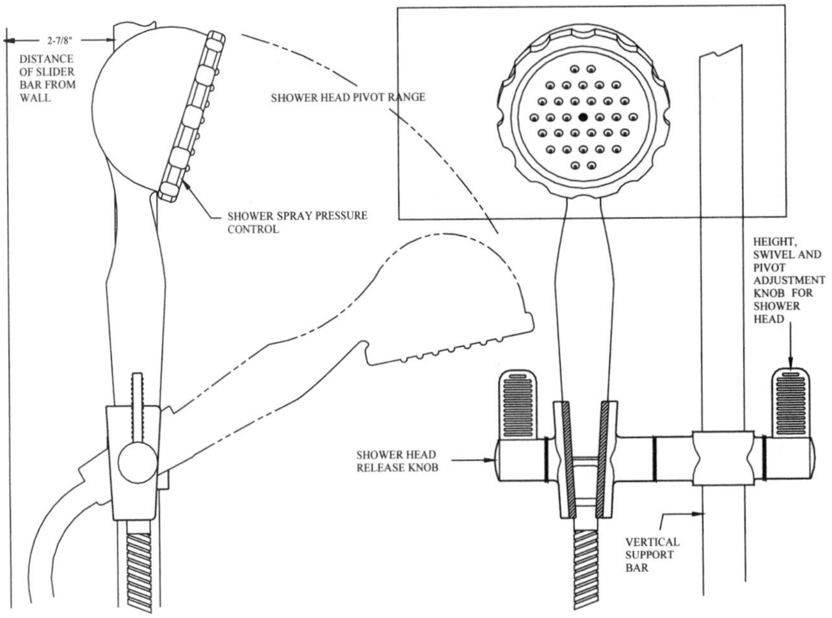

Figure 2 – Zoom Exercise

Solution

1. Invoke the Zoom command. Type **Z** and then use the scroll wheel on the mouse to zoom in and out.

2. *Press ESC or ENTER to exit, or right-click to display shortcut menu.*
   Press the LMB in the middle of the drawing and drag down to zoom out of the drawing.

3. *Press ESC or ENTER to exit, or right-click to display shortcut menu.*
   Press <ENTER> to end the command.

4. Invoke the Zoom Window command (z or zoom and <ENTER> once).

5. *[All/Center/Dynamic/Extents/Previous/Scale/Window/Object] <real time>:*
   Create a window with your mouse that will represent the area to zoom in on. Position your mouse inside a corner of the red box and click the LMB. Move the mouse diagonally to another corner of the box and click the LMB again. Notice how the Arcs and Circles are represented by small straight segments.

Extra: *From the <VIEW<ZOOM pull-down experiment with all the different zoom options available; Scale, Dynamic, Center, In, Out, Previous and All. Which method of viewing your drawing is the easiest?*

- *You can invoke the Zoom Window function directly by typing Z <ENTER> and specifying the opposite corners of the Zoom Window (the Window option is the default).*

Command Exercise

Exercise 2-3 – Modifying the View Ribbon

Drawing Name: **zoom1.dwg**
Estimated Time to Completion: 5 Minutes

Scope

Activate the View Ribbon.
Modify which tabs and panels are available.

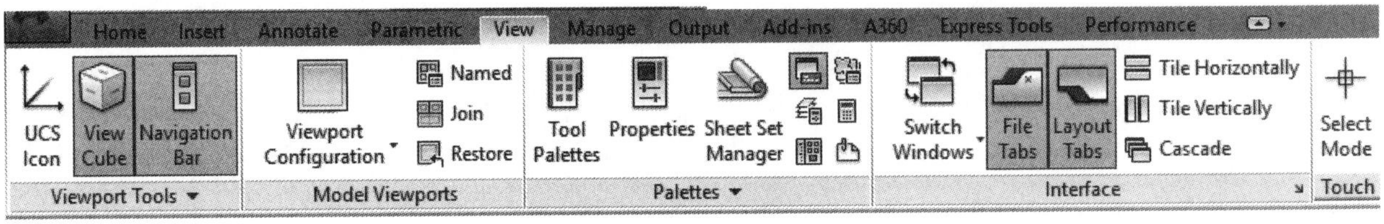

Figure 3 – View Ribbon

Solution

1.

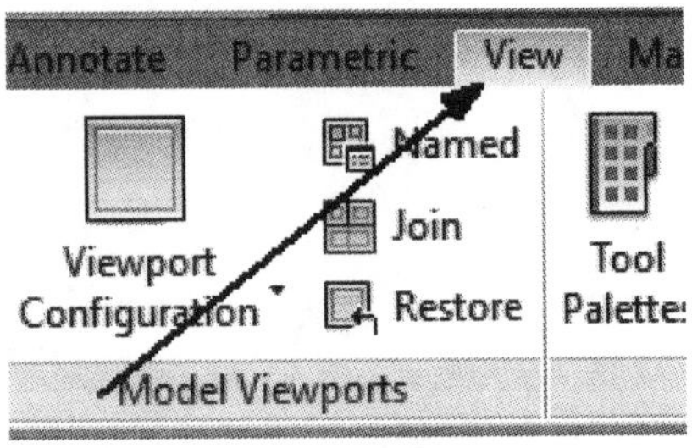

Select the **View** tab on the ribbon.

This activates the View ribbon.

2.

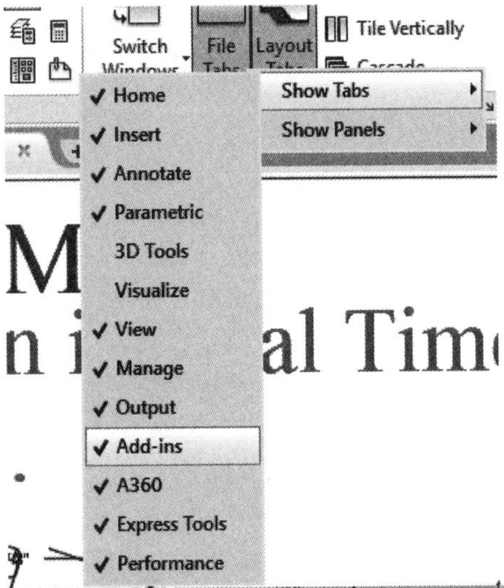

RMB anywhere on the ribbon.

If you expand the Show Tabs menu, you see the different tabs available for the ribbon.

Uncheck **Add-Ins.**

3.

Notice the Add-Ins tab no longer appears.

4. 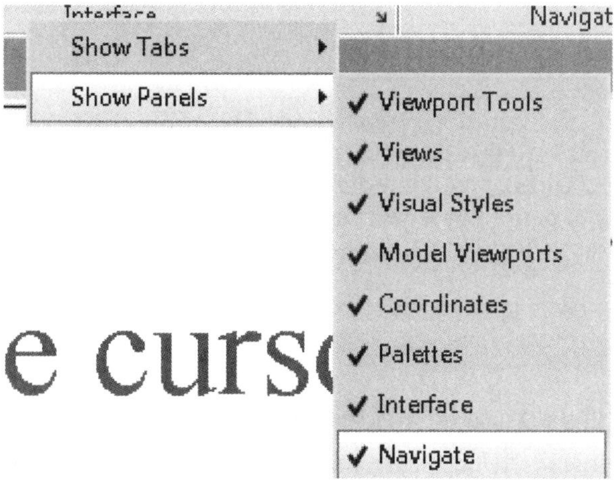

RMB on the ribbon again.

This time expand the Show Panels menu.

Place a check next to each name.

Observe how each panel is added to the ribbon.

> *Changes to the ribbon – like activating tabs and panels – are drawing-independent. Meaning when you change the ribbon, the changes remain regardless of which drawing file you are working on.*

Named Views

Command Locator

Command	**View**
Alias	**V**
Dialog Box	**View**
Ribbon	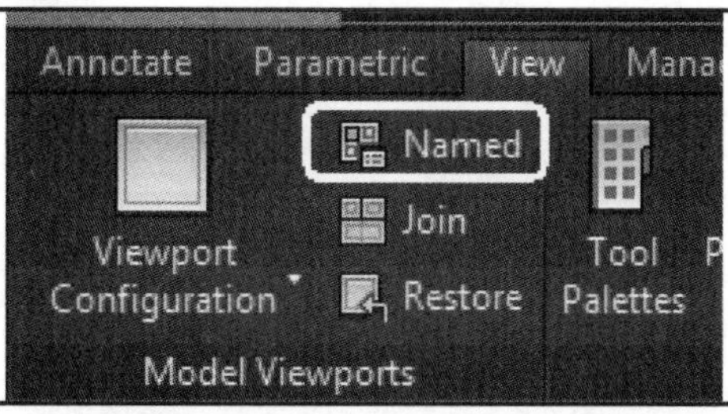

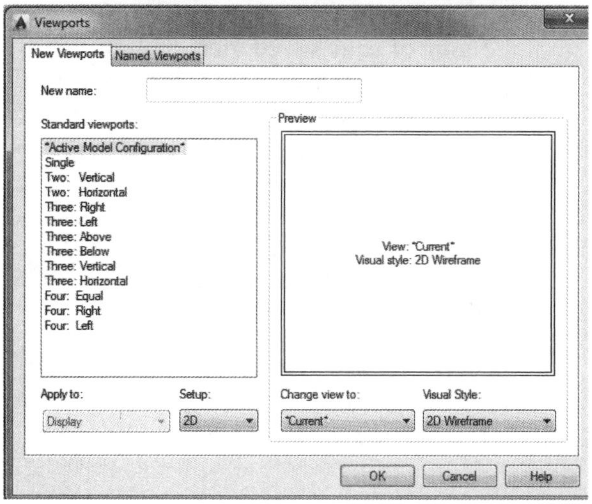

Viewports Dialog Box

Command Overview

Views can be saved and restored with the Named View command. This will save the time it takes to zoom out and in to a frequently selected view. This tutorial will focus on the Named Views area of the View dialog box. New views can be Named as the Current display or defined by a new view (Define Window). Named Views from the list can be selected and set as the Current view.

General Procedures

1. Begin the Named Views command. Highlight 'Current' and select 'New'.
2. In the New View window, type the view name. Select 'Current display' or 'Define Window'. If Define Window is selected, select the cursor arrow and make a window around the desired view in the drawing. If this view is okay, select OK, otherwise try again.
3. Named Views can now be selected from the list and "Set Current."
4. To Delete or Rename a Named View, select it, then right click (RMB) and select the desired option.

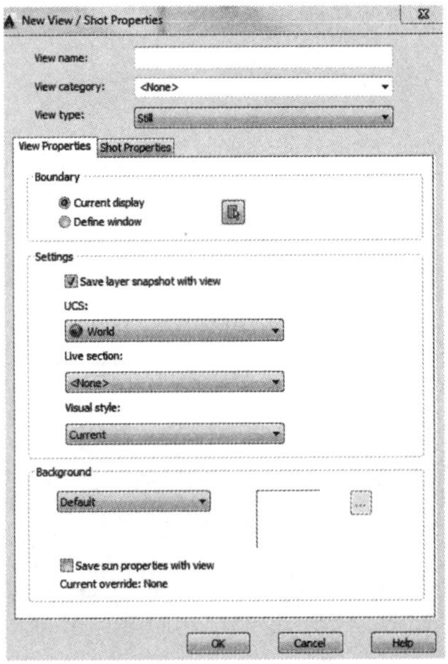

New Named View

View Name	Name of your saved view
View Category	The category is used in the Sheet Set Manager to organize your views. You can add a category or select one from the list. This entry is optional.
View Type	Options are Still, Cinematic and Recorded Walk.
Boundary	Sets the limits of the view.
Save layer snapshot View	Saves the current layer settings.
UCS Name	Allows you to set the view to a specific UCS.
Live section	Displays the live section applied when the view is restored. This option is only available when in the Model space.
Visual Style	Allows you to specify a visual style to be assigned to a view.
Background	Allows you to set a different background color than the current setting. This can only be done for model space views in shaded mode.

Command Exercise

Exercise 2-4 – Saving Named Views

Drawing Name: **nview1.dwg**
Estimated Time to Completion: 5 Minutes

Scope

Zoom into the specified area. With the Named Views command, name the view BALLAST and save it. Zoom All, then restore the named view.

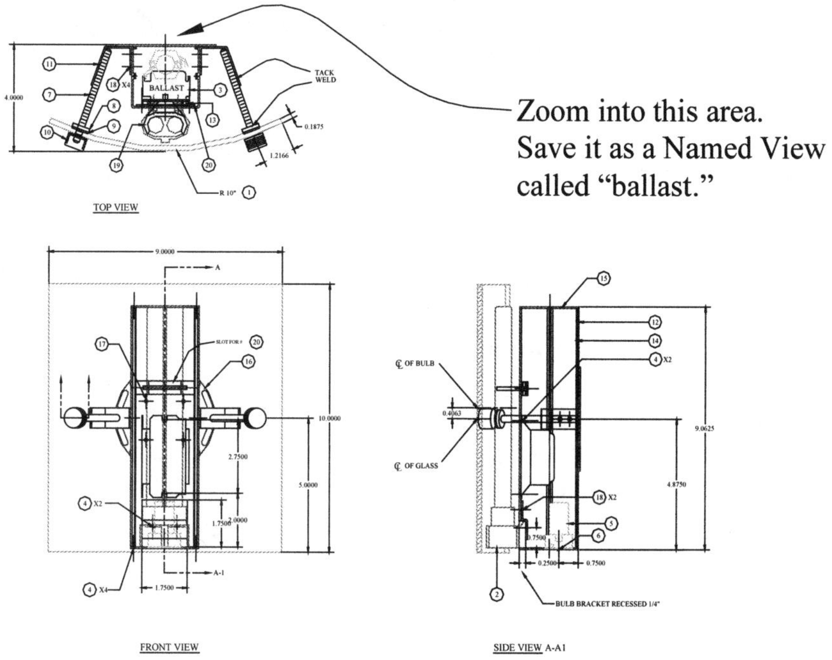

Figure 4 – Named View Exercise

Solution

Enable the Views panel on the ribbon in order to access the proper tools.

1. Invoke the Zoom Window command (z or zoom).

2. *[All/Center/Dynamic/Extents/Previous/Scale/Window/Object] <real time>:*
   Create a window around the desired area of the screen (upper left corner).

3. Invoke the Named Views command (view).
4. Activate the View ribbon and select **View Manager**.

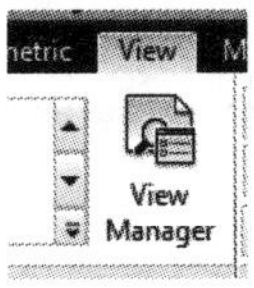

5. Press the **New** button.

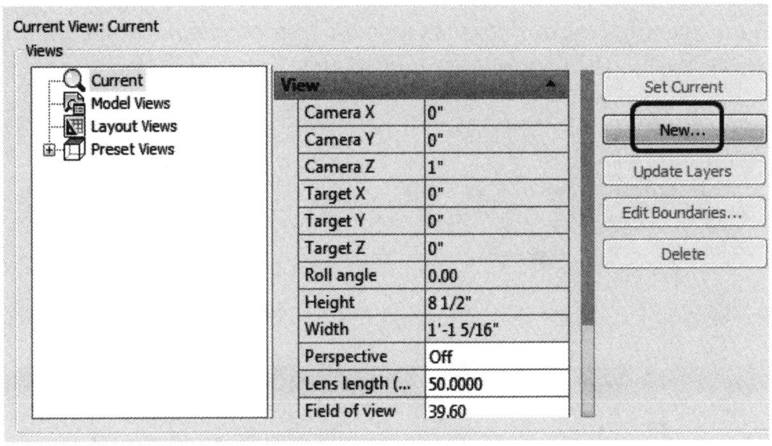

View Manager Dialog Box

6. In the New View dialog box, fill out the information as shown in the next figure and press **Apply**.

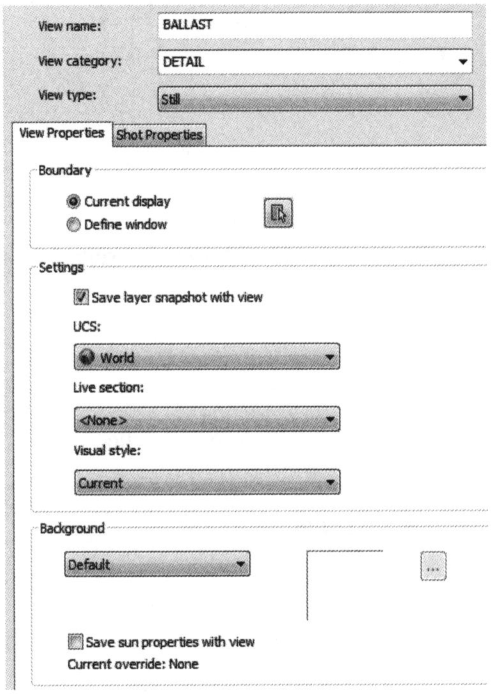

New View Dialog Box

7. Close the View dialog box by pressing **OK**. You have just saved a view that can be recalled at any time. We will zoom out and then restore the view you have just created called **BALLAST**.

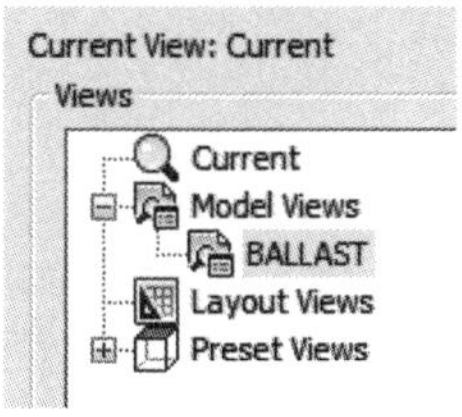

The view you created is listed in the View Manager.

Press **OK** to close the View Manager dialog.

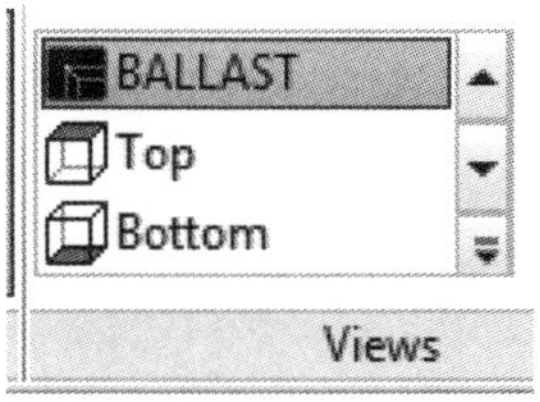

8. Notice that the view name appears in the view list on the ribbon.

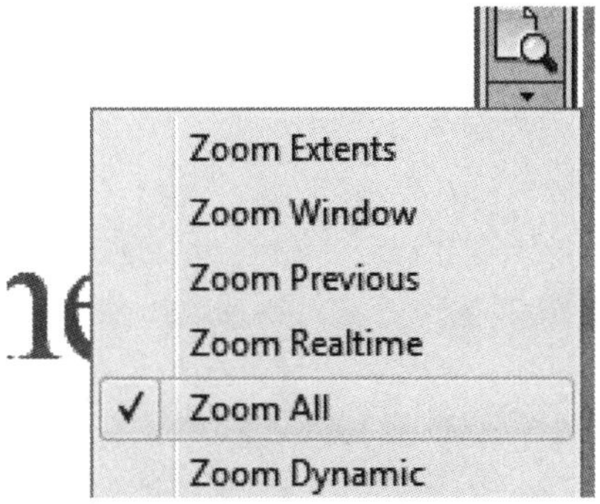

9. Use the dropdown list on the View Navigation bar as shown to invoke the Zoom All command (z or zoom, option a). Notice that the entire drawing is now visible in the drawing window.

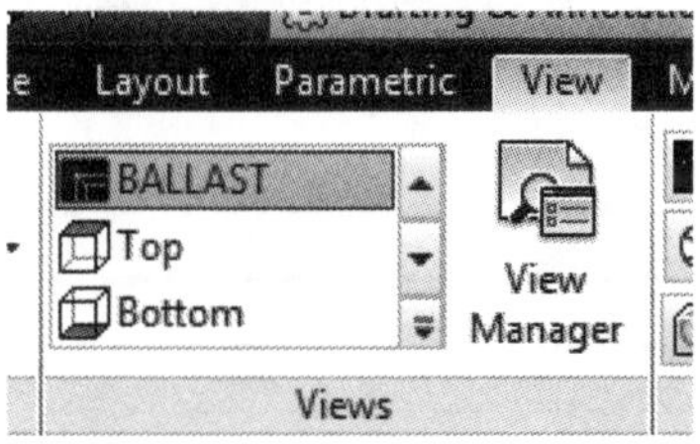

10. Double left click on the BALLAST name in the Views list on the ribbon.

11. Notice how the drawing window now displays the BALLAST view you created at the beginning of the exercise.

Extra: *Practice saving other views in the drawing.*

Tips & Tricks

- Named Views are saved with the drawing file.
- Certain characters are not allowed for the View name.
- Remember to select Current display or Define window for the New Named View.
- You can save layer settings with Named Views to create different views for your layouts.
- The name can be up to 255 characters long and contain letters, digits, and the special characters dollar sign ($), hyphen (–), and underscore (_).
- Named Views can be placed on sheets.

Multiple Viewports

Command Locator

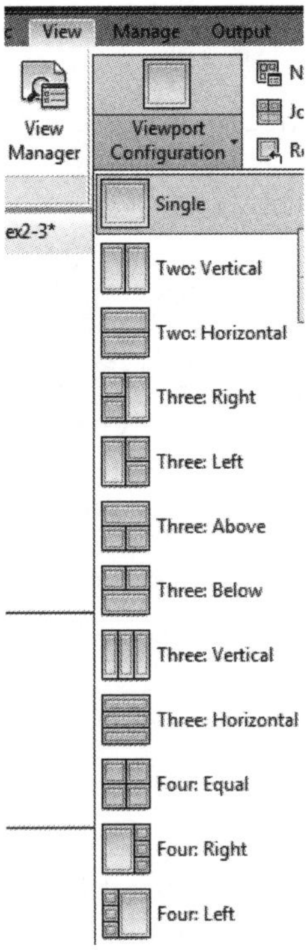

Command	**Viewports**
Alias	**Vports**
RMB Shortcut Menu	**List box**
Dialog Box	**Viewports**
Ribbon	**View/Model Viewports**

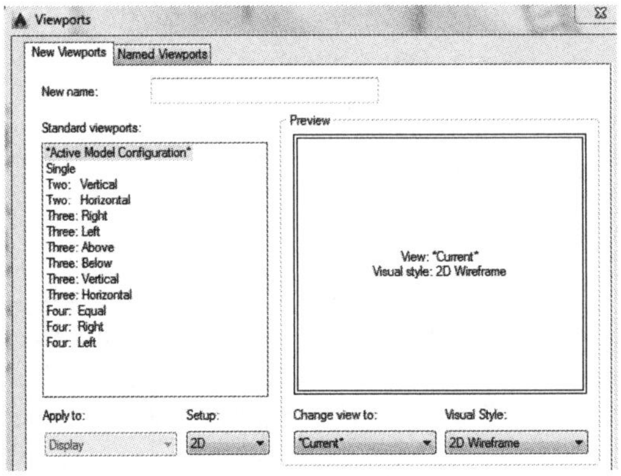

Viewports Dialog Box

Command Overview

The Model view of the drawing can be divided into Multiple Viewports. Each viewport can display a different part of the drawing; however, only one viewport may be active. Tiled viewports configurations, including the views within each viewport, can be named and selected to be current later in the drawing.

General Procedures

To create one, two, three, etc. viewports:

1. Select the desired number of viewports from the Pull-Down (POP) menu, View / (select 1, 2, 3, or 4 viewports).
2. Follow the command line prompts. For three viewports, "Right" is the default location for the largest viewport.

To create viewports using the Viewports dialog box:

1. Type vports, or select the POP option View / Viewports / New Viewports…
2. Select the viewport configuration from the list.

To use Multiple Viewports:

1. Select a viewport to make it active.
2. Use any of the Zoom commands. To draw between viewports, click on one viewport and pick a point, then click on the other viewport to continue drawing the object.

To Save a Viewport Configuration:

1. From the Viewport dialog box, select the New Viewports tab.
2. Type in the New name for the current viewport configuration.
3. This name will appear in the list, and later can be selected and made current.

Tips & Tricks

- An active viewport is the one with the bolder border around it. The cursor crosshairs will also be visible in the active viewport.
- Named Viewport configurations are saved with the drawing file.

Command Exercise

Exercise 2-5 – Multiple Viewports

Drawing Name: **vport1.dwg**
Estimated Time to Completion: 10 Minutes

Scope

Create four tiled viewports. Restore a named view in each viewport. Save the viewport configuration as V1. Join two adjacent views and save this as V2. Change to a single viewport. Restore the Saved viewport configurations.

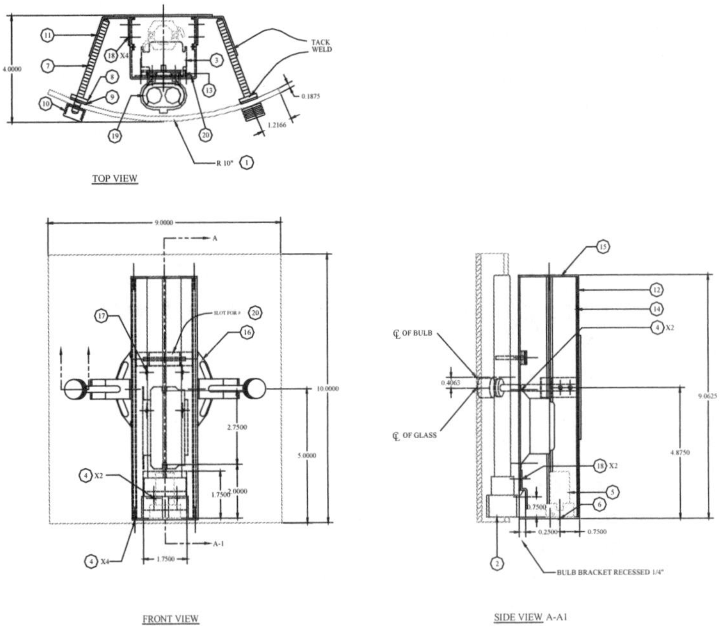

Figure 5 – Multiple Viewports Exercise

Solution

1. Start the exercise by creating four tiled viewports.

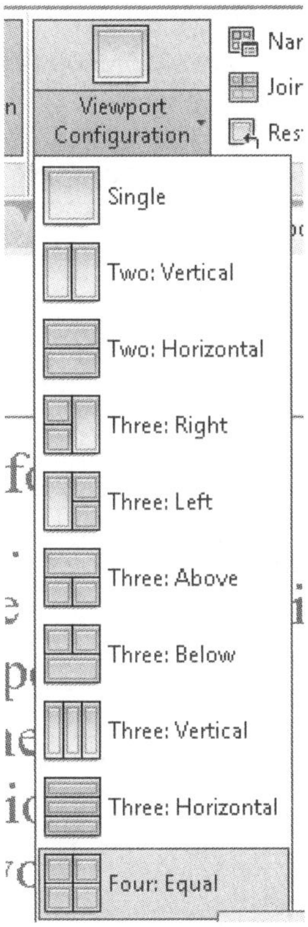

On the View ribbon:

Select Viewport Configuration→Four:Equal.

2. Notice how the drawing window is divided into 4 viewports. The same view is displayed in all four viewports. We will now restore different Named Views in each viewport.

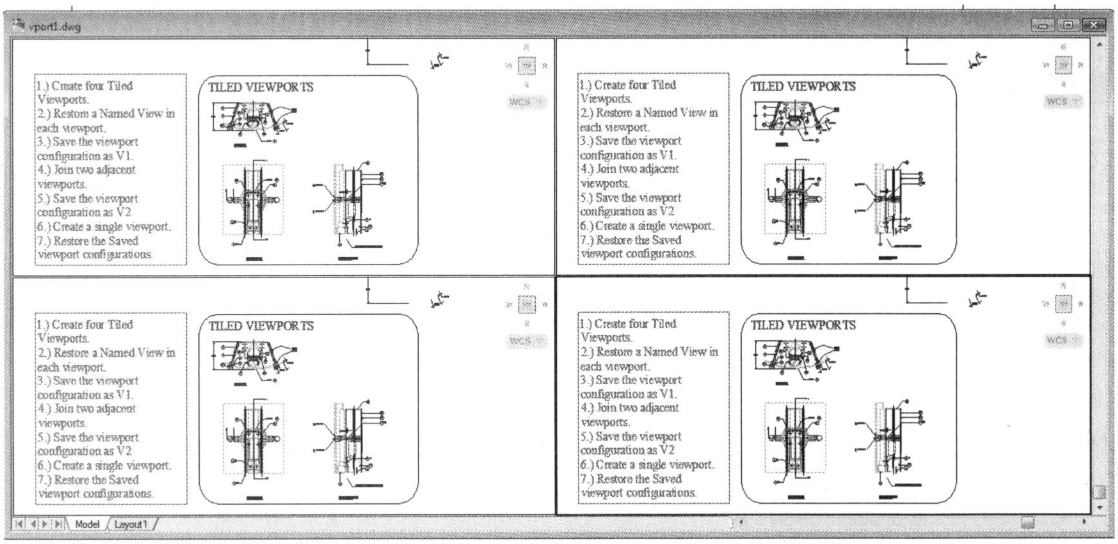

Four Viewports

3. Move your pointer to the upper left corner viewport and activate the viewport by clicking inside it with your LMB.

4. On the View ribbon, locate the View Manager with the view names listed.

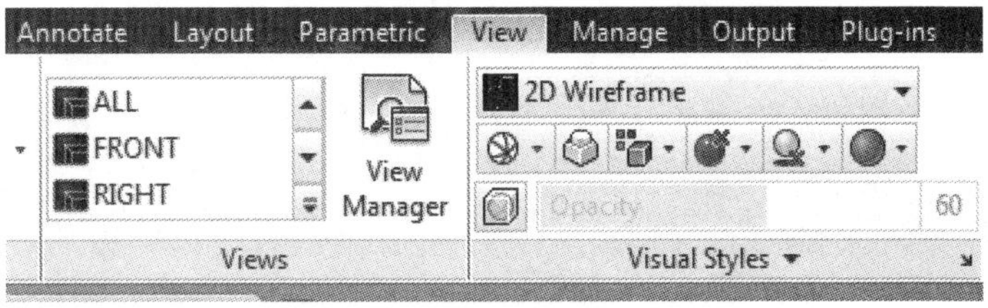

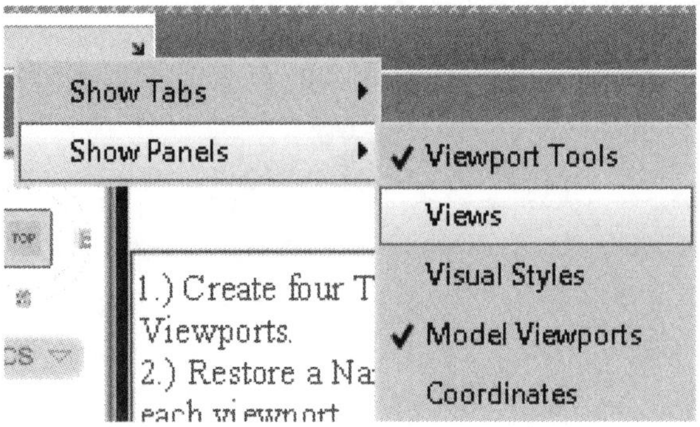

If you do not see the Views panel on the ribbon, you need to enable it.

Right click on the ribbon and select **Show Panels→Views**.

5. In the View list, double-click on 'TOP' to set it current for the viewport.

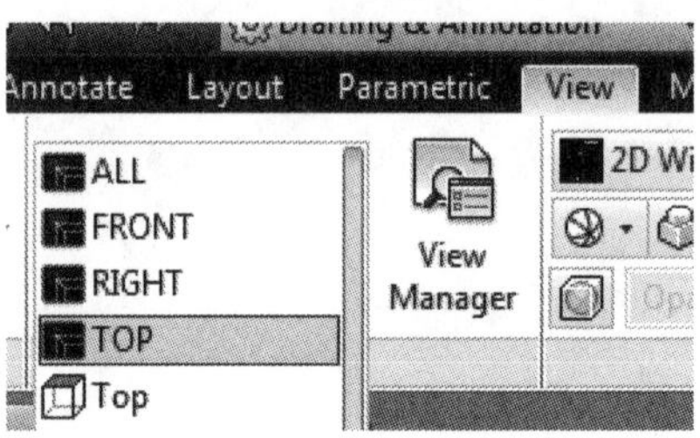

View Dialog Box

6. Move your cursor to the bottom left corner viewport and activate the viewport by clicking inside it with your LMB.

7. Double left click on the FRONT view to assign it to the bottom left viewport.

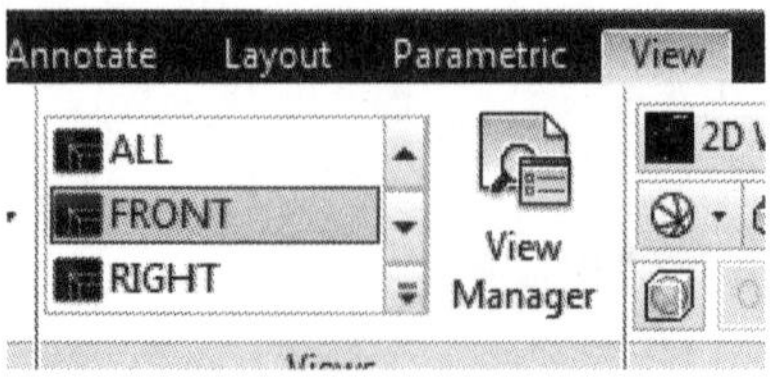

8. Move your cursor to the bottom right corner viewport and activate the viewport by clicking inside it with your LMB.

9. Double left click on the RIGHT view to assign it to the bottom left viewport.

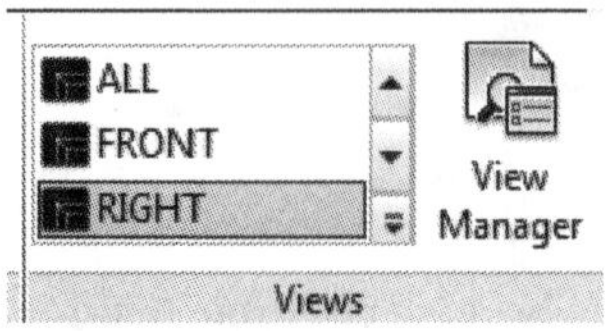

10. Your drawing may look similar to the next figure.

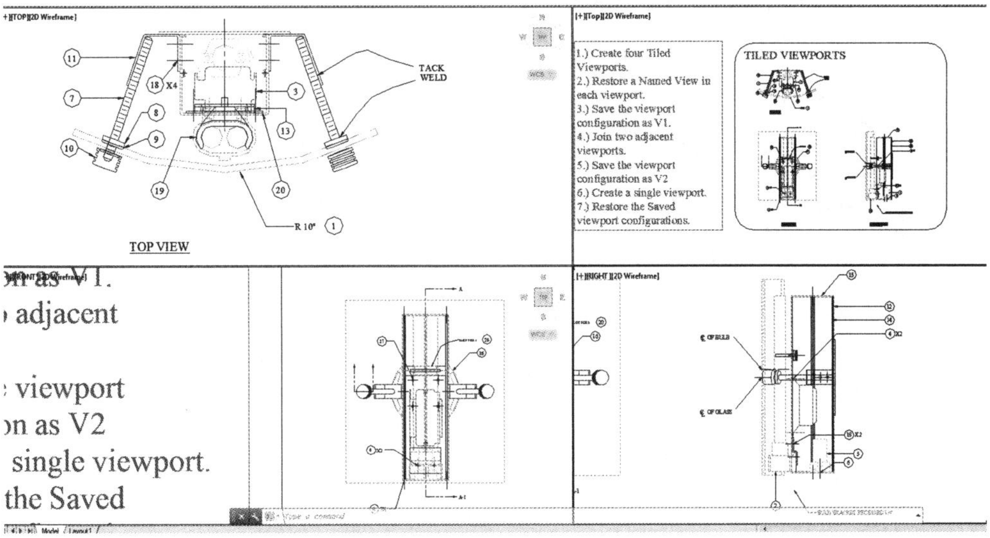

Four Viewports after Changing the Views

11. Once you have created the layout above, save the configuration. Select **Named** on the Model Viewports panel from the View ribbon.

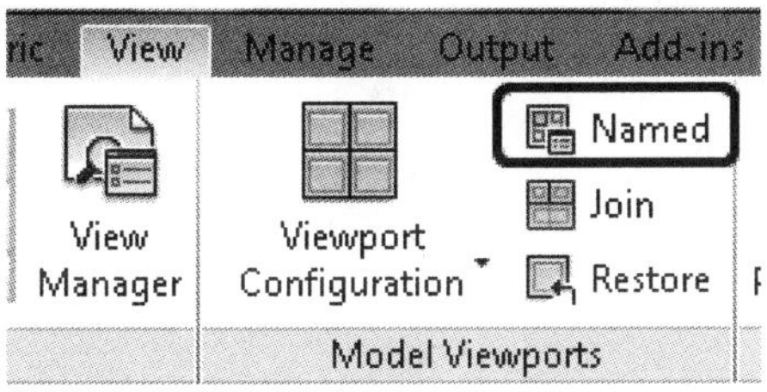

12. In the Viewports dialog box enter the information displayed in the following figure. Enter **V1** for the new name. Press **OK** to save. You have just saved a viewport configuration that can be restored at any time.

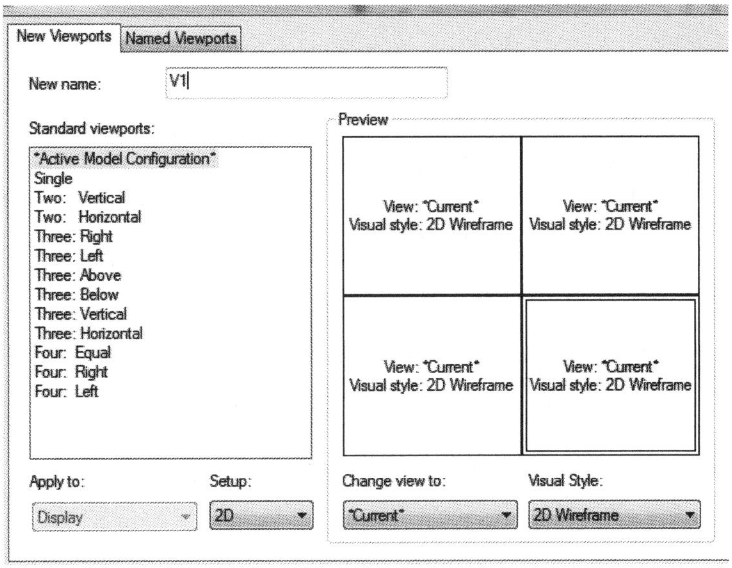

Viewports Dialog Box

13. Click on the **Restore** button on the ribbon.

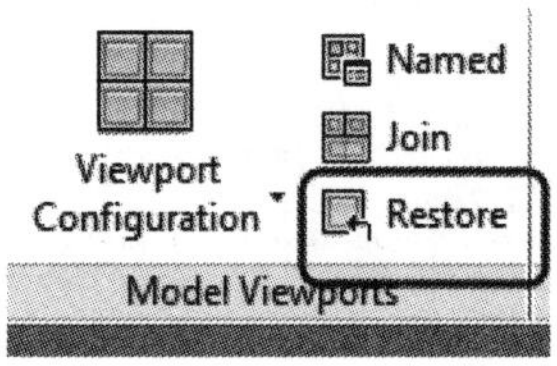

14. The display changes back to a single viewport.

15. Select **Named**.

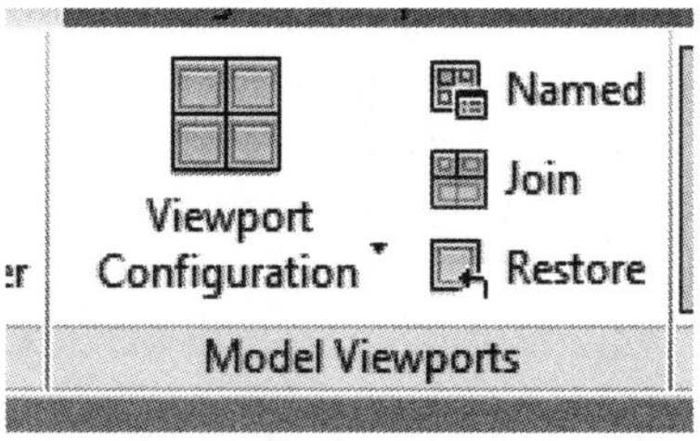

16. Left click on V1 – the named configuration you just created with four viewports. Press **OK**.

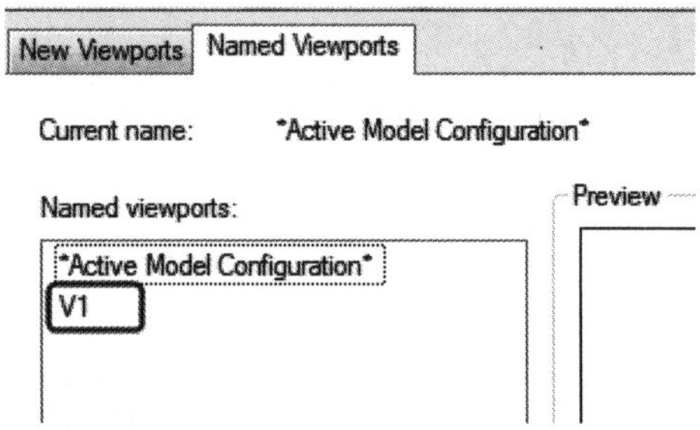

17. The V1 configuration is restored.

➢ *Use your RMB to activate a pop up dialog box that will allow you to delete or rename your viewport configurations (Named Viewports) in the Viewports dialog box.*

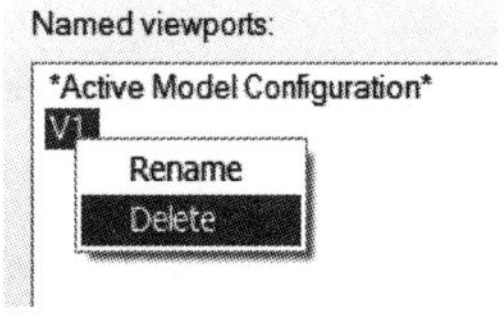

Lesson Exercise

Exercise 2-6

Viewing Drawings

Drawing Name: **Lesson 2 MCAD.dwg**
Estimated Time to Completion: 15 Minutes

Scope

Use the commands you have learned in the past Lesson to view the drawing. Determine which viewing commands are easier for you to use. Locate information on the drawing and fill out the table below. Follow the instructions on the drawing for creating a named view and tiled viewport layout. Save the file as Lesson 2 MCAD_complete.dwg.

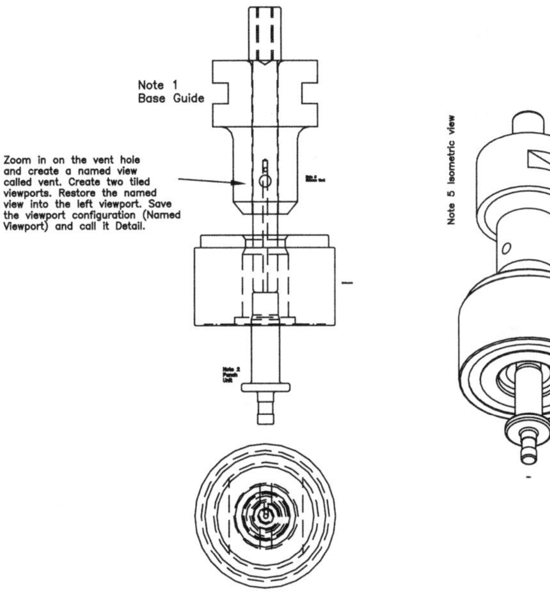

Figure 6 – Viewing Drawings

Hints

1. Choose a zoom command you feel comfortable with. The author likes the Zoom Window and Zoom Previous commands.
2. Note 6 is under the Isometric drawing. Note 7 is under the number 6 in Note 6.
3. Use the named views command and named viewports command to complete the second part of the exercise.

Lesson Exercise

Exercise 2-7

View Commands

Drawing Name: **Lesson 2 aec.dwg**
Estimated Time to Completion: **15 Minutes**

Scope

Using the commands learned in this Lesson, zoom and pan around the drawing. Examine the named views in the drawing and create named views of the kitchen, bath and small bedroom. View the drawing with multiple viewports.

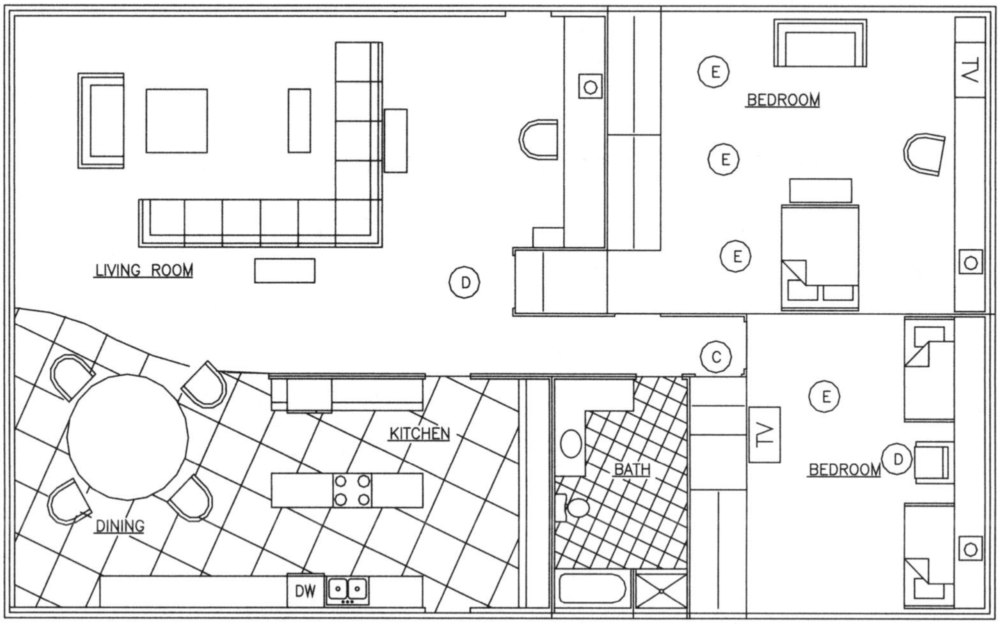

Figure 7 – View Commands Lesson Exercise

Hints

1. Use the different zoom options to become familiar with all of them.
2. Zoom in on the kitchen and create a named view of it. Do the same for the bathroom and small bedroom.
3. Use the Viewports command to bring up multiple viewports and show a different room in each viewport.

Review Questions

1. Identify the following icons by writing the command:

   Command

   a.  ______________________

   b.  ______________________

   c.  ______________________

   d.  ______________________

   e.  ______________________

   f.  ______________________

   g.  ______________________

2. What is the difference between Zoom Extents and Zoom All?

3. Which Zoom tools are available on the right click shortcut menu?

4. How do you make a viewport active? How can you tell that a viewport is active?

5. How many viewports can be active at the same time?
   - ❑ 1
   - ❑ 2
   - ❑ 3
   - ❑ As many as the user decides.

6. Can you create a new Viewport configuration (Named Viewport) if you activate the Viewport dialog box by selecting <VIEW<VIEWPORTS<NAMED VIEWPORTS… and Not <VIEW<VIEWPORTS<NEW VIEWPORTS…?

Review Answers

1. Identify the following icons by writing the command and the toolbars where they can be found:
   a. *Named View / Standard*
   b. *Pan Real-time / Standard*
   c. *Zoom / Standard*
   d. *Zoom Window / Standard & Zoom Toolbar*
   e. *Zoom Previous / Standard*
   f. *Zoom All / Standard & Zoom Toolbar*
   g. *Zoom Extents / Standard & Zoom Toolbar*

2. What is the difference between Zoom Extents and Zoom All?

   Zoom Extents will zoom only all of the geometry in the drawing. Zoom All will zoom everything - the drawing geometry and the drawing limits (grid area).

3. Which Zoom tools are available on the right click shortcut menu?

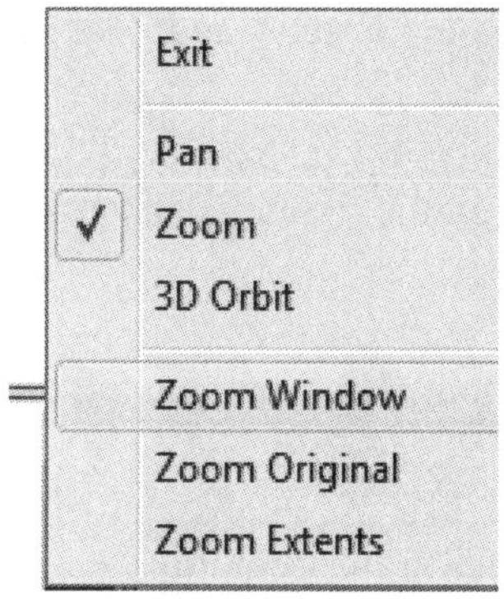

   Zoom Window, Zoom Original, and Zoom Extents

4. How do you make a viewport active? How can you tell that a viewport is active?

   a. To make a viewport active, place the cursor in the viewport and select the left button on the mouse (LMB).

   b. An active viewport will have a slightly bolder border around it, and will show the cursor crosshairs in it.

5. How many viewports can be active at the same time?

   ■ 1
   ❑ 2
   ❑ 3
   ❑ As many as the user decides.

   Only one viewport can be active in AutoCAD at one time.

6. Can you create a new Viewport configuration (Named Viewport) if you activate the Viewport dialog box by selecting <VIEW<VIEWPORTS<NAMED VIEWPORTS… and Not <VIEW<VIEWPORTS<NEW VIEWPORTS…?

   Yes, The viewport dialog box has two tabs: Named Viewports and New Viewports. Users can switch to either tab no matter how the dialog box was activated.

Lesson 3.0 – Drawing Lines

Estimated Class Time: 2 Hours

Objectives

This section introduces AutoCAD commands for creating a simple drawing. Starting with a New drawing, the user will learn to draw lines using different methods.

- **Start From Scratch**
  Use the New command to begin a new drawing from "scratch."
- **Line**
  Draw line segments
  Using Direct Distance Method
  Using Polar Tracking
  Using Cartesian Coordinates
  Absolute Coordinates
  Relative Coordinates
  Polar Coordinates
  Drag Method
- **Coordinate Entry**
- **Erase**
  Deleting AutoCAD entities
- **Constraints**
  Managing Geometric Constraints

Start from Scratch

Command Locator

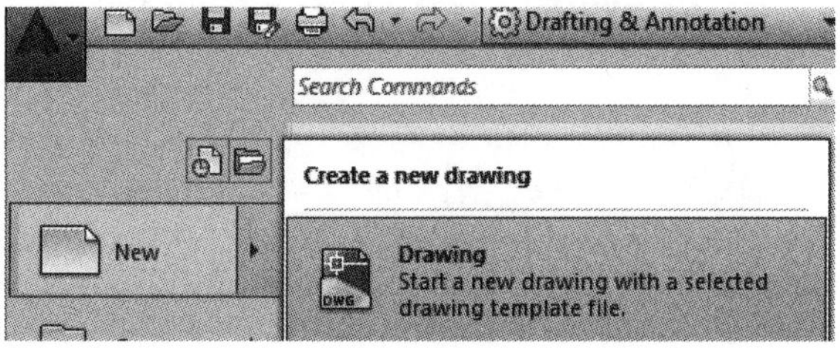

Command	**New**
Alias	**Ctrl+N**

For the exercises in this section, we will be using the *acad.dwt* template. This template setting was made when AutoCAD was installed. If you want to set a different default template to be used, go to the **Options** dialog and select the default template you wish to use.

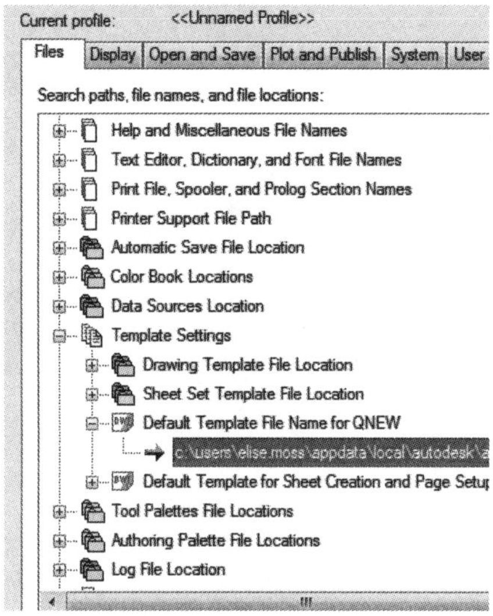

The Options Dialog

Command Overview

To Create a New drawing, choose New. Every time the New drawing command is invoked, a new drawing is created with the title Drawing1, Drawing2, Drawing3, etc.

General Procedures

1. Select the New button from the Standard Toolbar.

- Make it a habit to select the New file icon from the Quick Access Toolbar. This is a quicker way to access the command than from the Applications menu.
- Close drawings that are not being used.

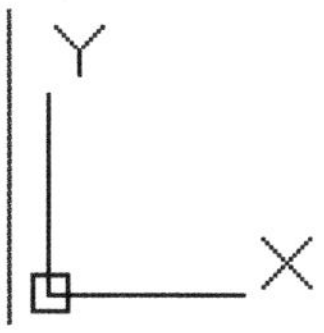
Y
X

The graphics window uses a Cartesian coordinate system. The lower left corner of the screen shows a UCS (user coordinate system) icon. The icon shows x for horizontal and y for vertical. The z-axis is pointed toward the user. The UCS is located at the 0,0 or origin point.

1.6898, 14.1004, 0.0000 MODEL

In the middle of your screen, you will see some numbers. These numbers reflect the coordinate point (x, y) of your mouse. Move your mouse around and note how the coordinate values change.

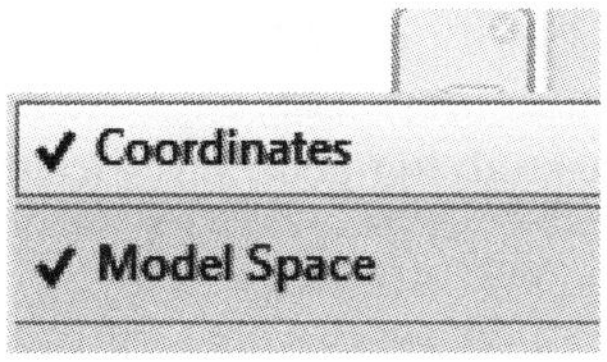
✓ Coordinates
✓ Model Space

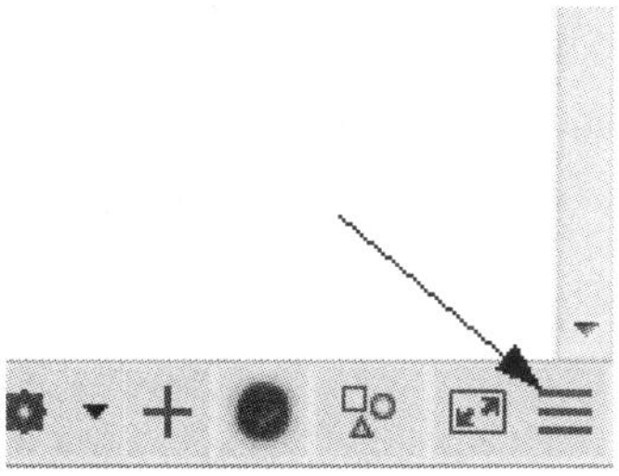

- To toggle the display of coordinates, left click on the Customize tool in the lower left of the screen and left click on Coordinates in the list.

Your graphics window in AutoCAD emulates a piece of paper. LIMITS controls the size of your piece of paper. When you start a new file, you can specify the size of paper you want to draw on using Wizards or Templates. AutoCAD really doesn't care where you draw in your graphics window. You can draw outside the limits with impunity.

AutoCAD allows you to draw geometry using four methods:

- Absolute Coordinates
- Relative Coordinates
- Polar Coordinates
- Direct Entry

Absolute Coordinates use absolute values relative to the origin.

Relative Coordinates use coordinates relative to the last point selected.

Polar Coordinates use a distance and angle relative to the last point selected.

Direct Entry allows the user to set ORTHO on (this is like using a ruler to draw a straight line), move the mouse in the desired direction, and then enter in the desired distance.

AutoCAD allows you to draw geometry using four methods:

- Absolute Coordinates
- Relative Coordinates
- Polar Coordinates
- Direct Entry

Absolute Coordinates use absolute values relative to the origin.

Relative Coordinates use coordinates relative to the last point selected.

Polar Coordinates use a distance and angle relative to the last point selected.

Direct Entry allows the user to set ORTHO on (this is like using a ruler to draw a straight line), move the mouse in the desired direction, and then enter in the desired distance.

There are two types of parametric constraints:

1. Geometric constraints control the shape of elements, such as lines and arcs, and their relationship to each other. For example, a horizontal constraint on a line ensures the line will be straight/ orthogonal and parallel/coincident to the x-axis. A vertical constraint ensures a line will be straight/orthogonal and parallel/coincident to the y-axis. I tease my students that they should have paid better attention when they were studying geometry because all those geometric symbols - parallel, perpendicular, tangent - make an appearance and are used for geometric constraints.

2. Dimensional constraints control the distance, length, angle, and radius values of elements.

Line

Command Locator

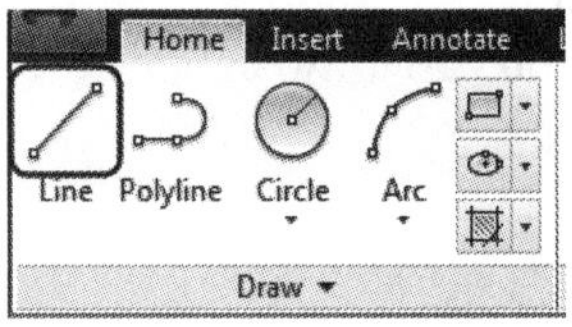

Command	**Line**
Alias	L

Command Overview

A line is defined by two endpoints. A line has 0 width and 0 thickness. When drawing a line, specify the first point, then specify the next point. Press the enter button on the mouse (with the cursor in the drawing window) to access the Line Shortcut menu. Type C to close two or more line segments. Use the LMB to pick the points.

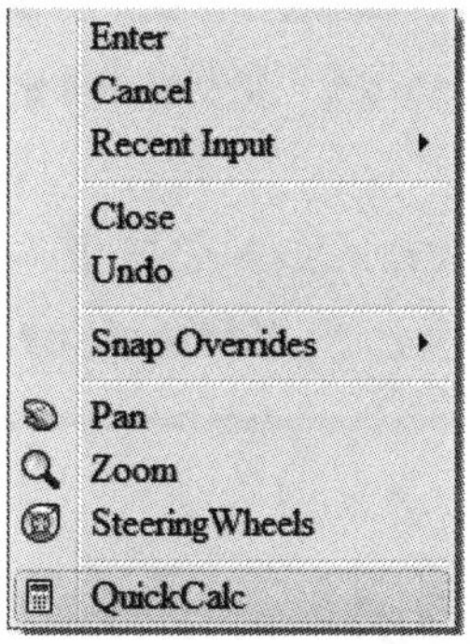

Line Shortcut Menu

Line Shortcut Menu Option:	Overview
Enter	Select to exit the Line command.
Cancel	Cancels the command.
Recent Input	Lists the most recently entered point coordinates.
Close	Closes the line to form a closed polygon.
Undo	Undoes the last segment of the line.
Snap Overrides	Allows the user to select a snap.
Pan	Begins Real-Time Pan.
Zoom	Begins Real-Time Zoom.
Steering Wheels	Launches the Steering Wheel control.
QuickCalc	Launches a calculator.

General Procedures

1. Begin the line command by selecting the line icon in the Draw panel on the ribbon or typing L at the blank command prompt.
2. Select the first point, select the next point, and continue selecting the endpoints of each successive line segment.
3. Press the <ENTER> button on the mouse (with the cursor in the drawing window), then select <ENTER> to end the Line command.
4. Press <ENTER> to Repeat the Line command.

Tips & Tricks

- Move the mouse after selecting each endpoint of the line. This will make it easier to see the last line segment created.
- Double click on ORTHO in the Status Bar (or press F8) to alternate between drawing straight or angled line segments.
- Typing U for Undo in the middle of the line command will undo the last line segment. Typing U after completing line segments (at the blank command prompt) will Undo the entire line command.

Command Exercise

Exercise 3-1— Line using Direct Distance Method

Drawing Name: **Begin a new drawing**
Estimated Time to Completion: 10 Minutes

Scope

Start a New drawing. Enable DYN. With ORTHO on, draw the object below. Drag the line in the desired direction and type the distance. Do not add the dimensions.

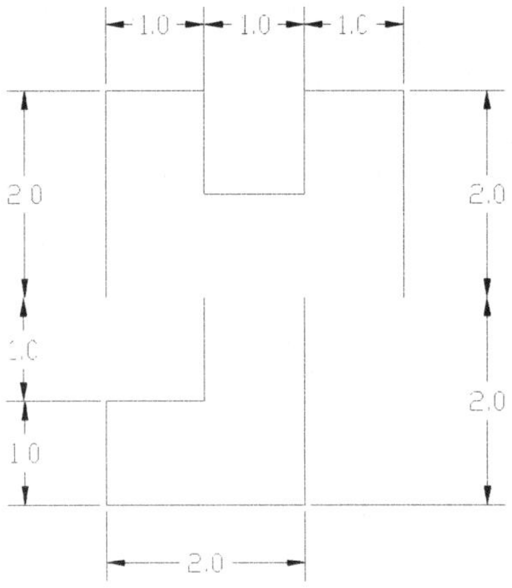

Figure 1 – Line Exercise

Solution

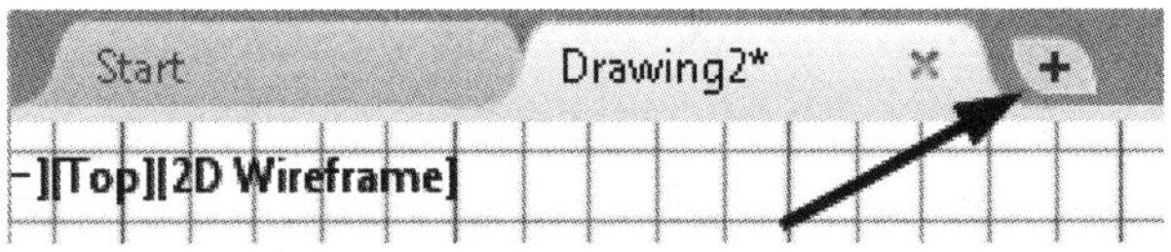

1. Start a New drawing by pressing the + tab.

2. Turn **ORTHO** on by pressing <F8> until the command line says '<Ortho on>'.

3. To see the geometric constraints as they are added, enable **Infer Constraints** or press **Ctrl+Shift+I**.

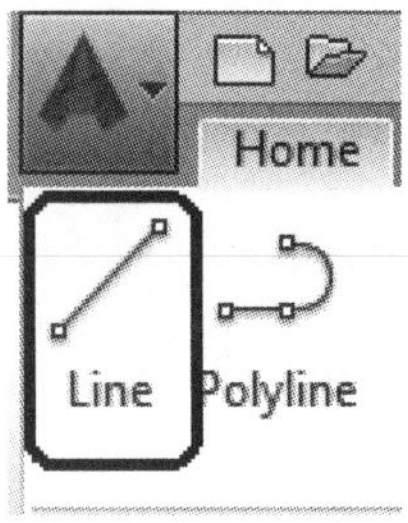

4. Invoke the **Line** command (l or line) on the Home ribbon.

5. *Specify next point or [Undo]:*
   Type **2.5** for the X-coordinate.
   Use the TAB key to advance to the Y-coordinate square.
   Type **3.5** for the Y-coordinate. Press <**ENTER**>.

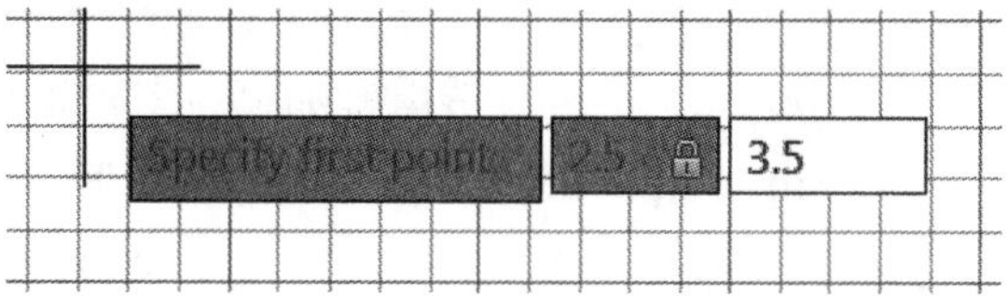

6. *Specify next point or [Undo]:*
   Drag the cursor downward and type **2.00** and press <ENTER>.

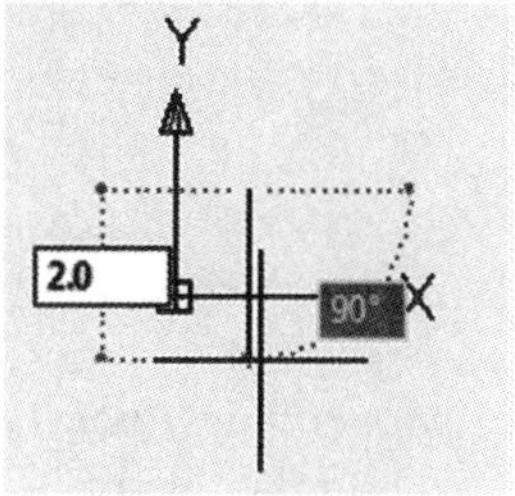

You will see a small icon next to the line. This is a geometric constraint.

A geometric constraint controls the geometry of an element. In this case, the symbol indicates that the line is vertical.

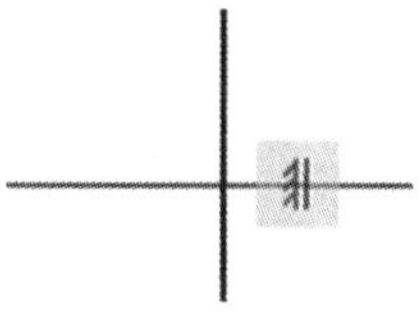

7. *Specify next point or [Undo]:*
   Drag the cursor to the right and type **1.00** and press <ENTER>.

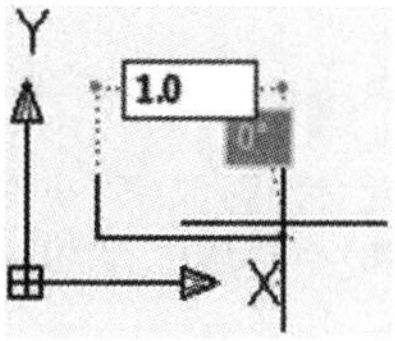

You should see another geometric constraint. This symbol indicates that the two lines are perpendicular to each other. Perpendicular means two lines form a 90°angle.

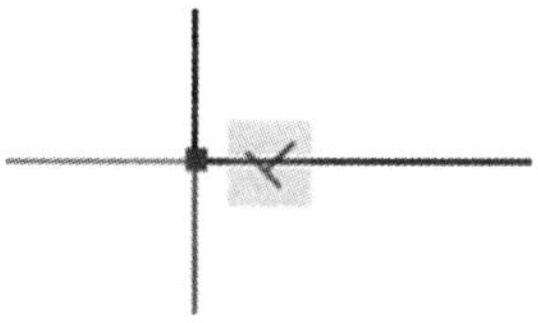

8. *Specify next point or [Close/Undo]:*
   Drag the cursor downward and type **1.00** and press <ENTER>.

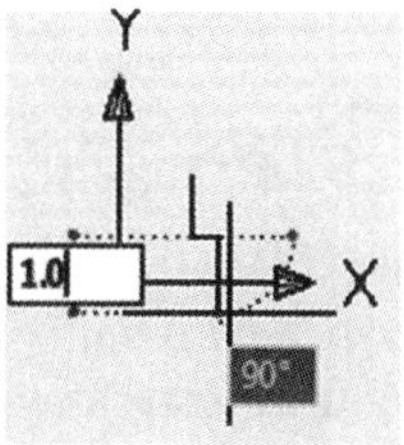

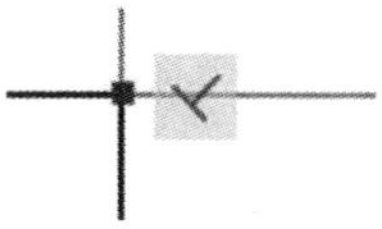

Another perpendicular symbol is added.

9. *Specify next point or [Close/Undo]:*
   Drag the cursor to the left and type **1.00** and press <ENTER>.

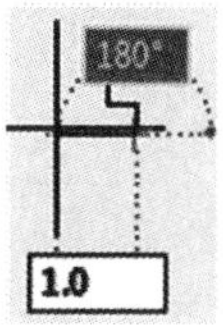

10. *Specify next point or [Close/Undo]:*
    Drag the cursor downward and type **1.00** and press <ENTER>.

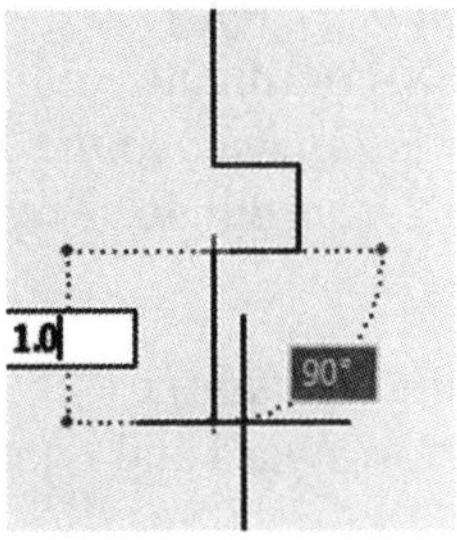

11. *Specify next point or [Close/Undo]:*
    Drag the cursor to the right and type **2.00** and press <ENTER>.

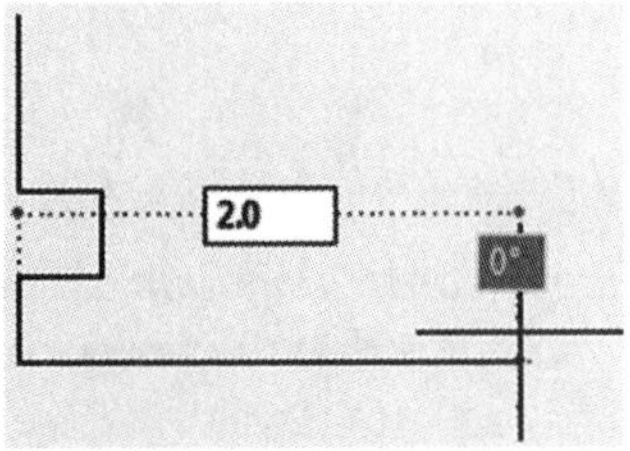

12. *Specify next point or [Close/Undo]:*
    Drag the cursor up and type **2.00** and press <ENTER>.

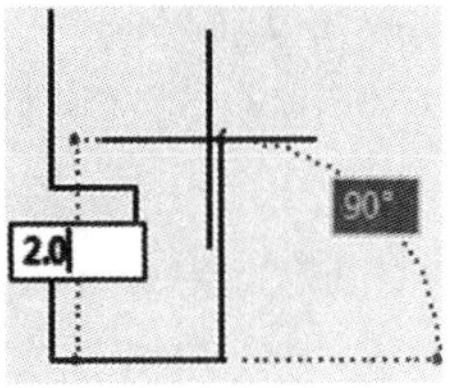

13. *Specify next point or [Close/Undo]:*
    Drag the cursor to the right and type **1.00** and press <ENTER>.

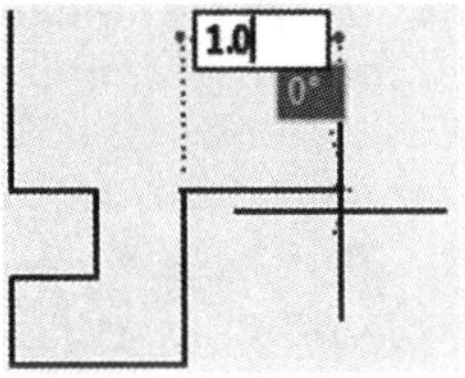

14. *Specify next point or [Close/ Undo]:*
    Drag the cursor upward and type **2.00** and press <ENTER>.

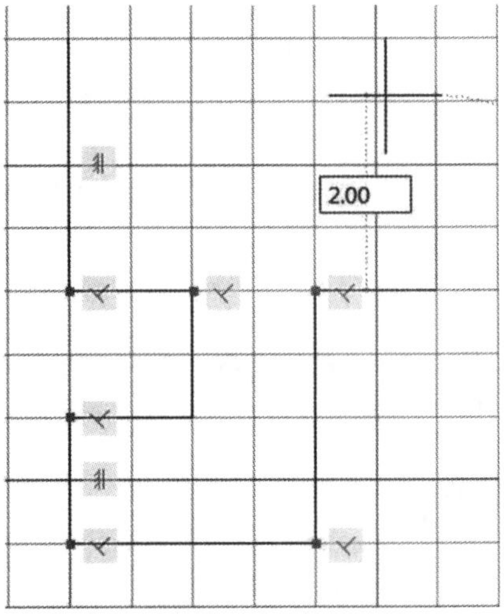

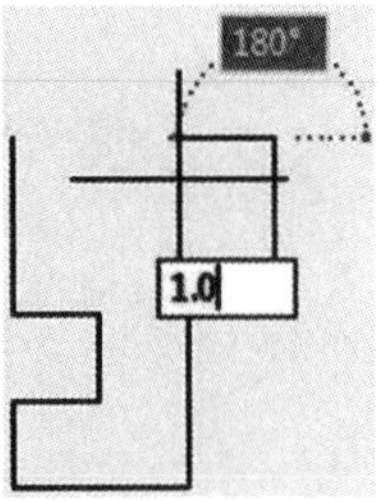

15. *Specify next point or [Close/Undo]:*
    Drag the cursor to the left and type **1.00** and press <ENTER>.

16. *Specify next point or [Close/Undo]:*
    Drag the cursor downward and type **1.00** and press <ENTER>.

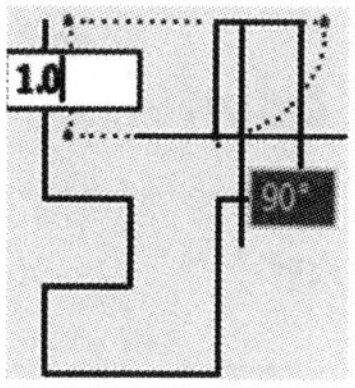

17. *Specify next point or [Close/Undo]:*
    Drag the cursor to the left and type **1.00** and press <ENTER>.

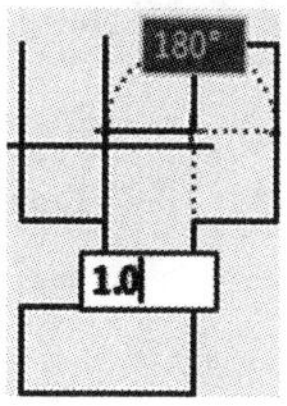

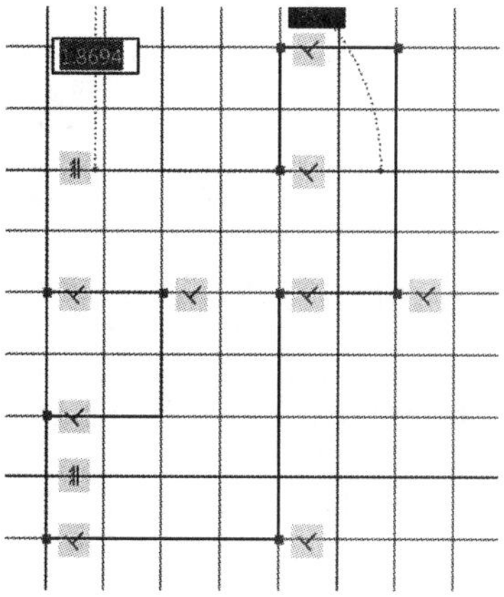

18. *Specify next point or [Close/Undo]:*
    Drag the cursor upward and type **1.00** and press <ENTER>.

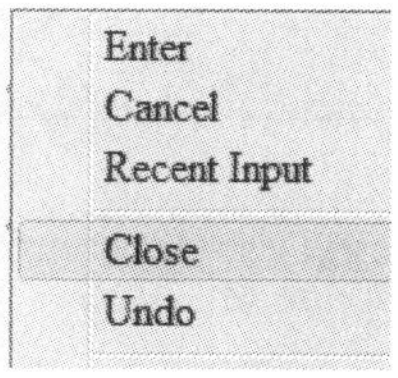

19. *Specify next point or [Close/Undo]:*
    Right-click in the drawing area and select 'Close' or type 'C' and press <ENTER>.

The Close command will only work if you created a continuous line. If you exited the line command and started again, then you have to manually close the figure.

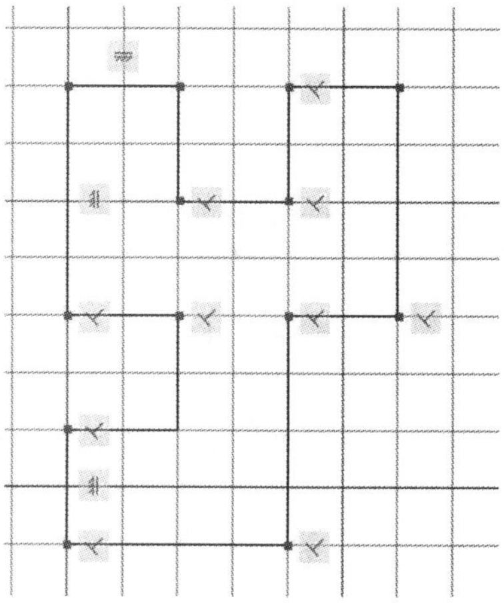

Your completed figure should look like this.

See if you can identify the different geometric constraints. You should see constraint symbols for vertical, horizontal and perpendicular.

If the lines look crooked, then ORTHO is not on. You must begin again. Try to draw all of the line segments without starting and stopping the line command.

*The **Close** option only works if you draw in one continuous line. Otherwise, you can simply draw a closing line from endpoint to endpoint.*

Parametric Constraints

Command Locator

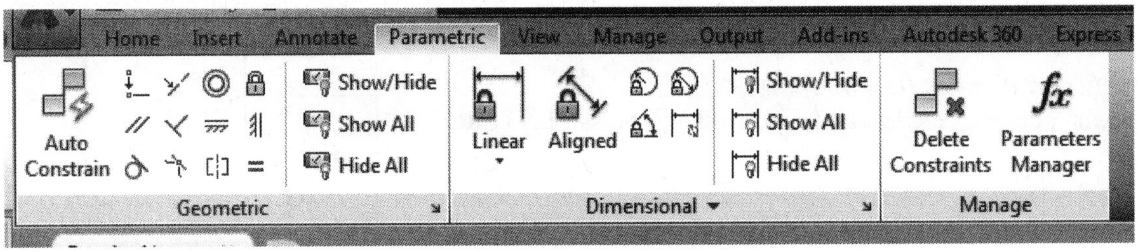

Parametric Ribbon	**Parametric**
Command	**Geomconstraint**

Command Overview

To see the parametric constraints ribbon, you should have the Drafting & Annotation Workspace enabled.

General Procedures

1. To apply a geometric constraint, select the type of geometric constraint desired, then select the element(s) to be constrained.

Tips & Tricks

- Use inferred constraints - these are constraints which are automatically added as you draw.
- Hide geometric constraints when you are not actively constraining your sketch.
- Typing U for Undo in the middle of the line command will undo the last line segment. Typing U after completing line segments (at the blank command prompt) will Undo the entire line command.
- You can prevent constraints from automatically being applied by toggling OFF inferred constraints on the status bar or using the shortcut Ctl+Shift+I.

Command Exercise

Exercise 3-2 – Parametric Constraints

Drawing Name: **constraints1.dwg**
Estimated Time to Completion: 10 Minutes

Scope

Open 'constraints1.dwg.' Mouse over a constraint. Show all Constraints. Add a constraint. Delete a constraint. Hide all Constraints.

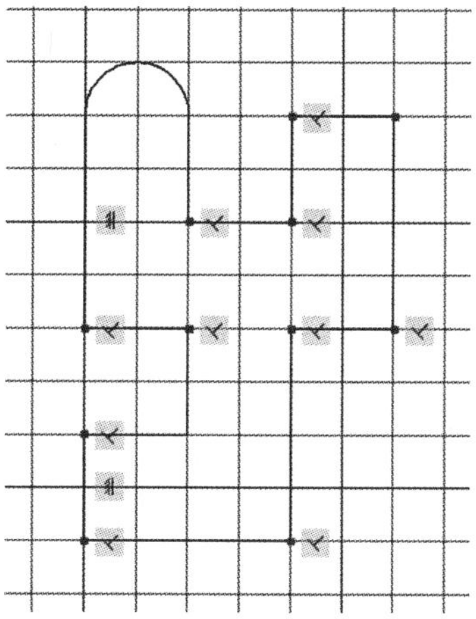

Solution

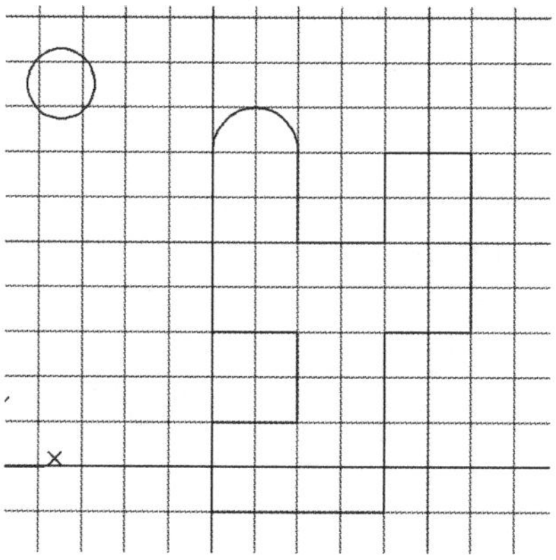

When the drawing is first opened, you should not see any geometric constraints.

The geometric constraints have been hidden. Their display has been turned OFF.

1. Mouse your cursor over the drawing WITHOUT selecting anything. Don't left click. As you mouse over the lines, you should see a small symbol. The symbol indicates that a geometric constraint exists for that line. If no geometric constraint exists, you will not see the symbol. Mouse over the small circle and notice that no symbol appears.

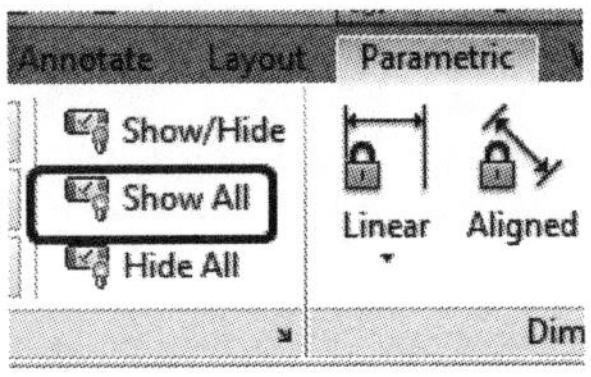

2. Activate the Parametric ribbon.

3. Select **Show All** to display all the geometric constraints currently applied.

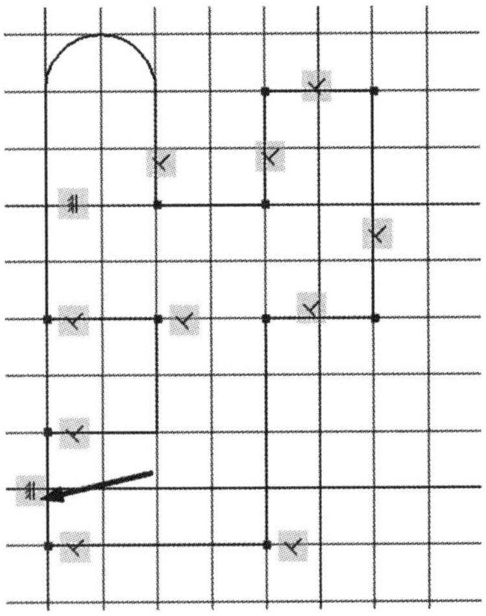

4. Use your left mouse button to rearrange the geometric symbols.

5. Hold down the left mouse button and drag the symbol to a new position.

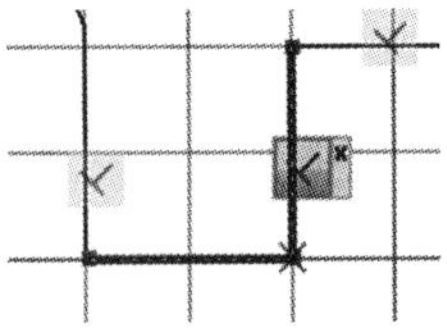

6. Press down with the left mouse button on one of the perpendicular symbols.

Notice that it will display the two lines that are perpendicular.

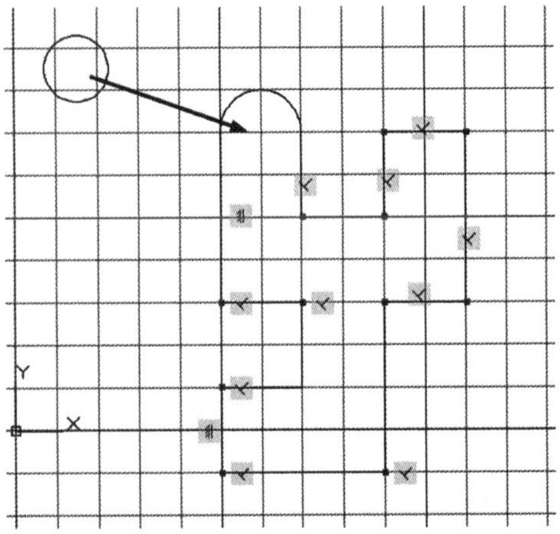

Let's move the small circle so it is concentric to the arc using a geometric constraint.

A concentric constraint means that two or more arcs/circles share the same center point. The elements can have different radii.

When you apply a geometric constraint, the FIRST element remains fixed and the SECOND element moves to be constrained.

On the Parametric ribbon:

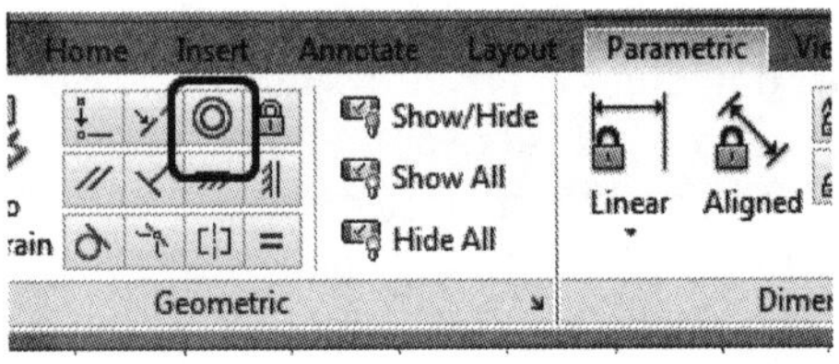

7. Select the **Concentric** constraint.

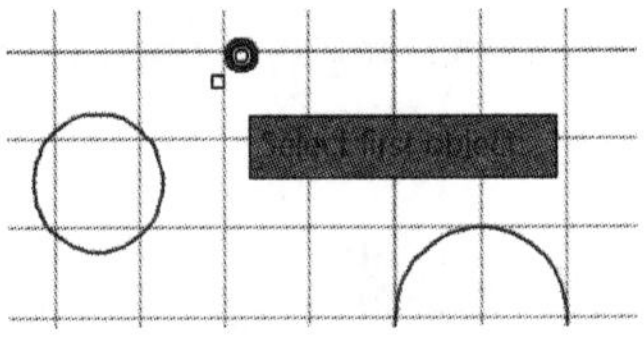

You will see a small Concentric symbol indicating that you are going to be applying that constraint type.

There is a prompt asking you to select the elements to be used for the constraint.

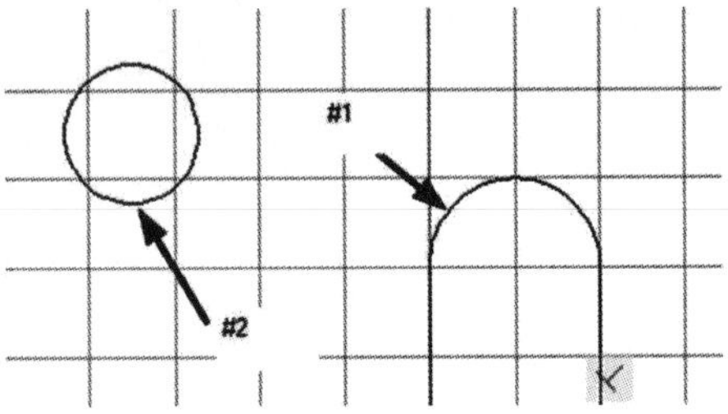

8. Select the arc first and then the circle.

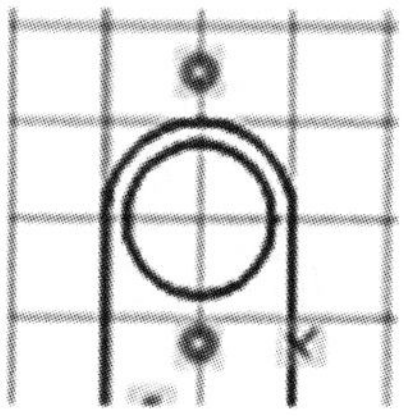

The circle popped into the correct position.

You also see the concentric symbol on the arc and the circle.

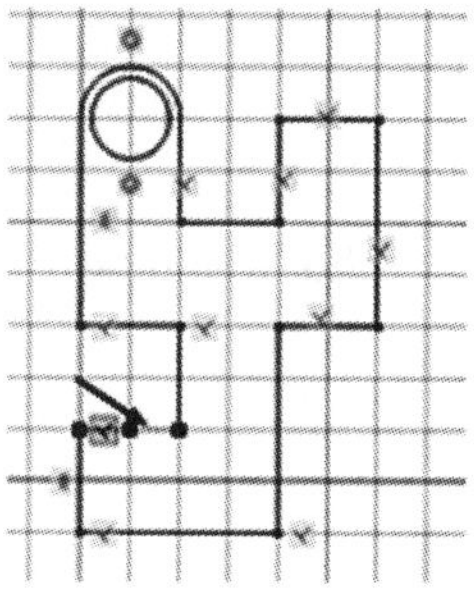

9. Select the line indicated.

On the ribbon:

10. Select **Delete Constraints**.

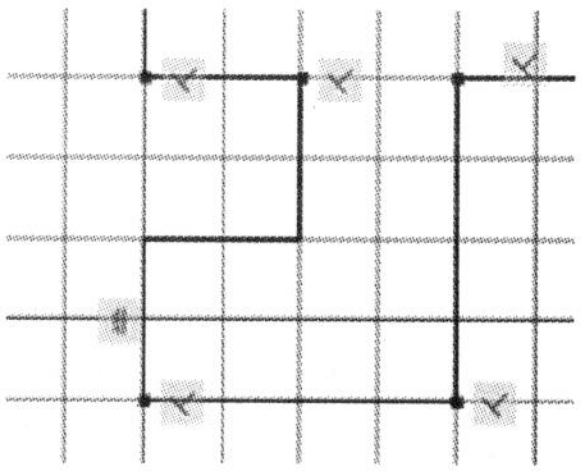

The perpendicular constraints on the selected line are deleted.

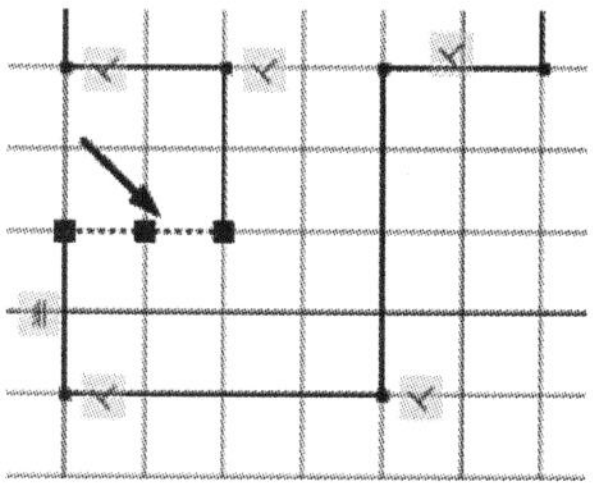

11. Select the same line.

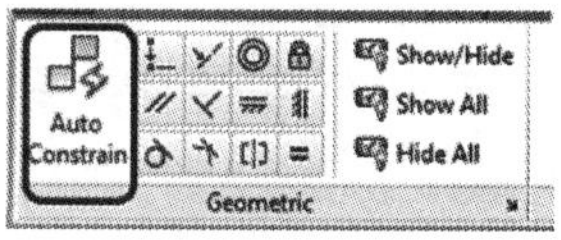

12. Select **Auto Constrain** from the ribbon.

This will add constraints to the selected line.

What constraints do you think will be added?

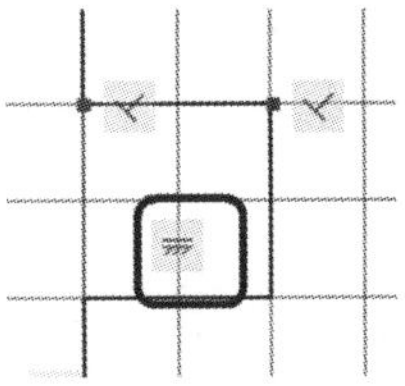

13. A horizontal constraint is added.

In order to add a perpendicular constraint - you need to select TWO lines.

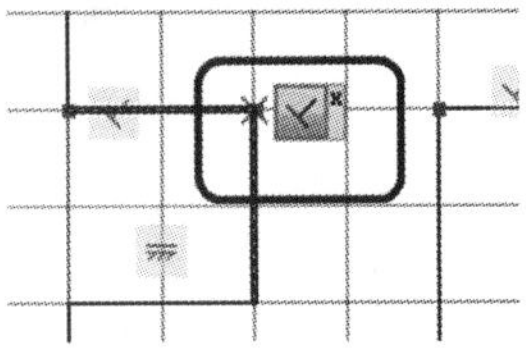

14. Select the perpendicular constraint.
15. Select the small x in the symbol box.

This hides the perpendicular constraint.
It does not delete it.

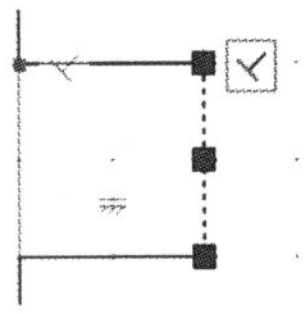

16. Select the vertical line.

The perpendicular symbol will appear while the line is selected.

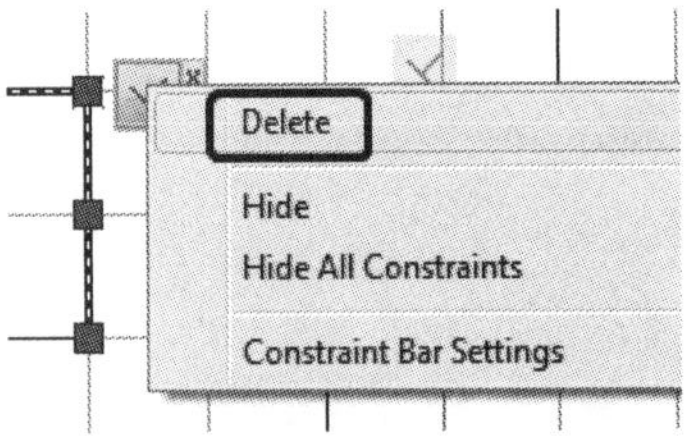

17. To delete the perpendicular constraint, select it, right click and select **Delete**.
18. *Press ESC to release the selection.*

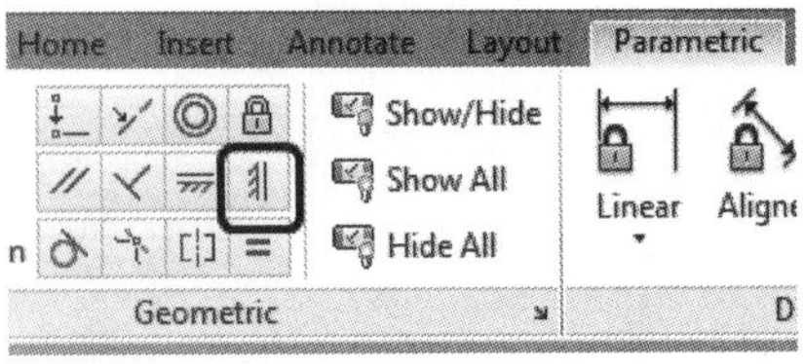

19. Select the vertical constraint.

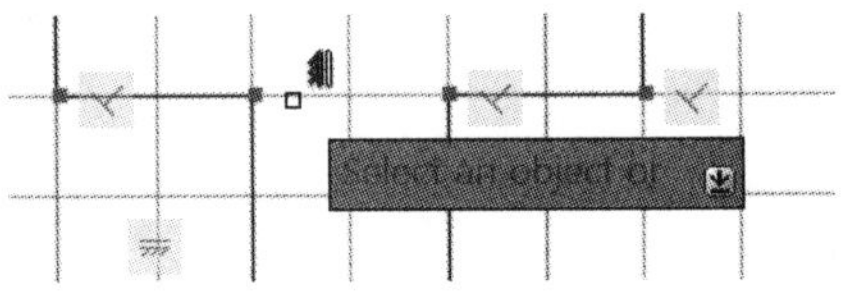

You will see the Vertical constraint icon and a prompt to select the element where the constraint is to be applied.

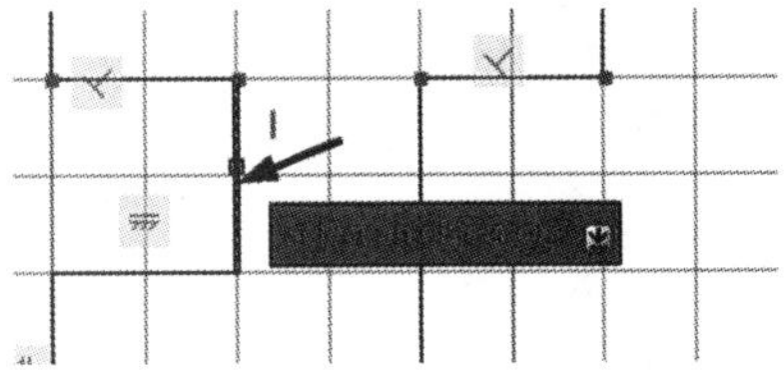

20. Select the vertical line.

You see a vertical constraint has been applied.

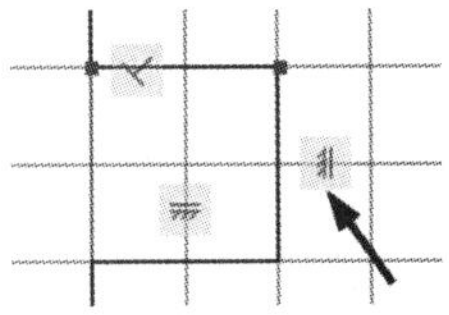

You can only apply a vertical constraint if the perpendicular constraint has been removed. Too many geometric constraints on the same element is not allowed.

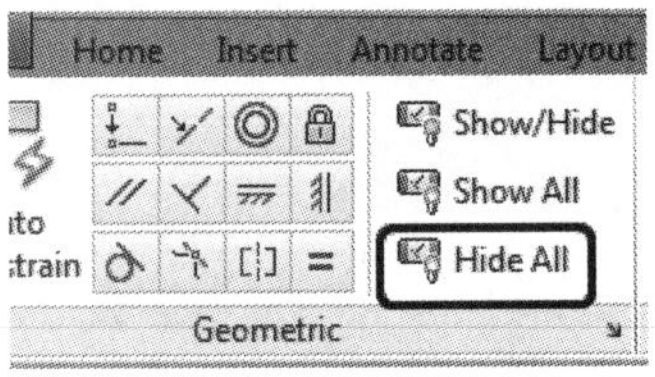

21. Select **Hide All.**

This hides all the geometric constraints.

22. Close without saving.

Command Exercise

Exercise 3-3 – Line Using Polar Tracking

Drawing Name: **Line2.dwg**
Estimated Time to Completion: 10 Minutes

Scope

Open 'line2.dwg' and draw the object shown in the example using the line command with POLAR enabled. Polar settings have already been made to create the necessary angles. When you have completed the third segment, type C to close the object. Press <ENTER> to repeat the line command, press <ENTER> again, and see that the line picks up from the last point selected.

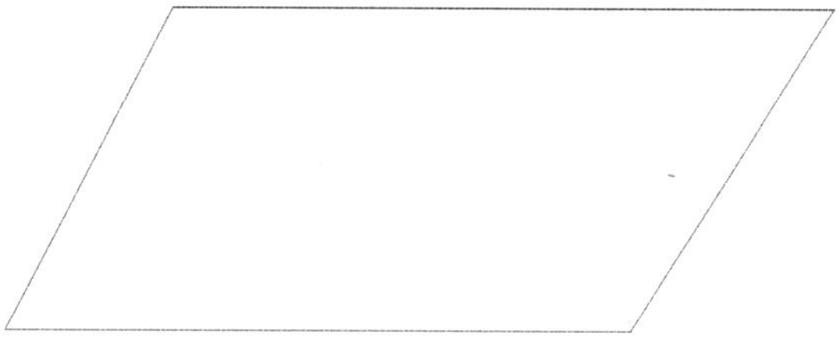

Solution

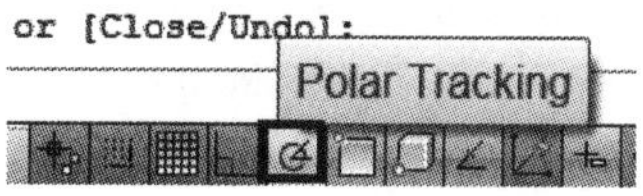

1. Turn **POLAR** on.

2. Left click on the down arrow next to the Polar Tracking icon.
3. Enable the 57.00 polar values.

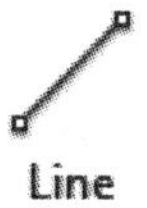

4. Invoke the **Line** command (l or line).

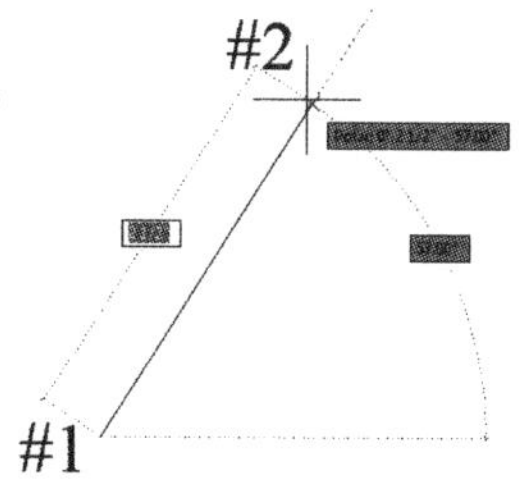

5. *Specify first point:*
   Pick a start point of the line with your left mouse button near the #1 on the drawing.

6. *Specify next point or [Undo]:*
   Pick a second point near the #2 on the drawing.

As you draw your line up to the #2, look for the Tooltip indicating the 57-degree angle.

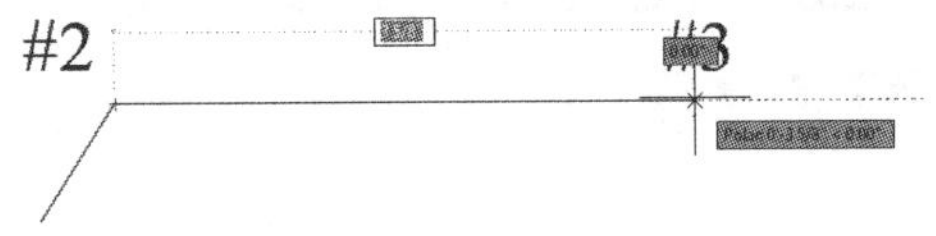

7. *Specify next point or [Undo]:*
Move your mouse near #3 and click to complete the second line segment.

As you draw your line up to the #3, look for the Tooltip indicating the 0-degree angle.

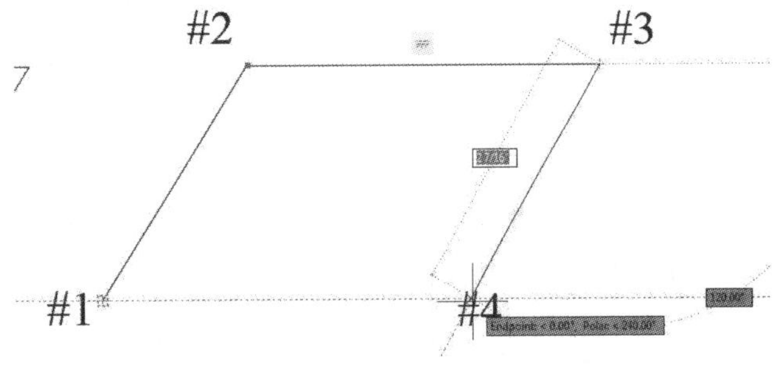

8. *Specify next point or [Close/Undo]:*
Use Object Tracking to line up your end point and set the Polar Angle to 240-degrees.
9. *Specify next point or [Close/Undo]:*
Right-click in the drawing area and select **Close** or type 'C' or 'CLOSE' and press <ENTER> at the command line to create the final line segment.

- When you closed your object did it complete the parallelogram? If not, you may have stopped and restarted the line sequence, in which case the close option will refer to the new start point.
- Move your mouse as you work to see what line segments you have just completed.
- Click on ORTHO in the Status bar, or press the <F8> function key, whichever is more convenient at the time to create straight lines.
- Make a habit of using the <ENTER> key to complete your AutoCAD commands, and to repeat the last command used. Alternately, you may click the right mouse button and select the Repeat option.
- In order for Polar Tracking to click to specific angle values, you have to have them set. Use Settings in the Polar Tracking dialog to add angles you want to use in your drafting.

Command Exercise

Exercise 3-4 – Line Using Cartesian Coordinates

Drawing Name: **Begin a new drawing**
Estimated Time to Completion: 10 Minutes

Scope

Start a New Drawing using the acad.dwt template and draw the object shown in the example using the line command with Cartesian Coordinates. When you have completed the third segment, type C to close the object. Press <ENTER> to repeat the line command, press <ENTER> again, and see that the line picks up from the last point selected. Turn DYN off and ORTHO on for this exercise.

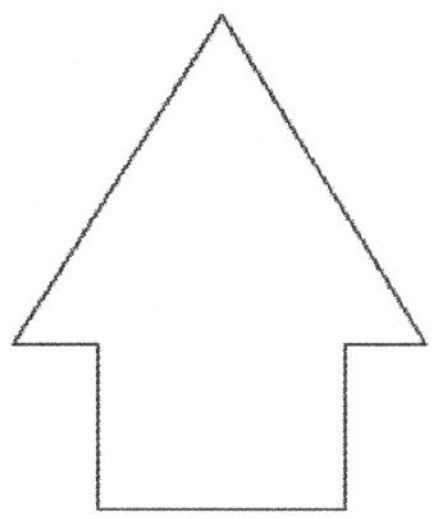

Solution

1. Invoke the **Line** command (l or line).

2. *Specify first point:* Type **0,0** at the command line.
3. *Specify next point or [Undo]:* Type **3,0**.
4. *Specify next point or [Undo]:* **3,2**
5. *Specify next point or [Close/Undo]:* **4,2**
6. *Specify next point or [Close/Undo]:* **1.5,6**
7. *Specify next point or [Close/Undo]:* **-1,2**
8. *Specify next point or [Close/Undo]:* **0,2**
9. *Specify next point or [Close/Undo]:*
   Right-click in the drawing area and select 'Close' or type 'C' or 'CLOSE' and press <ENTER> at the command line to create the final line segment.

> *If your drawing did not turn out properly, make sure you had DYN OFF. To check your data entry, press F2 and the text window will open and you can review your entries.*

Coordinate Entry

Command Overview

Once the Units have been established, coordinates can be typed to specify points or distances. Always draw full scale. There are four ways to specify coordinates: absolute, relative, polar, and direct distance.

Coordinate Entry Method	*Overview*	*Examples*
Absolute Coordinates	The x and y coordinates are determined by an absolute Origin point of 0,0.	X,Y 1,5
Relative Coordinates	The x and y coordinates reference the last point selected in the drawing.	@x,y @3,5
Polar Coordinates	The distance and angle specified references the last point selected in the drawing.	@distance<angle @5<45
Direct Distance	Select the first point, then drag the cursor in the desired direction and type the	Type the distance 4

General Procedures

Using Absolute Coordinates:
1. When prompted to specify a point, type the Absolute coordinates for x and y (x,y).
2. Type the Absolute Coordinate for each successive point (x,y).
   Typical Example: Inserting a Title Block or an Externally Referenced Drawing at a specific location.

Using Relative Coordinates:
1. When prompted to specify a point, select a point in the drawing.
2. Type the Relative Coordinate for each successive point (@x,y).
   Typical Example: Drawing a Rectangle.

Using Polar Coordinates:
1. When prompted to specify a point, select a point in the drawing.
2. Type the Polar Coordinate for each successive point (@distance < angle).
   Typical Example: Drawing lines or moving objects at a specified distance and angle other than orthogonal angles.

Using Direct Distance:
1. When prompted to specify a point, select a point in the drawing.
2. Turn ORTHO on and drag the cursor in the desired direction.
3. Type the distance and press <ENTER>.
   Typical Example: Drawing lines or using the Move, Copy or Stretch commands.

- Always use object snap for selecting specific points in the drawing.
- Remember to separate the x and y coordinates by a comma. Example: 1,5 means the absolute coordinate where x=1 and y=5.
- It is not necessary to type the z coordinate when z = 0.
- Angles are typically measured counter-clockwise. Angle 0 is typically East.
- Precede Relative and Polar coordinate information with an @ sign (over the number 2 on the keyboard).
- ORTHO should be on when using the direct distance method.
- When drawing lines, or moving objects at specific angles (other than with ORTHO on), type the polar coordinate (example: @10<45) or use Polar Tracking Settings.
- Typing the minimum number of keystrokes is important for drawing efficiently. AutoCAD will fill in leading and trailing zeros and the appropriate Unit endings.
- AutoCAD will convert decimal equivalents to feet and inches.
- AutoCAD will assume inches, unless the foot mark ' is typed.
- The Coordinates Display can be turned on or off from the Status Bar by double clicking on it (LMB). If in the middle of a Draw or Modify command, a third option will display the distance and <angle.
- The DYN toggle can be used to display and enter coordinates.

Command Exercise

Exercise 3-5 – Absolute Coordinates

Drawing Name: **entry1.dwg**
Estimated Time to Completion: 5 Minutes

Scope

Start the line command. Draw the objects using the absolute coordinates in the order indicated. Connect the points using only the keyboard. Turn DYN off and ORTHO on.

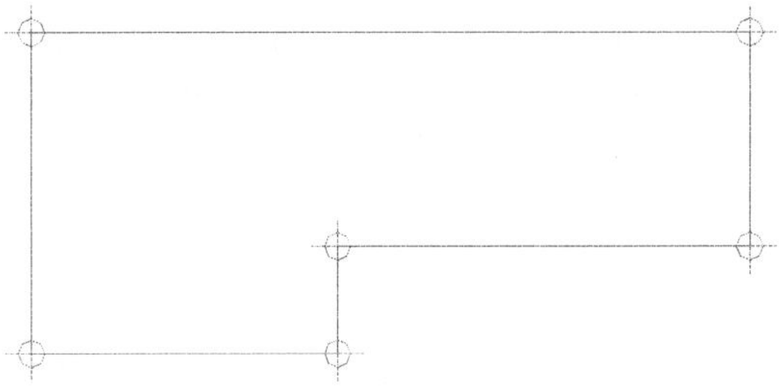

Solution

1. 

Invoke the **Line** command (l or line).

2. *Specify first point:*
Type **1,1** at the command line and press <ENTER>. Notice where the first point of the line is created.
3. *Specify next point or [Undo]:*
Type **4,1** at the command line and press <ENTER>.
4. *Specify next point or [Undo]:*
Type **4,2** at the command line and press <ENTER>.
5. *Specify next point or [Close/Undo]:*
Type **8,2** and press <ENTER>.
6. *Specify next point or [Close/Undo]:*
Type **8,4** and press <ENTER>.
7. *Specify next point or [Close/Undo]:*
Type **1,4** and press <ENTER>.
8. *Specify next point or [Close/Undo]:*
Type **1,1** and press <ENTER>.
9. *Specify next point or [Close/Undo]:*
Press the <ENTER> key to end the command.

Tips & Tricks

- *You can also use the close option to complete the exercise rather than typing in the final '1,1'.*

Command Exercise

Exercise 3-6 – Relative Coordinates

Drawing Name: **entry2.dwg**
Estimated Time to Completion: 5 Minutes

Scope

Start the line command. Draw the objects using the relative coordinates in the order indicated. Connect the points using only the keyboard.

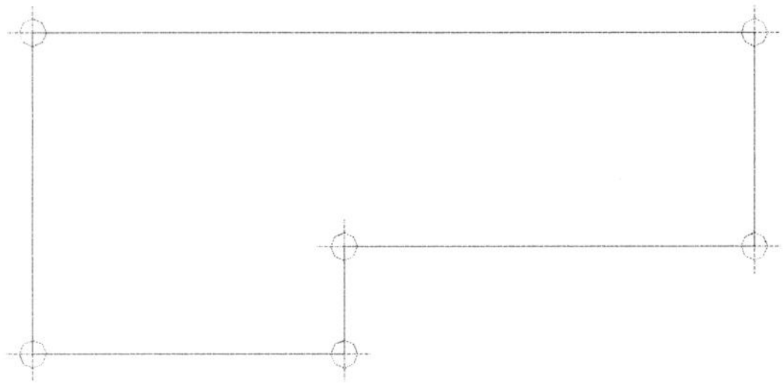

Solution

1. 

Invoke the **Line** command (l or line).

2. *Specify first point:*
   Type **1,1** at the command line and press <ENTER>.

   Notice where the first point of the line is created.
3. *Specify next point or [Undo]:*
   Type **@3,0** at the command line and press <ENTER>.
4. *Specify next point or [Undo]:*
   Type **@0,1** at the command line and press <ENTER>.
5. *Specify next point or [Close/Undo]:*
   Type **@4,0** and press <ENTER>.
6. *Specify next point or [Close/Undo]:*
   Type **@0,2** and press <ENTER>.
7. *Specify next point or [Close/Undo]:*
   Type **@-7,0** and press <ENTER>.
8. *Specify next point or [Close/Undo]:*
   Type **@0,-3** and press <ENTER>.
9. *Specify next point or [Close/Undo]:*
   Press the <ENTER> key to end the command.

Extra: *What would you type in to create the shape in a clockwise fashion instead of counterclockwise direction? Try it.*

Command Exercise

Exercise 3-7 – Polar Coordinates

Drawing Name: **entry3.dwg**
Estimated Time to Completion: 5 Minutes

Scope

Start the line command. Draw the objects using polar coordinates in the order indicated. Connect the points using only the keyboard.

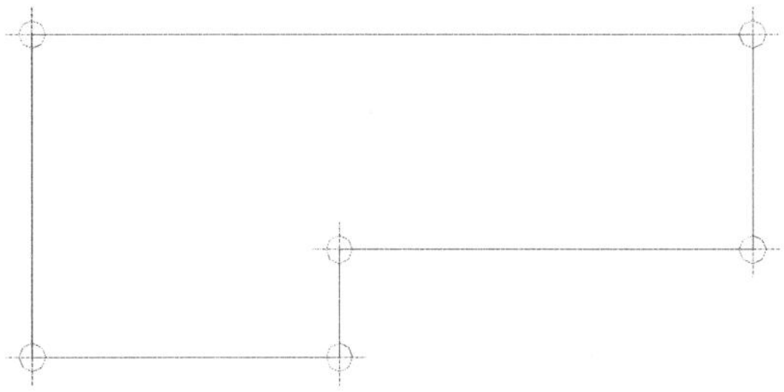

Solution

1. 

Invoke the **Line** command (l or line).

2. *Specify first point:*
Type **1,1** at the command line and press <ENTER>.

   Notice where the first point of the line is created.

3. *Specify next point or [Undo]:*
Type **@3<0** at the command line and press <ENTER>.

4. *Specify next point or [Undo]:*
Type **@1<90** at the command line and press <ENTER>.

5. *Specify next point or [Close/Undo]:*
Type **@4<0** and press <ENTER>.

6. *Specify next point or [Close/Undo]:*
Type **@2<90** and press <ENTER>.

7. *Specify next point or [Close/Undo]:*
Type **@7<180** and press <ENTER>.

8. *Specify next point or [Close/Undo]:*
Type **@3<270** and press <ENTER>.

9. *Specify next point or [Close/Undo]:*
Press the <ENTER> key to end the command.

Extra: *What would happen if you typed @-3<180 in step 3 in the exercise? Try it.*

Command Exercise

Exercise 3-8 – Drag Method

Drawing Name: **entry4.dwg**
Estimated Time to Completion: 5 Minutes

Scope

Start the line command. Draw the objects using the direct distance method.

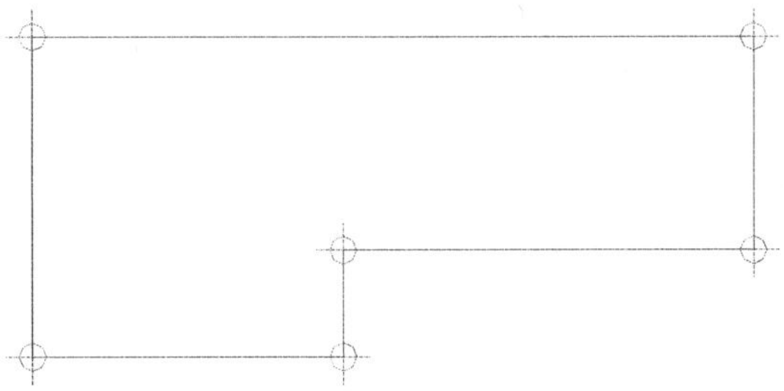

Solution

1. 

Invoke the **Line** command (l or line).

2. *Specify first point:*
Type **1,1** at the command line and press <ENTER>.

   Notice where the first point of the line is created.

3. *Specify next point or [Undo]:*
Toggle ORTHO ON at the Status bar.

4. *Specify next point or [Undo]:*
Drag the mouse to the right, type **3** and press <ENTER>.

5. *Specify next point or [Close/Undo]:*
Drag the mouse upward, type **1** and press <ENTER>.

6. *Specify next point or [Close/Undo]:*
Drag the mouse to the right, type **4** and press <ENTER>.

7. *Specify next point or [Close/Undo]:*
Drag the mouse upward, type **2** and press <ENTER>.

8. *Specify next point or [Close/Undo]:*
Drag the mouse to the left, type **7** and press <ENTER>.

9. *Specify next point or [Close/Undo]:*
Drag the mouse downward, type **3** and press <ENTER>.

10. *Specify next point or [Close/Undo]:*
Press the <ENTER> key to end the command.

Erase

Command Locator

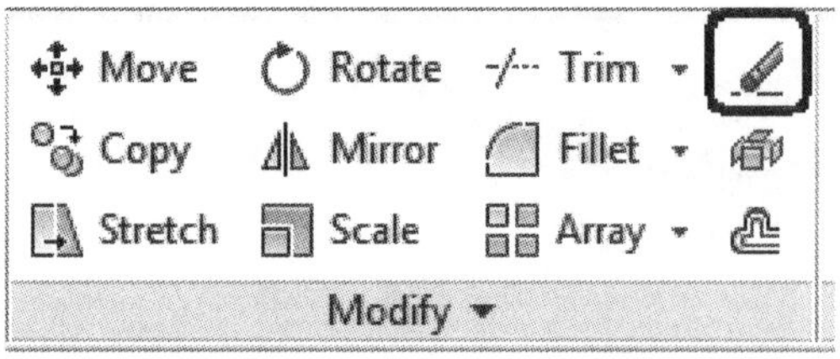

Home/Modify Panel	Erase
Command	**Erase**
Alias	**E**

Command Overview

Erase deletes selected objects. Press <ENTER> after selecting the objects to erase to execute the command. Type OOPS to bring back the last set of erased objects, even if other objects were drawn since the last erase.

General Procedures

1. Begin the erase command by selecting the Erase icon from the Modify Toolbar/Ribbon or typing E at the blank command prompt.
2. Place the cursor over the objects to erase and pick (LMB).

Tips & Tricks

- If the cursor is not over an object, a selection window will appear. Make the other corner of the selection window.
- A Selection Window made from Left to Right will select only the objects completely in the window. *This is called a selection window.*
- A Selection Window made from Right to Left will select all objects the window crosses. *This is called a selection crossing.*
- Typing All (and pressing <ENTER>) will select all objects in the drawing to erase. Press <ENTER> to execute the command.

Command Exercise

Exercise 3-9 – Erase

Drawing Name: **erase1.dwg**
Estimated Time to Completion: 5 Minutes

Scope

Erase the objects in the drawing. Draw some more lines. Type OOPS to bring back the last set of erased objects.

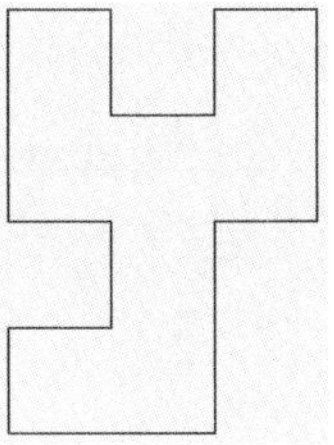

Solution

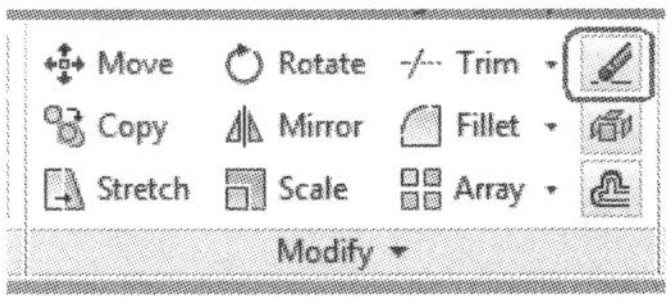

1. Invoke the **Erase** command (e or erase) on the Home ribbon.

2. *Select objects:*
   Select the objects by typing **ALL** and pressing <ENTER>, picking each line individually, or using the Window method. When all the objects are highlighted, press <ENTER> to execute the Erase command.

3. Invoke the **Line** command (l or line).

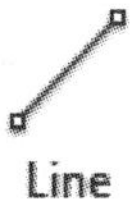

4. *Specify first point:*
   Use your LMB to pick the start point of a line segment. Select any location on the drawing.

5. *Specify next point or [Undo]:*
   Continue to use the LMB to create lines on the drawing.

6. *Specify next point or [Close/Undo]:*
   Press the <ENTER> key to end the line command.

7. Type **OOPS** at the command line and press the <ENTER> key.

Tips & Tricks

➢ *Select all the objects to erase, then press <ENTER> to execute the command. To remove an object from the selection set, hold down the shift key and select the object again. See that it is removed from the selection set. Then press <ENTER>.*

Review Questions

1. How do you turn on the display of the coordinates in the status bar?
2. A user enters LINE 1,1 and then @0,2 ….what type of coordinates is she using?
3. To make sure you will always draw a straight line, what tray button should be enabled?
4. When using the POLAR method of coordinate entry, which tray button should be enabled?
5. When entering direct coordinates, which tray button should be disabled?
6. What is the difference between OOPS and UNDO?

Review Answers

1. How do you turn on the display of the coordinates in the status bar?
   Left click on the STATUS bar options icon and enable Coordinates

2. A user enters LINE 1,1 and then @0,2 ….what type of coordinates is she using?
   Relative

3. To make sure you will always draw a straight line, what tray button should be enabled?
   ORTHO

4. When using the POLAR method of coordinate entry, which tray button should be enabled?
   POLAR

5. When entering direct coordinates, which tray button should be disabled?
   DYN

6. What is the difference between OOPS and UNDO?
   UNDO reverses the last command entered. OOPS restores the last item(s) erased or deleted from the drawing.

Notes:

Lesson 4.0 – Draw Commands

Estimated Class Time: 4 Hours

Objectives

This section introduces AutoCAD commands for creating a simple drawing. The user will learn to use the commands on the Draw toolbar.

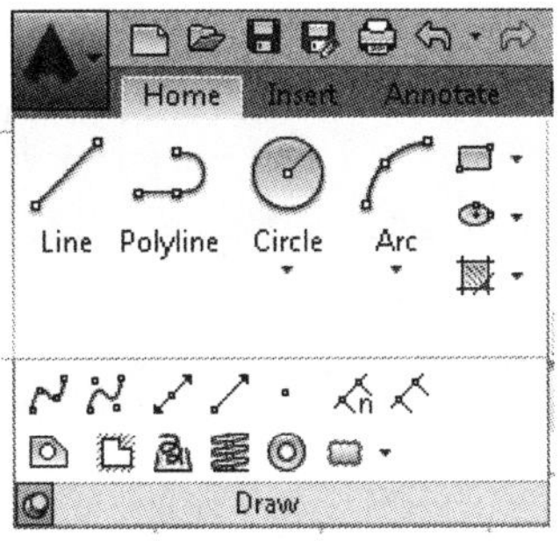

- **Polyline**
  Draw polylines.
- **Polygon**
  Draw multi-sided polylines.
- **Rectangle**
  Draw rectangular polylines.
- **Arc**
  Draw arcs several different ways.
- **Circle**
  Draw circles using six different methods.
- **Donut**
  Draw a donut – a circle with a thick outline.
- **Spline**
  Draw splines by using Points to control the spline shape.
- **Ellipse**
  Draw ellipses using two different methods.
- **Ellipse Arc**
  Draw an elliptical arc.
- **Add Selected**
  Adds selected elements using source properties.
- **Hatch**
  Adds a selected pattern to a closed boundary or region.

Polyline

Command Locator

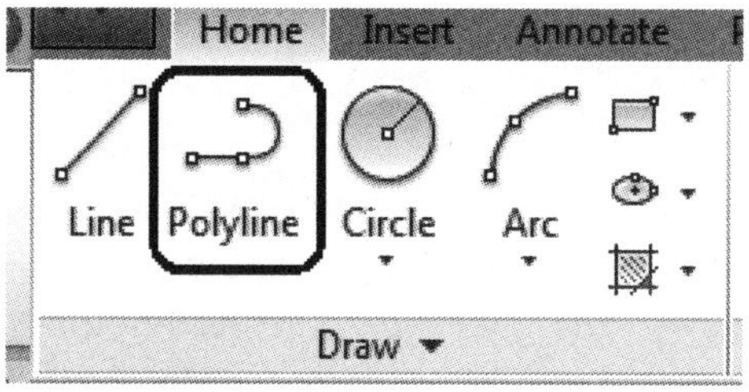

Home Ribbon	**Draw Panel/ Polyline**
Command	**Pline**
Alias	**PL**
RMB Shortcut Menu	**Drawing Window**

Command Overview

Polylines are essential to drawing in AutoCAD. Polylines are line and arc segments with common endpoints that are joined to make one object. A rectangle is an example of a polyline. Polylines can be more efficient because selecting one polyline segment will automatically select the entire polyline, and offsetting a Polyline will Offset all of the segments equally. Sometimes it is necessary to  explode a Polyline, then use the  Edit Polyline command to *join* all the line and arc segments. When drawing a Polyline, the user will be presented with many command line options; however, for all practical purposes, drawing a Polyline is much like drawing line segments.

Primarily, GIS drafters and architects use polylines. Mechanical drafters use polylines to create drawing borders, arrows and cutting plane lines. Cutting plane lines are used for section views.

A polyline is similar to a line but it can have thickness. Additionally, you can "join" or connect more than one line to create a single object. Polylines can have varying thickness or widths.

You can draw your object using lines and arcs and convert it to polyline using the polyline edit command. You can convert polylines and polyarcs back to lines and arcs using the EXPLODE command.

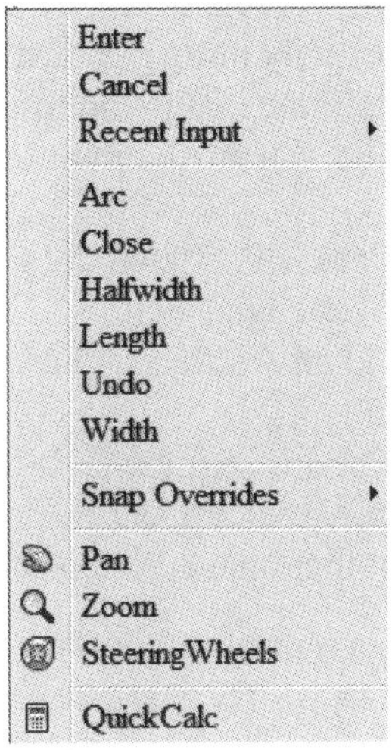

Polyline Option	**Overview**
Specify next point	This is the default option. Simply pick the next polyline point, much like drawing line segments.
Arc	This option, used within the Polyline command, will invoke the polyline Arc option, creating a Polyarc. There are a few ways to draw a polyline arc; one way is to simply drag the cursor in the desired direction (ORTHO on or off) and type the distance, then type L to return to the Polyline Line segment option.
Close	This option closes a polyline so that the first and last points are connect-ed.
Halfwidth	This option will make the polyline width half the designated distance.
Length	The length option will extend the polyline being drawn a designated length.
Undo	The Undo option will undo the last polyline segment.
Width	Type W for width, then specify a start width and an ending width.

General Procedures

1. Invoke the Pline command.
2. Specify a start point.
3. Type W for width (and <ENTER>).
4. Specify a starting width (and <ENTER>) and an ending width (and <ENTER>). The default ending width is usually equal to the starting width, unless drawing an object such as an arrowhead.
5. Specify the next point using the methods learned in drawing line segments.
6. Optional: Type U (and <ENTER>) to Undo the last polyline segment without exiting the polyline command.
7. Optional: Type A (and <ENTER>) to go invoke the Arc option without exiting the polyline command. Type L (and <ENTER>) to return to the Line mode.
8. Optional: Type C (and <ENTER>) to Close the polyline.

- It is more typical, and usually more practical, to draw regular line and arc segments and then use the Edit Polyline command to join them (see next section).
- When drawing a Polyline, the most common options used are Width and "Specify next point."
- The default polyline width is 0. When the width is changed, it will remain the latest width setting until changed again.
- Polyline starting and ending widths can be specified by picking points in the drawing window.
- Draw polylines in continuous segments. If the polylines are drawn as separate segments, the intersections will appear jagged. If the polyline is not closed, there will be a jagged edge at that opened intersection.
- Do not cross polyline segments. Example: 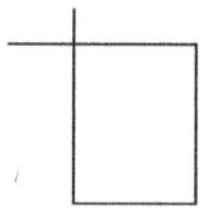

Sometimes it is easier for the beginner drafter to create the geometry using standard lines and arcs and then convert the geometry into polylines and polyarcs. To change a regular line to a polyline, use the PEDIT command. PEDIT can also be used to modify the width to an existing polyline and append geometry.

The Polyline Edit command can be initiated as follows:

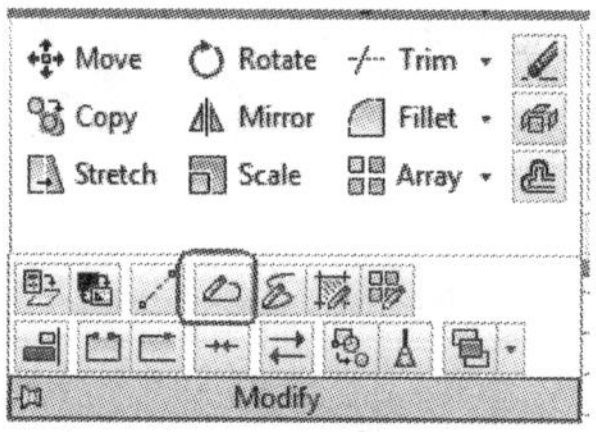

Home Ribbon	**Modify Panel/ Edit Polyline**
Command	**Pedit**
Double Click	**Double left mouse click on polyline**
Alias	**PE**

The PEDIT command has several options:

```
Enter an option [Close/Join/Width/Edit vertex/Fit/Spline/Decurve/Ltype gen/Reverse/Undo]:
```

Close	Creates the closing segment of the polyline, connecting the last segment with the first. AutoCAD considers the polyline open unless you close it using the Close option.
Join	Adds lines, arcs, or polylines to the end of an open polyline and removes the curve fitting from a curve-fit polyline. For objects to join the polyline, their endpoints must touch unless you use the Multiple option at the first PEDIT prompt. In this case, you can join polylines that do not touch if the fuzz distance is set to a value large enough to include the endpoints.
Width	Specifies a new uniform width for the entire polyline.
Edit Vertex	Marks the first vertex of the polyline by drawing an X on the screen. If you have specified a tangent direction for this vertex, an arrow is also drawn in that direction.

Fit	Creates a smooth curve consisting of pairs of arcs joining each pair of vertices. The curve passes through all vertices of the polyline and uses any tangent direction you specify.
Spline	Uses the vertices of the selected polyline as the control points, or frame, of a curve. The curve passes through the first and last control points unless the original polyline was closed. The curve is pulled toward the other points but does not necessarily pass through them. The more control points you specify in a particular part of the frame, the more pull they exert on the curve. The technical term for this type of curve is *B-spline*. AutoCAD can generate quadratic and cubic spline-fit polylines.
Decurve	Removes extra vertices inserted by a fit or spline curve and straightens all segments of the polyline. Retains tangent information assigned to the polyline vertices for use in subsequent fit curve requests. If you edit a spline-fit polyline with commands such as BREAK or TRIM, you cannot use the Decurve option.
Ltype gen	Generates the linetype in a continuous pattern through the vertices of the polyline. When turned off, this option generates the linetype starting and ending with a dash at each vertex. Ltype Gen does not apply to polylines with tapered segments.
Reverse	Reverses the direction of the polyline.
Undo	Reverses operations as far back as the beginning of the PEDIT session.

- *The PLINEGEN system variable controls the linetype pattern display around and the smoothness of the vertices of a 2D polyline. Setting PLINEGEN to 1 generates new polylines in a continuous pattern around the vertices of the completed polyline. Setting PLINEGEN to 0 starts and ends the polyline with a dash at each vertex. PLINEGEN does not apply to polylines with tapered segments.*
- *PLINETYPE controls both the creation of new polylines with the PLINE command and the conversion of existing polylines in drawings from previous releases.*
- *0 Polylines in older drawings are not converted when opened; PLINE creates old-format polylines*
- *1 Polylines in older drawings are not converted when opened; PLINE creates optimized polylines*
- *2 Polylines in older drawings are converted when opened; PLINE creates optimized polylines*
- *The CONVERT command can be used to optimize polylines created in AutoCAD R13 or earlier.*

Command Exercise

Exercise 4-1 – Polyline

Drawing Name: **pline1.dwg**
Estimated Time to Completion: 10 Minutes

Scope

Using the Polyline command with the Width, Arc and Line options, draw the object as indicated with a polyline width of '0.3'. Ortho should be on.

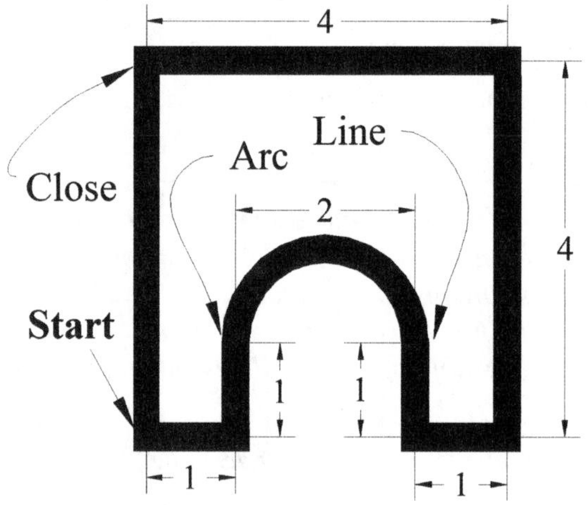

Solution

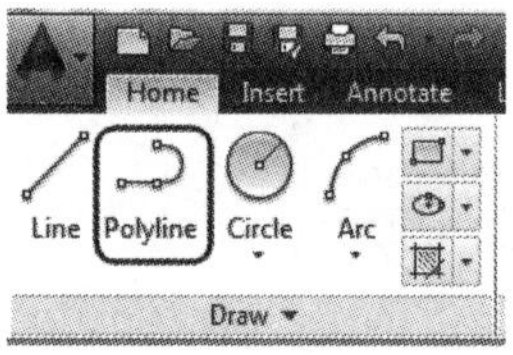

1. Invoke the Polyline command (pl or pline).
2. *Specify start point:*
   Pick the start point with the LMB.
3. *Specify next point or [Arc /Halfwidth/Length/Undo/Width]:*

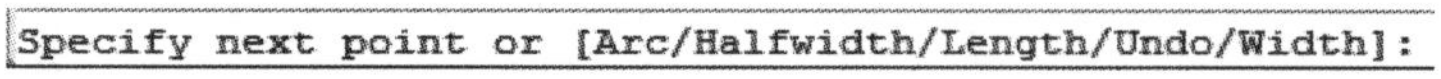

Right-click in the drawing window and select 'Width' or type 'W' for width and press <ENTER>.

4. *Specify starting width <0.0000>:*
   Type '0.3' and press <ENTER>.

5. *Specify ending width <0.3000>:*
   Press <ENTER>.
6. *Specify next point or [Arc/Close/Halfwidth/Length/Undo/Width]:*
   Make sure ORTHO is ON. Drag the mouse to the right. Type '1' and press <ENTER>.
7. *Specify next point or [Arc/Close/Halfwidth/Length/Undo/Width]:*
   Drag the mouse upward. Type '1' and press <ENTER>.
8. *Specify next point or [Arc/Close/Halfwidth/Length/Undo/Width]:*
   Right-click in the drawing window and select 'Arc' or type 'A' for arc and press <ENTER>.
9. *Specify endpoint of arc or [Angle/CEnter/CLose/Direction/Halfwidth/Line/Radius/Second pt/ Undo/ Width]:*
   Drag the mouse to the right. Type '2' and press <ENTER>.
10. *Specify endpoint of arc or [Angle/CEnter/CLose/Direction/Halfwidth/Line/Radius/Second pt/ Undo/ Width]:*
    Type 'L' for line and press <ENTER>.
11. *Specify next point or [Arc/Close/Halfwidth/Length/Undo/Width]:*
    Drag the mouse downward. Type '1' and press <ENTER>.
12. *Specify next point or [Arc/Close/Halfwidth/Length/Undo/Width]:*
    Drag the mouse to the right. Type '1' and press <ENTER>.
13. *Specify next point or [Arc/Close/Halfwidth/Length/Undo/Width]:*
    Drag the mouse upward. Type '4' and press <ENTER>.
14. *Specify next point or [Arc/Close/Halfwidth/Length/Undo/Width]:*
    Drag the mouse to the left. Type '4' and press <ENTER>.
15. *Specify next point or [Arc/Close/Halfwidth/Length/Undo/Width]:*
    Right-click in the drawing window and select 'Close' or type 'C' for close to complete the exercise.

As the figure is created, you will see small symbols indicating geometric constraints which are automatically applied.

	Vertical
	Perpendicular
	Tangent

Extra: *Explode the polyline. What happens? Undo the explode command. Move the objects by selecting the arc only. Notice that the entire polyline is selected.*

Tips & Tricks

- *Do not start and stop the polyline segments. Use the polyline UNDO option if an incorrect endpoint is selected.*

Command Exercise

Exercise 4-2 – Polyline

Drawing Name: **new drawing**
Estimated Time to Completion: 10 Minutes

Scope

Using the Polyline command with the Width and Line options, draw an arrow. ORTHO should be enabled.

Solution

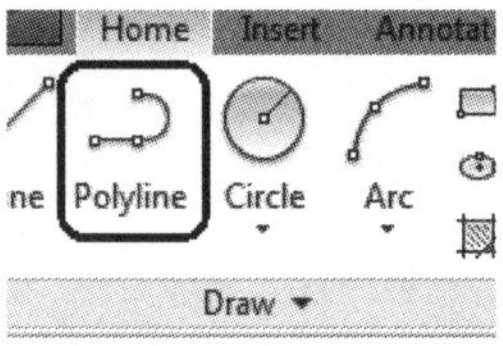


```
Command: _pline
Specify start point: 2,2
Current line-width is 0.4000
Specify next point or [Arc/Halfwidth/Length/Undo/Width]: W
Specify starting width <0.4000>: 0
Specify ending width <0.0000>: 0.8
Specify next point or [Arc/Halfwidth/Length/Undo/Width]: .75
Specify next point or [Arc/Close/Halfwidth/Length/Undo/Width]: W
Specify starting width <0.8000>: 0.4
Specify ending width <0.4000>: 0.4
Specify next point or [Arc/Close/Halfwidth/Length/Undo/Width]: 5
Specify next point or [Arc/Close/Halfwidth/Length/Undo/Width]:
```

1. Invoke the Polyline command (pl or pline).
2. When prompted for the start point, enter **2,2**.
3. Right click and select **W** for width.
4. Set the starting width to **0**.
5. Set the ending width to **0.8**.
6. Specify the next point as **.75**. (Move the cursor towards the right.)

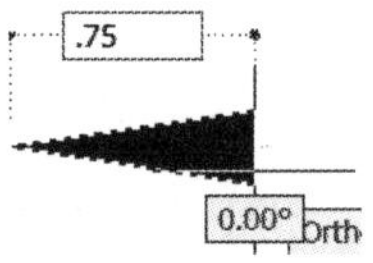

7. Right click and select **W** for width.
8. Set the starting width to **0.4**.
9. Set the ending width to **0.4**.
10. Set the distance to **5**. (Move the cursor towards the right.)

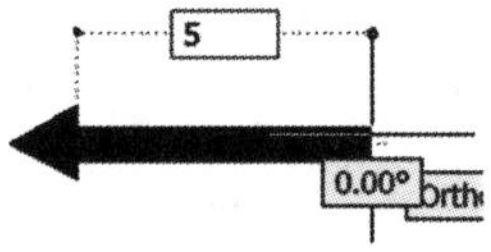

11. Press <**ENTER**> to exit the command.
12. You will see the icons for geometric constraints indicating horizontal constraints.

Polygon

Command Locator

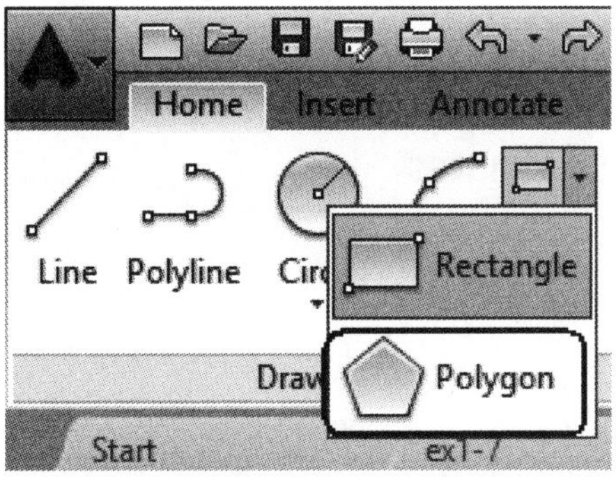

Home Ribbon	**Draw Panel/ Polygon**
Command	**Polygon**
Alias	**Pol**

Command Overview

Polygons are polylines with equal line segments. First determine the number of sides for the polygon then select a center point. A polygon may be either Inscribed (I) within or Circumscribed (C) around an imaginary circle. Typing the radius of this circle will determine the size of the polygon. A Polygon may also be constructed using the Edge option and specifying the length of the Polygon Edge.

General Procedures

1. Begin the Polygon command. Type the number of sides, and press <ENTER>.
2. Specify the center of the Polygon.
3. Determine whether it is Inscribed (I) or Circumscribed (C) about the radius of the circle.
4. Specify the radius.

- After specifying the number of sides to the polygon, type E (for Edge mode) to specify the length and direction of the polygon edge.
- There is no polygon Center. Use the Tracking Object Snap or draw a construction line.

Command Exercise

Exercise 4-3 – Polygon

Drawing Name: **poly1.dwg**
Estimated Time to Completion: 5 Minutes

Scope

Practice the options for drawing a polygon:
1.) Draw a 6-sided polygon making the overall radius 2, using the Inscribed option.
2.) Draw a 6 sided polygon making the overall radius 2, using the Circumscribed option.
3.) Draw a 6 sided polygon using the Edge option, with a length of 1. Notice that the angle of the polygon is determined by the cursor direction as it is dragged from the first pick point.

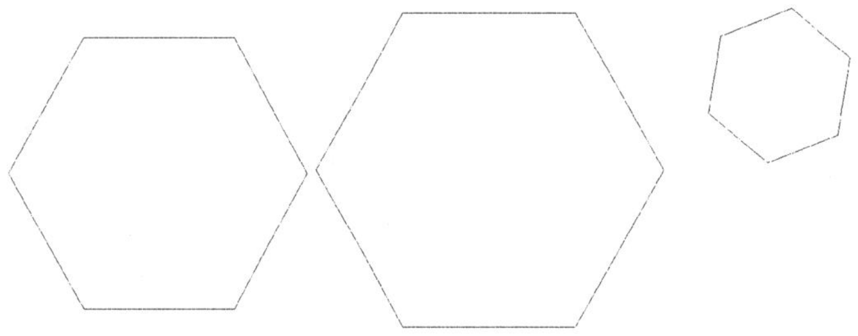

Solution

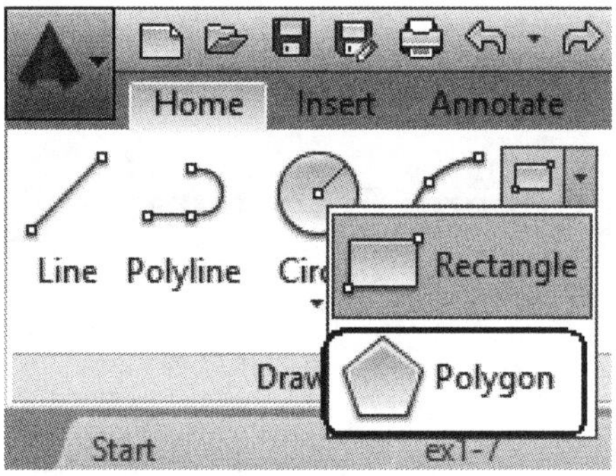

1. Turn ORTHO ON by pressing F8.
2. Invoke the Polygon command (polygon).

Enter number of sides <4>:
3. Type '6' at the command line for the number of sides and press <ENTER>.

Specify center of polygon or [Edge]:
4. Pick a point on your drawing with the LMB.

Enter an option [Inscribed in circle/Circumscribed about circle] <I>:
5. If the default value is <I> for inscribed, press <ENTER> to accept this value, right-click in the drawing window and select 'Inscribed in circle' or type 'I' and press <ENTER>.

Specify radius of circle:
6. Type '2' and press <ENTER> for the radius in which the polygon is inscribed.

7. Repeat the Polygon command with the RMB.

8. *Enter number of sides <6>:*
   Press <ENTER> to accept the default.

9. *Specify center of polygon or [Edge]:*
   Pick a point with your LMB.

10. *Enter an option [Inscribed in circle/Circumscribed about circle] <I>:*
    Right-click in the drawing window and select 'Circumscribed about circle' or type 'C' at the command line and press <ENTER>.

11. *Specify radius of circle:*
    Type '2' and press <ENTER> for the radius of the circle about which the polygon is circumscribed.

12. Repeat the Polygon command with the RMB.

13. *Enter number of sides <6>:*
    Press <ENTER> to accept the default.

14. *Specify center of polygon or [Edge]:*
    Right-click in the drawing window and select 'Edge' or type 'E' and press <ENTER> for the edge option.

15. *Specify first endpoint of edge:*
    Pick the first point with the LMB.

16. *Specify first endpoint of edge:*
    To specify second endpoint of the edge, drag the mouse away from the first point and type '1' at the command line and press <ENTER>. Notice what happens as the cursor is dragged if ORTHO is ON or OFF.

Tips & Tricks

> *Can the Center Object Snap be used to select the center of the polygon? Try it. How would you draw a line from the center point of one polygon to the next?*

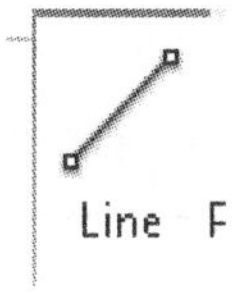

17. Select the LINE command.

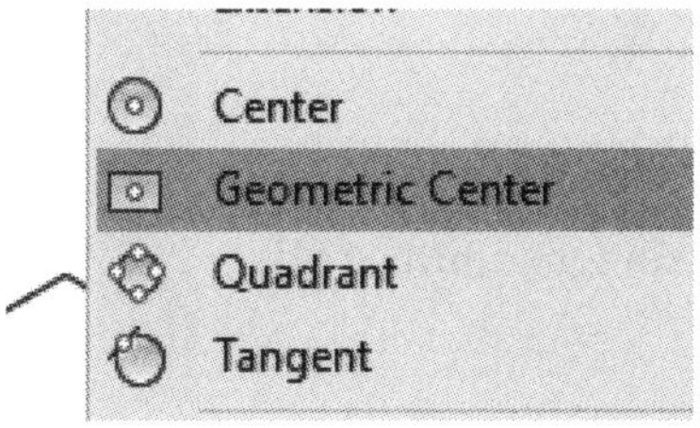

18. Press Shift + RMB to access the shortcut menu.

19. Select Geometric Center to activate the center object snap.

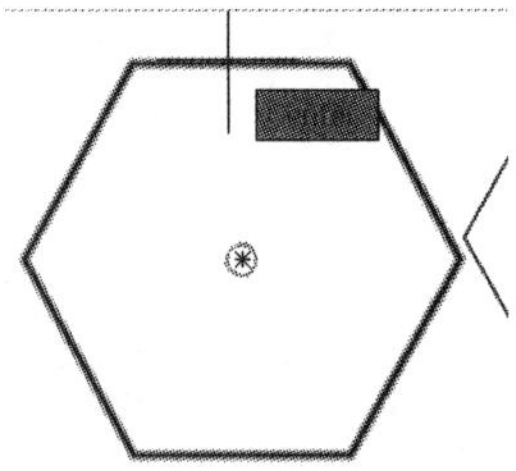

20. Mouse over one of the polygon edges and you should see the center point snap "wake up."

Select the center point snap as the start point of the line.

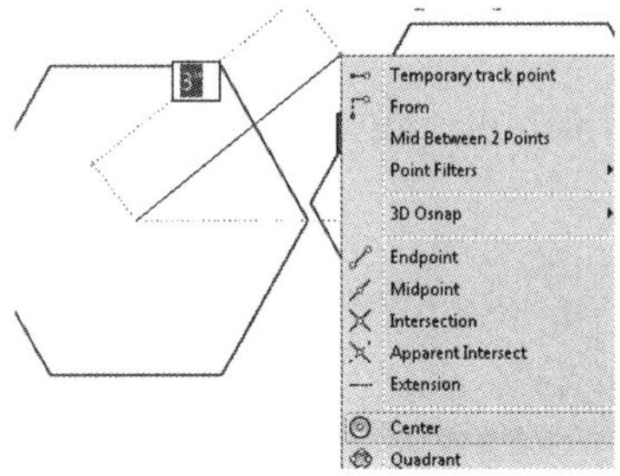

21. Press Shift + RMB to access the shortcut menu.

22. Select Geometric Center to activate the center object snap.

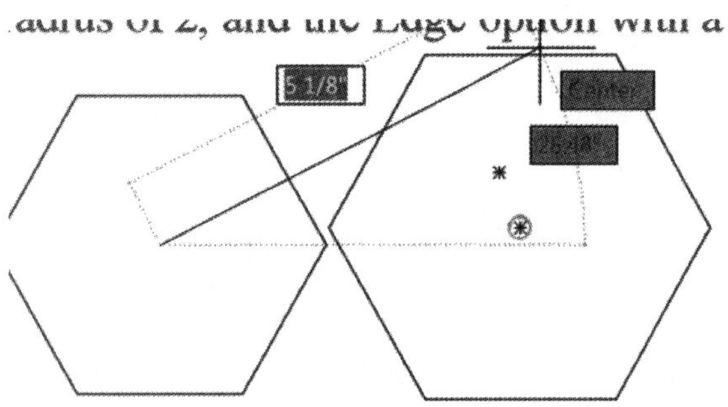

23. Mouse over one of the polygon edges for the second polygon and you should see the center point snap "wake up."

Select the Geometric center point snap as the start point of the line.

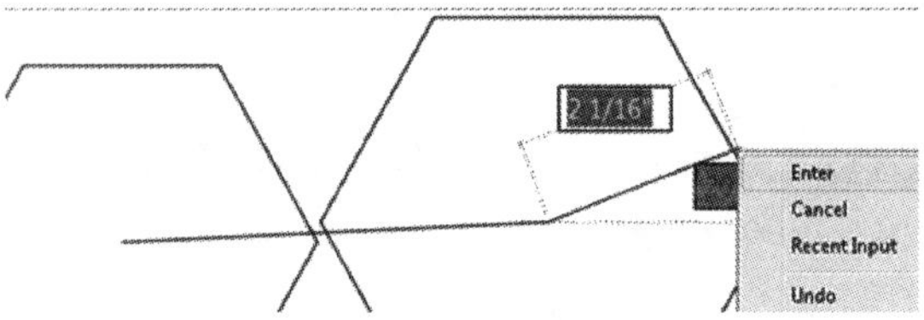

24. RMB and select ENTER to exit the LINE command.

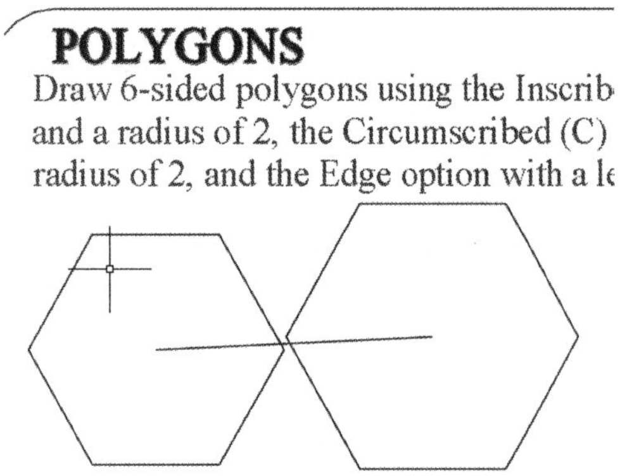

You were able to place a line at the center of two polygons using the Shift+RMB object snap menu.

Rectangle

Command Locator

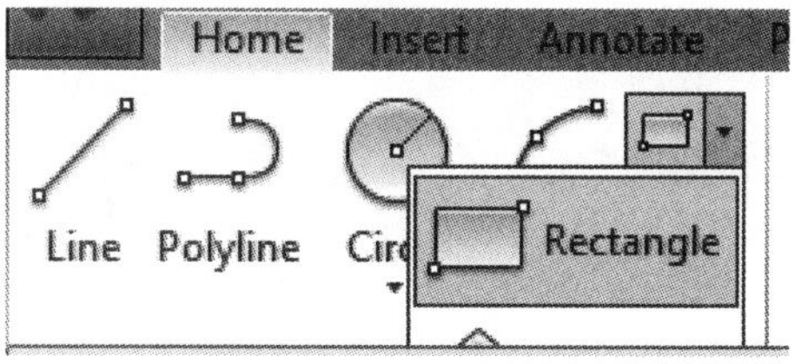

Home Ribbon	**Draw / Rectangle**
Command	**Rectangle**
Alias	**Rectang**
RMB Shortcut Menu	**Drawing Window (before select the first corner point)**

Command Overview

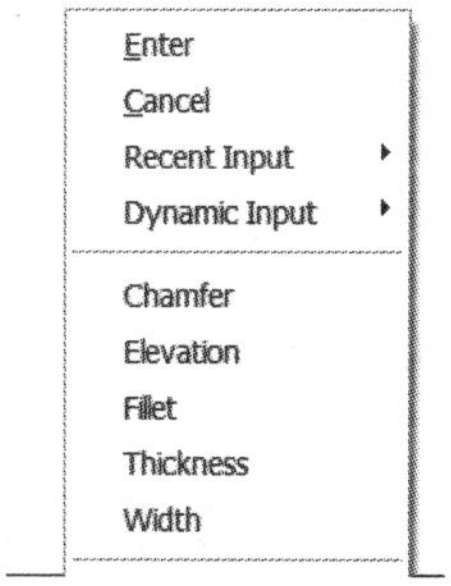

RMB Shortcut Menu for the Rectangle Command Before Selecting a Point

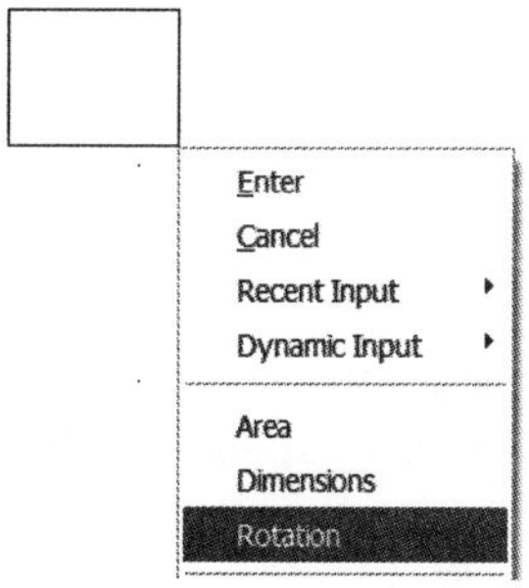

RMB Shortcut Menu for the Rectangle Command After Selecting a Point

Rectangles are polylines. All of the line segments are connected. Draw rectangles by designating the opposite corners.

General Procedures

To draw a rectangle by picking opposite corners:

1. Begin the rectangle command, and pick the first corner.
2. Drag the mouse and pick the opposite corner.

To draw a rectangle using coordinates:

1. Begin the rectangle command, and pick the first corner.
2. Type '@5,3' to create a 5 x 3 rectangle. The @ means "relative to the last point picked"; the first number is the distance in the x direction, and the second number is the distance in the y direction. The rectangle will be drawn 5 units to the right, and up 3 units. If a negative coordinate is typed, i.e. @-5,-3, the rectangle will be drawn to the left and down from the point picked.

Command Exercise

Exercise 4-4 – Rectangle

Drawing Name: **rect1.dwg**
Estimated Time to Completion: 5 Minutes

Scope

Draw rectangles as they are in the example. Turn Snap on to make the small rectangles. Turn Snap off to make the large rectangle.

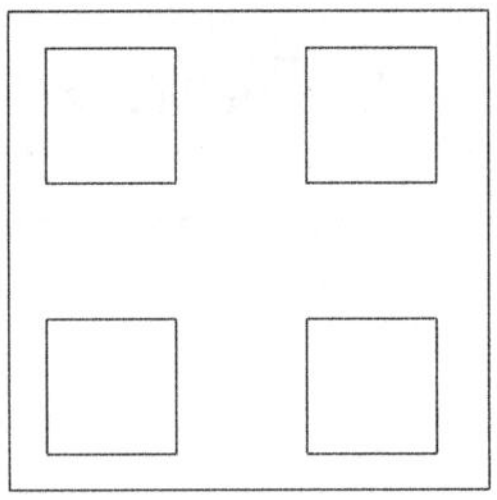

Drawing Rectangles

Solution

1. Start by creating the small rectangles. Turn <Snap on> by pressing the <F9> key, or use your LMB to toggle SNAP on at the Status Bar.
2. Invoke the **Rectangle** command (rectang).

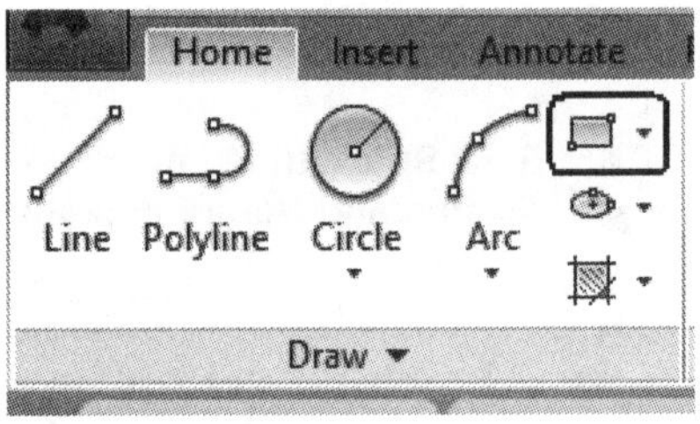

3. *Specify first corner point or [Chamfer/Elevation/Fillet/Thickness/Width]:*
   Position your pointer to the desired location and pick the first point with your LMB.
4. *Specify other corner point:*
   Move your pointer diagonally to the second desired location and pick the point with your LMB.
5. Repeat the Rectangle command by pressing the RMB or the <ENTER> key. Select the first corner of for the rectangle and then the second corner. Repeat the command to finish the small rectangles.
6. Turn Snap off by pressing the <F9> key or using the LMB to toggle snap off at the Status Bar.
7. Repeat the Rectangle command by right-clicking in the drawing area and selecting 'Repeat'.
8. *Specify first corner point or [Chamfer/Elevation/Fillet/Thickness/Width]:*
   Pick the first corner of the large rectangle with your LMB.
9. *Specify other corner point:*
   Pick a second diagonal corner to complete the large rectangle.

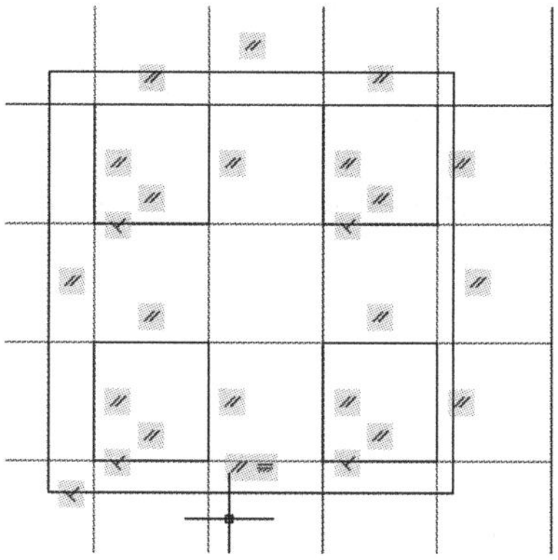

Geometric constraints will automatically be added as you draw.

You should see symbols for parallel, perpendicular, and horizontal constraints.

- Use the Rectangle command rather than drawing four separate line segments. This is quicker to make, and a more efficient object, since it is a polyline.
- Beginners should ignore the other Rectangle options, which appear at the command line, until they have had more experience using AutoCAD. The Chamfer and Fillet options will automatically add those features to the corners of the rectangle. Width will change the width of the rectangle's lines. Thickness and Elevation are for 3D drawing. Area allows the user to set the area of the rectangle. The user is still prompted for the length of one side of the rectangle and AutoCAD performs the calculation to determine the length of the other side based on the area provided. Rotation allows you to create a rectangle at an angle.
- *You can toggle the SNAP on and off in the middle of the rectangle command. Try it.*
- You can use the Shift+RMB Center Object Snap to snap to the center of a rectangle.

Arc

Command Locator

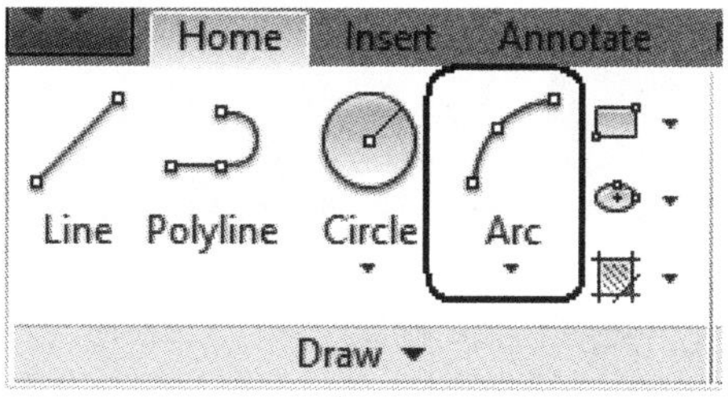

Home Ribbon	**Draw Panel/ Arc**
Command	**Arc**
Alias	**A**
RMB Shortcut Menu	**Drawing Window**

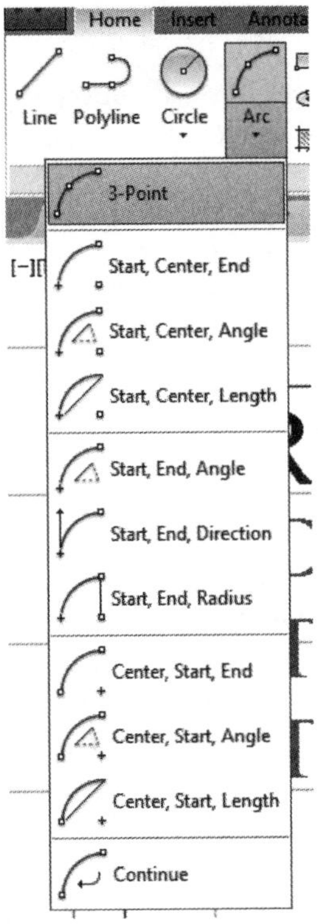

Arc options from the Draw (Arc) Pull-Down Menu

Command Overview

There are many arc options. We will look at the following Arc options: '3 points', 'Start, Center, End', and 'Start, End, Radius'. These Arc options will work in most instances.

Invoke the Arc command from the toolbar or by typing A at the command line. This will draw a '3-point' Arc through three consecutive points. Other Arc options can be selected from the Pull-Down menu. Arcs are constructed in a counterclockwise direction, except when drawing a 3-point Arc.

General Procedures

1. Begin the Arc command from the toolbar to draw a 3-point arc, or select one of the Arc options from the Pull-Down Menu.
2. Follow the Command Line prompts.
3. Press the RMB, with the cursor in the Drawing Window, to repeat the Arc command.

Tips & Tricks

- Arcs are constructed in a counterclockwise direction, except when drawing a 3-point Arc.
- Press the right button on the mouse to repeat the Arc command.
- When the cursor is in the Drawing Window, the Shortcut Menu (RMB) will provide an option to repeat the same Arc command.
- When the cursor is over the Command Line, the shortcut Menu (RMB) will provide and option to repeat the Arc command, but it will be the generic 3-point Arc.

Command Exercise

Exercise 4-5 – Arc

Drawing Name: **arc1.dwg**
Estimated Time to Completion: 10 Minutes

Scope

Draw the object on the left using the appropriate Arc and Object Snap options. Use running object snaps (Endpoint and Midpoint).

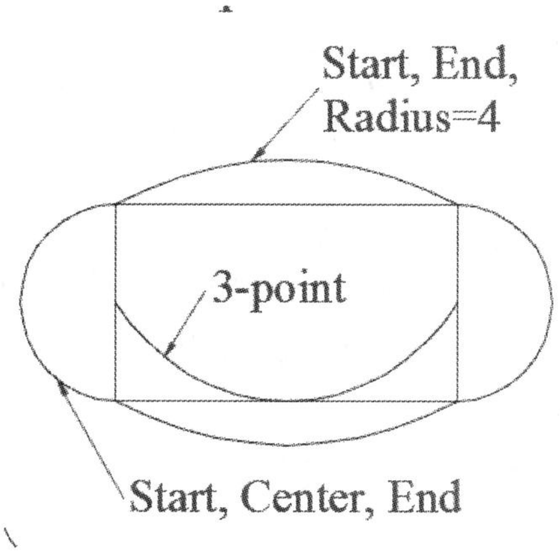

Drawing Arcs

Solution

1. Start by toggling OSNAP on. Press the **OSNAP** button on the Status Bar.

2. Right click on the Object Snap Tracking button on the Status Bar. Select **Object Snap Settings**.

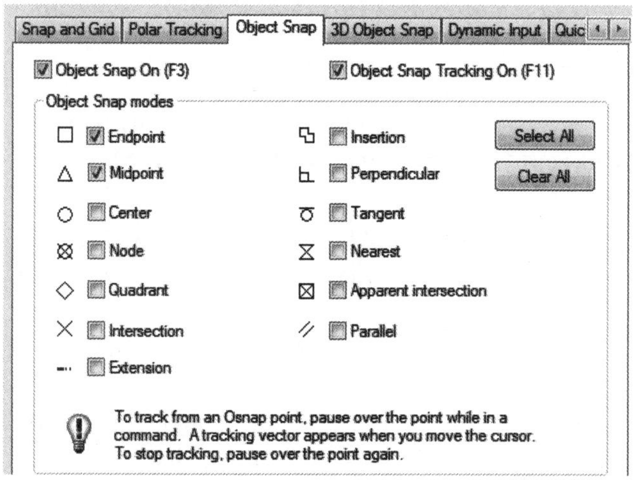

3. Enable **Midpoint** and **Endpoint** running object snaps as shown below.

4. Clear all the selections and enable Endpoint and Midpoint.

5. Verify that both Object Snap On and Object Snap Tracking is enabled.

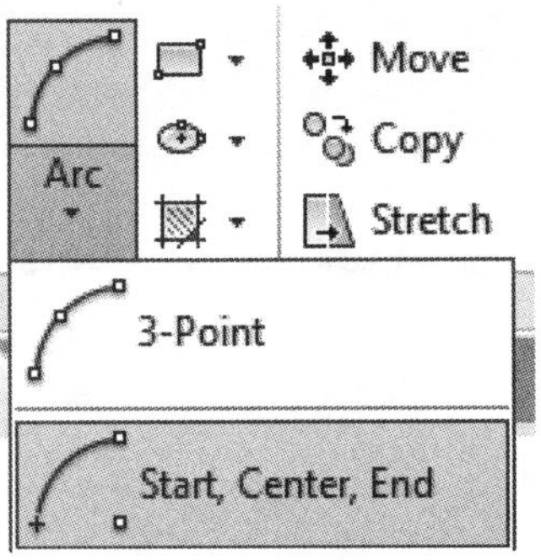

6. Invoke the Start, Center, End ARC command from the pull-down menu on the ribbon. (<DRAW<ARC<START,CENTER,END…).
7. *Specify start point of arc or [CEnter]:*
   Move near the upper left corner of the box until the desired Object Snap Marker appears. Select the point with the LMB.
8. *Specify second point of arc or [CEnter/ENd]: _c Specify center point of arc:*
   Move the pointer near the middle of the left side of the box until the Midpoint Object Snap appears. Select the point with the LMB.
9. *Specify end point of arc or [Angle/chord Length]:*
   Move near the bottom left corner of the box. Use your LMB when the Endpoint Object Snap appears.
10. Repeat the Start,Center,End Arc command with the RMB.
11. *Specify start point of arc or [CEnter]:*
    Repeat the exact procedure for the right side of the box but start the arc at the lower right corner.

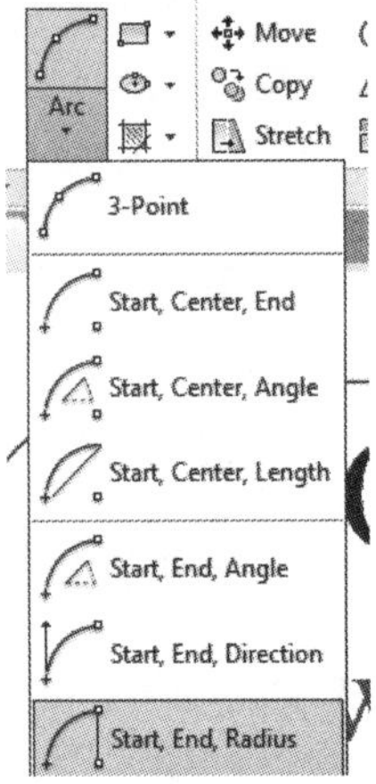

12. Invoke the Start, End, Radius Arc command from the pull-down menu on the ribbon(<DRAW PANEL<ARC<START,END,RADIUS).
13. *Specify start point of arc or [CEnter]:*
    Select a point near the upper right corner of the box. Remember to use the LMB when the desired Endpoint Object Snap Marker appears.
14. *Specify second point of arc or [CEnter/ENd]:*
    Select the end point of the arc at the upper left corner of the box.
15. *Specify center point of arc or [Angle/Direction/Radius]: _r Specify radius of arc:*
    Type '4' for the radius of the Arc.
16. Repeat the Start, End, Radius Arc command with the RMB. Repeat the process above. Start your Start, End, Radius Arc at the lower left corner of the box.

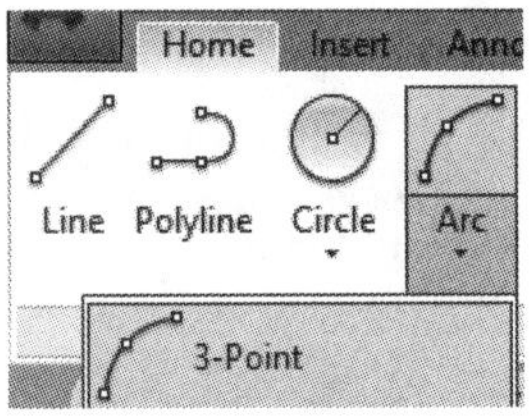

17. Invoke the Three Point Arc command by selecting it from the tool ribbon or by typing 'A' or 'ARC' at the command line and pressing <ENTER>.

18. *Specify start point of arc or [CEnter]:*
    Pick the midpoint of the right side of the box.
19. *Specify second point of arc or [CEnter/ENd]:*
    Pick the midpoint of the bottom of the box.
20. *Specify end point of arc:*
    Pick the midpoint of the left side of the box. This will complete the arc.

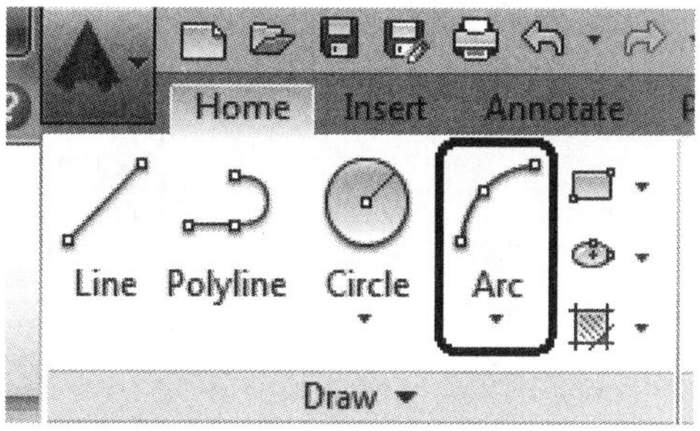

Tips & Tricks

> *Notice how the first two sets of arcs were created in a counterclockwise fashion. What happens if they were created in a clockwise fashion? Try it.*

Circle

Command Locator

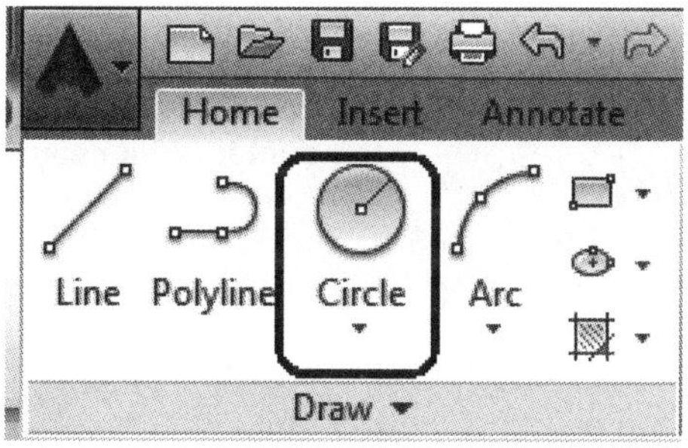

Ribbon Home	**Draw / Circle (select option)**
Command	**Circle**
Alias	**C**
RMB Shortcut Menu	**Drawing Window**

Command Overview

There are several ways to draw a Circle. The most common way is to pick the center point then designate a radius. Right click to view the shortcut menu for options. If a center point is selected first, the shortcut menu option for circle is Diameter. If no center point is selected, the shortcut menu will display other options.

Circle Options	**Overview**
Radius / Diameter	If a center point is selected, type or pick the Radius. Right-click to select the Diameter option or type D and <Enter>.
3P	Draws a circle by selecting 3 Points on the circumference.
2P	Draws a circle by selecting 2 Points on the diameter.
TTR	Draws a circle by selecting two Tangents and typing a radius.
Tangent, Tangent, Tangent	(Accessed from the Draw Pull-Down menu only.) Draws a circle by selecting three Tangents.

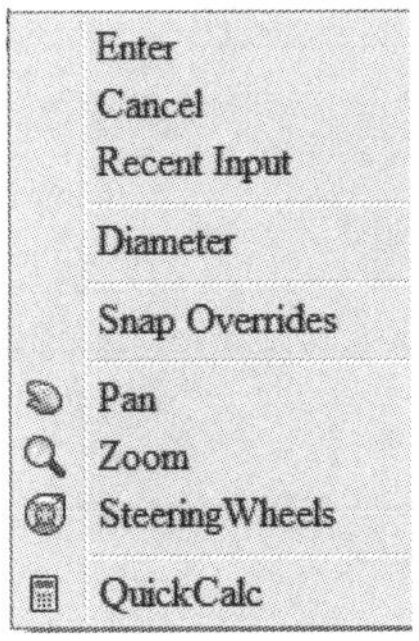

Circle Shortcut Menu (center point selected)

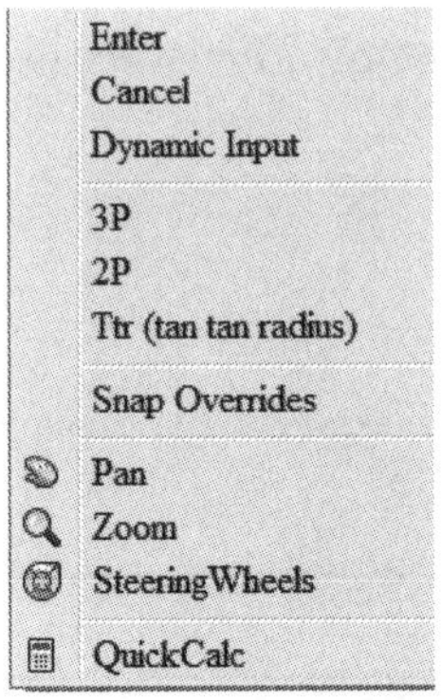

Circle Shortcut Menu (no center point selected)

General Procedures

1. Begin the Circle command, and pick the center point.
2. Type the radius, or press <ENTER> and select the Diameter option. Then type the diameter.

Donut

Command Locator

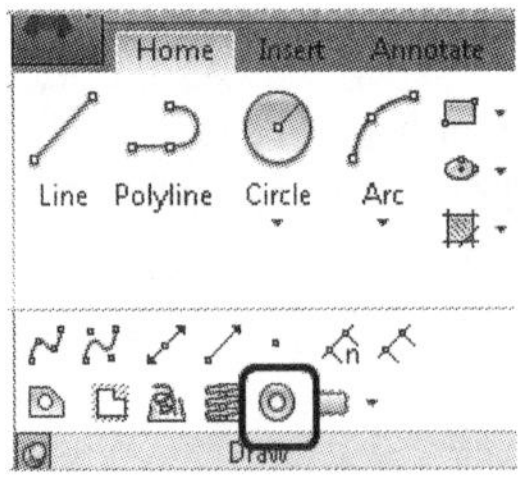

Home ribbon/Draw Panel	
Pull Down Menu	**Draw / Donut**
Command	**Donut**
Alias	**DO**

Command Overview

A Donut has an inner diameter and an outer diameter. When prompted for inner and outer diameters, type it, or press <ENTER> to accept the default.

General Procedures

1. Begin the Donut Command by typing DO (and <ENTER>) or selecting it from the Draw Pull-Down Menu.
2. Type the inside diameter or press <ENTER> to accept the *default.*
3. Type the outside diameter or accept the *default.*
4. Specify the center of the donut by picking in the drawing window. <ENTER> to exit.

Tips & Tricks

- For a solid filled Donut, make the inner diameter zero (0).
- The diameters can also be determined by picking two points in the AutoCAD Window.

Command Exercise

Exercise 4-6 – Circle and Donut

Drawing Name: **circle1.dwg**
Estimated Time to Completion: 10 Minutes

Scope

Draw the large circle using the Tan, Tan, Tan option. With Snap On, draw the inner ring using the Center, Diameter (3) option. With Snap On, draw four circles the same size using the Center, Radius (0.25) option. Place a donut with an inside diameter of 0 and an outside diameter of 0.5 as designated.

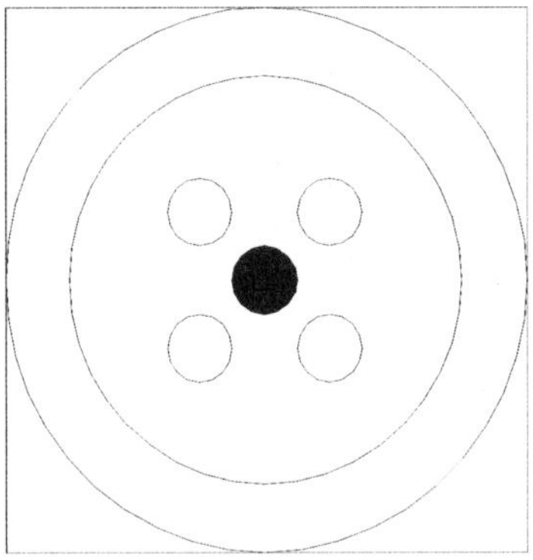

Circles and Donuts

Solution

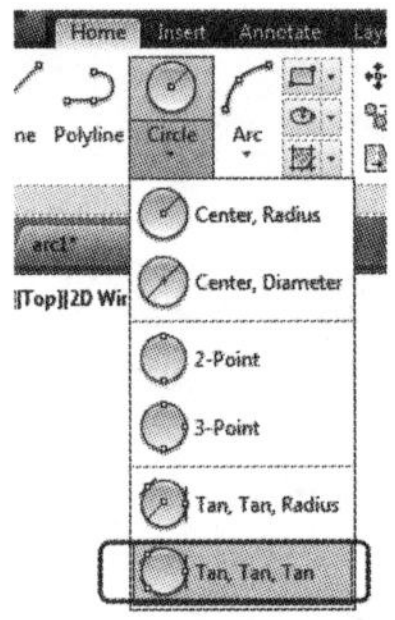

1. Invoke the circle command by using the **DRAW→CIRCLE→TAN, TAN, TAN** command from the Home ribbon.
2. *Specify first point on circle: _tan to*
   Select the top line segment of the box with the LMB. You will notice a symbol appearing when your pointer is on the line segment.
3. *Specify second point on circle: _tan to*
   Select the left or right side of the box with the LMB. (Notice the symbol that appears.)
4. *Specify third point on circle: _tan to*
   Select the bottom of the box with the LMB. (Notice the symbol that appears.) The Circle is automatically drawn.
5. Turn Snap on with the <F9> key or use your mouse to toggle snap on at the Status Bar.
6. Invoke the circle command by using the **DRAW→CIRCLE→ CENTER, DIAMETER** command from the pull-down menu.

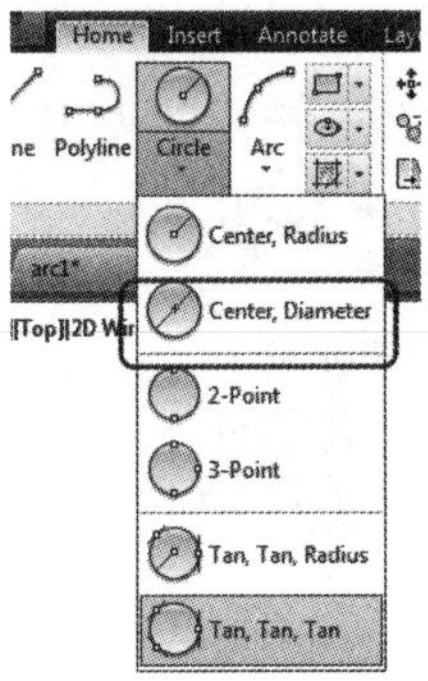

7. *Specify center point for circle or [3P/2P/Ttr (tan tan radius)]:*
   Pick in the center of the box.
8. *Specify diameter of circle:*
   Type '3' at the command line and press <ENTER>.

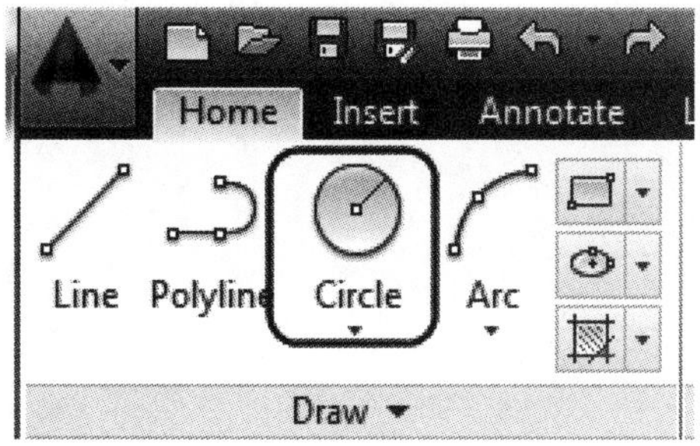

9. Invoke the circle command from the toolbar or by typing **C** or **CIRCLE** at the command line and pressing <ENTER>.
10. *Specify center point for circle or [3P/2P/Ttr (tan tan radius)]:*
    Use your LMB to pick the desired center point of the first small circle.
11. *Specify radius of circle or [Diameter] <1.5000>:*
    Type **0.25** at the command line and press <ENTER>.
12. Repeat the Circle command by pressing <ENTER> or the RMB.
13. *Specify center point for circle or [3P/2P/Ttr (tan tan radius)]:*
    Select the desired center point for the second small circle.
14. *Specify radius of circle or [Diameter] <0.2500>:*
    Press <ENTER> to accept the radius setting of 0.25.
15. Repeat the command to complete the remaining circles.

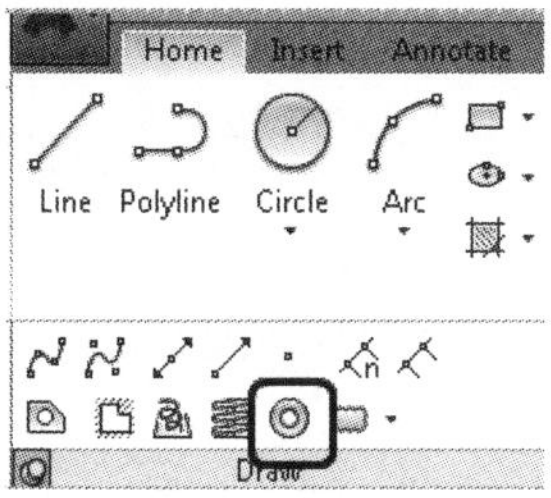

16. Invoke the Donut command by selecting Donut from the Draw panel on the Home ribbon or type **DO**.
17. *Specify inside diameter of donut <0.5000>:*
    Type **0** and press <ENTER>.
18. *Specify outside diameter of donut <1.0000>:*
    Type **0.5** and press <ENTER>.
19. *Specify center of donut or <exit>:*
    Use your LMB to pick the center point for the donut.
20. *Specify center of donut or <exit>:*
    Press <ENTER> to end the command.

Tips & Tricks

- *AutoCAD remembers the radius of the last circle that was created. If you start the Circle command by typing 'C' or 'Circle' you can enter a radius by default. If you would like to enter a diameter, type 'D' and press <ENTER> after you have selected the center point of the circle and then enter the diameter of the circle.*

Spline

Command Locator

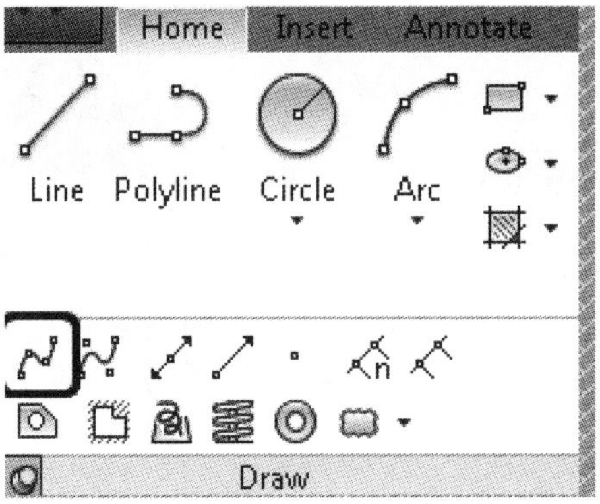

Home Ribbon	**Draw / Spline**
Command	**Spline**
Alias	**spl**

Command Overview

You can make a spline from a polyline using the Pedit command. An easy way to create a spline is to define the points where the arcs (both concave and convex) are to be placed and use those points to control your spline's shape.

General Procedures

1. Begin the Spline command.
2. Pick a point.
3. Pick a second point.
4. You can right click at this point to see the spline options.
5. Continue picking points until you are done. Press <ENTER> or 'Close' to exit the command.

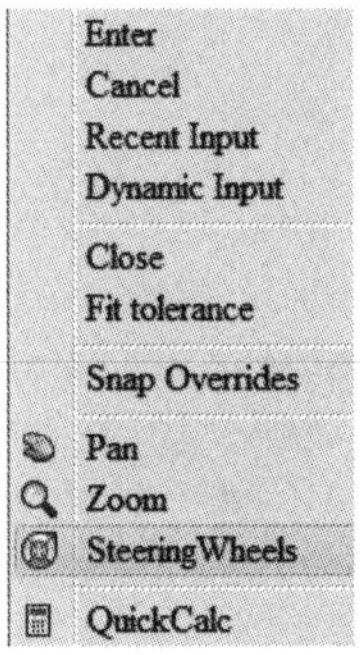

Spline Shortcut Menu Options

You can use the Fit tolerance option to define a spline using points. If you set the fit tolerance to 0, then the spline will pass through the selected points. If you set the fit tolerance to a number greater than 0, it will create a spline using the tolerance to get as close to the points as the tolerance allows. Dynamic Input only appears in the shortcut menu if the DYN button is enabled.

Command Exercise

Exercise 4-7 – Spline

Drawing Name: **spline1.dwg**
Estimated Time to Completion: 5 Minutes

Scope

Use the points to assist you in creating your spline.

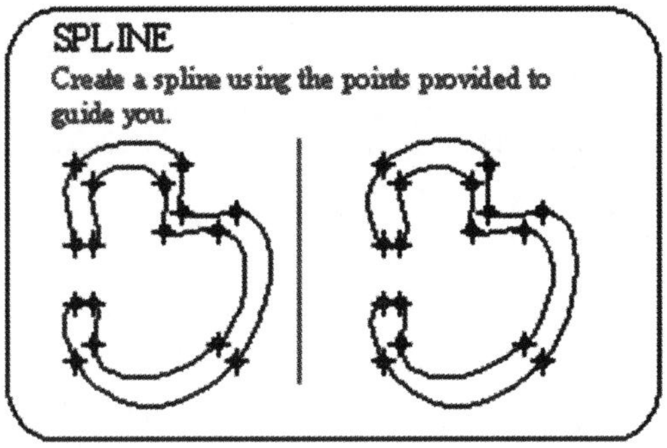

Drawing a Spline

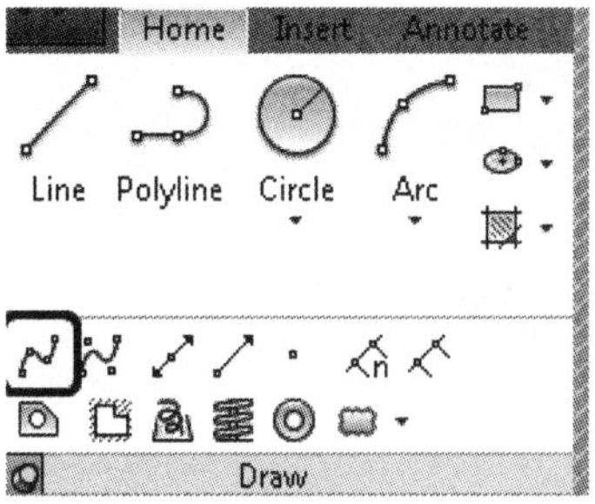

Solution

1. Invoke the **Spline** command.
2. Select a point.
3. Follow the points along to create your spline object.
4. At the last point, right click and select **Close** and then <ENTER>.

Ellipse

Command Locator

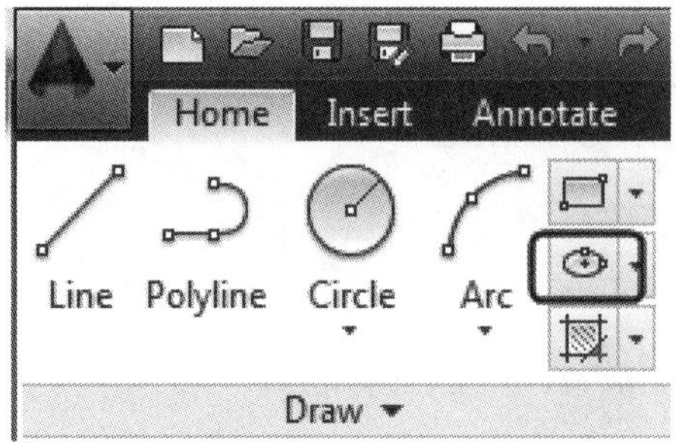

Home Ribbon	**Draw / Ellipse**
Command	**Ellipse**
Alias	**el**

Command Overview

The Ellipse command prompts for a center point, an axis end point, and then a radius distance to the perpendicular axis. Users can also determine the size of the ellipse based on rotation. Ellipse Arc allows the user to create a partial ellipse.

General Procedures

1. Begin the Ellipse command.
2. Pick a center point.
3. Pick a second point to indicate one axis end of the ellipse.
4. Move the mouse in a perpendicular direction from the second point to set the second axis. Enter a radius distance or select a point.

Command Exercise

Exercise 4-8 – Ellipse and Ellipse Arc

Drawing Name: **ellipse1.dwg**
Estimated Time to Completion: 5 Minutes

Scope

Use the points to assist you in creating your ellipse.

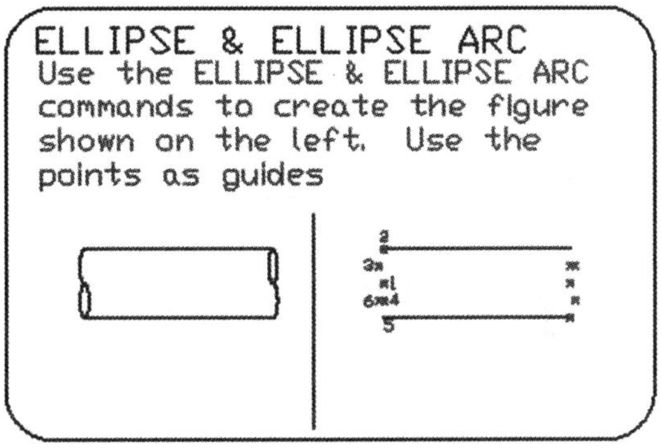

Drawing an Ellipse

1. Invoke the **Ellipse** command.

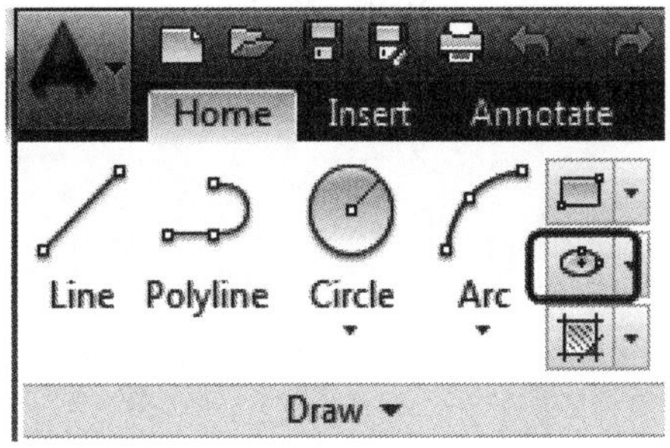

2. Select Point 4.

The NODE OSNAP should be enabled to assist you in selecting the points.

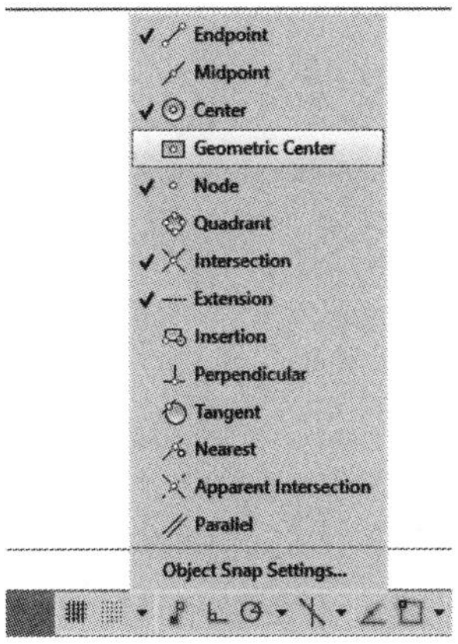

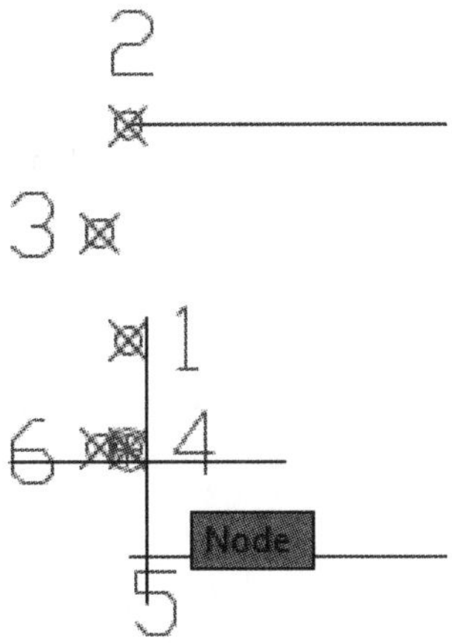

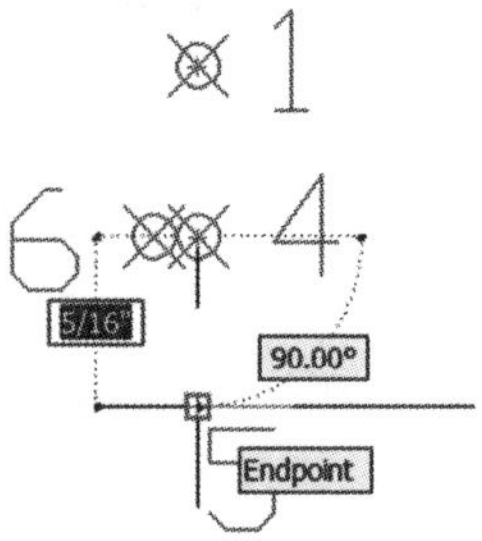

3. Select the endpoint located at Point 5.

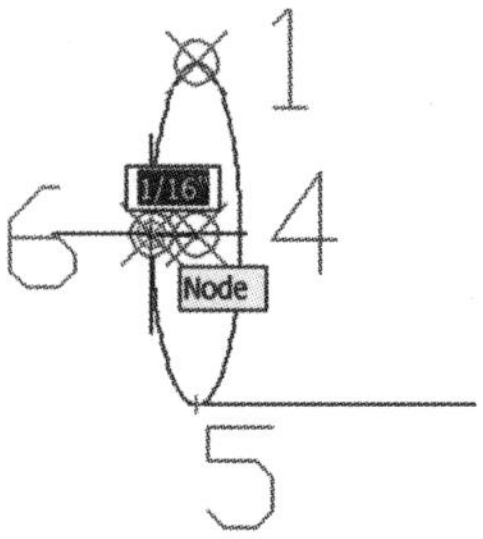

4. Select Point 6 when prompted for the distance to the other axis.

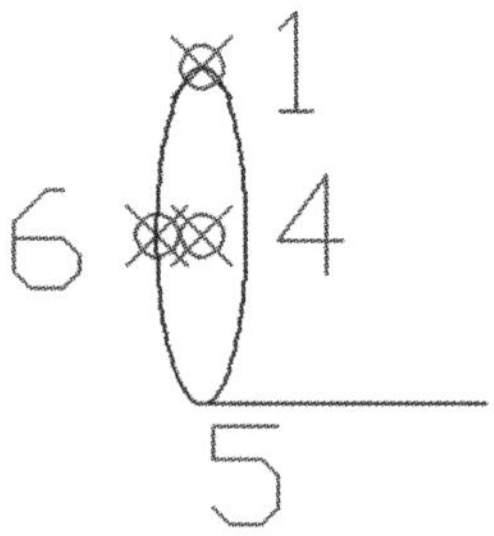

The ellipse is placed.

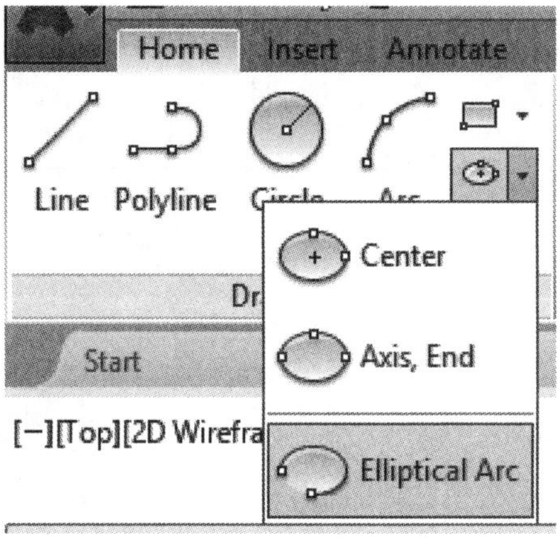

5. Select the Elliptical Arc tool.

6. Select Point 1.

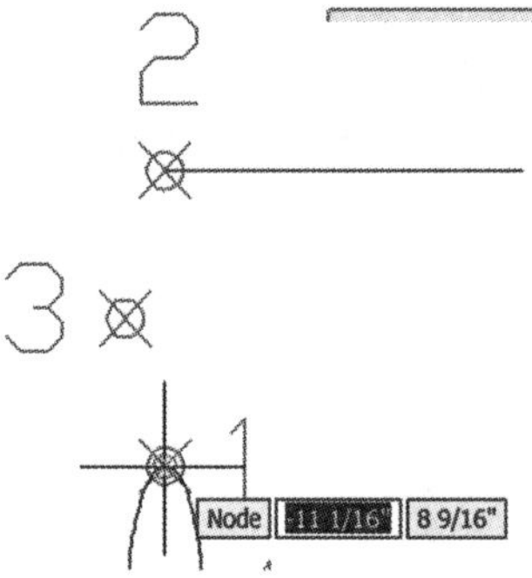

7. Select Point 2.

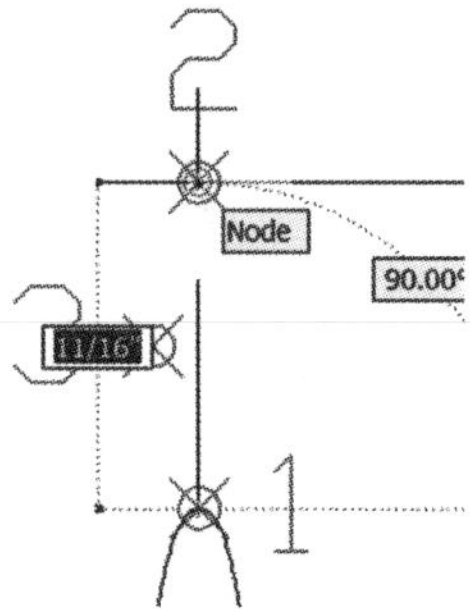

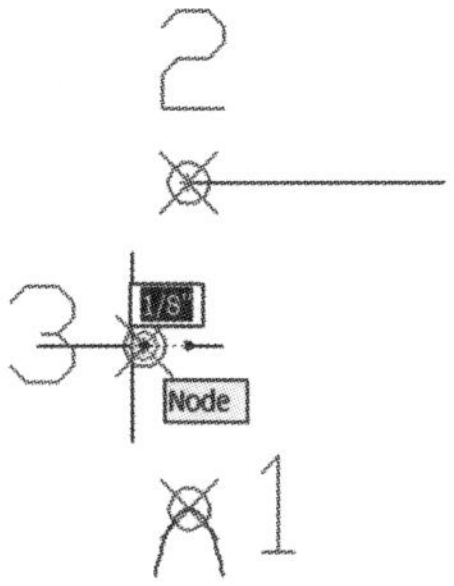

8. Select Point 3.

You will be prompted for the start and end points for the angle for the ellipse.

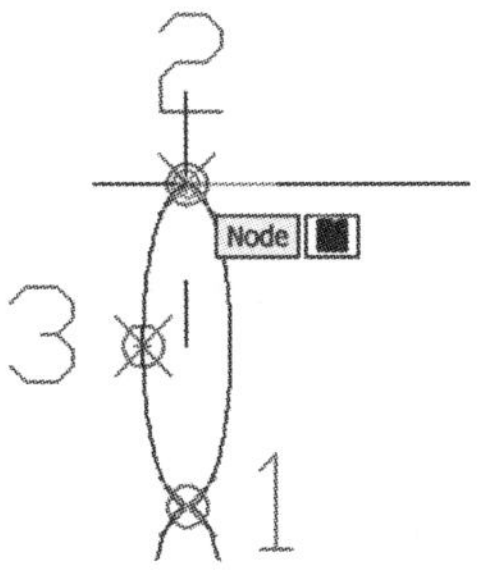

9. Select Point 2 as the start point for the ellipse.

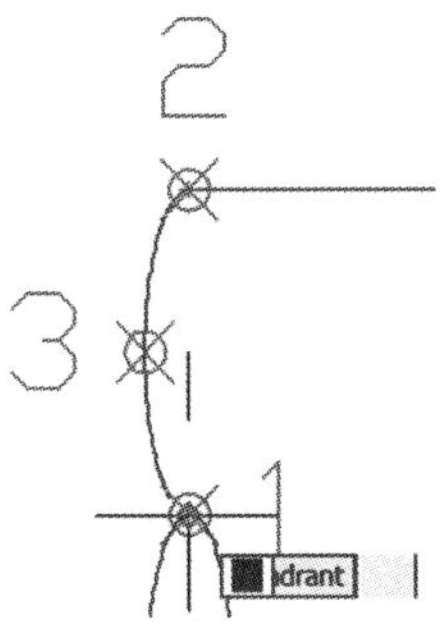

10. Select Point 1 as the end point for the angle.

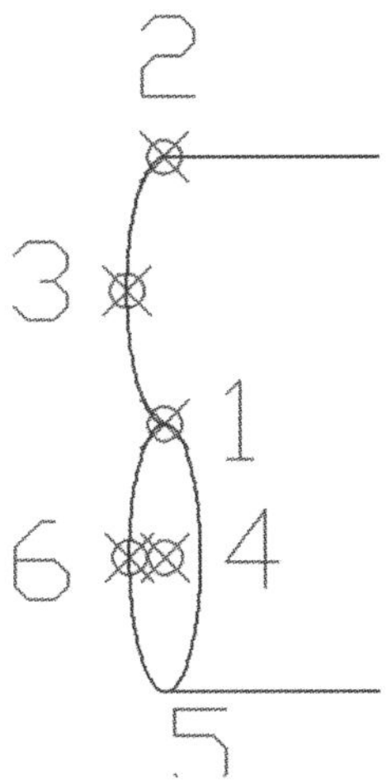

One end of your wire is completed.

11. Repeat the steps for the other side.

Add Selected

Command Locator

Shortcut Menu	**Select an object, right click and select Add Selected**
Command	**Add Selected**

Command Overview

With the ADD SELECTED command, you can create a new object using a source object. The new object will have the same layer, color, and line type as the source object; however, the user can define new location points and new sizes.

General Procedures

1. Select an object.
2. The command which is used to create the selected object is initiated.
3. Create a new object.
4. The new object has the same layer, color, linetype, etc. as the source object.

Command Exercise

Exercise 4-9 – Add Selected

Drawing Name: **Add Selected.dwg**
Estimated Time to Completion: 5 Minutes

Scope

Use Add Selected to add lines and a circle.
Note that the new entities have the same properties as the source entities: layer, color, etc.

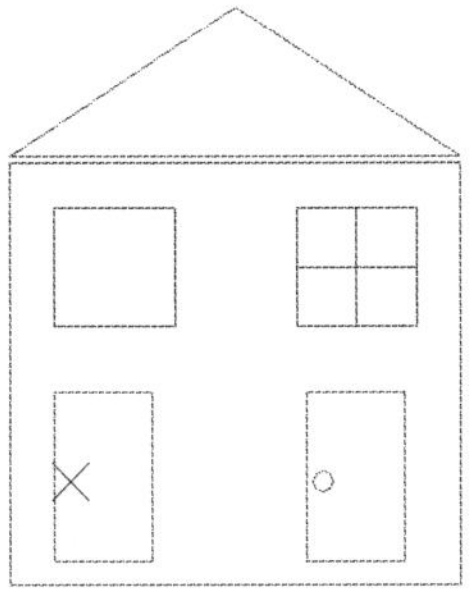

Add Selected Exercise

Solution

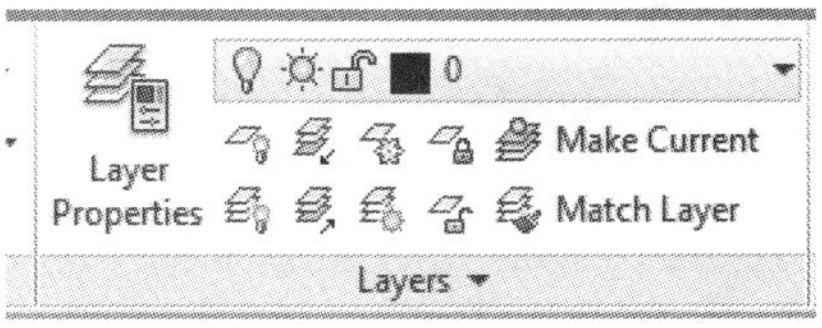

Note that the current layer is 0.

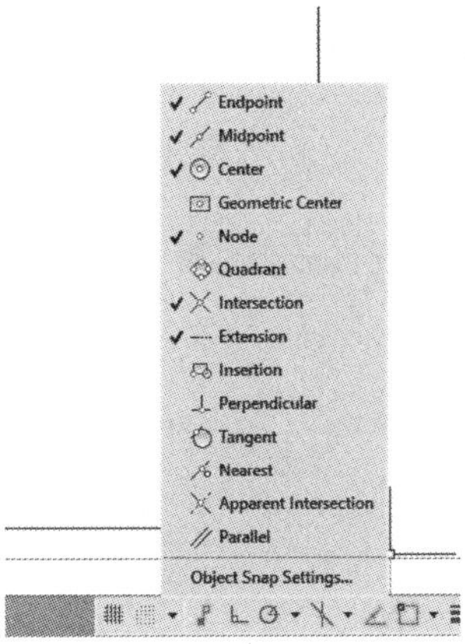

Right click on the OSNAP settings on the status bar.

Verify that the Midpoint OSNAP is enabled.

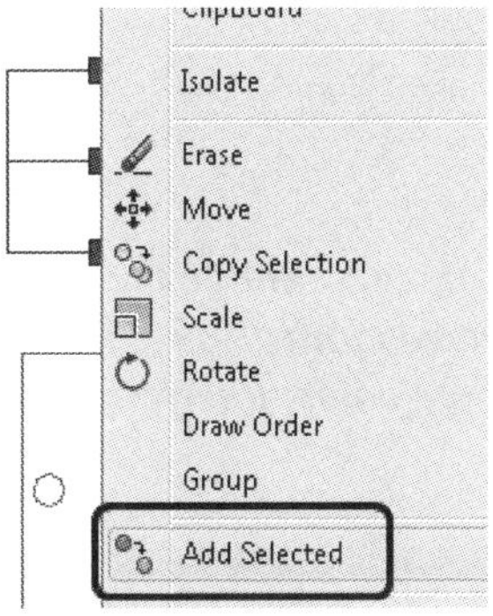

1. Select the vertical blue line.
2. Right click and select **Add Selected**.

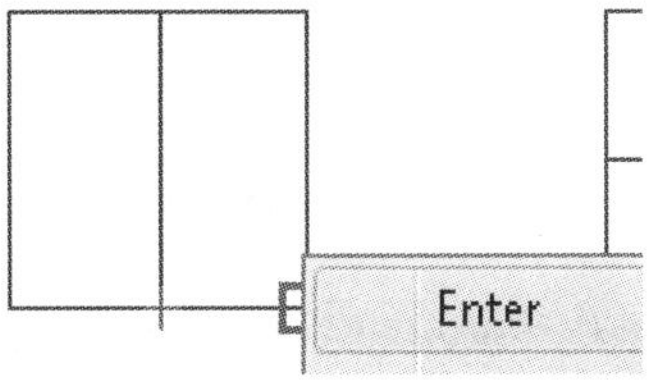

3. Select the top and bottom midpoints to place the new line.
4. Right click and select ENTER to exit ADD SELECTED mode.

Note that the new line is placed on the same layer and is the same color as the line selected.

Verify that the current layer is still layer 0.

5. Repeat to place the horizontal blue line.

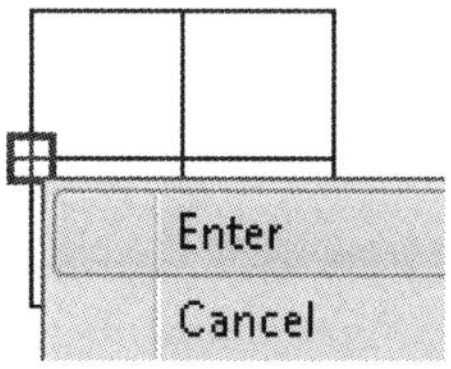

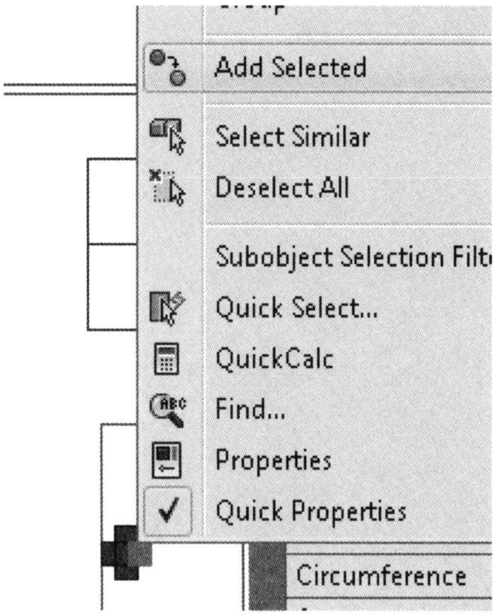

6. Enable the NODE object snap.
7. Select the orange circle.
8. Right click and select **Add Selected**.

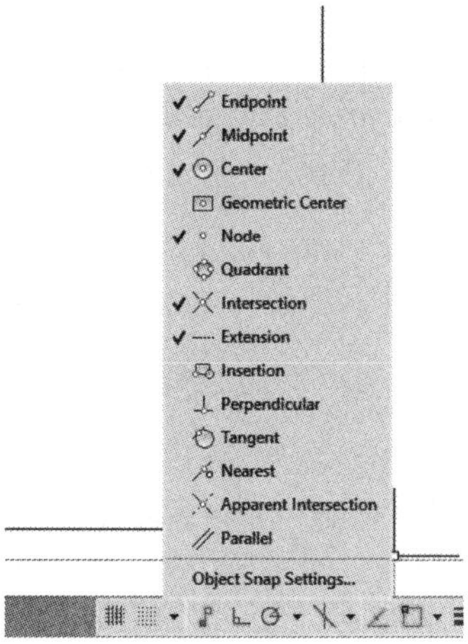

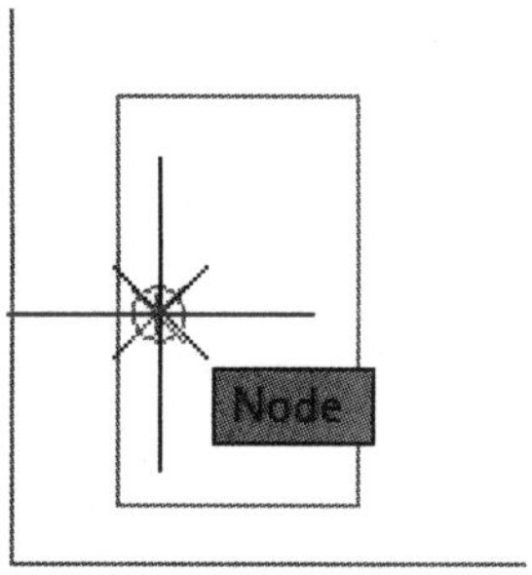

9. Select the point in the left-side door to place the circle.
10. Specify a radius of 1/8″.

Note: You can change the radius of the circle. AddSelected controls the type of object—circle, line, etc. and the color, linetype, and properties—but not the size.

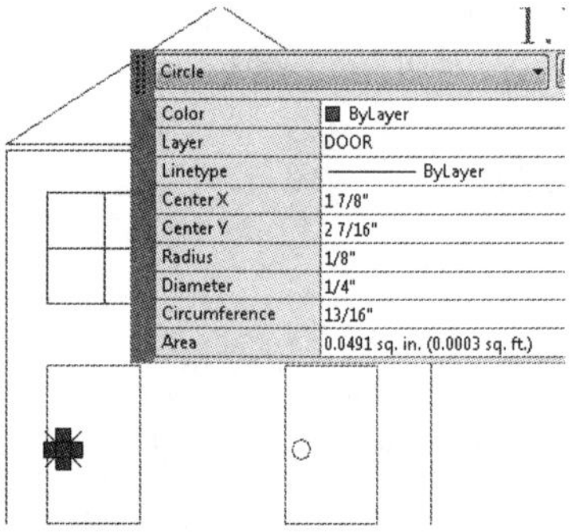

Note that the new circle has the same properties as the selected circle.

Verify that the current layer is still layer 0.

Section Exercise

Exercise 4-10 – Standard Bracket

Drawing Name: **create a new drawing**
Estimated Time to Completion: **15 Minutes**

Scope

Use the commands you have learned in the past section to create the three view orthographic drawing of the bracket in the figure below. Do not worry about a title block, drawing dimensions or hidden lines. Try to place the polygon and circle in the middle of the upper and lower plates. Remember to use the most efficient commands (i.e. Running Object Snap or Geometric Center).

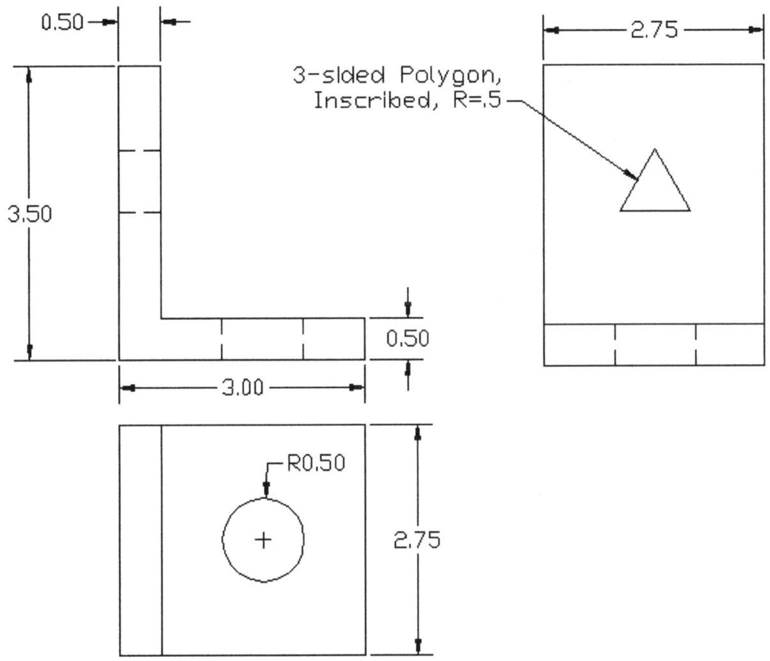

Standard Bracket

Hints

1. Start by setting the Endpoint, Midpoint, Intersection and Quadrant Running Object Snaps. Turn OTRACK on.
2. Try to use the Line and Rectangle commands to create the overall geometry. Try the Polygon command to create the Triangle, and the circle command to make the hole.
3. Use the ORTHO mode to create vertical and horizontal lines.

Section Exercise

Exercise 4-11 – Simple House

Drawing Name: **create a new drawing**
Estimated Time to Completion: **15 Minutes**

Scope

Using the commands learned in this section, draw this simplified house.

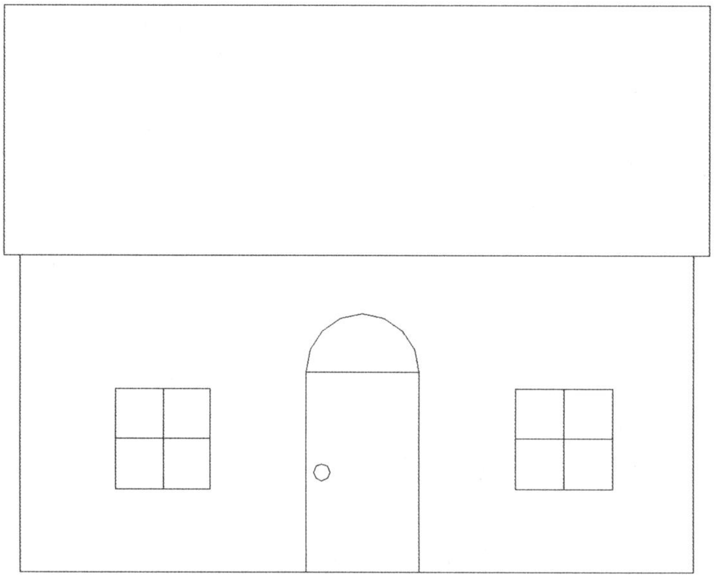

Simple House

Hints

1. Use Rectangles for the basic shapes.
2. Use lines with midpoint object snaps for the window frames.
3. Draw extra shapes with the polygon command and then erase them.

Hatch

Command Locator

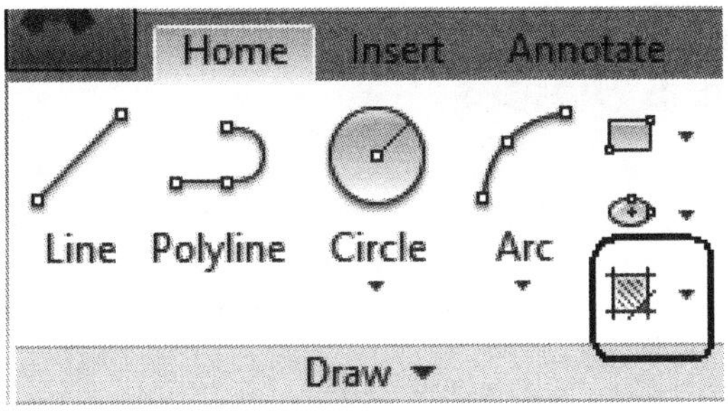

Home Ribbon	Draw/Hatch
Shortcut	**HA**
Command	**Hatch**

Command Overview

Hatch adds a pattern to a closed region or polygonal shape. Hatching is used to delineate materials or differentiate from one area to another.

General Procedures

1. Start the Hatch command.
2. Select the desired pattern from the ribbon.
3. Set the angle and scale as desired.
4. Select inside the area desired.
5. The area will preview.
6. If the result is OK, then press ENTER or Close Hatch Creation on the ribbon.

Tips & Tricks

- *Use a Solid Hatch to completely fill an area.*

Command Exercise

Exercise 4-12 – Hatch

Drawing Name: **hatch1.dwg**
Estimated Time to Completion: **5 Minutes**

Scope

Use the Hatch Command to add a roof shake pattern to the roof on this house.

Add a roof shake to the house

Solution

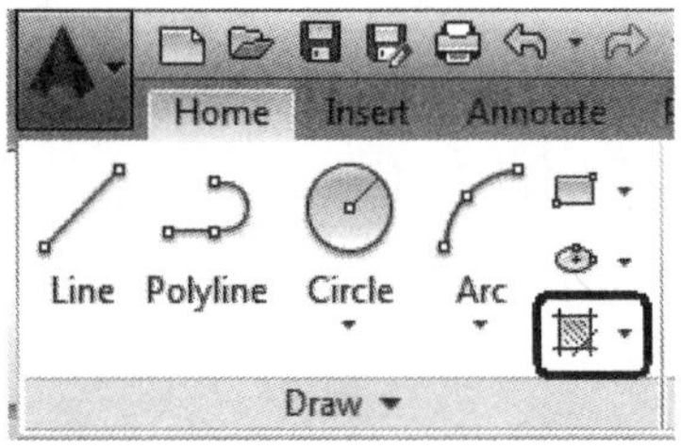

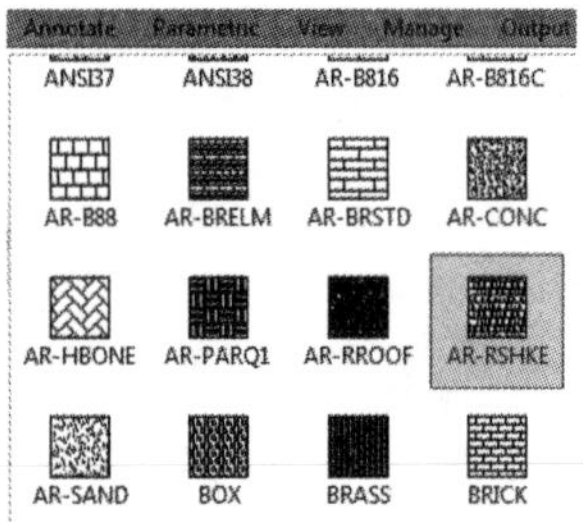

1. Select the Hatch command.
2. Locate the AR-RSHKE hatch pattern on the ribbon or right click and select Settings.

The settings dialog will allow you to select the pattern and color to be used for the Hatch pattern.

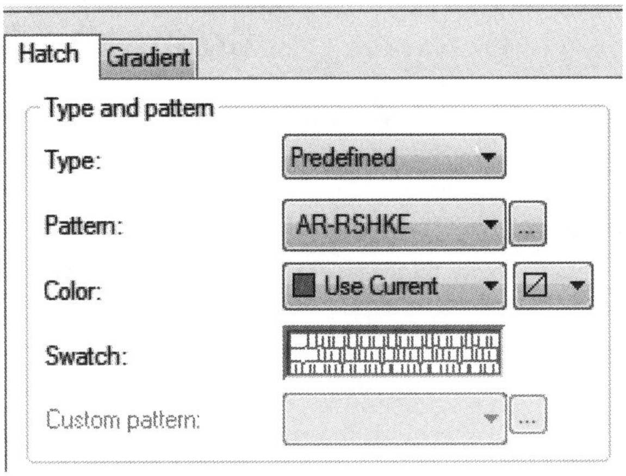

3. Pick a point on the roof.
4. You should see a preview of the roof hatch pattern.

5. RMB and select ENTER or press Close Hatch on the ribbon.

Command Exercise

Exercise 4-13 – HPLAYER

Drawing Name: **hplayer.dwg**
Estimated Time to Completion: **20 Minutes**

Scope

Use the new HPLAYER system variable to set a layer as the default layer for new hatches and fills.

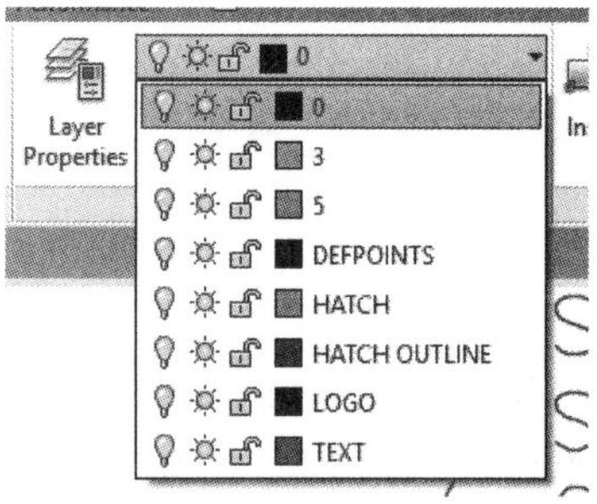

1. Go to the Layers list and check to see which layers are available. Notice that one of the layers is called HATCH.
2. Verify that the current layer is 0.

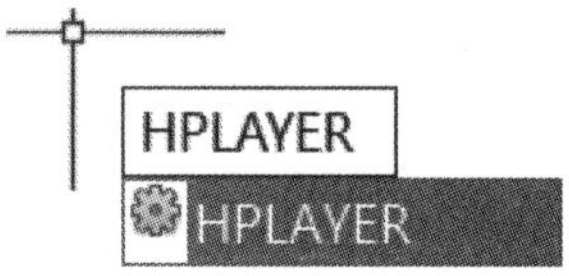

3. Type HPLAYER.

4. Type HATCH when prompted for the layer to be assigned for hatches.
5. Press ENTER.

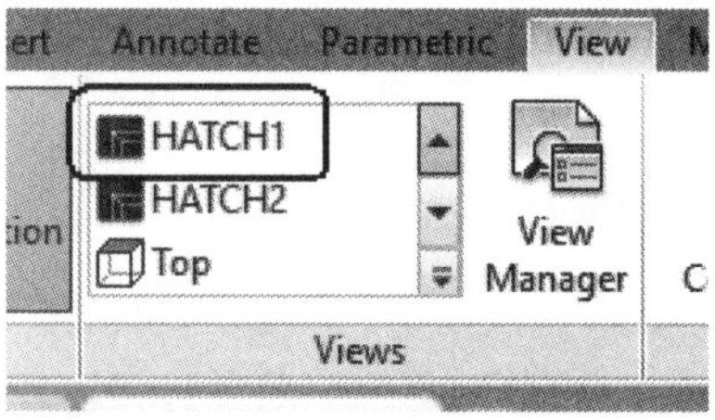

6. Activate the View ribbon.
7. Double left click on the HATCH1 named view to display.

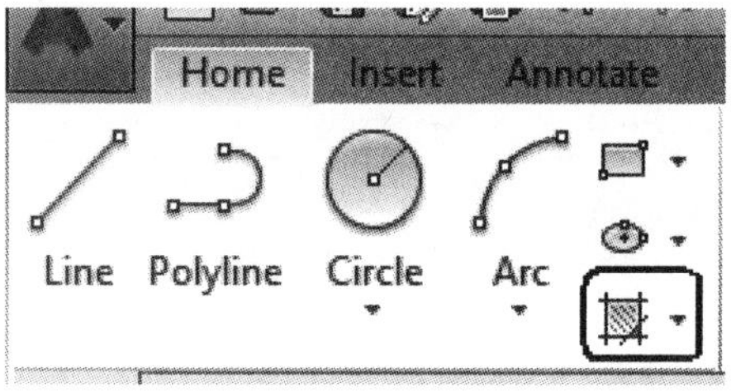

8. Activate the Home ribbon.
9. Select the HATCH tool.

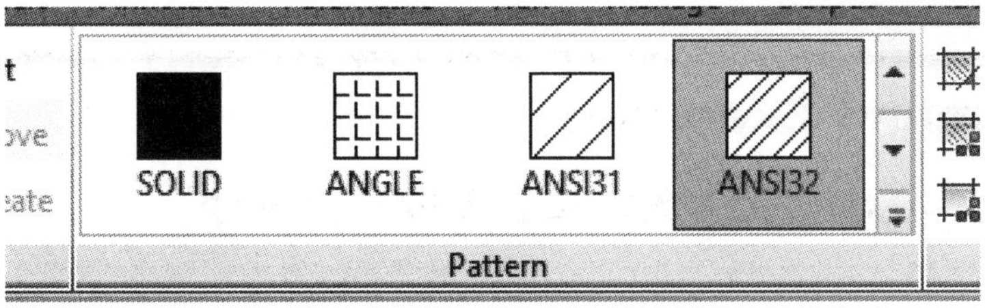

10. Select the ANSI32 hatch pattern.

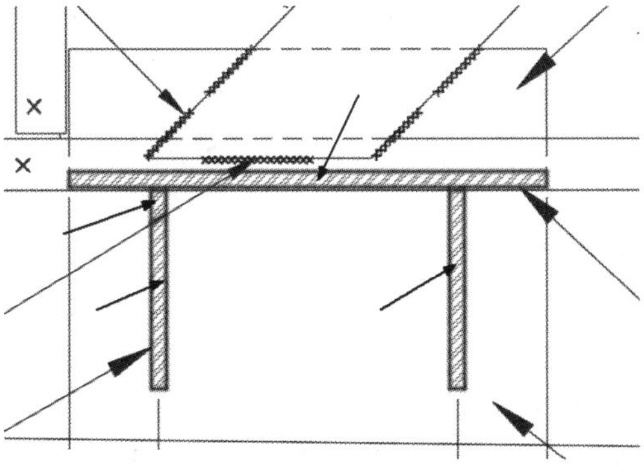

11. Left click inside the four areas indicated. These are steel plates.

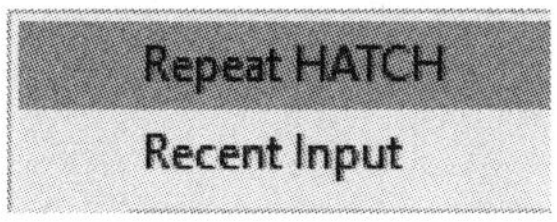

12. Right click and select **Repeat HATCH**.

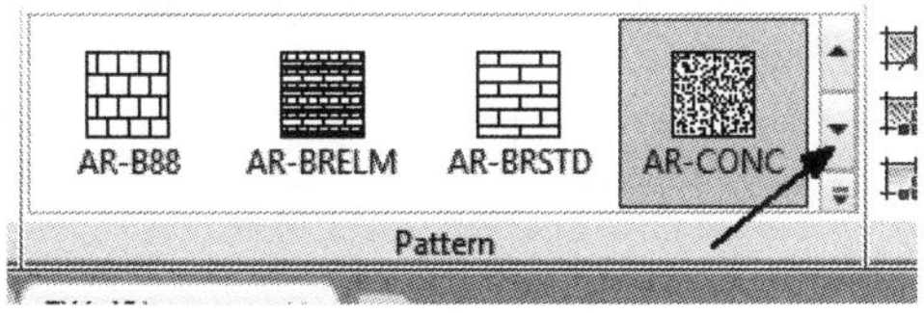

13. Use the scroll down arrow to scroll down the list of hatch patterns.

14. Select AR-CONC.

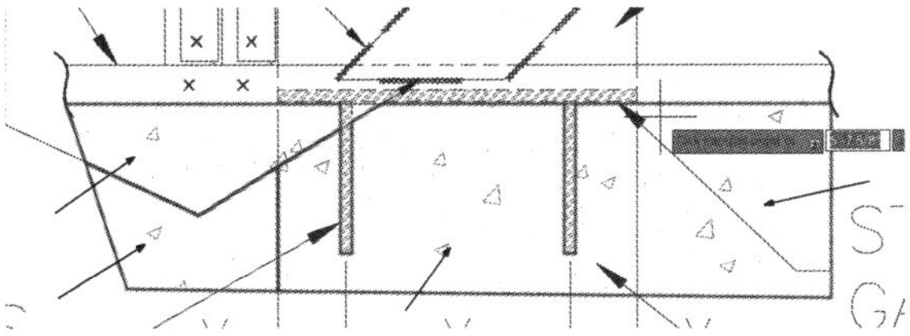

15. Left pick in the areas shown to place the hatch pattern.

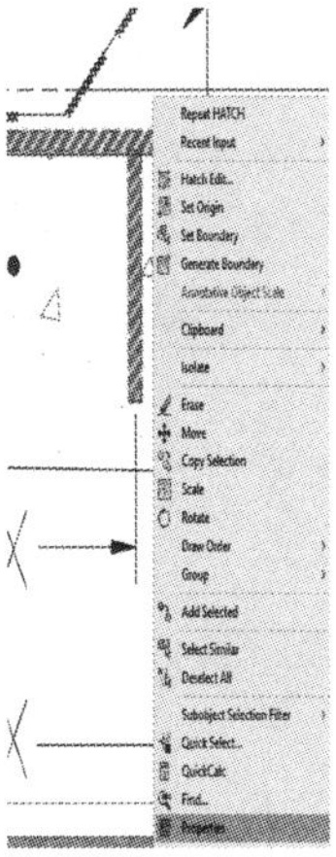

16. Select the hatch pattern placed on the plates.

17. Right click and select Properties.

18. Verify that the hatch was placed on the HATCH layer—which was assigned using HPLAYER. Note that the hatch pattern name is listed correctly as ANSI32.

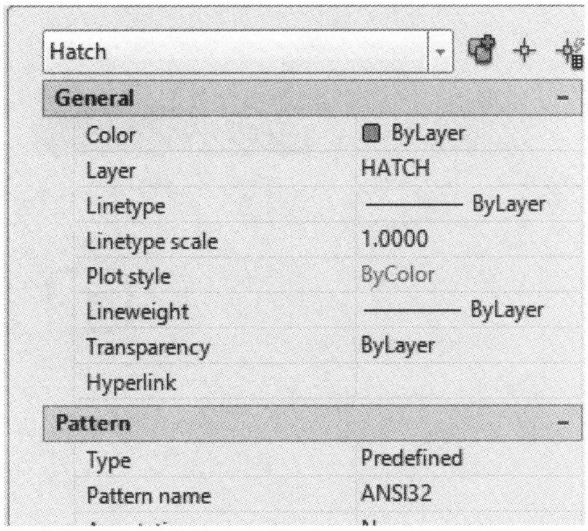

Command Exercise

Exercise 4-14 – HPLAYER REPRISED

Drawing Name: **hplayer2.dwg**
Estimated Time to Completion: **15 Minutes**

Scope

Use the new HPLAYER system variable to create a new layer and set it as a layer to be used as the default layer for new hatches and fills. The new layer uses the properties of the current layer; i.e. color and linetype.

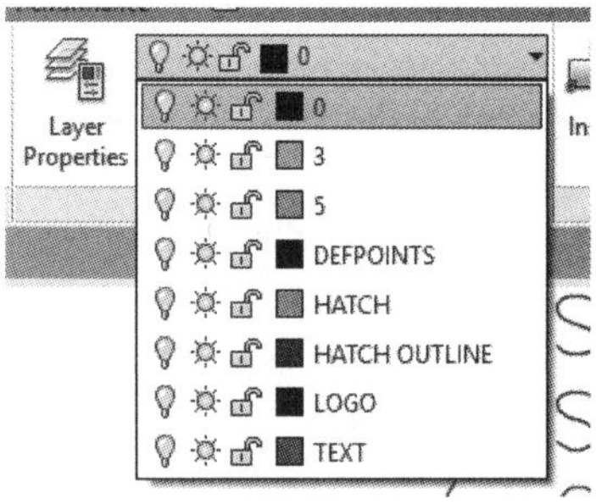

1. Go to the Layers list and check to see which layers are available. Notice that there is no layer called HATCH2.
2. Verify that the current layer is 0.

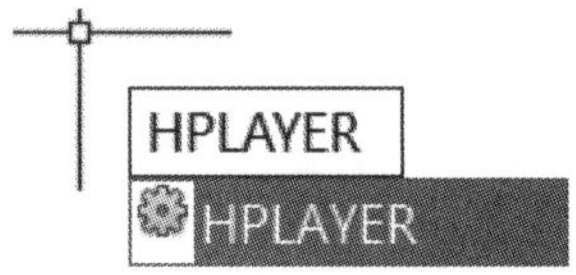

3. Type HPLAYER.

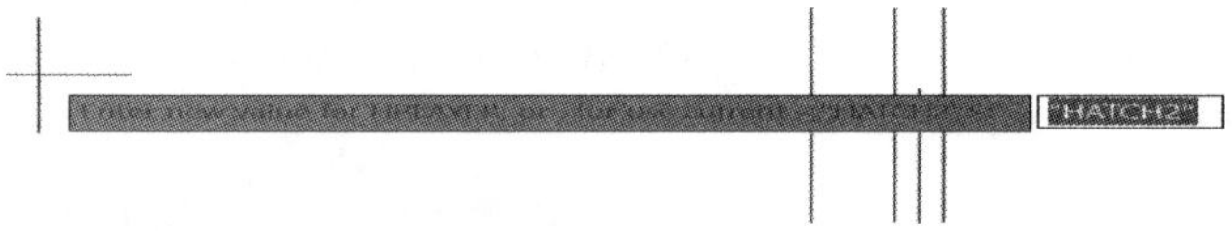

4. Type HATCH2 when prompted for the layer to be assigned for hatches.
5. Press ENTER.

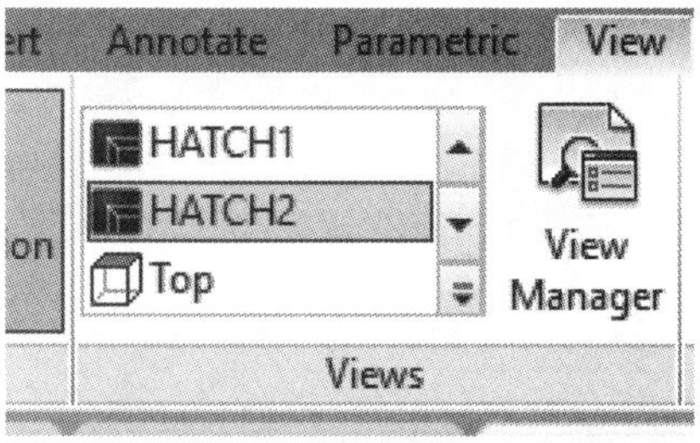

6. Activate the View ribbon.
7. Double left click on the HATCH2 named view to display.

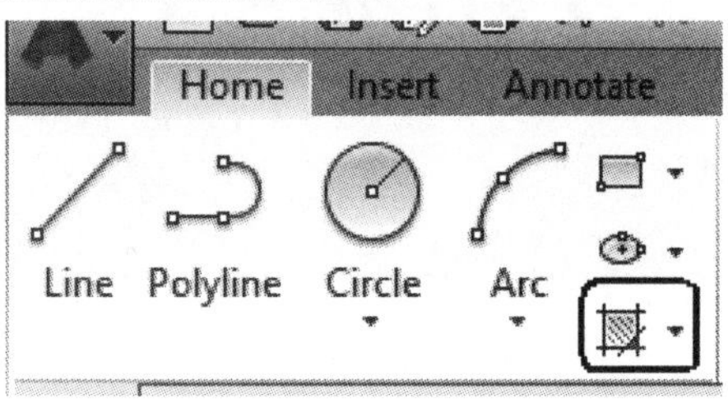

8. Activate the Home ribbon.
9. Select the HATCH tool.

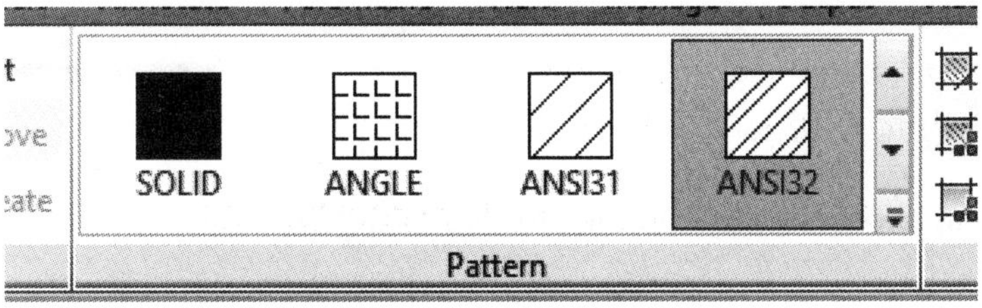

10. Select the ANSI32 hatch pattern.

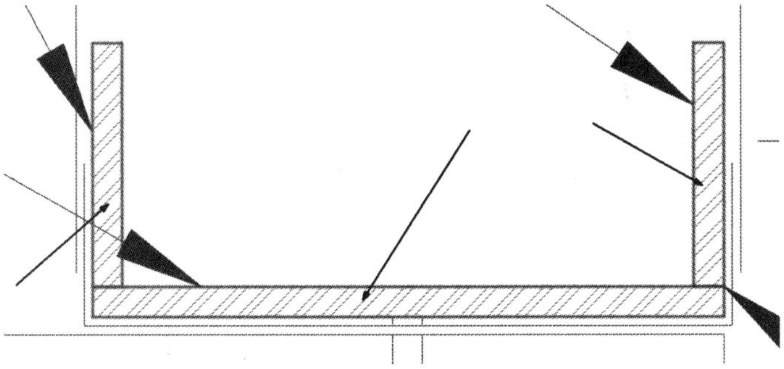

11. Left click inside the three areas indicated. These are steel plates.
12. Press ENTER to continue.

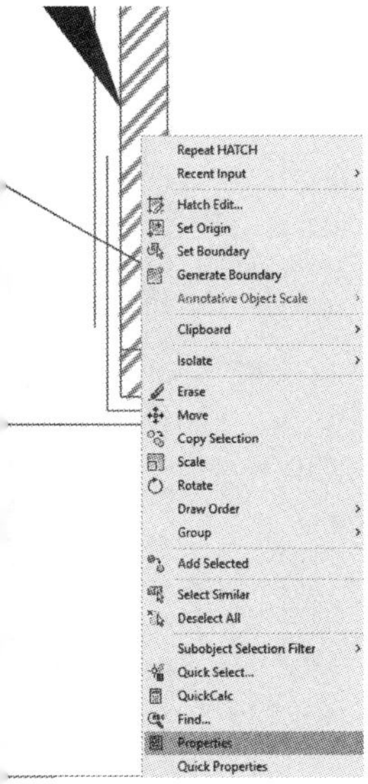

13. Select the hatch pattern placed on the plates.
14. Right click and select Properties.

15. Verify that the hatch was placed on the HATCH layer—which was assigned using HPLAYER. Note that the hatch pattern name is listed correctly as ANSI32.

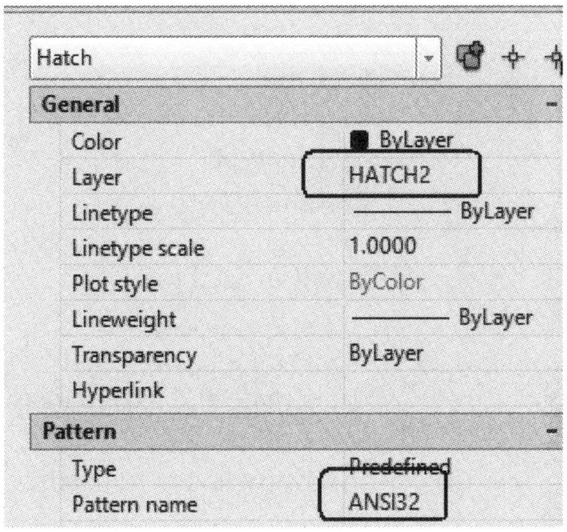

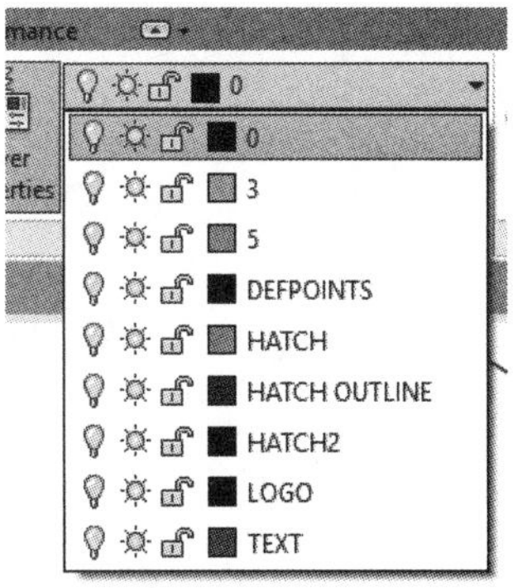

16. Check in the layers drop-down to see there is now a layer called HATCH2.

Review Questions

1. Identify the following icons by writing the name of the command and the toolbar where it can be found. *Extra: Write the command line shortcut, or alias.*

Command

 ____________________

 ____________________

 ____________________

 ____________________

 ____________________

2. Name the six options for creating a circle.

3. Name three options for creating an arc.

4. You construct a circle using the 2P option. What does this option prompt you for?

5. **T F** Using Add Selected automatically changes the active layer.

6. Identify the properties which are copied when using **Add Selected.**

   a) Color
   b) Layer
   c) Linetype
   d) Location

7. HPLayer is used to:

   a) Print a layer
   b) Create and assign a layer for hatches
   c) Add hatches
   d) Copy layers to hatches

Review Answers

1. Identify the following icons by writing the name of the command.

   Line / Draw / L

   Rectangle / Draw / REC

   Circle / Draw / C

   Arc / Draw / A

   Polygon / Draw / POL

2. Name the six methods for creating a circle.

   Center, Radius

   Center, Diameter

   2P

   3P

   Tan, Tan, Tan

   Tan, Tan, Radius

3. Name three methods for creating an arc.

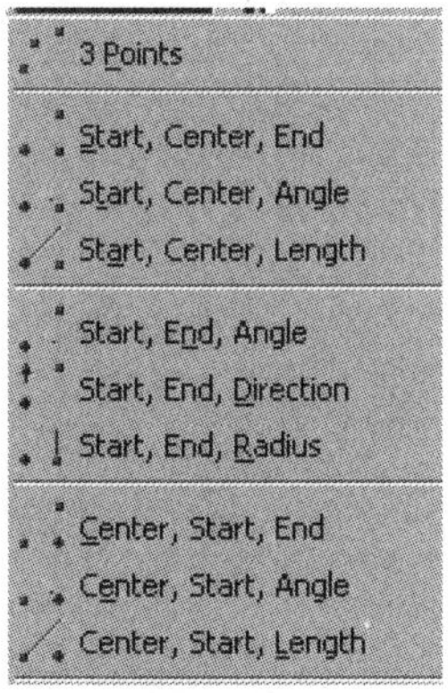

4. You construct a circle using the 2P option. What does this option prompt you for?

   The two end points of the diameter

5. *False*

6. *a, b, c*

7. *b*

Notes:

Lesson 5.0 – Modify Commands

Estimated Class Time: 2 Hours

Objectives

This section introduces AutoCAD commands for modifying objects in a simple drawing. This lesson reviews the following commands on the Modify toolbar:

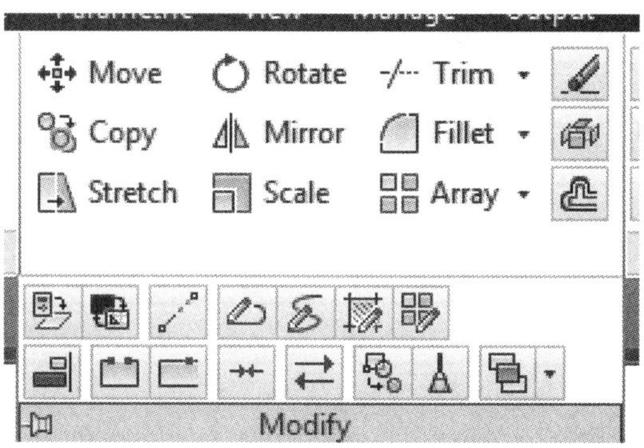

- **Copy**
  Copy selected objects to a new location.
- **Mirror**
  Mirror selected objects about a mirror line.
- **Offset**
  Offset selected objects a set distance.
- **Array**
  Rectangular and Polar Arrays.
- **Move**
  Move selected objects to a new location.
- **Rotate**
  Rotate selected objects to a new angle.
- **Scale**
  Scale objects to make them larger or smaller.
- **Stretch**
  Use stretch to lengthen and widen geometry.
- **Trim**
  Trim objects to a cutting edge.
- **Extend**
  Extend objects to a selected boundary.
- **Fillet**
  Use fillets.
- **Undo and Redo**
  Undo previous commands and redo the "undo."

Copy

Command Locator

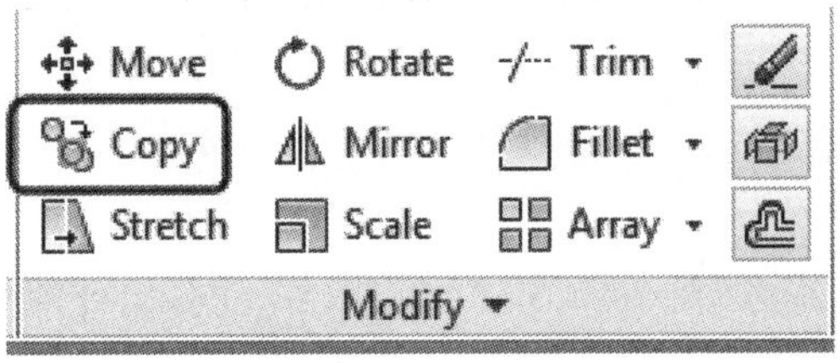

Home Ribbon	**Modify/Copy**
Command	**Copy**
Alias	**CO or CP**
RMB Shortcut Menu	**Drawing Window**

Command Overview

To Copy an object, pick the base point, drag the mouse and pick the location for the copied object. Copy is automatically set to make multiple copies. You will continue to place copies until you press <ESC> or <ENTER>.

General Procedures

To Create a single copy:

1. Invoke the Copy Command.
2. Select the objects to Copy, and press <ENTER>.
3. Pick a point on or near the object as the base point.
4. Drag the mouse and pick the location for the copied object.
5. Press <ESC> to exit the command or right click and select <ENTER>.

Tips & Tricks

- Use Object Snaps for picking the base point and the new location.
- If using direct distance to relocate the object, be sure ORTHO is ON.
- Remember to use the LMB to pick the base point and the new location of the object.
- Be sure SNAP (in the Status Bar) is off when selecting objects.
- The Copy command is automatically in MUTLIPLE mode.

Command Exercise

Exercise 5-1 – Copy

Drawing Name: **copy1.dwg**
Estimated Time to Completion: 5 Minutes

Scope

Copy the objects in the rectangle on the left into the rectangle on the right

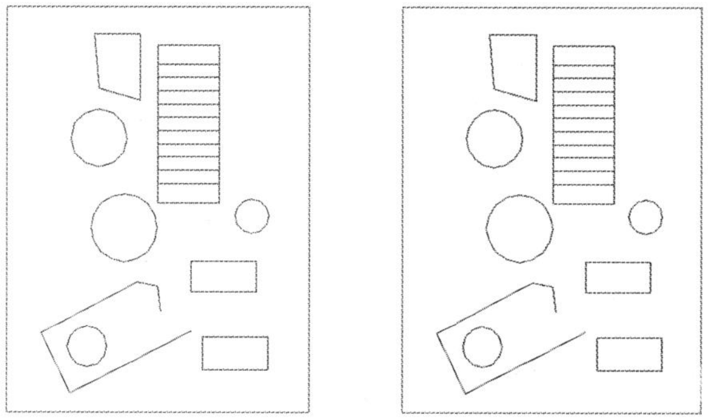

Copy Exercise

Solution

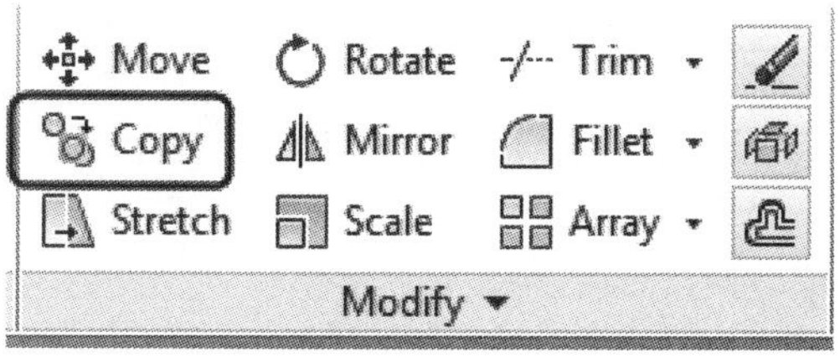

1. Invoke the Copy command (co or copy).

2. *Select objects:*
   Select all of the objects using a window inside the red box.

3. *Specify base point or displacement:*
   You may want to turn OSNAP off. Use your LMB to select in the middle of the red box with the objects somewhere. This is the point from which the objects will be copied.

4. *Specify second point of displacement or <use first point as displacement>:*
   Move your mouse to position the rectangles in the red box on the right and press the LMB to specify the second point of displacement.

5. Press **<ESC>** to exit the command.

> *You may also leave OSNAP on, and snap to a corner of the left red box for the base point and the same corner of the right red box for the second point of displacement.*

Command Exercise

Exercise 5-2 – Copy Multiple

Drawing Name: **copy2.dwg**
Estimated Time to Completion: 5 Minutes

Scope

Decorate the tree on the right by making multiple copies of the star as indicated in the drawing on the left.

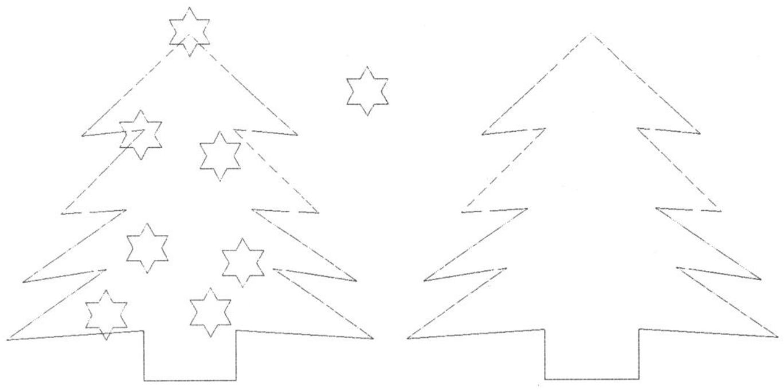

Copy Multiple Exercise

Solution

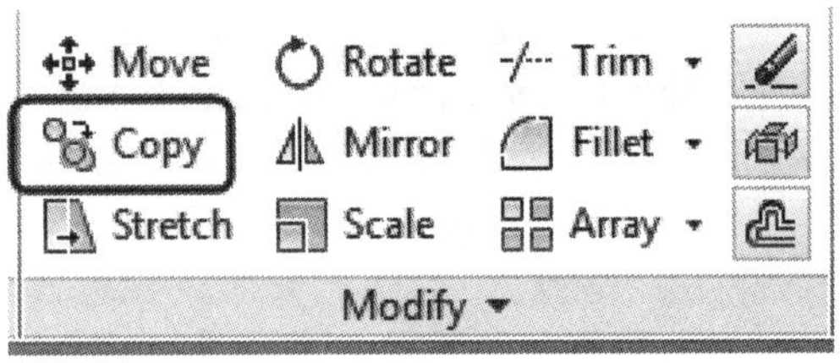

1. Invoke the Copy command (cp or copy).
2. *Select objects:*
   Select the star between the trees with the LMB. Close the selection set with the <ENTER> key or RMB.
3. *Specify base point:*
   You may want to turn OSNAP off. Use your LMB to select in the middle of the selected star. This is the point from which the stars will be copied multiple times.
4. *Specify second point of displacement or <use first point as displacement>:*
   Move your mouse to position the star on the tree on the right and press the LMB to specify the second point of displacement. Move your mouse to another location and press the LMB to copy another star. Repeat the process to decorate the tree. Right click and select <ENTER> to exit the command.

***Extra:** What happens when you use the Undo command after making multiple copies? Try making multiple copies of multiple objects.*

Mirror

Command Locator

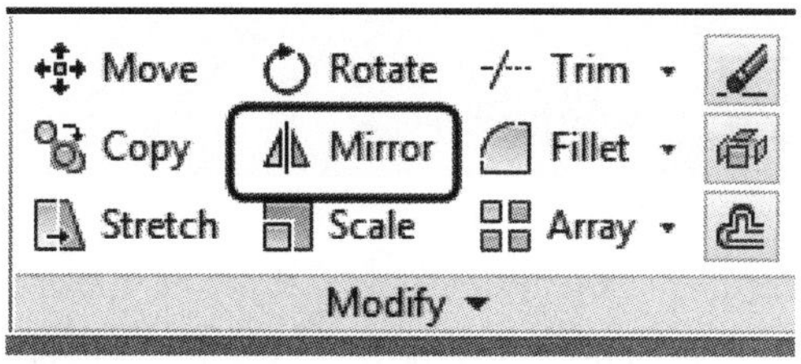

Home Ribbon	**Modify / Mirror**
Command	**Mirror**
Alias	**MI**
RMB Shortcut Menu	**Drawing Window**

Command Overview

Mirror selected objects around a mirror line with ORTHO on or off. Use the MIRRTEXT system variable to control whether text will mirror or not.

General Procedures

To use the Mirror command:

1. Invoke the Mirror Command.
2. Select the objects to mirror, and press <ENTER>.
3. Pick the first point of the mirror line. Drag the mouse and pick the second line.
4. At the prompt Delete source objects? [Yes/No] <N>, press <ENTER> to accept the default or type Y to delete the source objects.

To use the Mirror command without mirroring text:

1. Type MIRRTEXT, and press <ENTER>.
2. Type 0 to turn MIRRTEXT off.
3. Proceed with the Mirror command.

Command Exercise

Exercise 5-3 – Mirror

Drawing Name: **mirror1.dwg**
Estimated Time to Completion: 5 Minutes

Scope

Mirror the lines below using the endpoints of the upper and lower lines for the Mirror Line.

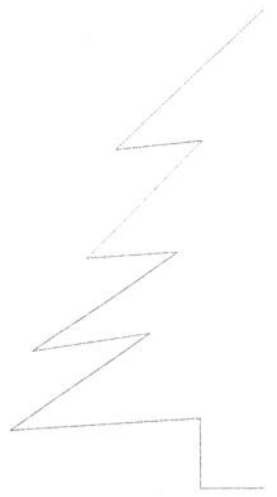

Mirror Exercise

Solution

1. Invoke the Mirror command (mirror).

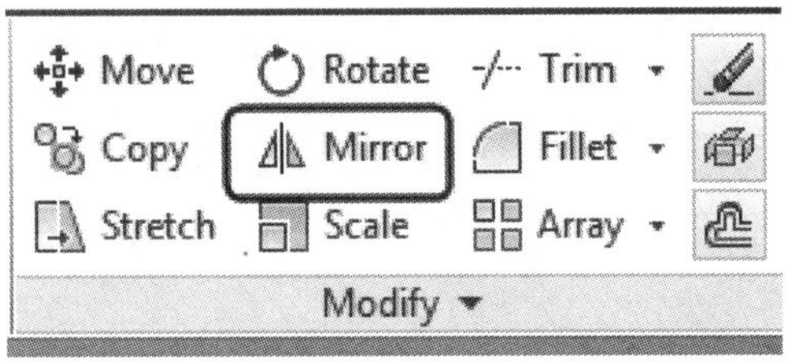

2. *Select objects:*
   Select the left side of the tree and press <ENTER> to end the selection.
3. *Specify first point of mirror line:*
   Make sure OSNAP is on. Pick the endpoint of the line that will represent the top of the tree with the LMB.
4. *Specify second point of mirror line:*
   Use the LMB and object snap to select the end point that represents the bottom of the tree.
5. *Erase source objects? [Yes/No] <N>:*
   Right-click in the drawing area and select 'No' or just press <ENTER> to accept the default (N).

Extra: *Mirror the word MIRROR. Type 'MIRRTEXT' at the command line and press <ENTER>. Type 0 <ENTER>. Mirror the word MIRROR again. What is the difference? Try it.*

Extra: *On the Certification exam, you may be asked to mirror some elements and then measure the distance between two points to verify that you have mirrored the object properly.*

General Procedures

To measure the distance between two points:

1. Type DIST for distance.
2. Select the first endpoint.
3. Select the second endpoint.
4. The distance value will display.

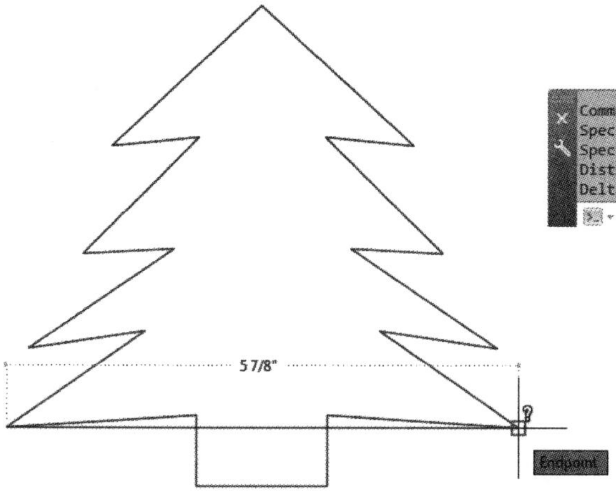

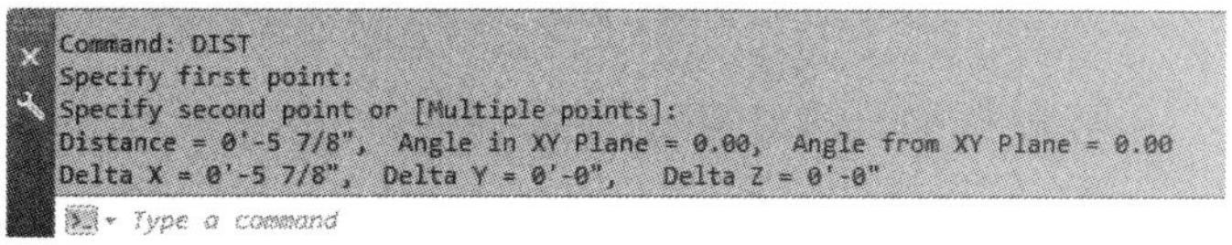

Verify that your distance value is 5 7/8".

Command Exercise

Exercise 5-4 – Mirror Text

Drawing Name: **mirror2.dwg**
Estimated Time to Completion: 5 Minutes

Scope

Turn the mirror text system variable MIRRTEXT off, and mirror the objects using the endpoints of the upper and lower lines for the mirror line.

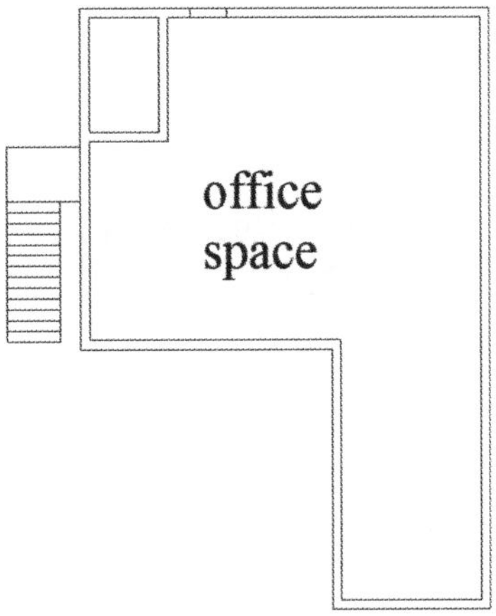

Mirror Text

Solution

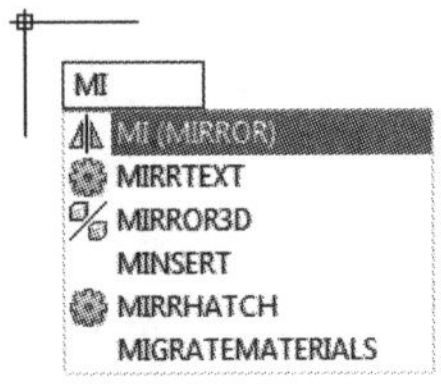

1. Start the exercise by making sure the Endpoint running object snap is activated.

2. Place the cursor anywhere in the drawing area. Type 'MI' and notice how AUTOCOMPLETE provides a list of commands that start with MI. Select MIRRTEXT from the list and press <ENTER>.

3. *Enter new value for MIRRTEXT <1>:*
   Type '0' and press <ENTER>.

4. Invoke the Mirror command (mirror).

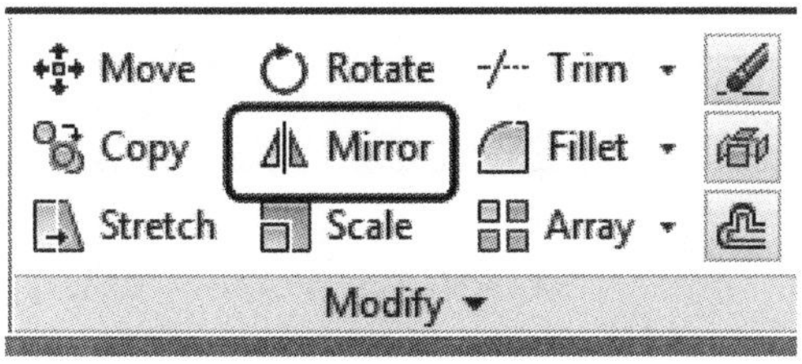

5. *Select objects:*
   Select the objects that make up the office space. Include the text.
6. *Select objects:*
   Close the selection set by pressing <ENTER>.
7. *Specify first point of mirror line:*
   Select the upper right hand corner of the office space. Remember to use the object snap.
8. *Specify second point of mirror line:*
   Toggle ORTHO on. Move the mouse near the bottom right corner of the office space and click the LMB.
9. *Erase source objects? [Yes/No] <N>:*
   Right-click in the drawing area and select 'No' or just press <ENTER> to accept the default option of 'No'.

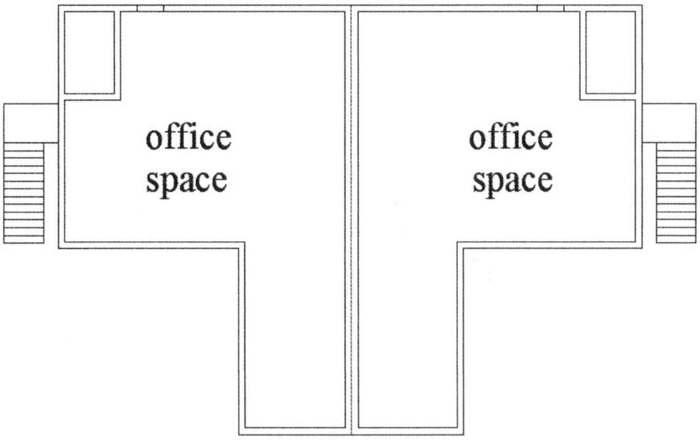

Offset

Command Locator

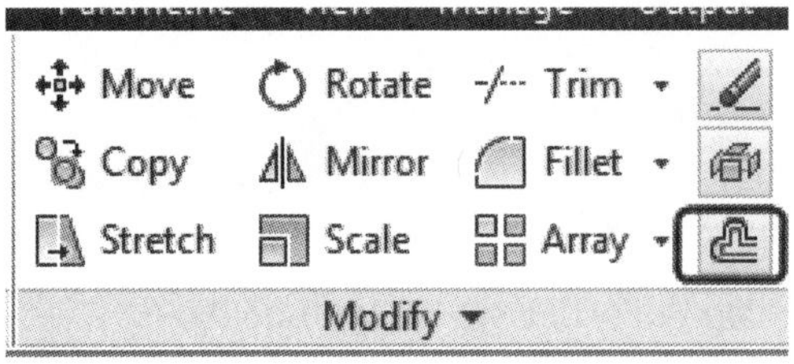

Home Ribbon	**Modify / Offset**
Command	**Offset**
Alias	**O**
RMB Shortcut Menu	**Drawing Window**

Command Overview

To Offset a single object, first set the offset distance by picking two points in the Drawing Window, or typing the offset distance. Select the object to offset and the side to offset.

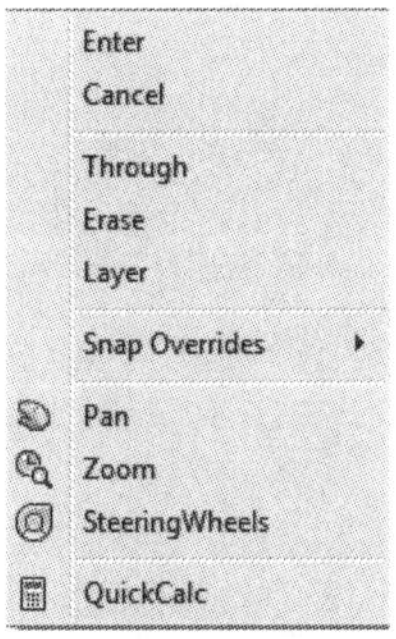

Offset Shortcut Menu

Offset Option	Overview
Through	Use this option to use a second object or point to set the distance for the offset.
Erase	Use this option to delete the source object after it is offset.
Layer	Use this option to set what layer the offset/new object will be assigned. You can set the new object to the current layer or the layer used by the source object.

General Procedures

1. Invoke the Offset Command.
2. Type the Offset distance.
3. Select the object to Offset, then pick the side to offset the object.

Tips & Tricks

- Offset lines, circles, arcs and polylines.

Command Exercise

Exercise 5-5 – Offset

Drawing Name: **offset1.dwg**
Estimated Time to Completion: 5 Minutes

Scope

Offset the objects with an offset distance of 0.25.

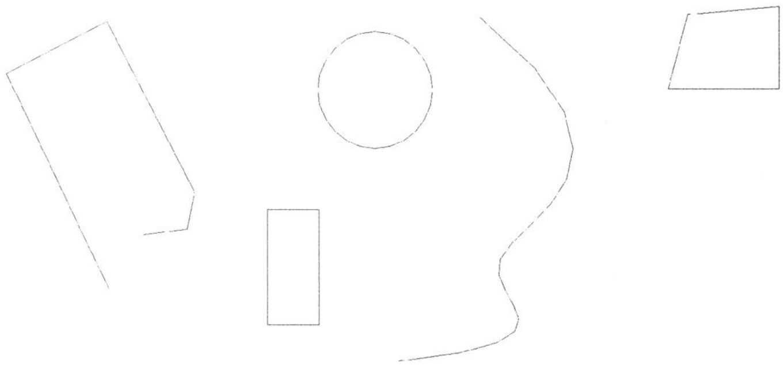

Offset Exercise

Solution

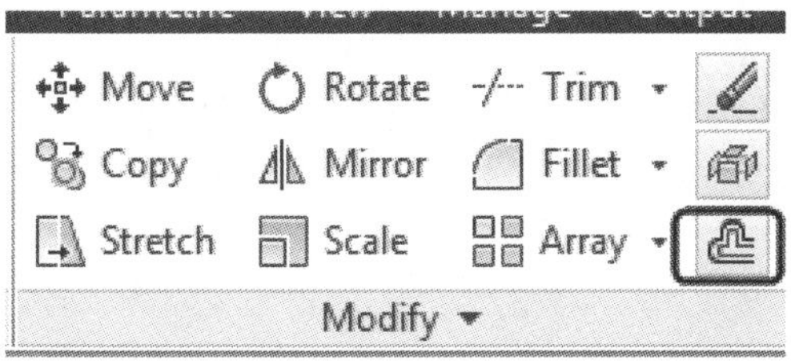

1. Start the Offset command (o or offset).
2. *Specify offset distance or [Through] <Through>:*
   Type '0.25' at the command line and press <ENTER>.
3. *Select object to offset or <exit>:*
   Select the desired object with the LMB.
4. *Specify point on side to offset:*
   Select the side of the object to create the offset on.
5. *Select object to offset or <exit>:*
   Repeat the process offsetting all the objects on the screen.

Array

Command Locator

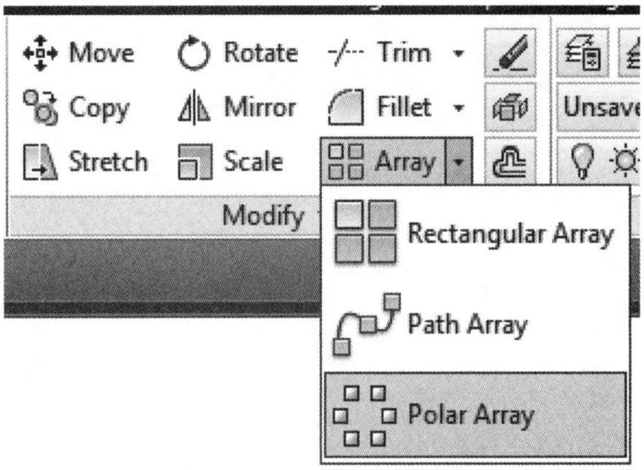

Home Ribbon	**Modify / Array**
Command	**Array**
Alias	**AR**
RMB Shortcut Menu	**Drawing Window**

Command Overview

A rectangular array copies the objects into rows and columns with designated distances between the objects. Columns are copied in the positive X direction, and Rows are copied in the positive Y direction. A negative distance will copy the objects in the negative X and Y directions, respectively.

A path array distributes an object along a line, arc, spline, or polyline at equal distances.

A polar array copies objects around a center point. Specify the total number of objects, the angle to fill (360 degrees or less) and whether the objects should be rotated.

General Procedures

To create a Rectangular Array:

1. Invoke the Array command.
2. Select the objects to Array and press <ENTER>.
3. Right click to set the number of rows.
4. Enter the number of rows, then enter the number of columns.
5. Right click and select Spacing.
6. Type the distance between the rows and the columns.
7. Press ENTER to accept the array that is previewed.

To create a Path Array:

1. Invoke the Array command.
2. Select the objects to Array and press <ENTER>.
3. Select the path.
4. Enter the number of elements to place.
5. Specify the distance between the elements or whether to divide the path distance by the number of elements (equal spacing).
6. Press ENTER to accept the array that is previewed.

To create a Polar Array:

1. Invoke the Array command.
2. Select the objects to Array and press <ENTER>.
3. Specify the center point of the array.
4. Enter the total number of items for the array or specify the angle to fill.
5. Press <ENTER> for 360, or type the angle.
6. Press <ENTER> to accept the default to rotate the arrayed objects.

- For Rectangular Array, a negative distance between columns will array the objects in the negative x (-x) direction (right to left). A negative distance between rows will arrays objects in the negative y (-y) direction (below one another).
- For Path Array, you can change the orientation so elements are tangent or centered on a path.
- For Polar Array, a negative angle arrays objects in a counterclockwise direction.
- For Rectangular Array, one row or one column will array objects in one direction only.
- The MINSERT command (typed) will insert blocks in rows and columns. Individual blocks cannot be deleted or Exploded.
- For Rectangular Array, you can set an angle to array from.

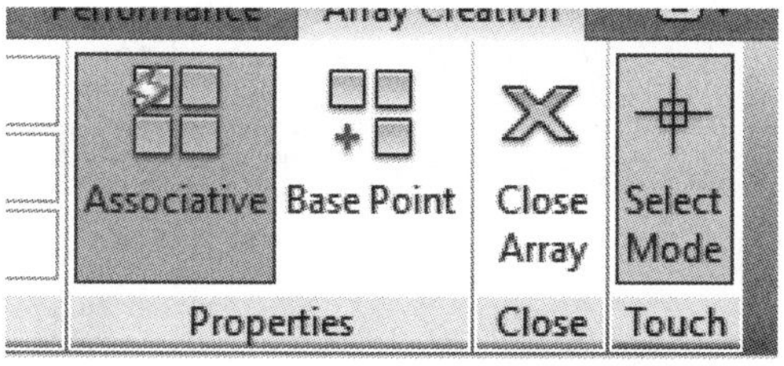

The Select Mode option is used when you are using a device with a touch screen, such as a tablet or smart phone. If Select Mode if enabled, then selections can be made by touching the screen.

Command Exercise

Exercise 5-6 – Rectangular Array

Drawing Name: **arrayr1.dwg**
Estimated Time to Completion: 5 Minutes

Scope

Create a 3 x 2 rectangular array of the object with a spacing of 1.5.

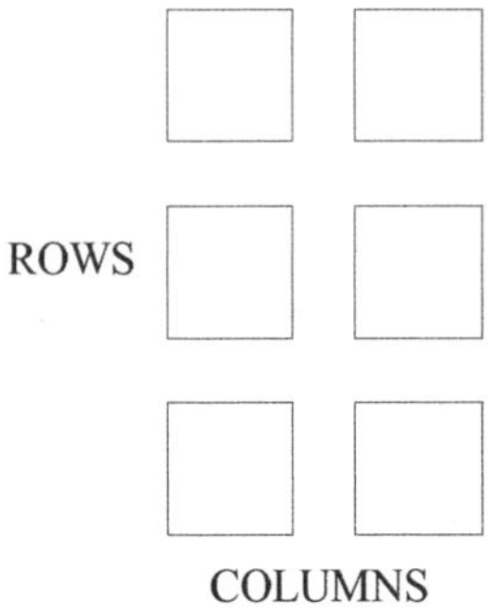

Solution

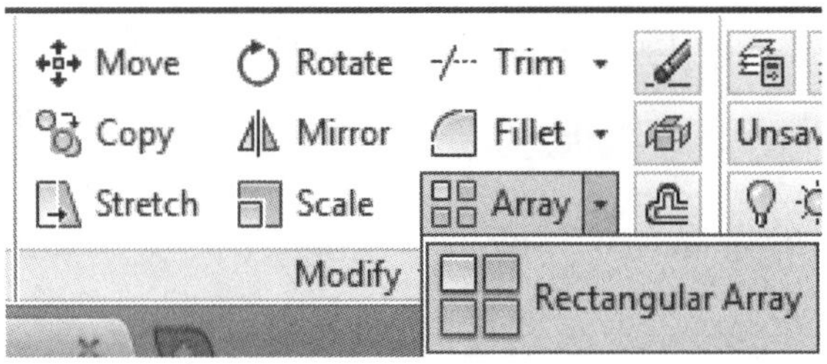

1. Invoke the Array command (array).
2. Select the rectangle on the right.
3. Press <ENTER> when it has been selected.
4. On the ribbon, set the Columns to 2.
5. Verify that the Rows are set to 3.

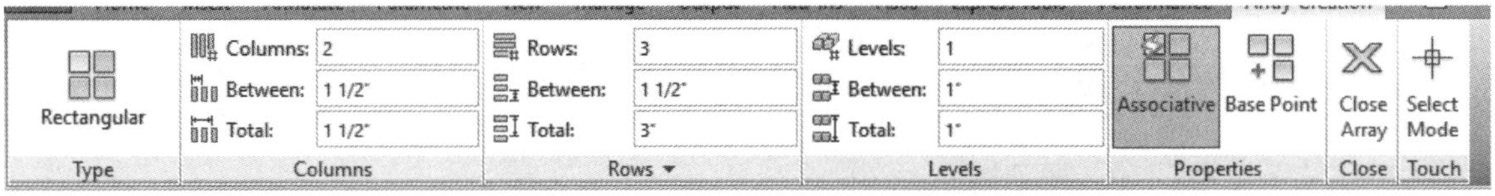

6. Verify that the distance between the rows and columns is set to 1 1/2″.
7. Select **Close Array** on the ribbon.
8. You are prompted for the distance between columns. Type '1.5' or press <ENTER> to accept the default value if it is correct.
9. If the array looks correct, press <ENTER>.

Command Exercise

Exercise 5-7 – Rectangular Array at an Angle

Drawing Name: **arrayr2.dwg**
Estimated Time to Completion: 5 Minutes

Scope

Create a 3 x 2 rectangular array of the object with a spacing of 1.5 at a 30-degree angle.
The ability to create a rectangular array at an angle is available using the "Classic" Array dialog box.

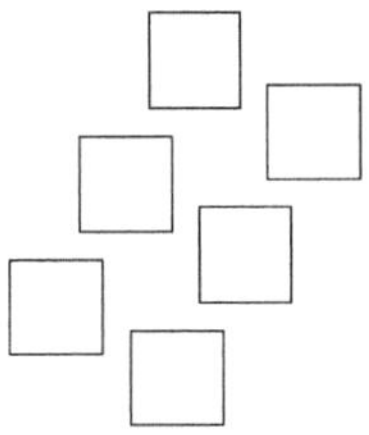

Array at an angle

Solution

1. Start typing anywhere in the window. Type ARRAY… and use the Auto-Fill to select **ARRAYCLASSIC**.

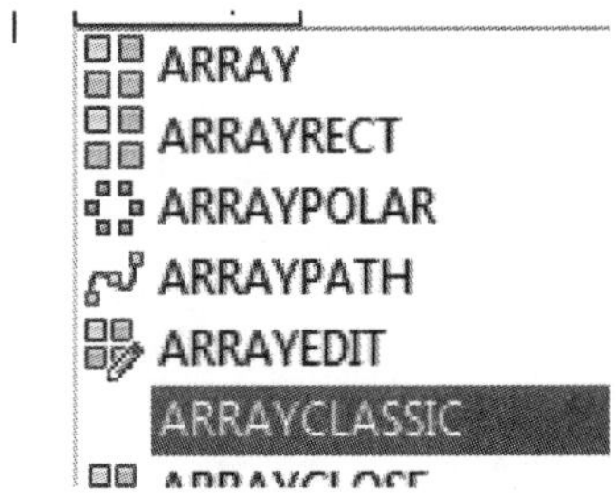

2. In the dialog box, select the **Select objects** tool.
   Select the rectangle on the right.
   Press <ENTER> when it has been selected.

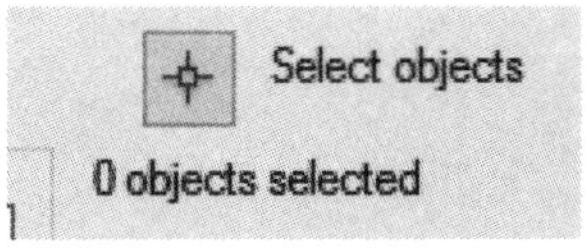

3. In the dialog box:
   Set the Rows to **3**.
   Set the Columns to **2**.
   Set the Row Offset to **1 1/2″**.
   Set the Column Offset to **1 1/2″**.
   Set the Angle of array to **-30.00**.
   Press the **Preview** button.

   Note the angle is a negative value.

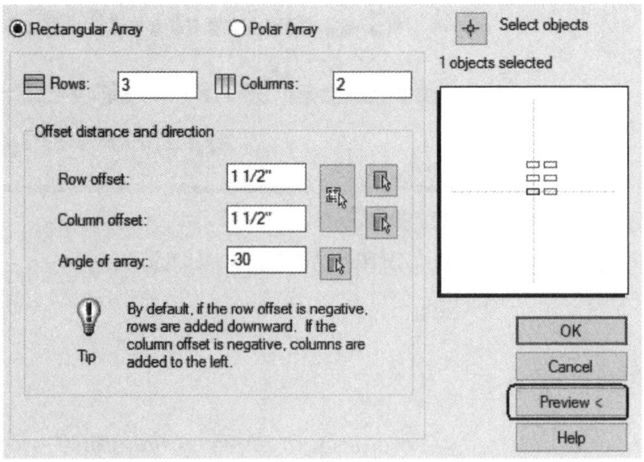

4. If the preview looks like the figure on the right, press the right mouse button to accept. If it doesn't, press ESC and double-check the settings in the dialog box.

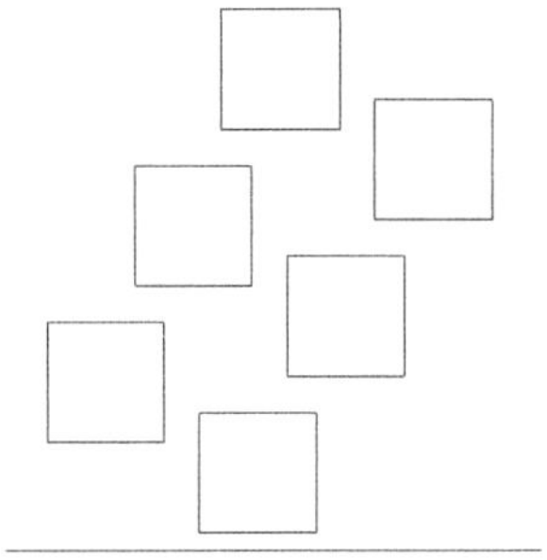

Command Exercise

Exercise 5-8 – Polar Array

Drawing Name: **arrayp1.dwg**
Estimated Time to Completion: 5 Minutes

Scope

Array the hex object using the polar array option as indicated in the drawing. The number of items is 8 (total).

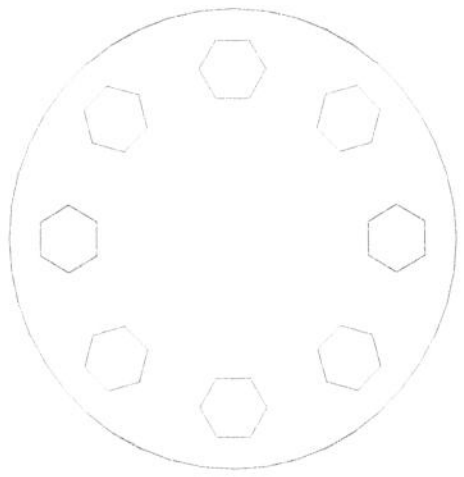

Polar or Circular Array

Solution

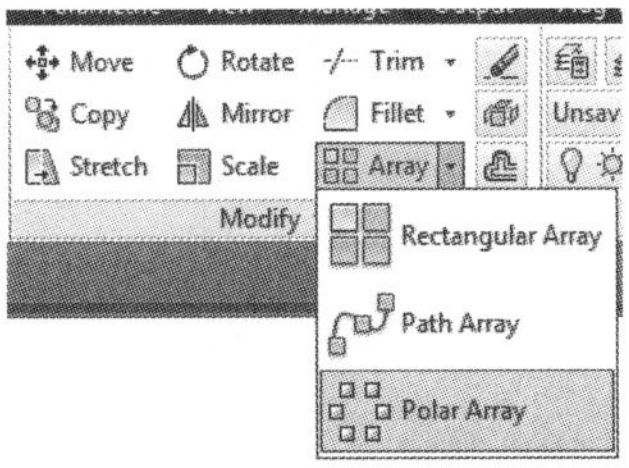

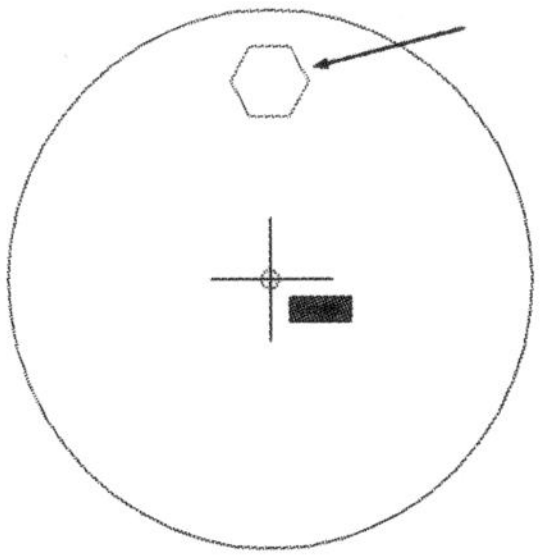

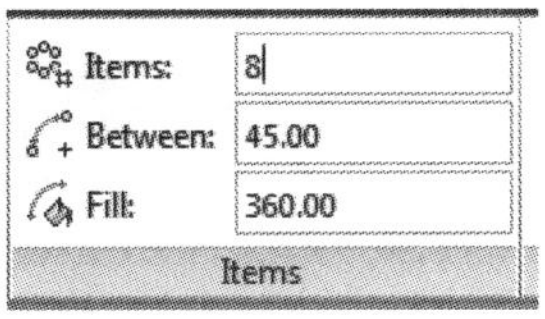

1. Invoke the Array command (array).
2. Select the polygon on the right.
   Press <ENTER> to complete the selection.
3. You are prompted to select the center point for the array.
4. Pick the center of the circle as the base point.
5. On the ribbon:
   Set the number of items to **8**.
   AutoCAD will automatically calculate the space between the objects.
6. Verify that the **Rotate items** button is shaded (enabled) on the ribbon.
7. Select **Close Array** or press ENTER to exit the command.

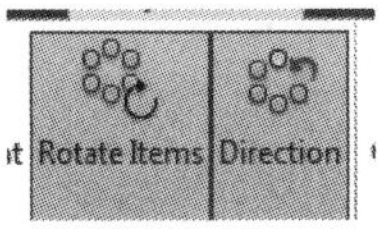

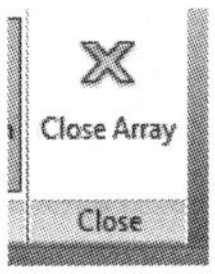

Extra: *Undo the polar array and repeat the exercise. Do not rotate the objects as they are copied.*

Command Exercise

Exercise 5-9 – Path Array

Drawing Name: **arraypath.dwg**
Estimated Time to Completion: 5 Minutes

Scope

Array the circle object using the path option as indicated in the drawing. The number of items is 6 (total).

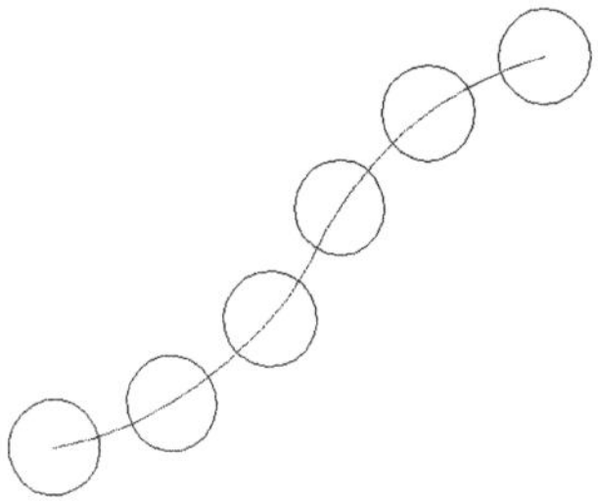

Array along a path

Solution

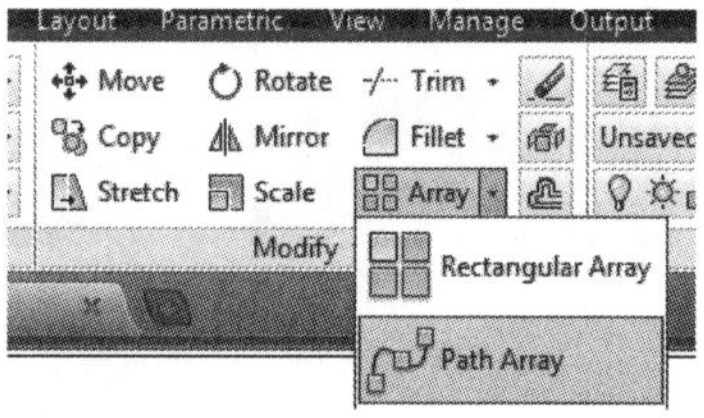

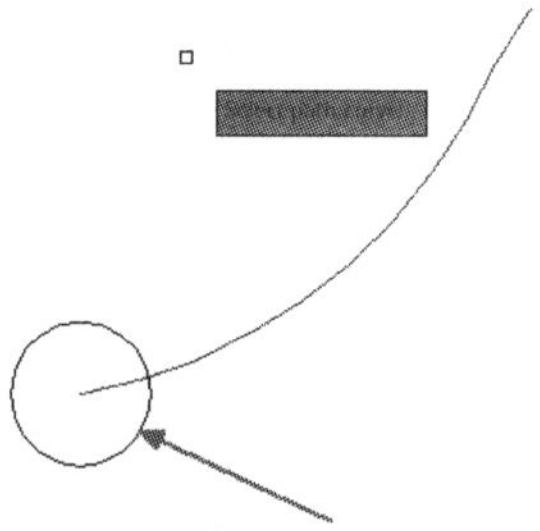

1. Invoke the Array command (array) using the Path option.

2. Select the circle on the right side of the view.

   Press <ENTER> to complete the selection.

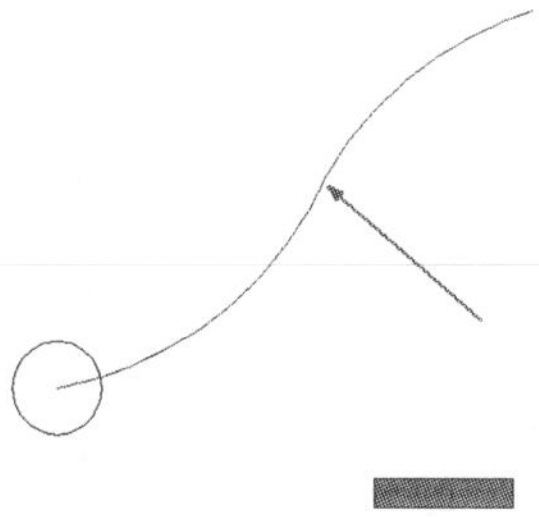

3. Select the path curve.

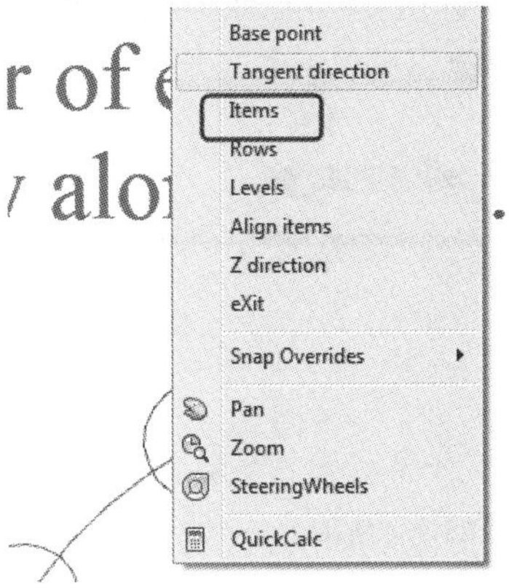

Base point
Tangent direction
Items
Rows
Levels
Align items
Z direction
eXit
Snap Overrides
Pan
Zoom
SteeringWheels
QuickCalc

4. Right click anywhere in the drawing window and select **Items** from the shortcut menu.

You'll be asked to specify the distance between items along the path.

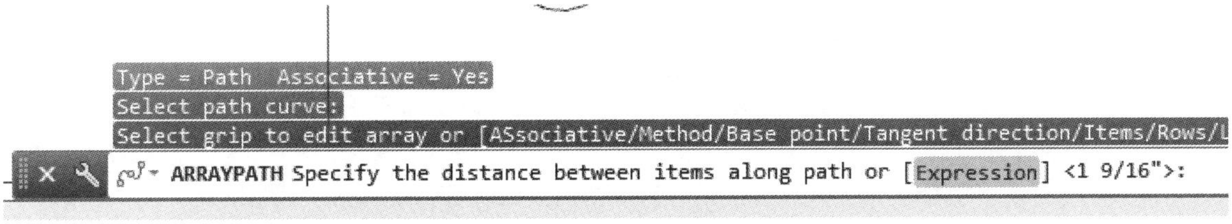

Type = Path Associative = Yes
Select path curve:
Select grip to edit array or [ASsociative/Method/Base point/Tangent direction/Items/Rows/L
ARRAYPATH Specify the distance between items along path or [Expression] <1 9/16">:

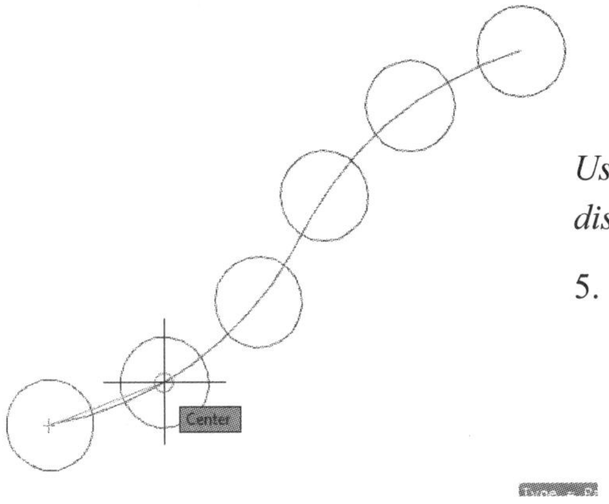

Center

Use the completed drawing on the left side to help set the spacing distance.

5. Select two center points on two of the circles on the path on the left to set the distance between the circles.

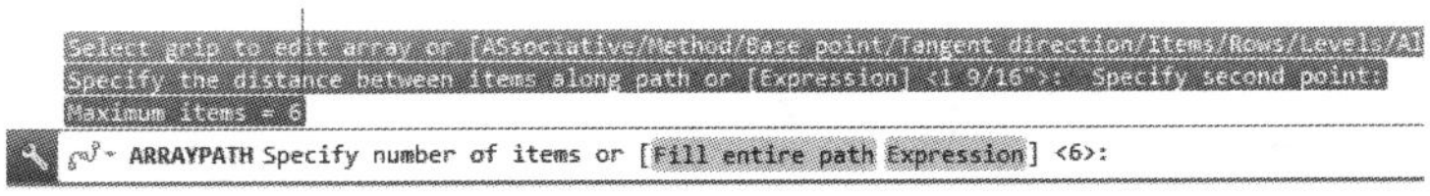

Select grip to edit array or [ASsociative/Method/Base point/Tangent direction/Items/Rows/Levels/Al
Specify the distance between items along path or [Expression] <1 9/16">: Specify second point:
Maximum items = 6
ARRAYPATH Specify number of items or [Fill entire path Expression] <6>:

You will then be offered the maximum number of items that will fill the path as 6.

6. Press <ENTER> to accept the default of spacing the items evenly along the path.

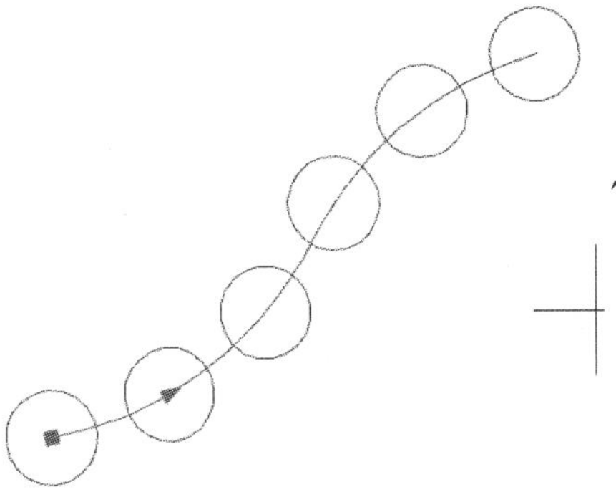

7. Press <ENTER> to accept the preview of the array and exit the command.

Command Exercise

Exercise 5-10 – Associative Array

Drawing Name: **assocarray.dwg**
Estimated Time to Completion: 10 Minutes

Scope

Array the square object using the rectangular array. Use the Associative option on the left side. Turn off Associative for the right array. Explore the difference.

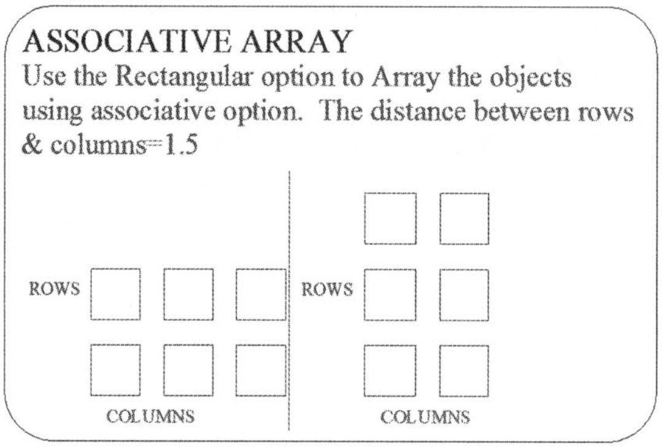

Associative Array

Solution

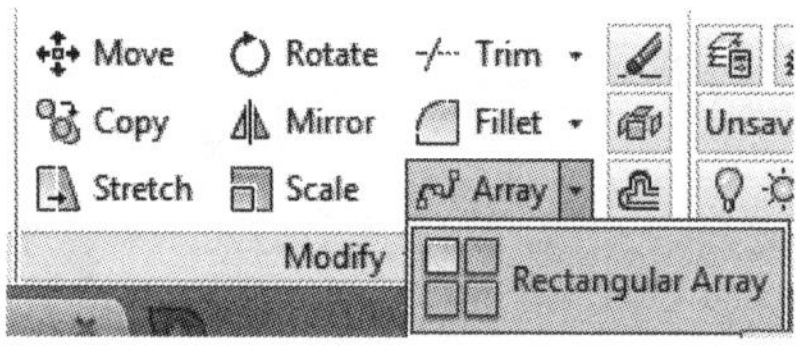

1. Invoke the Array command (array) using the Rectangular option.

2. Select the square on the left side of the view.

   Press <ENTER> to complete the selection.

3. On the ribbon:

   Set the Columns to 2.

   Set the Rows to 3.

   Set the distance between rows to 1 1/2″.

   Set the distance between columns to 1 1/2″.

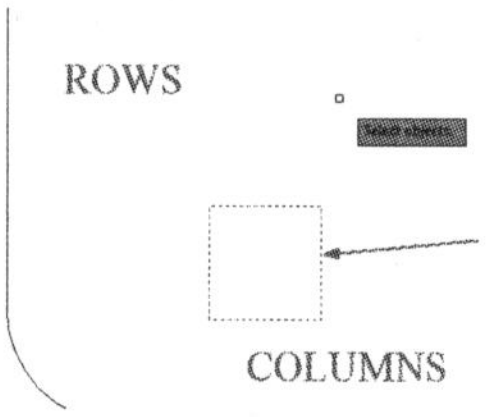

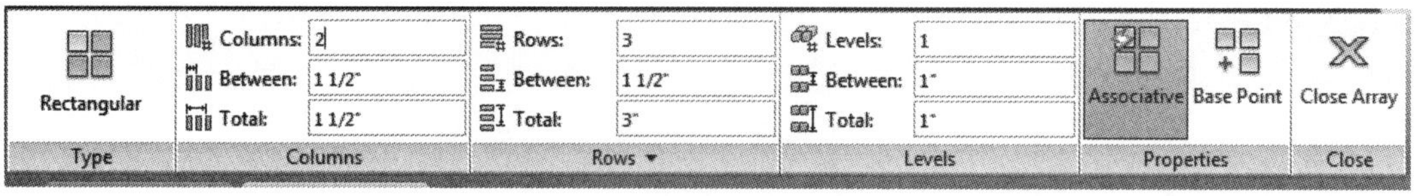

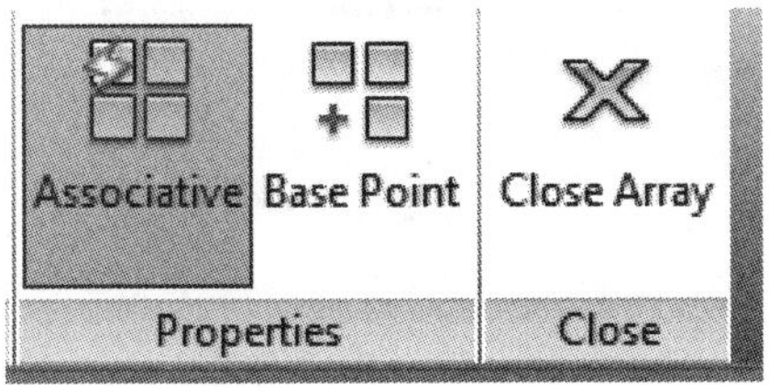
Associative
Base Point
Close Array
Properties
Close

4. Enable **Associative**.

   Press **Close Array**.

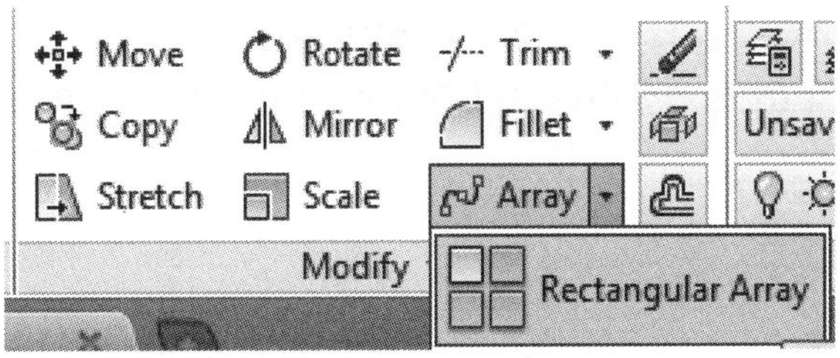
Move
Rotate
Trim
Copy
Mirror
Fillet
Stretch
Scale
Array
Modify
Rectangular Array

5. Invoke the Array command (array) using the Rectangular option.

6. Select the square on the right side of the view.

   Press <ENTER> to complete the selection.

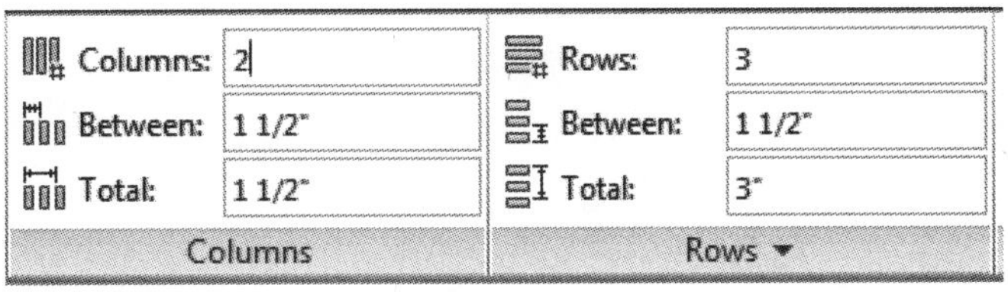
Columns: 2
Between: 1 1/2"
Total: 1 1/2"
Columns
Rows: 3
Between: 1 1/2"
Total: 3"
Rows

7. On the ribbon:

   Set the Columns to **2**.

   Set the Rows to **3**.

   Set the distance between rows to **1 1/2″**.

   Set the distance between columns to **1 1/2″**.

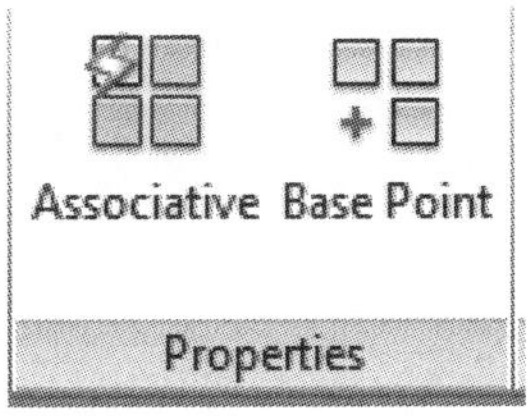
Associative
Base Point
Properties

8. Disable **Associative**.

   Press **Close Array**.

9. Select the array on the left (the array created as an associative array).

   The ribbon will allow you to modify the array.

10. Change the number of rows to **2**.

    Change the number of columns to **3**.

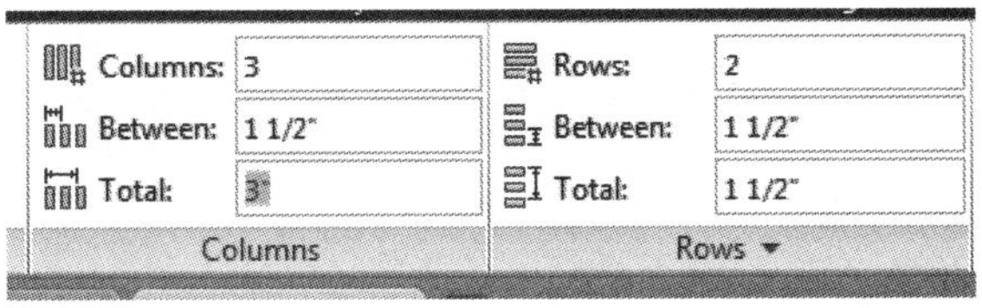
Columns: 3
Between: 1 1/2"
Total: 3"
Columns
Rows: 2
Between: 1 1/2"
Total: 1 1/2"
Rows

11. Close the Array to exit editing.

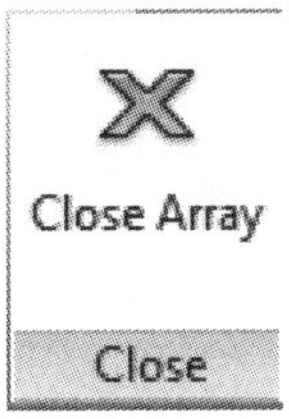
Close Array
Close

12. Select one of the squares on the right array (the array created as the non-associative array).

Note that it acts as an independent element. The array was created as a non-associative array.

Command Exercise

Exercise 5-11 – Polar Array Challenge

Drawing Name: **arrayp2.dwg**
Estimated Time to Completion: 10 Minutes

Scope

For the certification exam, you will be asked to array different objects and then measure the distance between one of the elements to another element. If you have performed the array correctly, the distance value should be correct.

Create a Polar Array of the chairs around the table. Use a fill angle of 150°, Non-associative, with four members. Then measure the distance between the two points indicated.

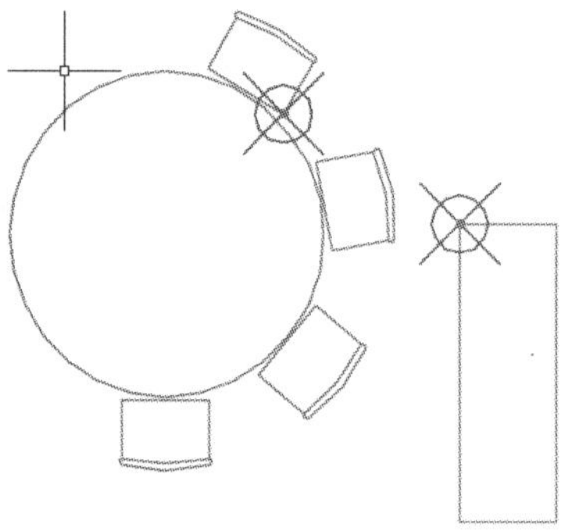

Polar Array

Solution

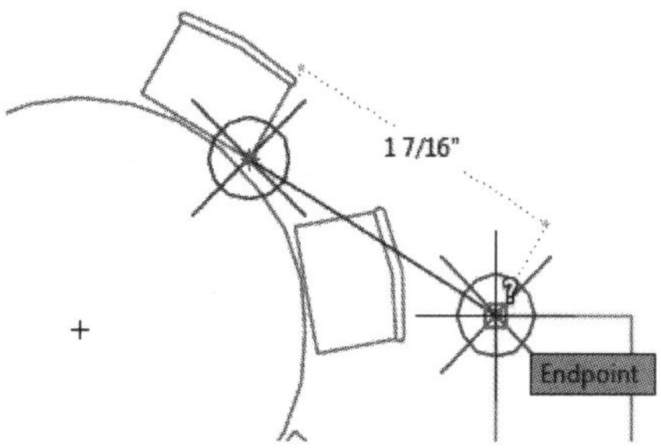

Using the DIST command, measure the distance between the two points.

Your distance should be 1 7/16".

```
Specify second point or [Multiple points]:
Distance = 0'-1 7/16",  Angle in XY Plane = 328.89,  Angle from XY Plane = 0.00
Delta X = 0'-1 1/4",  Delta Y = -0'-0 3/4",   Delta Z = 0'-0"
Command: DIST
Specify first point:
```

Move

Command Locator

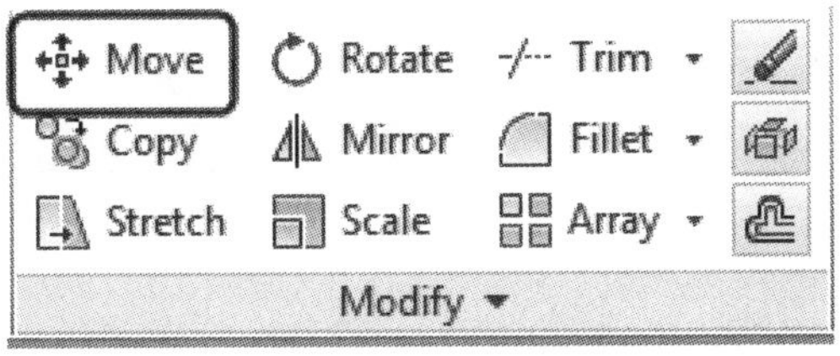

Home Ribbon	**Modify / Move**
Command	**Move**
Alias	**M**

Command Overview

To Move an object, pick the base point, drag the object and pick or use any of the methods previously discussed to input coordinates.

General Procedures

1. Invoke the Move Command.
2. Select the objects to Move, and press <ENTER>.
3. Pick a point on or near the object for the base point.
4. Drag the mouse and pick the new location or use absolute, relative coordinates, polar coordinates, or the direct distance method to relocate the object.

Tips & Tricks

- Use Object Snaps for picking the base point and the new location.
- If using the direct distance to relocate the object, be sure ORTHO is ON.
- Remember to use the pick button (LMB) to select the base point and the new location of the object.
- Be sure SNAP (in the Status Bar) is off when selecting objects.
- Use ORTHO TRACKING to help align objects being moved.

Command Exercise

Exercise 5-12 – Move

Drawing Name: **move1.dwg**
Estimated Time to Completion: 5 Minutes

Scope

Turn Snap off and Move the blue objects into the red rectangle.

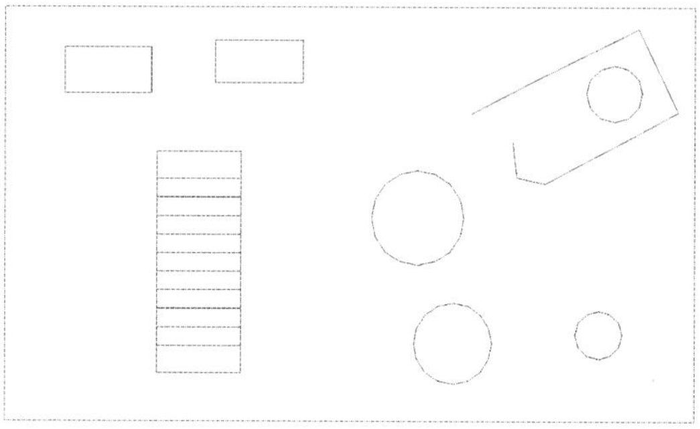

Move Exercise

Solution

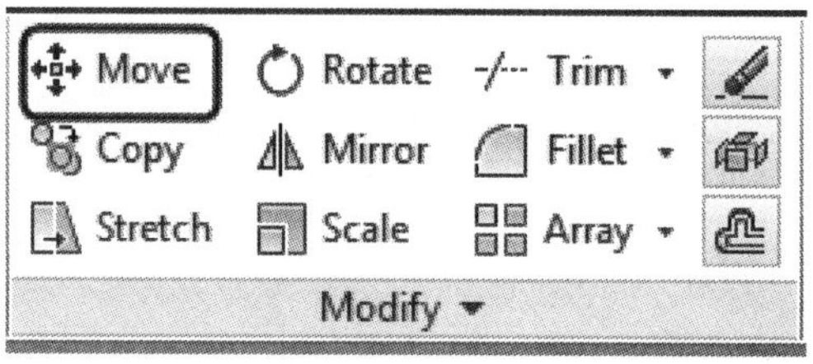

1. Invoke the Move command (m or move).
2. *Select objects:*
   Start by selecting one of the blue rectangles with the LMB. Close the selection set with the <ENTER> key or RMB.
3. *Specify base point or displacement:*
   You may want to turn OSNAP off. Use your LMB to select in the middle of the rectangle. This is the point from which the rectangle will be moved.
4. *Specify second point of displacement or <use first point as displacement>:*
   Move your mouse to position the rectangle in the red box and press the LMB to specify the second point of displacement.
5. Repeat the Move command with the RMB (m, move or <ENTER>).

6. *Select objects:*
   Select another object.
7. *Specify base point or displacement:*
   Pick near the middle of the object. This will be the point from which it is moved.
8. *Specify second point of displacement or <use first point as displacement>:*
   Select a point inside the red box for the second point.
9. Repeat the Move command with the RMB (m, move or <ENTER>) and move the rest of the objects into the red box, one at a time or in groups.

Extra: *Undo the command and repeat the exercise using different methods of selecting objects.*

Rotate

Command Locator

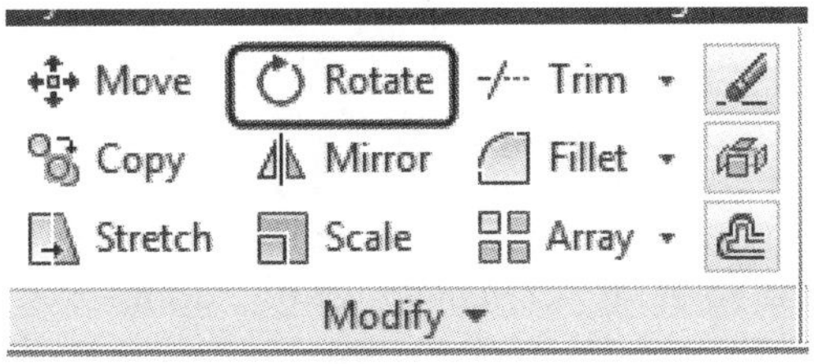

Home Ribbon	**Modify / Rotate**
Command	**Rotate**
Alias	**RO**
RMB Shortcut Menu	**Drawing Window**

Command Overview

Rotate selected objects in a counterclockwise direction with a positive rotation angle. Rotate in a clockwise direction with a negative angle. The Reference option permits the user to reference the angle of an existing line in the drawing and type a new angle.

General Procedures

To use the Rotate command:

1. Invoke the Rotate Command.
2. Select the objects to rotate, and press <ENTER>.
3. Pick a base point on or near the object.
4. Type the rotation angle or drag the mouse and pick the rotation angle.

To use the Rotate command with the Reference option:

1. Invoke the Rotate Command.
2. Select the objects to rotate, and press <ENTER>.
3. Pick a base point on or near the object. Type R for reference, or press the RMB and select Reference from the shortcut menu.
4. Using Object Snap, select the endpoints of the line to reference. This will determine the precise reference angle.
5. Type the new rotation angle.

- Turn ORTHO on to rotate in 90 degree increments, relative to the current rotation angle.
- When rotating the object with ORTHO on, keep the cursor close to the base point to make it easier to rotate the object.
- Toggle through the Coordinates display by selecting F6 or double clicking the coordinates in the Status Bar to view the distance and angle option.
- When using the Reference option to straighten objects, it is more accurate to reference the angle of a line in the drawing using the object snap than to try to find the angle of the line and rotate it in the negative direction.
- Objects will be rotated around the rotation base point.
- The Rotate Command now has a COPY option, so that you can create a copy in addition to rotating selected objects.

Command Exercise

Exercise 5-13 – Rotate

Drawing Name: **rotate1.dwg**
Estimated Time to Completion: 5 Minutes

Scope

Rotate the objects as indicated in the drawing.

Rotate Exercise

Solution

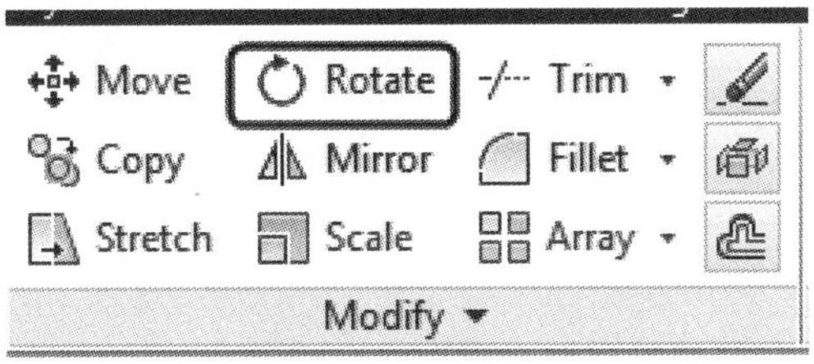

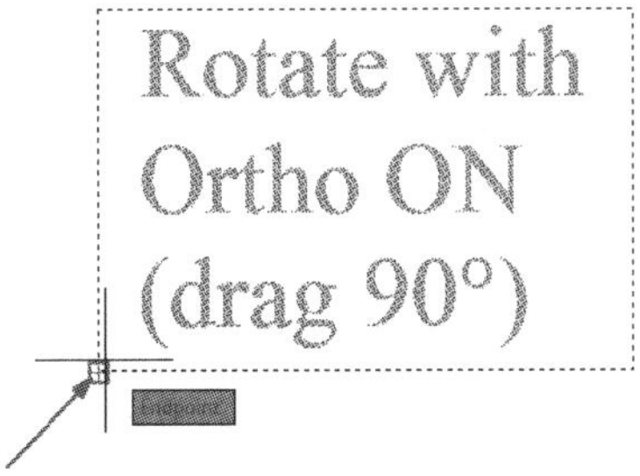

1. Invoke the Rotate command (rotate).
2. *Select objects:*
   Select the box and text on the left.
3. *Select objects:*
   Press <ENTER> to close the selection set.
4. *Specify base point:*
   Pick the left lower corner of the rectangle. This is the point about which the objects will be rotated.
5. *Specify rotation angle or [Reference]:*
   Type '45' and press <ENTER>.
6. The rectangle and text are rotated.

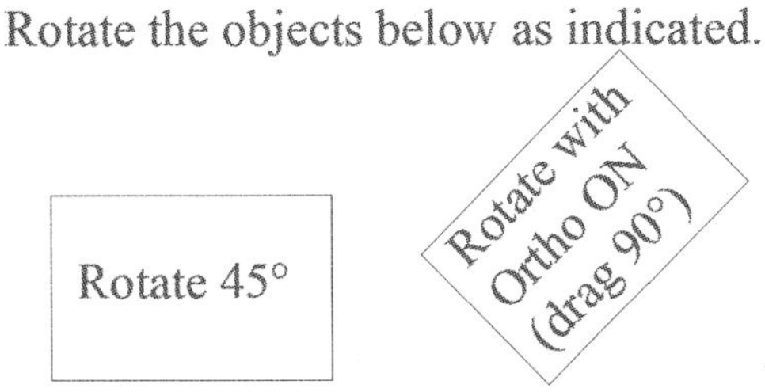

7. Repeat the Rotate command with the RMB (rotate or <ENTER>).

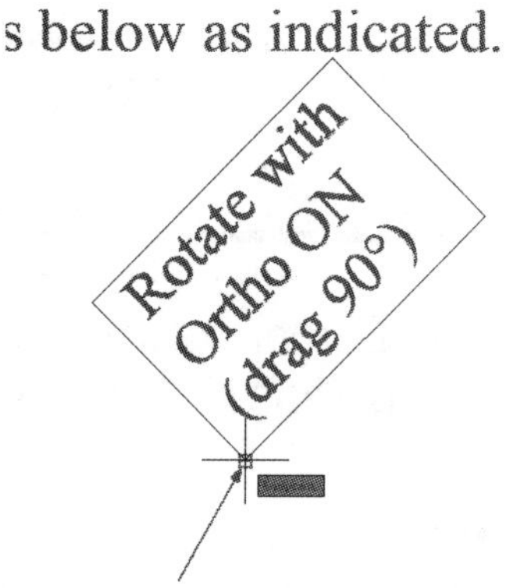

8. *Select objects:*
   Select the box and text on the right.
9. *Select objects:*
   Press <ENTER> to close the selection set.
10. *Specify base point:*
    Select the end point on the lower left as the base point.
11. Toggle ORTHO on. Pick a point inside the box on the right with the LMB.
12. *Specify rotation angle or [Reference]:*

    Drag the mouse upward and click to rotate the objects 90 degrees counterclockwise.

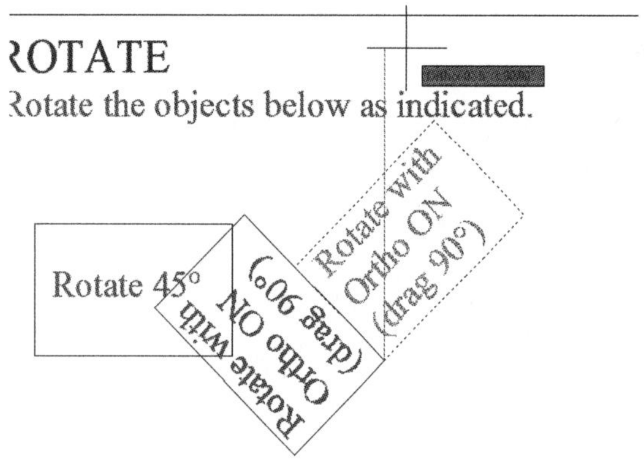

Command Exercise

Exercise 5-14 – Rotate Using Reference

Drawing Name: **rotate2.dwg**
Estimated Time to Completion: 5 Minutes

Scope

Straighten the object using the reference option with rotate.

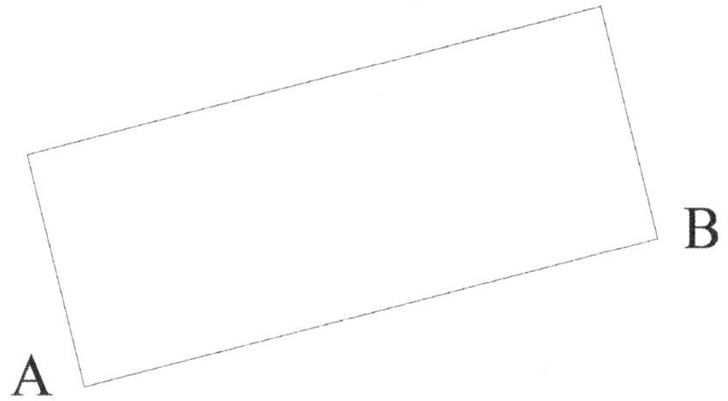

Rotate using a Reference

Solution

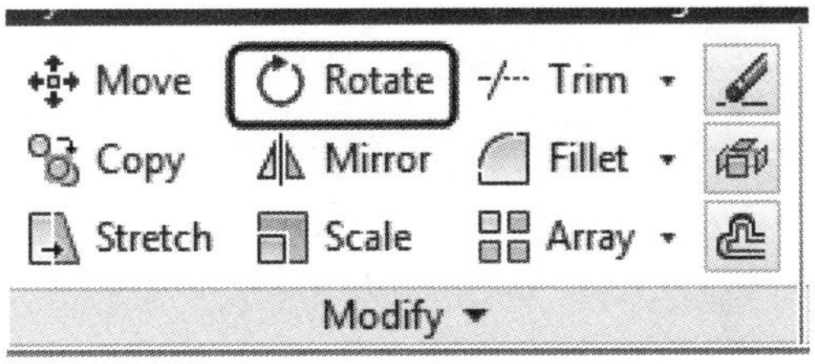

1. Invoke the Rotate command (rotate).
2. *Select objects:*
   Select the rectangle with the LMB.
3. *Select objects:*
   Close the selection set by pressing <ENTER>.
4. *Specify base point:*
   Pick the lower left corner of the rectangle (A). Remember to use Object Snaps.
5. *Specify rotation angle or [Reference]:*
   Right-click in the drawing area and select 'Reference' or type 'R' for Reference and press <ENTER>.
6. *Specify the reference angle <0>:*
   Pick the same point on the rectangle (A).
7. *Specify second point:*
   Pick the lower right corner of the rectangle (B).
8. *Specify the new angle or [Points] <0>:*
   Type '0' at the command line and press <ENTER>.
   (The Points option allows you to select two points to specify the new angle.)

Command Exercise

Exercise 5-15 – Rotate and Copy

Drawing Name: **rotate3.dwg**
Estimated Time to Completion: 5 Minutes

Scope

Use Rotate to Copy and Rotate an object.

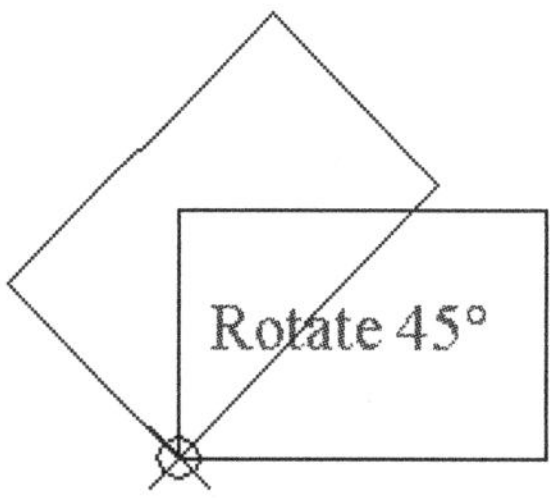

Copy and Rotate Exercise

Solution

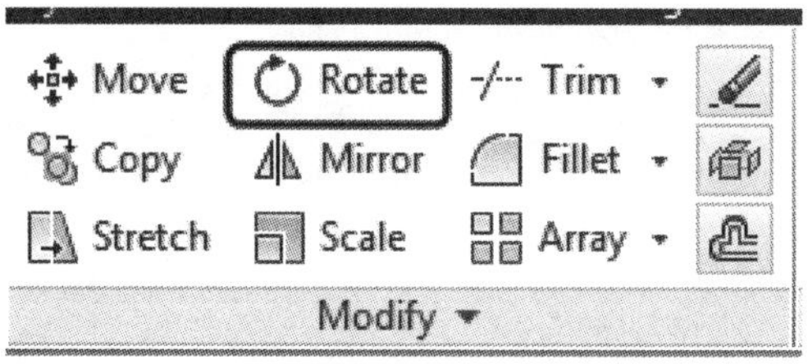

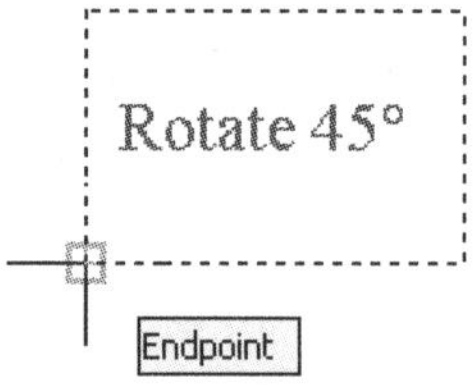

1. Invoke the Rotate command (rotate).
2. Select the rectangle on the left.
3. Press ENTER to indicate you are done with selecting objects.
4. Select the lower left corner as the base point.
5. Press the RMB and select **Copy** from the shortcut menu.
6. Type **45** as the rotation angle.
7. Press ENTER.

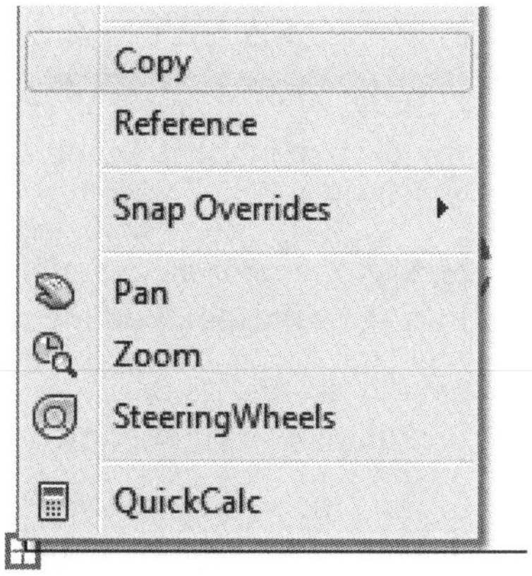

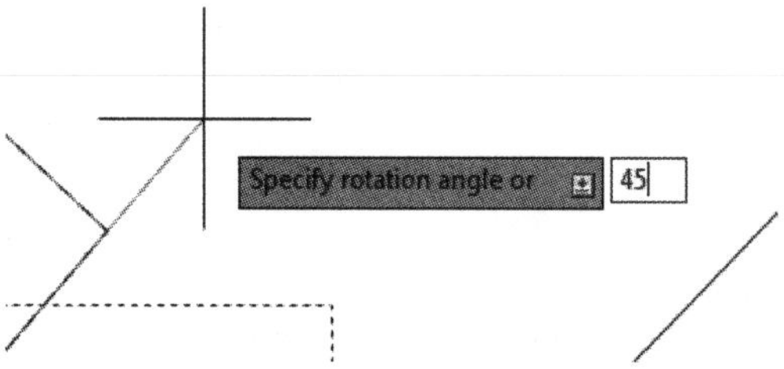

Challenge Exercise

Exercise 5-16 – Rotate Using Reference

Drawing Name: **rotate4.dwg**
Estimated Time to Completion: 5 Minutes

Scope

Rotate using a reference and then measure the distance between the points indicated.

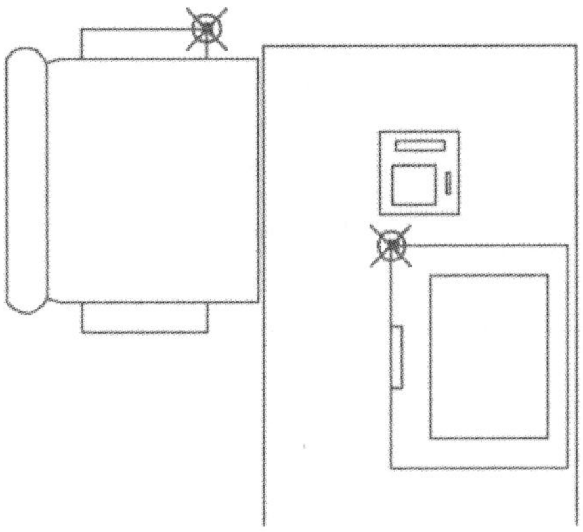

Solution

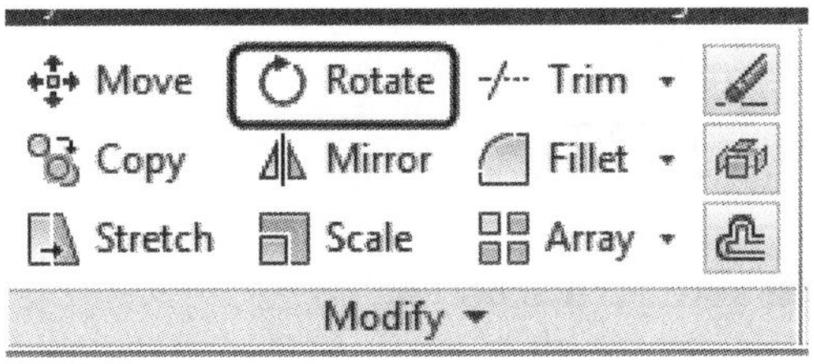

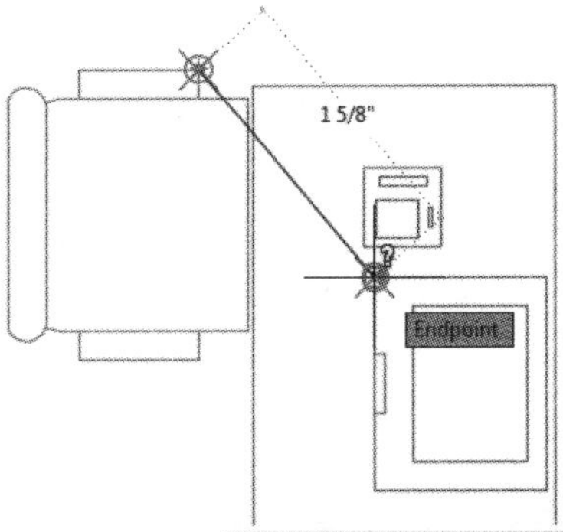

Distance should be shown as 1 5/8".

```
Command: DIST
Specify first point:
Specify second point or [Multiple points]:
Distance = 0'-1 5/8",  Angle in XY Plane = 311.07,  Angle from XY Plane = 0.00
Delta X = 0'-1 1/16",  Delta Y = -0'-1 3/16",   Delta Z = 0'-0"
```

Scale

Command Locator

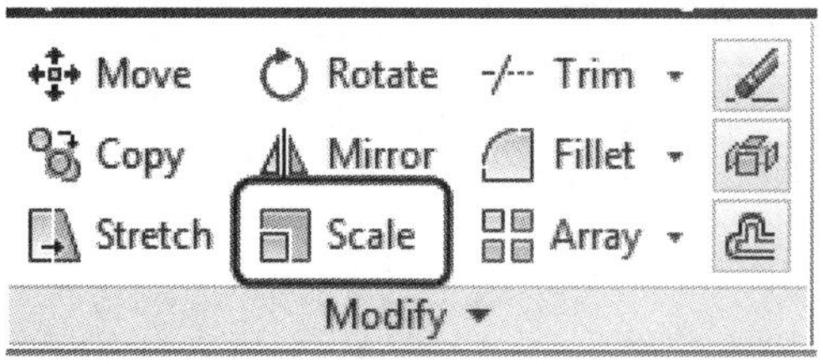

Home Ribbon	**Modify / Scale**
Command	**Scale**
Alias	**SC**
RMB Shortcut Menu	**Drawing Window**

Command Overview

Scale objects *up* or *down* from a selected base point. Use the Reference option to reference a known length, then type the new length to scale the object proportionately.

General Procedures

To use the Scale command:

1. Invoke the Scale Command.
2. Select the objects to Scale, and press <ENTER>.
3. Pick a base point on or near the object.
4. Type the Scale Factor and press <ENTER>.

To use the Scale command with the Reference option:

1. Invoke the Scale Command.
2. Select the objects to Scale, and press <ENTER>.
3. Pick a base point on or near the object. Type R for reference (and press <ENTER>), or press the RMB and select Reference from the shortcut menu.
4. Use Object Snaps to specify the reference length, or type the reference length, if known.
5. Type the new length.

Command Exercise

Exercise 5-17 – Scale

Drawing Name: **scale1.dwg**
Estimated Time to Completion: 5 Minutes

Scope

Scale the images as indicated in the drawing.

Scale Exercise

Solution

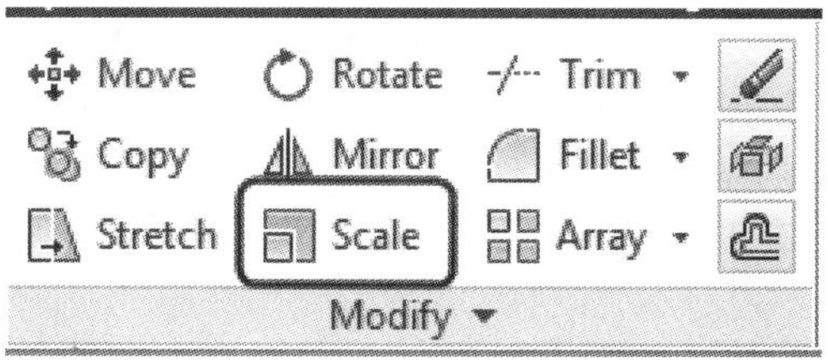

1. Invoke the Scale command (scale).
2. *Select objects:*
   Select the objects that make up the part on the left.
3. *Select objects:*
   Press <ENTER> to close the selection set.
4. *Specify base point:*
   Select a point near the base of the part.
5. *Specify scale factor or [Reference]:*
   Type **0.5** and press <ENTER>.
6. Repeat the Scale command with the RMB (scale or <ENTER>).
7. *Select objects:*
   Select the objects that make up the part on the right.
8. *Select objects:*
   Press <ENTER> to close the selection set.
9. *Specify base point:*
   Select a point near the base of the part.
10. *Specify scale factor or [Reference]:*
    Type **2** and <ENTER>.

Command Exercise

Exercise 5-18 – Scale Using Reference

Drawing Name: **scale2.dwg**
Estimated Time to Completion: 5 Minutes

Scope

Using the Reference option, scale the image so that the overall height is 4.

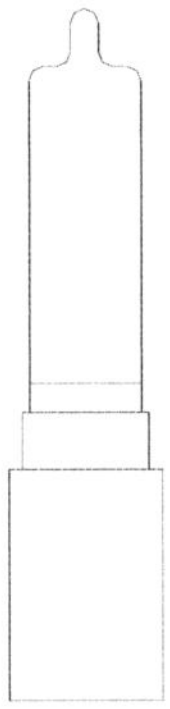

Scale Using Reference

Solution

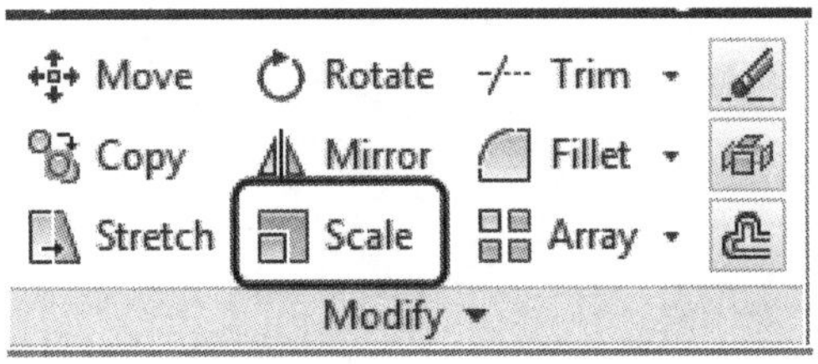

1. Invoke the Scale command (scale).
2. *Select objects:*
   Select the objects that make up the part.
3. *Select objects:*
   Press <ENTER> to close the selection set.
4. *Specify base point:*
   Select the Midpoint of the base with the LMB. Remember to use the Object Snap.
5. *Specify scale factor or [Reference]:*
   Right-click in the drawing window and select **Reference** or type **R** for Reference and press <ENTER>.
6. *Specify reference length <1>:*
   Pick the Midpoint or Quadrant of the top with the LMB.
7. *Specify second point:*
   Pick the Midpoint or Perpendicular to the bottom with the LMB. Remember to use the running object snap.
8. *Specify new length:*
   Type **4** and press <ENTER>.

Stretch

Command Locator

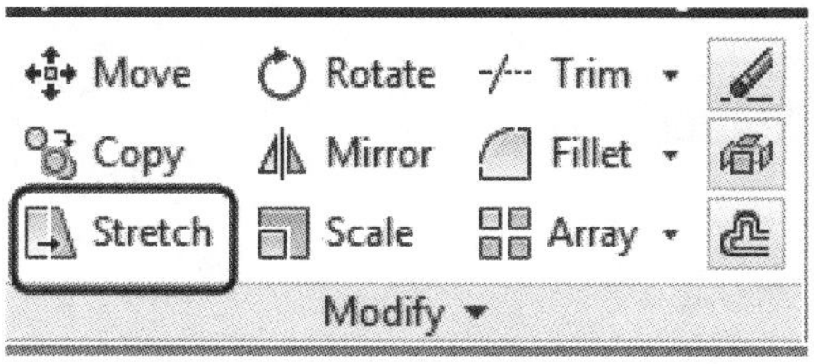

Home Ribbon	**Modify→Stretch**
Command	**Stretch**
Alias	**s**

Command Overview

Learning how to use the Stretch command is tricky at first. Always use a Crossing Window or Crossing Polygon to select the objects to stretch. The endpoints or vertices of the objects selected will be stretched, or *moved*, to a new location, while the objects outside of the selection window will remain anchored. Once the objects are selected, press <ENTER> and pick a base point, then with ORTHO on, drag the object in the desired direction and type a distance.

General Procedures

1. Begin the Stretch command.
2. Select objects using the automatic Crossing Window option (right to left). Frame the object so that the endpoints to be moved are completely within the selection box.
3. Pick a base point on or near the object.
4. Select the second point of displacement, drag the object in the desired direction (with ORTHO on) and type the distance.

Tips & Tricks

- Circles cannot be stretched with this command but can be stretched using grips (grips will be covered at the end of this chapter).
- Objects that are completely within the selection window will be moved.
- If a crossing window is not used, only the objects completely within the window will be moved, and not stretched.
- Blocks cannot be stretched.
- When selecting the Second point of displacement, use the direct distance method with ORTHO on. Drag the cursor in the desired direction and type the distance.
- When selecting points (base point or second point of displacement), picking points with or without Object Snap, Relative Coordinates, or Polar Coordinates are all acceptable methods. However, the direct distance with ORTHO on works best.

Command Exercise

Exercise 5-19 – Stretch

Drawing Name: **stretch1.dwg**
Estimated Time to Completion: 5 Minutes

Scope

Use the crossing window option to select objects to stretch.

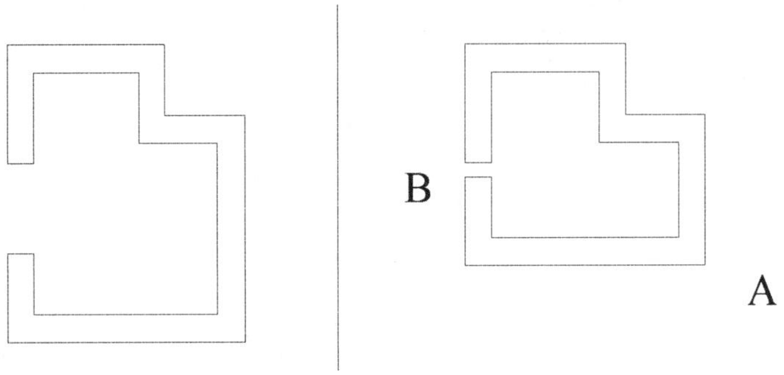

Stretch Using Crossing

Solution

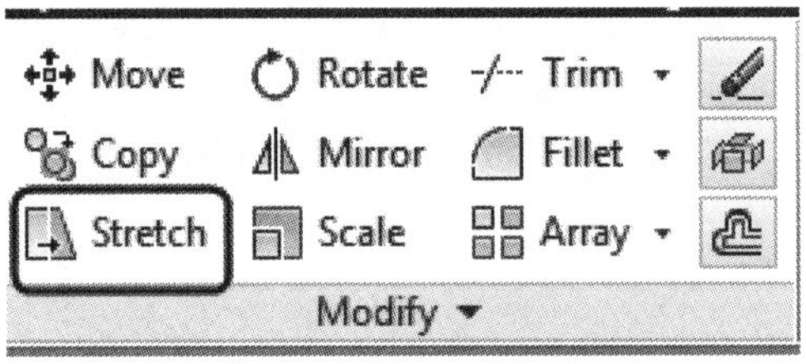

1. Invoke the Stretch command (stretch).
2. *Select objects:*
   Use a crossing window to select the lower half of the object.
3. LMB at Point A then LMB at Point B.

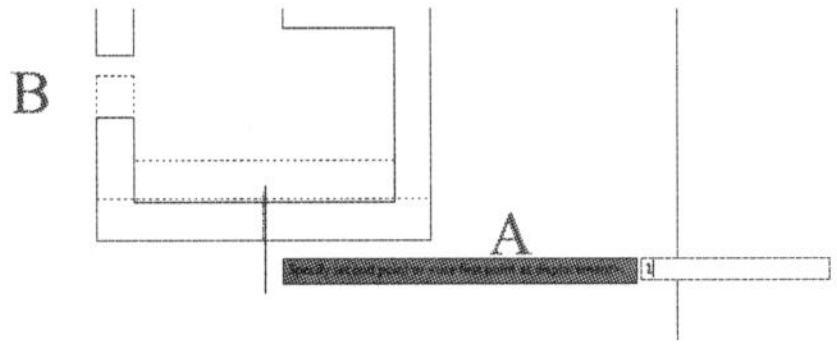

4. *Select objects:*
   Press <ENTER> to continue.
5. Specify base point or displacement:
   Turn ORTHO on and pick a point from which the part will be stretched with the LMB. ***(Hint:** Using the midpoint of the bottom horizontal line works well.)*
6. *Specify second point of displacement:*
   Drag the mouse downward. Type '1' at the command line and press <ENTER>.

➢ *Notice that the line segments that are fully contained in the crossing selection window are moved while the lines that are crossed are stretched.*

Challenge Exercise

Exercise 5-20 – Stretch

Drawing Name: **stretch2.dwg**
Estimated Time to Completion: 5 Minutes

Scope

Use the grips to stretch the polyline as shown.

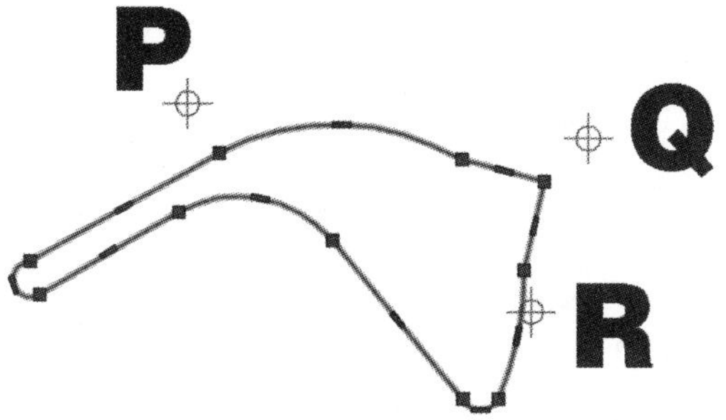

Stretch Using Grips

Solution

1. Select the polyline so it highlights.
2. *Select the vertex closest to P. Use the Node snap to place the vertex on the P node.*

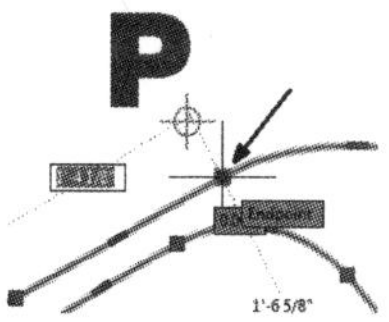

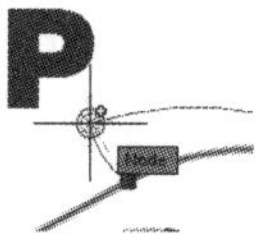

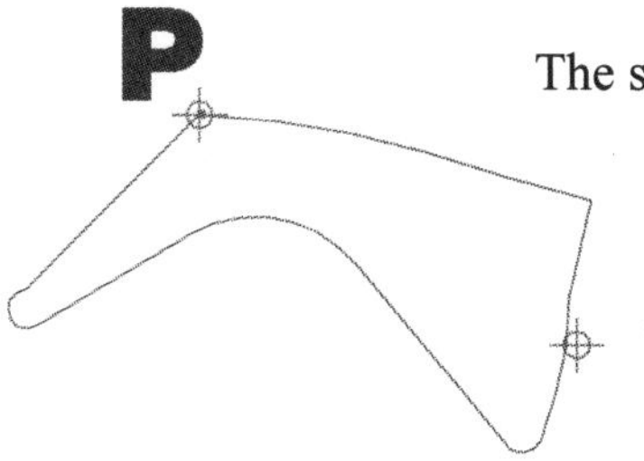

The shape should adjust as shown.

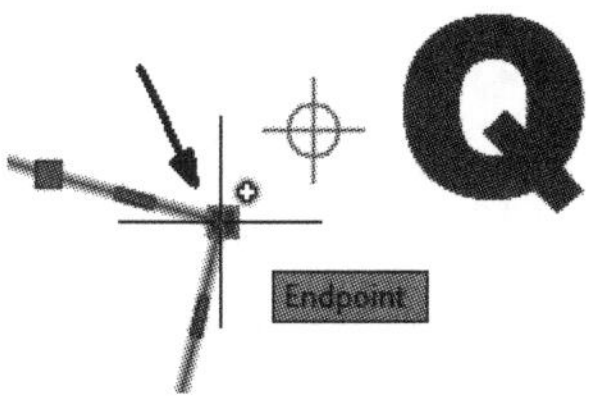

3. *Select the vertex closest to Q. Use the Node snap to place the vertex on the Q node.*

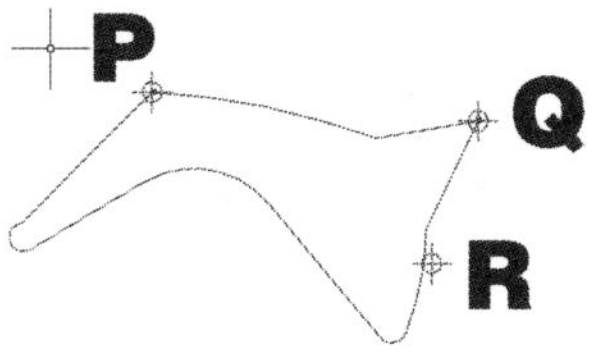

The shape should adjust as shown.

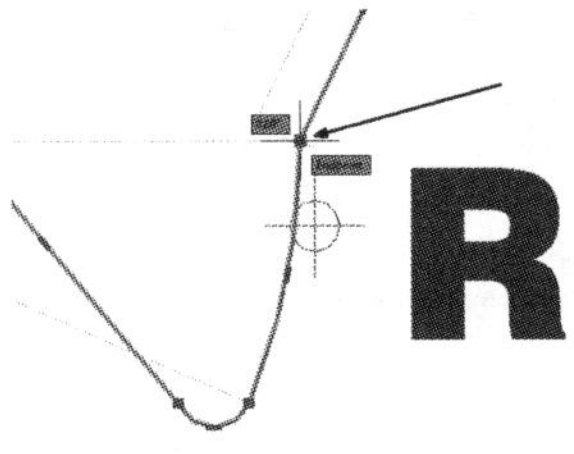

4. *Select the vertex closest/above to R. Use the Node snap to place the vertex on the Q node.*

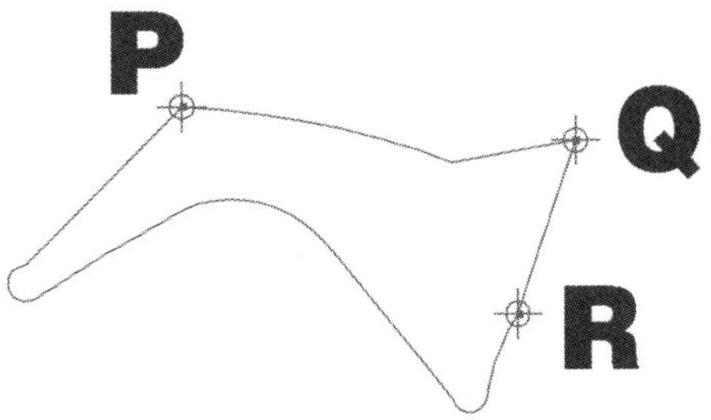

The shape should adjust as shown.

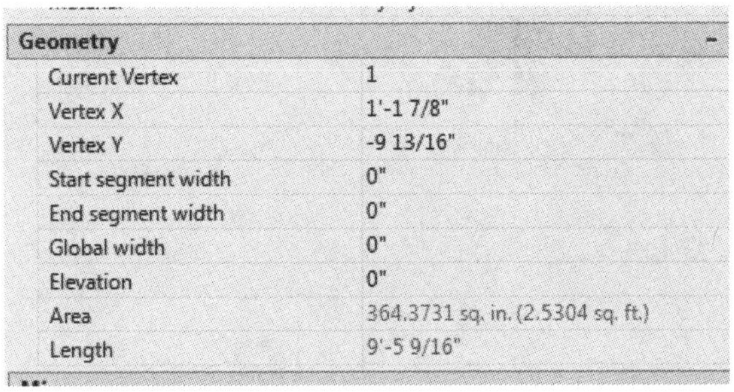

Geometry	
Current Vertex	1
Vertex X	1'-1 7/8"
Vertex Y	-9 13/16"
Start segment width	0"
End segment width	0"
Global width	0"
Elevation	0"
Area	364.3731 sq. in. (2.5304 sq. ft.)
Length	9'-5 9/16"

5. Select the polyline.
6. Right click and select Properties.
7. Determine the Length property for the polyline.

The new length should be 9' - 5 9/16".

Trim

Command Locator

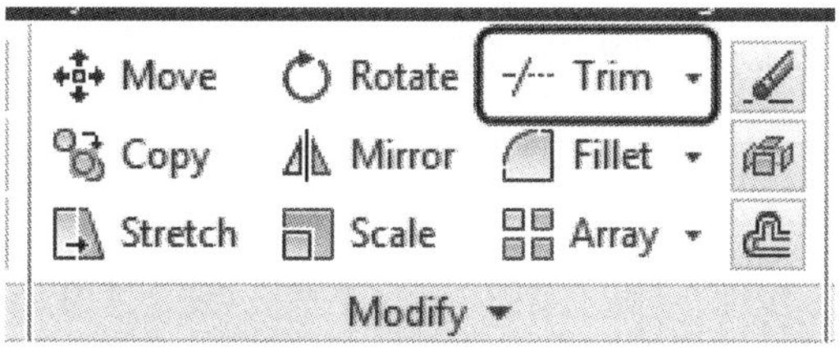

Home Ribbon	**Modify / Trim**
Command	**Trim**
Alias	**TR**
RMB Shortcut Menu	**Drawing Window**

Command Overview

Trim objects to a cutting edge. The cutting edge may or may not cross the object to trim. If the objects do not cross or intersect, the Edge mode must be set to "Extend." The Project option is for 3D. Undo is an option that can be used within the Trim command, without completely exiting the command.

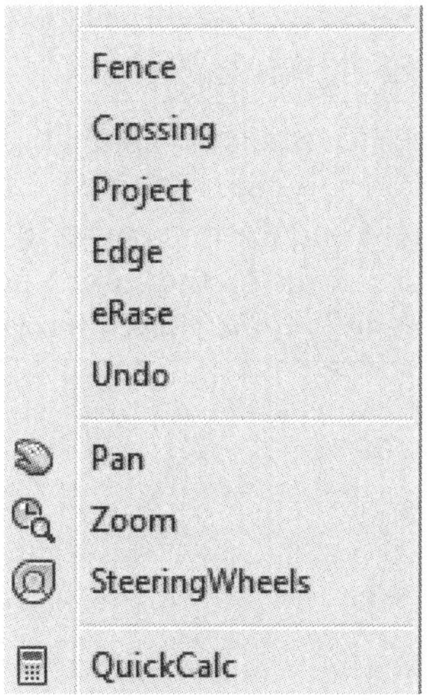

Trim Shortcut Menu

Trim Option	Overview
Fence	*When this option is selected, the user draws an imaginary fence line that is used as the cutting edge.*
Crossing	*The crossing option is used to designate the objects which are to be retained following the Trim operation.*
Project	*The Project option is used when you are working in 3D space and you wish to trim using objects which may be at a different elevation or work plane.*
Edge	*The Edge object is also used when working in 3D space to designate either a projected edge or an edge which is actually intersecting the object to be trimmed.*
Erase	*Deletes selected objects – temporarily suspends the trim command to allow the user to erase unwanted objects and then returns to the Trim command.*

General Procedures

Regular Trim (No Extend):

1. Invoke the Trim command.
2. Select the cutting edges, and press <ENTER>.
3. Select the objects to trim.

Trim using the Extend option:

1. Invoke the Trim command.
2. Select the cutting edges, and press <ENTER>.
3. Type E (for Edge) and press <ENTER>.
4. Type E (for Extend) and press <ENTER>.
5. Select the objects to trim.

Tips & Tricks

- Selecting Multiple lines to trim is acceptable, such as lines that trim to each other.
- An object must be crossed by the cutting edge to be trimmed (unless the Edge mode Extend option is selected and the object would cross the cutting edge if extended).
- A circle must be crossed twice by the cutting edge in order to be trimmed.
- The object will be trimmed on the side of the cutting edge where it is selected.

Command Exercise

Exercise 5-21 – Trim

Drawing Name: **trim1.dwg**
Estimated Time to Completion: 5 Minutes

Scope

Trim the lines outside the red box and select the line individually. Repeat the exercise but select the lines to trim using the Fence (F) option.

Trim Using Fence

Solution

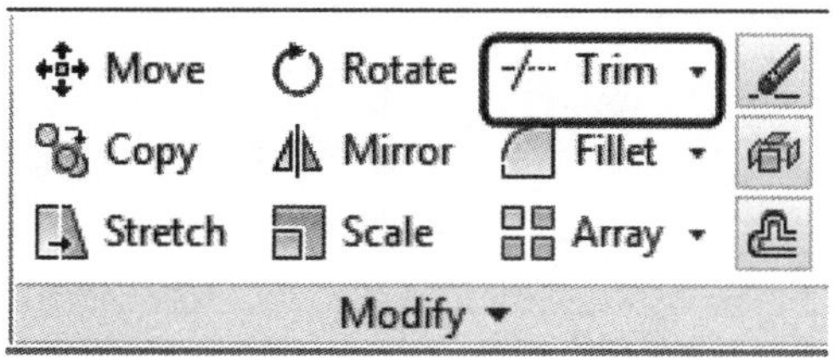

1. Invoke the Trim command (trim).
2. *Select objects:*
   Use the LMB to select the red box as the cutting edges.
3. *Select objects:*
   Press <ENTER> to finish selecting cutting edges.
4. *Select object to trim or [Project/Edge/Undo]:*
   Use the left mouse button to select the portion of the top black line that extends outside the left side of the red box.
5. *Select object to trim or [Project/Edge/Undo]:*
   Repeat the process for all the lines along the left side of the red box. Press <ENTER> when finished.
6. Repeat the Trim command with the RMB (trim or <ENTER>).
7. *Select objects:*
   Use the LMB to select the red box as the cutting edges.
8. *Select objects:*
   Press <ENTER> to finish selecting cutting edges.
9. *Select object to trim or [Project/Edge/Undo]:*
   Type 'F' at the command line for Fence and press <ENTER>.
10. *First fence point:*
    Create a fence line that cuts all the line segments that extend outside the red box on the right.

11. *Specify endpoint of line or [Undo]:*
    Finish creating the fence and press <ENTER> to trim the selected line segments.
12. *Select object to trim or [Project/Edge/Undo]:*
    Press <ENTER> to finish the exercise.

Extra: *Undo all the trimming and try removing the lines inside the red box. Undo again. Can a cutting edge be trimmed? Try it. Select all lines as the cutting edge, then trim the red rectangle and the lines.*

Extend

Command Locator

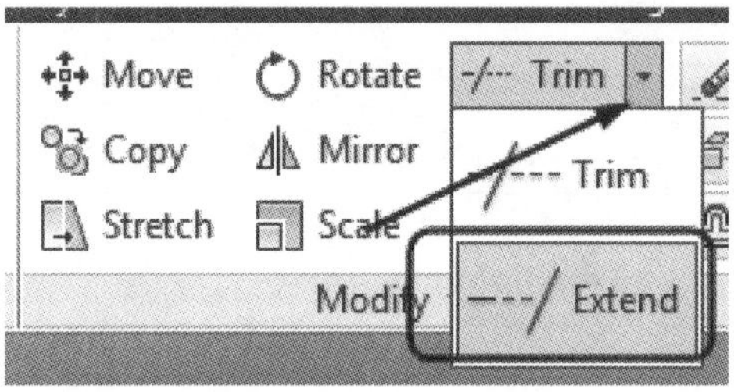

Home Ribbon	**Modify / Extend**
Command	**Extend**
Alias	**EX**
RMB Shortcut Menu	**Drawing Window**

Command Overview

Extend objects to a boundary by selecting the object towards the end to be extended. The boundary may or may not reach the object being extended. If the objects do not reach the boundary, the Edge mode must be set to "Extend." Typically this option is set to "No Extend." The Project option is for 3D. Undo can be used as an option within the Extend command without completely exiting the command.

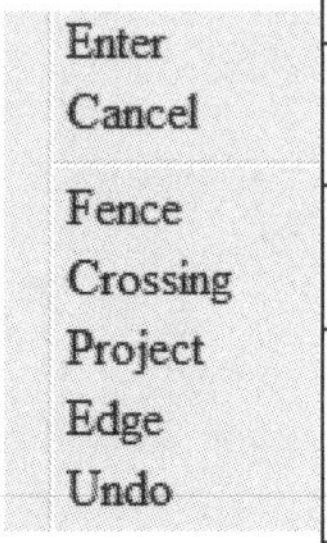

Extend Option	Overview
Fence	When this option is selected, the user draws an imaginary fence line that is used as the cutting edge.
Crossing	The crossing option is used to designate the objects which are to be retained following the Trim operation.
Project	The Project option is used when you are working in 3D space and you wish to trim using objects which may be at a different elevation or work plane.
Edge	The Edge object is also used when working in 3D space to designate either a projected edge or an edge which is actually intersecting the object to be trimmed.

Extend Shortcut Menu

General Procedures

Regular Extend (No Extend):

1. Invoke the Extend command.
2. Select the boundary edges, and press <ENTER>.
3. Select the objects to extend towards the boundary edge.

Trim using the Extend option:

1. Invoke the Extend command.
2. Select the boundary edges, and press <ENTER>.
3. Type E (for Edge) and press <ENTER>.
4. Type E (for the Extend option) and press <ENTER>.
5. Select the objects to extend towards the boundary edge.

Tips & Tricks

- The Undo option will undo one step at a time without exiting the Extend command.
- An object must be able to meet the boundary edge to be trimmed (unless the Edge mode Extend option is selected and the object would meet the boundary edge if extended).
- Select the object to Extend anywhere on the half that is closest to the boundary.

Command Exercise

Exercise 5-22 – Extend

Drawing Name: **extend1.dwg**
Estimated Time to Completion: 5 Minutes

Scope

Extend the horizontal line to the sides of the red rectangle.

Extend Exercise

Solution

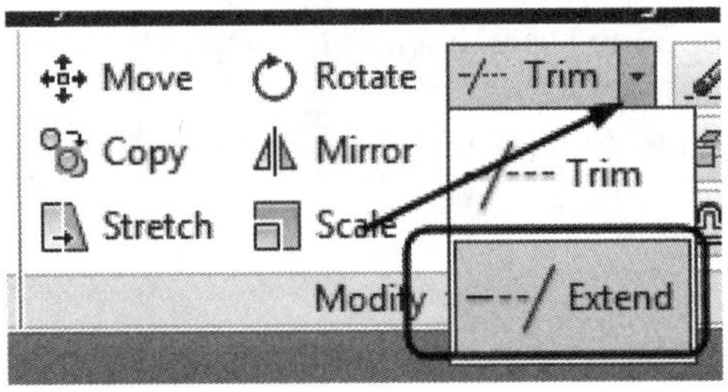

1. Invoke the Extend command (extend).
2. *Select objects:*
   Pick the red rectangle with the LMB as the boundary edge.
3. *Select objects:*
   Close the selection of boundary edges by pressing <ENTER>.
4. *Select object to extend or [Project/Edge/Undo]:*
   Pick on the left side of the top dark line. Notice that the line extends from the side of the line you have selected.
5. *Select object to extend or [Project/Edge/Undo]:*
   Pick the other side of the same line.
6. Select object to extend or [Project/Edge/Undo]:
   Repeat the process with the rest of the lines to finish the exercise.

Extra: *Create a line segment that is outside the red box. Start the Extend command and use the red box as the boundary edge. Extend the line to the outside of the rectangle and then extend the line through the rectangle to the opposite side.*

Tips & Tricks

- *You can extend Arcs to a boundary. Try it.*

Fillet

Command Locator

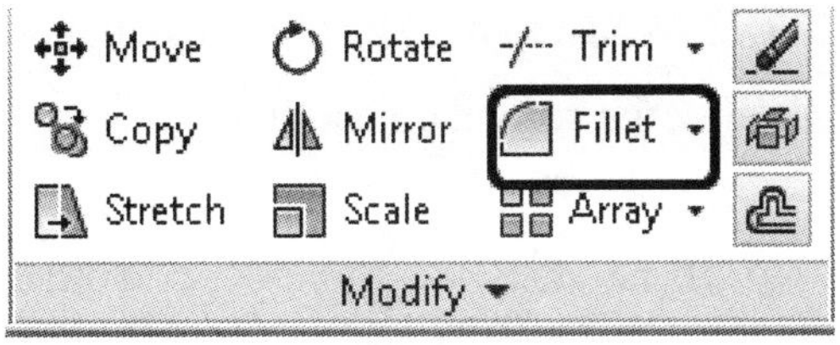

Home Ribbon	**Modify / Fillet**
Command	**Fillet**
Alias	**F**
RMB Shortcut Menu	**Drawing Window**

Command Overview

Radius corners with the FILLET command. Clean up corners with the Fillet radius set to 0.

Fillet Option	Overview
Select first object	This is the default selection. Select the first object towards the corner to fillet.
Select second object	Select the second object towards the corner to fillet. This object must be adjacent or parallel to the first line selected.
Polyline	Type P to fillet all of the corners of a polyline at once.
Radius	Type R to change the Radius of the fillet. This setting remains until it is changed again. The default radius setting when starting a new drawing is .50.
Trim	Type T to invoke the Trim or No Trim options. No trim (N) will leave the original lines when making a fillet.
Multiple	Type U to create more than one fillet. Works similar to the Multiple option of the Copy command.

Fillet RMB Options

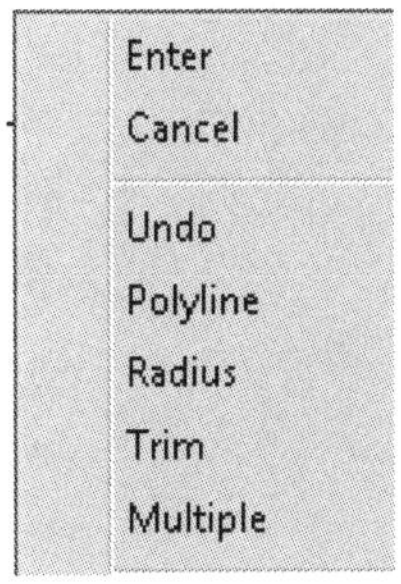

General Procedures

1. Begin the Fillet command.
2. To change the current radius, type R (and <ENTER>). Type the desired radius (and <ENTER>). Press <ENTER> to repeat to the Fillet command.
3. Select the first object, then select the second object.

- It is not necessary to set the radius to fillet parallel lines.
- Fillet can be used on any lines or arcs that are separate polylines, or at the arc intersections of polylines.
- Set a Radius value of 0 to create a 90-degree angle and trim corners.
- You cannot select all of the segments in one step. You must repeat the fillet command for each corner, unless the object is a polyline and the Fillet command is used with the Polyline option. Try it on a rectangle.

Command Exercise

Exercise 5-23 – Fillet

Drawing Name: **fillet1.dwg**
Estimated Time to Completion: 5 Minutes

Scope

Use the fillet command with a fillet radius of 0 to clean up the corners of the lines as indicated. Remember to change the fillet radius first.

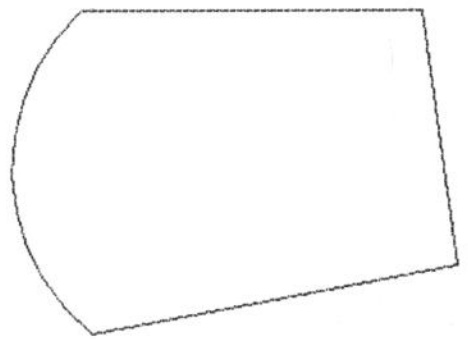

Fillet Exercise

Solution

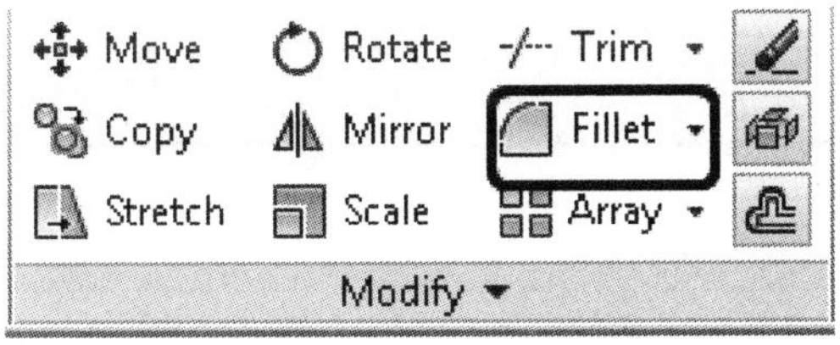

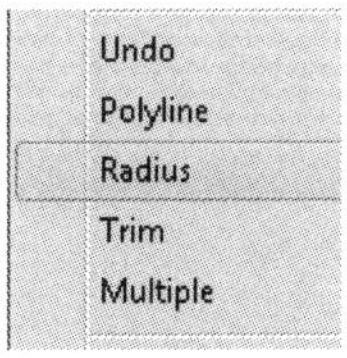

1. Invoke the Fillet command (f or fillet).
2. *Select first object or [Polyline/Radius/Trim]:*
   Right-click in the drawing window and select 'Radius' or type 'R' for Radius and press <ENTER>.
3. *Specify fillet radius <0.5000>:*
   Type '0' and press <ENTER>.

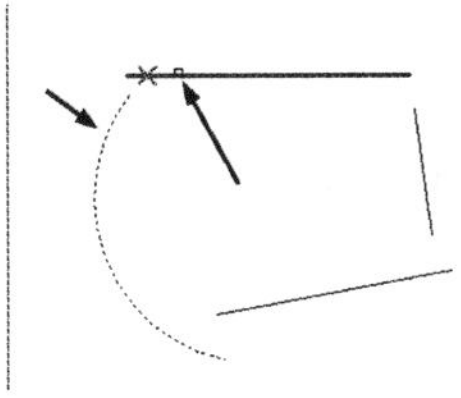

4. *Select first object or [Polyline/Radius/Trim]:*
   Use the LMB to select the arc.
5. *Select second object:*
   Use the LMB to select the top line segment.
6. Repeat the Fillet command with the RMB (f, fillet or <ENTER>).

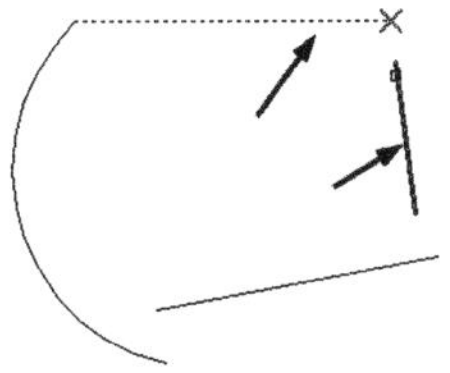

7. *Select first object or [Polyline/Radius/Trim]:*
   Select the top line with the LMB.
8. *Select second object:*
   Pick the line on the right side with the LMB.
9. Continue the process of repeating the fillet command, selecting two adjacent segments to clean up the corners of the object.

Undo and Redo

Command Locator

Home Ribbon	**Edit / Undo and Edit / Redo**
Command	**Undo or Redo**
Alias	**U (no alias for redo)**
RMB Shortcut Menu	**Drawing Window (for Undo options)**
Shortcut Keys	**Ctrl+Z for Undo, Ctrl+Y for Redo**

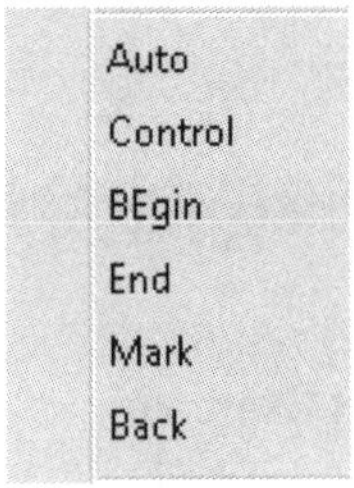

Undo RMB Options

Command Overview

Type U for undo or select the button  in the Standard Toolbar. This will reverse previous commands. Undo can be taken all the way back to the beginning of the drawing. Redo  must immediately follow the Undo command and will reverse the last Undo commands in order.

General Procedures

1. Select the Undo button or type U at the command line, and press <ENTER>.
2. Press the <ENTER> key to repeat the undo command until satisfied.

Tips & Tricks

- Be careful not to press the <ENTER> key too many times.
- Use U rather than typing the entire UNDO command.
- The Undo shortcut menu appears only when the entire word 'UNDO' is typed.
- Use the **Mark** option for Undo to mark a point before you start an edit sequence. You can then undo back to the point you have bookmarked.

Command Exercise

Exercise 5-24 – Undo and Redo

Drawing Name: **undo1.dwg**
Estimated Time to Completion: 5 Minutes

Scope

Draw several lines, circles and rectangles. Undo your drawing several steps back. Next try to Redo several steps. Notice that both Undo and Redo keep track of the commands issued.

Solution

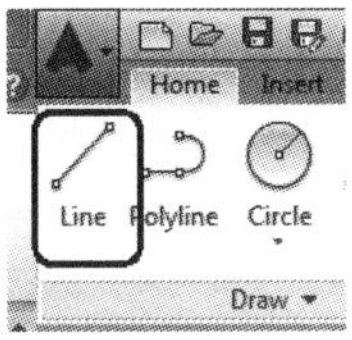

1. Invoke the **Line** command (l or line) and create several lines on the drawing.
2. Invoke the **Circle** command (c or circle) and create several circles on the drawing.

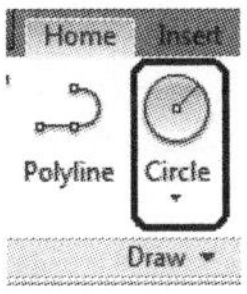

3. Invoke the **Rectangle** command (rectang) and create several rectangles on the drawing.
4. Invoke the **Erase** command (e or erase) and erase one or two of the objects you have just created.

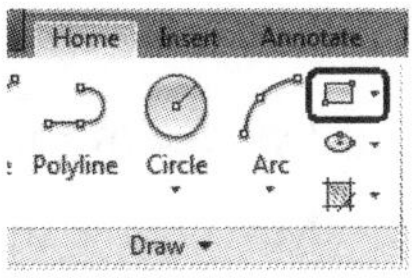

5. Invoke the **Undo** command by using the standard Windows icon at the top of the screen or typing 'U' at the command line.
6. Repeat the command until about half of your objects are gone.
7. Invoke the **REDO** command by using the standard Windows icon at the top of the screen.

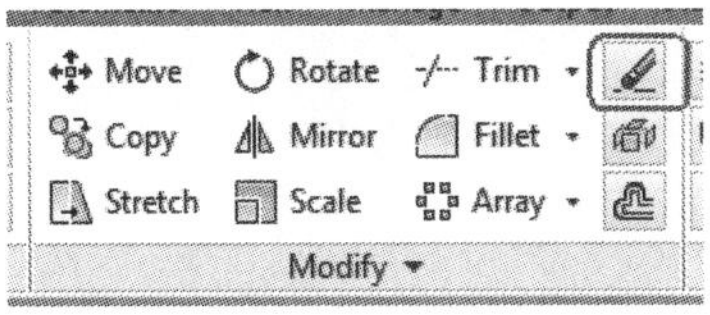

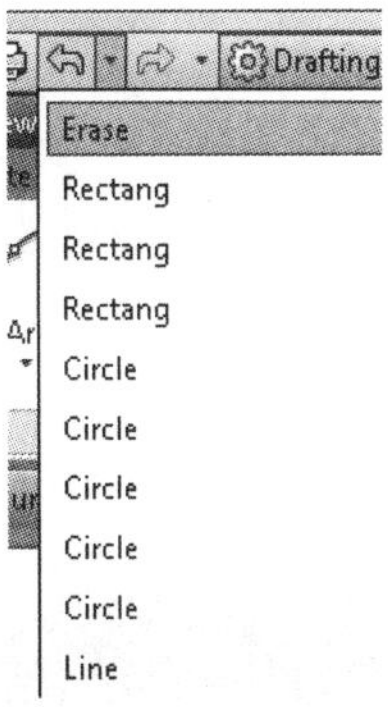

➢ Both the Undo and Redo commands have a drop-down list so you can see how far back or forward you want to go.

Section Exercise

Exercise 5-25 – Modify Commands

Drawing Name: **Lesson 5 AEC.dwg**
Estimated Time to Completion: 15 Minutes

Scope

Using the modify commands, furnish the apartment as shown.

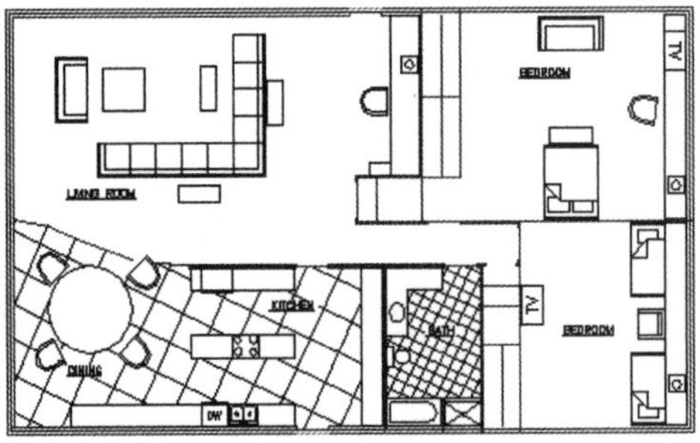

Modify Commands Exercise

Hints

1. Copy the chairs and sofa sections.
2. Use the mirror command to create the second single bed.
3. Move most of the pieces into place.
4. Use the Array command to array the chairs around the dining table.

Area

Command Locator

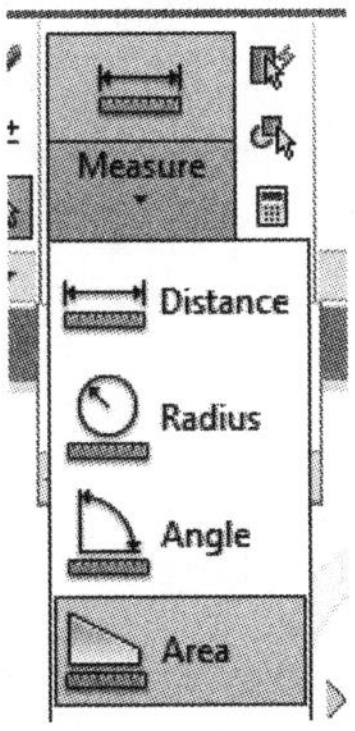

Home Ribbon	**Utilities / Area**
Command	**Area**
RMB Shortcut Menu	**Drawing Window**

Command Overview

Calculates the area and perimeter of objects . You can use the shortcut menu to add and subtract areas.

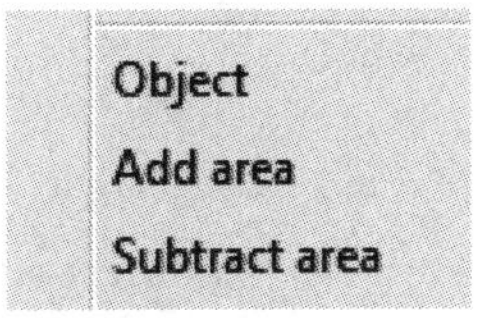

Area Option	**Overview**
Object	Selects a closed polygon or region.
Add	Select one or more objects to include.
Subtract	Select one or more objects to exclude.

Area RMB Options

Challenge Exercise

Exercise 5-26 – Area

Drawing Name: **Area.dwg**
Estimated Time to Completion: 15 Minutes

Scope

Calculate the area of a region. Subtract area L from Area A.

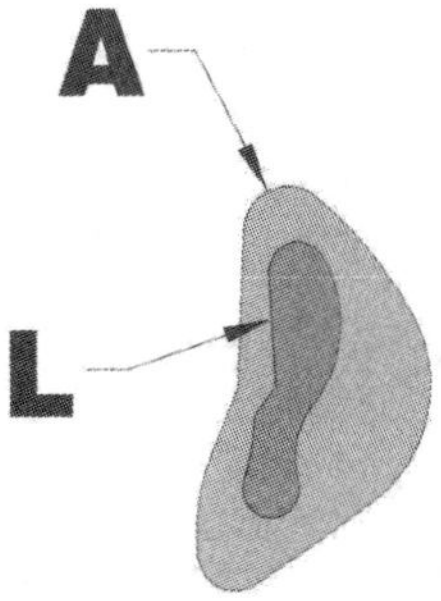
A
L

Area Exercise

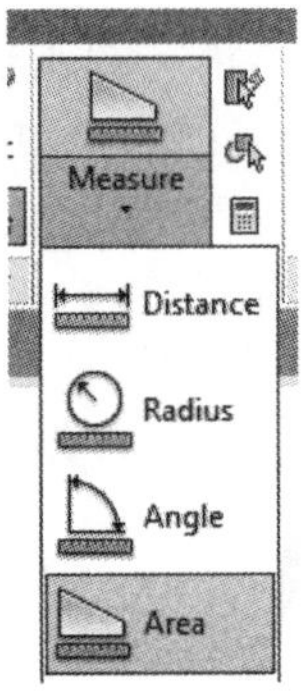
Measure
Distance
Radius
Angle
Area

Solution

1. Type AREA or select the AREA tool from the Utilities pane on the Home ribbon.
2. RMB and select Add area.
3. RMB and select Object.
4. Select polyline A.
5. Right click to complete the selections being added.

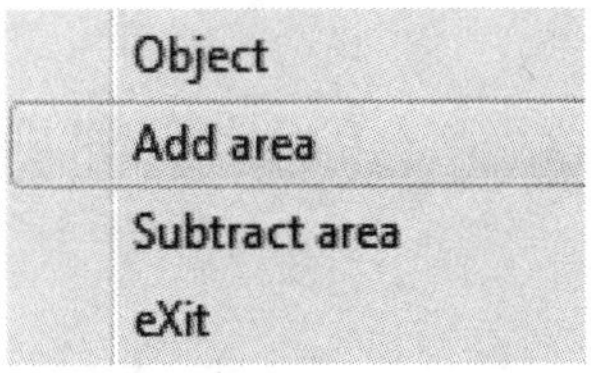
Object
Add area
Subtract area
eXit

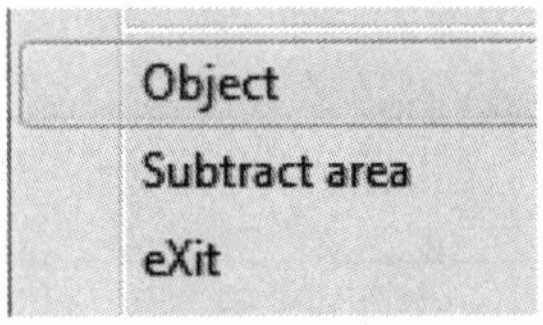
Object
Subtract area
eXit

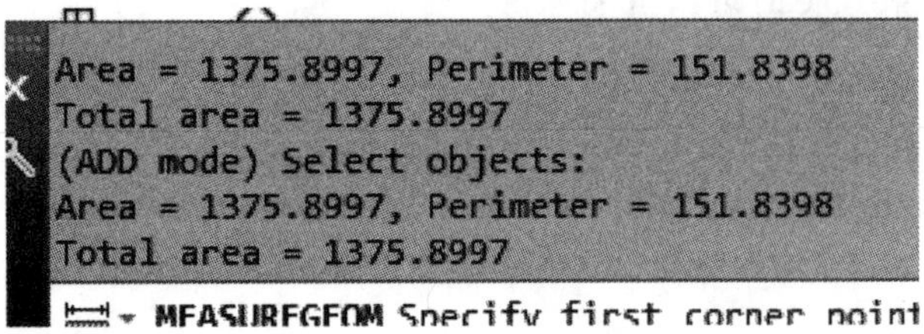
Area = 1375.8997, Perimeter = 151.8398
Total area = 1375.8997
(ADD mode) Select objects:
Area = 1375.8997, Perimeter = 151.8398
Total area = 1375.8997

You will see the area and perimeter value for polyline A.

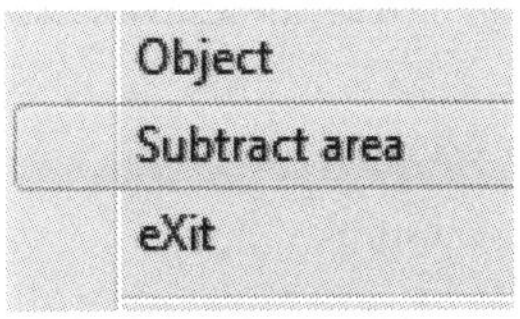
Object
Subtract area
eXit

6. RMB and select Subtract area.
7. RMB and select Object.
8. Select polyline L.
9. Right click to complete selecting objects.

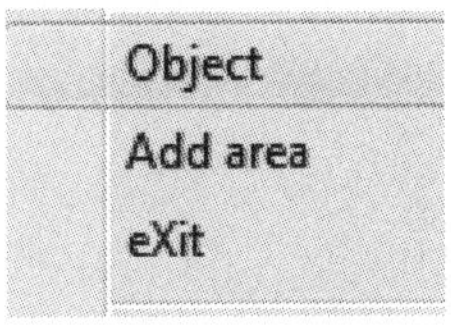
Object
Add area
eXit

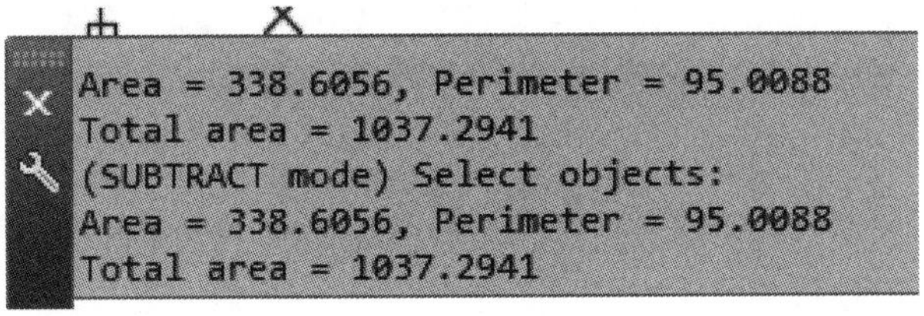
Area = 338.6056, Perimeter = 95.0088
Total area = 1037.2941
(SUBTRACT mode) Select objects:
Area = 338.6056, Perimeter = 95.0088
Total area = 1037.2941

AutoCAD will subtract Area A (1375.8997) from Area L (338.6056) and calculate the total: 1037.2941.

Review Questions

1. You construct a circle. You now want to copy the circle. What option can you use at the Select objects prompt to select the last object you created?

2. You wish to mirror some text. What value should MIRRTEXT be set to to ensure that the text mirrors properly?

3. You need to duplicate an object in a rectangular pattern. What command allows you to do this?

4. You enter the TRIM command. When prompted to select the cutting edges, you press the <ENTER> key. What is the result?

5. You wish to offset an object and delete the source object. What is the best way to do this?

6. Identify the following icons that are all located in the Modify Toolbar:

   a.  ____________________

   b.  ____________________

   c.  ____________________

   d.  ____________________

   e.  ____________________

   f.  ____________________

   g.  ____________________

   h.  ____________________

   i.  ____________________

7. Typing the letter R at the command line invokes which command?
   - ❑ Scale
   - ❑ Rotate
   - ❑ Redraw
   - ❑ Regen

8. What does the R option stand for in the Scale command?

9. What does the U option stand for in the trim and extend commands?

10. Explain the similarities between the Copy and Move commands.

11. Can you trim a line that is acting as a cutting edge? Try it.

Review Answers

1. *Type L at the command line to select the last object created.*

2. *Set **MIRRTEXT** to 1.*

3. *ARRAY*

4. *All objects in the drawing may now be used as a cutting edge.*

5. *Use the **ERASE** option for OFFSET.*

6.
   a. erase
   b. copy
   c. mirror
   d. offset
   e. move
   f. scale
   g. rotate
   h. trim
   i. Extend

7. *Redraw*

8. *Reference*

9. *Undo*

10. *The steps to move an object are similar to copying an object. The major difference is that the copy command leaves the original object in place.*

11. *Yes. Cutting edges can be trimmed as long as they cross another object.*

Lesson 6.0 – Selecting Objects

Estimated Class Time: 1 Hour

Objectives

This section introduces different methods of selecting objects and what to do with the objects once they are selected.

- **Selecting Objects**
- **Quick Select**
- **Quick Properties**

Selecting Objects

Command Overview

Knowing how to select objects is an important aspect to being able to manipulate objects inside of AutoCAD. Typically one begins with a specific Modify command, then selects the objects to modify. When an object is selected, it will be highlighted. Continue to select (or de-select) objects at the "Select objects" prompt, then press <ENTER> to continue. Objects can be selected individually, with the selection window, or by invoking one of the options at the *Select object* prompt.

Select Object Option	Key	Overview
Pick		Place the cursor over the object and pick it using the LMB.
Window (Left to Right)		Making a selection window from left to right will create a window in which only the objects that are completely within the window will be selected. Place the cursor in the blank area of the drawing to the left of the objects to select and pick (LMB). Drag the mouse to the right to display the selection window, and pick the opposite corner.
Window (Right to Left)		Making a selection window from right to left will create a crossing window. All objects that are crossed by this window will be selected. Place the cursor in the blank area of the drawing to the right of the objects to select and pick (LMB). Drag the mouse to the left to display the selection window, and pick the opposite corner.
Deselecting objects		To deselect a previously selected object, press the shift key and select it again using any of the selection methods.
Last	L	At the Select objects prompt, type L to select the last object drawn.
All	ALL	At the Select objects prompt, type ALL to select all objects in the drawing.
Fence	F	At the Select objects prompt, type F to initiate the Fence option. All objects crossed by the fence line will be selected.
Window Polygon	WP	At the Select objects prompt, type WP to initiate a Window Polygon. Create the polygon by picking points around the objects to select. This will be easier if ORTHO is off. Only objects completely within the Window Polygon will be selected.
Crossing Polygon	CP	At the Select objects prompt, type CP to initiate a Crossing Polygon. Create the polygon by picking points that cross the objects to select. This will be easier if ORTHO is off. All objects crossed by the Polygon will be selected.
Previous	P	At the Select objects prompt, type P to select the Previous objects selected.

General Procedures

1. Select a Modify Command.
2. At the Select object prompt, initiate a Selection option (remember to press <ENTER>).
3. When all of the desired objects have been selected, press <ENTER> to continue with the Modify Command.

- After objects have been selected, press <ENTER> to continue, even if all objects have been selected.
- If the selection window is accidentally initiated, try to utilize the crossing window to select the object. If there is no way to properly cross the object with a window to select it (right to left), make a window that selects nothing and try to select the object again without exiting the modify command.
- It is very difficult to select objects if SNAP is ON.
- Objects may also be selected first, then a Modify command can be selected. When objects are selected first, they will be highlighted and will display small boxes at various points of the object. These boxes are called Grips and will be covered in greater detail in the section on Advanced Commands.
- At the Select objects prompt, type S to view the list of command line options. Type the capitalized letter(s) of the Select Object option, and press <ENTER>. It is not necessary to view this list in order to invoke the select object option.
- If you want to select all the similar objects (for example, all circles), select one circle, right click and use 'Select Similar'.

AutoCAD uses cursor badges to provide contextual feedback.

A selection badge indicates when you are creating a crossing or window selection.

The green window with the symbol on the left indicates a crossing selection and the blue window with the symbol on the right indicates a window selection.

If you prefer not to see the cursor badges, you can turn off the display by typing CURSORBADGE. Enter 1 to turn OFF the display. Enter 2 to turn ON the display.

Command Exercise

Exercise 6-1 – Selecting Objects

Drawing Name: **select1.dwg**
Estimated Time to Completion: 5 Minutes

Scope

Using the erase command, practice selecting the blue and red objects in the drawing. Optional: use the select objects as indicated. Use the fence (F) option to select the red lines on the left. Use the Window Polygon (WP) to select the blue objects on the right.

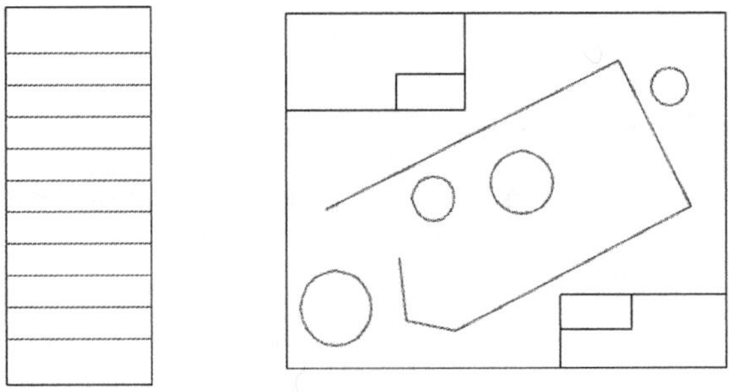

Selecting Objects Exercise

Solution

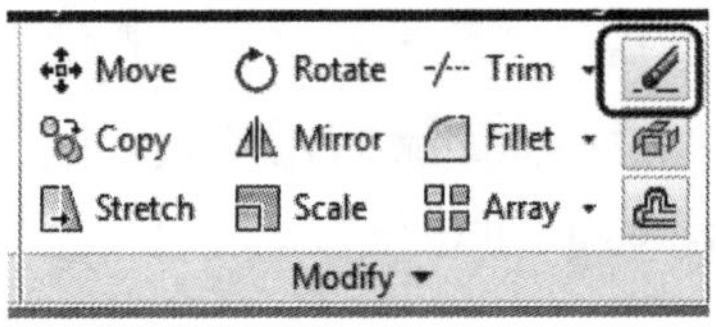

1. Invoke the Erase command (e or erase).
2. *Select objects:*
   Activate the Fence option by typing ‘F’ and pressing <ENTER>.
3. *First fence point:*
   Pick just above the top red line with the LMB. You may want to toggle OSNAP off.
4. *Specify endpoint of line or [Undo]:*
   Pick just below the bottom red line with the LMB. Press <ENTER> to close the selection set.
5. *Select objects:*
   Press <ENTER> again to erase the selected lines.
6. *Specify endpoint of line or [Undo]:*
   Press the <ENTER> key to close the selection set.

7. Repeat the Erase command with the RMB (e, erase or <ENTER>).
8. *Select objects:*
   Activate the Window Polygon option by typing 'WP' and pressing <ENTER> (make sure ORTHO is off).
9. *First polygon point:*
   Create a polygon around the blue objects similar to that shown in the figure to the right. Select the objects with a window polygon.

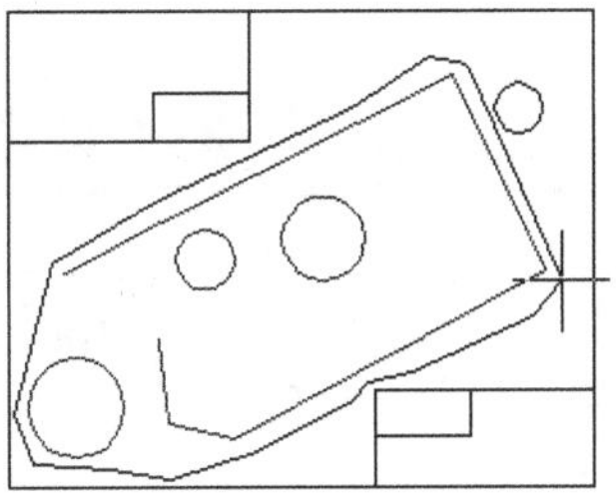

10. *Select objects:*
    Press the <ENTER> key again to complete the exercise by erasing the selection set.

Extra: *Use the Undo Command to bring the erased objects back. Experiment with different methods of selecting objects. Can you use the Fence selection method followed by the Crossing Polygon method to create a single selection set? Try it. Use the <Shift> key to remove an object from your selection set.*

Dashed lines displayed on the screen when using selection methods indicates that objects that are touched or crossed are selected. Solid lines indicate that only objects fully contained will be selected.

Command Exercise

Exercise 6-2 – Selecting Objects Using Properties

Drawing Name: **select2.dwg**
Estimated Time to Completion: 5 Minutes

Scope

Use the Properties dialog to filter out selected objects.

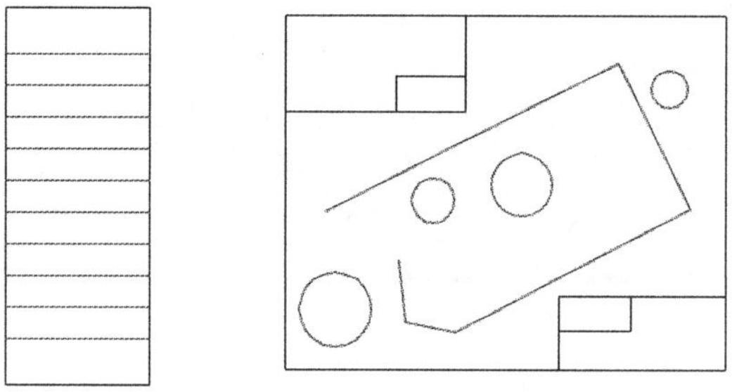

Selecting Objects Exercise

Solution

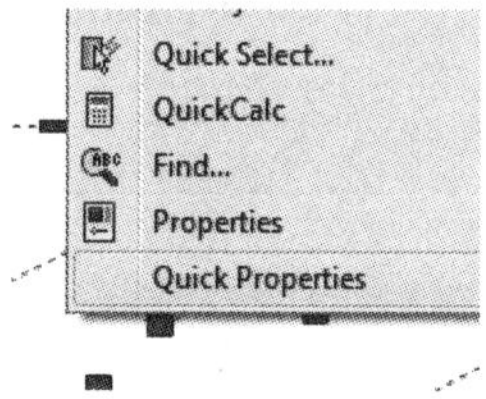

1. Window around all the objects so that they are highlighted.

2. Right click and select 'Quick Properties'.

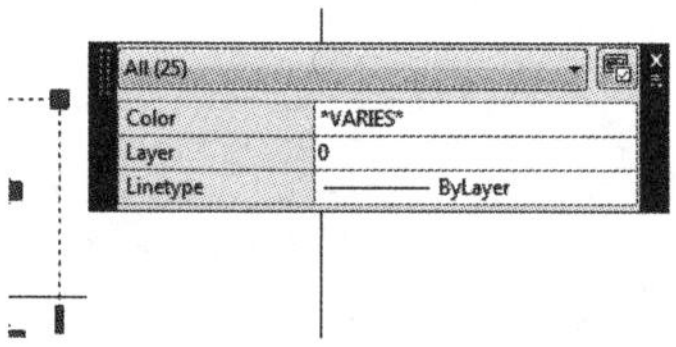

3. A small dialog will appear.

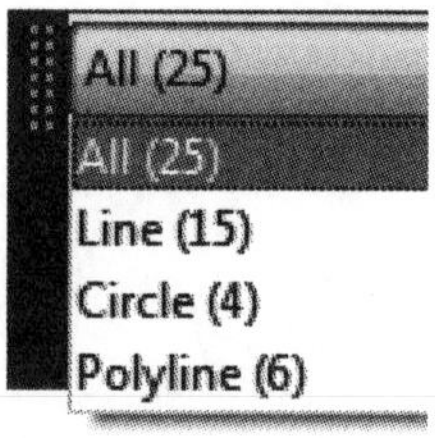

4. From the drop-down list, select **Circle**.

5. Select the **Circle** layer from the drop-down list for layers.

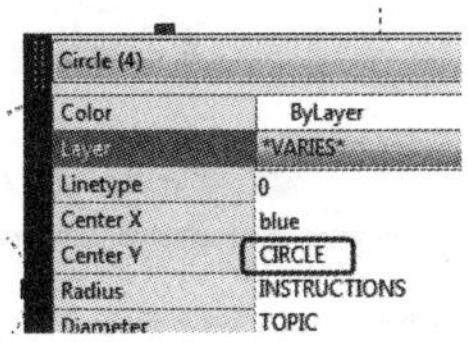

6. The circles will be moved to the circle layer.

- If you have a partially opened drawing, only objects that are currently loaded can be selected with the Quick Select command. Any objects in the drawing that are not currently loaded cannot be found by the command.
- You can also access the Quick Select filter using the Properties dialog.
- If you select more than one object accidentally, you can use the drop-down list in the Properties dialog to select the desired object.

Command Exercise

Exercise 6-3 – Select Similar

Drawing Name: **select3.dwg**
Estimated Time to Completion: 5 Minutes

Scope

Use Select Similar to target similar objects.

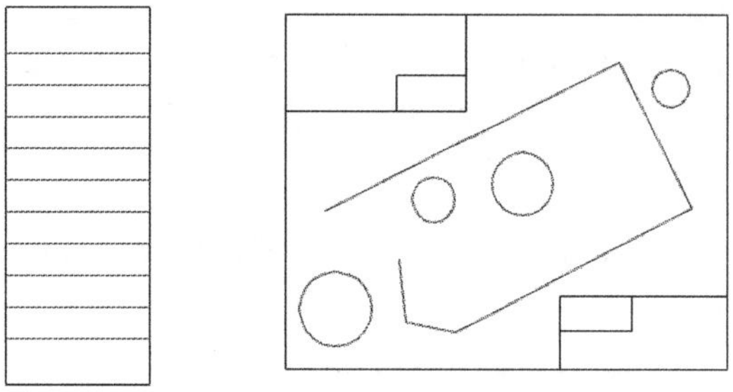

Select Similar Objects Exercise

Solution

1. Select the black circle located on the far right.

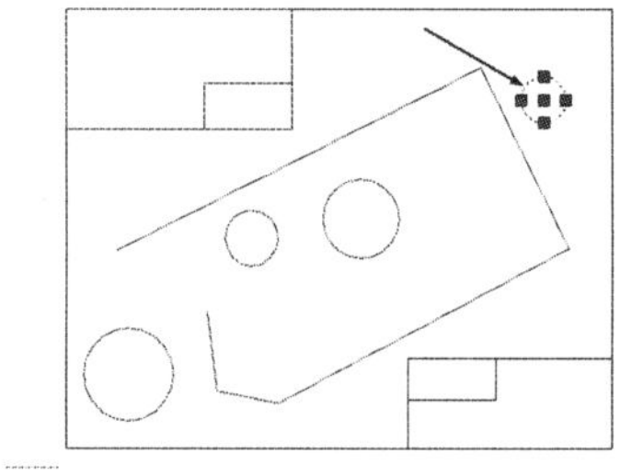

2. Right click and left pick on 'Select Similar'.

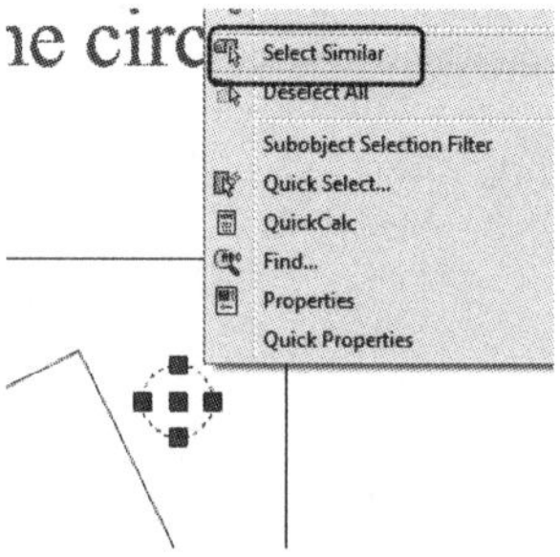

3. Note that none of the other circles are selected.

4. Press ESC to deselect the black circle.

5. Select the lower blue circle. Right click and left pick on 'Select Similar'.

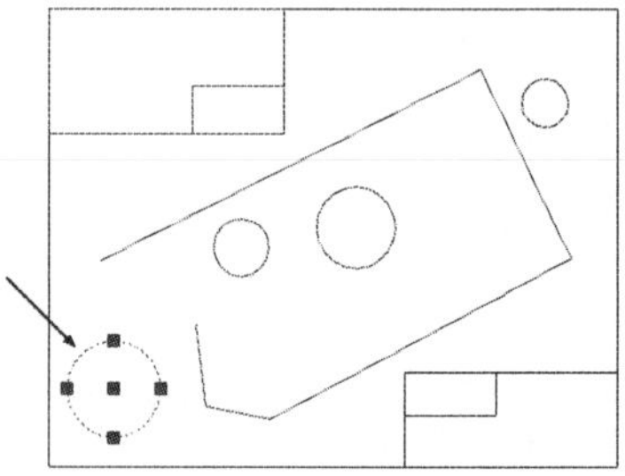

6. All the blue circles should highlight. Press ESC to release the selection set.

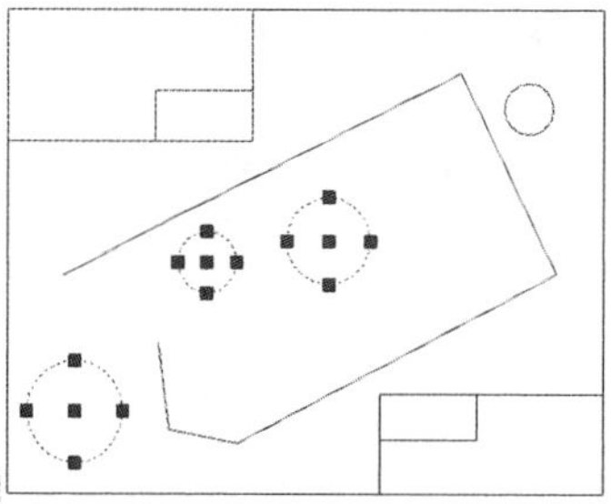

7. Right click and select 'Recent Input →SELECTSIMILAR'.

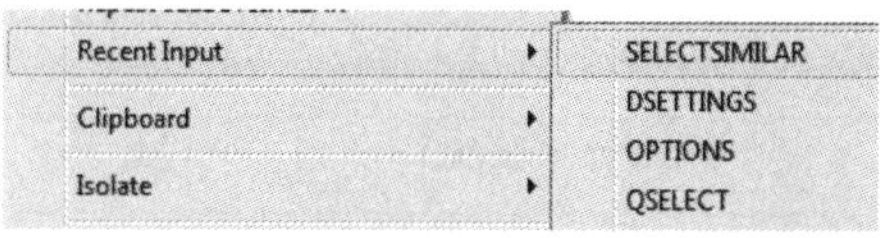

8. Right click and select 'Settings'.
9. Uncheck all the choices except for Name. Press 'OK'.

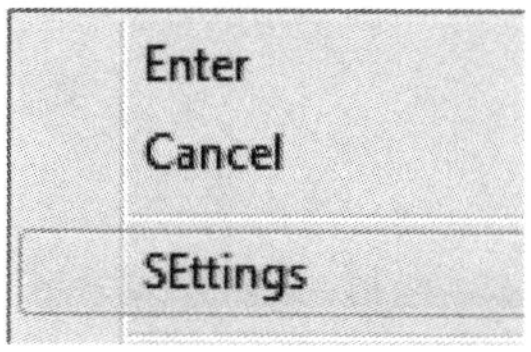

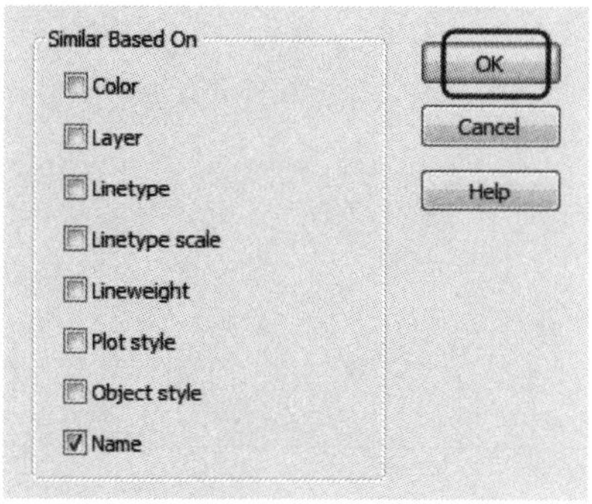

10. Select the lower blue circle. Press 'ENTER'. Now all the circles are selected.

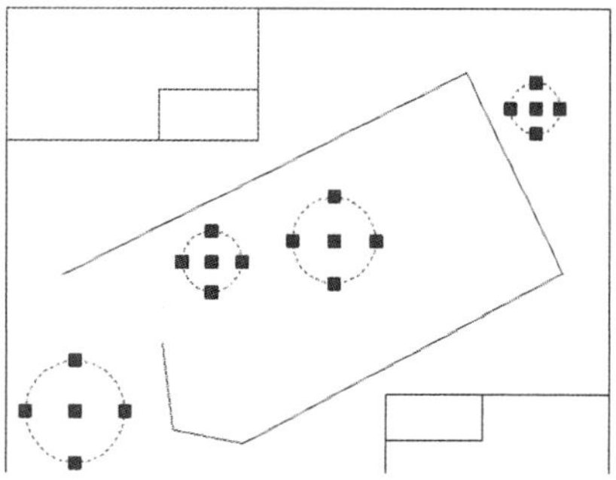

11. Select the CIRCLE layer from the drop-down layer list on the ribbon. Note that the circles all change color to match the layer.

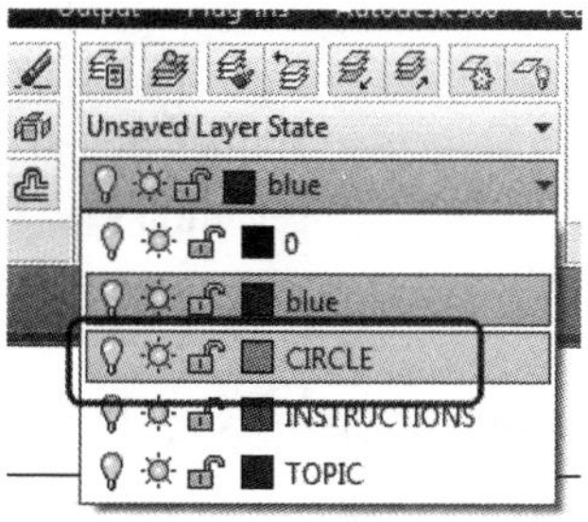

Tips & Tricks

➢ *You can only change the settings for SELECTSIMILAR when nothing is selected.*

Quick Select

Command Locator

Command	**qselect**
RMB Shortcut Menu	**Quick Select...**
Dialog Box	**Quick Select**

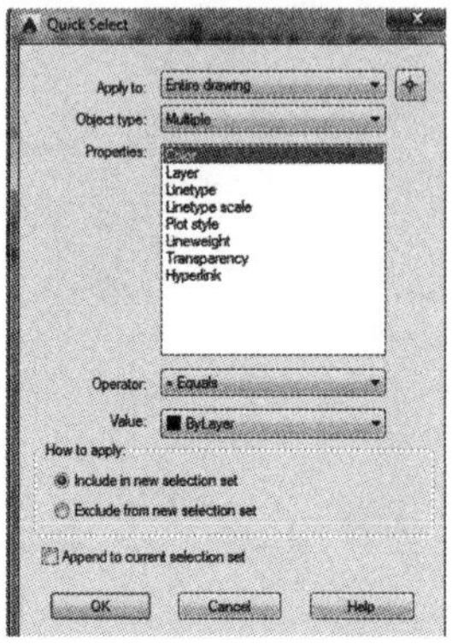

Quick Select Dialog Box

Command Overview

The Quick Select command allows you to specify filtering criteria and then decide how you want AutoCAD to create the selection set from that criterion. You are given the option to restrict the filter selection to currently selected entities or allow it to apply to the entire drawing. The Quick Select dialog box then presents you with the option to choose the object type. These options are "Multiple," or choose the drop down list which will display every type of entity currently in the drawing. After selecting the object type, you can further filter the selection set by choosing one of the entity's properties and then selecting an operator and value for that property. You are then given the option of how to apply this filter to the current selection set. You can choose to Include or Exclude the filter entities from the current selection set. Lastly you can decide whether or not to append to the current selection set.

General Procedures

Using Quick Select to create a filtered selection set:

1. Invoke the Quick Select command.
2. In the Quick Select dialog box, select the entity type in the Object Type drop down list.
3. In the Properties list, if applicable select a specific property for the objects being selected and set the operator and value fields accordingly.
4. Select whether to "Include objects in new selection set" or "Exclude objects from new selection set."
5. Select whether or not to "Append to current selection set."
6. Press 'OK'.

Command Exercise

Exercise 6-4 – Quick Select

Drawing Name: **qselect1.dwg**
Estimated Time to Completion: 10 Minutes

Scope

Using Quick Select, select all lines in the drawings and place on the lines layer. Next select all polylines in the drawing and place on the polyline layer. Repeat the process for all Mtext, Text, and blocks.

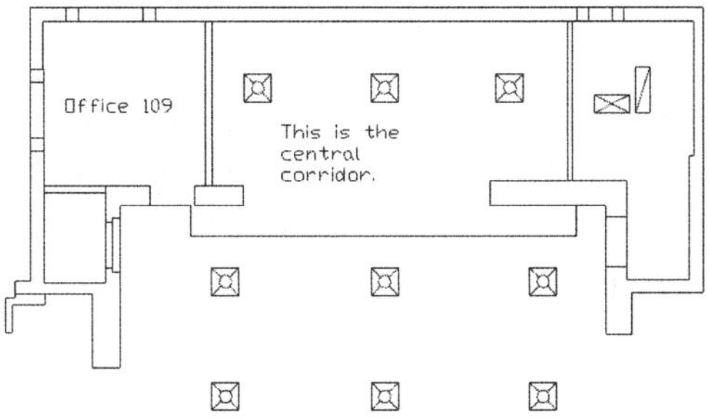

Quick Select Exercise

Solution

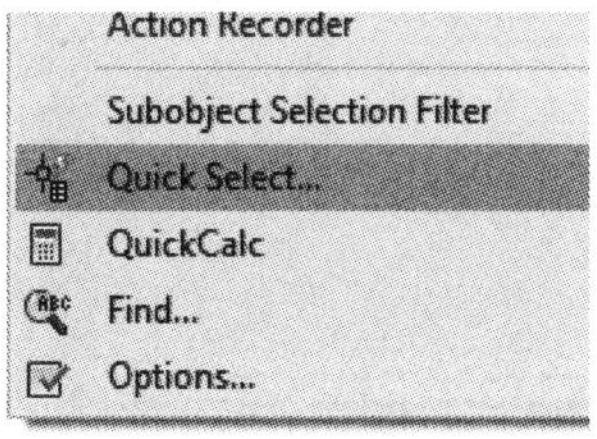

1. Right click in the window and select **Quick Select**.
2. Select 'Line' in the Object Type drop down list.

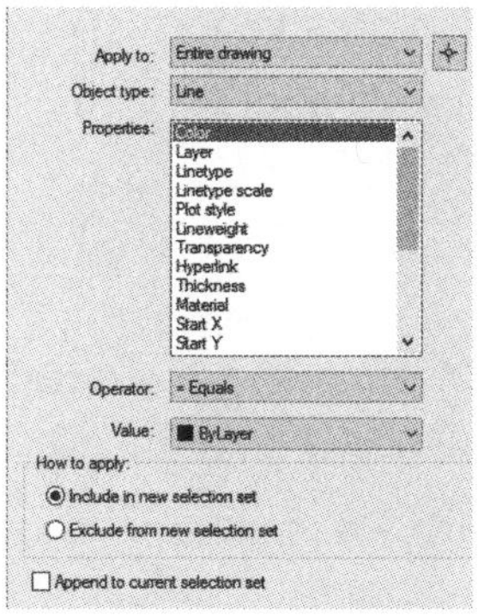

3. In the properties section, select 'Color', 'Equal =' as Operator, and 'Bylayer' as value.
4. In the 'How to apply' section, choose 'Include in new selection set.'
5. Uncheck the 'Append to selection set' if it is currently checked and select 'OK'.

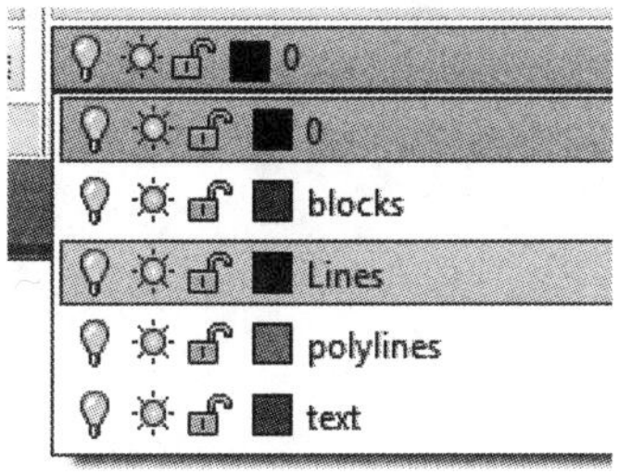

6. With all the lines selected in the drawing, use the Layer drop down list on the object properties tool bar and select the Lines layer. This will place the selected entities on the Lines layer.
7. Press <ESC> to clear the selection set.
8. Repeat the above process for Polylines, Text, Mtext, and Blocks.

***Extra:** You select several objects, including lines, circles, and rectangles. How can you filter the selection so that you change the layer of only the rectangles?*

Quick Properties

Command Locator

Status Toolbar	**Quick Properties toggle**
Command	**Quickproperties**
RMB Shortcut Menu	**Quick Properties…**
Shortcut Key	**Ctl+Shift+P**
Dialog Box	**Quick Properties**

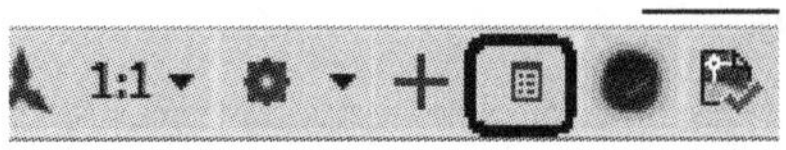

To enable Quick Properties, use the Quick Properties toggle located on the Status Bar. In order to enable the Quick Properties toggle, it needs to be enabled on the status bar first. To add Quick Properties to the status bar, left click on the customization button on the far right of the status bar and enable Quick Properties. You can also type QPMODE on the command line and type 1 to enable.

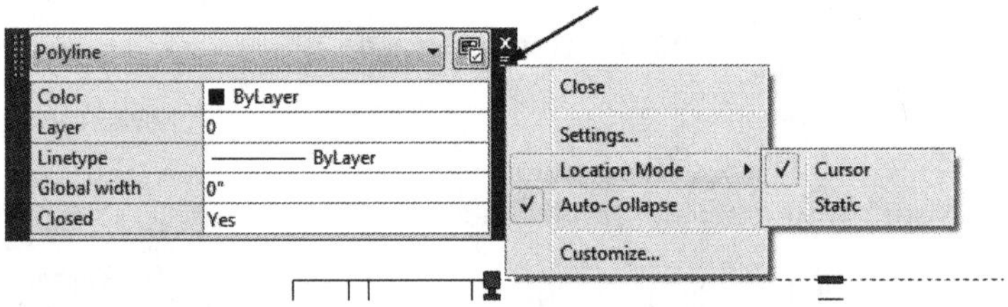

If no selection is made, the Quick Properties dialog is not available. You can customize what Properties are displayed/included in the dialog. The Options buttons allow you to control where the dialog will appear when any object is selected.

Command Exercise

Exercise 6-5 – Customize Quick Properties

Drawing Name: **qprops1.dwg**
Estimated Time to Completion: 5 Minutes

Scope

Learn how to set which fields will appear in the Quick Properties dialog.

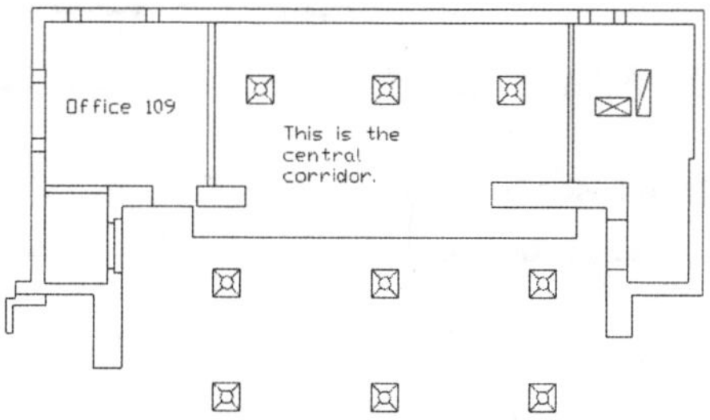

Quick Properties Exercise

Solution

1. Toggle **Quick Properties** ON using the Status Bar button.

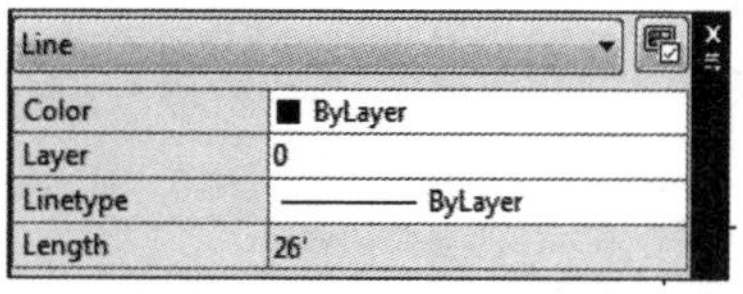

2. Select a line in the drawing.

The Quick Properties dialog will display information about the line.

Note which properties are listed: Color, Layer, Linetype, etc.

3. Select the **Customize** button.

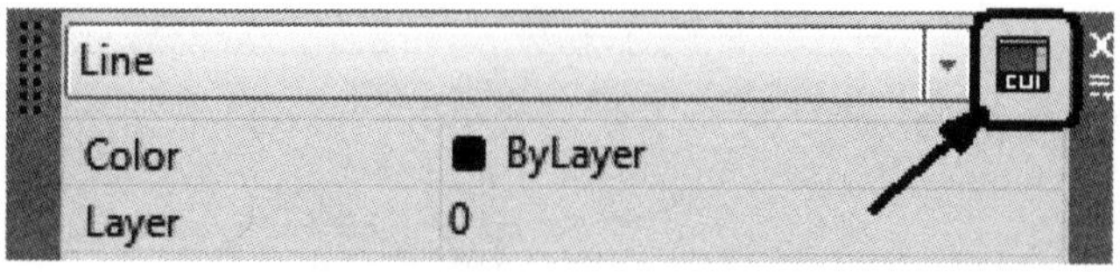

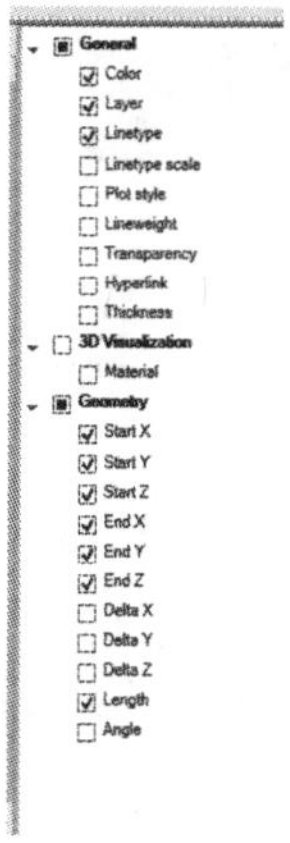

4. In the right hand pane, you see a list of properties that can be displayed in the Quick Properties dialog. A checkmark indicates it will be displayed.
5. Place a check mark in front of the Start X, Start Y, Start Z, and End X, End Y, End Z and Length.

These display the start and end coordinates of the selected line.

6. Press **Apply** and **OK** to close the dialog.

7. Select a line again. Press ENTER to complete the selection.
8. Notice how the Quick Properties have changed.

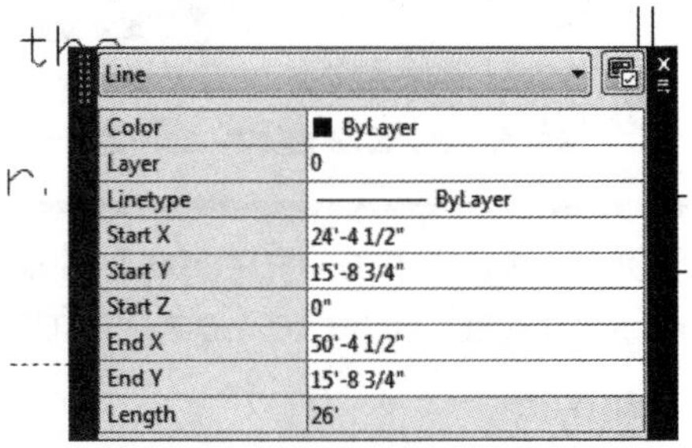
Line
Color
ByLayer
Layer
0
Linetype
ByLayer
Start X
24'-4 1/2"
Start Y
15'-8 3/4"
Start Z
0"
End X
50'-4 1/2"
End Y
15'-8 3/4"
Length
26'

9. Select a line again.
10. Quick Properties displays the selected properties.
11. Close the file without saving.

Note: Your Quick Properties may show different values depending on which line you selected.

Command Exercise

Exercise 6-6 – Use Quick Properties

Drawing Name: **qprops2.dwg**
Estimated Time to Completion: 5 Minutes

Scope

Learn how to use Quick Properties to modify objects easily.

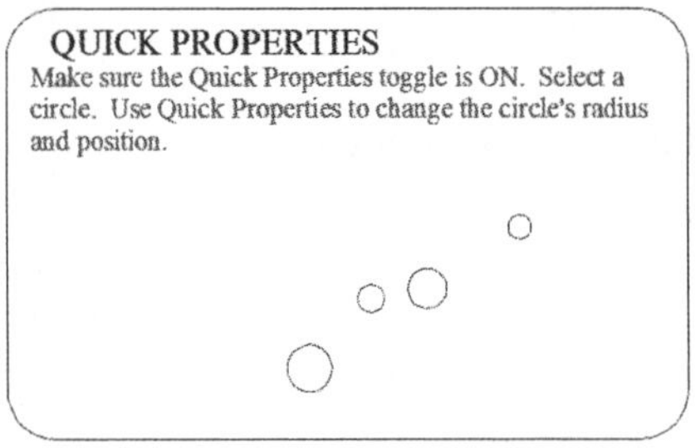
QUICK PROPERTIES
Make sure the Quick Properties toggle is ON. Select a circle. Use Quick Properties to change the circle's radius and position.

Quick Properties Exercise

Solution

Layout1

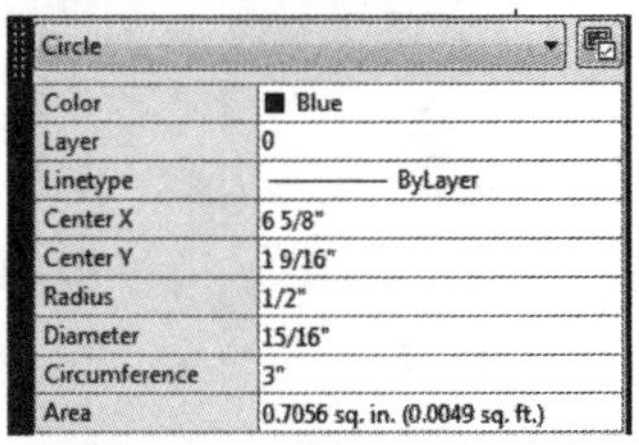
Circle
Color
Blue
Layer
0
Linetype
ByLayer
Center X
6 5/8"
Center Y
1 9/16"
Radius
1/2"
Diameter
15/16"
Circumference
3"
Area
0.7056 sq. in. (0.0049 sq. ft.)

1. Verify that the Quick Properties toggle is set to ON in the status toolbar.
2. Select a circle.
   The Quick Properties dialog should pop up immediately.
3. Change the Color to **Red**.
4. Change the Diameter to **2″**.
5. Try this with the other circles.
6. Close without saving.

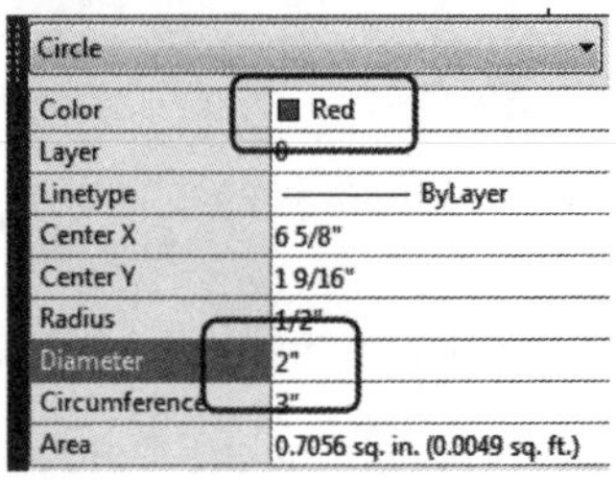
Circle
Color
Red
Layer
Linetype
ByLayer
Center X
6 5/8"
Center Y
1 9/16"
Radius
Diameter
2"
Area
0.7056 sq. in. (0.0049 sq. ft.)

Selection Cycling

Command Locator

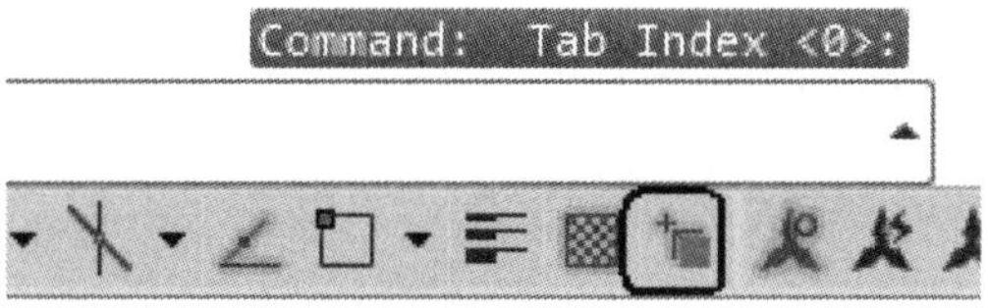

Selection cycling is used when creating or modifying a 3D model. Some edges or faces are often hidden. Rather than rotate the model, the user can use selection cycling to pick the desired entity.

To use selection cycling, toggle the Selection Cycling button on the Status Bar. You can also type SUBOBJSELECTIONMODE on the command prompt and enter 1 to enable.

As you position your cursor, a dialog will appear to aid you in your selection by displaying the object's information.

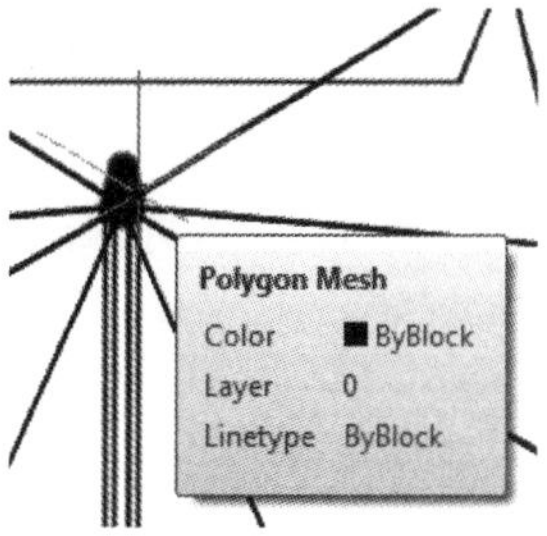

You can use the short cut keys in the list to the right to help filter your selections.

	Vertex filtering is on	Shift + F2
	Edge filtering is on	Shift + F3
	Face filtering is on	Shift + F4
	History subobject filtering is on	Shift + F5
⊘	Subobject filtering is off	Shift + F1

To set the Selection Cycling settings, you can access the Drafting Settings dialog and select the Selection Cycling tab. To launch the Drafting Settings dialog, type DS on the command prompt.

You can also right click on the status bar icon and select Selection Cycling Settings...

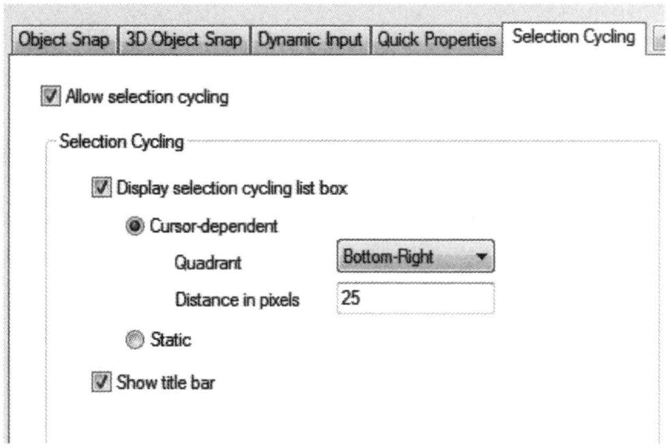

Command Exercise

Exercise 6-7 – Selection Cycling

Drawing Name: **selcycling1.dwg**
Estimated Time to Completion: 5 Minutes

Scope

Use Selection Cycling to select each letter and modify it to a number.

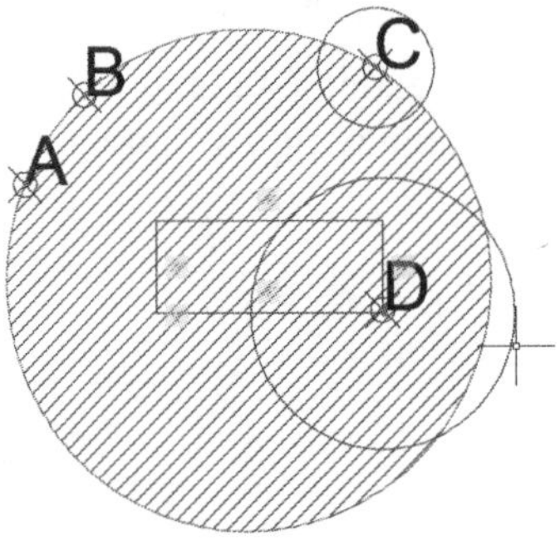

Selection Cycling Exercise

Solution

1. Verify that the Selection Cycling toggle is set to ON in the status toolbar.

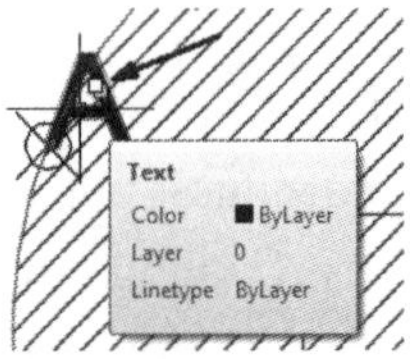

2. Hover your cursor over the letter A. You should see a dialog showing Text. You also should see a double rectangle indicating that the Text is lying on top of other objects.
3. Left click on the **A.**
4. A list will appear with the objects that can be selected in the area where you clicked. Left click on **Text** to modify the text.

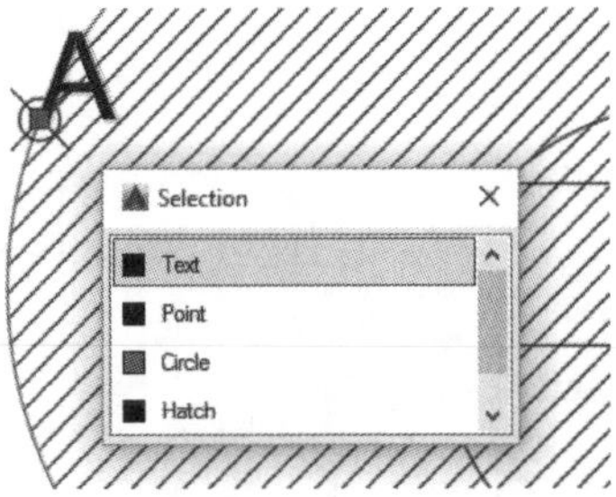

5. In the Quick Properties dialog, change the Contents of the Text to **1.**

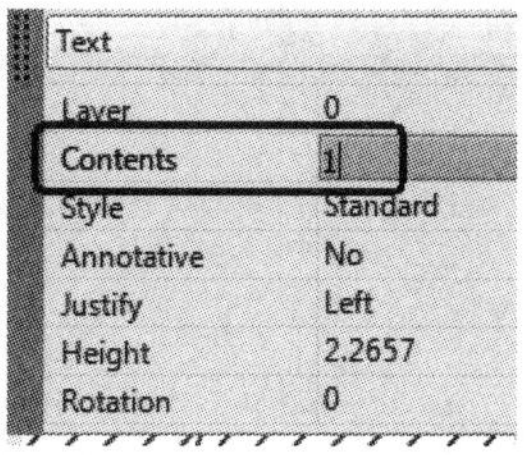

6. Press **ENTER** and the value will update and the selection will be released.

7. Repeat to change B to 2, C to 3, and D to 4.

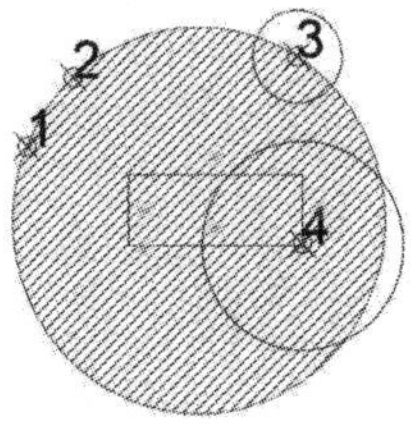

Review Questions

1. Name three methods of selecting an object.

2. Quick Select is used to filter through a drawing or selection to quickly select objects. Which object in the list below can be selected using the Quick Select dialog?
   a. Lines
   b. Circles
   c. Dimensions
   d. Polygons
   e. All of the above

3. To customize the properties in the Quick Properties dialog:
   a. Go to Options and select the Properties
   b. Go to Settings and select the Quick Properties tab
   c. Right click on the Quick Properties dialog and select Customize
   d. All of the above

4. True or False:
   You can determine where the Quick Properties will appear when an object is selected.

5. In order to change the settings for Select Similar:
   a. You cannot have anything selected
   b. Right click on the Select Similar toggle and choose 'Settings'
   c. Right click in the Graphics window and choose 'Options'
   d. B or C.

6. To deselect an object:
   a. Press Esc
   b. Press the Shift and pick the object again
   c. Press Enter
   d. A and B

Review Answers

1. Name three methods of selecting an object.

   Pick, Window, Crossing, Fence

2. Quick Select is used to filter through a drawing or selection to quickly select objects. Which object in the list below can be selected using the Quick Select dialog?

   e. All of the above.

3. To customize the properties in the Quick Properties dialog:

   c. Right click on the Quick Properties dialog and select Customize.

4. True or False:
   You can determine where the Quick Properties will appear when an object is selected.
   True

5. In order to change the settings for Select Similar:

   a. You cannot have anything selected.

6. To deselect an object:

   d. Press Esc and/or Press the Shift and pick the object again.

Notes:

Lesson 7.0 – Object Properties

Estimated Class Time: 3 Hours

Objectives

This section will focus on the Object Properties Toolbar. Object properties include Color, Layer, Linetype, Linetype Scale, Lineweight, and Thickness. The Match Properties and Properties commands can be used to change specific features as well as the properties of a selected object. Layers will help keep the drawing information organized. Use the drop down Layer Control list to make a layer current or change a layer state. Use the Layer Properties Manager dialog box to create new Layers. These settings can be saved to a drawing that can be used as a prototype or template for other drawings.

- **Layer Manager**
  Control the Layer states from this drop down list.
- **Make an Object's Layer Current**
  Select an object in the drawing and make the layer it is on the current layer.
- **Color Control**
  Control the Color of the objects being drawn.
- **Linetype Control**
  Control the Linetype of the objects being drawn.
- **Lineweight Control**
  Control the Lineweight of the objects being drawn.
- **Layer Properties Manager**
  Use the Layer Properties Manager dialog box to create a system of layers for the current drawing.
- **Match Properties Command**
  Match the properties of a selected object to other objects.
- **Properties Command**
  Change the object properties as well as specific features of a selected object.

When you start AutoCAD, the only line type available is CONTINUOUS. This is the linetype used primarily for object lines. In order to keep file sizes small, the user must load any other desired linetype before he can draw using that line style.

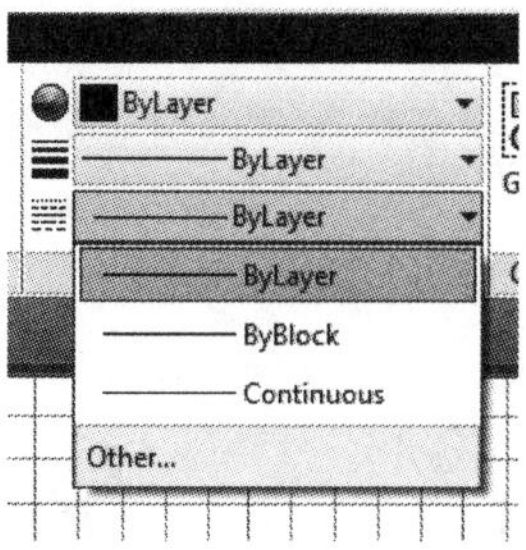

Once you load a linetype it remains in the drawing's database even if you don't have any geometry with that linetype. To keep your file size small, you should routinely run the PURGE command to eliminate unused linetypes and layers.

The architectural industry has set up layer standards defining colors and linetypes to be used when creating drawings. The mechanical engineering industry has not developed a standard to be used for layers. Each company usually creates their own standards to be used for all technical documents. This ensures that the drawings have a uniform appearance.

One method to ensure that all drafters comply with a company's standards is to use a template set up with layers and linetypes. Use of templates is discussed later in this text.

AutoCAD 2004 and above come with a CAD Standards tool to help you ensure that drawings meet company standards.

Layers are used to organize your drawing. Industry standard is to place object lines, hidden, dimensions, etc. each on a separate layer. Many drafters organize their drawings by placing object types on separate layers. For example, fasteners, doors, walls, gears might each be placed on a separate layer. Layer names should be short but easy to understand.

You can use the Layer Control and Linetype control to set up your layers to use the different linetypes and colors.

Layer Manager

Command Locator

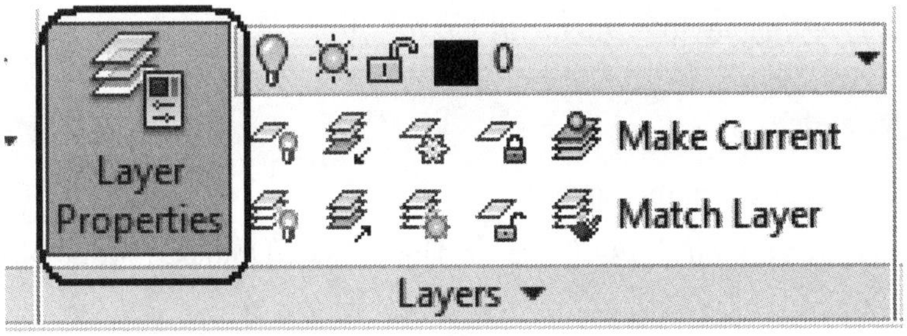

Command	**Layer**
Alias	**la**
Dialog Box	**Layer Manager**

Command Overview

Layers may be conveniently selected from the Layer Control drop down list. Layers may be made current, or the *layer state* may be changed. The options include On or Off, Freeze or Thaw, Lock or Unlock, and making a layer plottable or not. A layer may be made current by selecting it from the list. When the command line is blank, the properties of a selected object will be identified in the Object Properties Toolbar, and can be placed on a different Layer by selecting a different Layer from the drop down list. This feature applies to the Color, Linetype, and Lineweight Controls as well.

Layer State	Overview
Make a Layer Current	Select the name of the layer in the drop down list to make it current. Objects drawn on the current layer will have the properties assigned to that layer.
Turn a Layer On or Off	Select the light bulb to turn that layer on (yellow). Select it again to turn it off (gray). A layer is not visible when it is turned off; however, it may be current. A layer that is off and current at the same time would be odd, because the new objects drawn would be invisible until the layer is turned on again.
Freeze or Thaw in All Viewports	Select the sun to freeze that layer (snowflake). Select the snowflake to thaw that layer (sun). A layer is not visible when it is frozen. It is also completely ignored in a regeneration, which will make the regeneration time faster. A layer that is made current cannot be frozen.
Lock or Unlock a layer	Objects on a Locked layer can not be changed. When a layer is locked current, objects may be drawn on that layer, but cannot be changed.
Make a layer plottable or non-plottable	Whether a layer is plotted or not can be controlled by selecting this feature. This way the layer may be visible, but will not plot.

General Procedures

To make a Layer current:

1. Select the down arrow in the Layer list.
2. Select the layer (name) to make it current.

To change a Layer state:

1. Select the down arrow in the Layer list.
2. Select the desired option: On/Off, Freeze/Thaw, Lock/Unlock, Plot/no plot.

To move objects from one Layer to another:

1. With the Command Line blank (press Escape), select the objects to change.
2. Select the down arrow in the Layer list. And select the desired layer.
3. Press Escape two times to deselect the object and cancel the *grips*.

- If there are no objects on a layer, the layer key will appear grayed out.
- The Layer Control list will appear gray when in the middle of a command. Press Escape to cancel the command and the Layers Control list will be accessible.
- Use the Freeze option instead of Off. A frozen layer is completely ignored in a drawing regeneration and will therefore make a faster regeneration.

Command Exercise

Exercise 7-1 – Layer Control

Drawing Name: **layerc1.dwg**
Estimated Time to Completion: 15 Minutes

Scope

Using Layer Control drop down list, draw the objects on the appropriate layer. Make the layer current before you draw. Practice the Freeze and Thaw options.

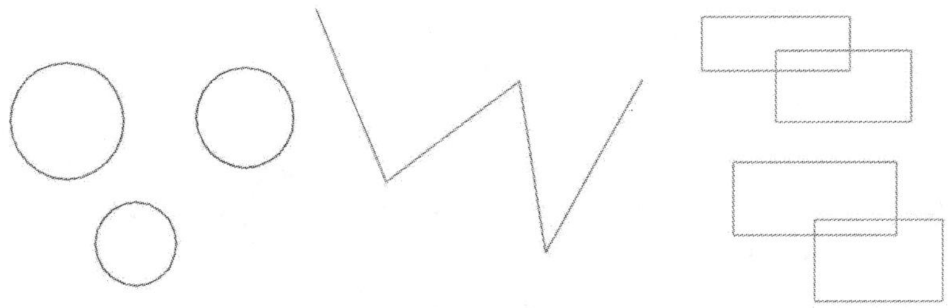

Layer Control Exercise

Solution

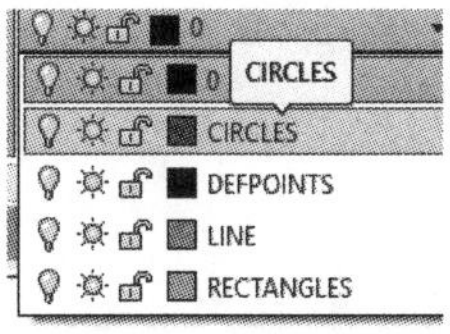

1. Start the exercise by selecting the **CIRCLES** layer in the Layer Control drop down list.

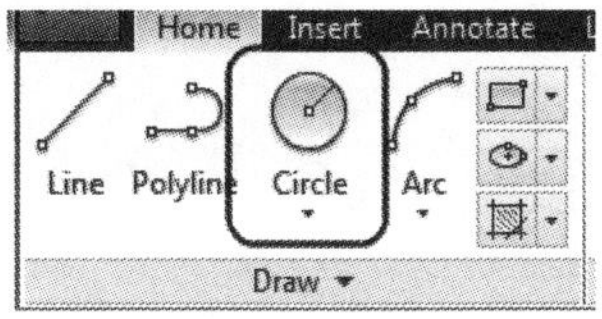

2. Invoke the **Circle** command (c or circle).

3. *Specify center point for circle or [3P/2P/Ttr (tan tan radius)]:*
   Pick a point on the screen with the LMB.

4. *Specify radius of circle or [Diameter]:*
   Use the LMB to determine the radius. Notice that the Circle is purple. This is a visual indicator that the Circle is located on the CIRCLES layer.

5. Repeat the circle command and create more circles on the Circles layer.

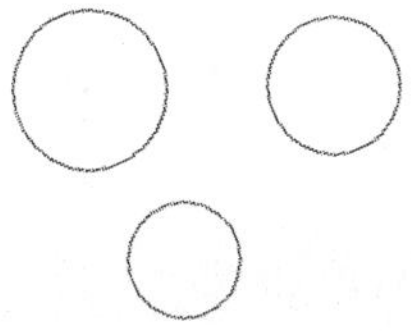

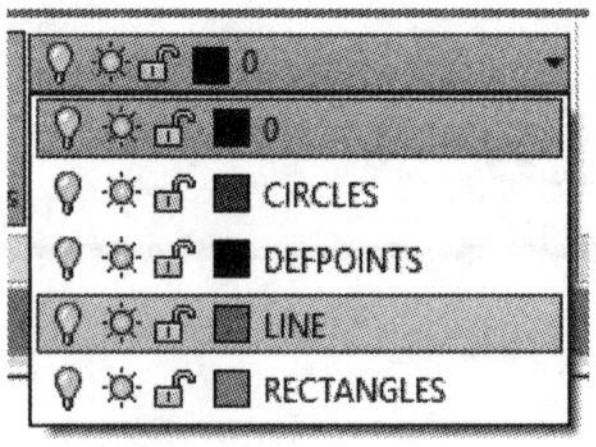

6. Use the Layer Control drop down list to select the LINE layer as the current layer.

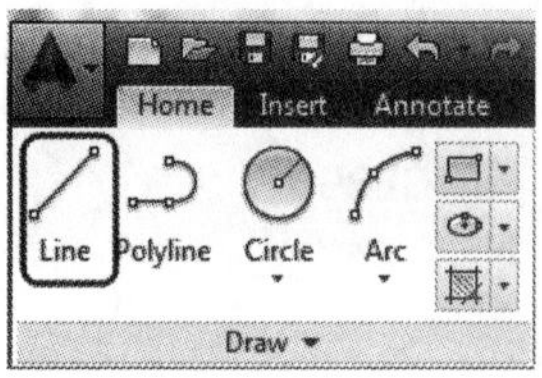

7. Invoke the **Line** command (l or line).
   Specify first point:
   Use the LMB to pick the first point.
8. *Specify next point or [Undo]:*
   Use the LMB to pick the second point.
   Notice that the line is green.

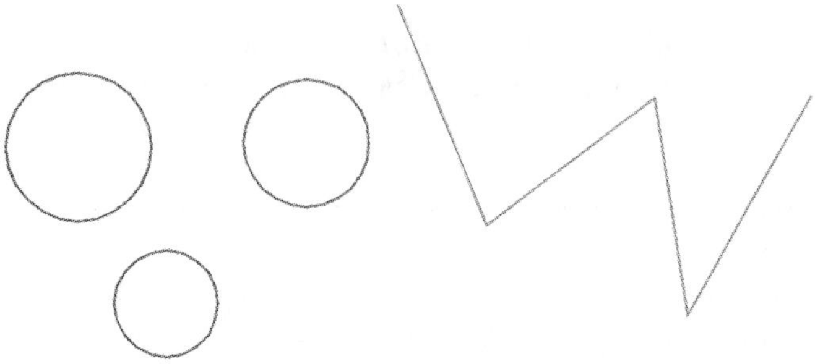

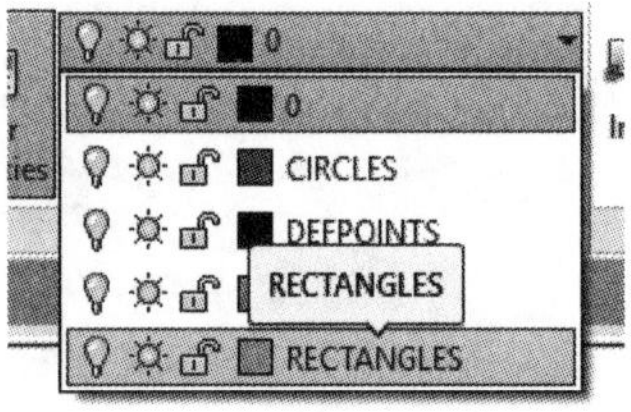

9. Create more line segments on the LINE layer and press <ENTER> to end the command.
10. Use the Layer control drop down list to select the **RECTANGLES** layer.

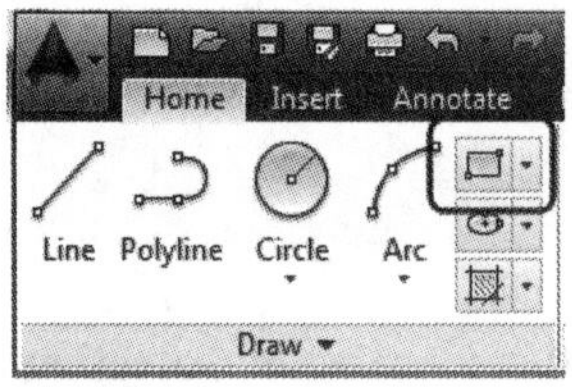

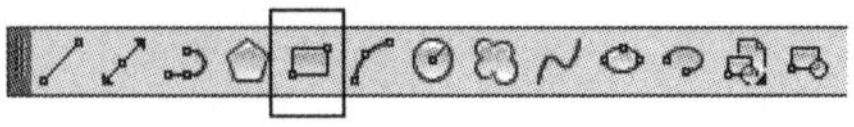

11. Invoke the **Rectangle** command (rectang).
12. *Specify first corner point or [Chamfer/Elevation/Fillet/Thickness/Width]:*
    Use the LMB to select the first corner of the rectangle.
13. *Specify other corner point:*
    Use the LMB to specify the second point of the rectangle.
14. Repeat the command to create multiple rectangles on the RECTANGLES layer.

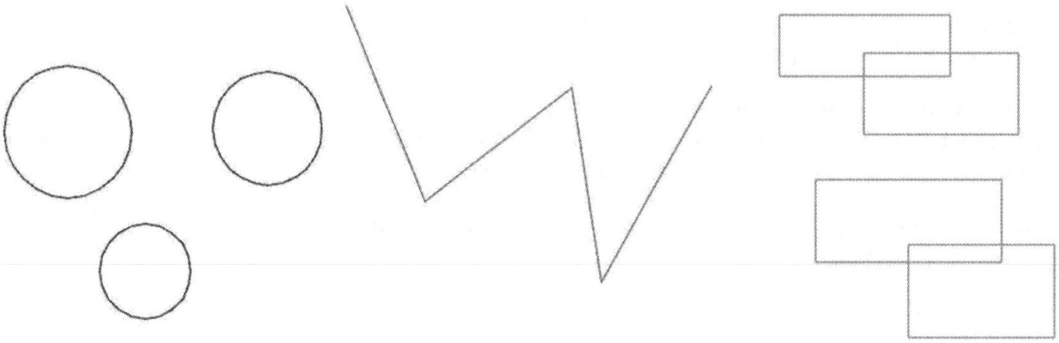

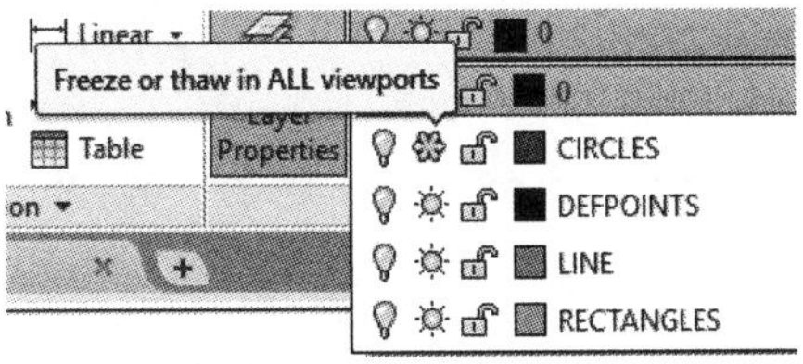

15. Freeze the CIRCLES layer by selecting the Layer Control drop down list and selecting the Freeze / Thaw icon for a layer that is not current.

Note that the icon changes to a snowflake.

Because the CIRCLES layer is frozen, the circles are no longer visible.

16. Left click on the Freeze/Thaw icon next to the Circles layer. This will thaw the layer and the icon will show as a sun.

Note that the circles are visible when the layer is thawed.

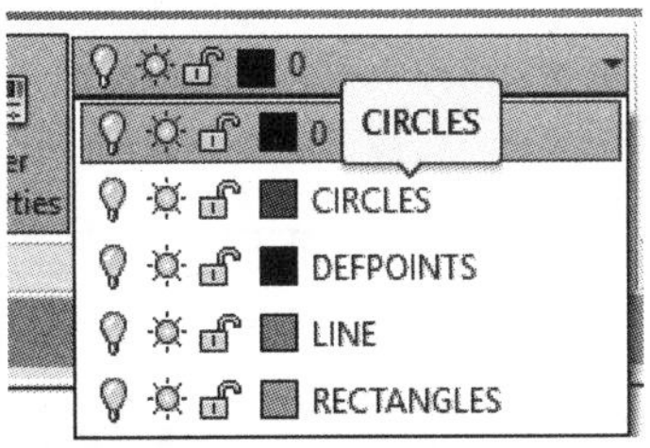

Extra: *Try freezing the current layer. What happens? Try turning a layer ON and OFF. Try drawing on a layer that is OFF. To toggle a layer ON/OFF, left click on the light bulb icon.*

Tips & Tricks

- *You can draw on a layer that is turned OFF. But you cannot draw on a layer that is frozen. AutoCAD will not REGEN objects on a frozen layer. Locking a layer is a good way to filter the selection of objects. Entities on a locked layer cannot be edited.*

Make an Object's Layer Current

Command Locator

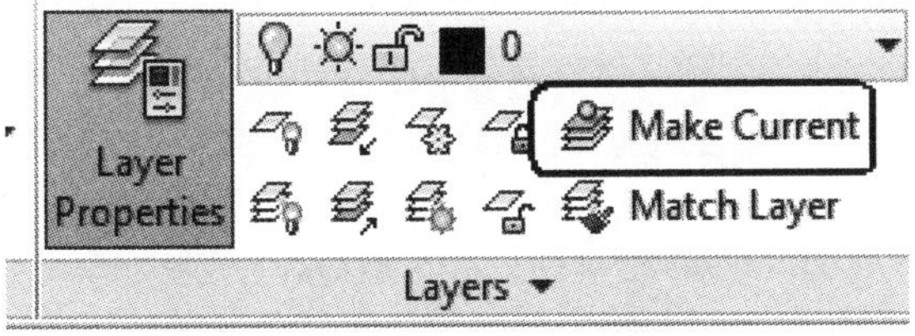

Command	**LAYMCUR**

Command Overview

Make a layer current by selecting an object in the drawing on that layer.

General Procedures

1. Select the Make Object's Layer Current button from the Properties toolbar.
2. Select the desired object.

Color Control

Command Locator

Command	**Color**
Alias	**COL**
Dialog Box	**Select Color**

Command Overview

This option controls the color of the objects currently being drawn. Typically, the colors of objects in the drawing should be determined *by the layer*, and it is not advisable to mix colors in the same layer. This is because the user will usually want to know at a glance that all objects that are Blue, for instance, are on a particular layer. Be sure that "ByLayer" appears in the Color Control box. When an object is selected with the Command Line blank, selecting a color from the drop down list will automatically apply the color to the selected object.

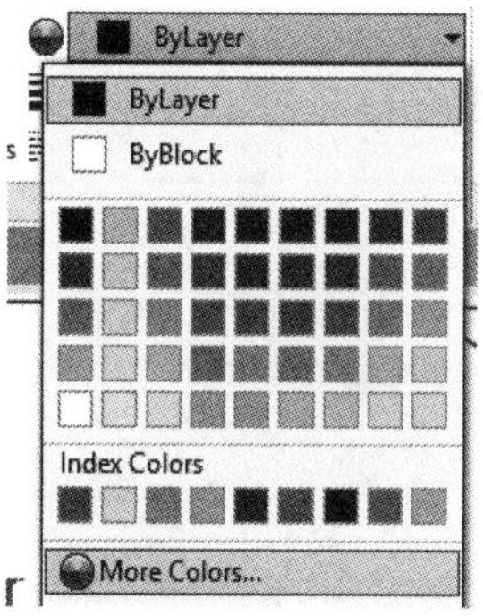

Color Control Drop-down List

General Procedures

1. Select the down arrow in the Color Control list.
2. Select "ByLayer."

- When drawing, make sure that the word "BYLAYER" appears in the Color Control window. This is a suggestion, but not the rule.
- The Color Control list will appear gray when in the middle of a command. Press Escape to cancel the command and the Color Control list will be accessible.
- Selecting "Other..." from the Color Control drop down list will display the Select Color dialog box and full Color Spectrum.

Linetype Control

Command Locator

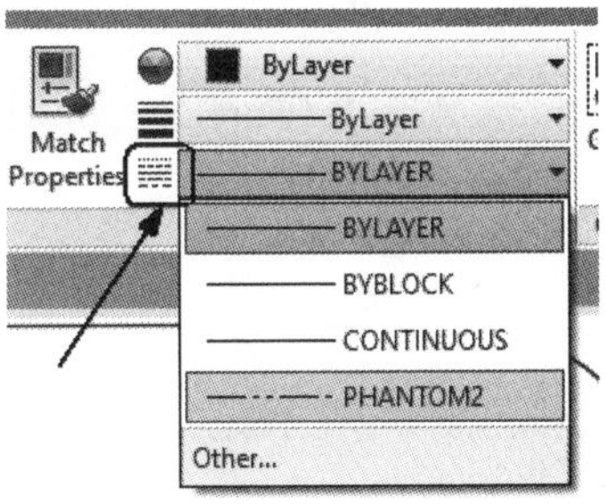

Command	**Linetype**
Alias	**LTYPE**
Dialog Box	**Linetype Manager**

Command Overview

This option controls the Linetype of the objects currently being drawn. It is typical that a variety of linetypes may be present on the same layer, such as Continuous, Center and Hidden. However, it is best to leave the Linetype Control setting to ByLayer. Selecting "Other…" from the drop down list will display the Linetype Manager dialog box. The user can load additional linetypes into the drawing using either this dialog box or the Layer Properties Manager dialog box.

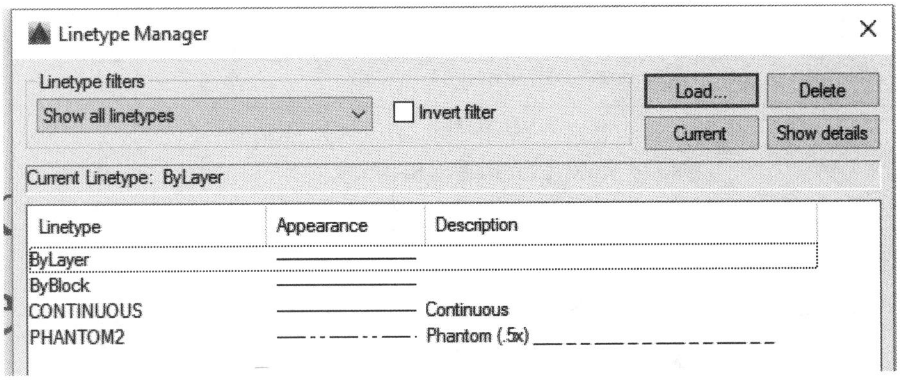

Linetype Manager Dialog Box

General Procedures

To load a linetype into the drawing:

1. Select the down arrow in the Linetype Control list.
2. Select "Other…"
3. From the Linetype Manager dialog box, select Load, then scroll through the list to find and select the linetypes to load into the drawing. Hold down the Control key to select alternate linetypes; hold down the Shift key to select several linetypes. Then select OK (two times) to exit.

- Be sure that the word "ByLayer" appears in the Linetype Control window. If making another linetype current for a specific reason, remember to change it back to ByLayer.
- Linetypes can be assigned to a Layer. This will be covered further on in this chapter.
- The system variable, LTSCALE, will globally control the scale of the linetypes in the drawing.
- Linetypes beginning with ACAD_ISO are for Metric drawings.

Lineweight Control

Command Locator

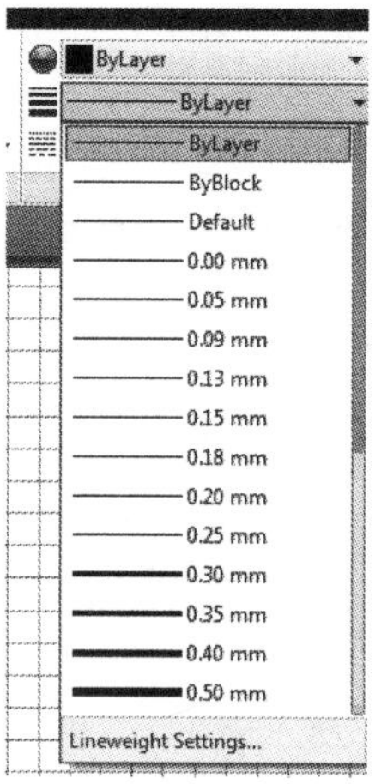

Command	**Lineweight**
Alias	**LWEIGHT**
Dialog Box	**Lineweight Settings**

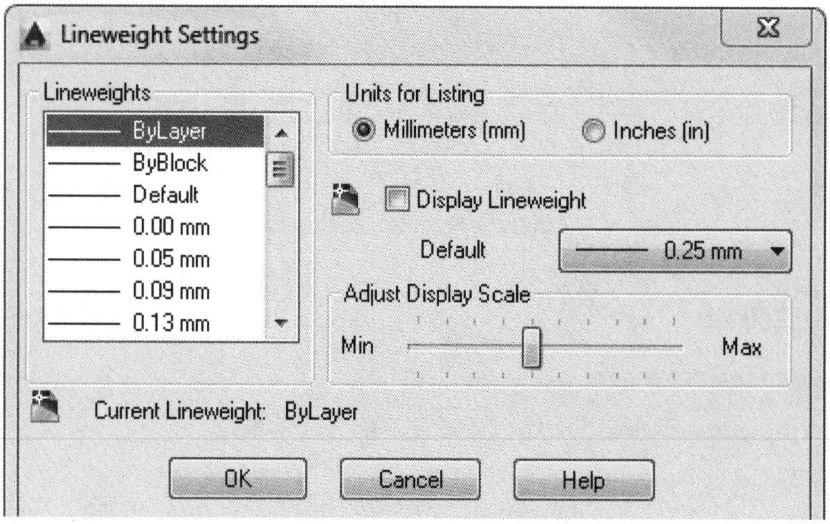

Lineweight Settings Dialog Box

Command Overview

The lineweight of the objects in the drawing can be controlled individually or by the Layer when set to ByLayer. You will learn how to determine linetypes by the Layer in the section that covers the Layer Properties Manager dialog box.

General Procedures

To make a lineweight the current setting:

1. Select the down arrow in the Linetype Control list.
2. Select the desired linewidth.

To change the lineweight of an existing object:

1. With the Command Line blank, select the objects in the drawing to change.
2. Select the down arrow in the Linetype Control list.
3. Select the desired linewidth. Once the lineweights of the objects have changed, press Escape two times to cancel the selection.

Tips & Tricks

- Be sure that the word "ByLayer" appears in the Lineweight Control window. If selecting another lineweight current for a specific reason, remember to change it back to ByLayer.
- Lineweights can be assigned to a Layer. This will be covered further on in this chapter.
- Lineweights will not be visible unless "Display Lineweight" is selected in the Lineweight Settings dialog box.

Layer Properties Manager

Command Locator

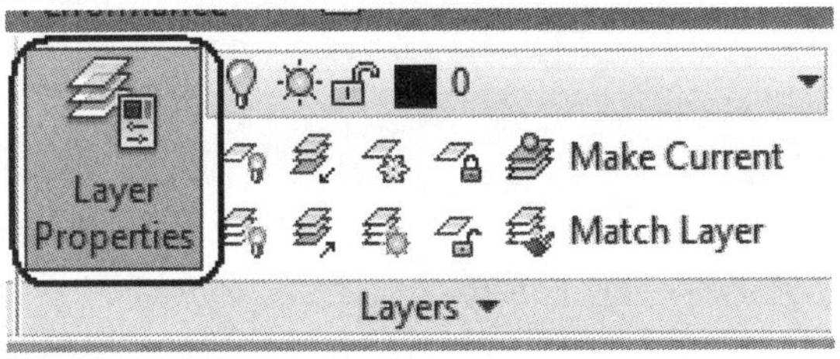

Command Overview

Use the Layer Properties Manager dialog box to create drawing Layers with specified Names, Colors, Linetypes, Lineweights, and Plot Styles (plot colors) and Plot variables (plottable or not). The layer lists may be sorted in ascending or descending order by double-clicking the heading, such as Name. Layer 0 is a default standard layer and cannot be renamed or deleted. This makes it a good "working layer." Other layers may only be deleted if there is no geometry on those layers and they are not "current." Layers may be made current, frozen, thawed, locked, unlocked, turned on or off from this dialog box. Once objects are created, they may be moved to other layers using the Match Properties, or the Properties commands (see next section), or by selecting the object with the Command line blank and selecting the layer to move it to from the drop down list (shown in the previous section). Create a system of layers to save as a prototype or template drawing.

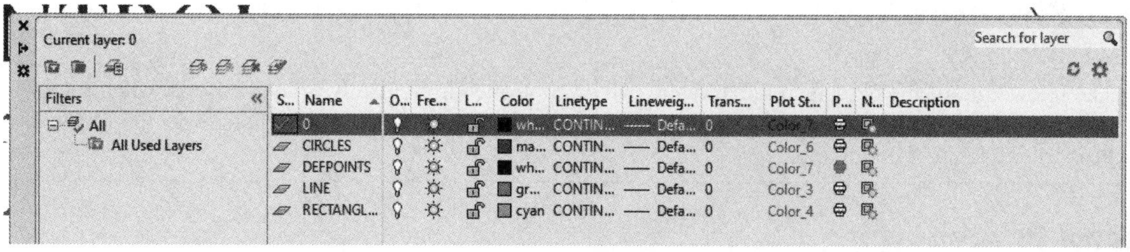

Layer Properties Manager

Command	**Layer**
Alias	**LA**
RMB Shortcut Menu	**In the list area of the Layer Properties Manager dialog box**
Dialog Box	**Layer Properties Manager**

Feature	**Overview**
Named Layer Filters	This section controls what layer names are visible. For all practical purposes, the words "Show all layers" should be visible in the text window and the Invert Filter and Apply to Object Properties toolbar options should not be checked.
New	Select this button to create a New layer. The default name will be Layer1, Layer2, Layer3, etc. Type in a different layer name, or select the layer name twice to rename it.
Delete	This option allows selected layers to be deleted, only if the layer contains no geometry, or is not current.
Current	Select this option to make a highlighted layer current. A layer that is current cannot be frozen. You can also use the "Make Object's Layer Current" icon found in the Object Properties Toolbar to make a layer current. Select the object whose layer will become current.

Layer List Heading	Icon	Overview
Name		Lists the layer name. Select two times to rename a layer. Spaces and certain characters are not allowed. To select a layer in the dialog box, pick it (LMB), to deselect it, pick it again, select another layer or pick in the blank area of the dialog box. To select all layers, right-click (RMB) in the blank area and choose "Select All."
On / Off		Turns selected layers on or off. A layer that is turned OFF may still be current but will not be visible. This is an odd state because objects drawn on that layer will not be seen until the layer is turned back on.
Freeze / Thaw in all VP	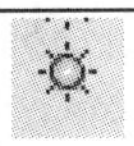	Freezes or thaws selected layers in all view ports. A frozen layer is not visible and cannot be made current.
Lock / Unlock		Locks or unlocks selected layers. It is possible to lock a current layer and draw on a locked layer, but not modify the objects on that layer until it is unlocked.
Color		Pick the color for the corresponding layer(s) to access the Select Color dialog box. Pick a color from the Standard Colors or the Full Color Palette to apply to a selected layer.
Linetype		Pick the linetype for the corresponding layer(s) to access the Select Linetype dialog box. Pick a linetype from "Loaded linetypes" list to apply to a selected layer. Select the Load button to access and select from the "Available linetypes" list.
Lineweight		Pick the lineweight for the corresponding layer(s) to access the Lineweight dialog box. Pick a lineweight from the list to apply to a selected layer.
Transparency		Sets the level of transparency for the layer; if level is set to 0, then layer is not transparent. Transparency can be set from 0 – 90, where 90 is fully transparent.
Plot Style		Controls how layers are plotted.
Plot		Makes a layer plottable or not.

General Procedures

1. Invoke the Layer command.
2. In the Layer Properties Manager dialog box, select New. Name the layer.
3. Select the corresponding color to access the Select Color dialog box, pick a color, then select OK.
4. Select the corresponding linetype to access the Select Linetype dialog box, and pick a linetype from the list. If the desired linetype is not in the list, select "Load…" and pick a linetype from the list. Select OK or Cancel to exit the Linetype dialog boxes.
5. Select OK to close the Layer Properties Manager dialog box.

Command Exercise

Exercise 7-2 – Drawing on Layers

Drawing Name: **layers1.dwg**
Estimated Time to Completion: 15 Minutes

Scope

In the layers dialog box, create the designated layers and draw the object using the appropriate layers. Do not simply copy the objects from the left side to the right side! Learn to create layers.

Layers Exercise

Solution

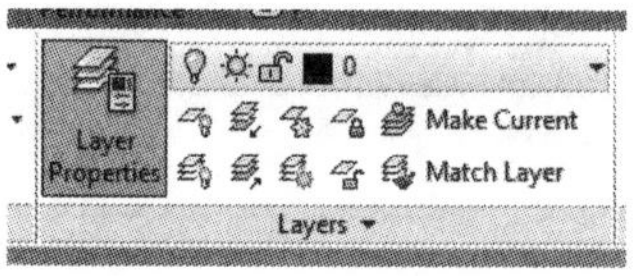

1. Invoke the **Layers** command (layer) to open the Layer Properties Manager.

2. In the Layer Properties Manager dialog box press the **New** button with the LMB. This will create a new layer called 'Layer1' in rename mode.

3. In the dialog box, rename LAYER1 to **BOX**.

4. Use the LMB to select the color box to change the color associated with the BOX layer.

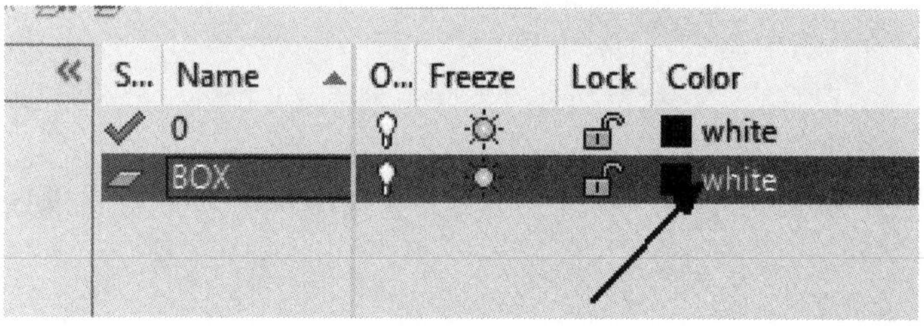

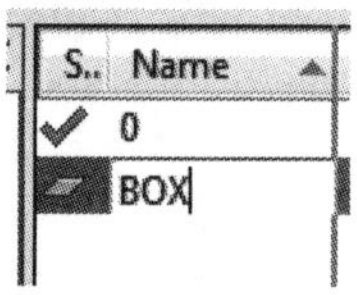

5. Use the LMB to select BLUE from the Standard Colors section in the Select Color dialog box.

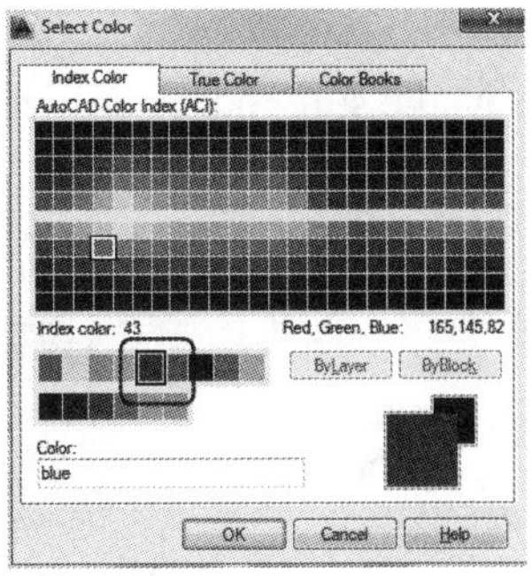

6. Press '**OK**' to complete the change.

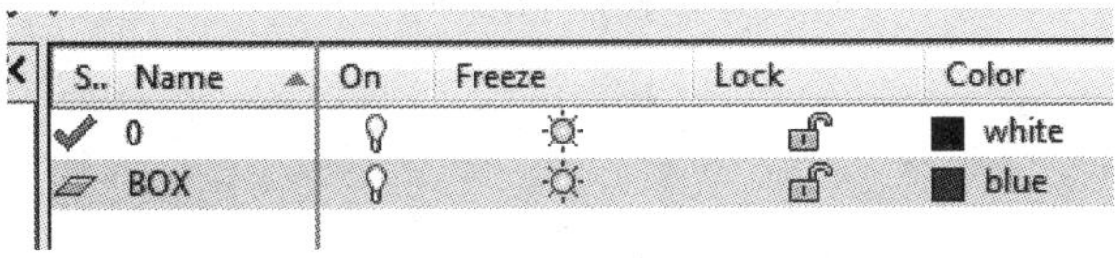

7. Create a third layer by pressing the **New** button in the Layer Properties Manager dialog box. Rename the new layer to **HIDDEN**. Set the color to **RED**.

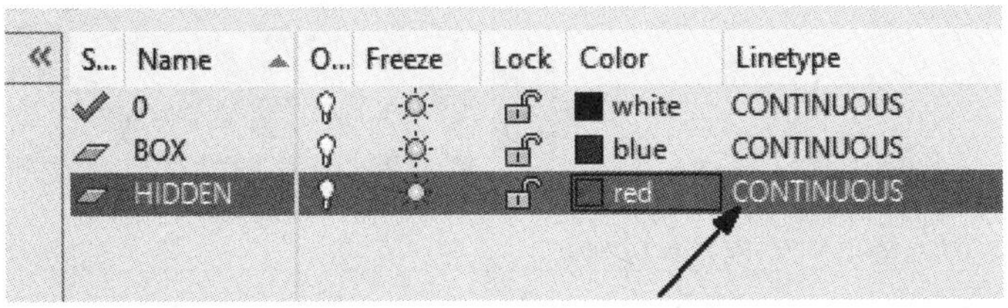

8. Use the LMB and press on the Word CONTINUOUS under Linetype for the HIDDEN layer. This will activate the Select Linetype dialog box.

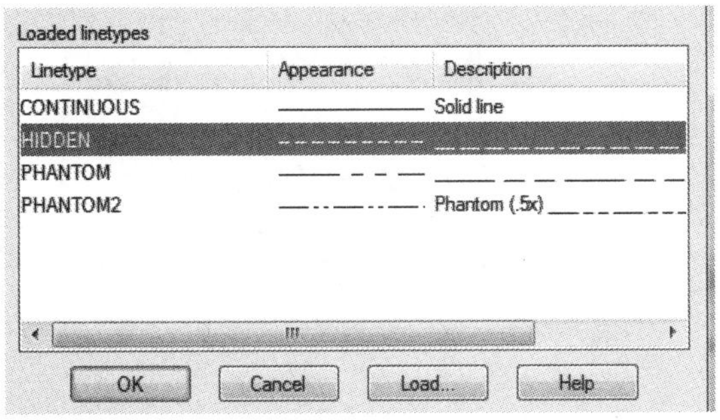

9. Use the LMB to select the **HIDDEN** Linetype.

10. Press 'OK'.

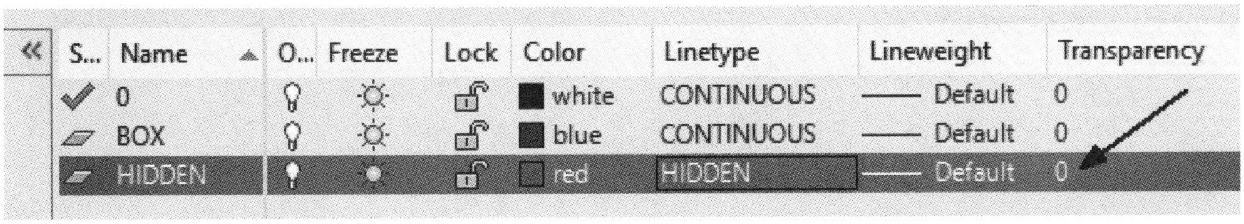

11. LMB on the **0** under the Transparency column.

12. Enter the value **50** in the dialog and press **OK** to continue.

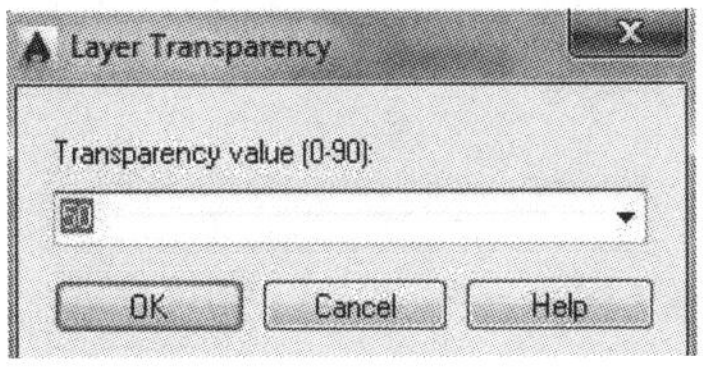

13. Create a layer called SUPPORT. Press the **New** button in the Layer Properties Manager dialog box and rename the new layer to **SUPPORT**. Change the color to green, and set the linetype to **PHANTOM**. Transparency should be set to 0.

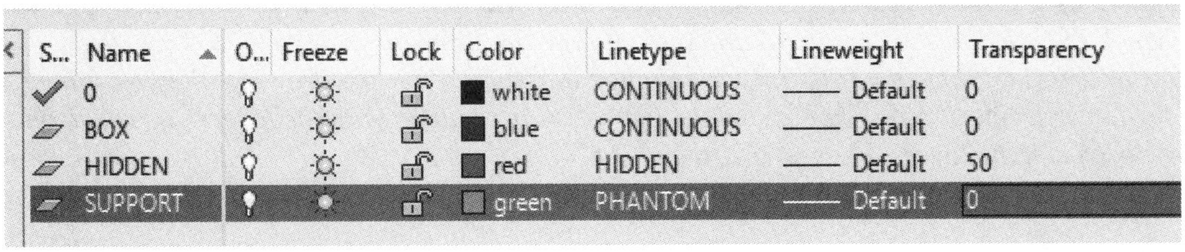

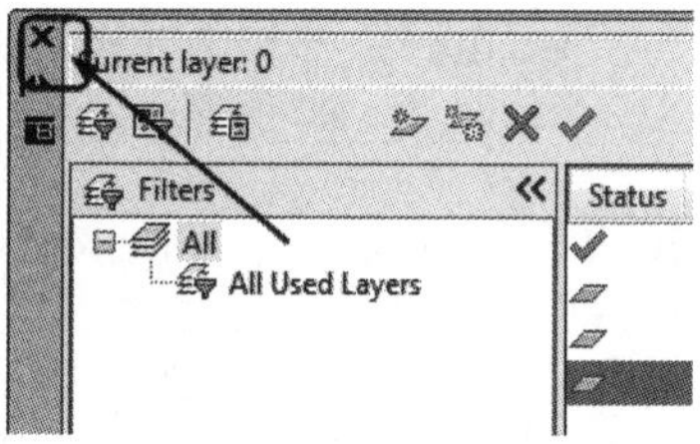

14. Make sure that your layers are UNLOCKED or you will not be able to edit any objects you place on that layer.

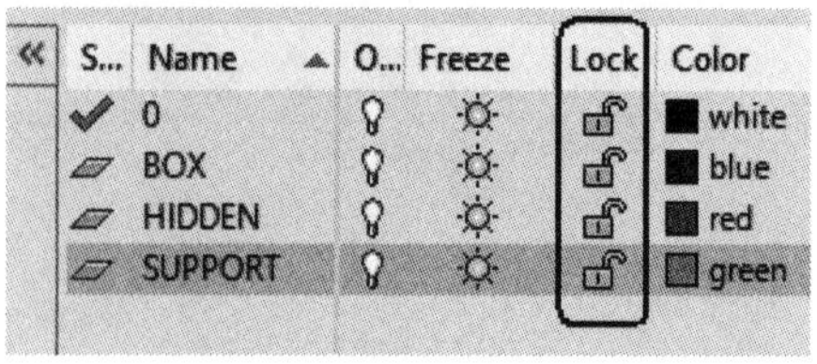

15. When you have finished creating the three layers, close the dialog box by pressing the 'x' button in the upper corner.

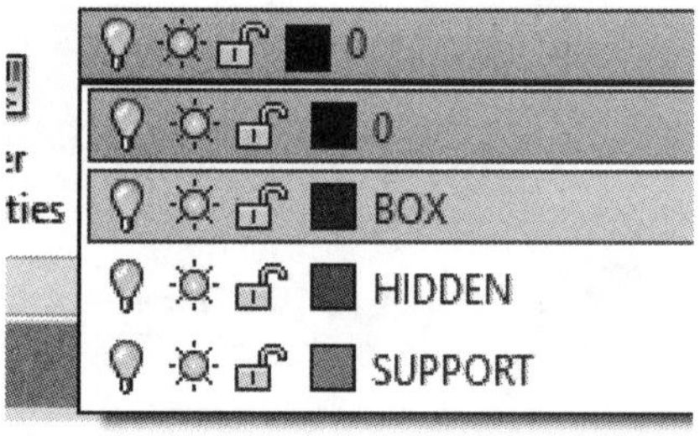

16. Start by setting the BOX layer current before you create the blue box. Select the BOX layer from the Layer Dropdown list in the Object Properties toolbar.

17. Invoke the **Rectangle** command (rectang).

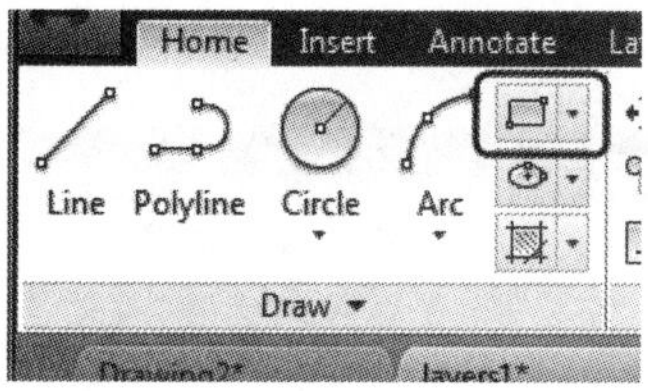

18. Use your mouse and LMB to create the blue rectangle.

19. Set the HIDDEN layer current.

20. Draw the two horizontal lines inside the blue rectangle.

21. Set the SUPPORT layer current.

22. Place two green rectangles.

EXTRA: *Type LTSCALE at the command line and change the linetype scale to 0.75. View the changes to your drawing. Repeat LTSCALE, and change it to 0.25. View the drawing, then set it back to 0.5. From the Layer Properties dialog box change the colors associated with the layers you created. Change the linetype of the layers. View your drawing.*

- Use the Freeze option instead of Off. Layers that are frozen are completely ignored in a regeneration, and hence will speed regeneration time.
- Deleting a selected Layer or linetype is similar to the PURGE command.
- A layer can be renamed any time. This will help to organize the information in the drawing.
- Layer 0 cannot be renamed or deleted.
- The Color, Linetype and Lineweight Control options in the Properties Toolbar should be set to Bylayer. In this way these options will be determined by the layer.
- The system variable LTSCALE controls the global scale of the linetypes in the drawing. The effects of LTSCALE apply to linetypes that contain spaces and dashes (i.e. the hidden or the center linetypes).
- Refer to Scale Factor Chart to help determine an appropriate LTSCALE.
- You can create more than one layer at a time by typing a comma at the end of your layer name.
- Transparency controls how bright objects appear.
- To rename a layer: double click on the name with the LMB to activate a cursor that will allow you to type a new name.
- Double clicking on a layer will also set it to be the current layer.
- Use the shortcut ALT+C to set a selected object's layer current.

Command Exercise

Exercise 7-3 – Creating Layers

Drawing Name: **new drawing** (use the acad.dwt template)
Estimated Time to Completion: 20 Minutes

Scope

Practice creating layers, loading linetypes and assigning linetypes and colors to the layers.

Solution

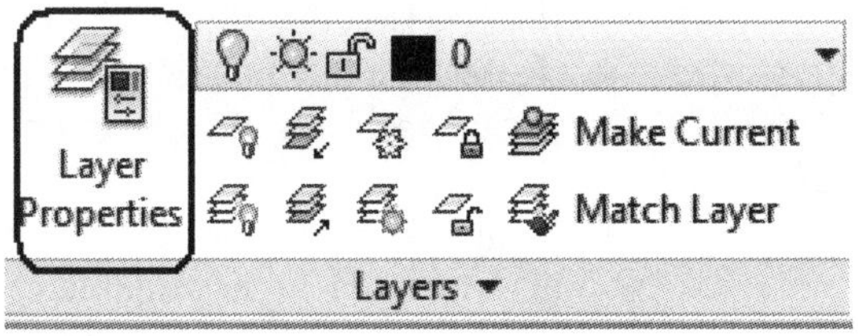

1. Select the **Layer Properties Manager** button.

2. Select the **New Layer** tool.

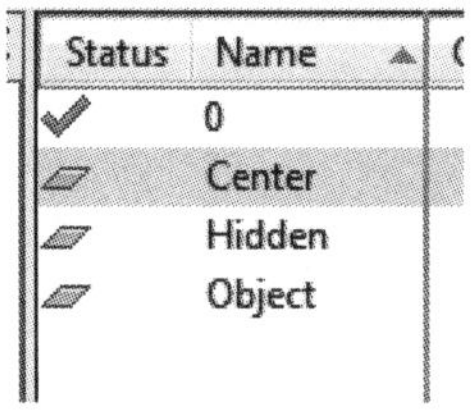

3. Create three layers:
   - Object
   - Hidden
   - Center

- *If you type a comma after you enter the layer name, AutoCAD will automatically drop a line so you can add the next layer.*
- *Your layers are automatically listed in alphabetical order.*

4. Highlight the **Hidden** layer. Pick the word **Continuous** to assign a different linetype.

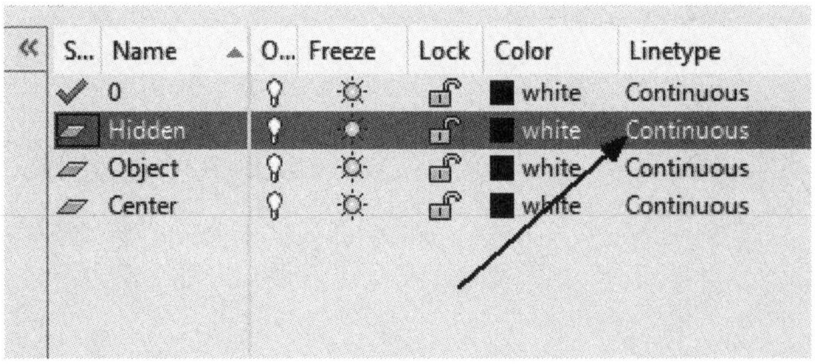

5. Press the **LOAD** button.

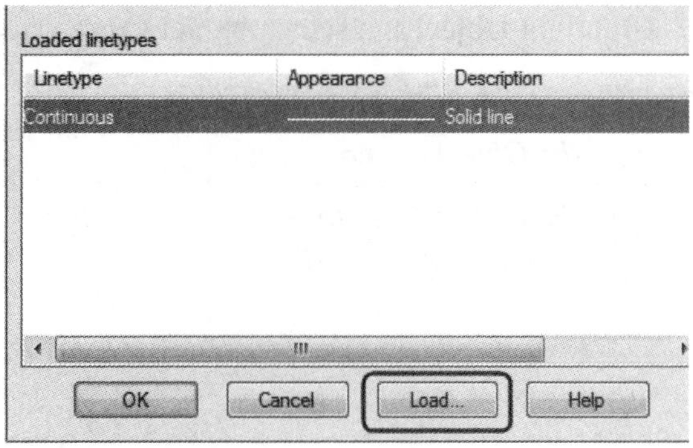

6. Use the scroll bar on the right side of the dialog to locate the Hidden linetype.
7. Select the **Hidden** linetype.
8. Press **OK**.

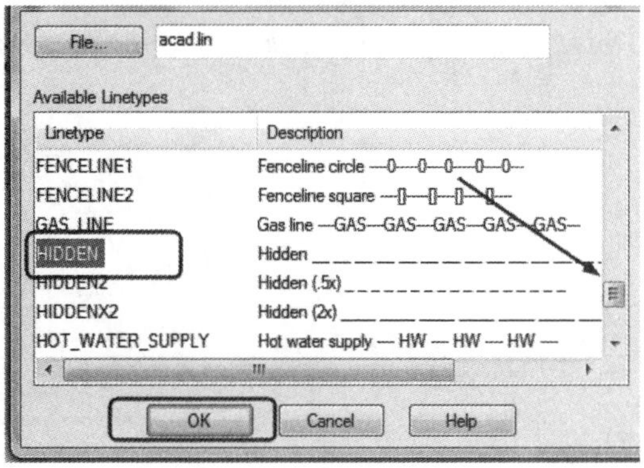

This loads the selected linetype into the active drawing.

You can select more than one linetype to load by holding down the ***Control*** *key.*

9. HIDDEN is now listed as a loaded linetype.
10. Highlight HIDDEN.
11. Press **OK**.

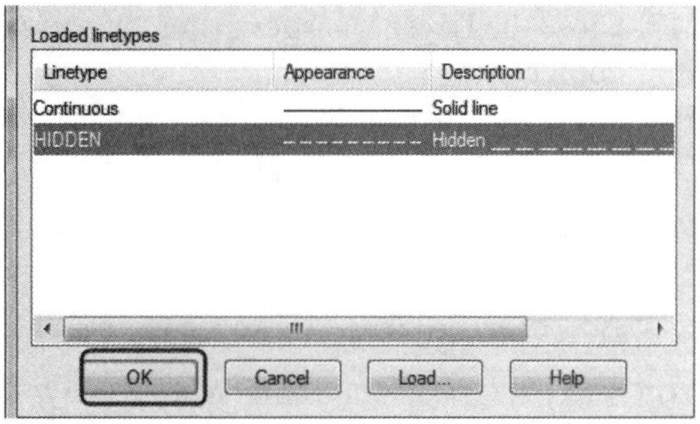

This assigns the HIDDEN linetype to the selected layer.

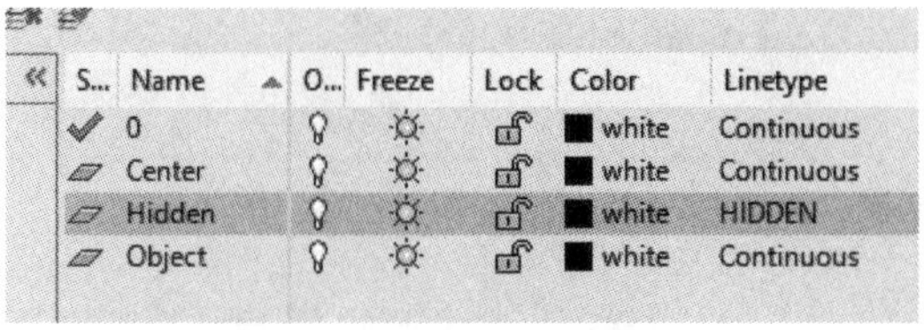

Note that the layer HIDDEN now has been assigned the HIDDEN linetype.

12. Highlight the HIDDEN layer.
13. Pick the Color button.
14. Select the **Cyan** color.
15. Press **OK**.

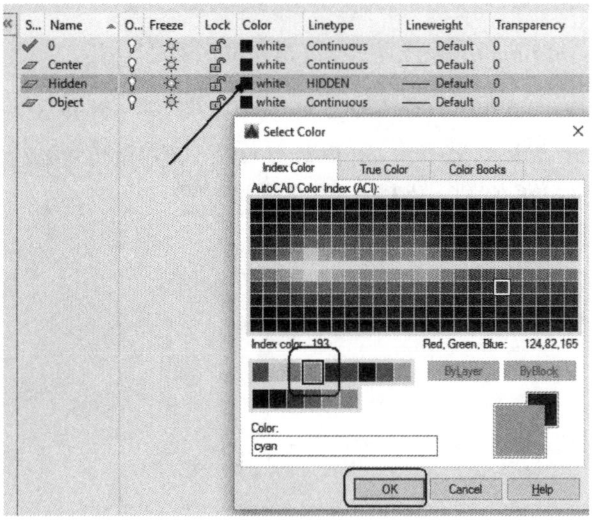

The Cyan color has now been assigned to the Hidden layer.

16. Highlight **Object** and select the Set Current icon.

You can also use Alt-C as a shortcut.

This sets the Object Layer current.

We want the Object layer to be the Current layer – the layer where any entities we create are placed.

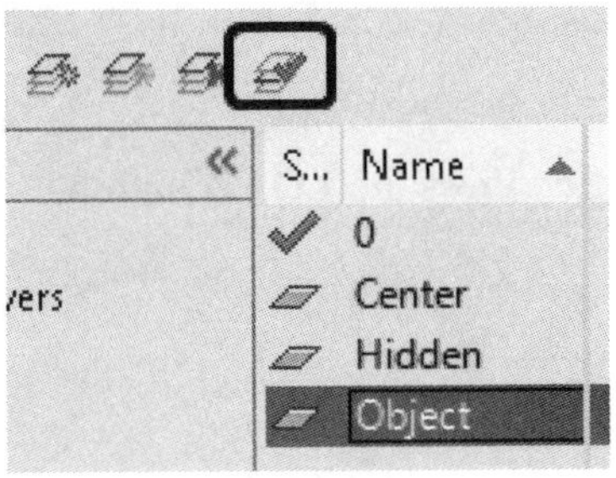

The Current Layer is noted at the top bar of the Layer dialog.

You also see a green check next to the current layer.

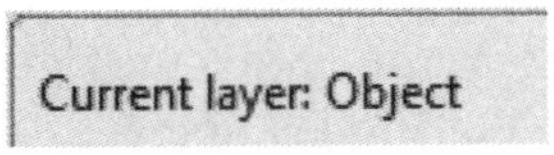

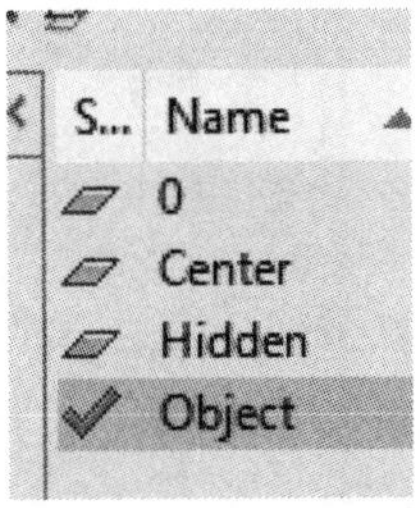

17. Close the Layer Manager dialog by pressing the 'X' in the dialog corner.

The current layer is shown in the layer drop-down list.

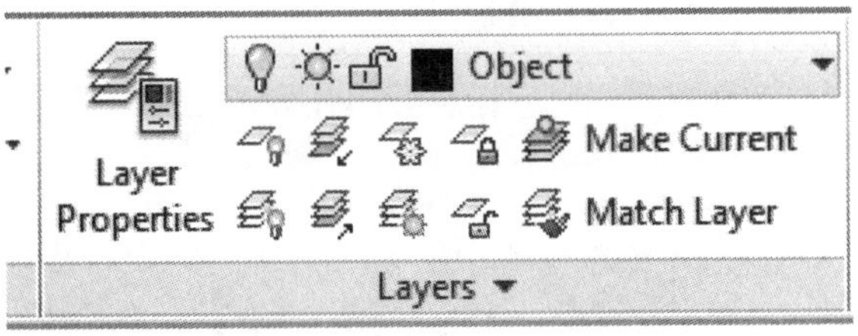

18. Left click on the drop-down arrow in the layer list.

Notice that the layers are listed in alphabetic order.

You can set a layer current by selecting it from the drop-down list.

You can quickly assign an object to a layer by selecting it and then selecting the layer from the drop-down list.

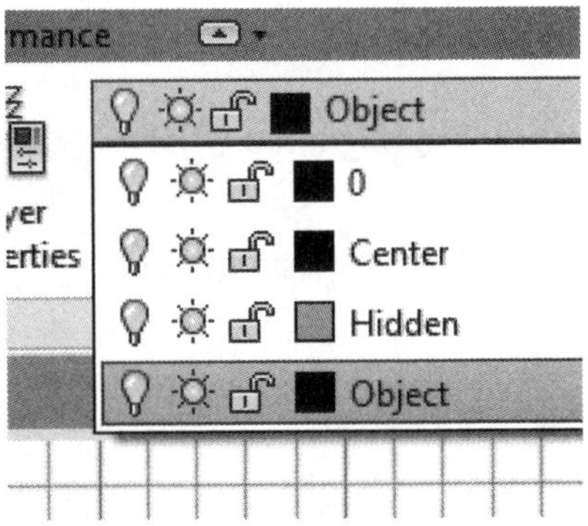

Command Exercise

Exercise 7-4 – Rename Layers

Drawing Name: **layers2.dwg**
Estimated Time to Completion: 5 Minutes

Scope

In the Layer Properties dialog box, Rename layer #1 to WINDOW. Make the House Layer current. Select all, then Freeze all.

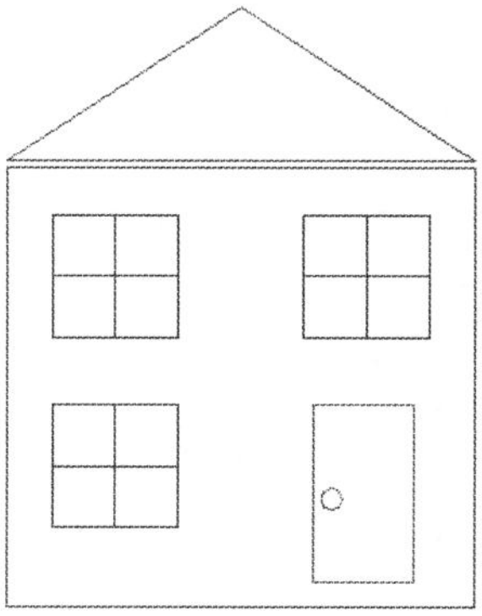

Layers Exercise

Solution

1. Invoke the Layers command (layer) to open the Layer Properties Manager dialog box.

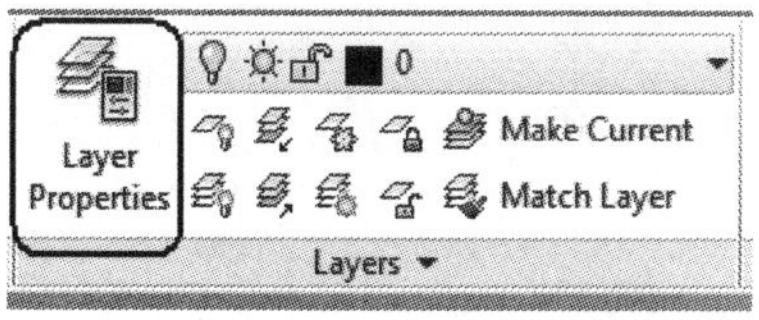

2. In the Layer Properties Manager, double click on the name of Layer '1' to rename it to **WINDOW**. You also can right click and select Rename Layer or press F2.

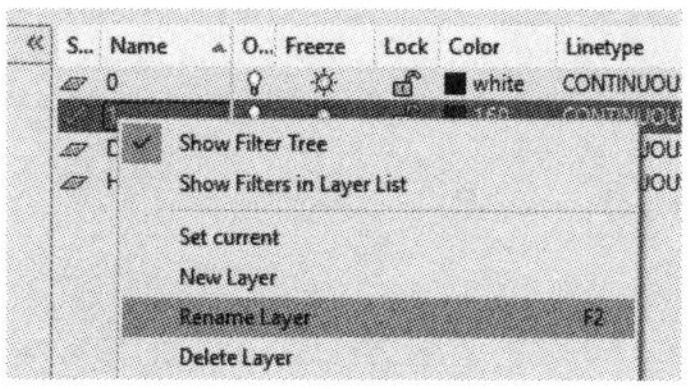

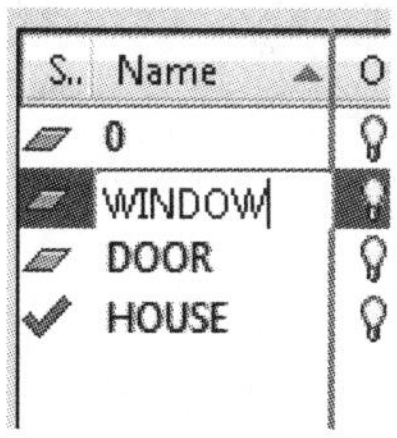

3. Select the HOUSE layer and set it current by pressing the 'Current' button.

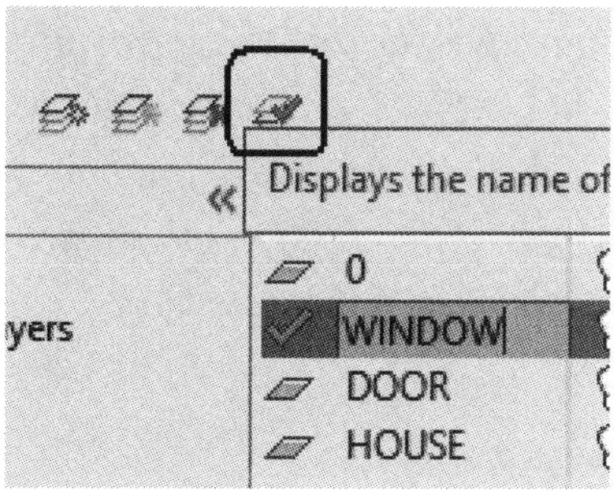

4. Hold down the <SHIFT> key to select all the layers so they are highlighted.

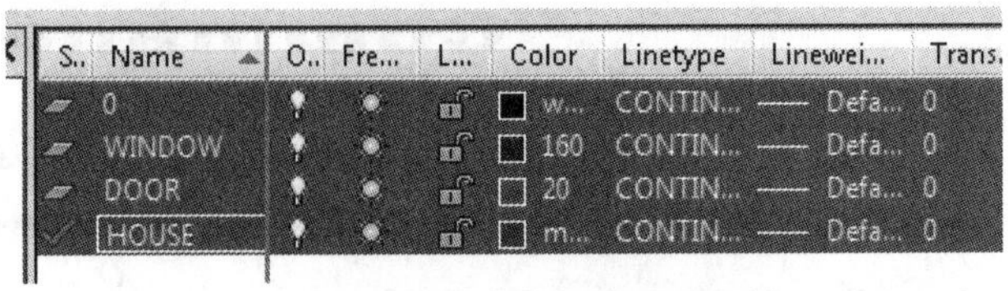

5. LMB click the sun in the Freeze column on the first row.

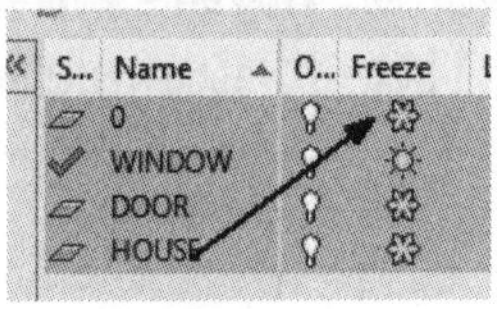

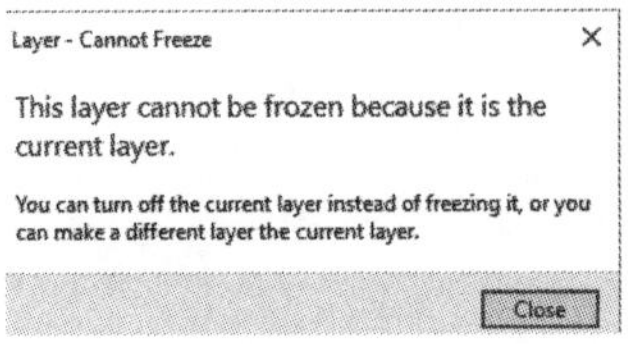

6. A warning message will appear.
7. Press **Close**.

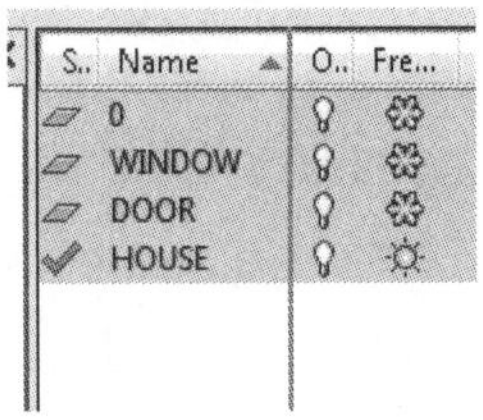

All the layers will be frozen except for the current layer – House.

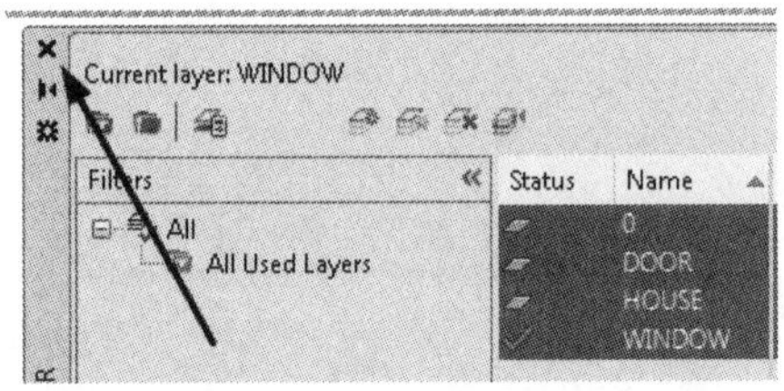

8. Close the layer properties dialog by pressing the X in the corner.

Extra: *Try Freezing and Thawing different layers. Try turning different layers ON or OFF.*

Tips & Tricks

- *Remember visually turning layers OFF is similar to Freezing, but time can be saved during regeneration if a layer is Frozen.*

When you first start out as a drafter, chances are you won't be creating drawings from scratch. Instead, you will be given legacy drawings to work on. (A legacy drawing is an older drawing that needs to be updated to comply with engineering changes or standards.) Your first step upon opening up a legacy drawing should be to identify how the drawing is organized; i.e. which objects are on which layers. Once you have determined how the drawing is organized, you may opt to move objects onto different layers to make it easier to work on the drawing or in order to comply with your company's CAD standards.

Command Exercise

Exercise 7-5 – Identifying Layers

Drawing Name: **Floor Plan.dwg**
Estimated Time to Completion: 10 Minutes

Scope

Use the Layer Translator to identify the layers in a drawing.

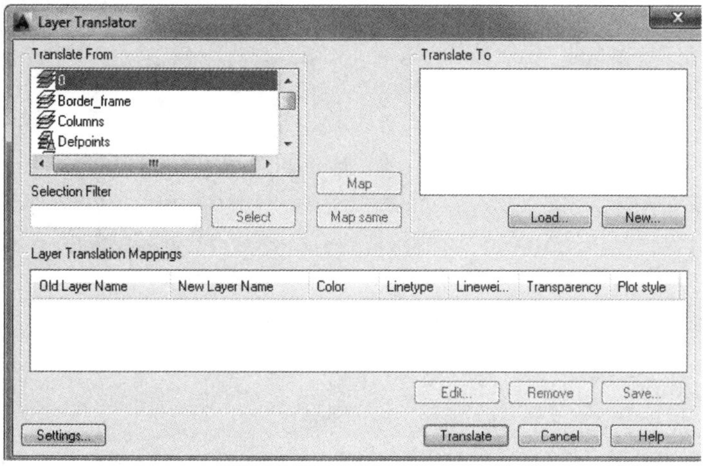

Layer Translator Dialog

Solution

1. Activate the **Manage** ribbon.
   Select the **Layer Translator** on the CAD Standards panel.

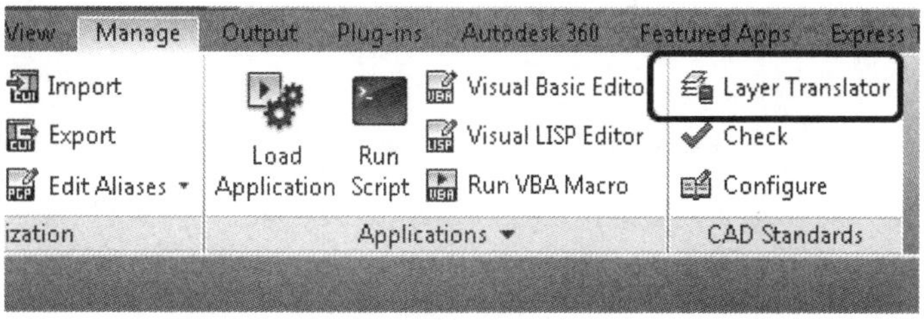

If you are using the AutoCAD Classic workspace: Go to ***Tools→CAD Standards→Layer Translator***.

2. Select **Settings**.

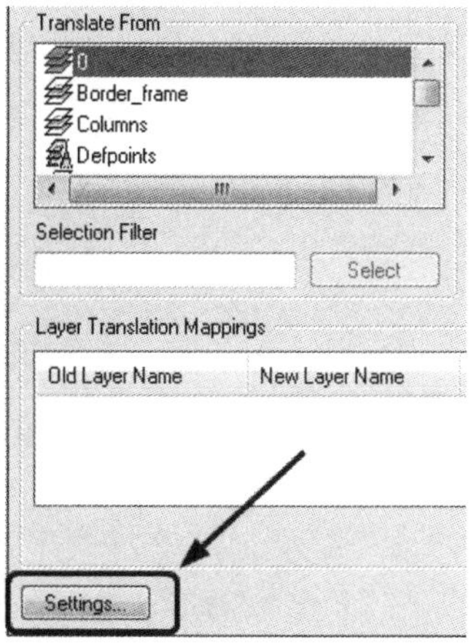

3. Enable **Show layer contents when selected.**

4. Press **OK.**

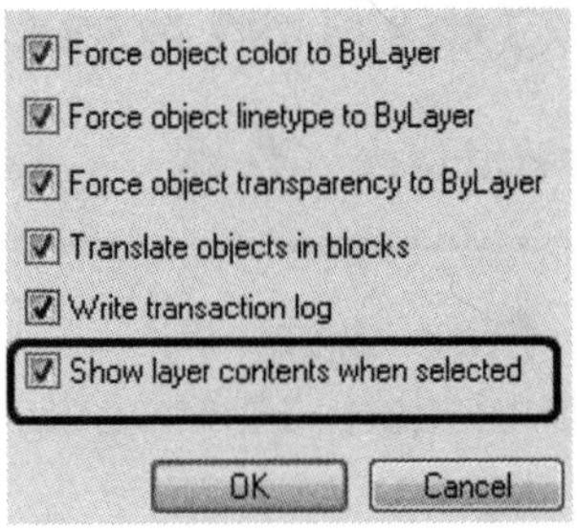

5. Move the Layer Translator dialog to the side so you can see the drawing.

6. Select each layer in the Translate From list. Note which objects are visible when which layers are highlighted.

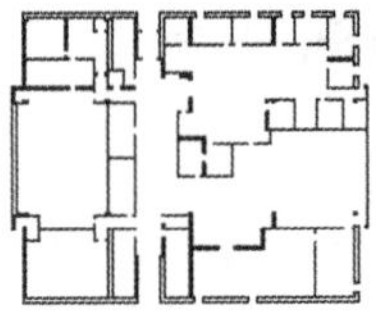

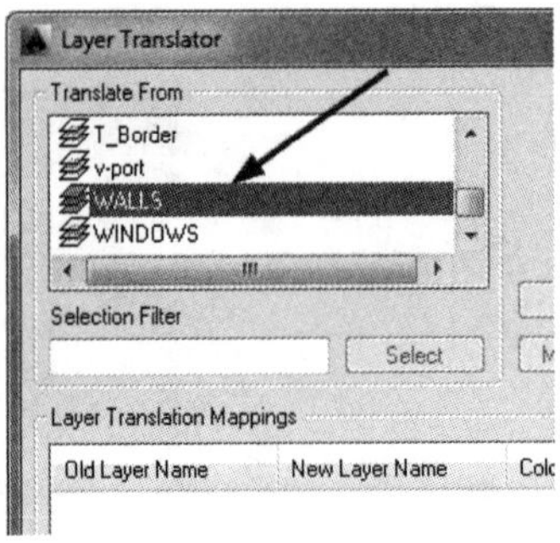

Note that several layers don't have anything on them.

7. Close the Layer Translator.

8. Close the file without saving.

Command Exercise

Exercise 7-6 – Using the Layer Translator

Drawing Name: **Elevation.dwg**
Estimated Time to Completion: 15 Minutes

Scope

Often you will work on a file with objects residing on the wrong layer. The Layer Translator makes it easy for you to organize drawings. In this exercise, you learn how to use the Layer Translator to organize objects on layers.

Solution

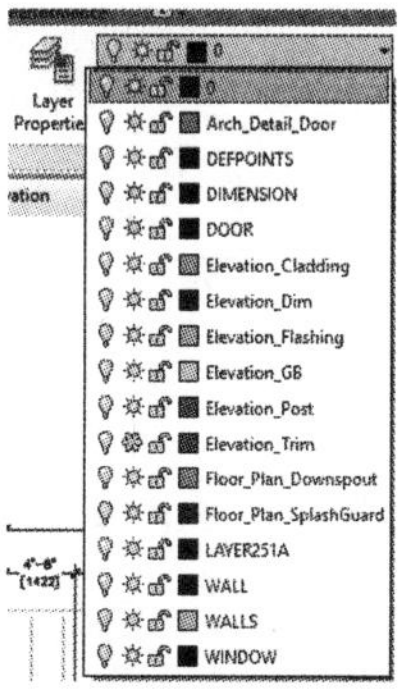

1. Check the layer drop-down list to see what layers currently exist in the drawing.

2. Activate the **Manage** ribbon.
   Select the **Layer Translator** on the CAD Standards panel.

*If you are using the AutoCAD Classic workspace: Go to **Tools→CAD Standards→Layer Translator**.*

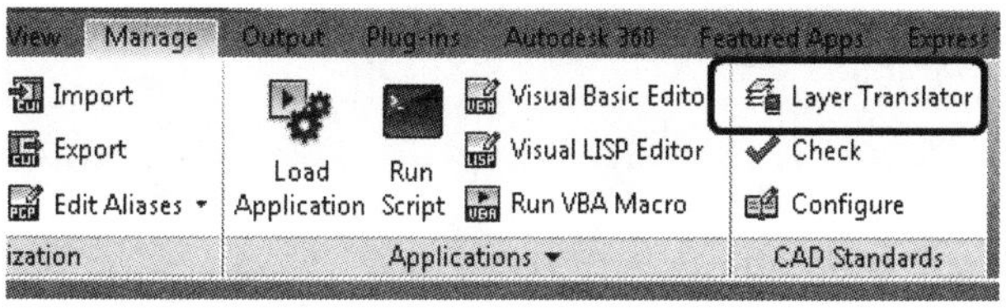

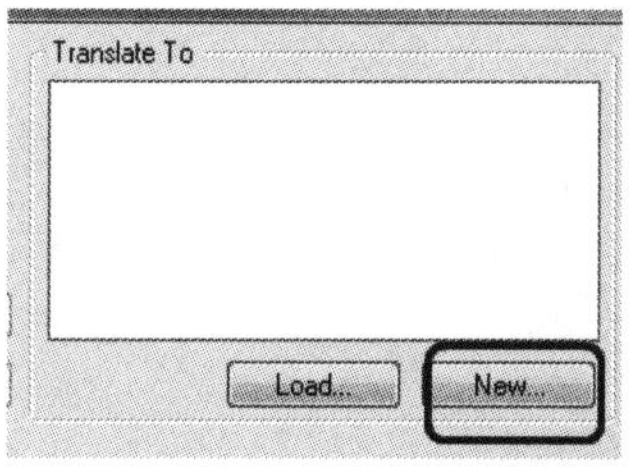

3. Select the **New** button.

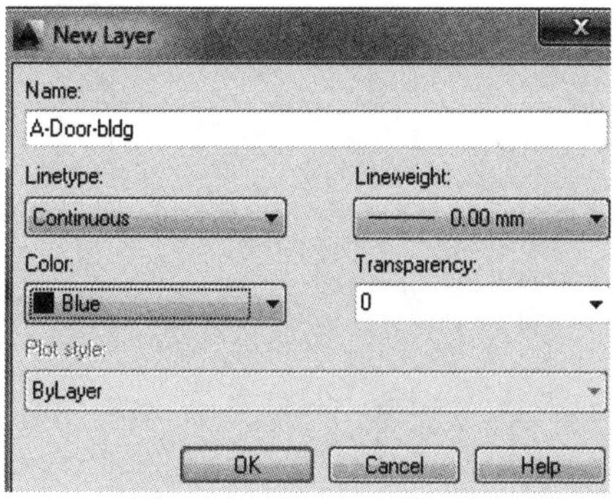

4. In the New Layer dialog:
   In the Name field, enter **A-Door-bldg**.

   Set the Color to **Blue**.

   Press **OK**.

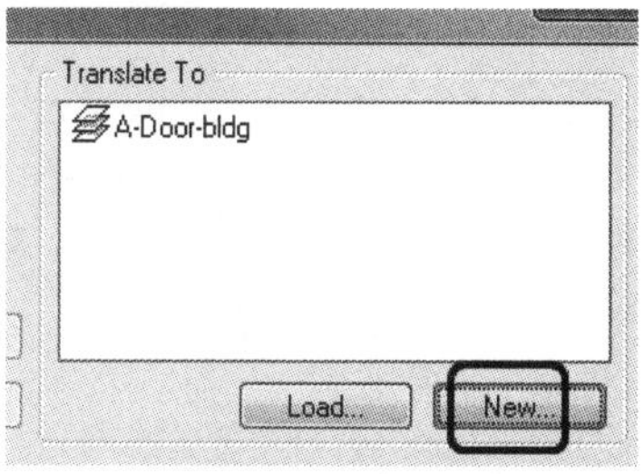

Note that the A-Door-bldg. layer is listed in the Translate To list.

5. Select the **New** button.

6. In the New Layer dialog:

   In the Name field, enter **A-Window-Elev**.

   Set the Color to **Magenta**.

   Press **OK**.

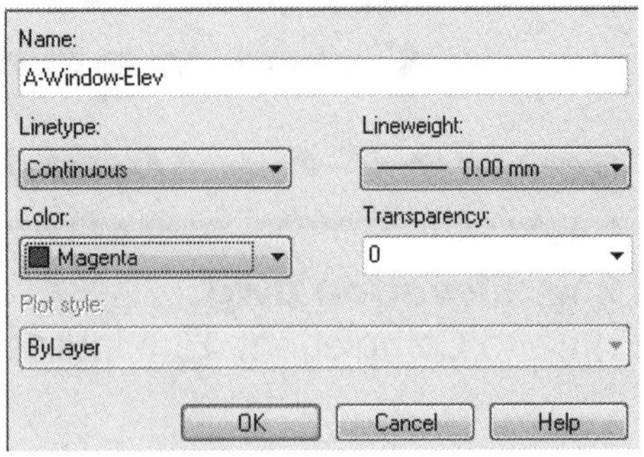

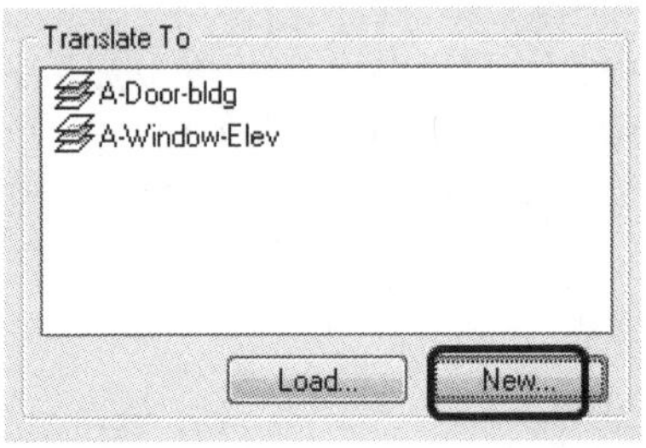

7. Select the **New** button.

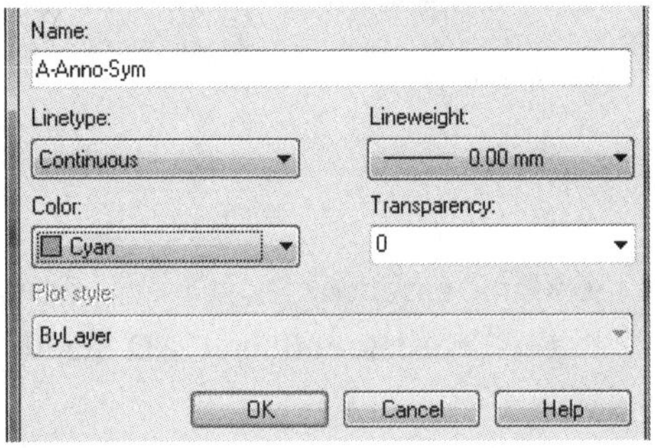

8. In the New Layer dialog:

   In the Name field, enter **A-Anno-Sym**.

   Set the Color to **Cyan**.

   Press **OK**.

9. Highlight **WINDOW** in the Translate From window.

   Highlight **A-Window-Elev** in the Translate To window.

   Select **Map**.

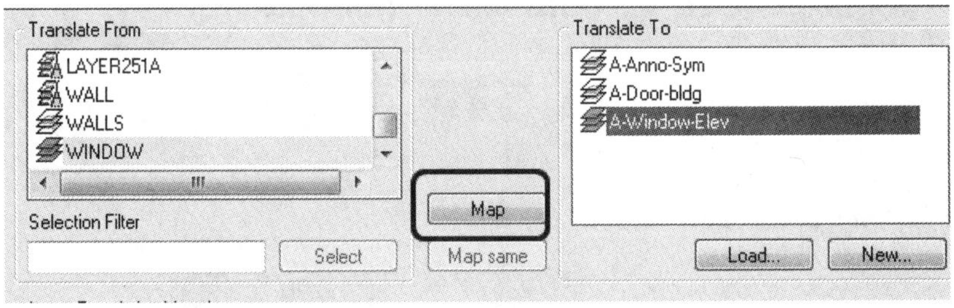

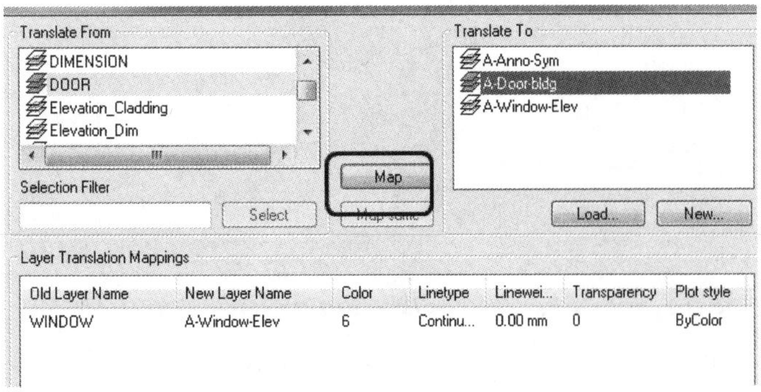

10. Highlight **DOOR** in the Translate From window.

    Highlight **A-Door-bldg** in the Translate To window.

    Select **Map**.

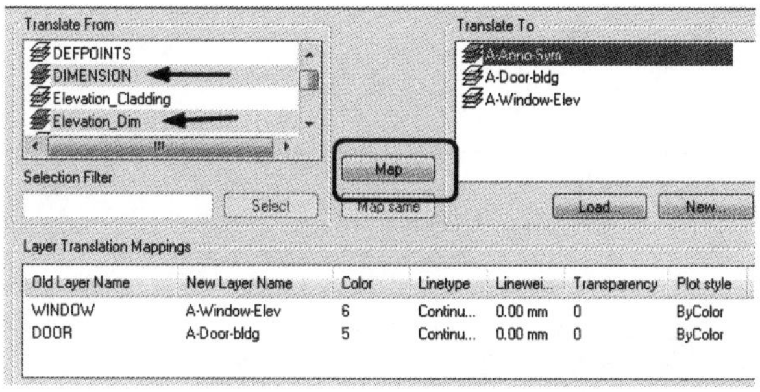

11. Hold down the Control key.

    Highlight **DIMENSION** and **Elevation_Dim** in the Translate From window.

    Highlight **A-ANNO-SYM** in the Translate To window.

    Select **Map**.

You can map more than one layer at a time.

The list of layers to translate are listed in the lower panel.

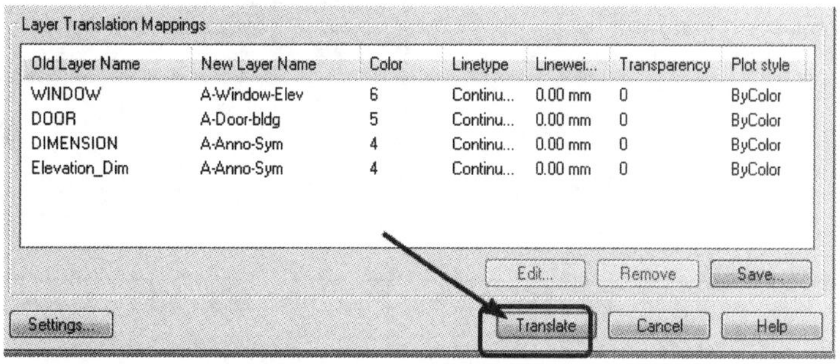

12. Select **Translate**.

13. Select **Translate Only**.

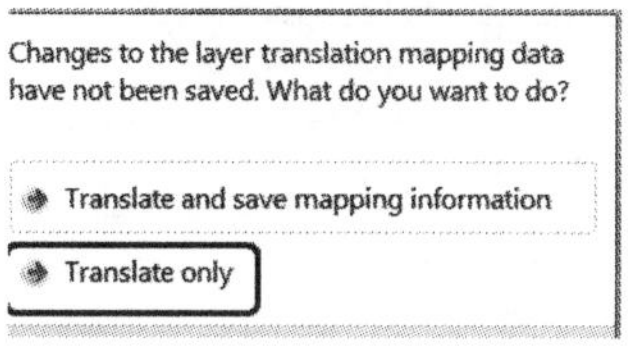

You may wish to Save your mapping settings if you plan to translate more than one drawing from the same source.

14. Check your layer drop-down list.

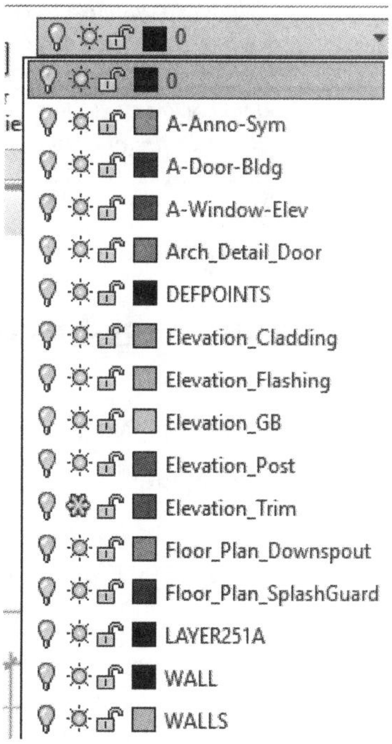

Note that the new layers have been created and that the Doors, Windows, Dimension and Elevation_Dim layers have been purged. The objects on those layers have been moved to the assigned layers.

15. Close the drawing without saving.

Extra: Create a new layer called A-Wall-bldg with the color Black and move objects on the WALL layer to the new layer using the Layer Translator.

Match Properties

Command Locator

Pull Down Menu	**Modify / Match Properties**
Command	**Matchprop**
Alias	**MA**
RMB Shortcut Menu	**Drawing Window**
Dialog Box	**Property Settings**

Command Overview

Object Properties of a selected object can be matched to other objects in the drawing. Select the Source object first, then select the destination object(s). The Matching Properties command will apply the Color, Layer, Linetype, Linetype Scale, Lineweight, Thickness (for 3D), and Dimension, Text, and Hatch styles. Type S to invoke the Settings option or press the RMB to access the shortcut menu and select Settings. Remove the checkmark from any items not to match.

General Procedures

1. Select the Match Properties command from the Properties panel on the Home ribbon.
2. Select the Source object.
3. Select the destination objects.
4. Press <ENTER> to Exit the command.

Tips & Tricks

- This option is similar to the Microsoft Word *Property Painter.*

Command Exercise

Exercise 7-7 – Match Properties

Drawing Name: **match1.dwg**
Estimated Time to Completion: 5 Minutes

Scope

Using the Match Properties command, match the properties of the colored objects to the similar objects on layer 0 (Black or White). Zoom Window for a close-up view of the drawing.

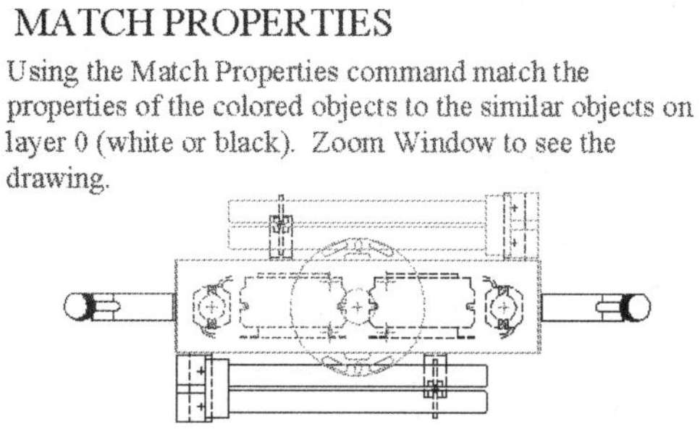

Match Properties Exercise

Solution

1. Invoke the **Match Properties** (matchprop) tool.
2. *Select source object:*
   Use the LMB to select the Cyan colored object at the top of the assembly.
3. *Select destination object(s) or [Settings]:*
   Pick the corresponding part at the bottom of the assembly.
4. *Select destination object(s) or [Settings]:*
   Press the <ENTER> key to end the command.
5. Repeat the process by repeating the Match Properties command. Select the source object first and then apply the properties of the source object to the desired part in the assembly.

Tips & Tricks

- *The properties of the dark blue object can be applied to multiple objects.*

Properties

Command Locator

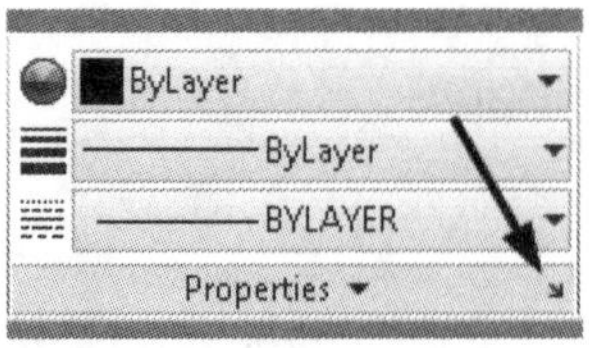

Pull Down Menu	**Modify / Properties**
Command	**Properties**
Dialog Box	**Properties**

Command Overview

The Properties of selected objects can be changed using the Properties command. The list in the Properties dialog box will correspond to the objects that are selected. Objects may be selected before or after the Properties command is invoked. The most common features to change are Layer and Linetype. When one item is selected, the Properties dialog box will display options relevant to the features of that object, such as the radius or diameter of a circle, or the contents of selected Text. The Properties dialog box can be moved to select items in the drawing that may appear behind it. Press Escape to deselect objects, and pick new objects to modify.

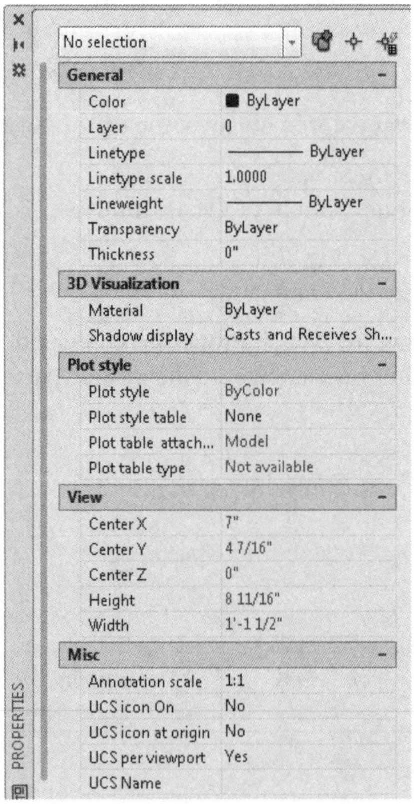

Properties Dialog Box

General Procedures

1. Invoke the Properties command, then select the object(s) to change.
2. Select the option to change from the list, and select or type the new option.
3. Press Escape to deselect the objects.
4. Select the X in the upper right-hand corner to close the dialog box.

Tips & Tricks

- The linetype scale will be multiplied by the global LTSCALE for the objects selected. This change will only affect linetypes other than Continuous.
- The beginners' rule is that the colors of objects should be set to BYLAYER.
- Only layers that are already created will be available in the Select Layer list.
- Only linetypes that have already been loaded will be available in the Select Linetype list.

Command Exercise

Exercise 7-8 – Properties

Drawing Name: **change1.dwg**
Estimated Time to Completion: 10 Minutes

Scope

Using the Properties command, place the shaft on the SHAFT layer, the bellows on the BELLOWS Layer, and the CV joints on the CV Layer.

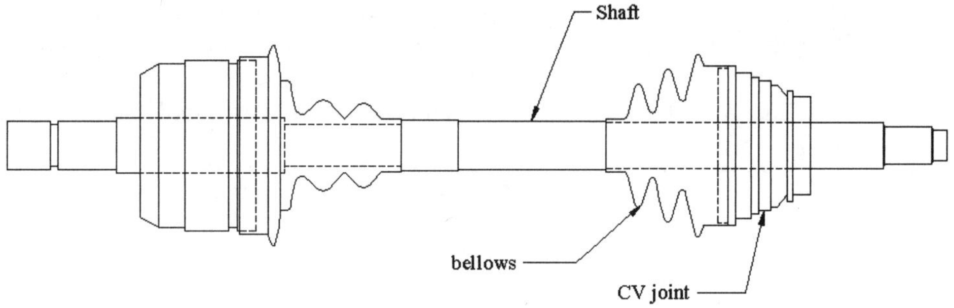

Properties Exercise

Solution

1. Launch the Properties palette (properties).

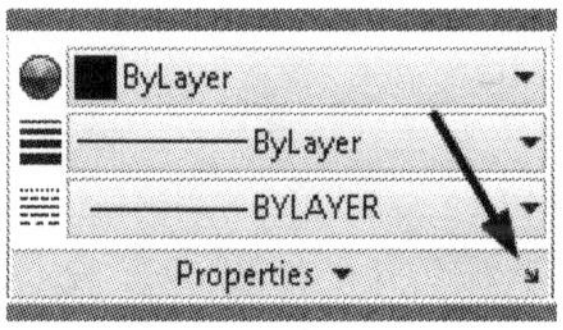

Your Properties palette will look similar to the following figure.

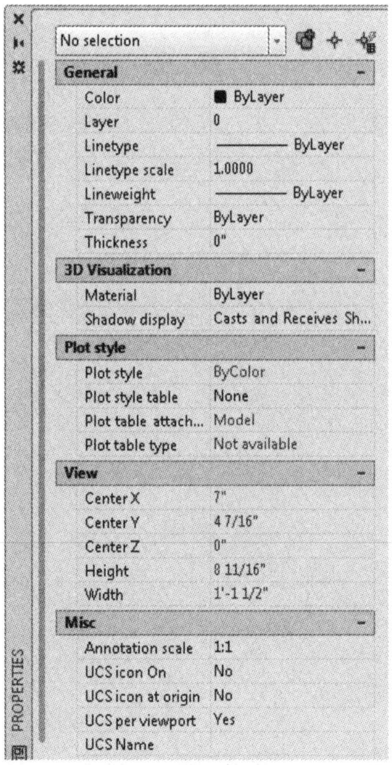

2. Use the LMB to select the Shaft.
   Notice that it is highlighted when selected and the information in the Properties Dialog box changes.

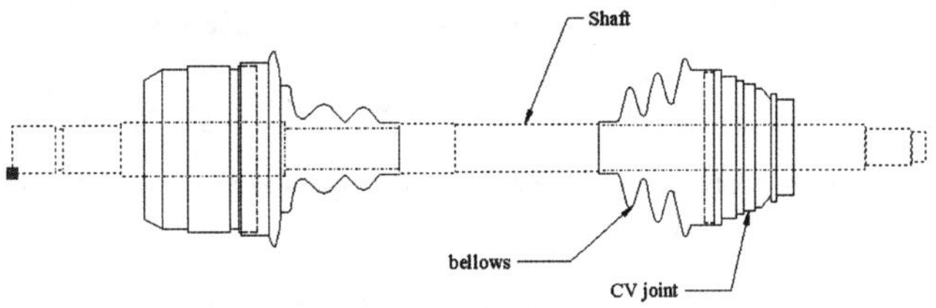

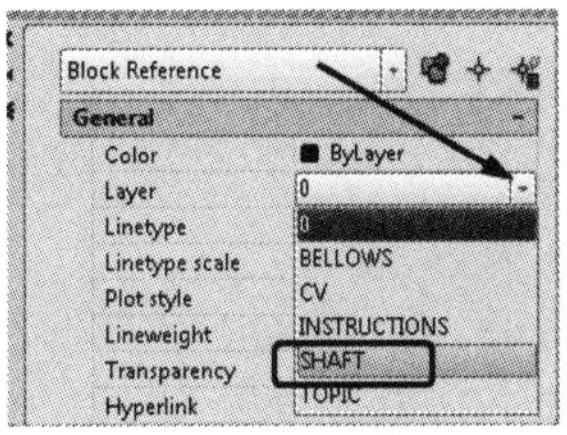

3. Change the layer the shaft is on to the SHAFT layer.

   Pick 0 next to the word Layer in the Properties dialog box.

   In the drop down list that appears select the SHAFT Layer.

   Notice that the Shaft changes color. Press the <ESC> key to clear the selection.

Press <ESC> to release the selection.

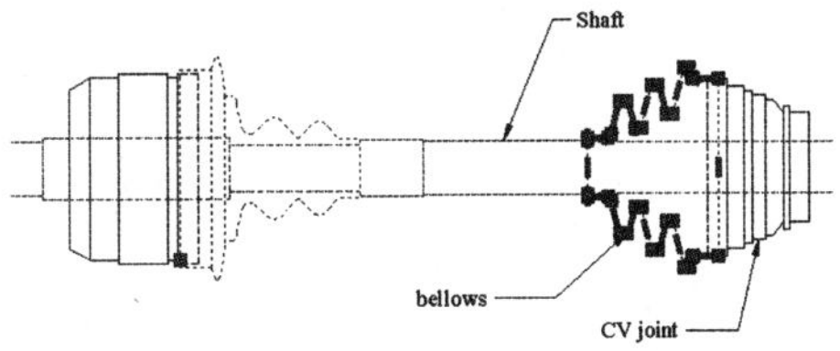

4. Select the two Bellows with the LMB.

   Notice how the information in the Properties Dialog box changes.

   Activate the Drop down list next to the word Layer and select BELLOWS.

   Note that the Properties dialog displays that two items have been selected.

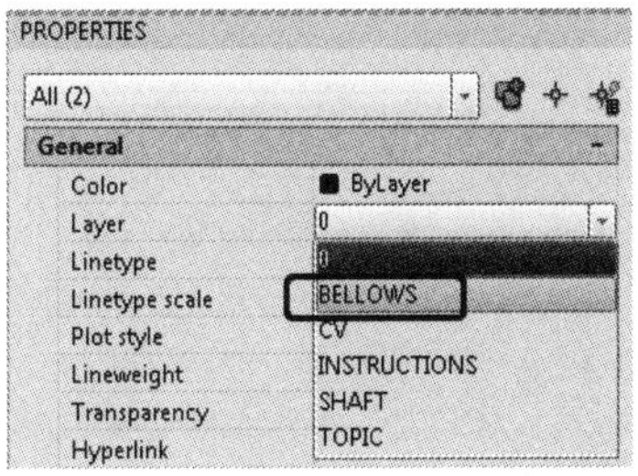

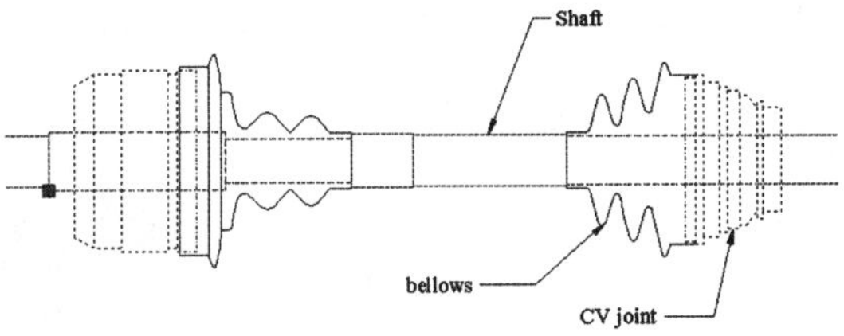

5. Press <ESC> to release the selection.
6. Select the two CV joints and change the layer in the Properties dialog box to CV.

7. Press <ESC> to release the selection.

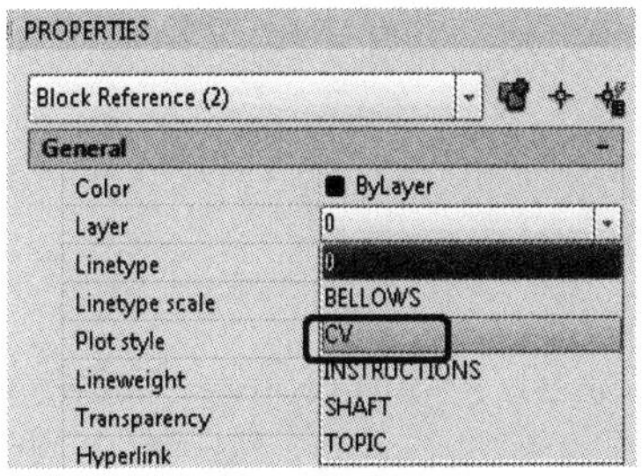

***Extra:** Try undocking the Properties dialog box from the side of the screen and float it in the drawing area. If it is already floating, try to dock it.*

Command Exercise

Exercise 7-9 – Change Properties

Drawing Name: **change2.dwg**
Estimated Time to Completion: 10 Minutes

Scope

Using the Properties command, change the radius of the circle to 2, the layer to "Circle" and the center point to the midpoint of the line. Perform all these changes in the Properties dialog box. Using the Properties dialog, switch between the circle and the line selection. Change the layer for the line.

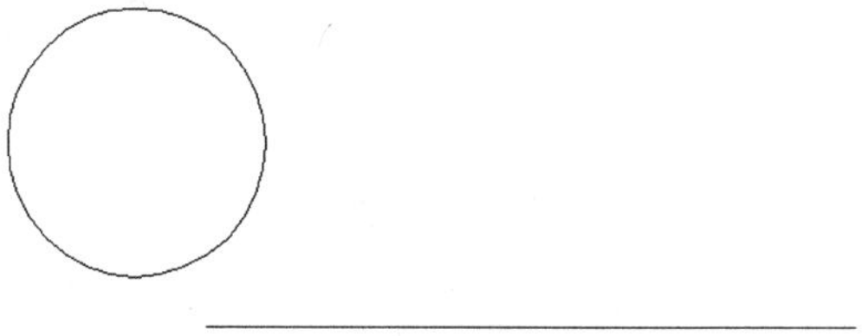

Properties Exercise

Solution

1. Open the Properties palette if it is not already open.

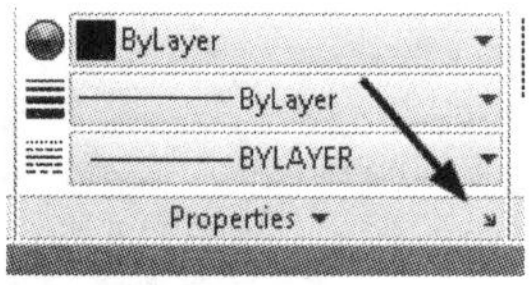
ByLayer
ByLayer
BYLAYER
Properties

2. Select the circle and the line using window or crossing.
3. Two items are listed in the Properties dialog.
   Select the drop-down arrow.
4. Select the Circle in the list.

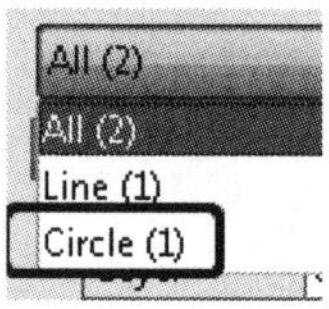
All (2)
All (2)
Line (1)
Circle (1)

5. Change the layer to the CIRCLE layer in the properties dialog box.

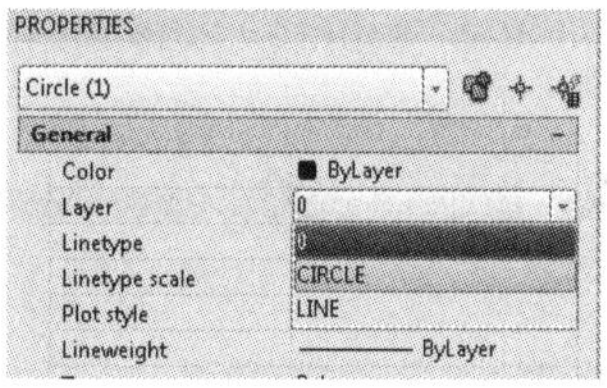
PROPERTIES
Circle (1)
General
Color
ByLayer
Layer
0
Linetype
0
Linetype scale
CIRCLE
Plot style
LINE
Lineweight
ByLayer

6. Select the Radius property and change it to 2".

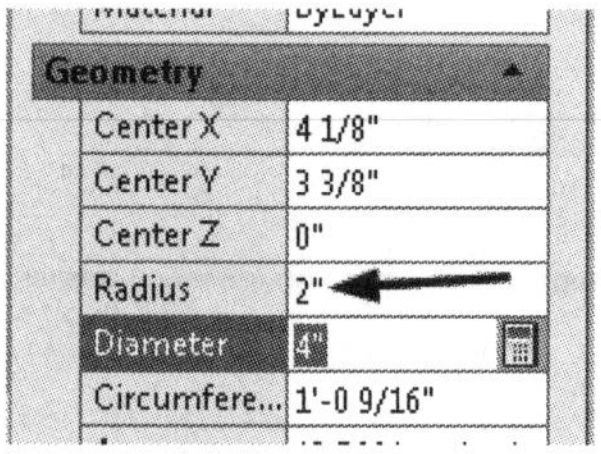
Geometry
Center X
4 1/8"
Center Y
3 3/8"
Center Z
0"
Radius
2"
Diameter
4"
Circumfere...
1'-0 9/16"

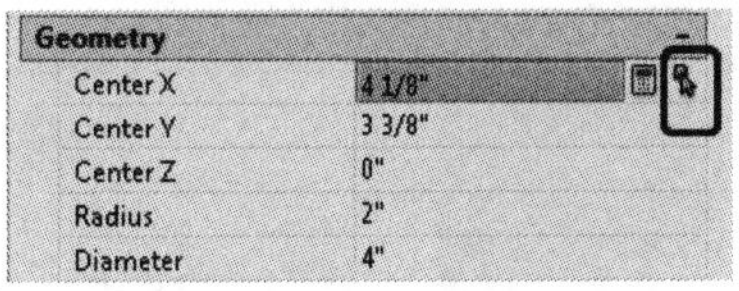
Geometry
Center X
4 1/8"
Center Y
3 3/8"
Center Z
0"
Radius
2"
Diameter
4"

7. Under the Geometry properties of the circle LMB inside the Center X property.
8. Pick the pointer icon that appears next to the Center X property in the dialog box.

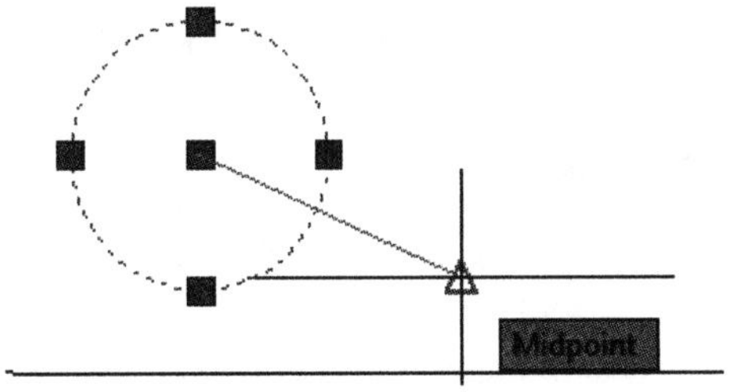
Midpoint

9. *Pick a point in the drawing.*
   Use your OSNAP to select the midpoint of the line.

Notice how the circle has been changed.

10. Select the Line from the drop-down list on the Properties dialog.

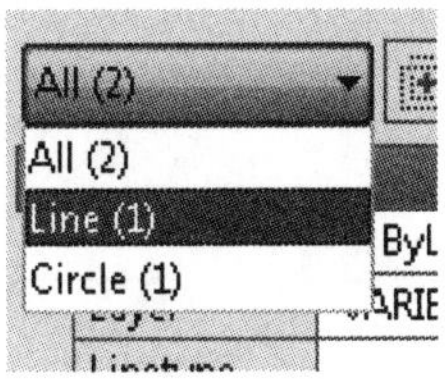
All (2)
All (2)
Line (1)
Circle (1)

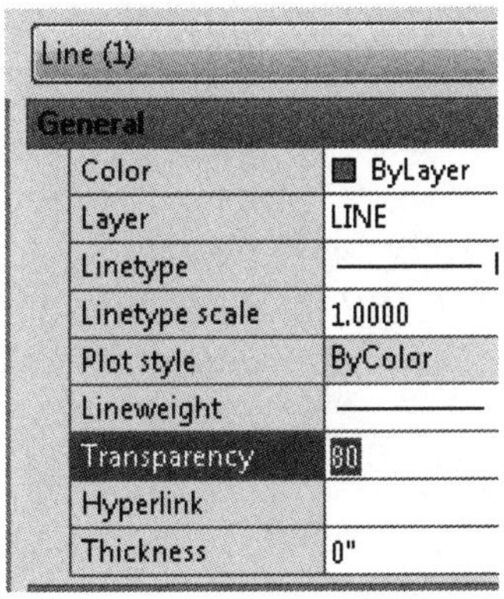
Line (1)
General
Color
ByLayer
Layer
LINE
Linetype
Linetype scale
1.0000
Plot style
ByColor
Lineweight
Transparency
80
Hyperlink
Thickness
0"

11. Assign the Line to the LINE layer.

12. Set the Transparency of the line to 80.

13. Press <ESC> to release the selection set.

Note how the objects have changed.

Extra: *Try changing the Area and Circumference of the circle using the Properties palette.*

Section Exercise

Exercise 7-10 – Organize Your Drawing

Drawing Name: **Lesson 7 MCAD.dwg**
Estimated Time to Completion: 15 Minutes

Scope

Use the commands you have learned in the past section to organize the drawing into different layers. Create a Layer for each part in the assembly. Use the Properties tools to place the corresponding part on the correct layer.

Layer Name:	*Color:*
NUT	*GREEN*
UPPERBODY	*RED*
LOWERBODY	*YELLOW*
POST	*91*
PLATE	*65*
SHOULDERSCREW	*CYAN*
BILL_OF_MATERIAL	*YELLOW*
TEXT	*250*

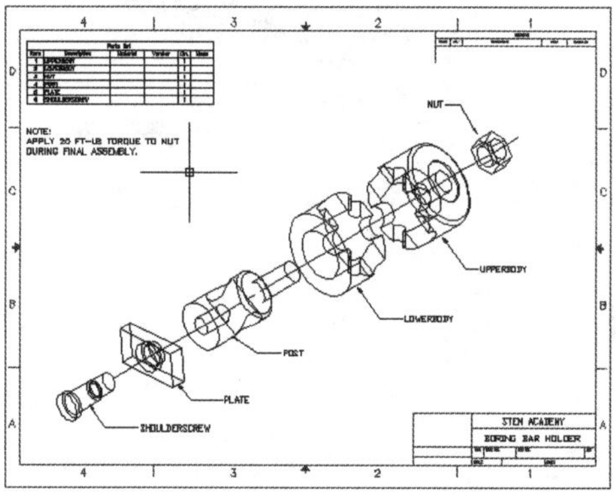

Object Properties MCAD Section Exercise

Solution

Hints

1. Start by creating the 8 new layers using the Layers Command. Notice that a layer for the title block already exists.
2. Use the Properties Command and different selection methods to make sure each part is on the correct layer.

Review Questions

1. Identify the following icons and briefly describe each function:

   A. 

   B. 

   C. 

2. What are the two options (what the image represents and its opposite) for the individual icons in the layers control dialog box?

   A.  ______________________________

   B.  ______________________________

   C.  ______________________________

3. What is the difference between FREEZE and OFF when controlling layers?

4. You can turn the current layer OFF. Can you FREEZE the current layer? Can you draw on a layer that is OFF? Try it.

5. What command will remove used layers thus decreasing the file size of your drawing?
   - ❑ CLEAN
   - ❑ DRAIN
   - ❑ PURGE
   - ❑ FLUSH

6. What does it mean to choose the color BYLAYER?
   - ❑ Objects choose their own color randomly
   - ❑ Objects default to the 0 layer and are black or white depending on the drawing window background color.
   - ❑ Objects take on the color of the current layer they are assigned to.
   - ❑ Objects take on an assigned color no matter what layer they are on.

7. What does the LTSCALE command do?

8. How can you control the Match Properties command so only specific features are matched like Line Type? Try it.

Review Answers

1. Identify the following icons and briefly describe each function:
   - A. *Layer Properties Command, opens the Layers dialog box*
   - B. *Match Properties, matches the properties of one or more objects to the first selected*
   - C. *Make Object's Layer Current, makes the layer of the selected object current*

2. What are the two options (what the image represents and its opposite) for the individual icons in the layers control dialog box?
   - A. *Freeze & Thaw*
   - B. *On & Off*
   - C. *Lock & Unlock*

3. What is the difference between FREEZE and OFF when controlling layers?

   The layers are not visible. Frozen layer is ignored in a regeneration (Saving time when you regen), and a layer that is simply turned Off will still be processed in a regeneration (saving no time in a regen). Therefore, use FREEZE instead of OFF.

4. You can turn the current layer OFF. Can you FREEZE the current layer? Can you draw on a layer that is OFF? Try it.

   You cannot FREEZE the current layer. You can turn OFF the current layer. You can draw on a layer that is turned OFF. It is not recommended to draw on layers that are turned off, though, because you cannot see what you are drawing.

5. What command will remove used layers thus decreasing the file size of your drawing?

   PURGE

   The Purge command will delete unused layers and other objects such as linetypes, blocks, etc. You may also delete unused layers and linetypes in the Layers dialog box.

6. What does it mean to choose colors BYLAYER?

   Objects take on the color of the current layer they are assigned to.

   Objects will take on the color of the current layer when the color control is set to ByLayer. In the Object Properties dialog box, selecting BYLAYER will assign color to the selected object according to the layer it is on.

7. What does the LTSCALE command do?

   LTSCALE is a system variable that controls the linetype scale.

8. How can you control the Match Properties command so only specific features are matched like Line Type? Try it.

   Right click and select Settings to enable/disable Match Property Options.

Lesson 8.0 – Drafting Settings and Object Snaps

Estimated Class Time: 2 Hours

Objectives

Students will practice setting different drafting and object snap settings and using the active settings to control how geometry is drawn.

- **Drafting Settings**
- **Object Snaps**
- **Creating Orthographic Views**

Drafting Settings

Command Locator

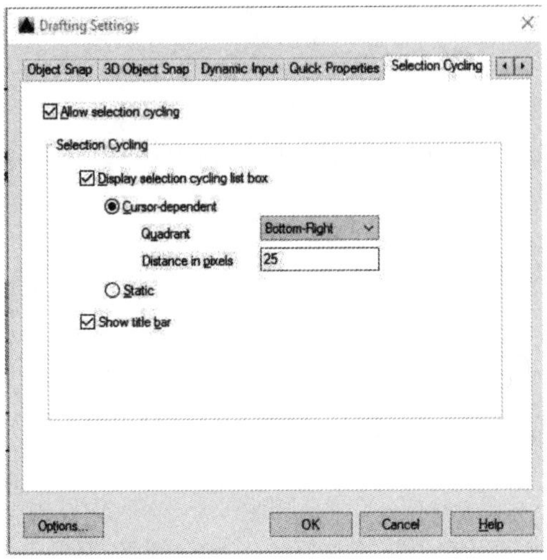

Command	**dsettings**
Alias	**ds**
RMB Shortcut Menu	**Over SNAP, GRID, POLAR, OSNAP or OTRACK in the Status Bar**
Dialog Box	**Drafting Settings**

Command Overview

The Drafting Settings dialog box contains seven tabs:

- Snap and Grid
- Polar Tracking
- Object Snap
- 3D Object Snap
- Dynamic Input
- Quick Properties
- Selection Cycling

Select the Status Bar option using the LMB to turn these functions ON or OFF. Use the RMB to access the Drafting Settings dialog box. You can quickly enable and disable object snaps by mousing over the OSNAP button and selecting/deselecting the preferred OSNAPs.

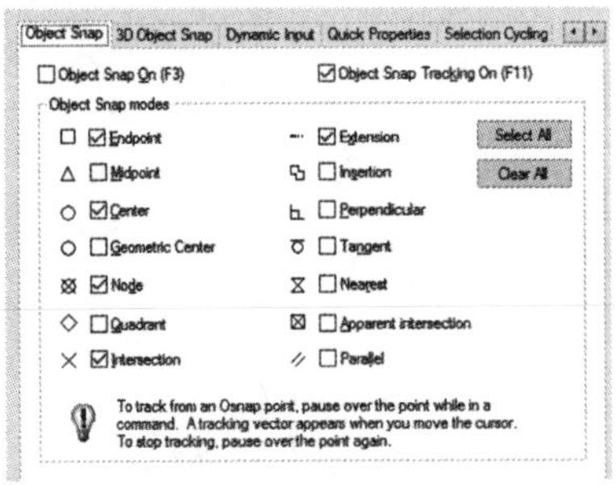

Drafting Settings Dialog Box, Object Snap Tab

Command Exercise

Exercise 8-1 – Drafting Settings

Drawing Name: **drsettings1.dwg**
Estimated Time to Completion: 5 Minutes

Scope

In the Drafting Settings dialog box, Set the Grid spacing to 0,0. Set the Snap Spacing to .5,.5. Turn the Snap and Grid ON. Select OK. Notice how the snap and grid spacing changes.

Solution

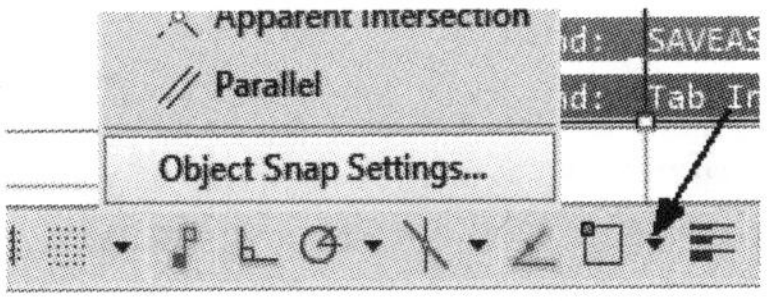

1. Activate the Drafting Settings dialog box by typing 'DSETTINGS' at the command line and pressing <ENTER> or select the down arrow next to the Object Snap icon on the task bar and select **Object Snap Settings.**

2. Select the Snap and Grid tab.

3. Fill out the settings in the dialog box as shown in the following figure.

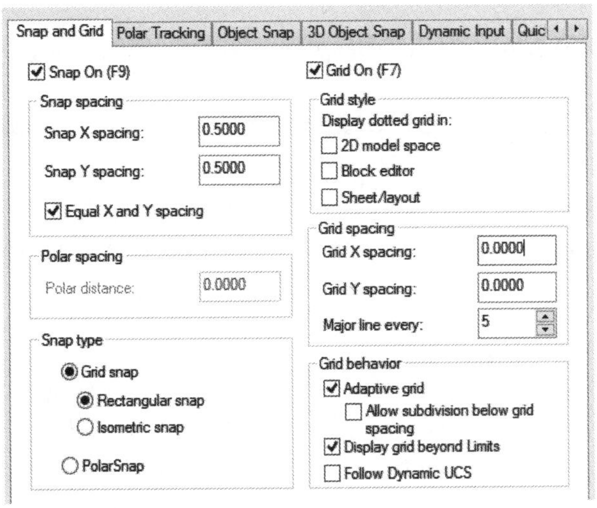

Drafting Settings Dialog Box

4. Press 'OK' to continue.
5. Notice how the Grid spacing defaults to the Snap spacing.

Extra: *What happens if you set the snap spacing to 1,1 and Grid spacing to .3,.3? Try it.*

Tips & Tricks

Use the Isometric Snap option in the dialog box above to create an isometric drawing. Turn Ortho ON and use the F5 function key or Ctrl+E to toggle through the isoplanes.

Drafting Settings: Polar Tracking Tab

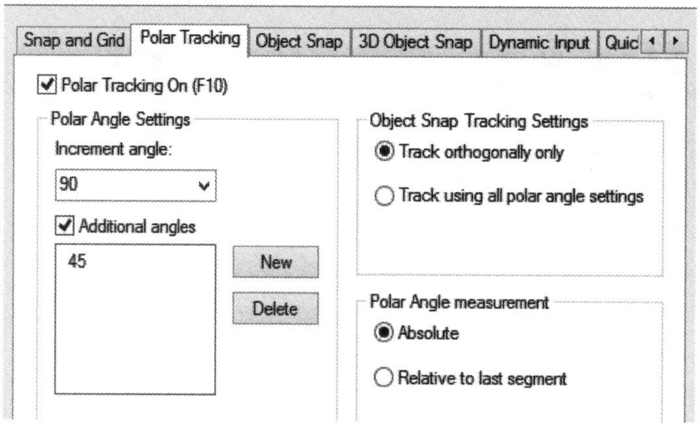

Drafting Settings Dialog Box, Polar Tracking Tab

Polar Snap works independently from SNAP. With Polar Snap turned ON incremental angles will be displayed as the line being dragged approaches that angle. Set the "Incremental angle" from the drop down list, or add "New" angles.

General Procedures

1. Right-click on POLAR in the Status Bar to open the Drafting Settings dialog box and select the Polar Tracking tab.
2. Select the desired "Incremental angle" from the drop down list. Check "Track orthogonally only" and "Absolute" Polar Angle measurement.
3. "Track orthogonally only" and "Absolute" Polar Angle measurement should also be selected.
4. Using the Line command, pick the first point, then drag the line to see the Polar Angle display.

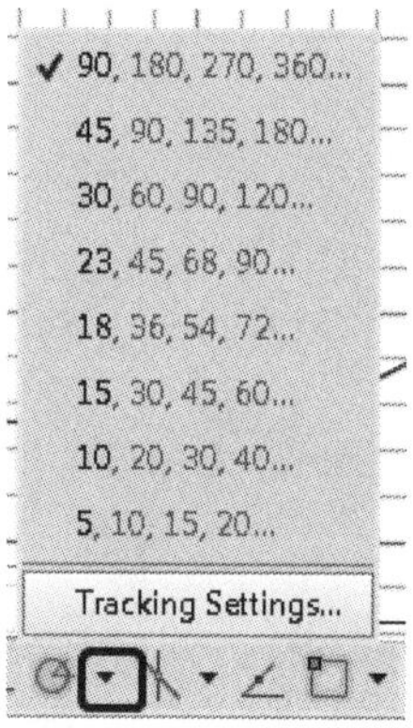

Selecting the Down Arrow next to the Polar icon on the Status Bar allows the user to select different combinations of angles to be used when tracking as well as creating new tracking settings.

Tips & Tricks

- With the desired polar angle displayed, type the length of the line and press the <ENTER> key.
- Select "Relative to last segment" to see the Polar Angle in relation to the angle of the last object drawn.

Drafting Settings: Object Snap Tab

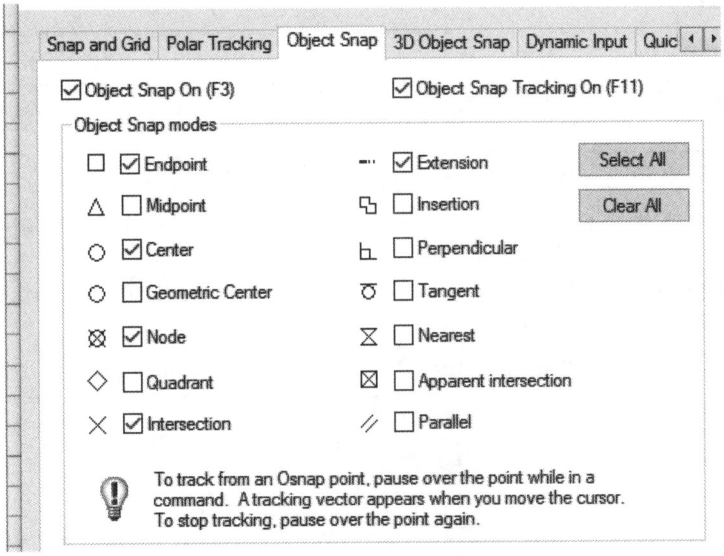

Drafting Settings Dialog Box, Object Snap Tab

When an Object Snap mode is selected, and a draw or modify command has been invoked, the OSNAP will be displayed as the cursor moves over a line or object. The cursor will want to "snap" to that point. If the cursor is held over that snap point, a label will display the snap mode. Once the cursor is moved away from that point, the Object Snap will no longer be displayed or selected. Toggle the OSNAP settings on and off from the Status Bar.

General Procedures

1. Right-click on OSNAP to open the Drafting Settings dialog box and select the Object Snap tab.
2. Select the desired Object Snap modes (i.e. Endpoint, Midpoint, and Intersection).
3. Select OK to exit the dialog box and draw using Object Snap.

Tips & Tricks

- OSNAP settings when selected will remain constant, or "running," if OSNAP is on. Object Snap options can be selected individually using the Object Snap toolbar (see next section), whether OSNAP is on or off.
- Object Snap will want to gravitate to the nearest OSNAP setting. When two options are selected that might make one option impossible to select (such as Center and Quadrant of a circle or arc), use the Tab key to toggle through the options. When the desired Object Snap is displayed, use the pick button to select it.
- Do not check all the Object Snap modes in the dialog box. This will make selecting objects tedious and no longer a handy tool.
- When no Object Snap modes are selected ("Clear All"), selecting OSNAP from the Status Bar will automatically open the Drafting Settings dialog box at the Object Snap tab. Once object snap modes are selected, OSNAP is an ON/OFF switch.
- Select Options from the dialog box to change the AutoSnap marker color and AutoSnap marker size.
- Type OS to open the Drafting Settings dialog box at the Object Snap tab.

Object Snap

Command Locator

Toolbar Menu	**Object Snap Fly-Out or Object Snap**
Alias	**End, mid, int, per, etc. (the first three letters of the option), then press <ENTER>**
RMB Shortcut Menu	**2-Button Mouse: Shift + <ENTER> with the cursor in drawing window** **3-Button Mouse: Middle button with the cursor in drawing window**

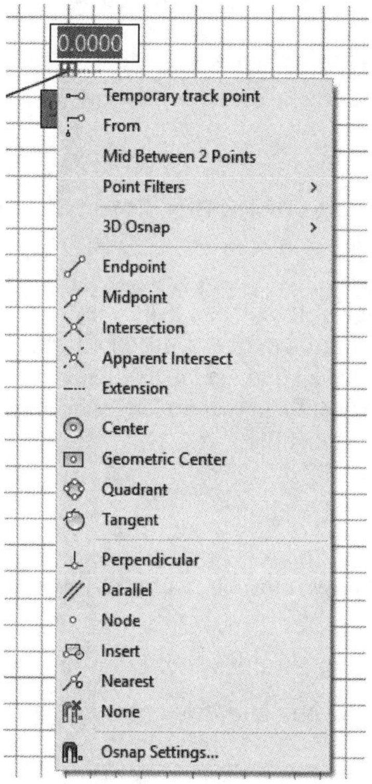

Object Snap Shortcut Menu

Command Overview

Object Snaps are used in combination with other commands. Use an object snap option when prompted to select a point and a specific object snap is desired. Unlike the OSNAP settings, which keep the OSNAP option "running," these object snaps are used for single selections.

Tips & Tricks

➢ *The Object Snap symbols help to indicate where the selection point will be placed. The Object Snap toolbar can also be used to select the desired Object Snap. Move your pointer near the circumference of a circle when using the Center Object Snap.*

Object Snap Option	Button	Overview
Endpoint	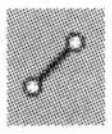	selects the endpoint of a line or arc.
Midpoint		selects the midpoint of a line or arc.
Intersection	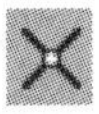	selects the intersection or projected intersection of two lines.
Apparent Intersect	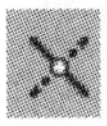	selects the virtual intersection of an existing line and the extension of another line.
Extension	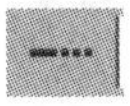	selects a point extending from a line's endpoint.
Center		selects the center of a circle or arc.
Geometric Center	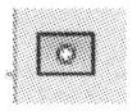	selects the center of a polygon.
Quadrant		selects one of the four quadrants of a circle or arc.
Tangent		makes the object drawn, tangent to the object selected.
Perpendicular		makes the object drawn perpendicular to the object selected.
Parallel	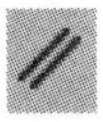	draws an object parallel to the selected object.
Node	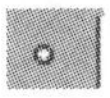	selects a point – you must have placed a point using the POINT command.
Insert	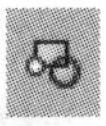	selects the point on the object where it was inserted –works for blocks, xrefs, and text.
Nearest		selects a point on the object selected at the location where it was picked.
None		turns off all active object snap settings during the active command.
OSNAP Settings		opens the Drafting Settings dialog box.

General Procedures

1. Begin a Draw (or Modify) command.
2. When prompted for a selection point, choose an Object Snap option.
3. Place the cursor over the object, and when the marker appears at the desired location, use the LMB to select.

Command Exercise

Exercise 8-2 – Object Snap

Drawing Name: **osnap1.dwg**
Estimated Time to Completion: 5 Minutes

Scope

Practice using single object snaps. Draw the objects shown using the object snaps as indicated.

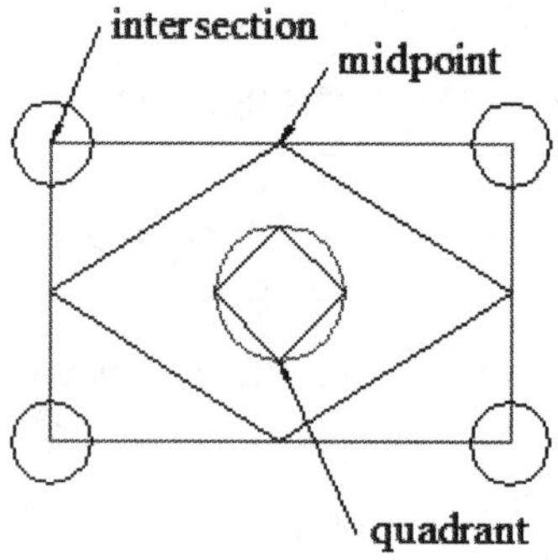

Object Snap Exercise

Solution

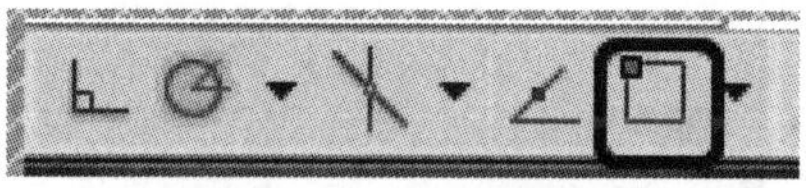

1. Make sure Running Object Snap is turned off. Use your LMB to toggle OSNAP off at the status bar. When OSNAP is off there is no blue indicator on the icon.

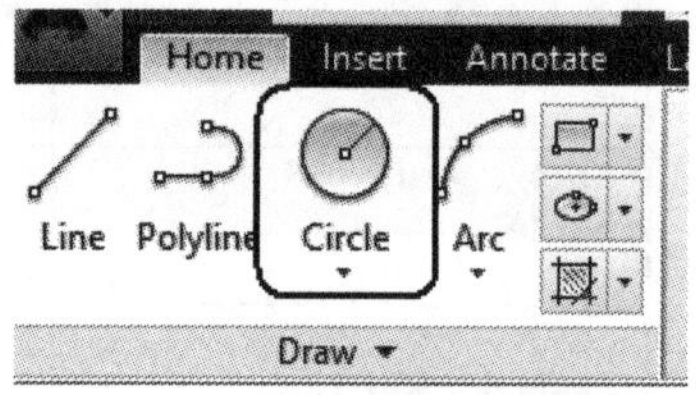

2. Create the four circles first. Invoke the Circle command (c or circle).

3. *Specify center point for circle or [3P/2P/Ttr (tan tan radius)]:*
   Before you pick the first center point of the circle hold your <Shift> key down and press the RMB to bring up the Object Snap shortcut menu. Select Intersection.

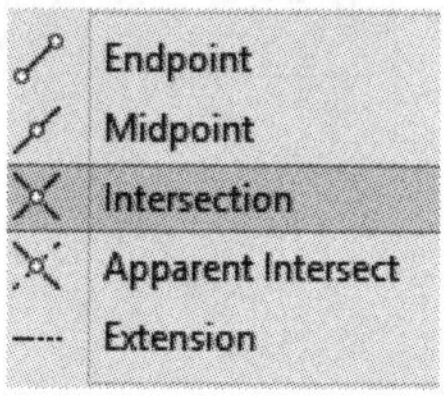

4. *Specify center point for circle or [3P/2P/Ttr (tan tan radius)]: _int of*
   Move your pointer near the desired intersection until the Intersection Object Snap Marker appears. Pick the point with your LMB. Notice how the center of the circle is exactly at the intersection of the 2 lines.

You should see a cursor badge indicating that you are selecting an intersection prior to the left picking.

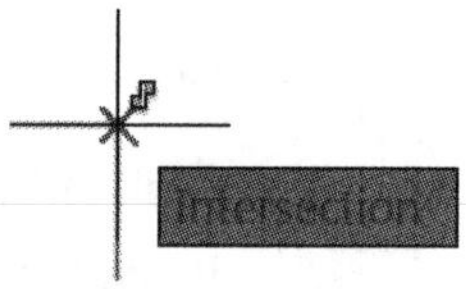

5. *Specify radius of circle or [Diameter]:*
   Type **0.5”.**

6. Repeat the process to complete the remaining circles. *You can press ENTER to accept the default value for the radius.*

7. Invoke the Line command (l or line).

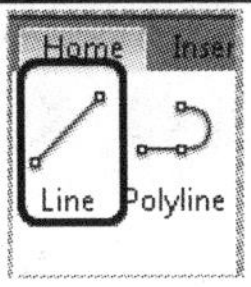

8. *Specify first point:*
   Before you pick the start point of the line hold your <Shift> key down and press the RMB. This will bring up the Object Snap shortcut menu. Select Midpoint.

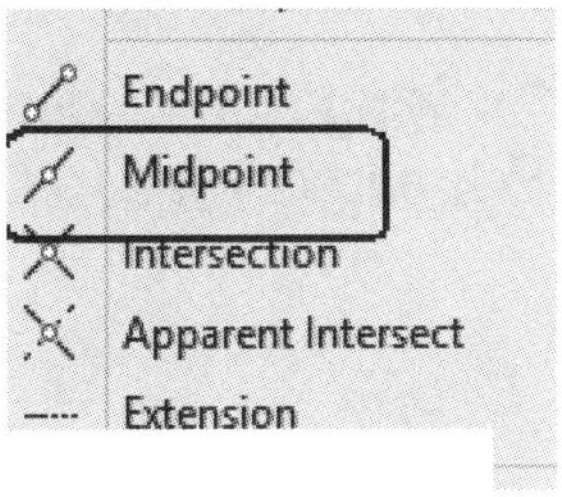

9. *Specify first point: _mid of*
   Move your pointer near one of the sides of the box until the Midpoint Object Snap Marker appears. Select the point with the LMB.
10. *Specify next point or [Undo]:*
    Hold your <Shift> key down and press the RMB to activate the Object Snap shortcut menu. Select Midpoint.

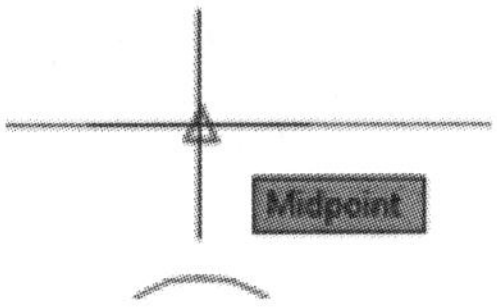

11. *Specify next point or [Undo]: _mid of*
    Move your pointer to the desired side of the box to compete the first line segment.
12. *Specify next point or [Close/Undo]:*
    Repeat the process using the midpoint object snap to finish the four line segments in the Box.
13. We will finish the exercise by creating the 4 line segments in the center circle. Invoke the Line command (l or line).

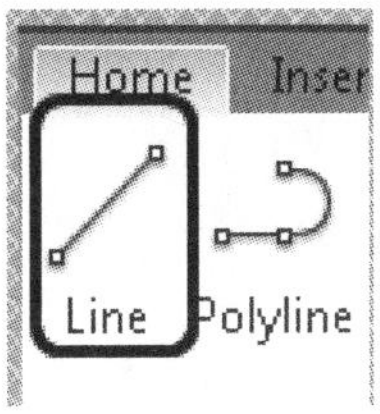

14. *Specify first point:*
    Hold the <Shift> key down and press the RMB to activate the Object Snap shortcut menu. Select the Quadrant object snap.

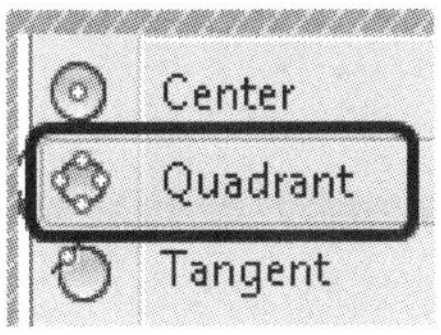

15. *Specify first point: _qua of*
    Move the pointer near the top of the center circle and press the LMB once; the Quadrant Object Snap Marker appears.
16. *Specify next point or [Undo]:* Repeat the process of using the <Shift> RMB to activate the shortcut menu. Remember to select the Quadrant Object Snap before selecting a point with the LMB.

You should see a cursor badge displaying the quadrant point prior to left picking.

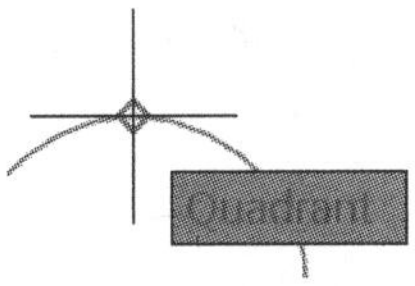

Tips & Tricks

- *AutoCAD will not display lines when using a Perpendicular or Tangent Object Snap until an end point is selected. This occurs because the first point is dependent on the second point selected when using Tangent and Perpendicular Object Snaps.*
- *Be aware of the cursor badges—they are there to help guide you and reinforce your selections to prevent you from making the wrong left pick.*

Command Exercise

Exercise 8-3 – Object Snap

Drawing Name: **osnap2.dwg**
Estimated Time to Completion: 5 Minutes

Scope

Using the single object snap option, draw the object on the left using the object snaps as indicated each time you select a point.

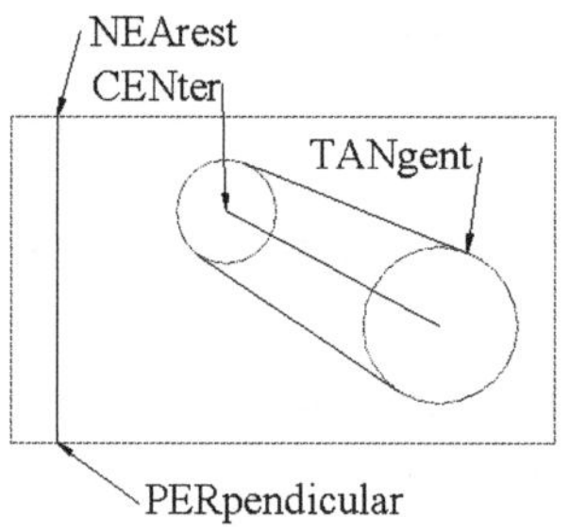

Object Snap Exercise

Solution

1. Start by creating the vertical line using the Perpendicular and Nearest Object Snaps. Invoke the Line command (l or line).

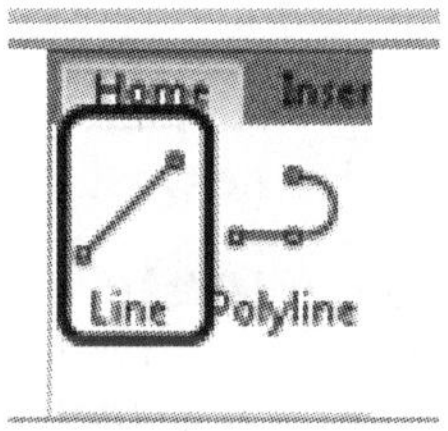

2. *Specify first point:*
   Hold the <Shift> key down and press the RMB to activate the Object Snap shortcut menu. Select the Nearest Object Snap.
3. *Specify first point: _per to*
   Move the pointer to the top of the box and press the LMB when the Nearest Object Snap Marker appears.
4. *Specify next point or [Undo]:*
   Hold the <Shift> key down and press the RMB to activate the Object Snap shortcut menu. Select the Perpendicular Object Snap.
5. *Specify next point or [Undo]: _nea*
   Move the pointer to the bottom of the box and select the desired point that will create the vertical line segment. Notice that the line is perpendicular to the bottom line segment and positioned at the second point you have selected.
6. Create the two lines that are tangent to the circles. Start by invoking the Line command (l or line).

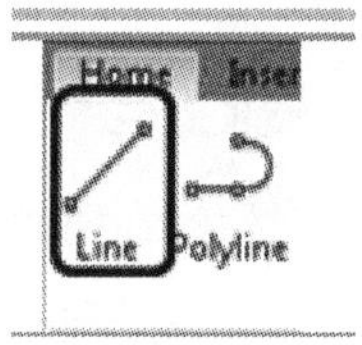

7. *Specify first point:*
   Hold your <Shift> key down and press the RMB to activate the Object Snap shortcut menu. Select Tangent.
8. *Specify first point: _tan to*
   Move the pointer to the general area for the start point of the line and press LMB when the Tangent Object Snap Marker appears.
9. *Specify next point or [Undo]:*
   Hold your <Shift> key down and press the RMB to activate the Object Snap shortcut menu.
10. *Specify first point: _tan to*
    Move the pointer to the general area for the end point of the line and press LMB when the Tangent Object Snap Marker appears. Repeat the process for the second line that is tangent to the 2 circles.
11. Finish the exercise by creating a line from the center point of the first circle to the center point of the second circle. Invoke the Line command (l or line).

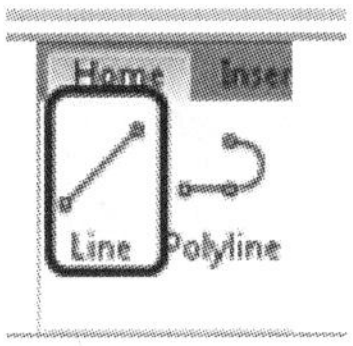

12. *Specify first point:*
    Hold your <Shift> key down and press the RMB to activate the Object Snap shortcut menu. Select Center.
13. *Specify first point: _cen to*
    Move the pointer to the center of the circle for the start point of the line and press LMB when the Center Object Snap Marker appears.
14. *Specify next point or [Undo]:*
    Hold your <Shift> key down and press the RMB to activate the Object Snap shortcut menu. Select Center.
15. *Specify next point or [Undo]: _cen of*
    Move the pointer to the center of the second circle for the end of the line. Press the LMB when the Center Object Snap Marker appears.

Command Exercise

Exercise 8-4 – Running Object Snap

Drawing Name: **osnap3.dwg**
Estimated Time to Completion: 5 Minutes

Scope

Draw the object on the left using Running Object Snaps. Double click on OSNAP, or select <TOOLS<DRAFTING SETTINGS. Activate the Endpoint, Midpoint and Quadrant running object snaps. Note that this exercise is similar to the previous single object snap exercise, except that Object Snap options will remain ON.

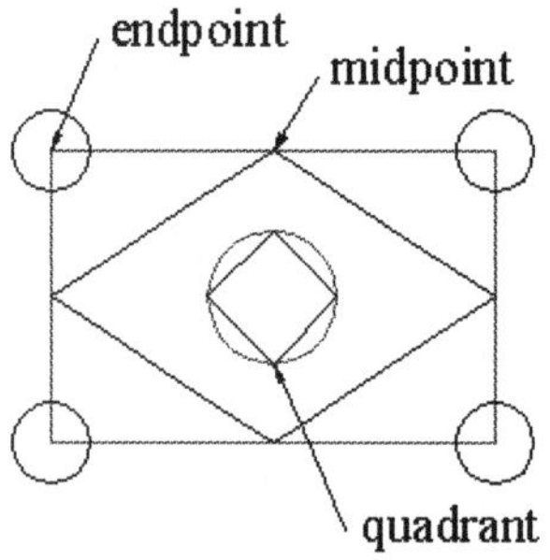

Running Object Snap Exercise

Solution

1. Start by making sure the Running Object Snaps are set. Use your LMB to toggle OSNAP on at the status bar. *When the OSNAP toggle is ON, it will show as blue.*

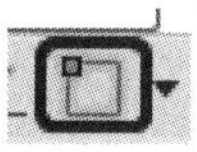

2. Set the correct running object snaps by left clicking on the down arrow next to the OSNAP icon.

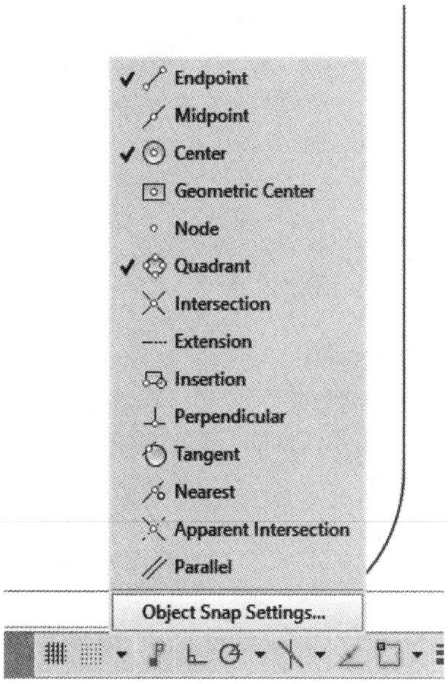

3. Enable Endpoint, Midpoint, and Quadrant by left clicking on those options. A check mark indicates the option is ENABLED.

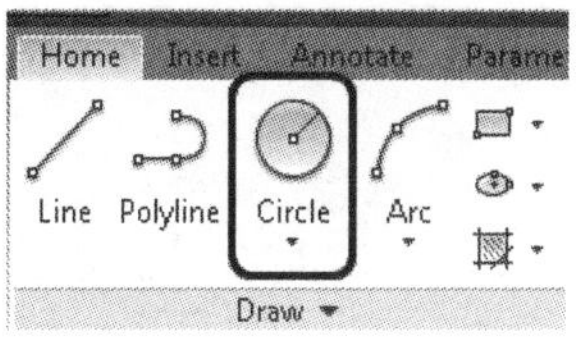

4. Press ‘OK’ to continue.
5. Invoke the circle command (c or circle).
6. *Specify center point for circle or [3P/2P/Ttr (tan tan radius)]:*
   Move your pointer to near one of the desired corners until the End Object Snap Marker appears. Pick the point with the LMB.
7. *Specify radius of circle or [Diameter]:*
   Use your mouse and LMB to finish the first circle.
8. Repeat the circle command by pressing <ENTER> or right-clicking in the drawing window and selecting ‘Repeat’.

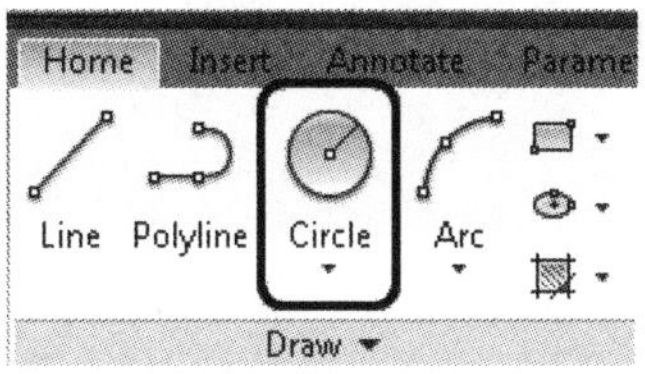

9. *Specify center point for circle or [3P/2P/Ttr (tan tan radius)]:*
   Move your pointer to the next corner until the desired End Object Snap Marker appears. Pick with your LMB.
10. *Specify radius of circle or [Diameter] <x.xx>:*
    Press <ENTER> to finish the second circle with the same radius. Repeat the process to complete the remaining circles.
11. Invoke the line command (l or line).

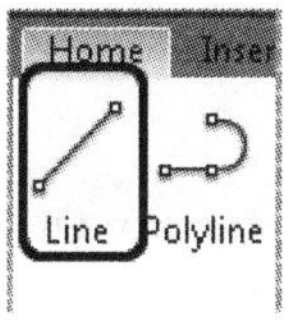

12. *Specify first point:*
    Move your pointer to one of the sides of the box. You will see the Midpoint Object Snap Marker appear. Pick with your left mouse button. This creates the start point of the line.
13. *Specify next point or [Undo]:*
    Move your pointer to another side to complete the first line segment. Remember to use your LMB when the desired object snap marker appears. Let the cursor *snap* into the Object Snap marker. Repeat the command to complete the four line segments.
14. Invoke the Line command (l or line) to finish the exercise by creating the diamond in the center circle.
15. *Specify first point:*
    Move your pointer near the top quadrant of the center circle. Press the LMB to select the start point of the line segment.
16. *Specify next point or [Undo]:*
    Repeat the process by moving the pointer near the desired quadrant and pressing the LMB when the Quadrant Object Snap appears.

Tips Tricks

- Before you start drafting, set running object snaps. Most commonly used object snaps are Endpoint, Midpoint, Intersection and Center. Use your <Tab> key to cycle through the different object snaps that overlap each other (i.e., Quadrant and Center or multiple object snap options that are close together).
- Remember to use the regular Intersection object snap to find the Intersection or Extended Intersection of two objects. Apparent Intersection is for 3D. Choosing an object snap option from the toolbar, shortcut menu, or by typing the alias will override Running Object Snap.

Command Exercise

Exercise 8-5 – Extended Intersection Object Snap

Drawing Name: **osnap4.dwg**
Estimated Time to Completion: 5 Minutes

Scope

Draw a circle with the Center at the projected intersection of the two lines as indicated in the figure below. Notice how the intersection option works in this exercise.

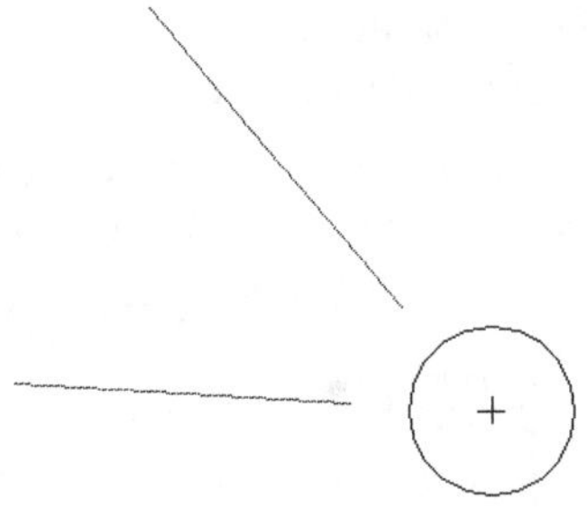

Extended Intersection Object Snap Exercise

Solution

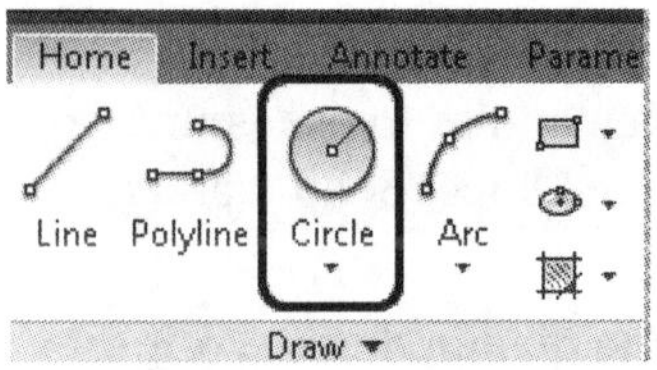

1. Invoke the circle command (c or circle).

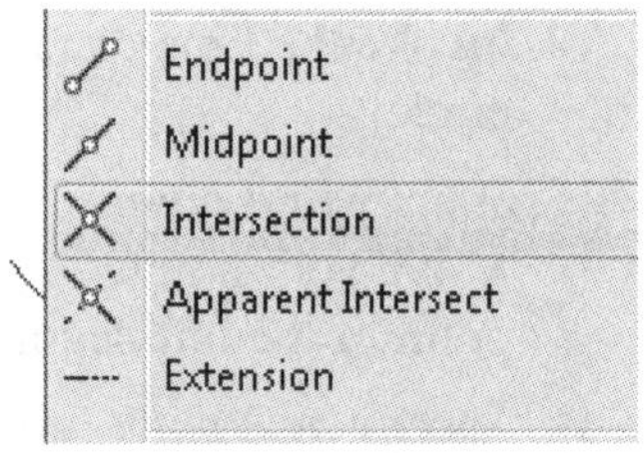

2. *Specify center point for circle or [3P/2P/Ttr (tan tan radius)]:*
   Hold the <Shift> key down and press the RMB to activate the Object Snap shortcut menu. Select Intersection.
3. *Specify center point for circle or [3P/2P/Ttr (tan tan radius)]: _int of*
   Move the pointer to the lower end of the top line and press the LMB. Notice the Object Snap tool tip will say "Extended Intersection." Click the LMB once.
4. *Specify center point for circle or [3P/2P/Ttr (tan tan radius)]: _int of and*
   Move the pointer near the end of the second line. Notice where the Intersection Object Snap appears. Press the LMB to select the center of the circle.
5. *Specify radius of circle or [Diameter]:*
   Type **9/16"** and **<ENTER>.**

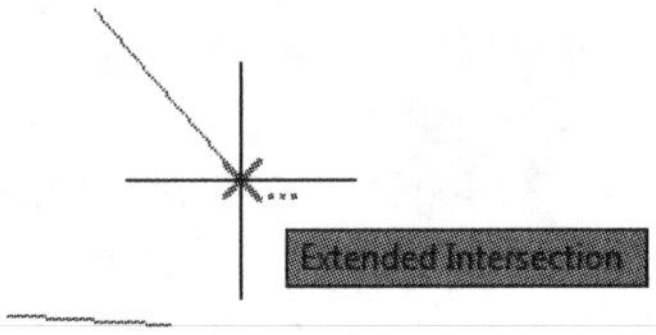

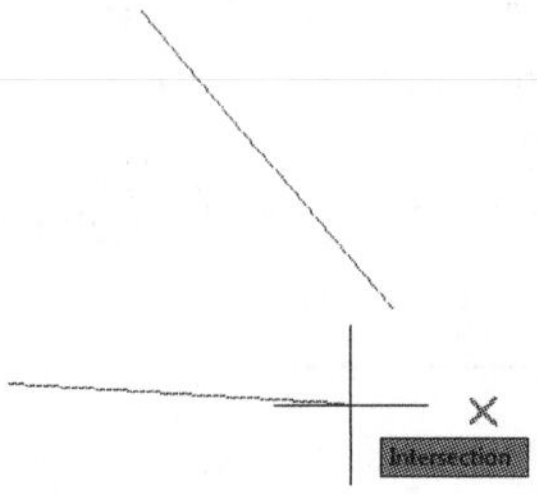

Command Exercise

Exercise 8-6 – Object Tracking

Drawing Name: **new drawing**
Estimated Time to Completion: 20 Minutes

Scope

Enable Object Snaps and Object Tracking in order to draw the figure. Enable ORTHO ON.

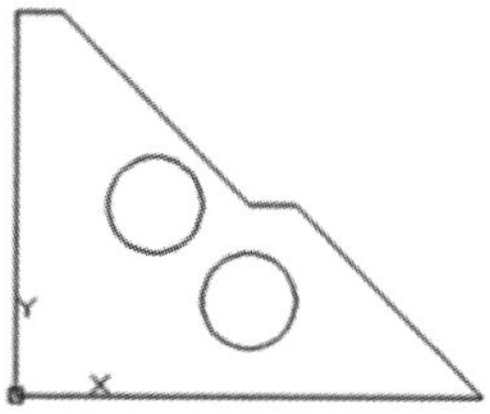

Object Tracking

Solution

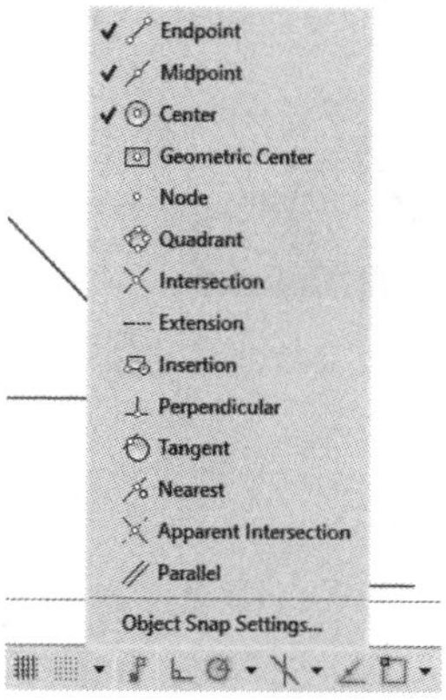

1. Start a new drawing using the *acad.dwt* template.
2. Left click on the down arrow next to the OSNAP tool on the status bar.
3. LMB on Endpoint, Midpoint, and Center to enable those OSNAPs.
4. Turn ORTHO **ON.**

You can press F8 to enable ORTHO.

The icon will display as blue when it is enabled.

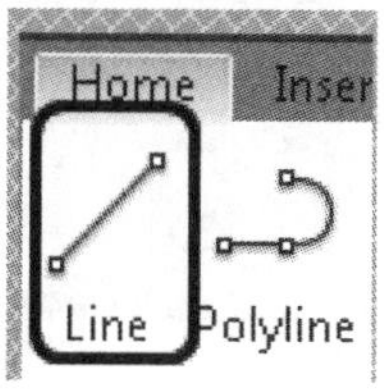

5. Start the **Line** command.
6. Specify the first point as **0,8**.
7. Move the cursor down and enter **8**.

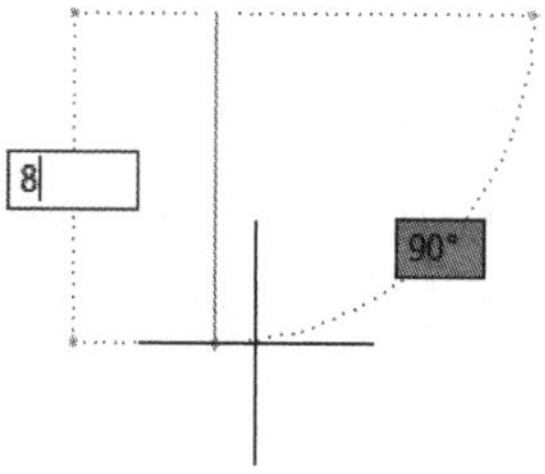

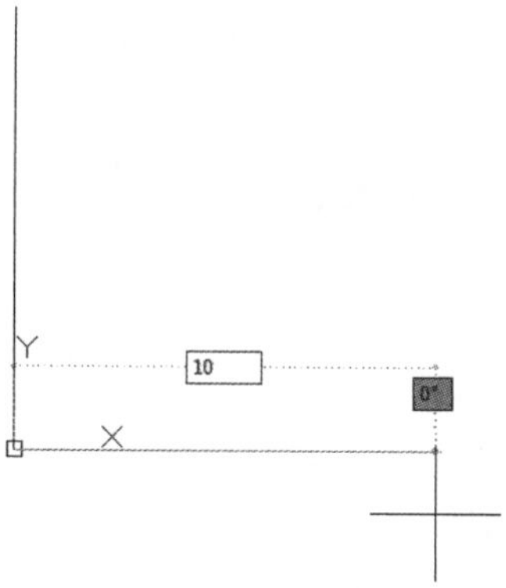

8. *Specify next point or [Undo]:*
   Move the cursor towards the right until a temporary polar tracking path of 0 degrees displays as shown in the next figure. Type **10** and press <ENTER> while this path is showing.

   Disable the ORTHO toggle.

   To disable, press F8 or left click on the ORTHO icon.

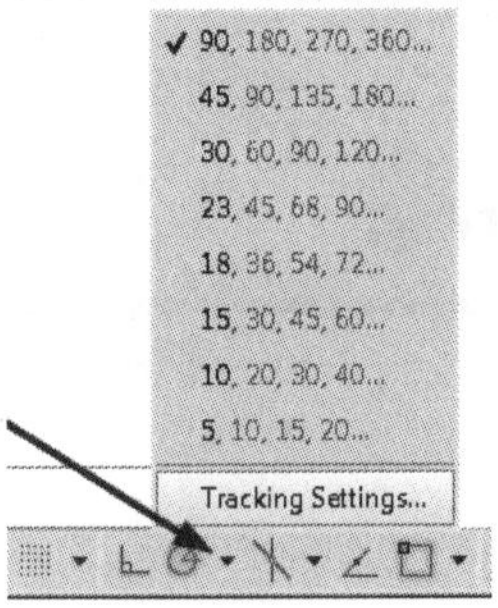

9. Left click on the down arrow next to the Polar Tracking icon.

10. Select **Tracking Settings....**

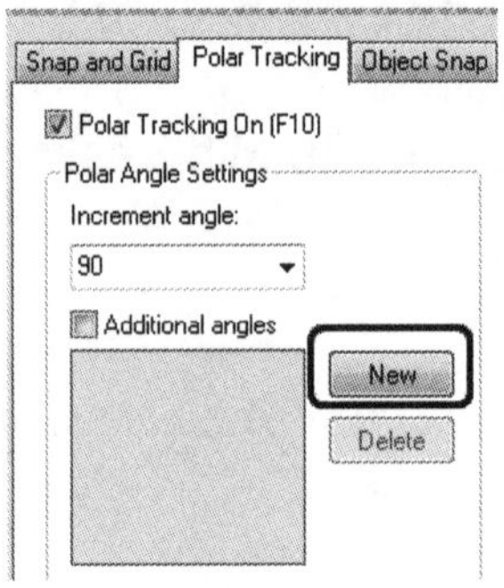

11. Press **New** to add an additional angle.

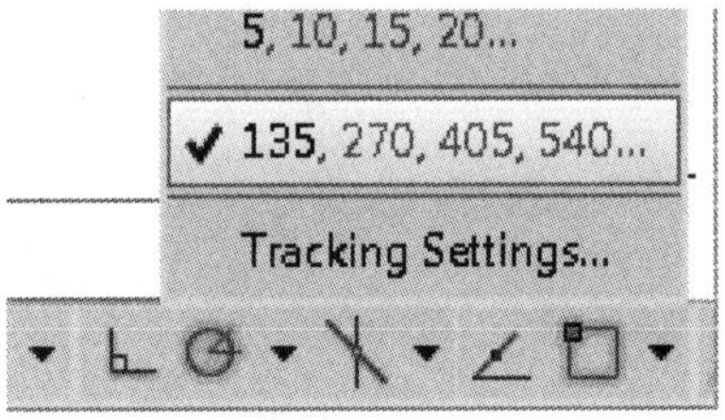

12. Type **135.**

13. Press **OK** to close the dialog box.

14. Enable the 135 setting on the Polar Tracking list.

This became available once you added it as a new setting.

15. Verify that Polar Tracking , Object Snap Tracking, and Object Snap are all enabled.

They should be displayed in blue.

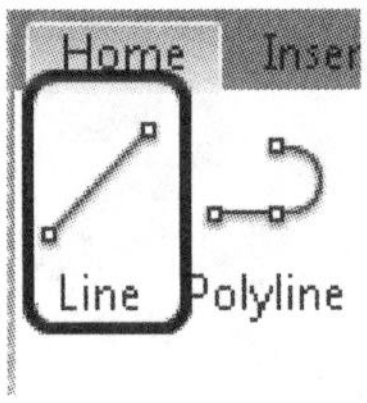

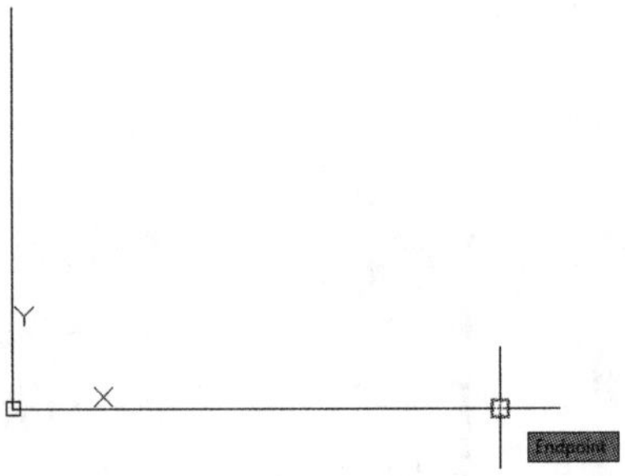

16. Start the Line command.

17. Start the line at the endpoint of the horizontal line.

If you press ENTER, the line should pick up where you left off.

18. *Specify next point or [Close/Undo]:* Move the cursor near the midpoint of the vertical line until it is acquired (a + sign shows up at the midpoint and a tooltip also appears). Then move the cursor to the right to display the tracking path through the midpoint until you also have a polar tracking path of 135 degrees. Then click to select that point.

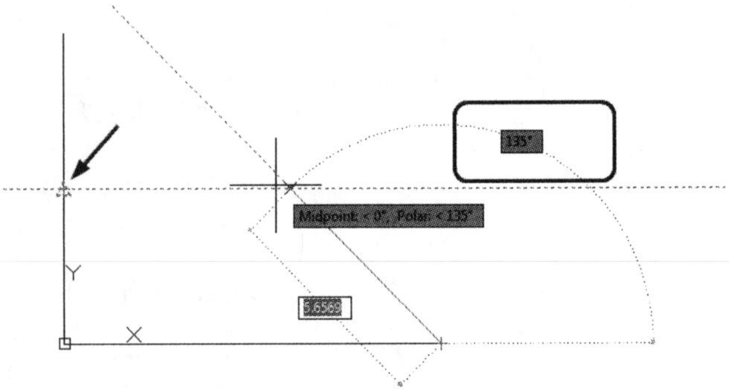

19. Switch the POLAR TRACKING settings to use the **90,180,270,360** option.

*To do this, just left click on the down arrow next to the Polar Tracking icon and then left click on the **90,180,270,360** option.*

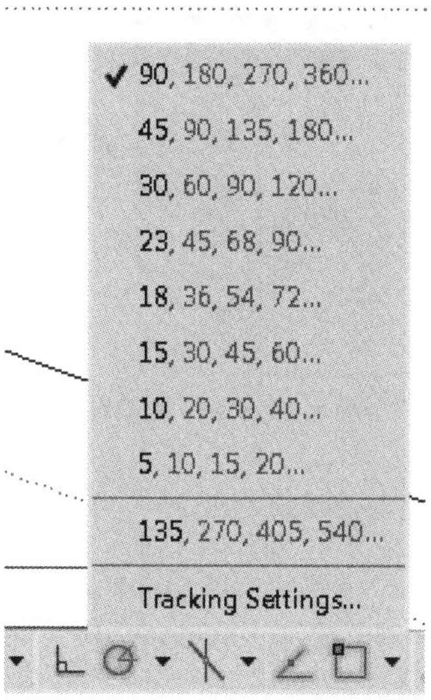

20. *Specify next point or [Close/Undo]:*
Move the cursor near the midpoint of the horizontal line until it is acquired (a + sign shows up at the midpoint and a tooltip also appears). Then move the cursor upward to display the tracking path through the midpoint until you also have a polar tracking path of 180 degrees as shown in the next figure. Then click to select that point.

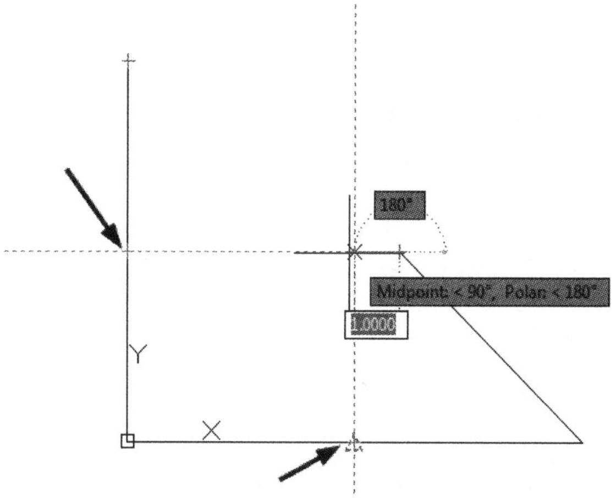

21. *Specify next point or [Close/Undo]:*
Move the cursor near the upper endpoint of the vertical line until it is acquired (a + sign shows up at the endpoint and a tooltip also appears). Then move the cursor to the right to display the tracking path through the endpoint until you also have a polar tracking path of 135 degrees. Then click to select that point.

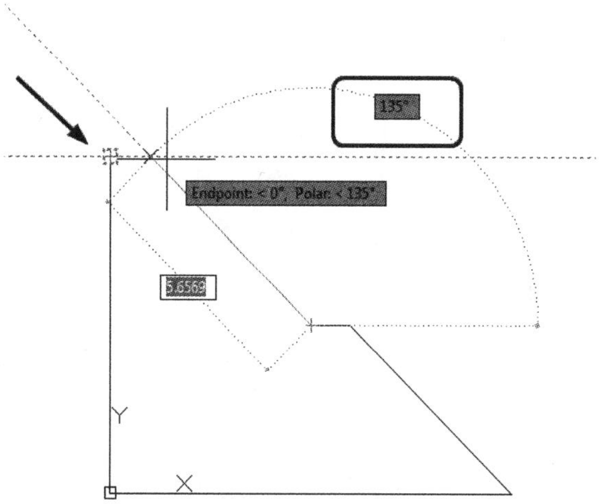

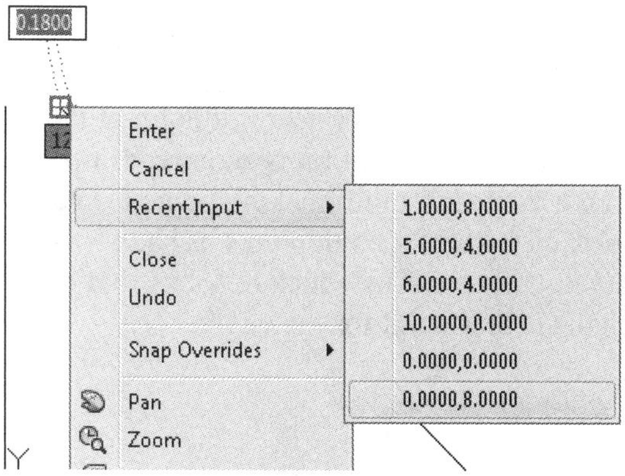

22. Right click and select **Recent Input**.

23. Select **0,8** as the closing point.

24. Press <ENTER> to exit the LINE command.

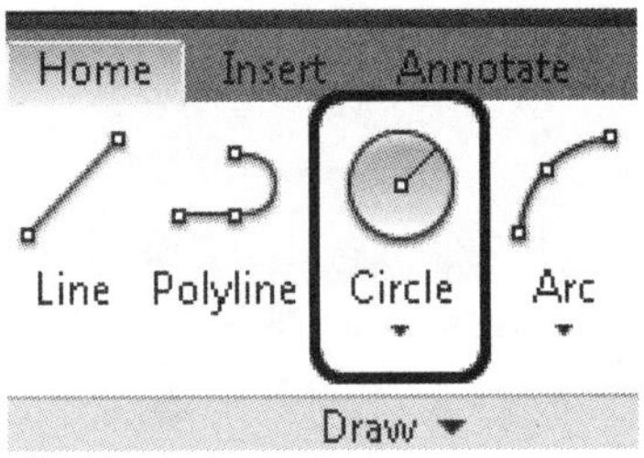

25. Invoke the **Circle** command (c or circle).

26. *Specify center point for circle or [3P/2P/Ttr (tan tan radius)]:*
    Move the cursor near midpoint of the vertical line until it is acquired (a + sign shows up at the midpoint and a tooltip also appears). Then move the cursor near midpoint of the upper inclined line until it is acquired. Finally, move downward until tracking paths display through both of the midpoints as shown in the next figure. Then click to select that point.

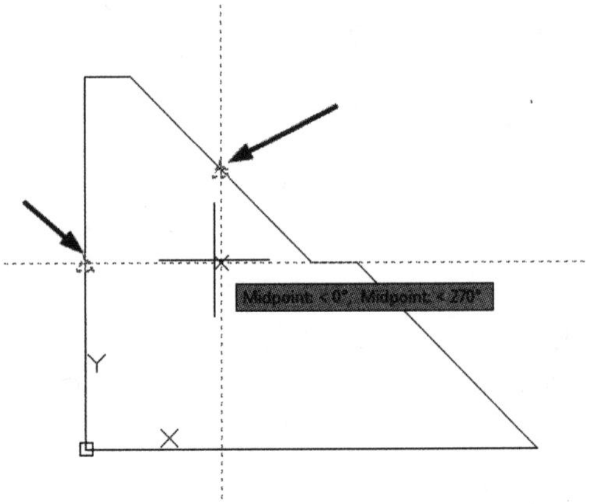

27. *Specify radius of circle or [Diameter] <x.xx>:*
    Type **1.0** and press <ENTER>.

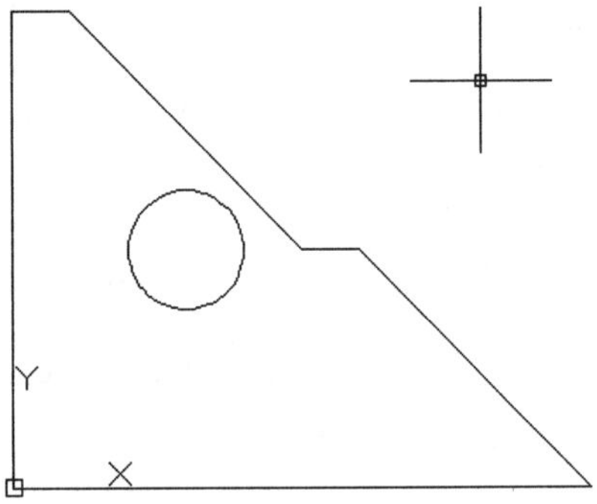

28. Invoke the **Circle** command (c for circle).

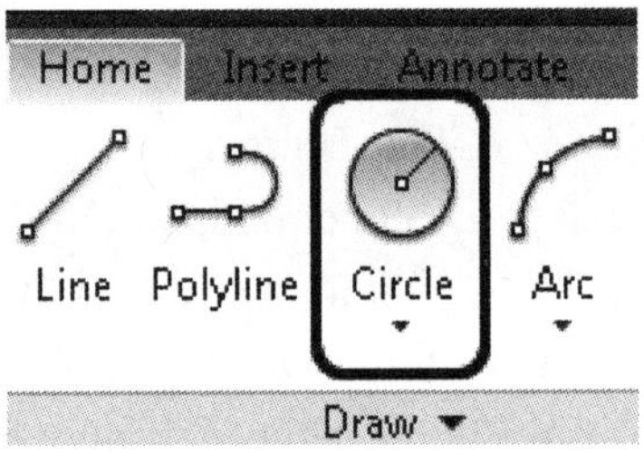

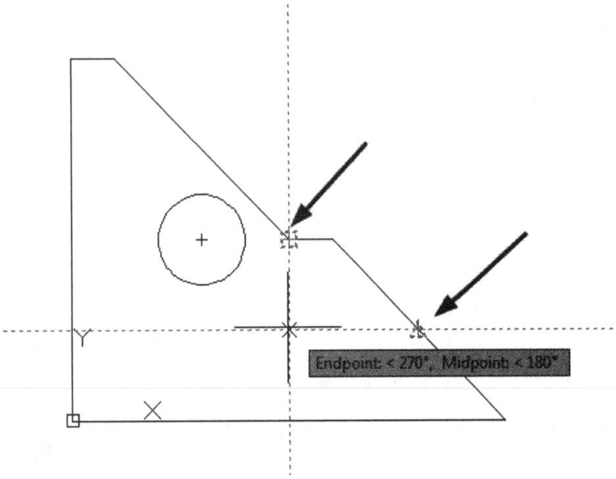

29. *Specify center point for circle or [3P/2P/Ttr (tan tan radius)]:*
    Move the cursor near endpoint of the upper horizontal line until it is acquired (a + sign shows up at the midpoint and a tooltip also appears).

    Then move the cursor near midpoint of the lower angled line until it is acquired. Finally, move to the left until tracking paths display through both of the midpoints as shown in the next figure. Then click to select that point as the center point for the circle.

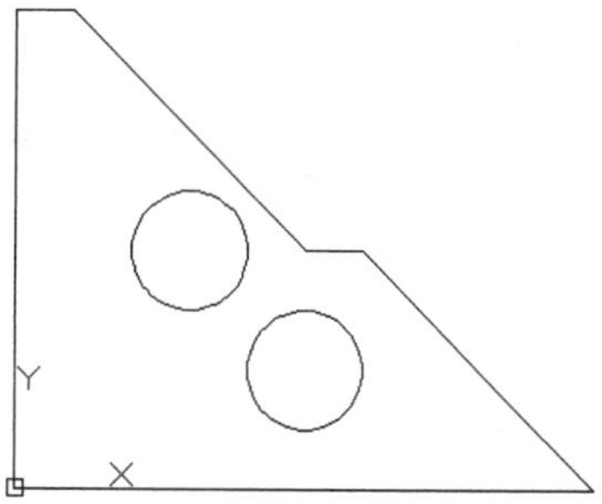

30. *Specify radius of circle or [Diameter] <x.xx>:*
    Type **1.0** and press <ENTER>.

Extra: Draw a line with a random angle, then draw another line that is parallel to it. Use the Parallel Object Snap option.

Command Exercise

Exercise 8-7 – Geometric Center

Drawing Name: **osnap5**
Estimated Time to Completion: 5 Minutes

Scope

Use the Geometric Center Osnap to place a triangle in the center of a octahedron.

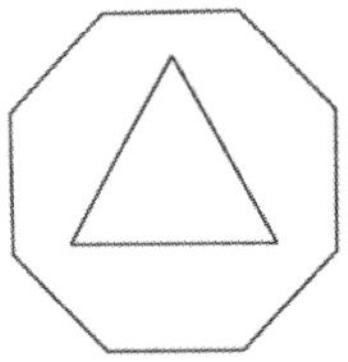

Geometric Center

Solution

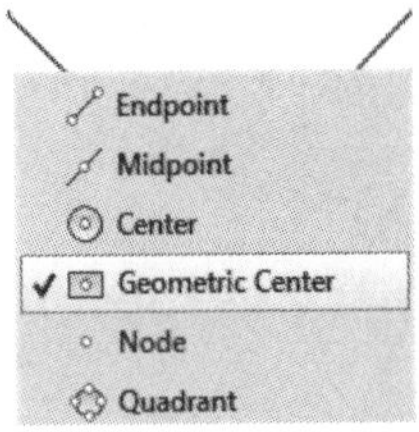

1. Left click on the down arrow next to the OSNAP tool on the status bar.
2. LMB on Geometric Center to enable.

3. Select the Move tool.
4. Select the triangle on the right.
5. Press ENTER.

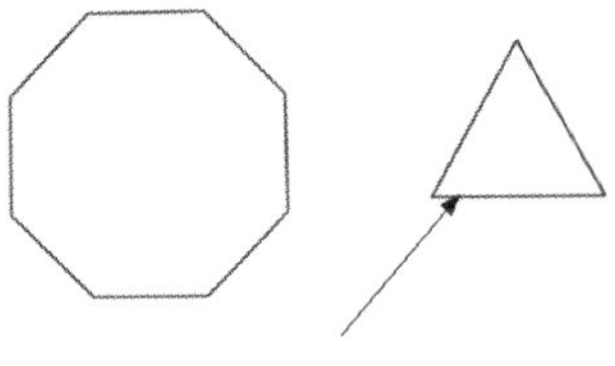

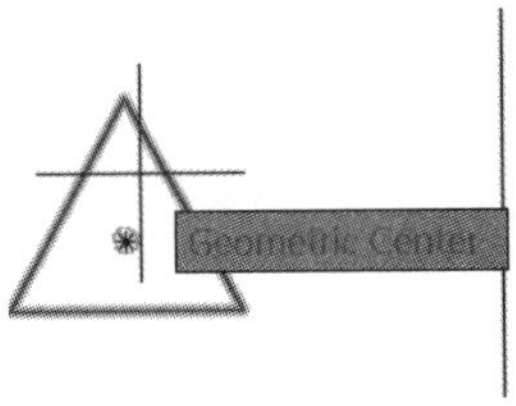

6. Hover the cursor over the triangle until the Geometric Center is shown. Left click to select.

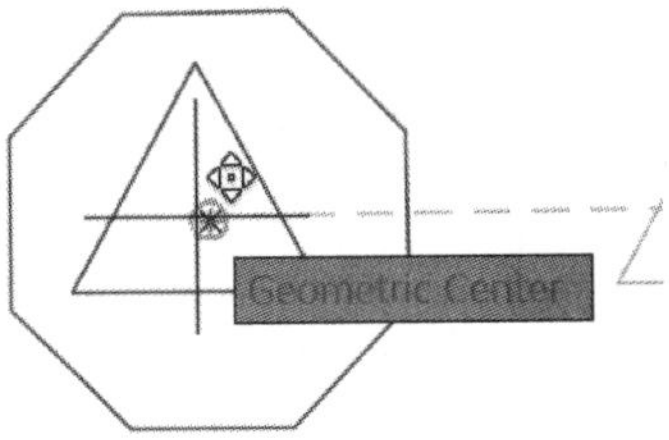

7. Move the cursor over the polygon. Left click when the Geometric Center is displayed.

Creating Orthographic Views

You can use the drafting settings to create the views required for a 2D drawing layout.

FIRST-ANGLE PROJECTION

The U.S. and Canada uses Third-Angle Projection.

The rest of the world uses first-angle projection.

All countries start with a FRONT VIEW.

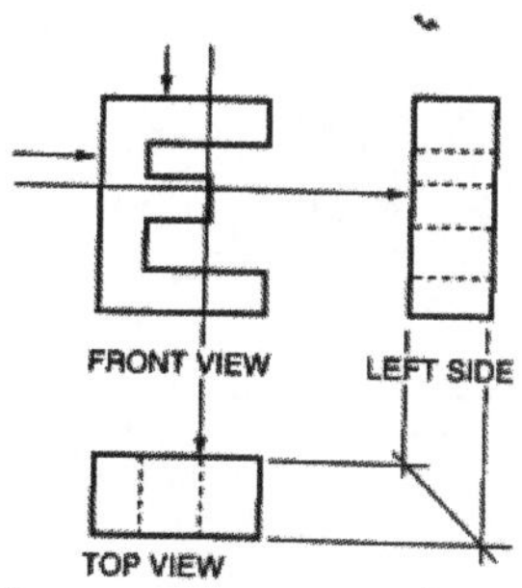

First-angle projection

You can view and download PowerPoints that I use in my lectures at:

laney.edu/wp/emoss

THIRD- ANGLE PROJECTION

THIS IS THE LAYOUT USED IN THE UNITED STATES & CANADA.

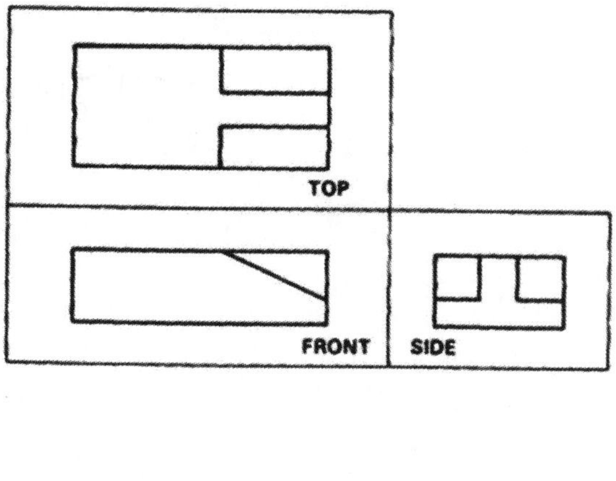

ORTHO LAYOUT WORKSHEET

SELECT THE CORRECT LAYOUT FOR THE THREE ISOMETRIC OBJECTS

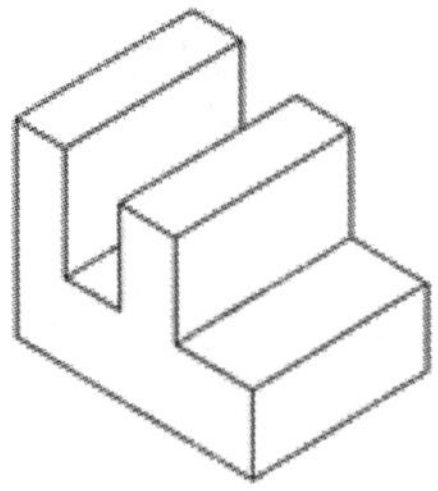

PROBLEM 1:

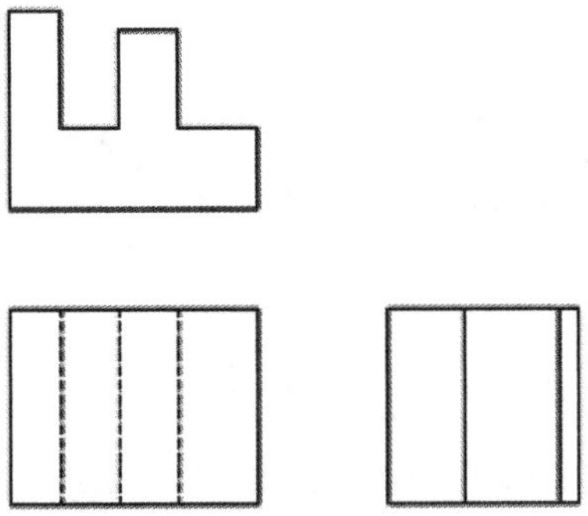

LAYOUT 1-A

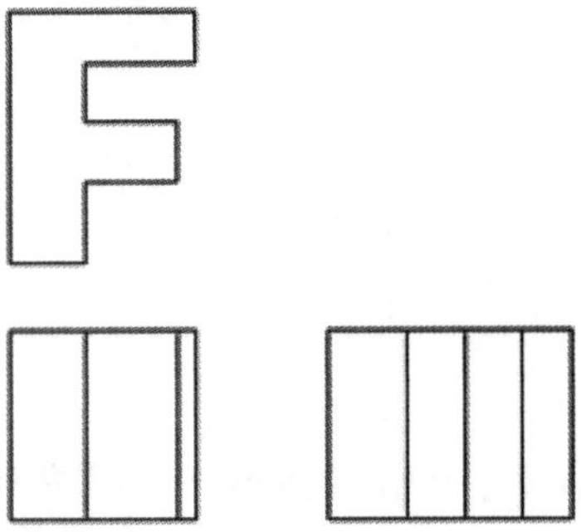

LAYOUT 1-B

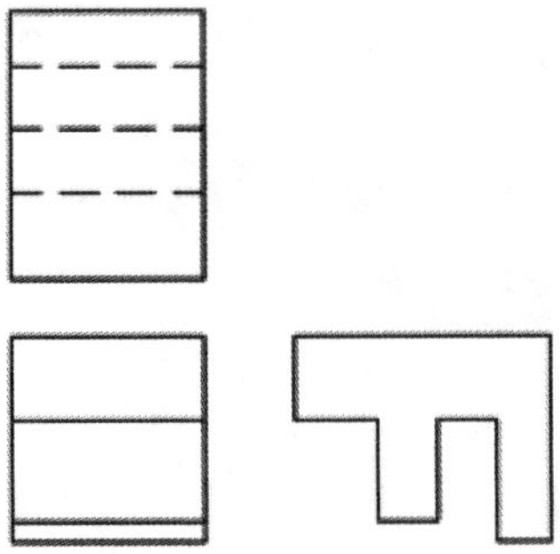

LAYOUT 1-C

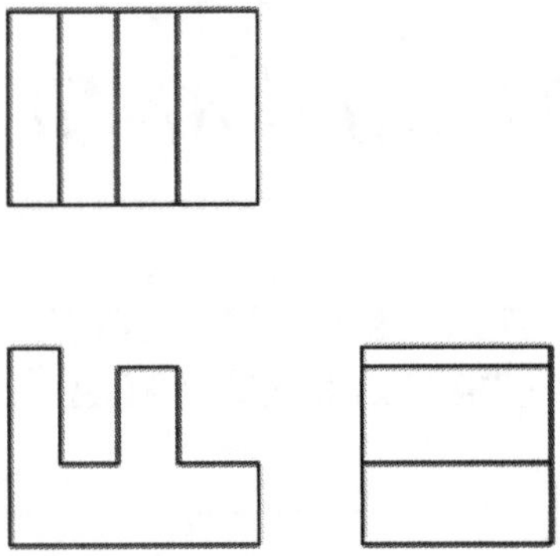

LAYOUT 1-D

SELECT THE CORRECT LAYOUT

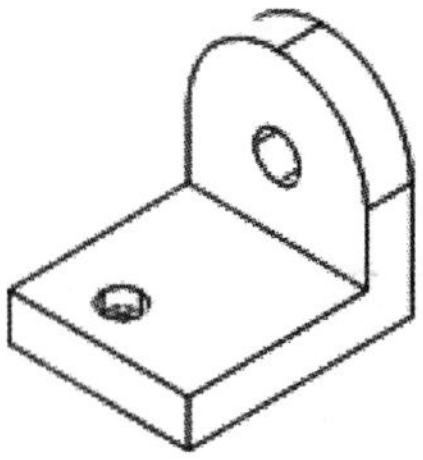

PROBLEM 2:

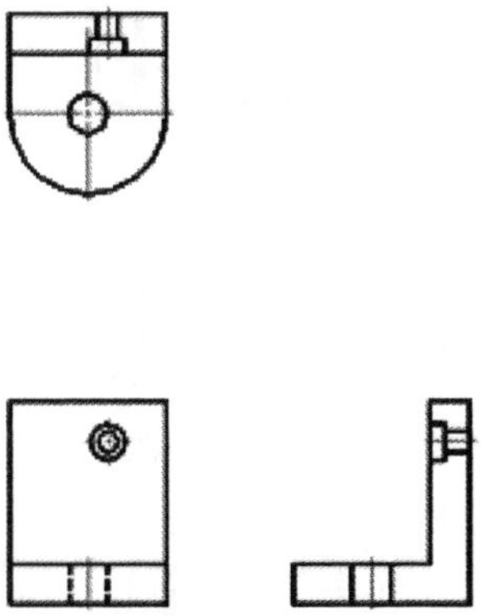

LAYOUT 2-A

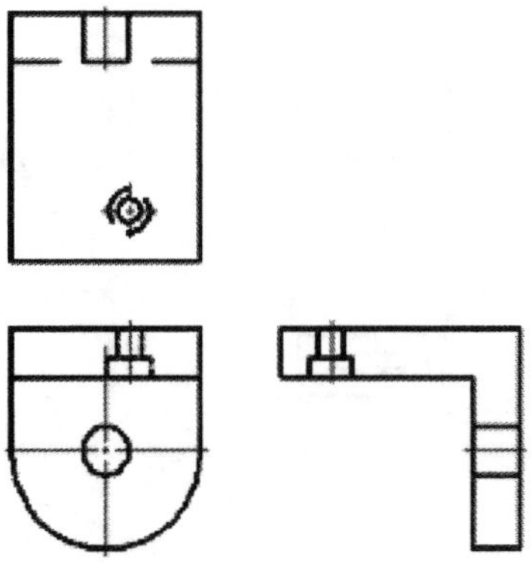

LAYOUT 2-B

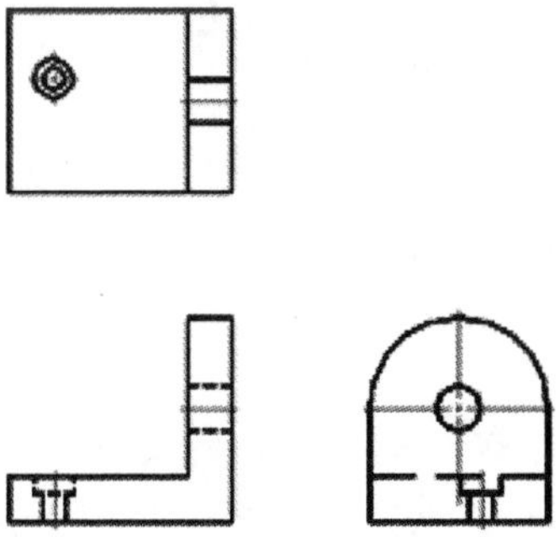

LAYOUT 2-C

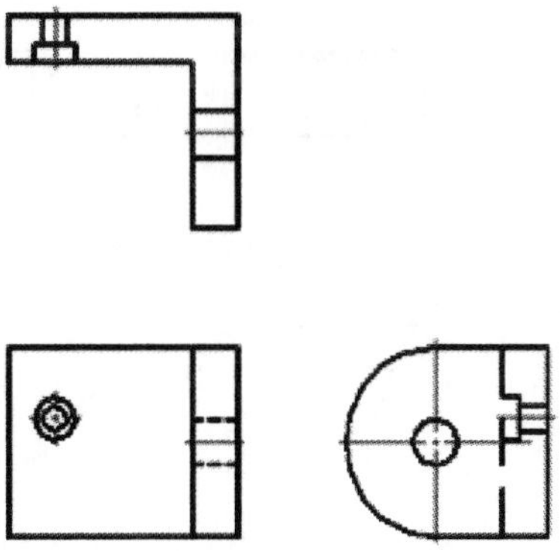

LAYOUT 2-D

SELECT THE CORRECT LAYOUT

PROBLEM 3

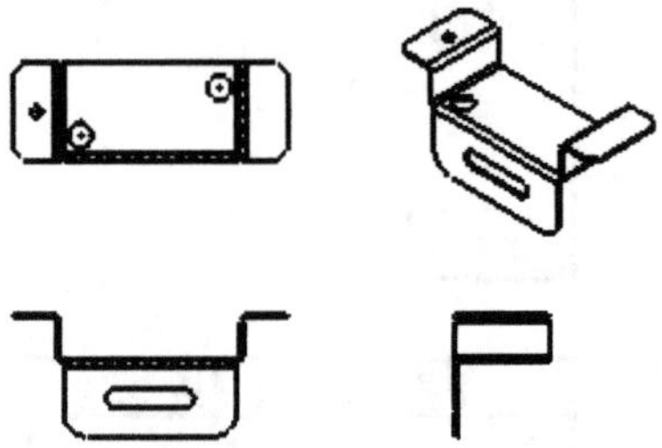

LAYOUT 3A

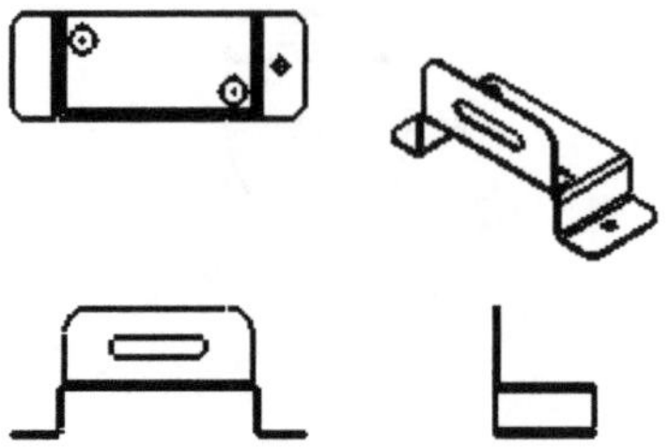

LAYOUT 3B

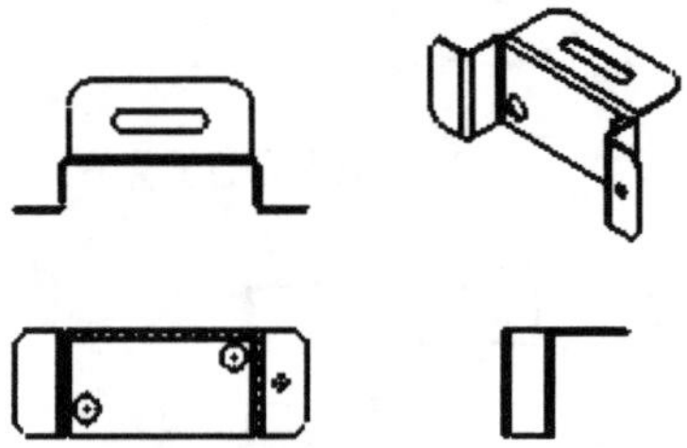

LAYOUT 3C

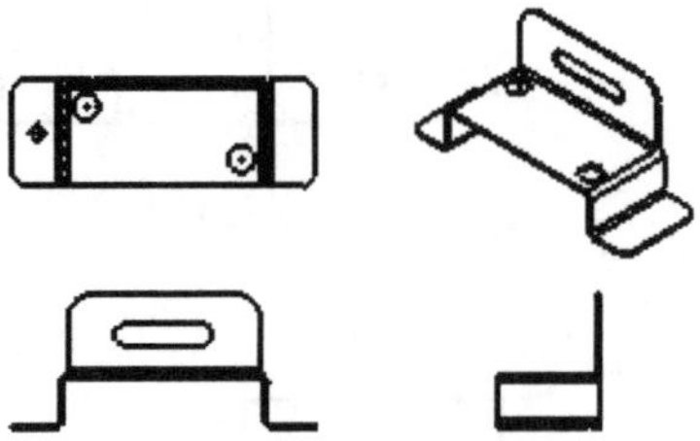

LAYOUT 3D

- Remember to select the Object Snap each time before picking a point.
- When specifying the center of a circle, be sure to pick the circumference.
- The "Apparent Intersection" Object Snap is for 3D modeling.
- Selecting two object snaps in a row, such as Endpoint and Midpoint, will cancel both Object Snap selections (it doesn't understand the "endpoint of the midpoint").
- If the wrong Object Snap option is mistakenly selected, pick in a blank area of the Drawing Window, then select the proper Object Snap option again.
- Single object snaps can be used in combination with the running OSNAP settings.

Section Exercise

Exercise 8-8 – Drawing Layout

Drawing Name: **new drawing**
Estimated Time to Completion: 20 Minutes

Scope

The goal of this exercise is to create an orthographic layout without using any construction lines. Use OTRACK, OSNAP, and OFFSET. If you have to draw and erase any lines, you have not done the exercise properly.

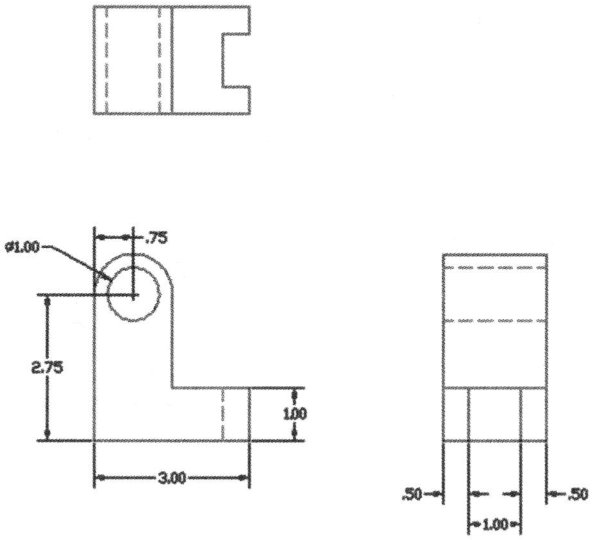

Orthographic Layout

Solution

1. Set up layers for object, hidden, center, and dimensions.

S.	Name	O.	F...	L...	Color	Linetype
✔	0				white	Continuous
	CENTER				yellow	CENTER
	DIMENSIONS				white	Continuous
	HIDDEN				cyan	HIDDEN
	OBJECT				green	Continuous

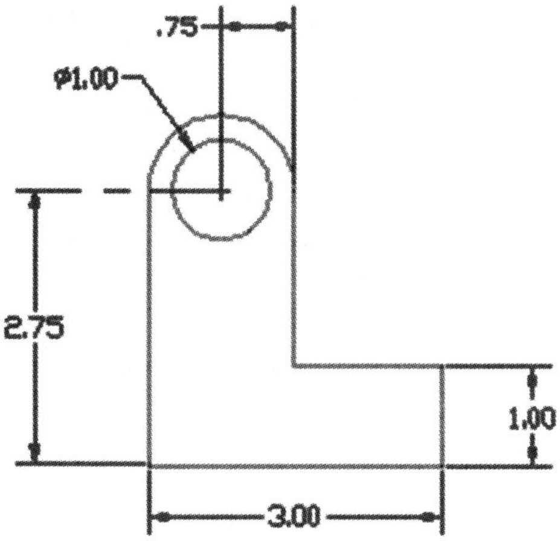

2. Draw the front view of this object.
3. Add dimensions.
4. Draw the top and right side views using object tracking and osnaps.

Review Questions

1. Identify the following object snap options:

   a. 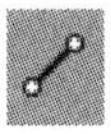

   b. 

   c. 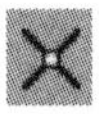

   d. 

   e. 

   f. 

   g. 

   h. 

   i. 

2. How can you access an object snap option for a single selection (not OSNAP)?

3. What control in the Status Bar turns the Object Snap Settings ON or OFF?

4. What does the DSETTINGS command do?
   - ❑ Invokes the Object Snap Pop up Menu
   - ❑ Allows you to adjust the running object snap settings
   - ❑ Toggles the OSNAP command on and off
   - ❑ Nothing

5. How would you select the exact center of a circle? How would you select the exact center of a 6 or 4 or 3 sided polygon? Try it.

Review Answers

1. Identify the following object snap options:
   - *a. Endpoint*
   - *b. Perpendicular*
   - *c. Intersection*
   - *d. Center*
   - *e. Nearest*
   - *f. Midpoint*
   - *g. Tangent*
   - *h. Quadrant*
   - *i. Object Snap Settings*

2. How can you access an object snap option for a single selection (not OSNAP)?

   Press the <Shift> key and RMB to access the Object Snap Pop up dialog box.

3. What control in the Status Bar turns the Object Snap Settings ON or OFF?

   OSNAP

4. What does the DSETTINGS command do?

   Invokes the Object Snap Pop up Menu
   Allows you to adjust the running object snap settings *(You can toggle OSNAP on and off)*
   Toggles the OSNAP command on and off
   Nothing

5. How would you select the exact center of a circle? How would you select the exact center of a 6, 4 or 3 sided polygon? Try it.

   Use the Geometric Center Osnap to select the center of a polygon. Use the Center Osnap to select the center of a circle.

Notes:

Lesson 9.0 – Dimensions

Estimated Class Time: 2 Hours

Objectives

Dimensioning a drawing is easy. If placed correctly, the dimensions will be as accurate as the drawing. Students will learn how to create Dimension Styles to suit the drawing specifications. Dimensions can be created in English/Standard or Metric units, or both. Edit selected dimensions or make changes to the Dimension Style for a global update.

- **Dimensions**
  Place dimensions using different dimension tools.
- **Ordinate Dimensions**
- **Dimension Space**
- **Dimension Break**
- **Dimension Style**
  Control the appearance of dimensions, including text color and size, arrowheads, and spacing.
- **Edit Dimension Location**
  Use grips to edit the placement of dimensions.
- **Edit Dimension Text**
- **Edit Dimension Properties**
  Edit dimensions globally by modifying the dimension styles or individually with the Properties command.
- **Dimensional Constraints**
- **Center Mark and Center lines**

  AutoCAD 2017 introduces new and improved functionality for center marks and center lines which allow users to reassociate and reset these annotations

Dimensions

If you are a mechanical drafter, you will be expected to use ANSI standards when applying dimensions. If you are an architectural drafter, you will be expected to apply AIA standards.

Architects will often create many different styles to manage the requirements of different counties and cities. Most mechanical drafters will create one style for standard (inch) dimensioning and one style for metric. Dimensioning styles for mechanical drawings are dictated by the American Society of Mechanical Engineers (ASME). A copy of the standards can be purchased through the ASME website at www.asme.org. The current dimensioning standards are ASME Y14.5M-2009. Most mechanical design jobs require drafters to be familiar with ANSI dimensioning standards.

Some simple rules to keep in mind when applying ANSI standards:

- Center the dimension. You can use GRIPS or DIMTEDIT to shift the dimension text position to get it centered.
- Always place your dimensions between views.
- Always place overall dimensions (length, height, and width).
- Place the shortest dimensions closest to the object.
- Never place dimensions on top or inside of the object.
- Leaders are placed at a 30, 45, or 60 degree angle.
- When dimensioning holes, use a diameter dimension NOT a radius.
- Never dimension to hidden or center lines.
- Do not double dimension (that is apply a dimension that is already shown in a different view or the same view).
- When using inches, suppress leading zeros.

Command Overview

Learn how to dimension a drawing using the dimension variables. Dimensions will be as accurate as the drawing, provided the objects were chosen correctly. To open the Dimension Toolbar, place the cursor over any icon and press the right button on the mouse, then place a checkmark before "Dimension." This section will cover individual dimension commands, how to select the object to dimension and pick the dimension location. The easiest way to adjust the dimension locations after they have been placed is to use the Grips. Some Dimension commands, such as Ordinate Dimensions and Tolerance, will not be covered in this Tutorial. Dimension Style and Edit Dimension commands and options will be covered in the next section.

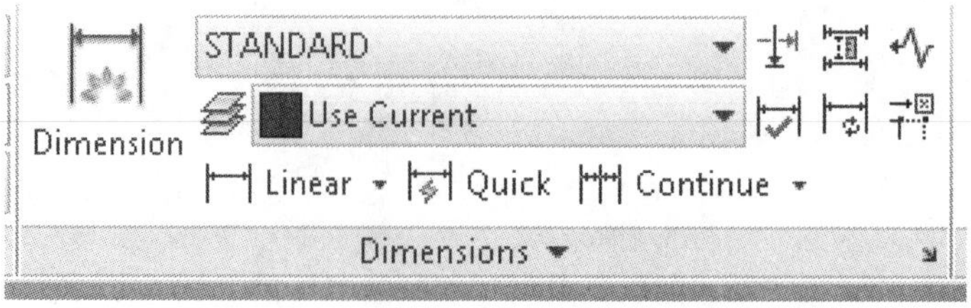

Dimension Command	**Button**	***Overview***
Linear Dimension		This option is for horizontal or vertical dimensions. Use object snap to select the first and second extension line origin or press return to select the object. Drag the cursor and pick to place the dimension.
Aligned Dimension		This option will align a dimension with an angled line. Use object snap to select the first and second extension line origin or press return to select the object. Drag the cursor and pick to place the dimension.
Arc Length		Dimension the length of an arc.
Ordinate Dimension		Places ordinate dimensions. Right click to select the Origin option to set the origin for the Ordinate Dimension.
Radius		Select a circle or arc for the Radius Dimension. Drag the cursor and pick to place the dimension.
Jogged		Places a jogged leader on a circle or arc.
Diameter Dimension		Select a circle or arc for the diameter dimension. Drag the cursor and pick to place the dimension.
Angular Dimension		This option will place an angular dimension between selected lines. Select two angular lines and pick the dimension location.
Quick Dimension		Quick Dimension (QDIM) allows the user to select an object that contains multiple lines and place multiple dimensions with the Continuous, Staggered, Baseline, Ordinate, Radius, Diameter, datum, Point, and Edit options.
Baseline Dimension		This option builds a baseline dimension from the first extension line of a linear, aligned or angular dimension. Begin with the linear, aligned or angular dimension first, using object snaps to select the origin points. Next invoke Baseline Dimension and select the next extension line origin. Continue then press <ENTER> to exit the command.
Continued Dimension		This option creates continuous dimensions from the second extension line of a linear, aligned or angular dimension. Begin with the linear, aligned or angular dimension first, using object snaps to select the origin points. Next invoke the Continued Dimension and select the next extension line origin. Continue then press <ENTER> to exit the command.
Dimension Space		Dimension Space allows you to quickly adjust the spacing between linear dimensions so that they do not overlap.
Dimension Break		This creates a gap in the extension line of a dimension. Select the dimension, then select the object (a line or point) where you wish to place the gap.
Tolerance		Places a GD&T symbol.
Center Mark		Select a circle or arc to place a center mark in the drawing. Center mark styles can be modified in the Dimension Style dialog box.
Inspection		Select existing dimensions to be used for inspection purposes.
Jogged Linear		Add a jog to an existing dimension so that it can be foreshortened as needed.
Dimension Edit		Shifts dimension text.
Dimension Text Edit		Edit the value of dimension text
Dimension Update		Update the dimension style applied to a dimension
Dimension Style drop-down		Use this drop-down box to select a dimension style on the fly.
Dimension Style		Launches the Dimension Style Manager dialog.

General Procedures

For Linear or Aligned dimensions:

1. Select the desired dimension command.
2. Use the appropriate Object Snaps to select the dimension line origin points. Drag the cursor and pick the dimension location.

Note: To dimension a single line segment, press <ENTER>, then select the line.

For Radius, Diameter, or Center Mark dimensions:

1. Select the desired dimension command.
2. Pick the Circle, Arc, or Line to dimension. Drag the cursor and pick the dimension location.

Note: Center Mark will simply be placed at the center.

For Baseline or Continued Dimensions:

1. Begin by placing a Linear, Aligned or Angular Dimension, using Object Snaps to select the origin points.
2. Invoke the Baseline or Continued Dimension. Using Object Snaps, pick the next dimension line origins. When finished, press <ENTER> to Exit the command.

For Quick Dimensions (QDIM):

1. Invoke the Quick Dimension command.
2. Window the objects to be dimensioned, or pick them individually, and press <ENTER>.
3. Specify the dimension line position by dragging in the desired direction. The default dimension option will appear in parentheses.
4. Pick to place the dimension, or type the capitalized letter of the desired option and <ENTER>. Then pick (LMB) to place the dimension.

Tips & Tricks

- Use Object Snaps or set the OSNAP settings when selecting dimension line origin points.
- Do not explode dimensions. Associativity to the object will be lost and the dimension will be broken into as many as 10 separate objects.
- Adjust dimension locations after they are placed using grips.
- Begin the Baseline and Continued dimensions by placing a Linear, Aligned or Angular dimension first.
- Leader text will have "no wrap" unless a width is specified.

Command Exercise

Exercise 9-1 – Linear and Aligned Dimensions

Drawing Name: **dim1.dwg**
Estimated Time to Completion: 5 Minutes

Scope

Dimension the object as indicated using Linear and Aligned Dimensions

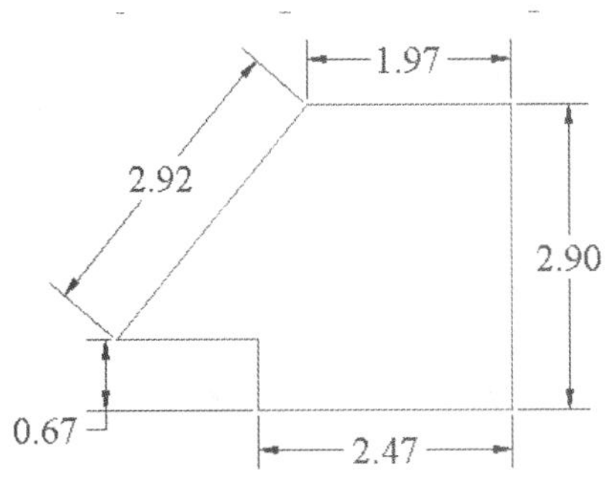

Dimensions Exercise

Solution

If you are still in the AutoCAD Classic workspace, we will now move over to the Drafting and Annotation workspace.

*Set **Drafting and Annotation** workspace current.*

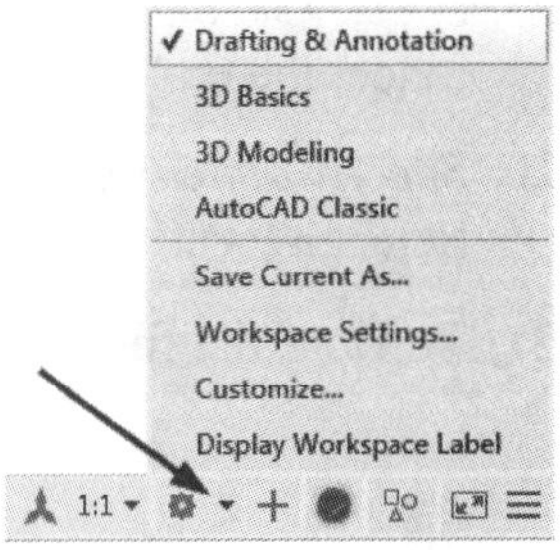

1. Invoke the Aligned Dimension command (dimaligned). On the Ribbon panel, locate the Aligned tool in the Annotations drop-down.

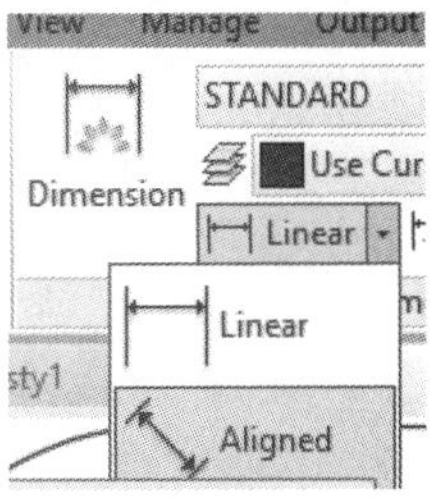

2. *Specify first extension line origin or <select object>:*
   Press <ENTER> to select the object.
3. *Select object to dimension:*
   Select the angled line between 1 and 2.
4. *Specify dimension line location or [Mtext/Text/Angle]:*
   Select a location for the dimension with the LMB.
5. Invoke the Linear Dimension command (dimlinear). Select the Linear Dimension command from the Annotate Ribbon tab.

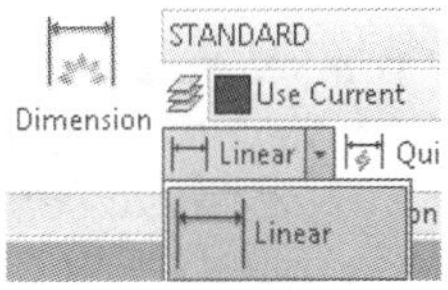

6. *Specify first extension line origin or <select object>:*
   Press <ENTER> to select the object.

7. *Select object to dimension:*
   Select the line between 2 and 3.
8. *Specify dimension line location or [Mtext/Text/Angle/Horizontal/Vertical/Rotated]:*
   Select a location for the horizontal dimension with the LMB.
9. Repeat the Linear Dimension command with the RMB (dimlinear or <ENTER>).
10. *Specify first extension line origin or <select object>:*
    Press <ENTER> to select the object.
11. *Select object to dimension:*
    Select the angled line between 3 and 4.
12. *Specify dimension line location or [Mtext/Text/Angle/Horizontal/Vertical/Rotated]:*
    Select a location for the vertical dimension with the LMB.
13. Repeat the Linear Dimension command with the RMB (dimlinear or <ENTER>).
14. *Specify first extension line origin or <select object>:*
    Press <ENTER> to select the object.
15. *Select object to dimension:*
    Select the angled line between 4 and 5.
16. *Specify dimension line location or [Mtext/Text/Angle/Horizontal/Vertical/Rotated]:*
    Select a location for the horizontal dimension with the LMB.
17. Repeat the Linear Dimension command with the RMB (dimlinear or <ENTER>).
18. *Specify first extension line origin or <select object>:*
    Select the endpoint of corner #5.
19. *Specify second extension line origin:*
    Select the endpoint of corner #1.
20. *Specify dimension line location or [Mtext/Text/Angle/Horizontal/Vertical/Rotated]:*
    Select a location for the vertical dimension with the LMB.
21. To close the file, go to **File→Close** or type **CLOSE**.

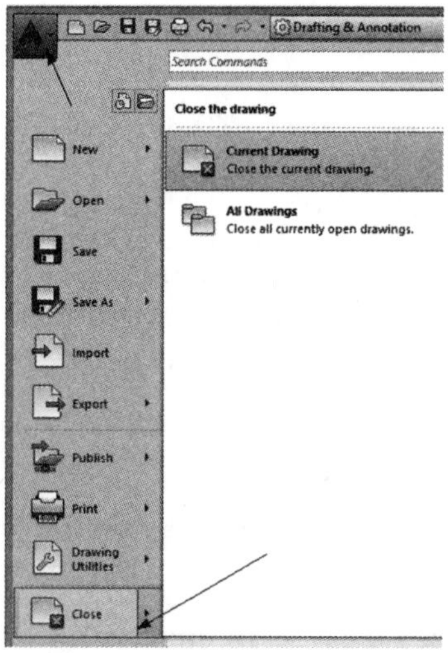

***Note:** If you select the entire line segment instead of the corners of the object for the first and second origin points, the dimension line will run over the object and no gap will be visible between the object and the dimension line.*

Command Exercise

Exercise 9-2 – Accessing the Dimension Toolbar

Drawing Name: **new drawing**
Estimated Time to Completion: 5 Minutes

Scope

Activate the AutoCAD Classic Workspace.
Activate the Dimension Toolbar.

Solution

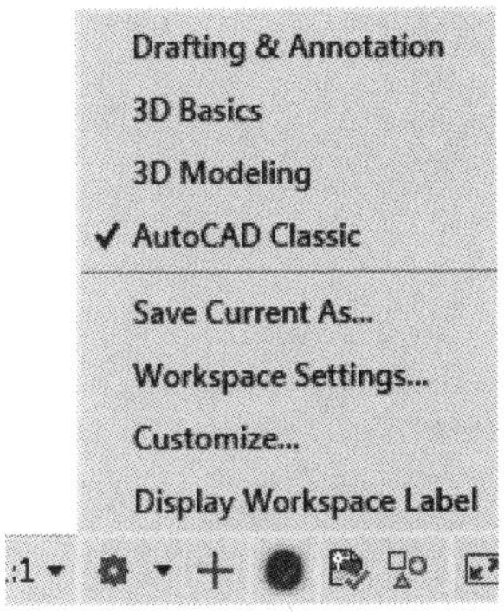

1. Select the **AutoCAD Classic** workspace from the drop-down list on the Workspace icon on the task bar.

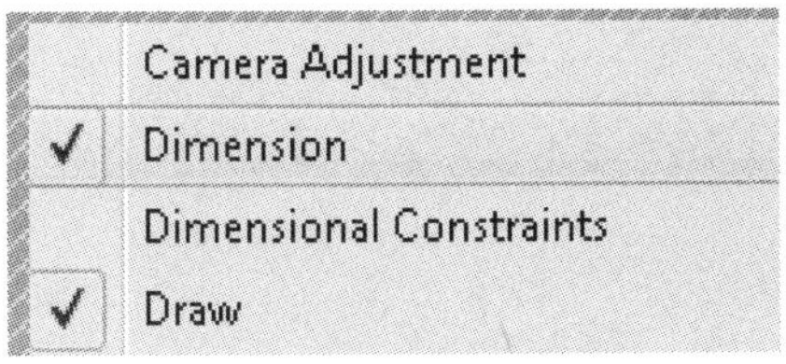

2. Right click on any toolbar.
3. Select **Dimension** to activate the Dimension toolbar. You may need to look closely at your screen to locate the toolbar.
4. Close the drawing without saving.

Command Exercise

Exercise 9-3 – Continuous and Baseline Dimensions

Drawing Name: **dim2.dwg**
Estimated Time to Completion: 5 Minutes

Scope

OSNAP should be enabled with ENDPOINT. Workspace should be set to Drafting & Annotation.

Dimension the object as indicated using Continuous and Baseline Dimensions.

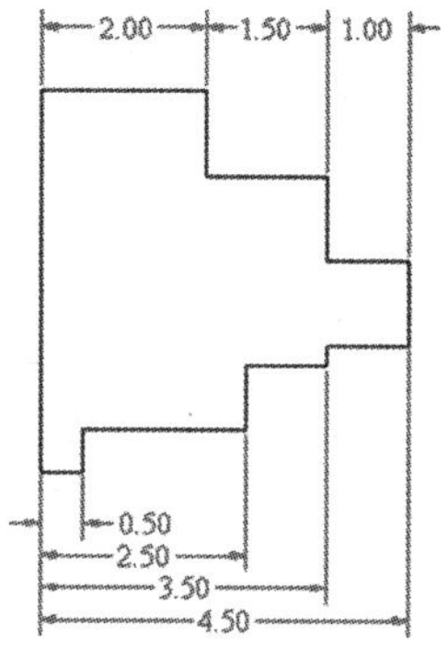

Dimensions Exercise

Solution

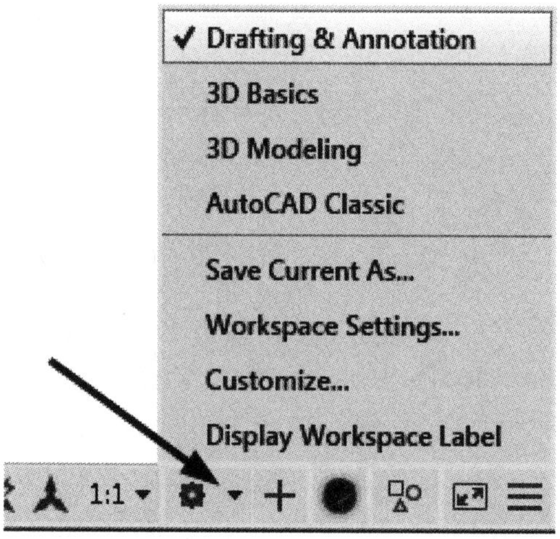

Verify that the workspace is set to Drafting & Annotation using the Workspace icon on the taskbar.

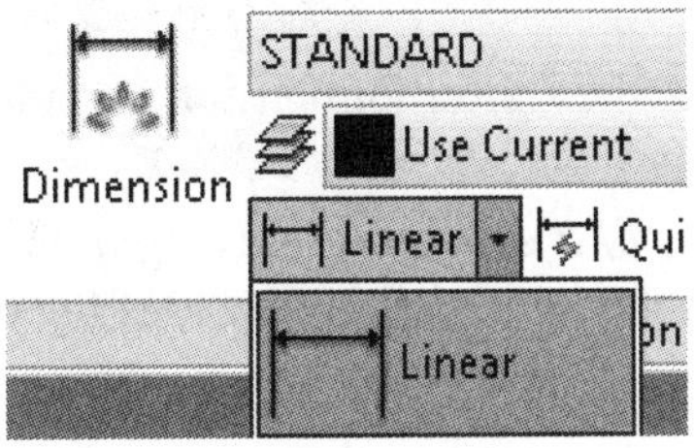

1. Activate the Annotate ribbon.

2. Select the **Linear Dimension** command from the Annotation panel on the ribbon.

3. *Specify first extension line origin or <select object>:*
   Make sure the Intersection Running Object Snap is active. Pick the upper left corner of the object A with the LMB.

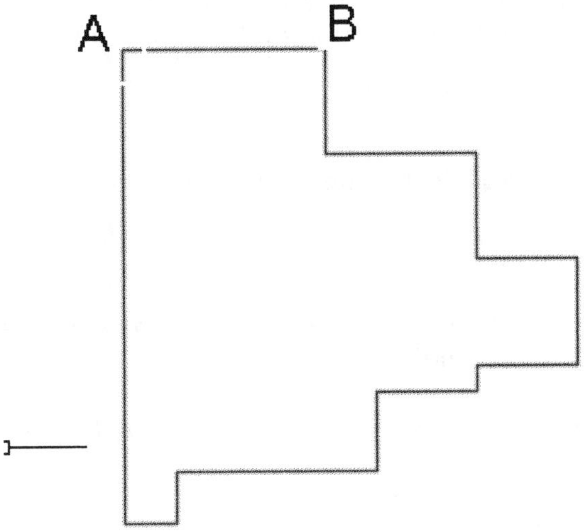

4. *Specify second extension line origin:*
   Pick corner B with the LMB.

5. *Specify dimension line location or [Mtext/Text/Angle/Horizontal/Vertical/Rotated]:*
   Select a location for the dimension with the LMB.

6. Invoke the Continue Dimension command (dimcontinue).

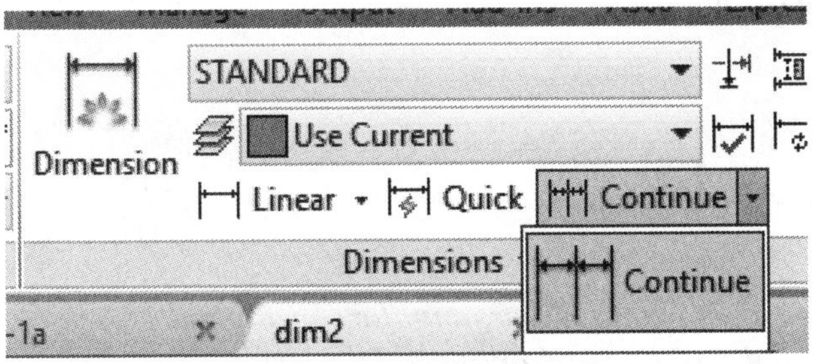

7. *Specify a second extension line origin or [Undo/Select] <Select>:*
   Select corner C.

8. *Specify a second extension line origin or [Undo/Select] <Select>:*
   Select corner D.

9. *Specify a second extension line origin or [Undo/Select] <Select>:*
   Right click and select <ENTER> to end the command.

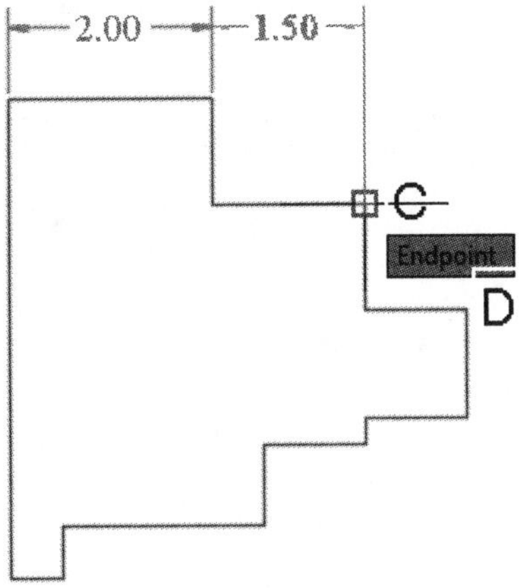

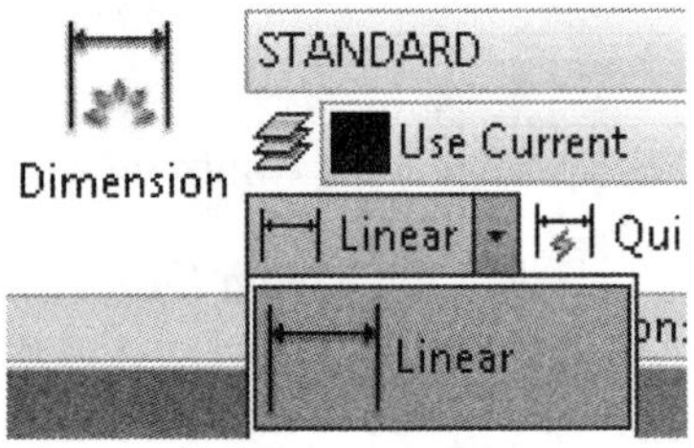

10. Invoke the Linear Dimension command (dimlinear).

11. *Specify first extension line origin or <select object>:*
    Select the lower left corner E of the object with the LMB.

12. *Specify second extension line origin:*
    Select corner F.

13. *Specify dimension line location or [Mtext/Text/Angle/Horizontal/Vertical/Rotated]:*
    Select a location for the dimension with the LMB.

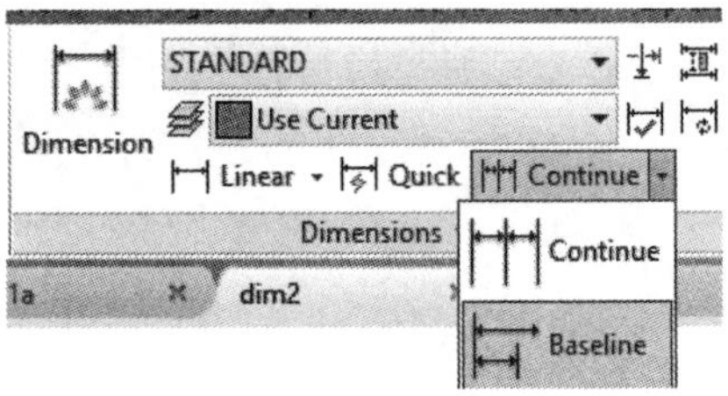

14. Invoke the Baseline Dimension command (dimbaseline).

15. *Specify a second extension line origin or [Undo/Select] <Select>:*
    Select corner G.

16. *Specify a second extension line origin or [Undo/Select] <Select>:*
    Select corner H.

17. *Specify a second extension line origin or [Undo/Select] <Select>:*
    Select corner I.

18. *Select base dimension:*
    Right click and select <ENTER> to end the command.

Note: *You will get the best results if you start with a linear, angular, or aligned dimension and immediately follow with the Baseline or Continued Dimension command.*

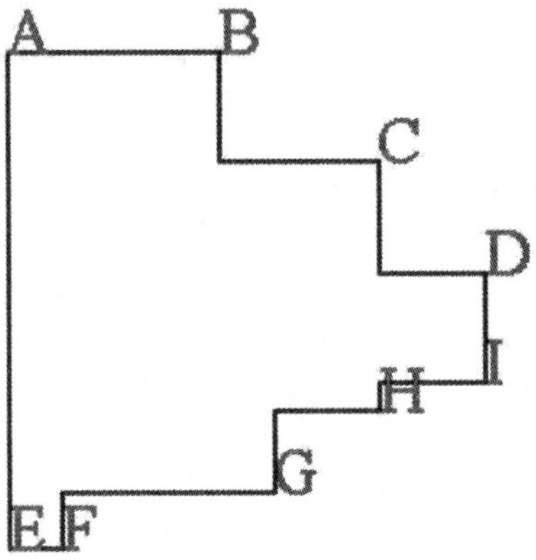

Command Exercise

Exercise 9-4 – Angular, Radius and Diameter Dimensions

Drawing Name: **dim3.dwg**
Estimated Time to Completion: 5 Minutes

Scope

Dimension the object as indicated using Angular, Radius, Diameter Dimensions, and Center Mark.

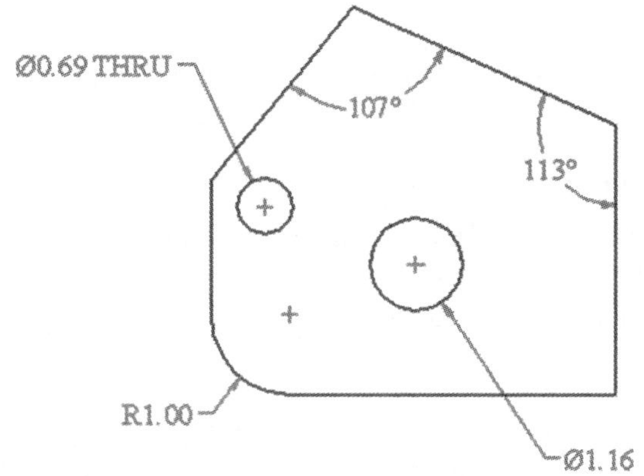

Dimensions Exercise

Solution

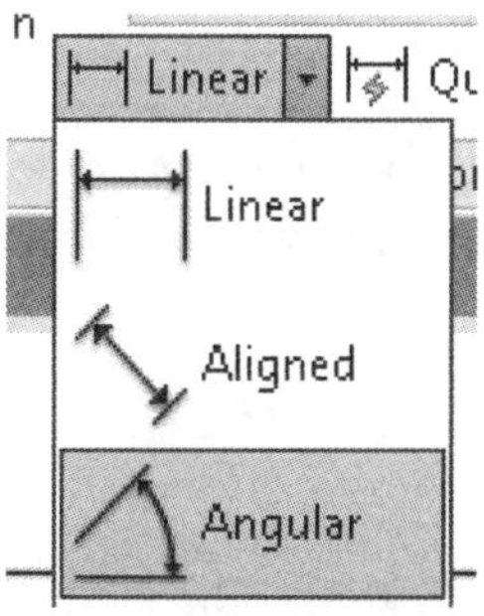

1. Invoke the Angular Dimension command (dimangular).
2. *Select arc, circle, line, or <specify vertex>:*
   Pick the line segment marked #1.
3. *Select second line:*
   Pick the line segment marked #2.
4. *Specify dimension arc line location or [Mtext/Text/Angle]:*
   Select a location for the dimension.
5. Repeat the Angular Dimension command with the RMB (dimangular or <ENTER>).
6. *Select arc, circle, line, or <specify vertex>:*
   Pick the line segment marked #3.
7. *Select second line:*
   Pick the line segment marked #2.
8. *Specify dimension arc line location or [Mtext/Text/Angle]:*
   Select a location for the dimension.

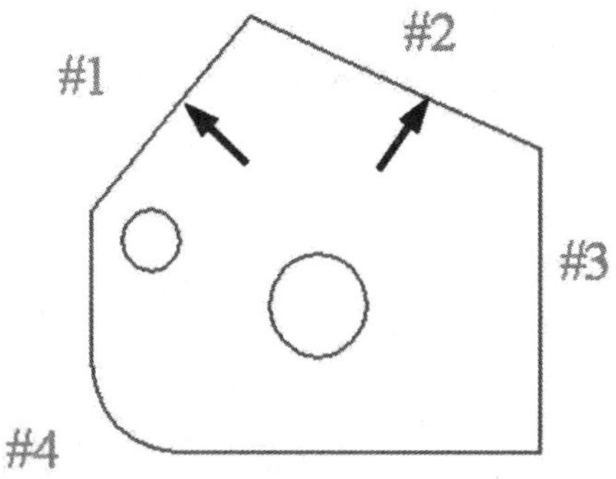

9. Invoke the Diameter Dimension command (dimdiameter).
10. *Select arc or circle:*
    Select the large circle.
11. *Specify dimension line location or [Mtext/Text/Angle]:*
    Select a location for the dimension.

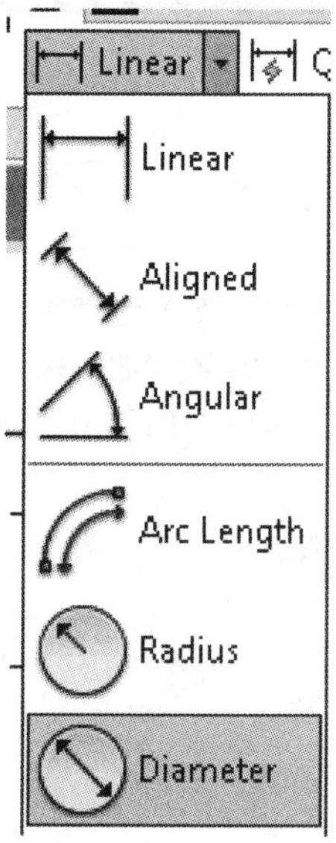

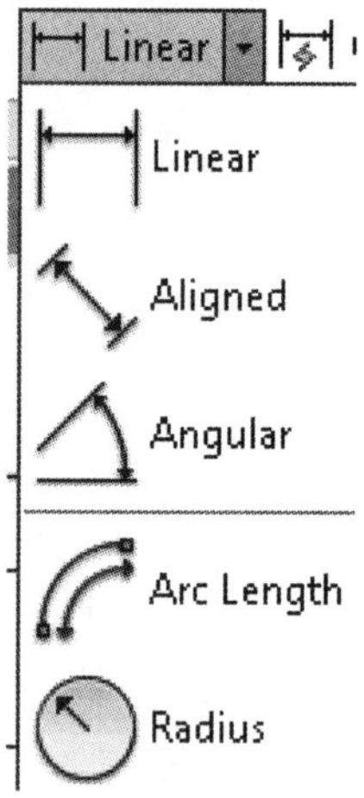

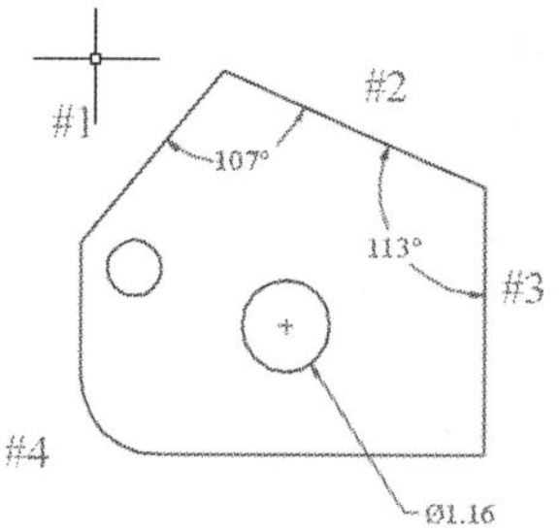

12. Invoke the Radius Dimension command (dimradius).
13. *Select arc or circle:*
    Select the arc marked #4.
14. *Specify dimension line location or [Mtext/Text/Angle]:*
    Select a location for the dimension.

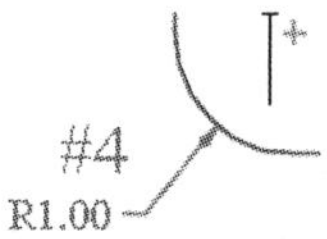

15. Invoke the Center Mark command (dimcenter).
16. *Select arc or circle:*
    Select the small circle.

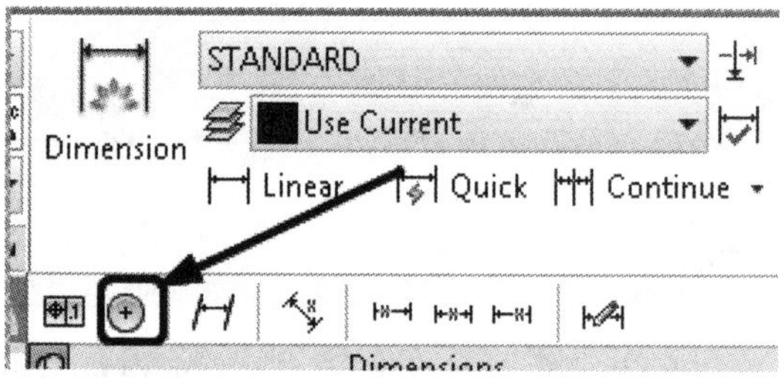

In the Drafting & Annotation workspace, you need to expand the Dimensions panel to see the Center Mark tool. To expand use the down arrow next to the word 'Dimensions'.

17. Invoke the Diameter Dimension command (dimdiameter).
18. *Select arc or circle:*
    Select the small circle.
19. *Specify dimension line location or [Mtext/Text/Angle]:*
    Select a location for the dimension.

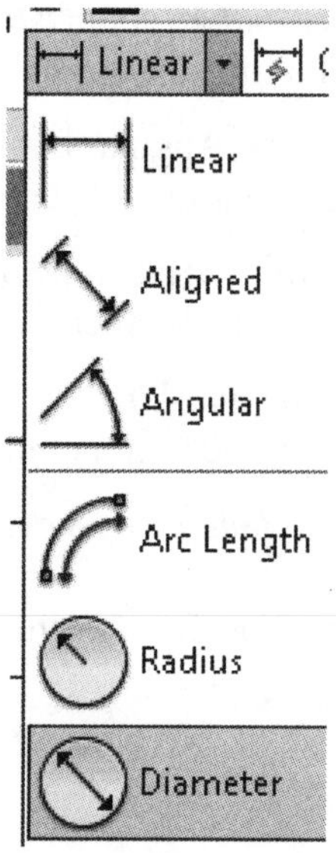

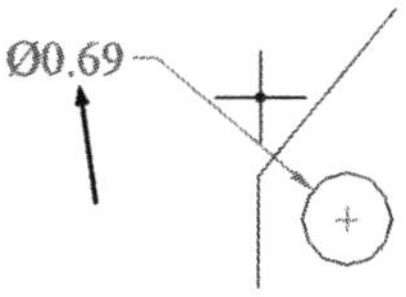
Ø0.69

20. Select the diameter dimension that was just placed.
21. Right click and select **Properties**.

Find...
Properties
Quick Properties

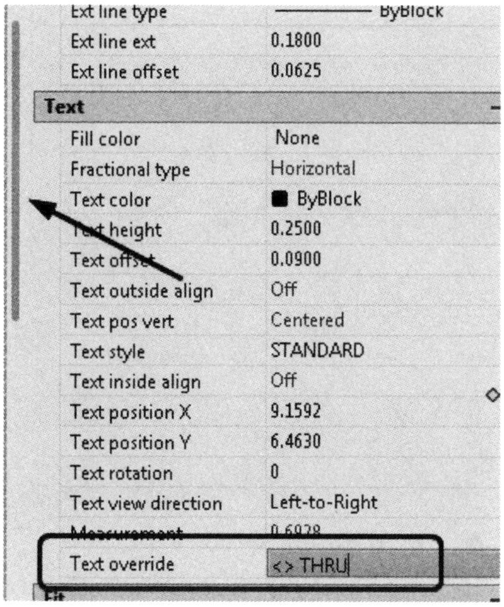
Ext line type ByBlock
Ext line ext 0.1800
Ext line offset 0.0625
Text
Fill color None
Fractional type Horizontal
Text color ByBlock
Text height 0.2500
Text offset 0.0900
Text outside align Off
Text pos vert Centered
Text style STANDARD
Text inside align Off
Text position X 9.1592
Text position Y 6.4630
Text rotation 0
Text view direction Left-to-Right
Text override <> THRU

22. Use the scroll bar to scroll down to locate the Text override field.
23. Type ‘<> THRU’ in the field. Press <ENTER>.
24. Press <ESC> to release the selection.

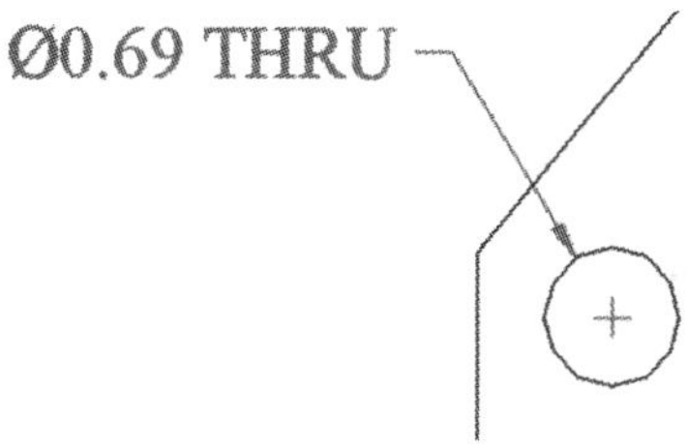
Ø0.69 THRU

The dimension updates.

25. Close without saving.

Tips & Tricks

<> is used to indicate the default text or dimension assigned to the object.

Command Exercise

Exercise 9-5 – Centerline Annotations

Drawing Name: **centerline.dwg**
Estimated Time to Completion: 25 Minutes

Scope

Add a centerline to the holes in the top and front view.
Set the layer to be used for the centerline using the CENTERLAYER command.

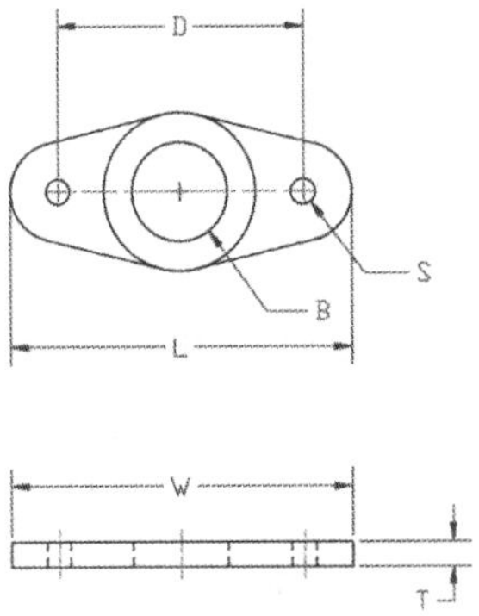

Centerline Exercise

Solution

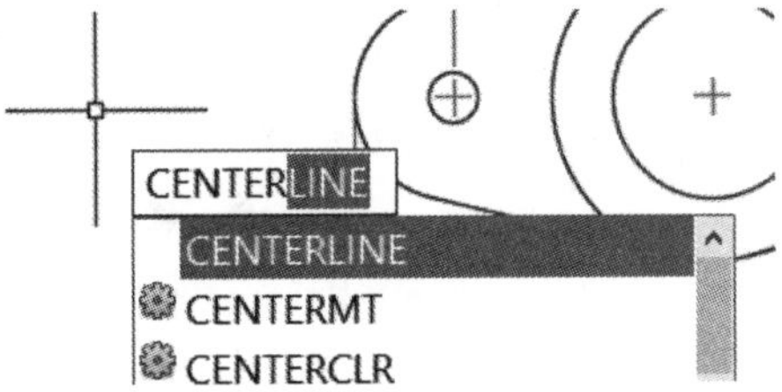

1. Type CENTERLINE at the command prompt.

   Autofill will display the command as you start typing.

2. Select the two hidden lines designating the left hole in the front view.

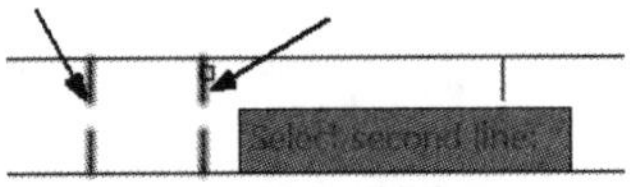

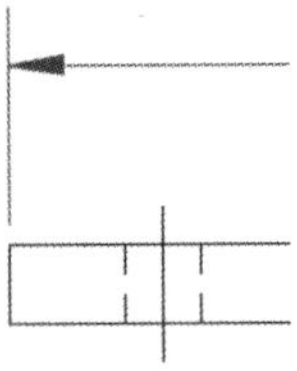

A center line is placed.

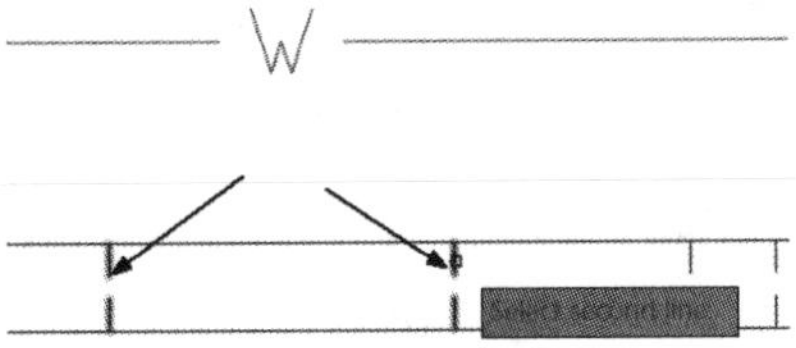

3. Type CENTERLINE at the command prompt.

   Autofill will display the command as you start typing.

4. Select the two hidden lines designating the middle hole.

5. Type CENTERLINE at the command prompt.

   Autofill will display the command as you start typing.

6. Select the two hidden lines designating the right hole.

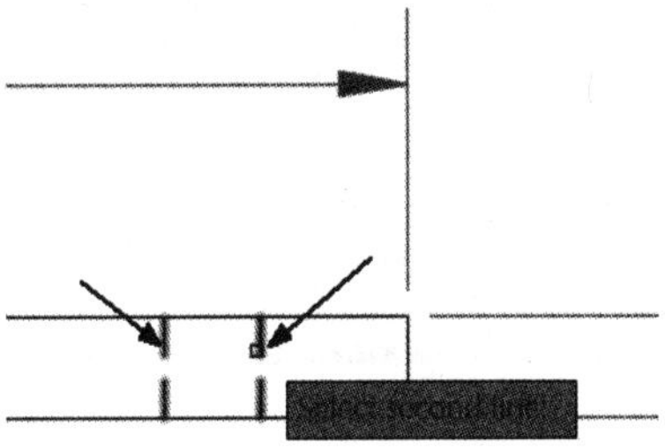

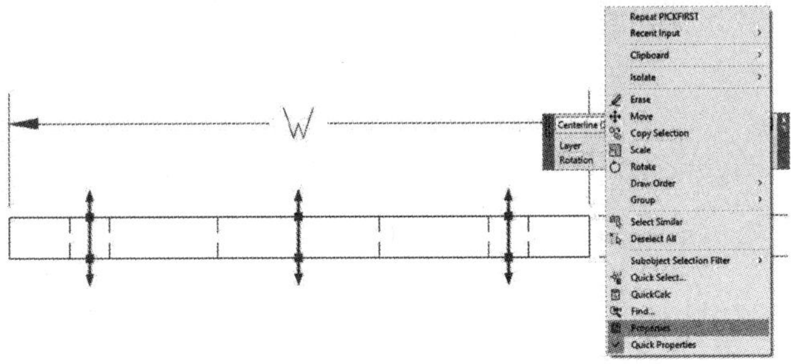

7. Select the three centerlines which were placed.

8. Right click and select 'Properties'.

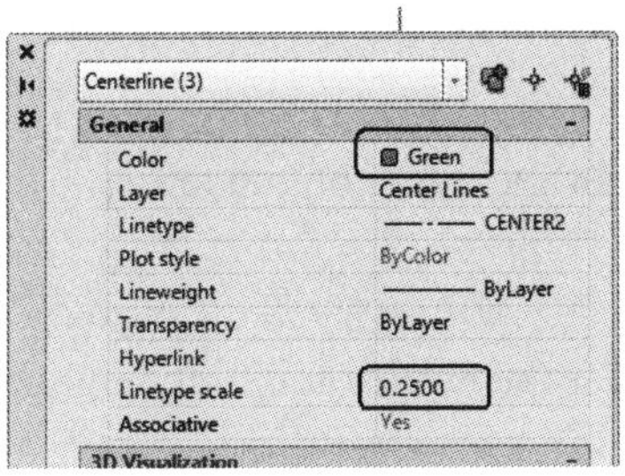

9. Change the color to Green.

10. Change the Linetype scale to 0.2500.

Notice that the center lines were automatically placed on a new layer called Center Lines with a CENTER2 linetype.

11. Press ESC to release the selection.

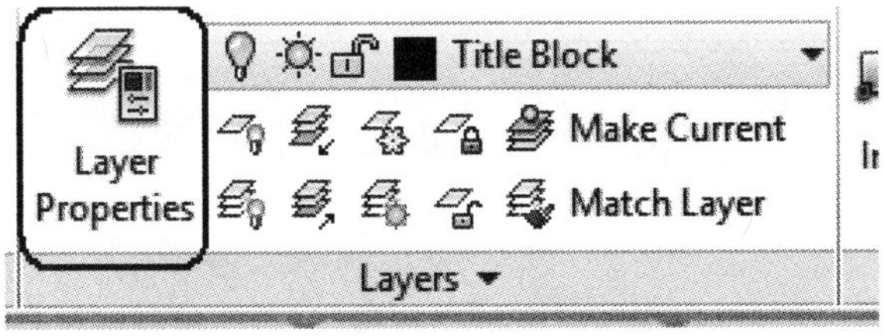

12. Select the Layer Properties tool on the Home ribbon.

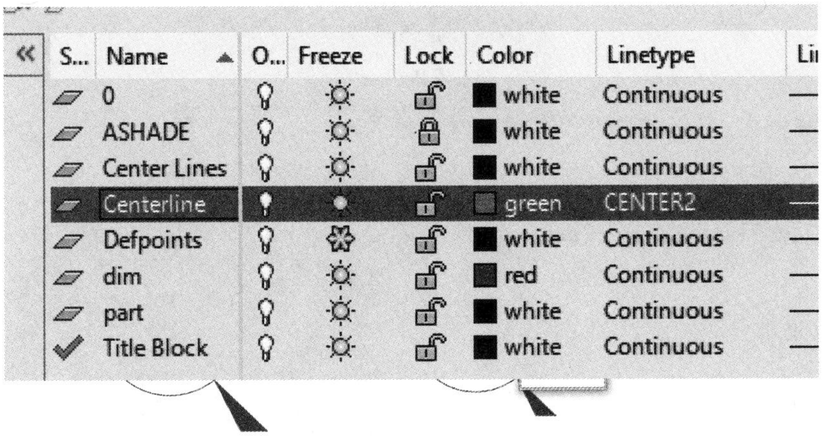

13. Note that there is a layer called Centerline that is set to use the Green color and the CENTER2 linetype.

14. Close the Layer Manager dialog.

15. Type CENTERLAYER at the command prompt.

16. Type Centerline and ENTER.

The CENTERLAYER tool allows you to set the layer for the new center line. It works similarly to the HPLAYER command.

Enter new value for CENTERLAYER, or . for use current <"Center Lines">:
Centerline

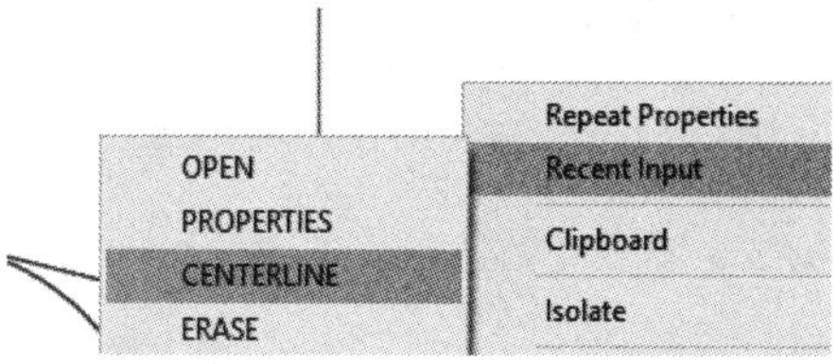
Repeat Properties
OPEN
Recent Input
PROPERTIES
Clipboard
CENTERLINE
ERASE
Isolate

17. Right click in the display window.

18. Select Recent Input → CENTERLINE.

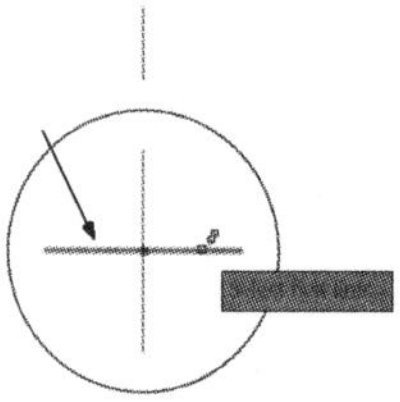

19. Select the horizontal line of the center mark for the circle on the left.

20. Pan over to the left hand side of the top view.

21. Select the horizontal line of the center mark for the circle on the right

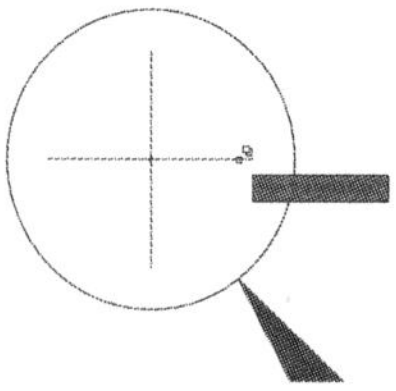

22. A list box will appear to allow the choice of overlapping elements. Select the line.

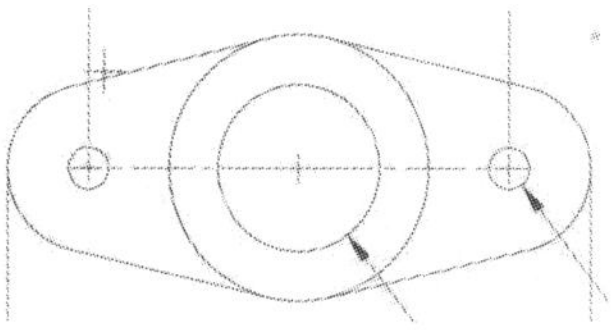

A centerline will be placed.

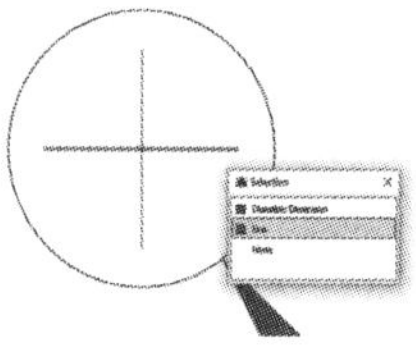

Find...
Properties
Quick Properties

23. Select the centerline.

24. Right click and select 'Properties'.

25. Verify that the centerline was placed on the correct layer and has the correct properties.

26. Press ESC to release the selection.

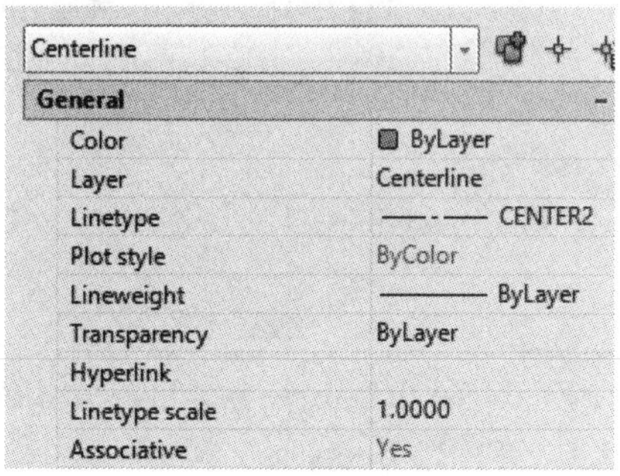
Centerline
General
Color
ByLayer
Layer
Centerline
Linetype
CENTER2
Plot style
ByColor
Lineweight
ByLayer
Transparency
ByLayer
Hyperlink
Linetype scale
1.0000
Associative
Yes

Command Exercise

Exercise 9-6 – Quick Dimensions

Drawing Name: **qdim.dwg**
Estimated Time to Completion: 10 Minutes

Scope

Use the Quick Dimension command to create continuous, staggered, baseline and ordinate dimensions of the same geometry under the appropriate headings. Select the geometry of the continuous set and remove one of the dimension points.

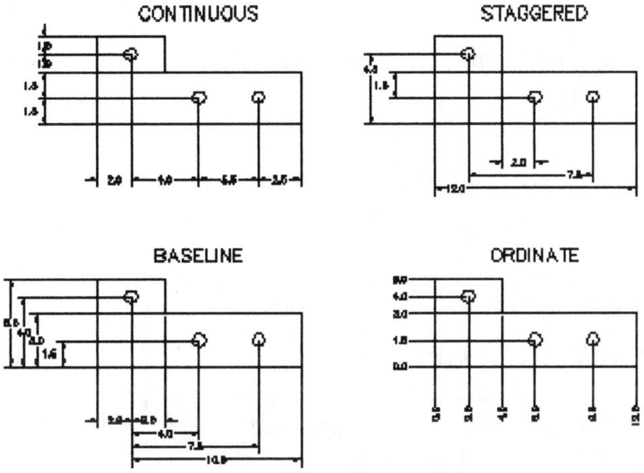

Quick Dimensions Exercise

Solution

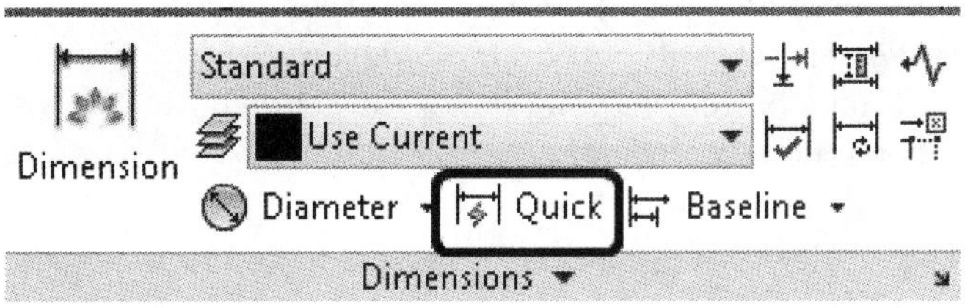

Continuous

1. Invoke the **Quick Dimension** command (qdim).
2. *Select geometry to dimension:*
   Select all of the geometry underneath the word 'CONTINUOUS'.
3. *Select geometry to dimension:*
   Press <ENTER> when all of the geometry is selected.
4. *[Continuous/Staggered/Baseline/Ordinate/Radius/Diameter/datumPoint/Edit] <Continuous>:*
   Select a placement point below the geometry to create the horizontal dimensions.

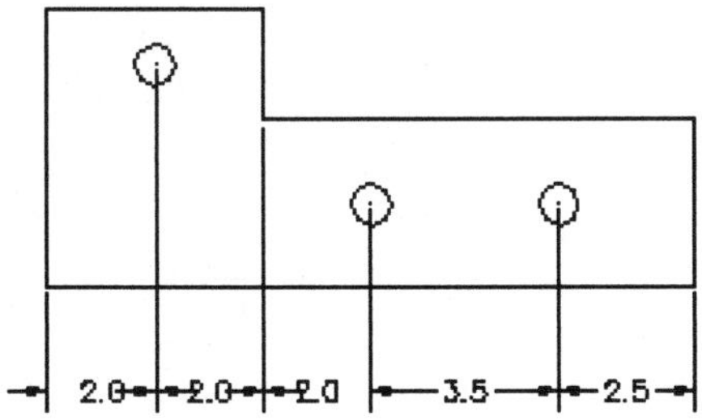

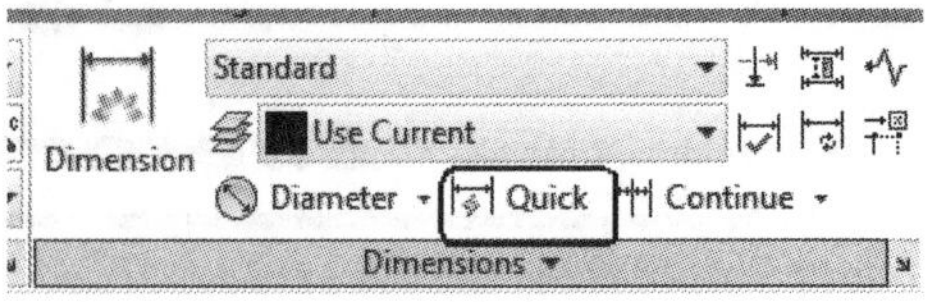

5. Repeat the **Quick Dimension** command with the RMB (press <ENTER> or qdim).
6. *Select geometry to dimension:*
   Select the same set of geometry (type 'P' and press <ENTER>).
7. *Select geometry to dimension:*
   Press <ENTER> when all of the geometry is selected.
8. *[Continuous/Staggered/Baseline/Ordinate/Radius/Diameter/datumPoint/Edit] <Continuous>:*
   Select a placement point to the left of the geometry to create the vertical dimensions.

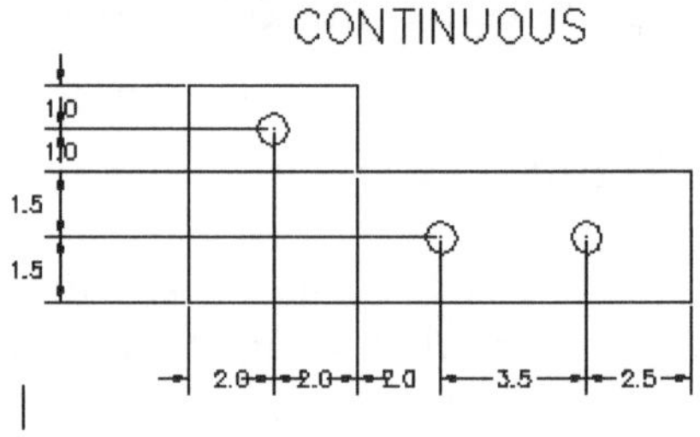

Staggered

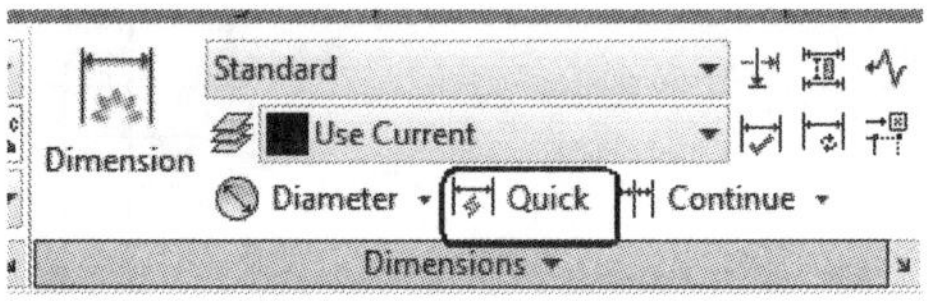

9. Repeat the **Quick Dimension** command with the RMB (press <ENTER> or qdim).
10. *Select geometry to dimension:*
    Select all of the geometry underneath the word 'STAGGERED'.
11. *Select geometry to dimension:*
    Press <ENTER> when all of the geometry is selected.
12. *[Continuous/Staggered/Baseline/Ordinate/Radius/Diameter/datumPoint/Edit] <Continuous>:*
    Right-click in the drawing area and select 'Staggered' or type 'S' and press <ENTER> to select staggered dimensions.
13. *[Continuous/Staggered/Baseline/Ordinate/Radius/Diameter/datumPoint/Edit] <Staggered>:*
    Select a placement point below the geometry to create the horizontal dimensions.

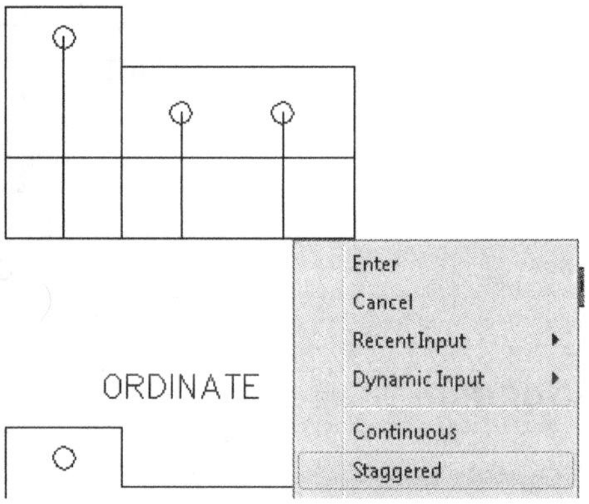

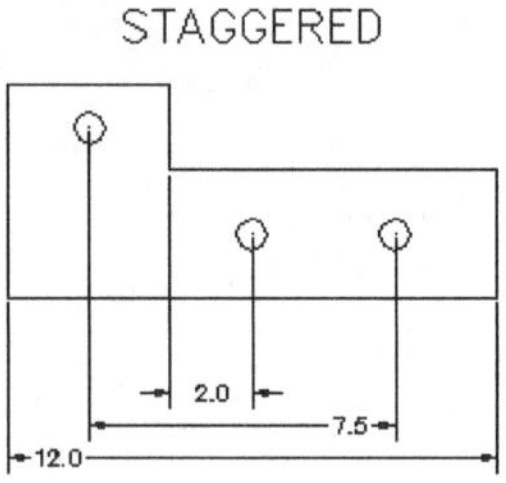

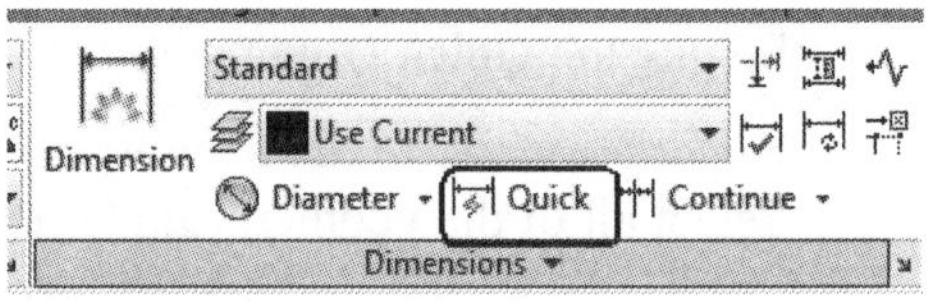

14. Repeat the **Quick Dimension** command with the RMB (press <ENTER> or qdim).
15. *Select geometry to dimension:*
    Select the same set of geometry (type 'P' and press <ENTER>).
16. *Select geometry to dimension:*
    Press <ENTER> when all of the geometry is selected.
17. *[Continuous/Staggered/Baseline/Ordinate/Radius/Diameter/datumPoint/Edit] <Staggered>:*
    Select a placement point to the left of the geometry to create the vertical dimensions.

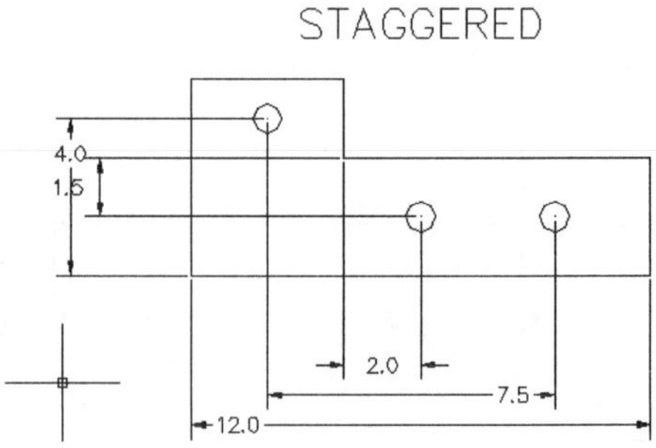

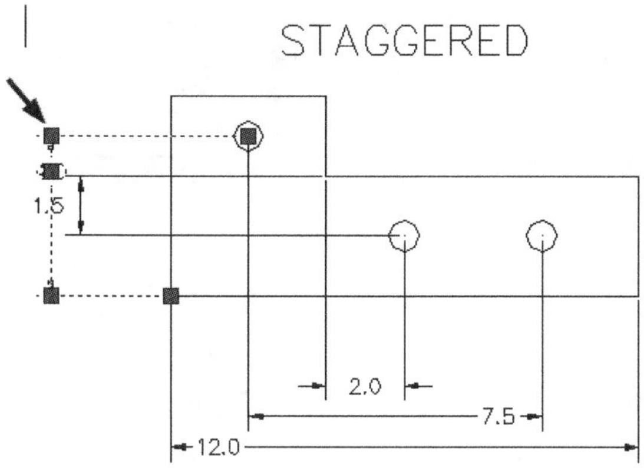

To adjust the position of the dimension:

18. Select the dimension so it highlights.
19. Select one of the end grips (blue square) and drag to a new position. LMB to place.

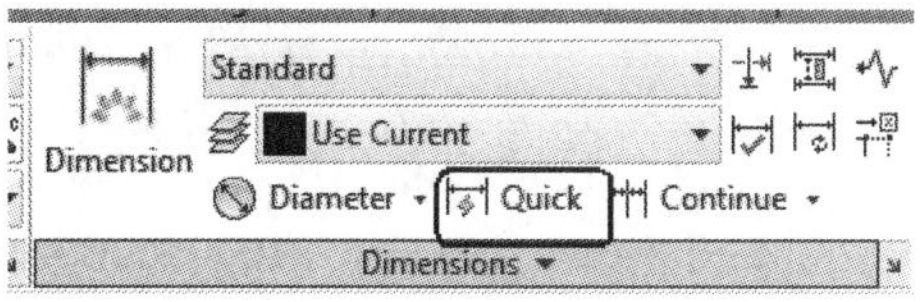

Baseline

20. Repeat the **Quick Dimension** command with the RMB (press <ENTER> or qdim).
21. *Select geometry to dimension:*
    Select all of the geometry underneath the word 'BASELINE'.
22. *Select geometry to dimension:*
    Press <ENTER> when all of the geometry is selected.
23. *[Continuous/Staggered/Baseline/Ordinate/Radius/Diameter/ datumPoint/Edit] <Staggered>:*
    Right-click in the drawing area and select 'Baseline' or type 'B' and press <ENTER> to select baseline dimensions.
24. *[Continuous/Staggered/Baseline/Ordinate/Radius/Diameter/ datumPoint/Edit] <Baseline>:*
    Select a placement point below the geometry to create the horizontal dimensions.

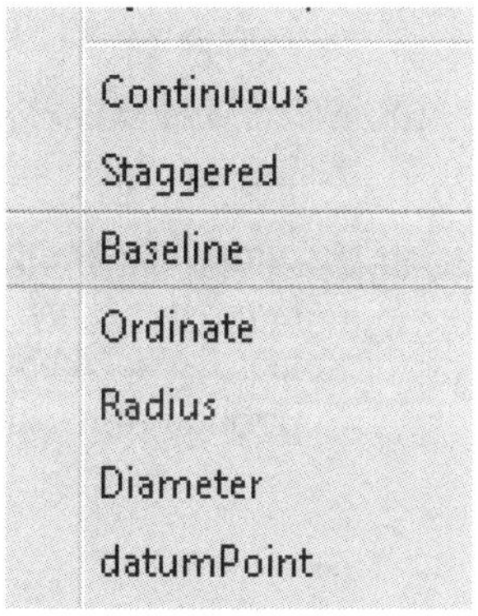

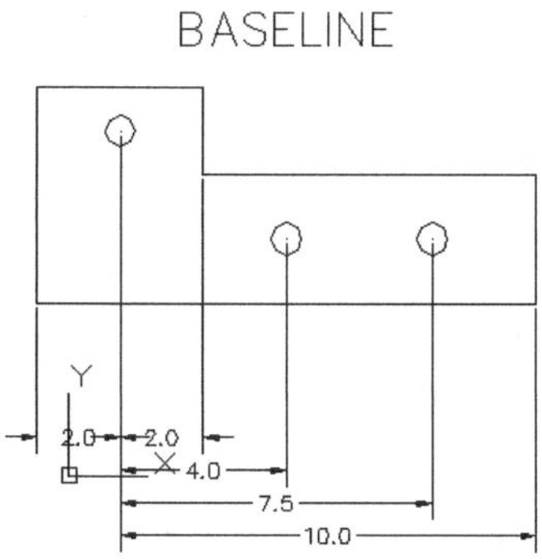

25. Repeat the **Quick Dimension** command with the RMB (press <ENTER> or qdim).
26. *Select geometry to dimension:*
    Select the same set of geometry (type 'P' and press <ENTER>).
27. *Select geometry to dimension:*
    Press <ENTER> when all of the geometry is selected.
28. *[Continuous/Staggered/Baseline/Ordinate/Radius/Diameter/ datumPoint/Edit] <Baseline>:*
    Select a placement point to the left of the geometry to create the vertical dimensions.
29. Use GRIPs to adjust the position of dimensions as needed.

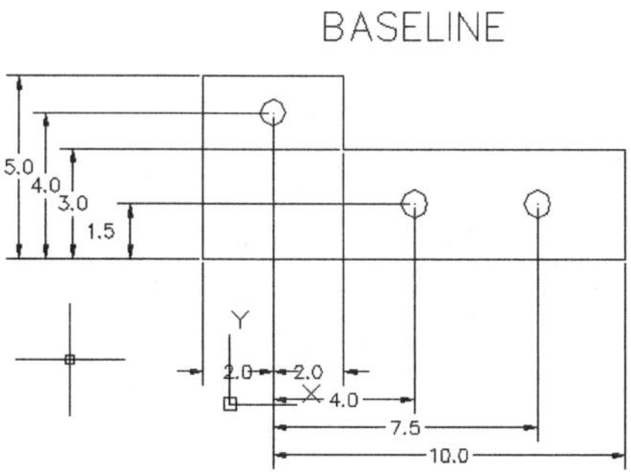

Ordinate

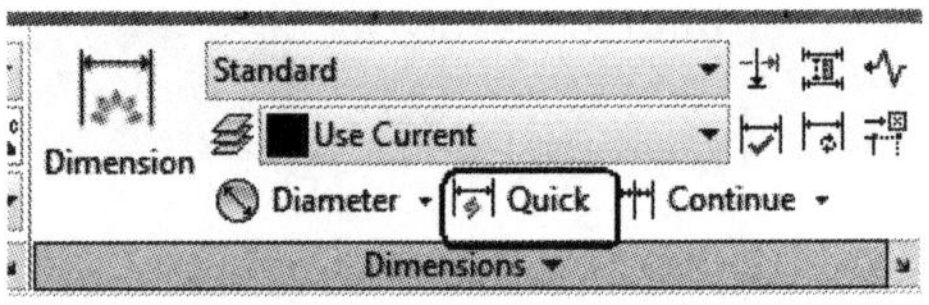

30. Repeat the **Quick Dimension** command with the RMB (press <ENTER> or qdim).

31. *Select geometry to dimension:*
Select all of the geometry underneath the word 'ORDINATE'.

32. *Select geometry to dimension:*
Press <ENTER> when all of the geometry is selected.

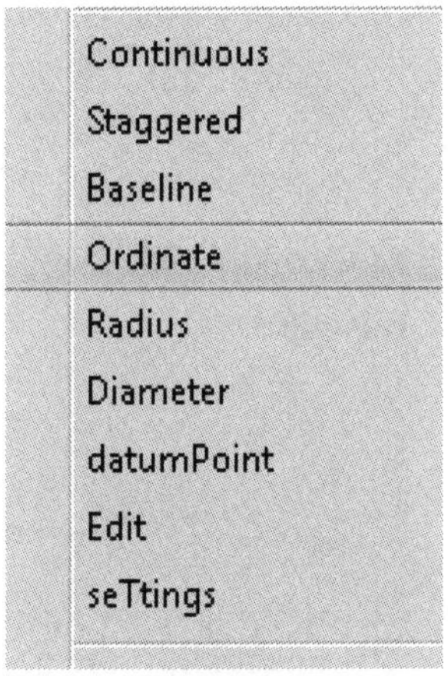

33. *[Continuous/Staggered/Baseline/Ordinate/Radius/Diameter/datumPoint/Edit] <Baseline>:*
Right-click in the drawing area and select 'Ordinate' or type 'O' and press <ENTER> to select ordinate dimensions.

34. *[Continuous/Staggered/Baseline/Ordinate/Radius/Diameter/datumPoint/Edit] <Ordinate>:*
Right-click in the drawing area and select 'datumPoint' or type 'P' and press <ENTER> to select a new datum point.

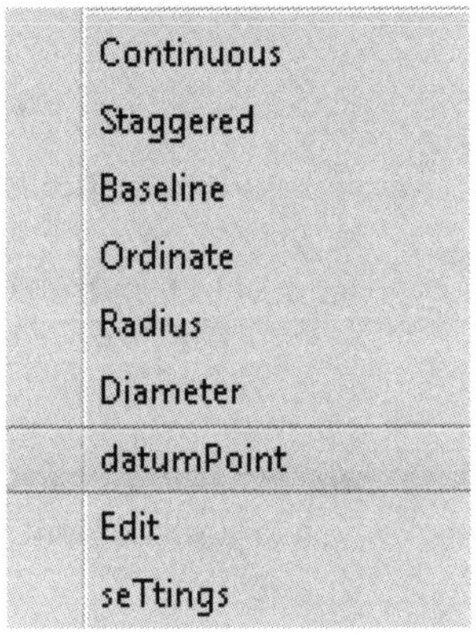

35. *Select new datum point:*
Using an object snap, select the lower left corner of the geometry.

36. *[Continuous/Staggered/Baseline/Ordinate/Radius/Diameter/datumPoint/Edit] <Ordinate>:*
Select a placement point below the geometry to create the horizontal dimensions.

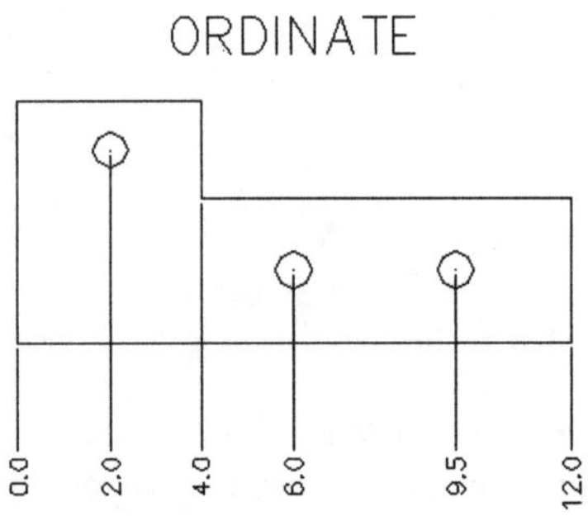

37. Repeat the **Quick Dimension** command with the RMB (press <ENTER> or qdim).

38. *Select geometry to dimension:*
Select the same set of geometry (type 'P' and press <ENTER>).

39. *Select geometry to dimension:*
Press <ENTER> when all of the geometry is selected.

40. *[Continuous/Staggered/Baseline/Ordinate/Radius/Diameter/datumPoint/Edit] <Ordinate>:*
Select a placement point to the left of the geometry to create the vertical dimensions.

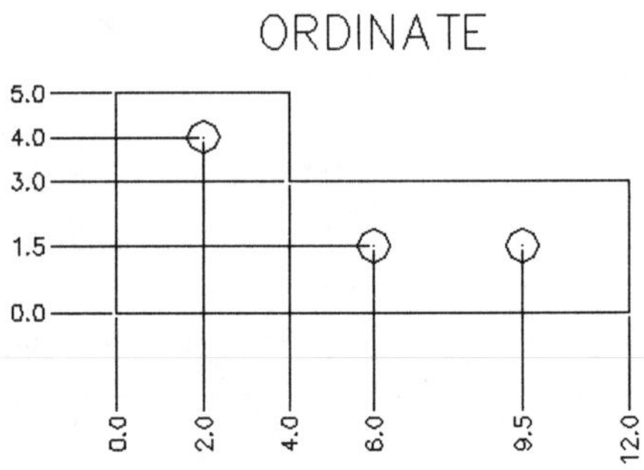

Remove a Dimension Point

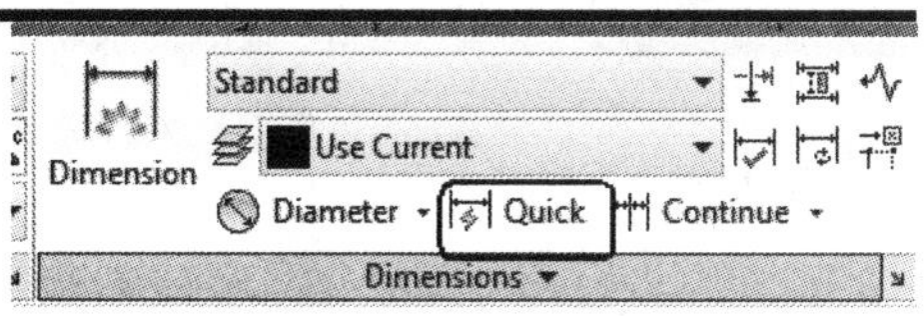

41. Invoke the **Quick Dimension** command (qdim).

If you are using the Drafting & Annotation workspace, you need to switch to the Annotate ribbon.

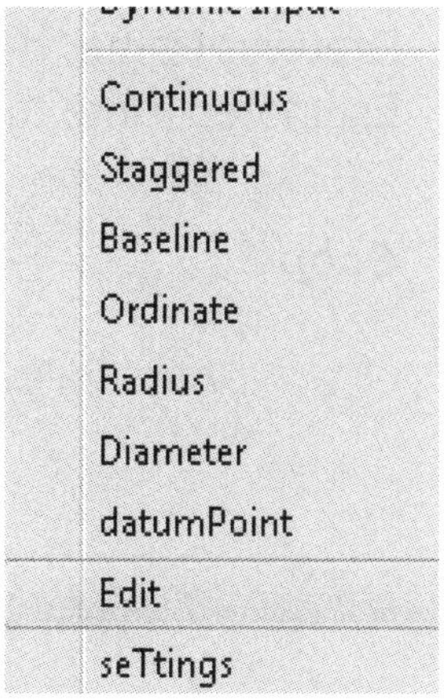

42. *Select geometry to dimension:*
    Select all of the geometry underneath the word 'CONTINUOUS'.
43. *Select geometry to dimension:*
    Press <ENTER> when all of the geometry is selected.
44. *[Continuous/Staggered/Baseline/Ordinate/Radius/Diameter/datumPoint/Edit] <Ordinate>:*
    Right-click in the drawing area and select 'Edit' or type 'E' and press <ENTER> to edit the dimension points.
45. *Indicate dimension point to remove, or [Add/eXit] <eXit>:*
    Select the two points indicated in the next figure.
46. Remove the Indicated Points.
47. *Indicate dimension point to remove, or [Add/eXit] <eXit>:*
    Press <ENTER> to exit edit mode.
48. *[Continuous/Staggered/Baseline/Ordinate/Radius/Diameter/datumPoint/Edit] <Ordinate>:*
    Right-click in the drawing area and select 'Continuous' or type 'C' and press <ENTER> to change back to continuous dimensions.
49. *[Continuous/Staggered/Baseline/Ordinate/Radius/Diameter/datumPoint/Edit] <Continuous>:*
    Select a placement point below the geometry to create the horizontal dimensions.

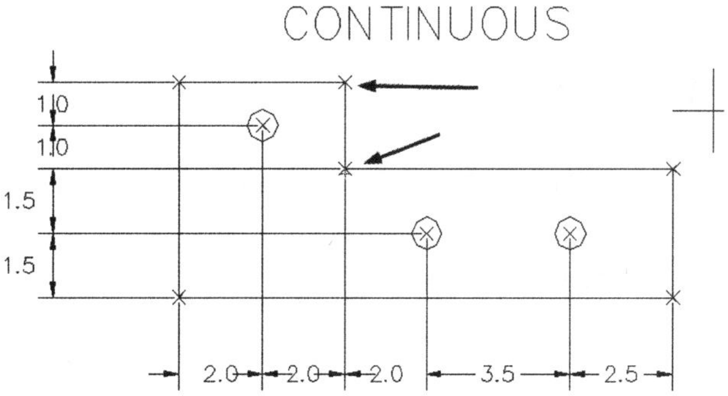

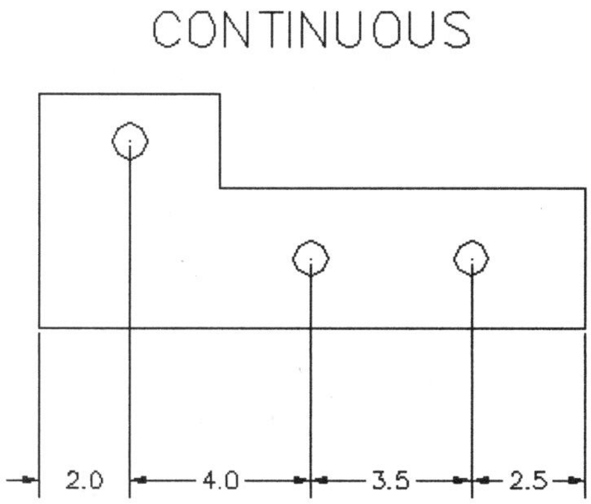

Note: You have to switch to the type of dimension style you want to use or whichever style was last selected is the default.

Command Exercise

Exercise 9-7 – Dimension

Drawing Name: **dim4.dwg**
Estimated Time to Completion: 5 Minutes

Scope

Dimension the object as indicated using the automatic dimension tool.

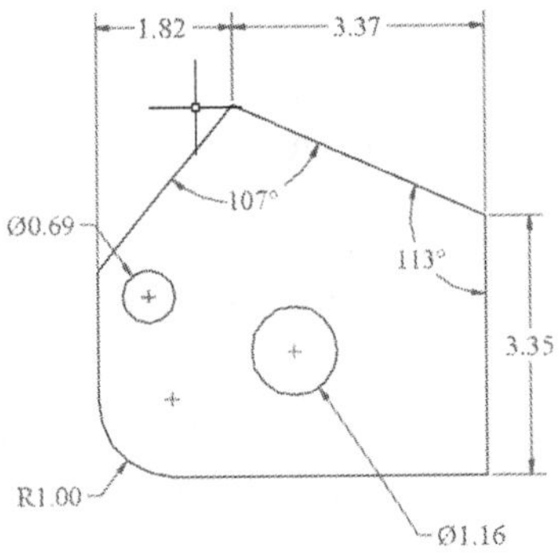

Dimensions Exercise

Solution

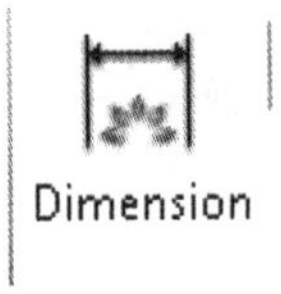

1. Invoke the Dimension command (dim) on the Annotate ribbon.
2. *Select arc, circle, line, or <specify vertex>:*
   Pick the line segment marked #1.
3. *Select second line:*
   Pick the line segment marked #2.
4. *Specify dimension arc line location or [Mtext/Text/Angle]:*
   Select a location for the dimension.

Note that you are still in the dimension command.

5. *Select arc, circle, line, or <specify vertex>:*
   Pick the line segment marked #3.
6. *Select second line:*
   Pick the line segment marked #2.
7. *Specify dimension arc line location or [Mtext/Text/Angle]:*
   Select a location for the dimension.

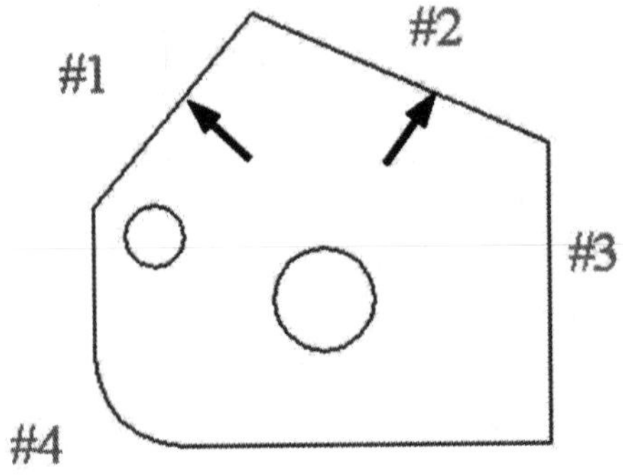

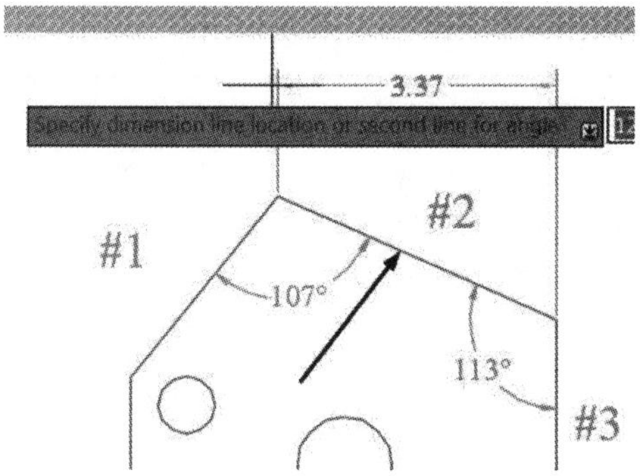

8. Select Line #2. Pull the dimension straight up and place.

Note that the direction you move the cursor will determine what type of dimension is placed—aligned, horizontal, or vertical.

nension tool.

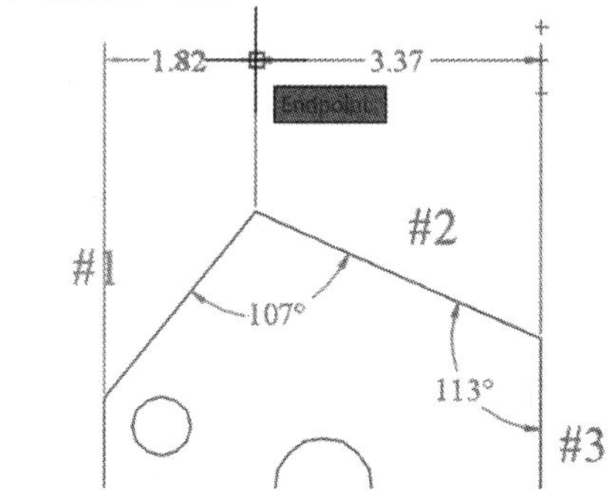

9. Select Line #1. Pull the dimension straight up and place.

Note that if you select the endpoint of the previous dimension you can align the two dimensions.

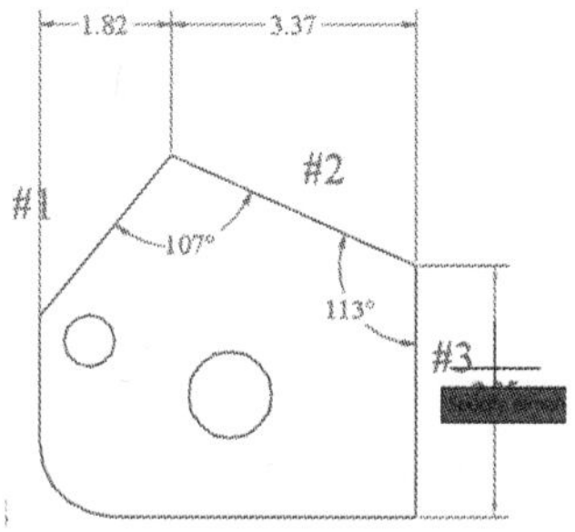

10. Select Line #3 and place a vertical dimension to the right of the line.

11. Select the large circle.

Select the outside circumference of the circle, not the center or inside the circle.

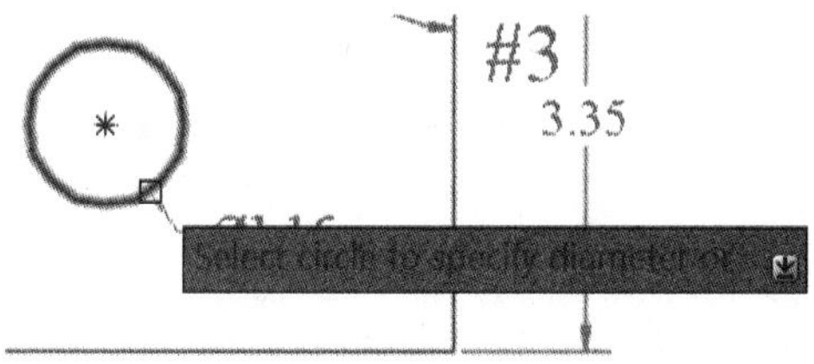

12. Place the dimension outside the figure.

13. Repeat for the small circle.

14. Select the radius of the fillet to place the last dimension. Left pick to place the dimension outside the figure.

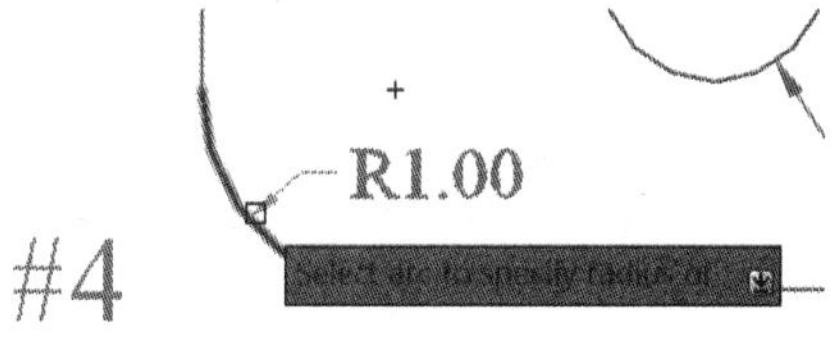

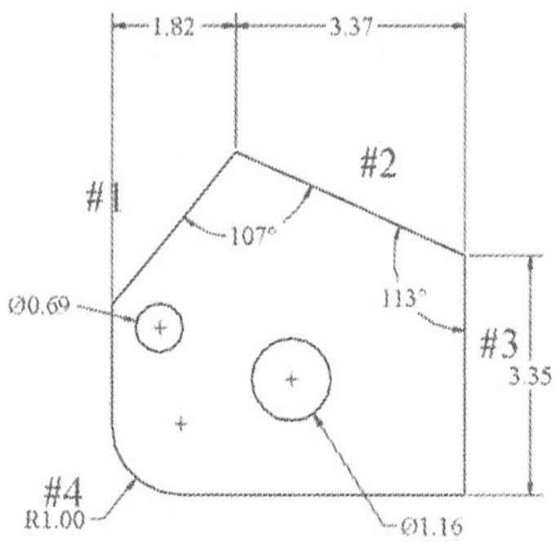

15. Close without saving.

Ordinate Dimension

Command Locator

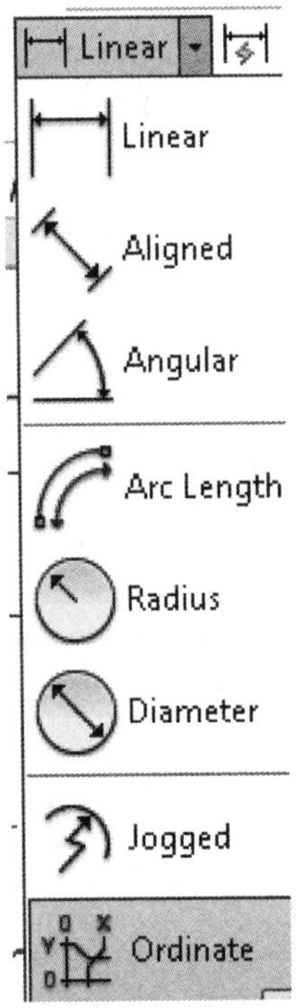

Toolbar Menu	**Dimension**
Pull Down Menu	**Dimension / Ordinate**
Command	**Dimord**
Alias	**D**

Command Overview

This dimension tool places ordinate dimensions in both the horizontal and vertical directions. You can add and delete points as well as set the origin.

Command Exercise

Exercise 9-8 – Ordinate Dimensions

Drawing Name: **dimord.dwg**
Estimated Time to Completion: 10 Minutes

Scope

Use the Ordinate Dimension tool to place vertical and horizontal dimensions. Set the Origin for the Ordinate Dimension by setting the UCS.

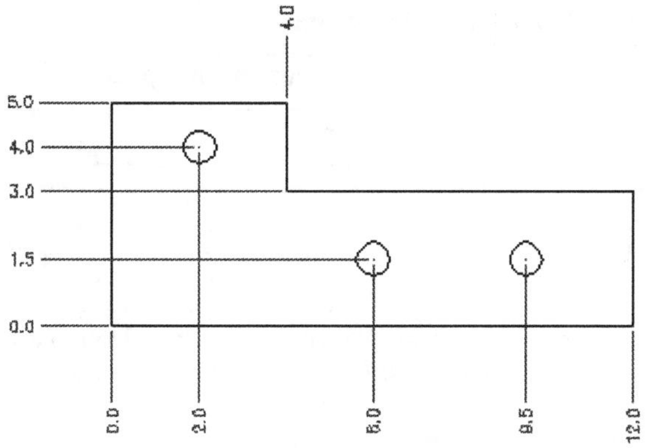

Ordinate Dimensions

Solution

1. Type **UCS** on the command line.
2. Select the lower left corner of the object to set the origin for the ordinate dimensions.
3. Press <ENTER> when prompted to specify the X-axis.
4. Select the Ordinate Dimension tool.

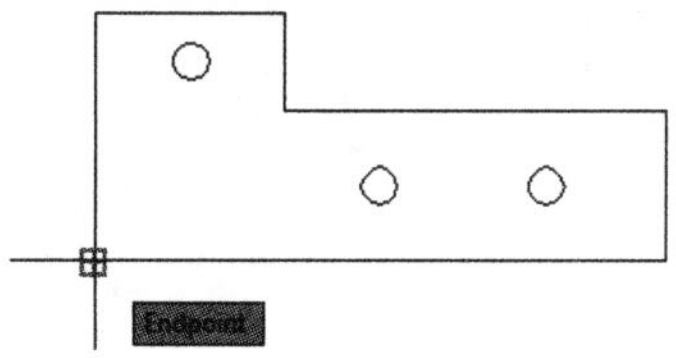

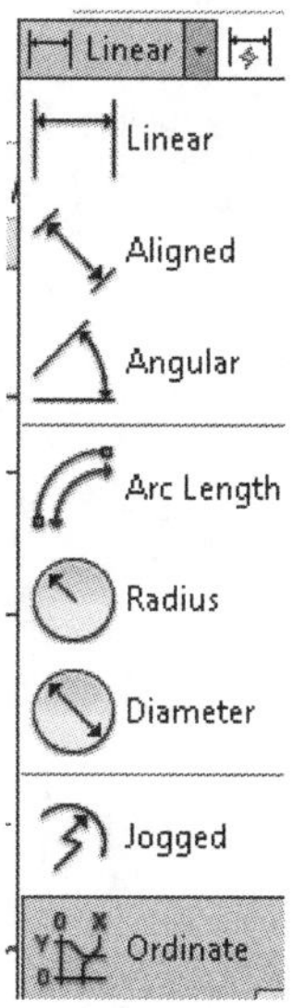

5. The prompt will ask you to select a feature.
6. Select the same point as the origin.
7. Bring the mouse down vertically to place the dimension. LMB to place.
8. Use Object Tracking to line up the next ordinate dimension.
9. Place the remaining dimensions.

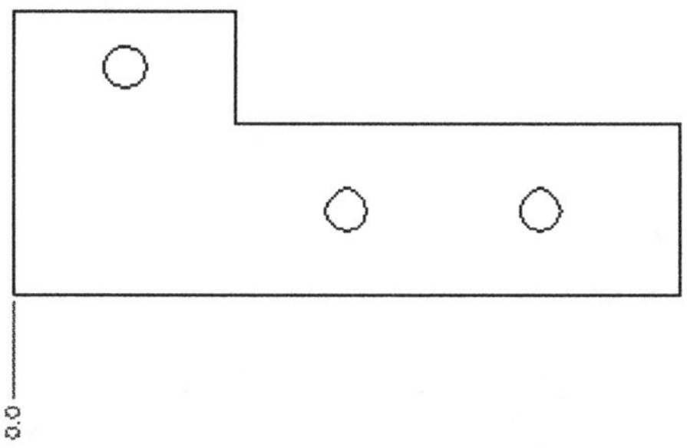

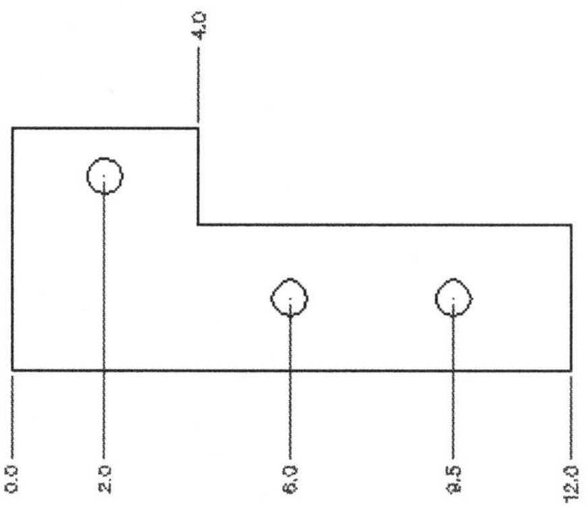

Dimension Space

Command Locator

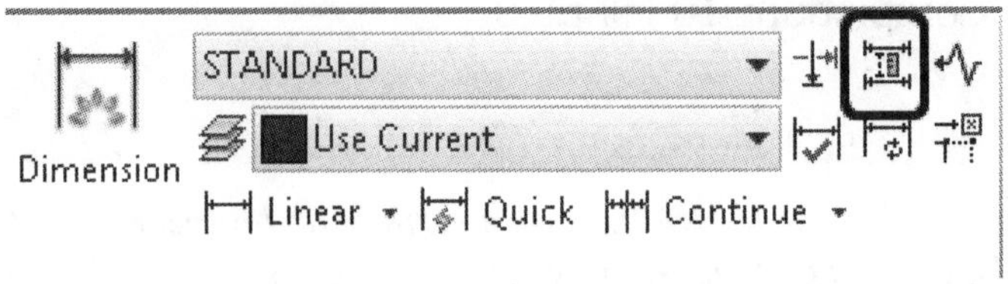

Toolbar Menu	**Dimension Space**
Pull Down Menu	**Dimension / Dimension Space**
Command	**DIMSPACE**

Command Overview

This dimension tool aligns and/or spaces linear and angular dimensions. It uses the spacing value set in the DIMDLI system variable. You can also set the spacing value within the command.

Command Exercise

Exercise 9-9 – Dimension Space

Drawing Name: **dimspace.dwg**
Estimated Time to Completion: 5 Minutes

Scope

Use the DIMSPACE tool to adjust the spacing of the overlapping linear dimensions.

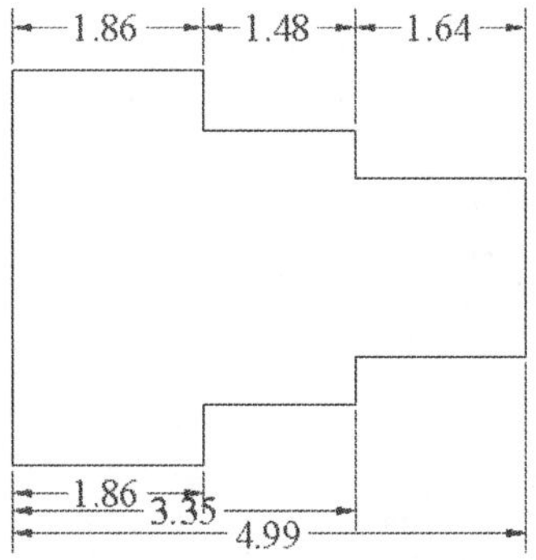

Dimspace Exercise

Solution

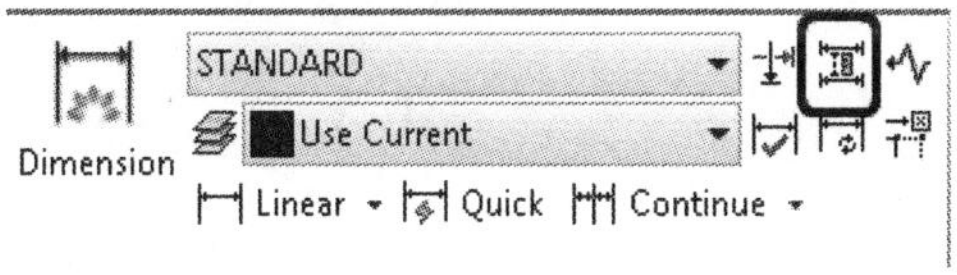

1. Select the DIMSPACE tool from the DIMENSION toolbar.
2. Select the lower 1.86 dimension. It will highlight when you mouse over it to indicate it will be selected.
3. Select the **3.35** dimension.
4. Select the **4.99** dimension.
5. You will be prompted to enter a spacing value or select Auto. Auto is the default and uses the value stored in the DIMDLI system variable.
6. Press **Enter** to accept the default value.

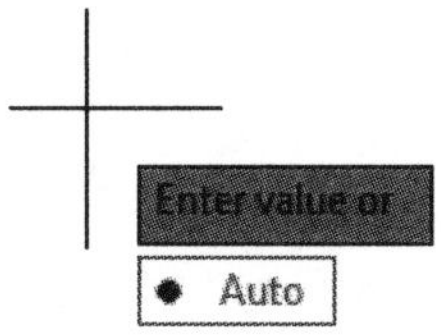

The dimensions will adjust to the correct spacing.

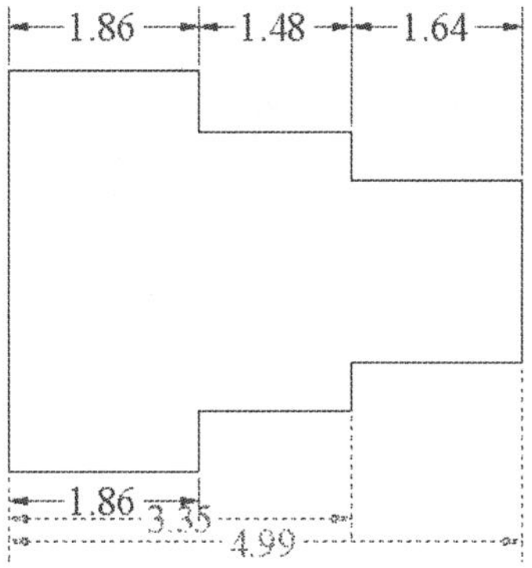

Dimension Break

Command Locator

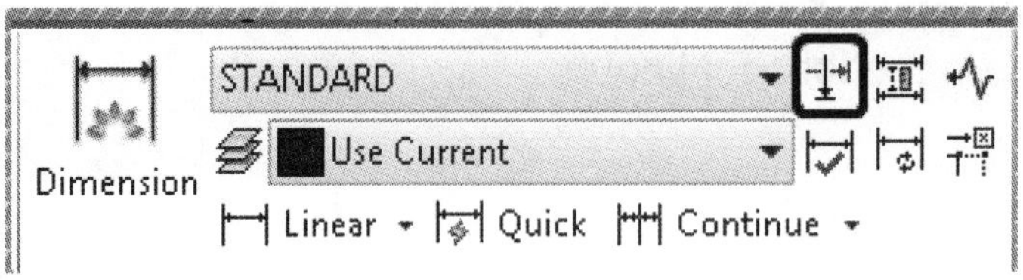

Toolbar Menu	**Dimension Break**
Pull Down Menu	**Dimension / Dimension Break**
Command	**DIMBREAK**
RMB Shortcut Menu	**Auto/Restore/Manual**

Command Overview

This dimension tool places or removes gaps in the extension lines of dimensions. This is used to create a cleaner drawing. The AUTO option requires the user to select an object such as a line to be used as the midpoint for the gap. The RESTORE option removes any breaks placed in the dimensions. The MANUAL option requires the user to select two points to define the gap. If the AUTO option is used, the gap will adjust if the selected object or the dimension is modified.

Command Exercise

Exercise 9-10 – Dimension Break

Drawing Name: **dimbreak.dwg**
Estimated Time to Completion: 15 Minutes

Scope

Use the DIMBREAK tool to place gaps in the extension lines using the AUTO and MANUAL methods. Use the RESTORE option to eliminate the breaks.

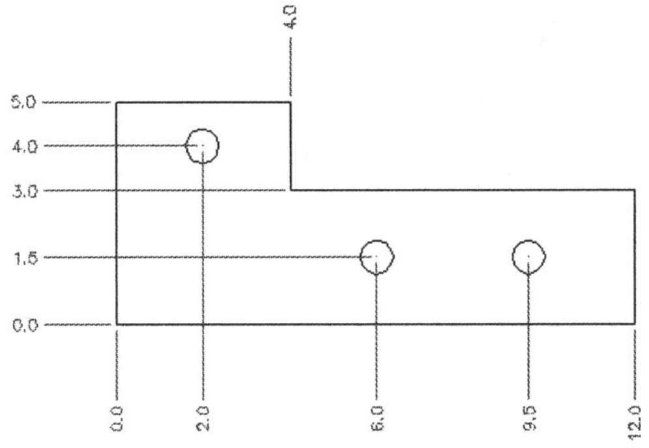

Dimbreak Exercise

Solution

1. Select the **DIMBREAK** tool from the Dimension toolbar.

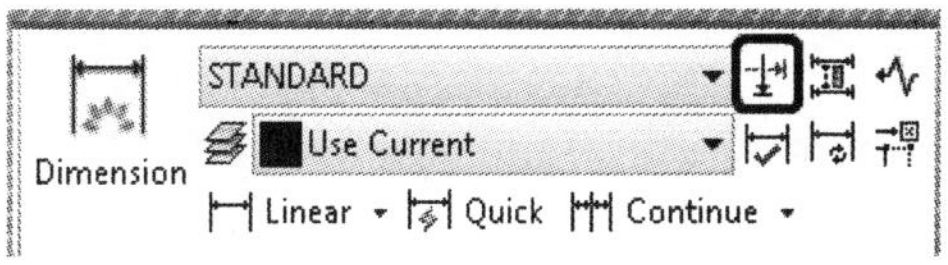

2. Select the 4.0 vertical dimension.
3. Select the polygon object.
4. A gap is placed in the dimension.
5. Press ENTER to exit the command.
6. Select the **DIMBREAK** tool again.
7. Select the 1.5 vertical dimension.
8. RMB and select **Manual**.

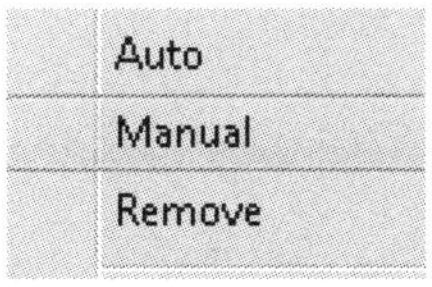

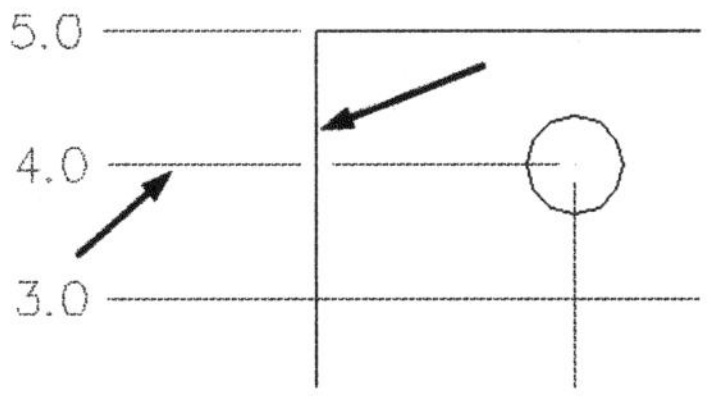

9. Select the horizontal dimension line between the circle and the 1.5 dimension as your first point. Refer to image.
10. Select the intersection between the object and the extension line as the second point. *Use an NEA osnap.*
11. Note the gap created.

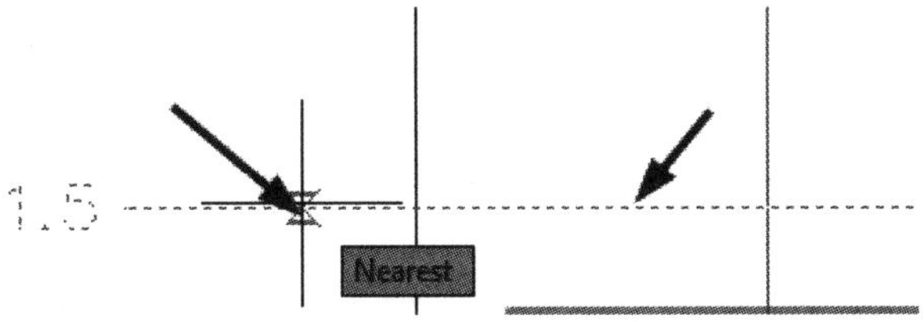

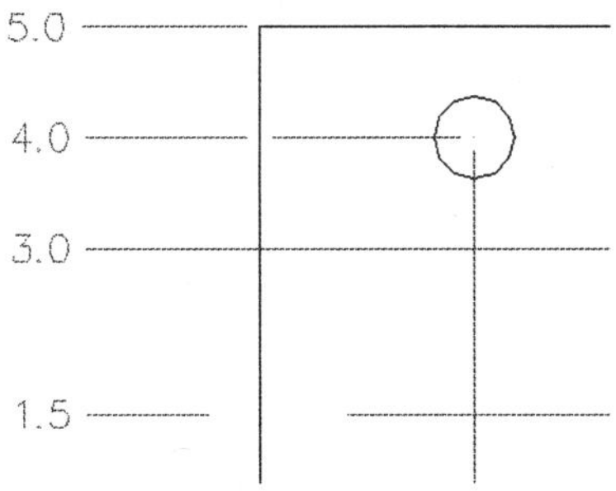

12. Select the **DIMBREAK** tool again.
13. Select the 1.5 vertical dimension you just modified.
14. RMB and select **Remove**.
15. The gap is removed.

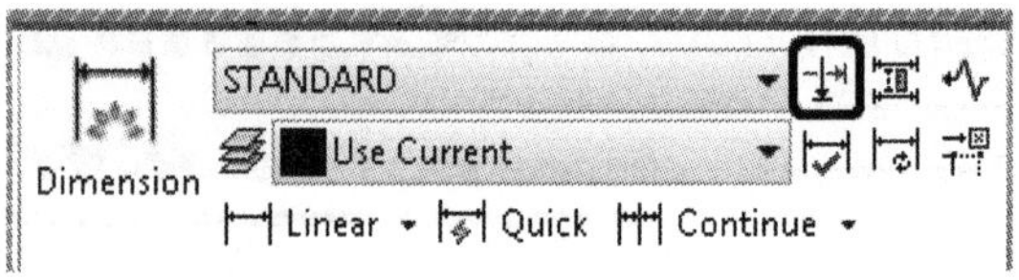

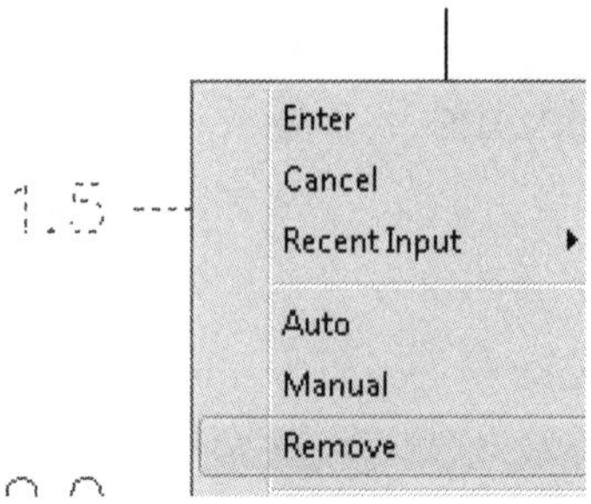

16. Select the **DIMBREAK** tool again.
17. RMB and select **Multiple**.
18. Select the three middle horizontal dimensions.

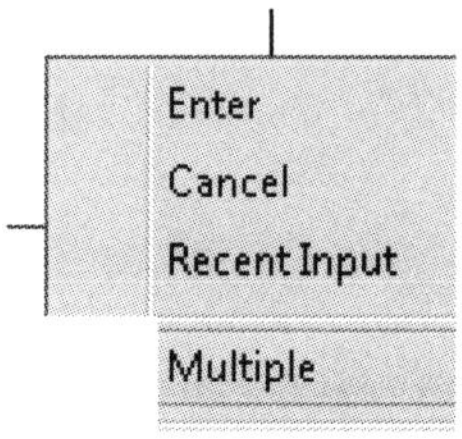

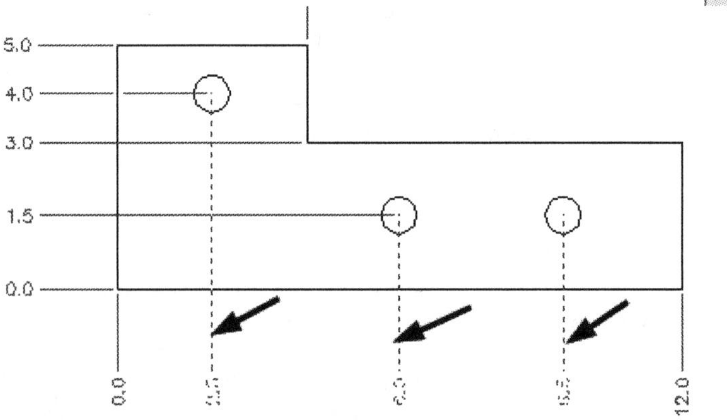

19. Press **ENTER**.
20. RMB and select **ENTER**.

A gap is automatically placed for all three dimensions without having to select the object.

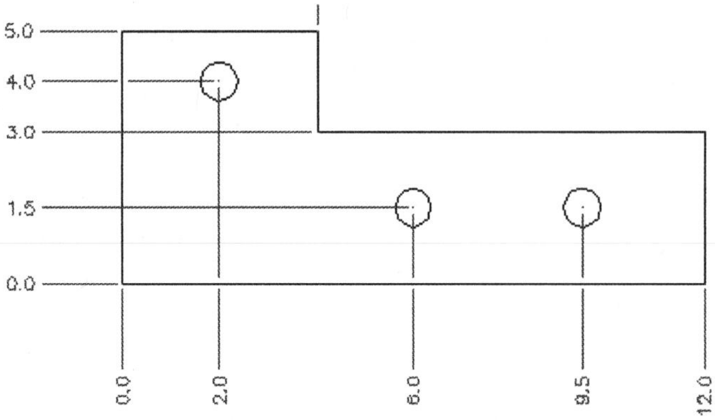

Dimension Style

Command Locator

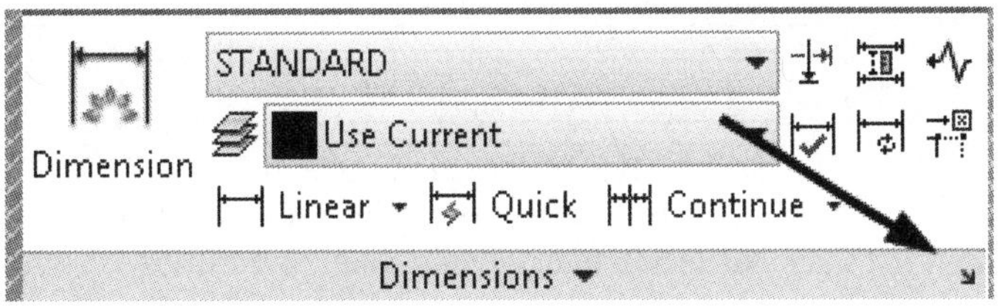

Toolbar Menu	**Dimension**
Pull Down Menu	**Dimension / Style...**
Command	**Dimstyle**
Alias	**D**
Dialog Box	**Dimension Style Manager**

Command Overview

The Standard Dimension Style is sufficient for most beginners. However, it may be necessary to make minor changes to the Standard Dimension Style or create additional Dimension Styles. The Dimension Style Manager dialog box lists and previews selected dimension styles. Select Modify to access the Modify Dimension Style options. Changes made to the Dimension Styles will globally affect the dimensions in the drawing that reference the style being modified, unless the change was made to an individual dimension. Only common modifications to dimension styles will be discussed in this tutorial.

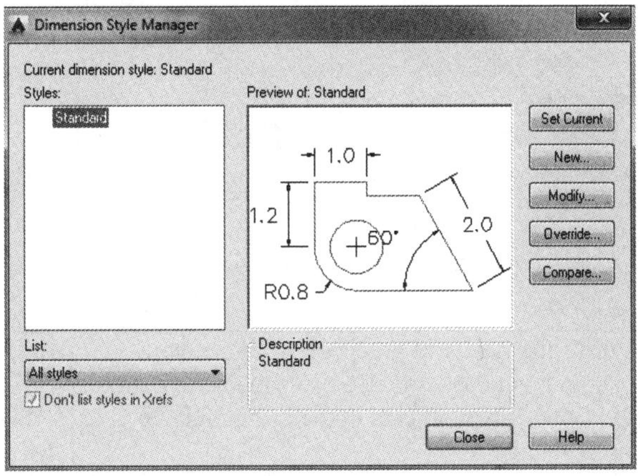

Dimension Style Manager Dialog Box

Use the **Dimension Style Manager** dialog box to make global changes to dimensions in the drawing. This will automatically apply modifications made to the dimension style. When creating a subset from a dimension style with changes to specific dimensions, select New, then choose the type of dimension from the list alongside "Use for." Then select Continue to make the desired changes.

Dimension Style Manager	Overview
Current Dimstyle	Displays the name of the current dimension style.
Styles:	Lists the dimension styles in the drawing.
List	Controls the display of either all dimension style names in the drawing or only the dimension styles in use.
Preview of : Standard	Shows a Preview image of the current [Standard] dimension style.
Set Current	Makes a selected dimension style current.
New…	Invokes the New Dimension Style dialog box where a new style name can be typed, starting with or based on a selected dimension style, for all or selected dimensions (linear, angular, radial…etc.).
Modify…	Invokes the Modify Dimension Style dialog box. Changes made to the current dimension style will be applied to dimensions placed in the drawing using that style (see next section).
Override…	Works similar to the Modify option; however, changes will be applied to dimensions placed after the Override modifications have been made.
Compare…	Compares selected dimension styles and displays the differences.

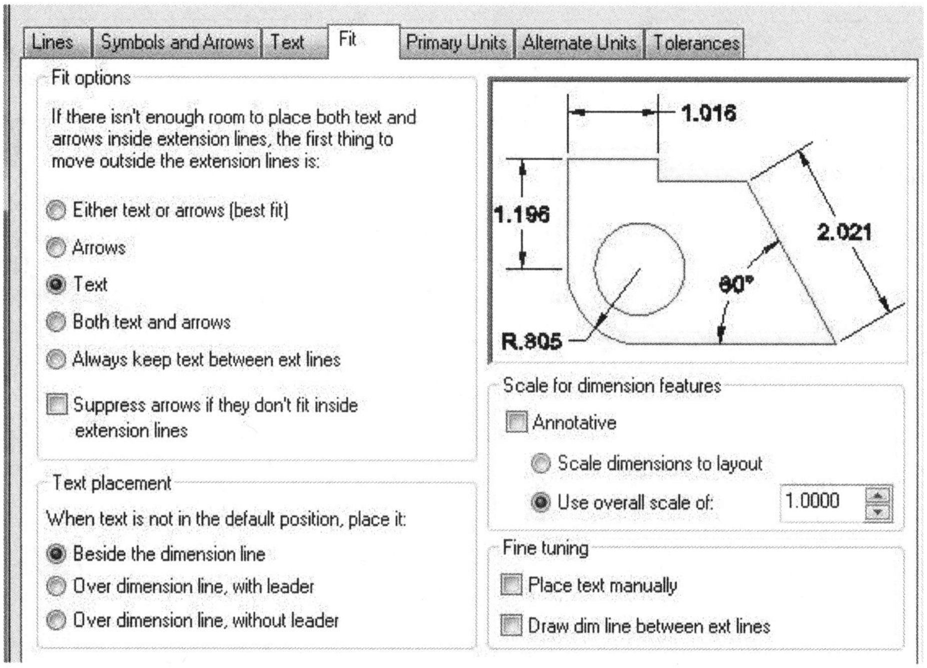

Dimension Style Modify Dialog

Primary Units	Controls the type and precision of dimension linear and angular units. Controls measurement scale factor when objects in the drawing have been scaled.	Linear Dimensions: Unit Format Precision Angular Dimensions: Units Format Precision Measurement Scale: Scale Factor
Alternate Units	Controls the display of Alternate Units, the Unit format, and the Multiplier for alternate units.	Display Alternate Units Precision
Tolerances	Controls Tolerance Format.	Tolerance Format Method Precision Values

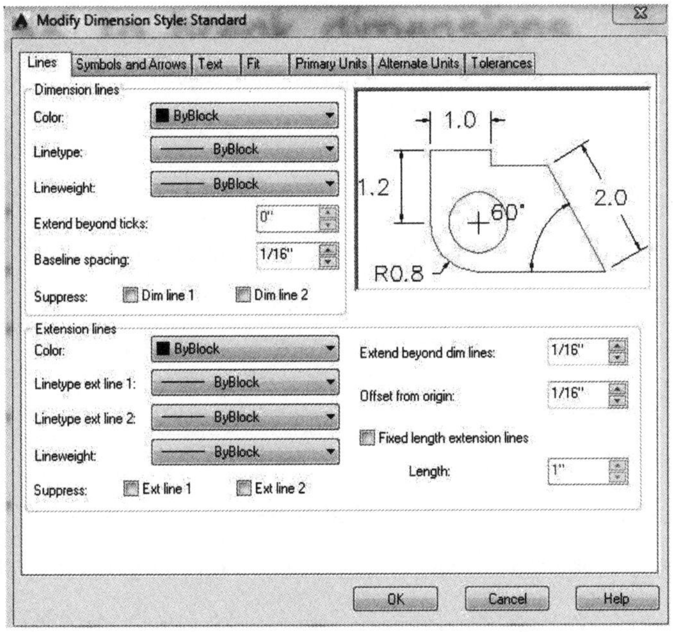

Modify Dimension Style Dialog Box

Modify Dimension Style dialog box tab	Overview	Typical Options to Change
Lines and Arrows	Controls the features of the Extension Lines and Arrowheads.	Offset from origin, colors, and linetype
Symbols and Arrows	Controls the size and the style of arrowheads.	Arrowhead style Center Marks for Circles
Text	Controls the text style, and where the text is located in relation to the dimension lines.	Text Alignment: Horizontal or Aligned with dimension line
Fit	Controls the placement of dimension text.	Sets text above, below, or beside dimension line Set the dimension as annotative
Primary Units	Controls the type and precision of dimension linear and angular units. Controls measurement scale factor when objects in the drawing have been scaled.	Linear Dimensions: Unit Format Precision Angular Dimensions: Units Format Precision Measurement Scale: Scale Factor
Alternate Units	Controls the display of Alternate Units, the Unit format, and the Multiplier for alternate units.	Display Alternate Units Precision
Tolerances	Controls Tolerance Format.	Tolerance Format Method Precision Values

General Procedures

To Create a New Dimension Style:

1. Invoke the Dimension Style command.
2. Select a dimension style to start with from the drop down list. Select the New button, then type the New Style Name, or accept the default name.
3. Select Continue to access the Modify Dimension Style dialog box.

To Modify a Dimension Style:

1. Invoke the Dimension Style command.
2. Select the dimension style, then select the Modify button.
3. Select the appropriate tab in the Modify Dimension Style dialog box. Select OK and Close to Continue.

To Delete a Dimension Style:

1. Invoke the Dimension Style command.
2. Select the dimension style from the list, then right-click (RMB) to access the shortcut menu.
3. Select delete. The dimension style will not be deleted if it is current, or if there are any dimensions in the drawing using that dimension style.

To make a change to a specific feature of an existing the Dimension Style Properties:

1. Invoke the Dimension Style command.
2. In the Dimension Style Manager box, select the dimension style to change then select the New button.
3. From the New Dimension Style dialog box select the dimension type (Angular, Radius, etc.) from the "Use for" list. Select Continue.
4. Select the options to change from the corresponding tab in the Modify Dimension Style dialog box. Then select OK to exit.

Tips & Tricks

- The Purge command can also be used to delete unreferenced Dimension Styles. Select File / Drawing Utilities / Purge (select option or All).
- The Standard Dimension Style will be adequate for most beginners.
- When creating a new dimension style, base the new style on Standard, and apply changes to it, leaving Standard alone, unless only minor changes are needed.
- Make global modifications to dimensions in the drawing by changing the Dimension Style. Existing dimensions should automatically update. If for some reason they do not update, select the dimension Update command from the Dimension toolbar or from the Dimension pull-down menu.

Command Exercise

Exercise 9-11 – Dimension Styles

Drawing Name: **dimsty1.dwg**
Estimated Time to Completion: 30 Minutes

Scope

Dimension the object on the left using the standard dimension style. Create a new Dimension Style called TEST based on the Standard dimension style with overall scale (Geometry) of 2 (remember to set current). Dimension the object on the right.

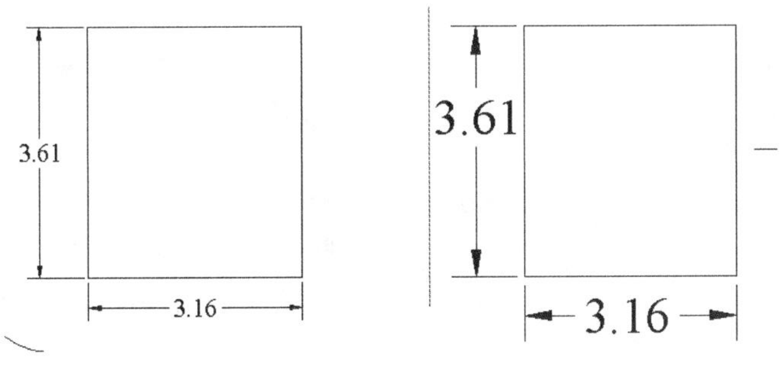

Dimension Styles Exercise

Solution

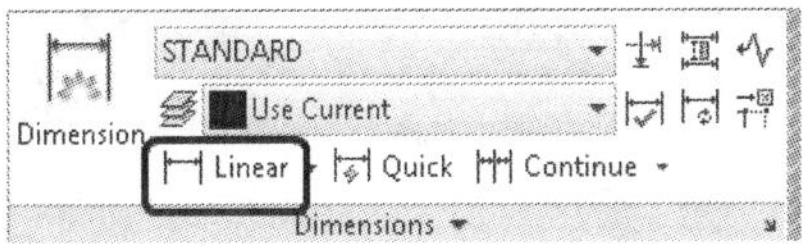

1. Invoke the **Linear Dimension** command (dimlinear).
2. *Specify first extension line origin or <select object>:*
   Press <ENTER> to select an object.
3. *Select object to dimension:*
   Select the left side of the left box.
4. *Specify dimension line location or [Mtext/Text/Angle/Horizontal/ Vertical/Rotated:*
   Select a location for the vertical dimension.
5. Repeat the Linear Dimension command with the RMB (dimlinear or <ENTER>).
6. *Specify first extension line origin or <select object>:*
   Press <ENTER> to select an object.
7. *Select object to dimension:*
   Select the bottom of the left box.

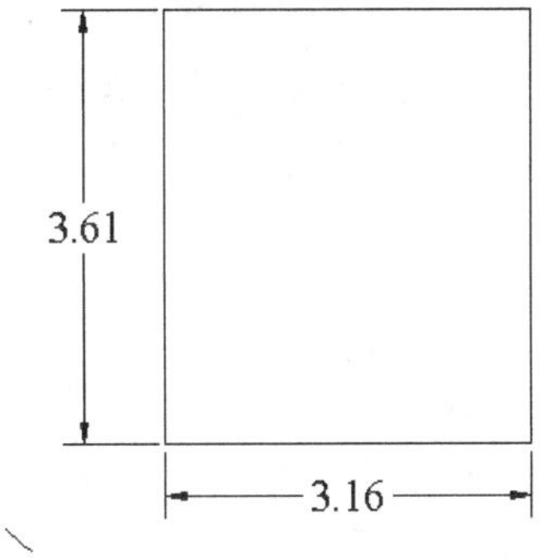

8. *Specify dimension line location or [Mtext/Text/Angle/Horizontal/Vertical/Rotated:*
   Select a location for the horizontal dimension.
9. Invoke the Dimension Style command (dimstyle).

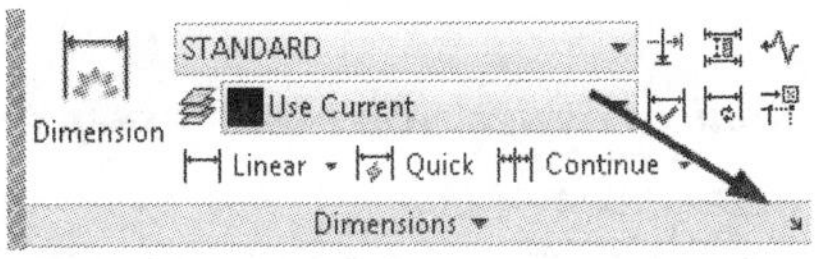

10. In the Dimension Style Manager dialog box, press **New...** to create a new dimension style.

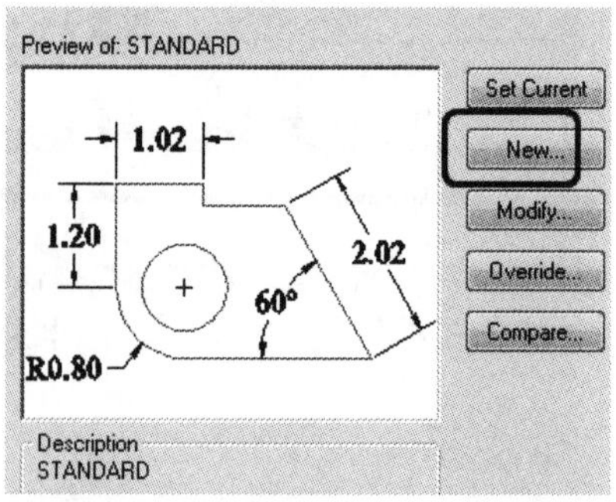

11. In the Create New Dimension Style dialog box, enter the new name **test** for the new dimension style based on the standard dimension style and press **Continue**.

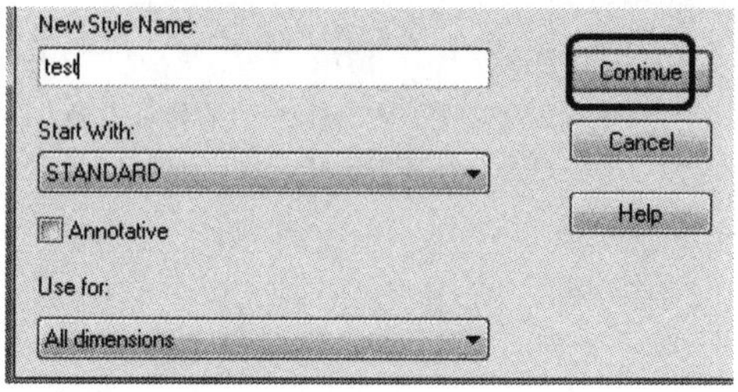

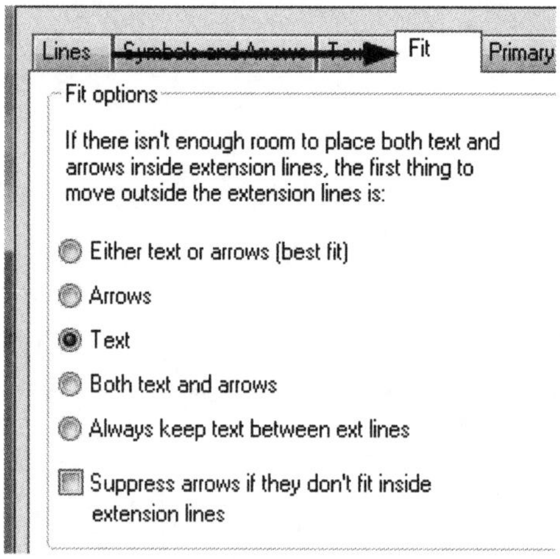

12. Select the Fit tab:

Under Fit options:

13. Enable **Text**.

Notice how the radial dimension changes in preview window.

Under Scale for dimension features:

14. Change the overall scale to **2**.

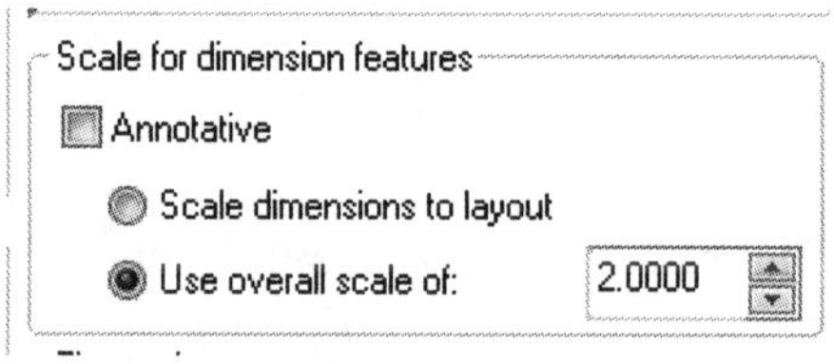

Under Text placement:

15. Enable **Beside the dimension line**.

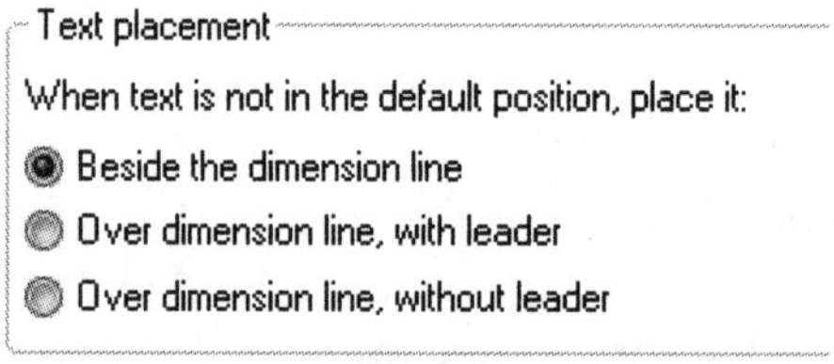

16. Select the Primary Units tab.

Under Linear Dimensions:

17. Set the Precision to **0.00**.

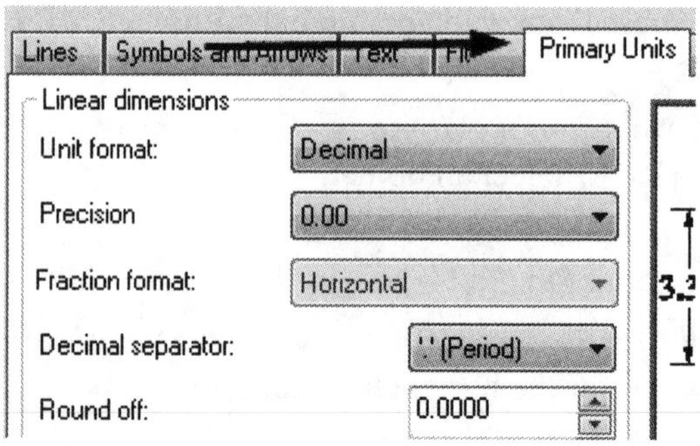

In mechanical design, you want to keep the precision for your dimensions to three decimal places or less. A good rule of thumb is that every decimal place adds 10% to the cost of fabrication.

Note how the Preview window display updates to reflect the changes.

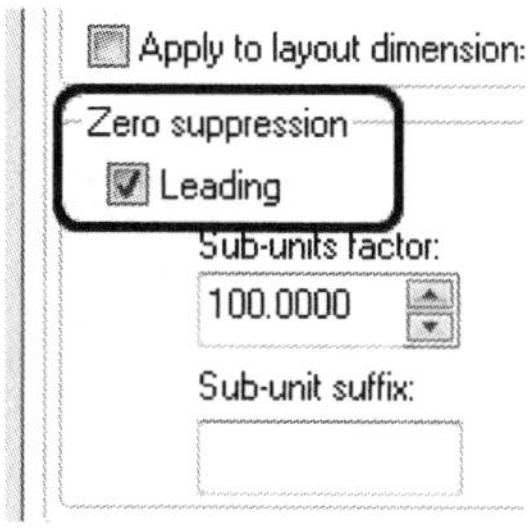

18. Enable **Leading** under Zero suppression.

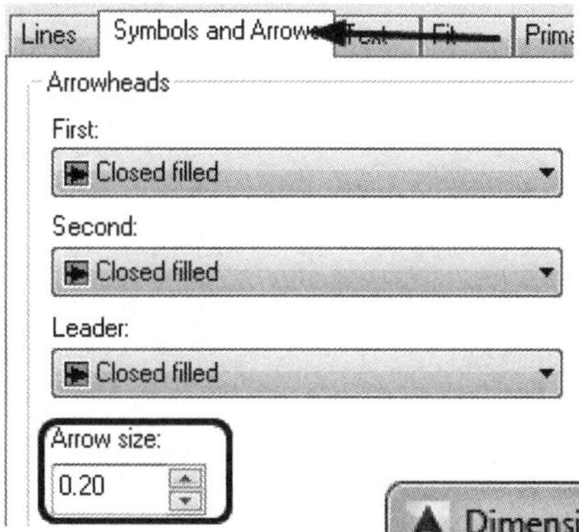

19. Select the Symbols and Arrows tab.

Under Arrowheads:

20. Set the Arrow size to **0.200**.

21. Press the **OK** button to continue.

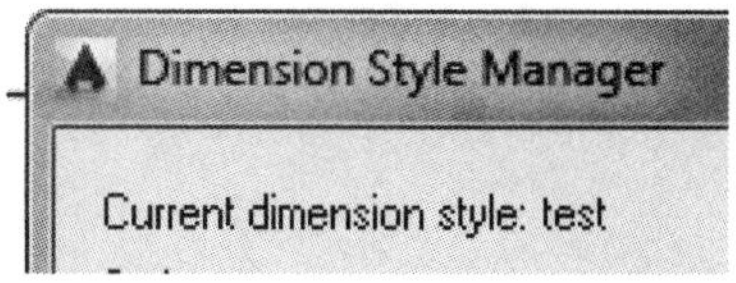

Note that the current dimension style is set to the new style.

22. Press **Close** to continue.

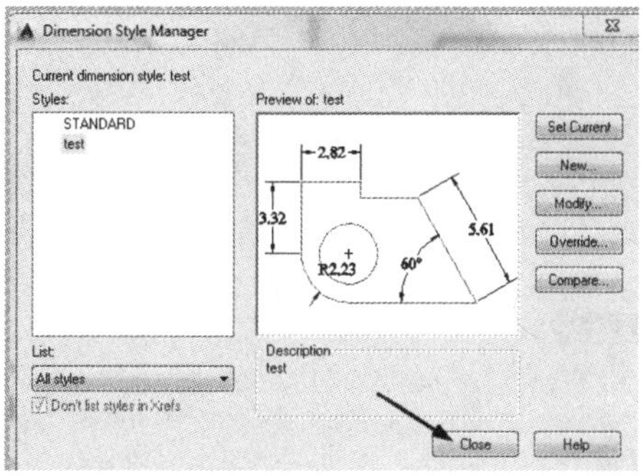

23. Invoke the Linear Dimension command (dimlinear).

24. *Specify first extension line origin or <select object>:*
Press <ENTER> to select an object.

25. *Select object to dimension:*
Select the left side of the box on the right.

26. *Specify dimension line location or [Mtext/Text/Angle/ Horizontal/Vertical/Rotated:*
Select a location for the vertical dimension.

27. Repeat the Linear Dimension command with the RMB (dimlinear or <ENTER>).

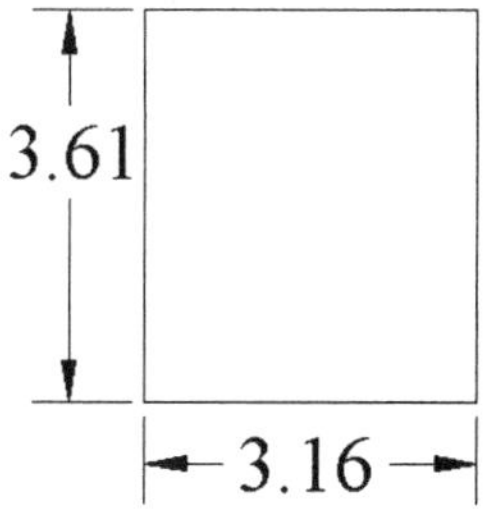

28. *Specify first extension line origin or <select object>:*
Press <ENTER> to select an object.

29. *Select object to dimension:*
Select the bottom of the box on the right.

30. Specify dimension line location or [Mtext/Text/Angle/Horizontal/ Vertical/ Rotated:
Select a location for the horizontal dimension.

Compare the two dimension styles.

Edit Dimension Location

Command Overview

The placement of the dimension lines and text can be adjusted using Grips. With the command line blank, select the dimension. Select the grip at either arrow point, or on the dimension text, drag the cursor then pick the new location. The location of the dimension text can be moved closer to one extension line or the other using the same method. This is also a good way to move the extension line origin points, should they be incorrectly selected.

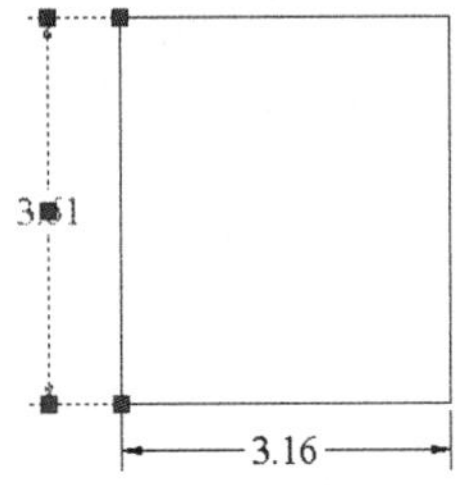

Grips on a Dimension Line

General Procedures

To move the dimension line:

1. With the Command line blank, select the dimension.
2. Select either the text, or arrowhead grip. The default grip mode will be Stretch.
3. Stretch the dimension line and pick the new location. Press Escape two times to cancel the grip selection.

To move the dimension text:

1. With the Command line blank, select the dimension.
2. Select the dimension text. The default grip mode will be Stretch.
3. Drag the dimension text toward one extension line or the other, or to a new location. Press Escape two times to cancel the grip selection.

To move a dimension origin point:

1. Zoom into the area where the dimension origin point should meet the object (intersection, endpoint...etc.). With the Command line blank, select the dimension.
2. Select the dimension origin point. The default grip mode will be Stretch.
3. Use Object Snap to drag the origin point to the correct location on the object. Press Escape two times to cancel the grip selection.

Note: *Sometimes both the object and the dimension may be selected and the origin point dragged to the grip of the object being dimensioned.*

Tips & Tricks

- Remember to press the Escape key two times to cancel the grip selection. Pressing <ENTER> will repeat the last command (which may have been the Erase command!).

Edit Dimension Text

Command Locator

Toolbar Menu	**Text/ Edit Text**
Pull Down Menu	**Modify / Text…**
Command	**Ddedit**
RMB Shortcut Menu	**Text area of the Multiline Text Editor**
Dialog Box	**Multiline Text Editor**

Command Overview

AutoCAD dimensions are *associated* with the object being dimensioned; therefore, if the dimension text appears to be incorrect, it is either because the dimension line origin points were incorrectly selected, or the drawing is incorrect. Check first to see that the origin points are at the correct location (see previous section). If this seems to be correct, then go back and correct the drawing. The Edit Text command (DDEDIT) should be used to add annotation to the dimension text and not to delete or overwrite existing dimension text. In the Multiline Text Editor, the dimension text will be represented as the *greater than* and *less than* symbols < >. Place the cursor before or after these symbols to type additional text. Do not overwrite or delete the < > symbols representing the dimension text. Deleting or typing over these symbols will break *associativity* between the dimension and the objects being dimensioned. It is better to make corrections to the geometry in the drawing. The Text Editor ribbon is a contextual ribbon that appears only when text is being edited.

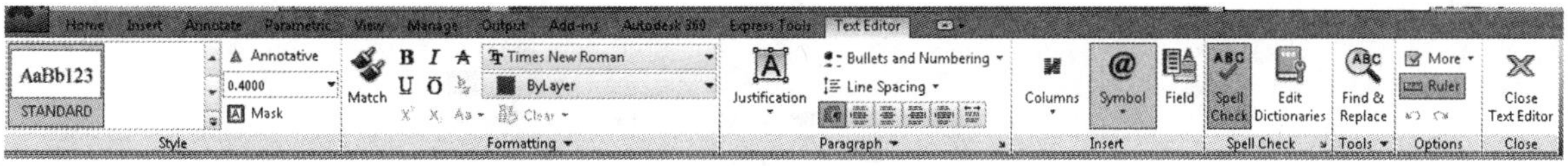

Multiline Text Editor Ribbon

General Procedures

1. Invoke the Edit Text command.
2. Select the dimension to edit.
3. Place the cursor before or after the < > symbols and type additional annotation. Select OK to exit.

Tips & Tricks

- Never delete these < > symbols, or type in between these symbols.
- By maintaining *associativity* between the dimension and the object being dimensioned, changes made to the object will automatically update the dimension text.
- If you ever accidentally delete or modify a dimension, you can select the dimension and type <> and the true dimension will automatically be recovered.

Edit Dimension Properties

Command Locator

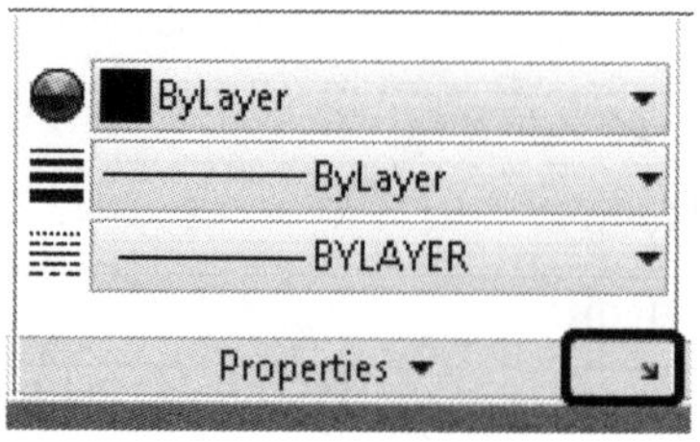

Toolbar Menu	**Standard** *(Select dimension first)*
Command	*(Select dimension first)* **Properties**
Dialog Box	**Properties**

Command Overview

When changing dimensions properties, decide first whether this change should apply globally to the dimension style, or to a single dimension.

For instance, if the precision of the primary units of a dimension style are set to four decimal places, and the user wants the precision of radial dimensions to always be two decimal places, then a subset style for Radius dimensions needs to be created from the original dimension style. Use the Dimension Style Manager dialog box to make the desired changes, and all of the radial dimensions in the drawing will be automatically updated to reflect the change.

If you want to change only a selected dimension in the drawing, use the Properties command. Changes made to individual dimensions will usually not update globally if a change is later made to that Dimension Style.

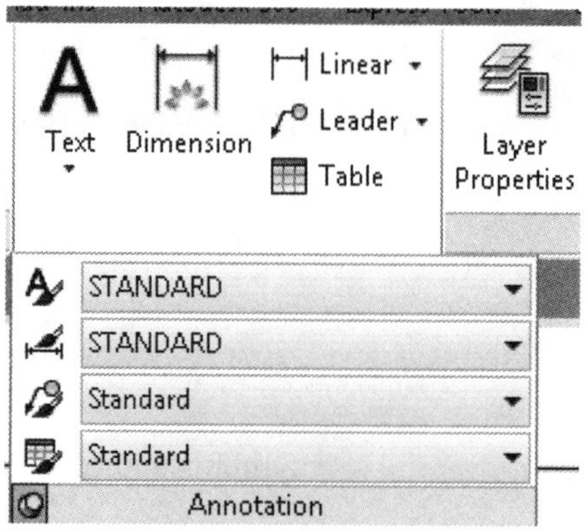

The Annotation Styles panel

The Styles panel is a drop down under Annotation on the Home ribbon. It allows you to select the current dimension style, the current text style and the current table style. Simply select the style you want to make active from the drop-down list.

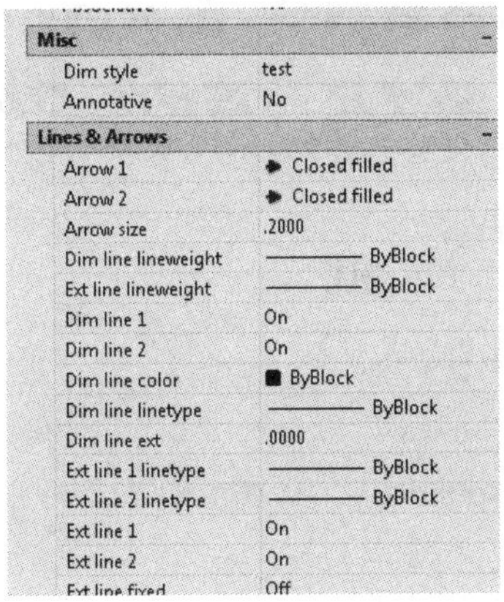

Properties

Use the **Properties** dialog box to change individual dimensions in the drawing. Select the dimension in the drawing to display the dimension properties in the dialog box. Select the plus sign + before the property to access the options to change.

General Procedures

To make a change to an individual dimension:

1. Invoke Properties command.
2. Select the dimension to change (move the Properties dialog box if necessary).
3. Select the option to change. If there is a plus + sign before the option to change, select the plus sign first, then select the option to change. Type or select the new option.
4. Select OK to exit.

Tips & Tricks

- When editing dimensions, determine whether you want to apply the change globally by making the change to the Dimension Style, or individually by using the Properties command.
- Changes made to individual dimensions will usually not update if a change is later made to that Dimension Style.

Command Exercise

Exercise 9-12 – Edit Dimension

Drawing Name: **dimedit1.dwg**
Estimated Time to Completion: 5 Minutes

Scope

Use the Properties command to modify the dimensions as indicated.

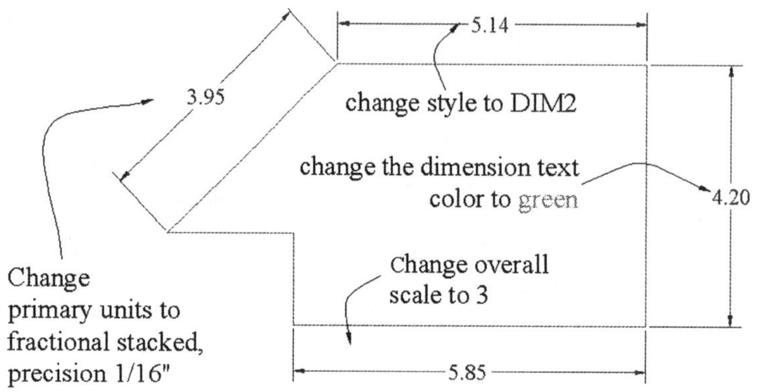

Edit Dimension Exercise

Solution

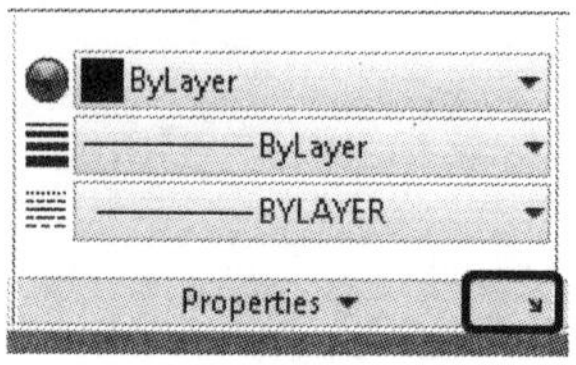

1. Launch the Properties palette on the Home ribbon.

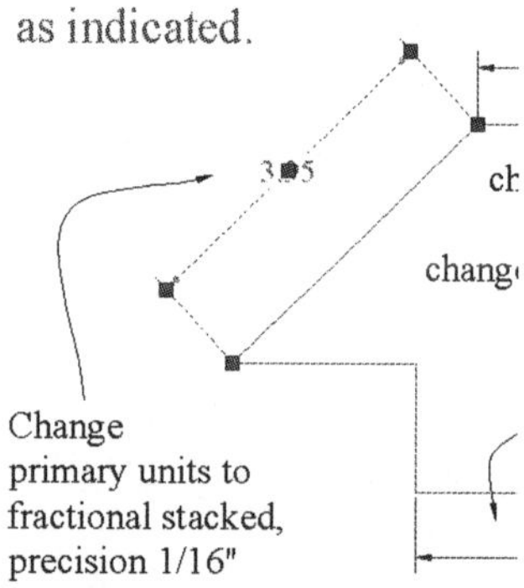

2. Select the aligned dimension that will be changed to fractional stacked.

3. In the Properties dialog box, scroll down and change the 'Dim units' to **Fractional**.

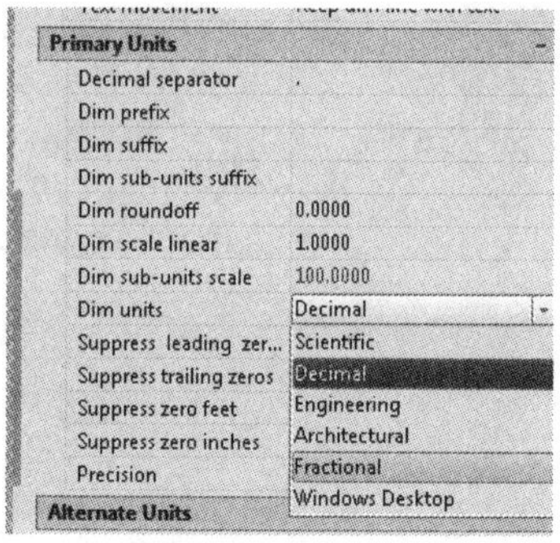

4. Change the 'Precision' to '**0 1/16**'.

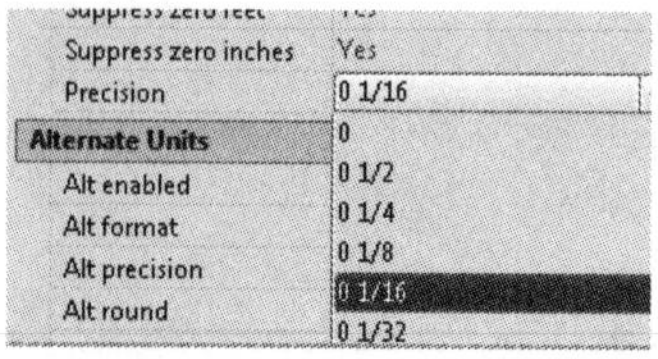

5. Click a point in the drawing window with the LMB.

Notice how the Dimension changes. Press the <Esc> key once to clear the selection.

6. Pick the top horizontal dimension that will have its style changed to DIM2.

7. Change the 'Dim style' to **DIM2** on the Annotation ribbon.

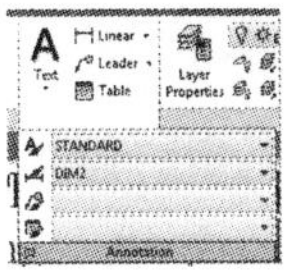

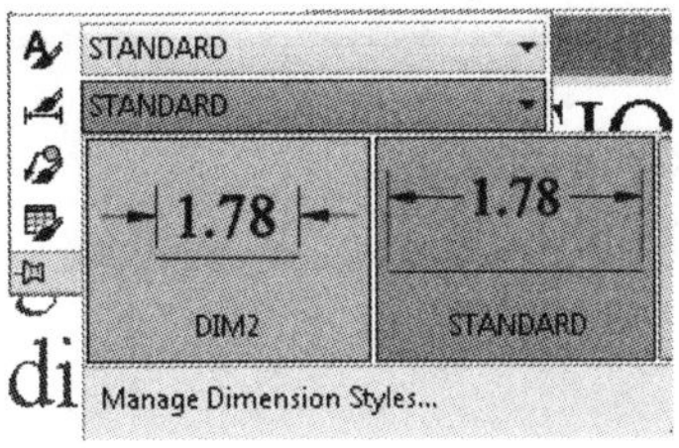
STANDARD
STANDARD
1.78
1.78
DIM2
STANDARD
Manage Dimension Styles...

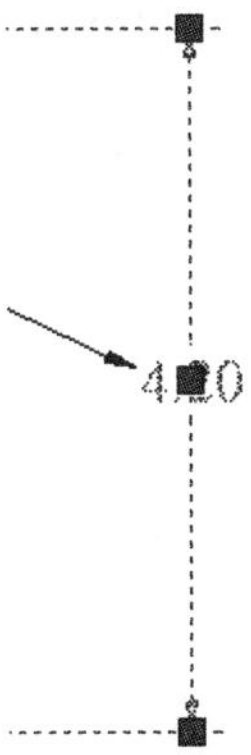

8. Notice how the Dimension changes. Press the <Esc> key once to clear the selection.

9. Pick the vertical dimension that will have its text color changed to green.

10. Scroll down the Properties palette to change the 'Text color' to **Green**.

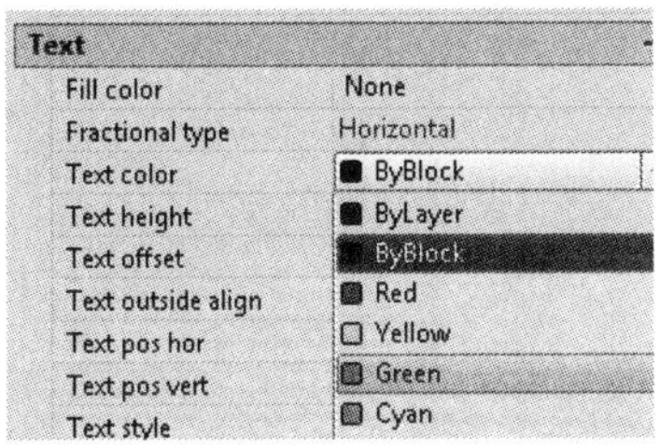
Text
Fill color
None
Fractional type
Horizontal
Text color
ByBlock
Text height
ByLayer
Text offset
ByBlock
Text outside align
Red
Text pos hor
Yellow
Text pos vert
Green
Text style
Cyan

Notice how the Dimension changes.

11. Press the <Esc> key once to clear the selection.

12. Pick the lower horizontal dimension that will have its overall scale changed to 3.

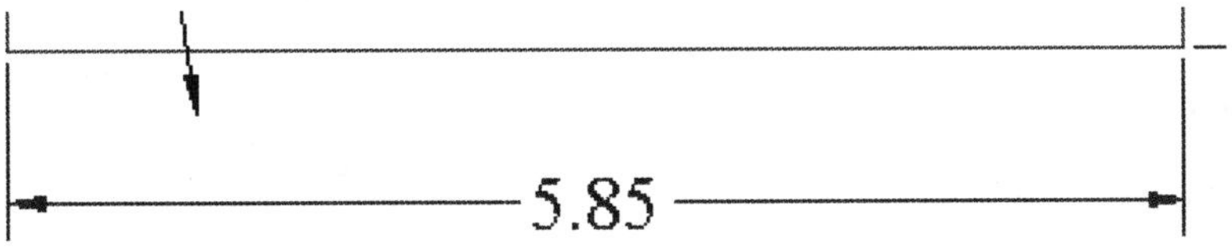
5.85

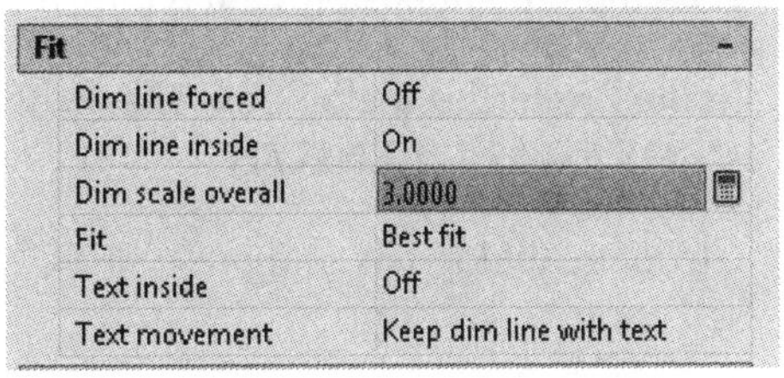
Fit
Dim line forced
Off
Dim line inside
On
Dim scale overall
3.0000
Fit
Best fit
Text inside
Off
Text movement
Keep dim line with text

13. Scroll down to the Fit heading and change the 'Dim scale overall' setting to **3**.

Notice how the Dimension changes.

14. Press the <Esc> key once to clear the selection.

15. Close the Properties palette.

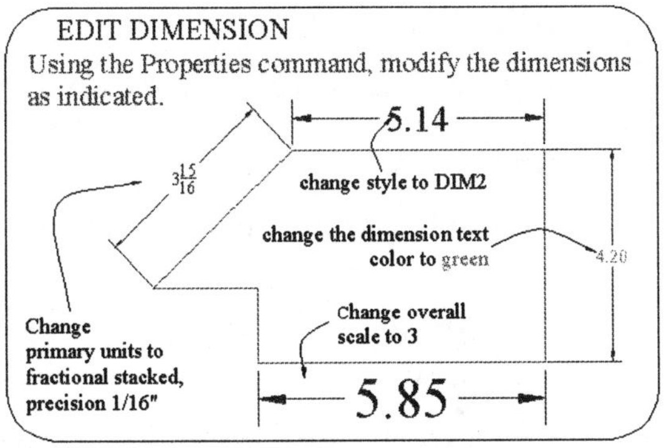
EDIT DIMENSION
Using the Properties command, modify the dimensions as indicated.
5.14
change style to DIM2
change the dimension text color to green
4.20
Change primary units to fractional stacked, precision 1/16"
Change overall scale to 3
5.85

Your drawing should look like this.

Command Exercise

Exercise 9-13 – Edit Dimension Text

Drawing Name: **dimedit2.dwg**
Estimated Time to Completion: 10 Minutes

Scope

Use the Properties command to edit the top dimension. Use the Edit Text command to make changes to the bottom dimension.

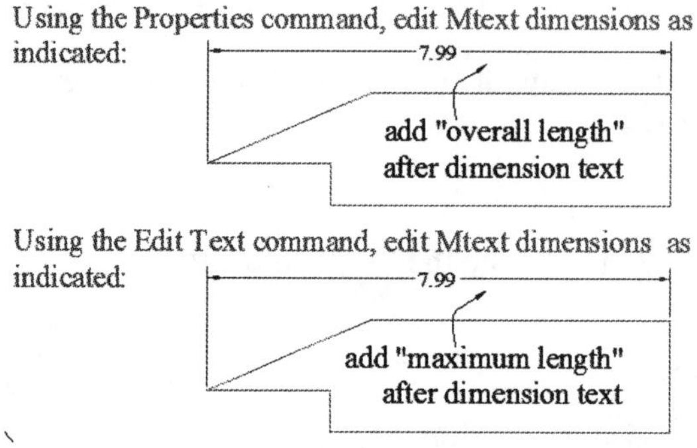
Using the Properties command, edit Mtext dimensions as indicated:
7.99
add "overall length" after dimension text
Using the Edit Text command, edit Mtext dimensions as indicated:
7.99
add "maximum length" after dimension text

Edit Dimension Exercise

Solution

ByLayer
ByLayer
BYLAYER
Properties

1. Launch the Properties palette from the Home ribbon.

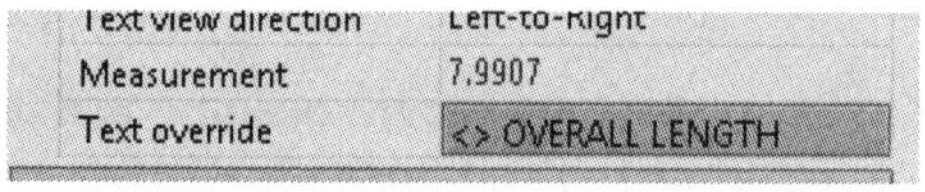
Text view direction
Left-to-Right
Measurement
7.9907
Text override
<> OVERALL LENGTH

2. Pick the top dimension with the LMB.
3. In the Properties dialog box, change the Text override to **<> OVERALL LENGTH.**
4. Close the dialog box and press <ESC> once to clear the selection.

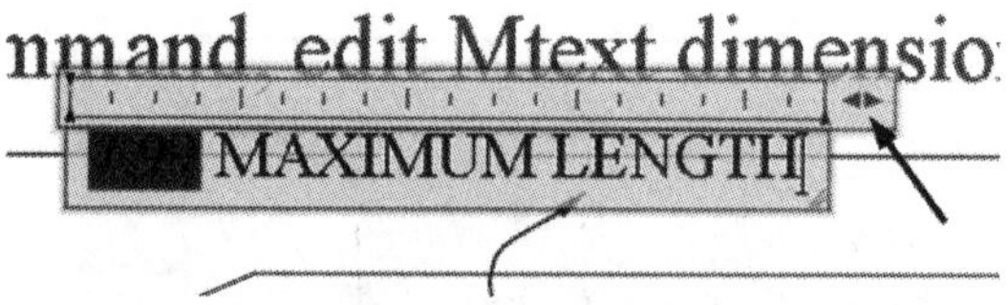
MAXIMUM LENGTH

5. *Type **TEXTEDIT.***

Select an annotation object or [Undo]:

<Select the lower dimension text>

6. Type in the desired text in the edit field. Use the arrows on the text box to expand the text box.
7. Select **Close Text Editor** on the ribbon.

Close
Text Editor
Close

Typing <> indicates the original dimension value.

Command Exercise

Exercise 9-14 – Edit Dimension Using Grips

Drawing Name: **dimedit3.dwg**
Estimated Time to Completion: 10 Minutes

Scope

Use the Align Text Option in the Dimensions Menu.
Use Grips to adjust the dimensions as indicated.

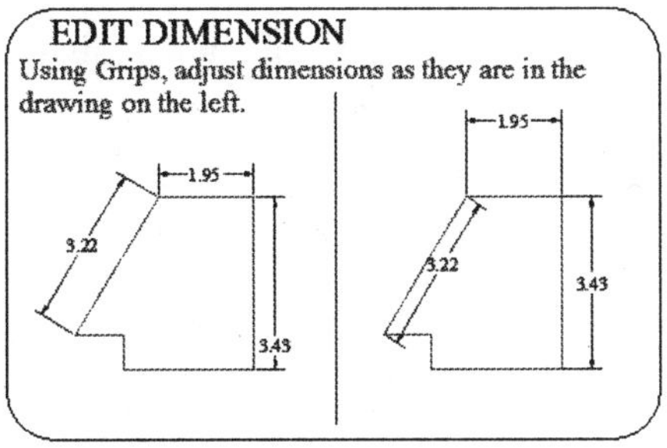

Edit Dimension Exercise

Solution

1. Pick the 3.43 vertical dimension on the right side figure.

Use the grip on the text to position the text.

Press <ESC> to release the selection.

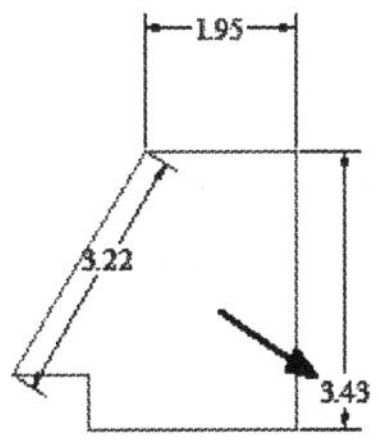

2. Pick the horizontal dimension at the top of the object on the right.

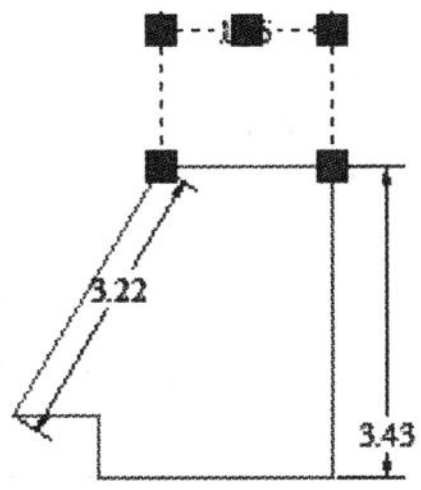

3. Select one of the end grips along the dimension line.
4. *Specify stretch point or [Base point/Copy/Undo/eXit]:*
   Move the dimension down closer to the top line segment and click again.
5. Press <ESC> once to clear the selection.

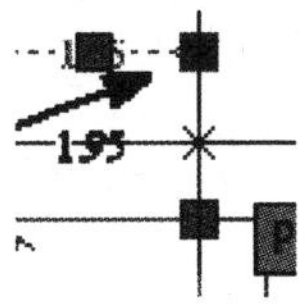

6. Pick the Aligned dimension.

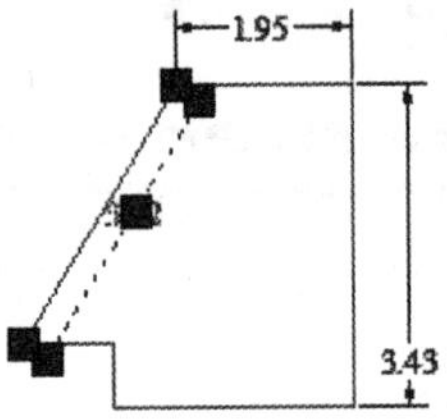

7. Select the grip over the text.

8. *Specify stretch point or [Base point/Copy/Undo/eXit]:*
   Move the dimension away from the line segment and click again to place.

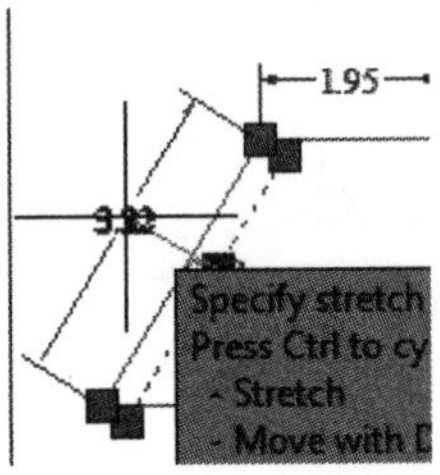

9. Press <ESC> to deselect.

Tips & Tricks

- When using the Stretch tool to modify objects, turn ORTHO ON.

Command Exercise

Exercise 9-15 – Edit Dimension Using Stretch

Drawing Name: **dimedit4.dwg**
Estimated Time to Completion: 10 Minutes

Scope

Use the Stretch command to modify the part. Notice that the dimensions will change automatically.

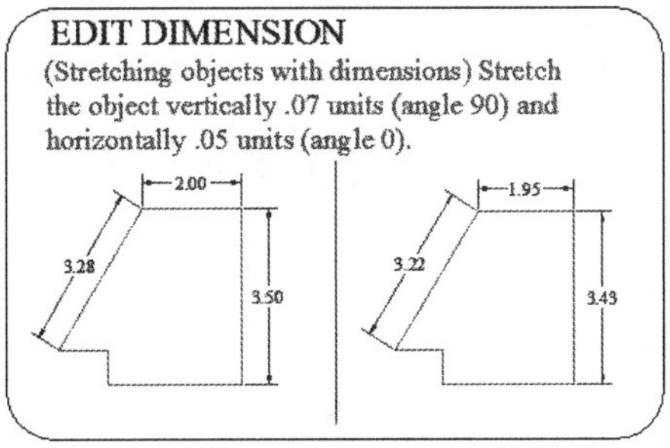

Edit Dimension Exercise

Solution

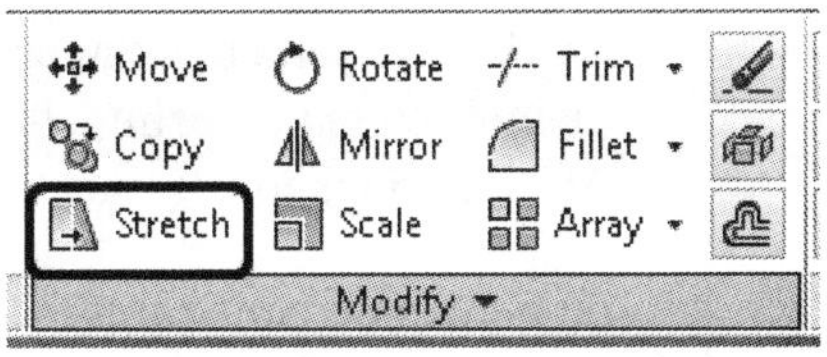

1. Invoke the Stretch command (stretch) on the Home ribbon.
2. *Select objects:*
   Using a crossing window, select the bottom portion of the part, and include crossing over the dimensions.
3. *Select objects:*
   Press <ENTER>

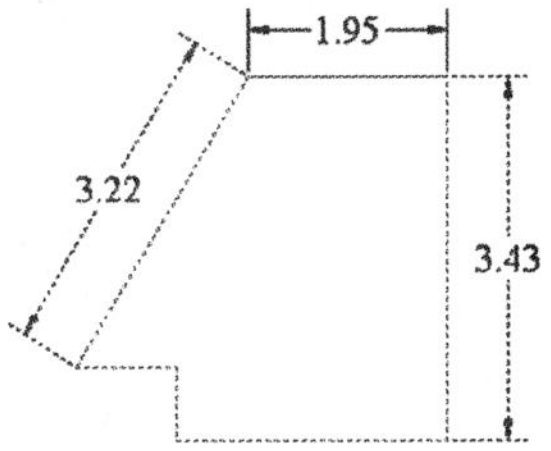

4. *Specify base point or displacement:*
   Pick a base point near the center of the object.
5. *Specify second point of displacement:*
   Drag the object down; type '0.07' and press <ENTER>. Notice how the part changes as well as the dimensions.

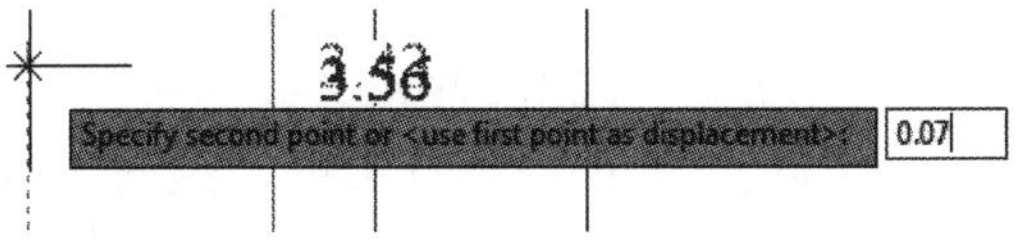

6. Repeat the Stretch command with the RMB (stretch or <ENTER>).
7. *Select objects:*
   Using a crossing window, select the right side, and include crossing over the horizontal dimension.

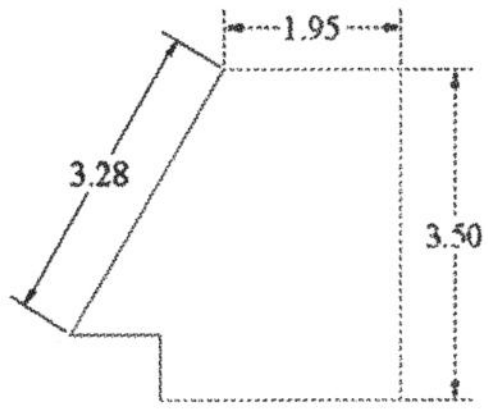

8. *Select objects:*
   Press <ENTER>
9. *Specify base point or displacement:*
   Pick a base point near the center of the object.
10. *Specify second point of displacement:*
    Drag the object to the right and type '0.05' and press <ENTER>.

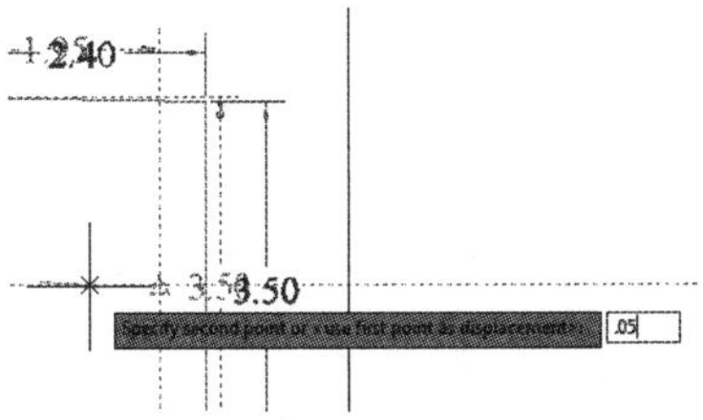

Dimconstraint

Command Locator

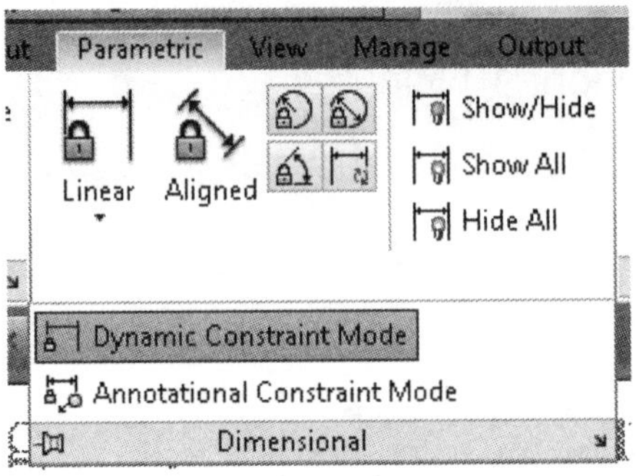

Toolbar Menu	**Parametric/DIMCONSTRAINT**
Command	*DIMCONSTRAINT*

Command Overview

Dimensional constraints control the lengths, radial sizes and angles of objects. They also control the distances or relation between objects.

By default, dimensional constraints are not plotted. If you wish to have dimensional constraints visible when you print, change the dimensional constraint to an annotational constraint. Annotational constraints are plotted, have a static size, and use the current dimension style.

Dimensional constraints are also called dynamic constraints because they can be modified and they control the size of the objects to which they are applied.

General Procedures

To add a dimensional constraint:

1. On the Dimensional panel, click Aligned.
2. Press ENTER to select an object to be dimensioned.
3. Select the object and then left click to place the dimension.
4. Press ENTER or left click anywhere outside the text box to accept the default value OR modify the value displayed and then press ENTER.

To modify a parametric dimension:

1. Double left click on the dimensional constraint to be changed.
2. Left click inside the text box and enter the new value.
3. Press ENTER or left click outside the textbox to complete the change.

To convert a parametric dimension to an annotational dimension:

1. Select a dimensional constraint.
2. In the Properties palette, set the Constraint to Annotational instead of Dynamic.

Tips & Tricks

- Add a FIX constraint at the desired base point of the sketch to prevent elements from moving around.
- Add geometric constraints BEFORE adding dimensional constraints.
- It is easier to go from BIG to SMALL than SMALL to BIG, so make your sketch bigger than desired if you plan to use dimensional constraints.
- Consider how the drawing might be changed in the future and apply dimensional constraints to control those changes.

Command Exercise

Exercise 9-16 – Dimension Constraints

Drawing Name: **dynconstraints1.dwg**
Estimated Time to Completion: 10 Minutes

Scope

Apply aligned and angular dimensional constraints. Use dimensional constraints to change elements.

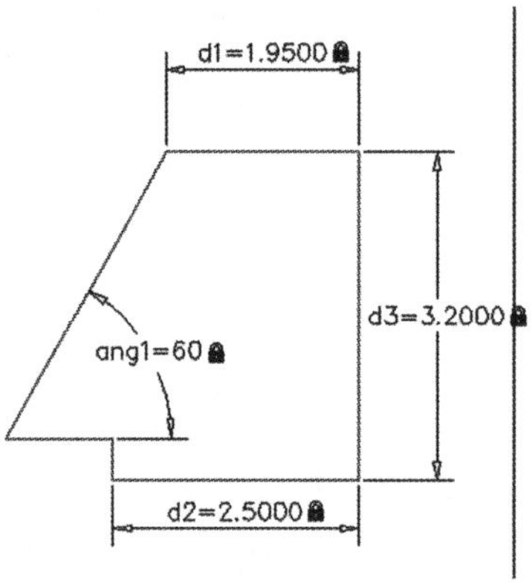

Dimension Constraints Exercise

Solution

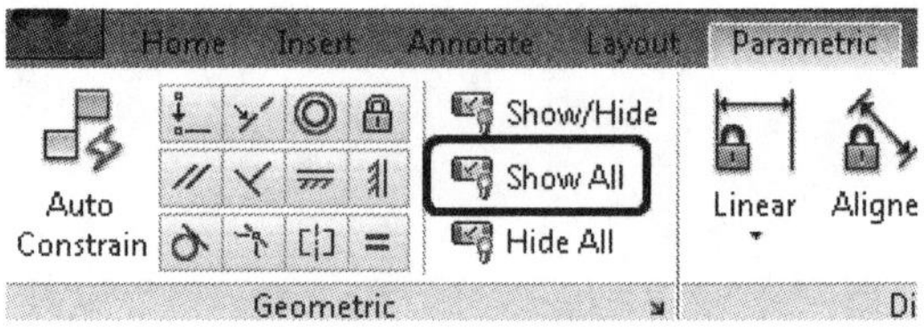

1. Activate the Parametric ribbon.

2. Select **Show All** to display any existing parametric dimensions.

3. Select the **ALIGNED** dimensional tool.

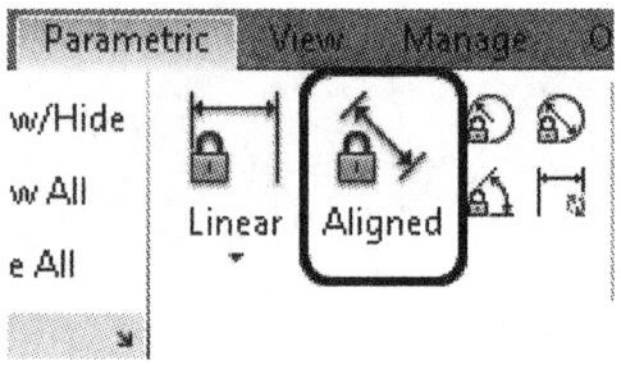

4. Press <ENTER> to select an object.

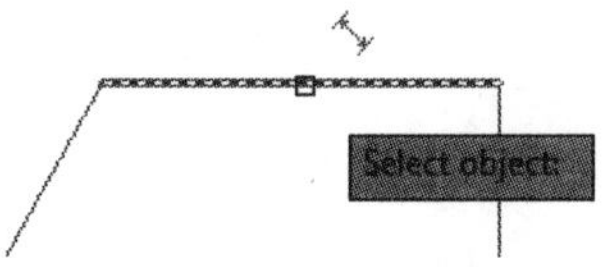

5. Select the top horizontal line on the right object.

6. Left click to place the dimension above the line.

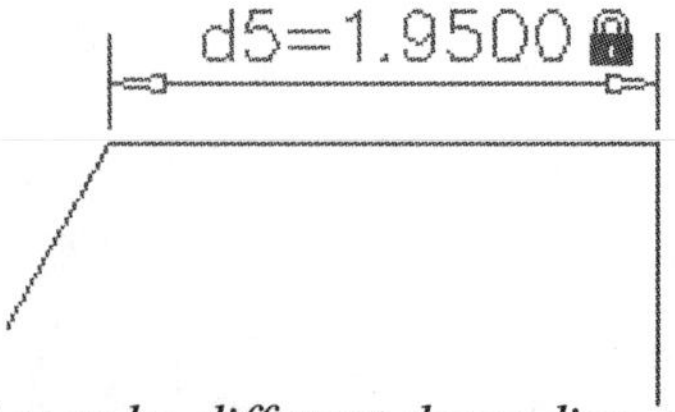

7. Left click anywhere outside the box to accept the dimension.

AutoCAD automatically assigns a d# to each dimension. Your d# may be different depending on how many dimensions have been placed.

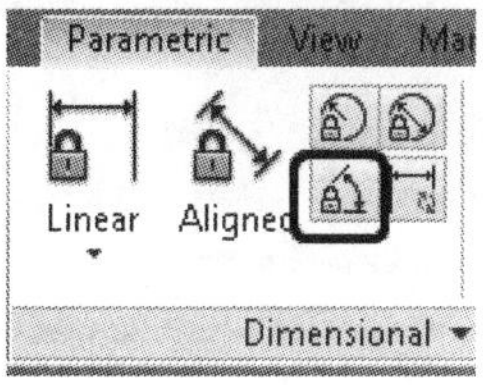

8. Select the **Angular** dimension from the Dimensional panel on the Parametric ribbon.

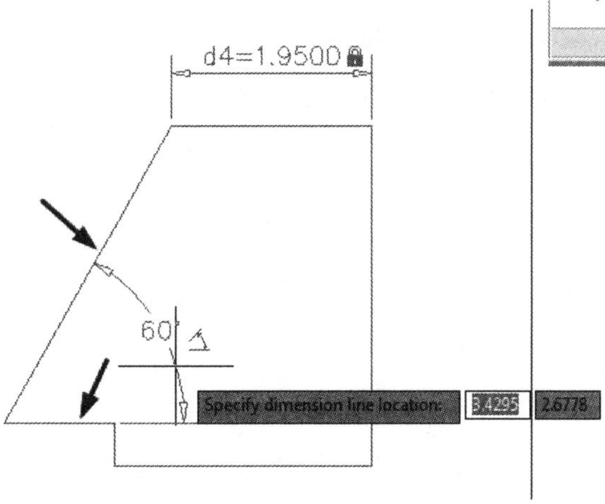

9. Select the Angled line indicated.

10. Select the short horizontal line.

11. Left click to place the dimension.

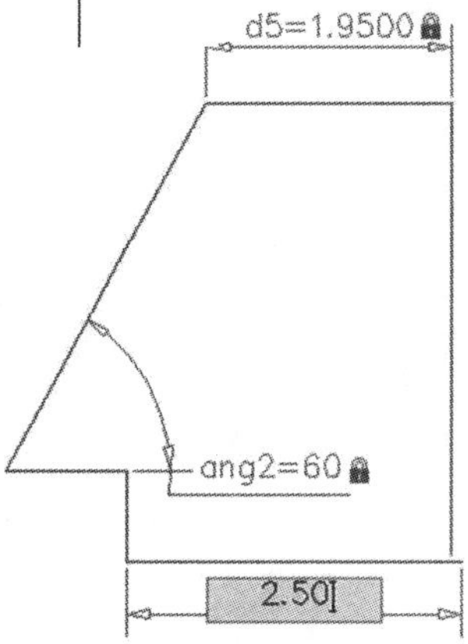

12. Left click inside the text box.

13. Change the dimension to **60**.

14. Left click outside the text box to accept the change.

15. Use the ALIGNED dimension tool to place a dimension on the bottom horizontal line. Change the dimension to **2.50**.

Note how the line adjusts.

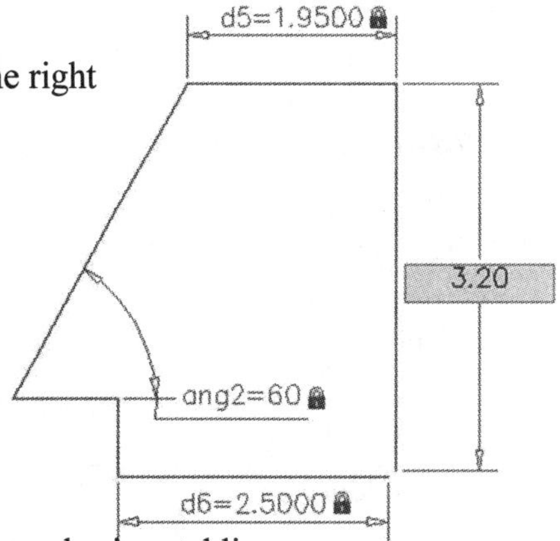

16. Use the ALIGNED dimension tool to place a dimension on the right vertical line. Change the dimension to **3.20**.

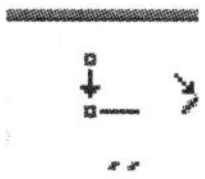

17. Select the **Coincident** tool on the Geometric panel.

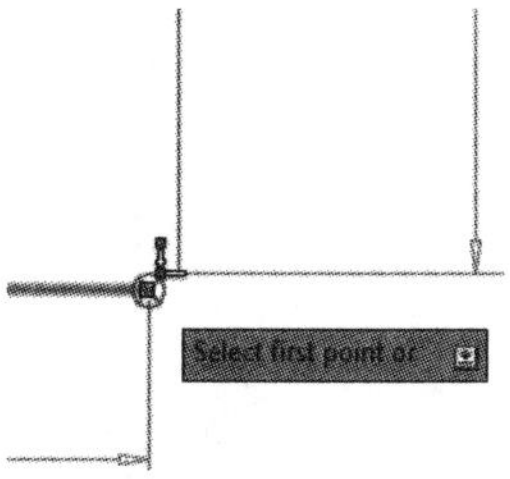

18. Select the right end point of the lower horizontal line.

19. Select the bottom end point of the right vertical line as the second point.

This joins/merges the two lines together without modifying any of the assigned dimensions.

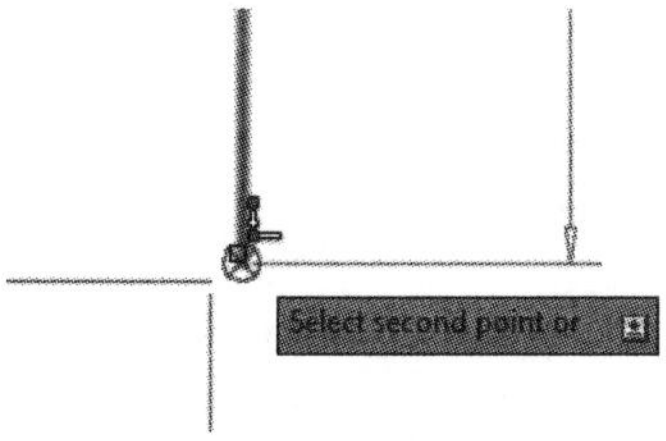

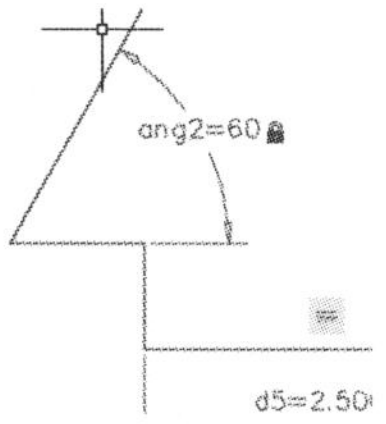

20. Use the TRIM tool to clean up the lines that form the angle.

Section Exercise

Exercise 9-17 – Dimension a Drawing

Drawing Name: **new drawing**
Estimated Time to Completion: 30 Minutes

Scope

Create a drawing from scratch using standard orthographic views and dimension.

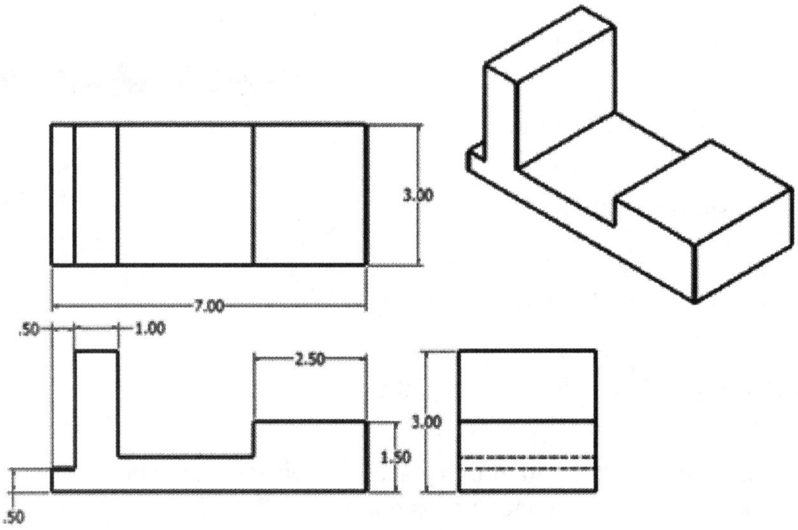

Dimension Drawing Exercise

Solution

1. Set Drawing Unit Precision to 2.

2. Create three layers:

Object	Green	Continuous
Hidden	Cyan	Hidden
Dimension	Red	Continuous

3. Draw a front, top, and right side view as shown.

Section Exercise

Exercise 9-18– Dimension a Drawing

Drawing Name: **new drawing**
Estimated Time to Completion: 30 Minutes

Scope

Create a drawing from scratch using standard orthographic views and dimension.

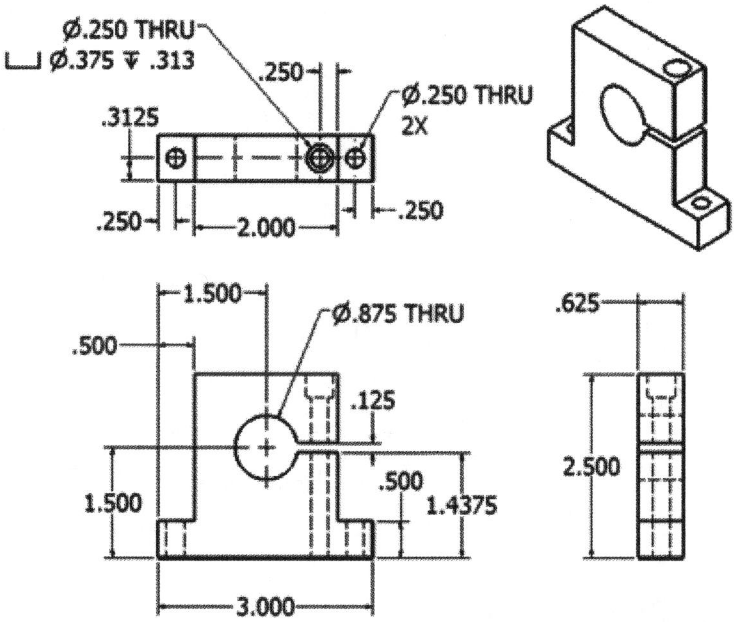

Dimension Drawing Exercise

Solution

1. Set Drawing Unit Precision to **3**.
2. Create three layers:

Object	Green	Continuous
Hidden	Cyan	Hidden
Dimension	Red	Continuous

3. Draw a front, top, and right side view as shown.

Command Exercise

Exercise 9-19 – Reassociate Dimensions

Drawing Name: **annotionmonitor.dwg**
Estimated Time to Completion: 10 Minutes

Scope

Use the Annotation Monitor to help re-associate dimensions.

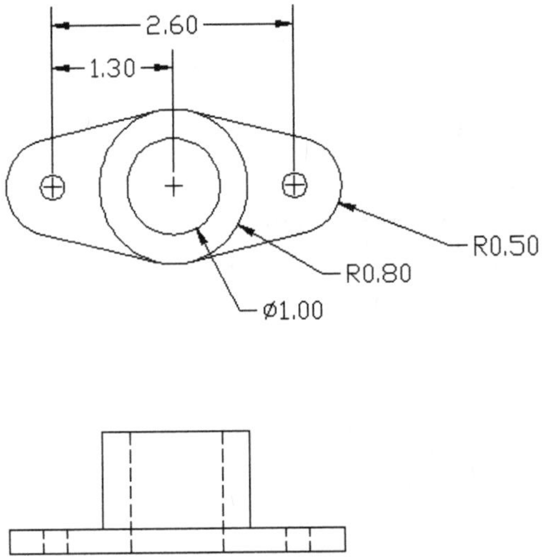

Reassociate Dimensions Exercise

Solution

1. Enable the **Annotation Monitor** on the status bar.

It will highlight in blue when it is ON.

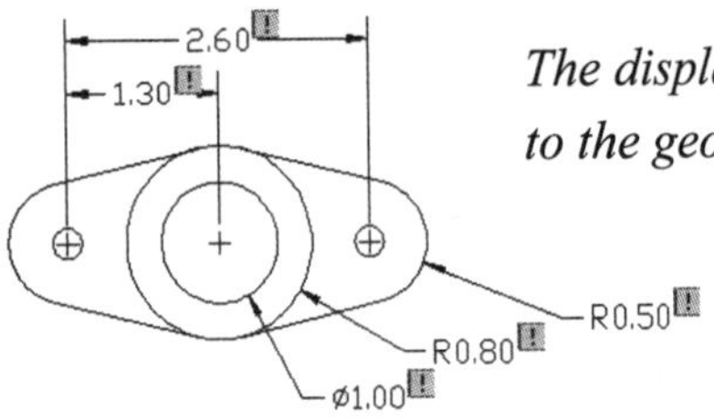

The display will update to indicate any dimensions which are disassociated to the geometry.

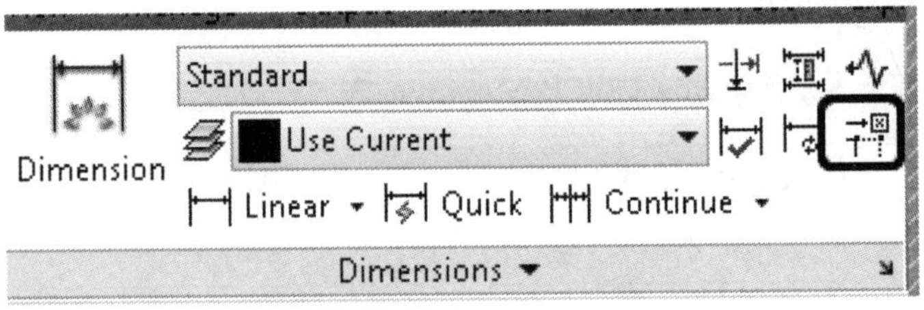

2. Select the **Re-Associate Dimension** tool on the Annotate ribbon.

3. Window around the entire top view.
   Press ENTER to complete the selection.

The 1.00 dimension will highlight.

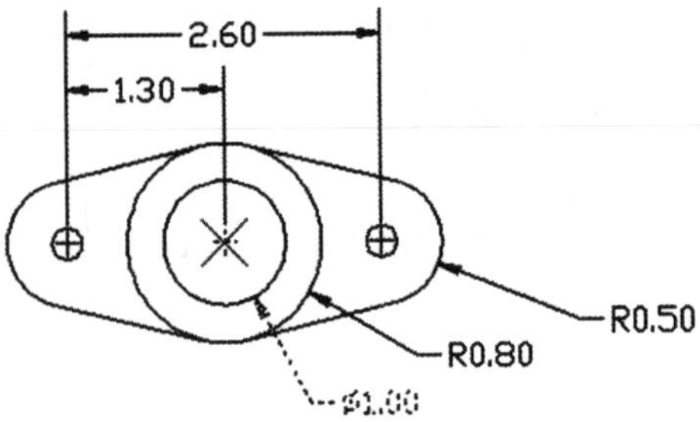

4. Select the circle that is associated with the 1.00 diameter dimension.

The next dimension that needs to be re-associated will highlight.

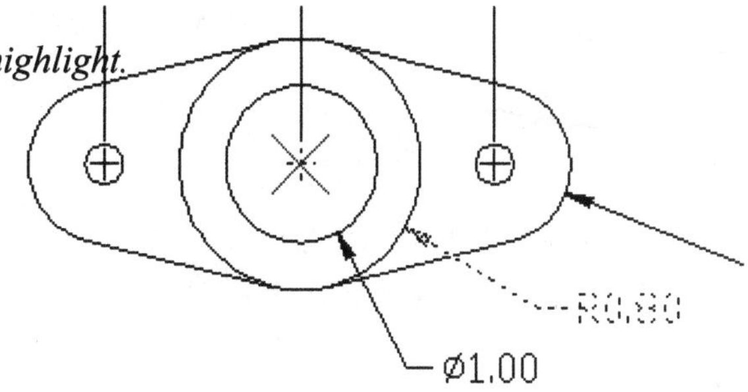

5. Select the circle associated with the dimension.

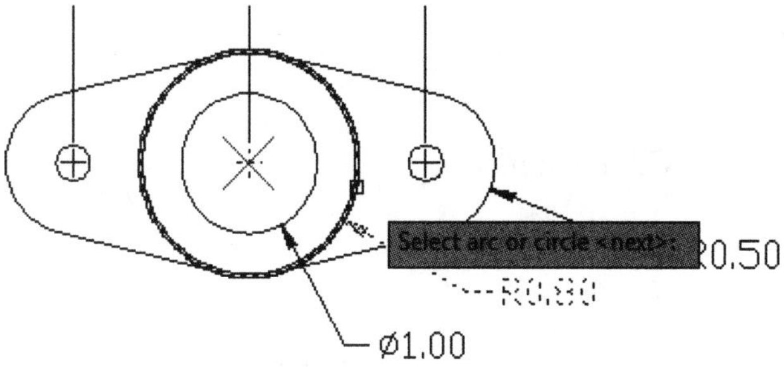

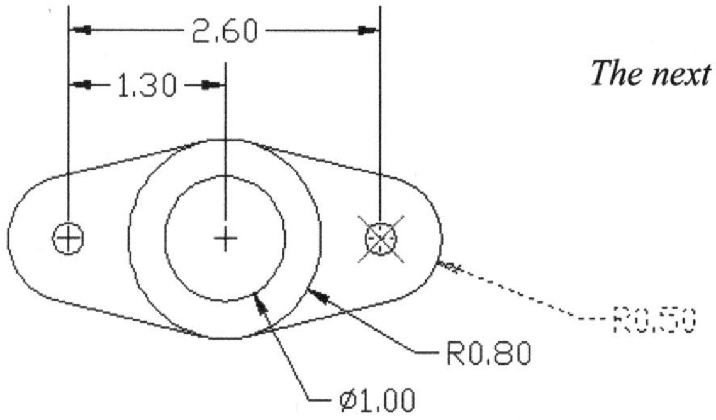

The next dimension that needs to be re-associated will highlight.

6. Select the arc associated with the dimension.

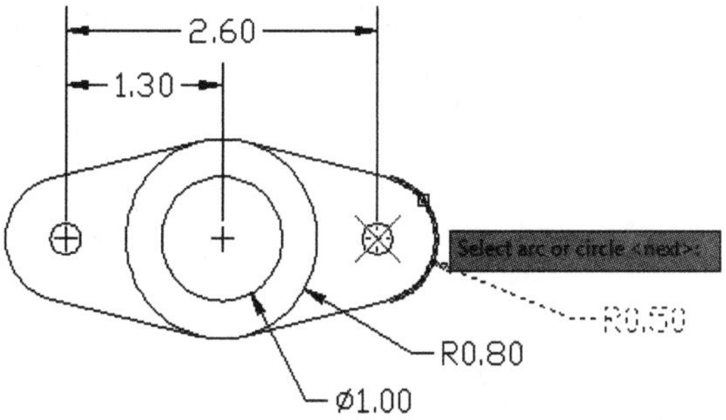

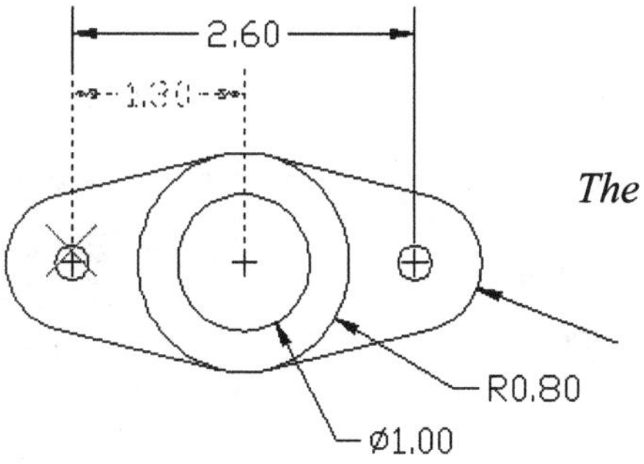

The next dimension that needs to be re-associated will highlight.

7. *You will be prompted to select the two points to associate the endpoints of the dimension.*

   Select the center of each circle.

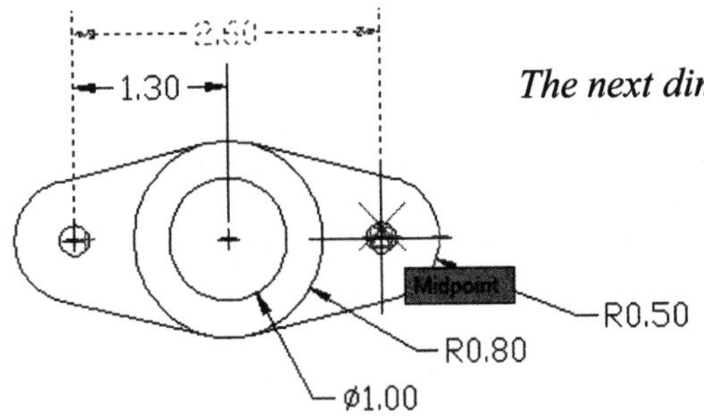

The next dimension that needs to be re-associated will highlight.

8. Select the center points for the circles associated with the dimension.

If any dimensions are still not associated, it will be indicated.

9. Use the Reassociate tool to re-associate any dimensions that need to be fixed.

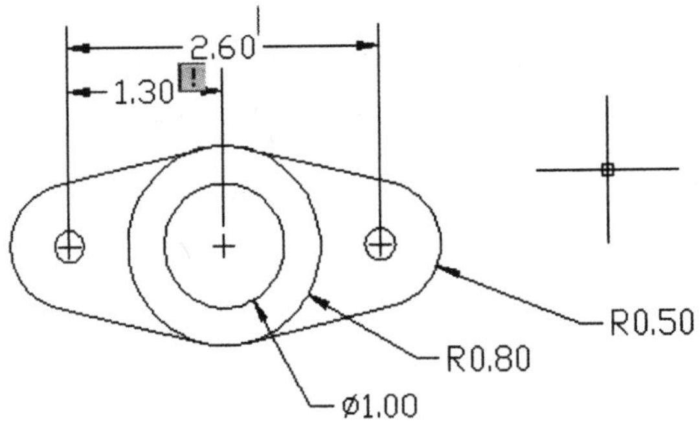

HINT: Right click and select Center to ensure the dimension re-associates to the center of the circles.

Tips & Tricks

- *If you select a dimension with Quick Properties enabled, you can verify that it is properly associated with the object. This means the dimension will update if the object is modified.*

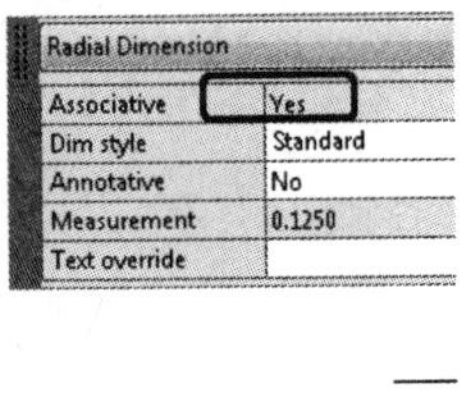

Review Questions

1. Which dimensioning units are most often used for Mechanical technical drawings?

   A. Decimal
   B. Engineering
   C. Architectural
   D. Scientific

2. The _______ dialog box is used to control dimension styles and variables.

   A. DIMENSION
   B. DIMSTYLE
   C. Dimension Style Manager
   D. STYLE

3. **T F** The DIMASO system variable governs the creation of associative dimensioning.

4. **T F** The size of dimension arrows cannot be modified.

5. The default dimension style is called:

   A. DEFAULT
   B. STANDARD
   C. OVERRIDE
   D. STYLE1

6. **T F** The DIMSTYLE command allows you to change the text style of the dimension.

7. **T F** Adding text to an existing dimension text is not possible.

8. **T F** Horizontal, vertical, aligned, and rotated dimensions cannot be associative dimensions.

9. **T F** You can trim and extend associative dimension extension lines.

10. **T F** Dimension Styles cannot be named.

11. In order to plot a dynamic constraint, you should set its properties to:

    A. DYNAMIC
    B. PLOT
    C. ANNOTATIONAL
    D. PARAMETRIC

Review Answers

1. Which dimensioning units are most often used for Mechanical technical drawings?

   A. Decimal

2. The _______ dialog box is used to control dimension styles and variables.

   C. Dimension Style Manager

3. **T F** The DIMASO system variable governs the creation of associative dimensioning.

   True

4. **T F** The size of dimension arrows cannot be modified.

   False

5. The default dimension style is called:

   B. STANDARD

6. **T F** The DIMSTYLE command allows you to change the text style of the dimension.

   True

7. **T F** Adding text to existing dimension text is not possible.

   False

8. **T F** Horizontal, vertical, aligned, and rotated dimensions cannot be associative dimensions.

   False

9. **T F** You can trim and extend associative dimension extension lines.

   False

10. **T F** Dimension Styles cannot be named.

    False

11. In order to plot a dynamic constraint, you should set its properties to:

    C. Annotational

Lesson 10.0 – Text Tools

Estimated Class Time: 2 Hours

Objectives

This section will cover how to use Text. Learn to type Text in either single or multiple lines, edit Text and check for spelling errors. Create Text Styles choosing from a variety of fonts.

- **Single Line Text**
  Type a single line of text for simple notes.
- **Multiline Text**
  Use the Multiline Text editor to create paragraphs of text or sentences that can be stretched into wider or narrower paragraphs using Grips.
- **Text Style**
  Create several Text Styles for specific text requirements.
- **Edit Text**
  Use the Edit Text command to change the content of Single Line or Multiline text. Use the Properties command to change other features of the text in the drawing.
- **Find and Replace**
  Use the Find and Replace to search and change text in the drawing.
- **Spell Check**
  Use the Spell command to check for spelling errors.
- **Fields**
  Fields are tied to drawing properties and can be used as a more dynamic and powerful version of attributes.
- **Tables**
  Tables may be used for tabulated drawings, parts lists, and material lists. Fields, attributes and texts can all be inserted into a table.

Single Line Text

Command Locator

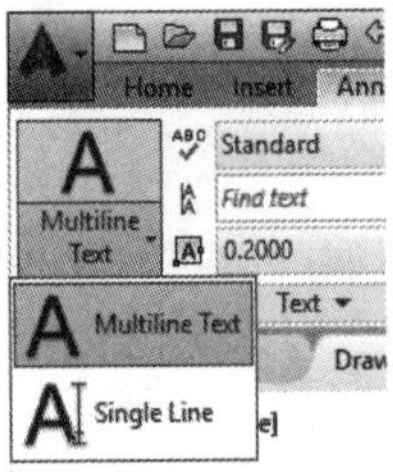

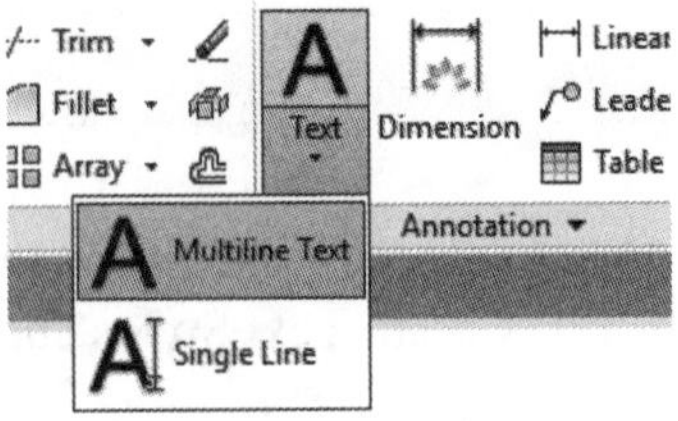

Text Toolbar Menu	
Pull Down Menu	**Draw / Text / Single Line Text**
Home or Annotate Ribbon	
Command	**Dtext**
Alias	**DT**
RMB Shortcut Menu	**Drawing Window**

Command Overview

Text can be typed as a single line at a time with the DTEXT command. Text can be moved, copied, rotated, scaled or changed after it has been placed in the drawing. When typing text, the spacebar will create a space, and the <ENTER> key will act as a carriage return and bring the cursor to the next line. The <ENTER> button on the mouse (RMB) will not work with text. Use the <ENTER> key on the keyboard. The easiest way to use the Single Line Text command is to pick a start point and follow the prompts for the Text height and Text rotation angle, then begin typing. It is important to press <ENTER> twice to end the DTEXT command. This is because the first time <ENTER> is pressed, the cursor will move to the next line, but the text will not be placed until <ENTER> is pressed again. Single Line Text is best when used for simple notes that contain only a few words or a short sentence.

DTEXT Option	Overview
Start point	Pick a start point for the text in the Drawing Window.
Specify height	Type in a height, or press <ENTER> to accept the default text height.
Specify rotation angle	Type in a rotation angle or press <ENTER> to accept the default rotation angle.

Two less common options within the DTEXT command are Justify and Style. Type J (and <ENTER>) to access the Justification options. The more common Justification options are Align, Fit, Center, Middle, and Right. The other options TL, TC, TR, for Top Left, Top Center, Top Right, etc., are more options than any beginner needs to know! Justifications will not display until the DTEXT command is completely executed. The default start point is Left Justification and need not be typed. The Text Style option will be covered in the next section.

Justification	Overview
Align	Aligns the text between two points, scaling the text height proportionately.
Fit	Fits the text between two points, maintaining the text height.
Center	Centers the text at the (bottom center).
Middle	Centers the text right in the middle of the text.
Right	Justifies the text to the right.

General Procedures

Typing Single Line Text:

1. Begin the Single Line Text command by typing DT (and <ENTER>).
2. Pick a start point in the Drawing Window.
3. Type the text height, or press <ENTER> to accept the default Text height.
4. Press <ENTER> to accept the default rotation angle (0) or type a new angle.
5. Type the first line of text. Press <ENTER>. Type the second line of text. Press <ENTER> twice to complete the dtext command.

Tips & Tricks

- Single Line Text (DTEXT) is referred to as dynamic or *displayed* text, because it is displayed on the screen as it is being typed.
- When the Dtext (Single Line Text) command is repeated, the last line of text will be highlighted to show the height and rotation. Pressing enter will automatically place the text cursor under the last line of text. The cursor can be moved at any time to locate new start points.
- Remember to press <ENTER> at the Keyboard.
- You will not be prompted for a text height if one is specified in the current text style.

Command Exercise

Exercise 10-1 – Single Line Text

Drawing Name: **text1.dwg**
Estimated Time to Completion: 5 Minutes

Scope

Create the two lines of text as indicated in the drawing using the Single Line text command.

Text Exercise

Solution

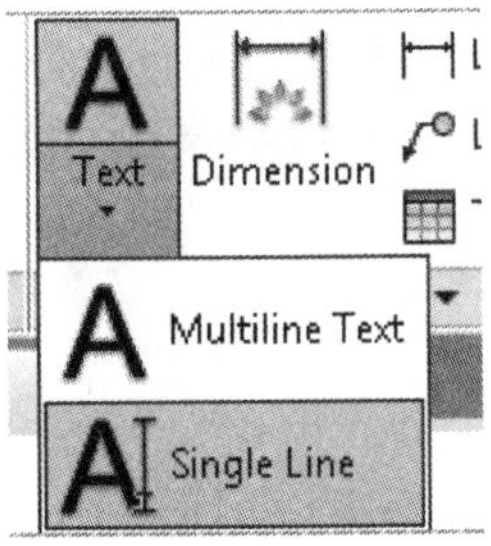

1. Invoke the Single Line Text command, and from the Annotation panel on the Home ribbon, select Text> Single Line Text (or type *dt, dtext* or *text*).

2. *Specify start point of text or [Justify/Style]:*
   Use the LMB to pick the start point of the text.

Remember that the text will be created from this pick point.

3. *Specify height <0.2000>:*
   Type **0.4** and press <ENTER>.

4. *Specify rotation angle of text <0>:*
   Type **0** and press <ENTER> or simply press <ENTER> to accept the default value.

5. Type the first line of text **HAVE A GOOD** and press <ENTER> once.

6. Type the second line of text **DAY!**.

7. LMB outside of the textbox and press <ESC> to exit the command.

Command Exercise

Exercise 10-2 – Single Line Text Options

Drawing Name: **text2.dwg**
Estimated Time to Completion: 15 Minutes

Scope

Recreate the single line text. Use the different methods of justifying the text. Note that the text justifications will not be displayed until the Enter key is pressed twice to complete the DTEXT command.

Text Exercise

Solution

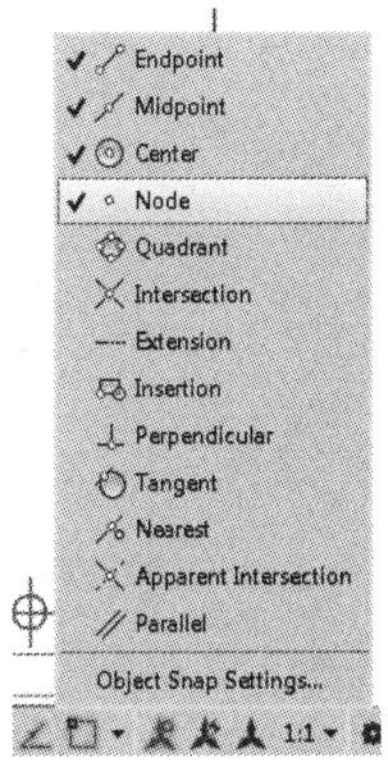

1. Enable the **Node** OSNAP.

2. Invoke the 'Single Line Text' command.

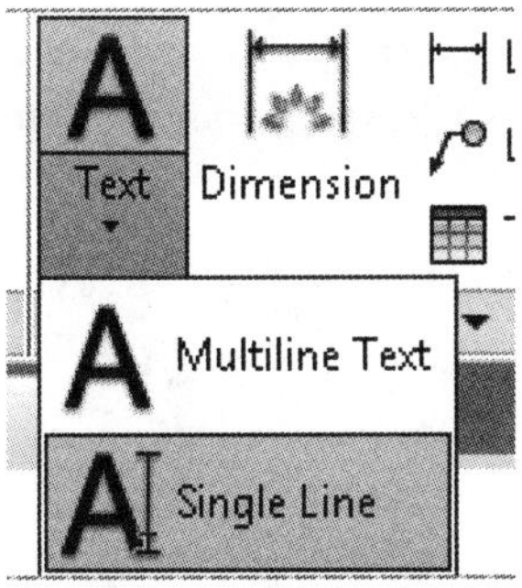

3. When prompted for a starting point, type **J** for justify or RMB and select 'Justify'.

A shortcut menu will appear.

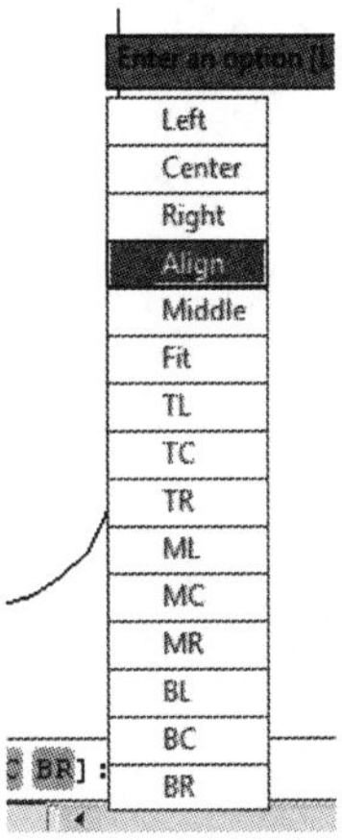

4. Select **Align**.

Specify first endpoint of text baseline:

5. Pick the first point with the LMB.

6. *Specify second endpoint of text baseline:*
   Select the second align point with the LMB.

7. Type **align** and LMB outside the text box.

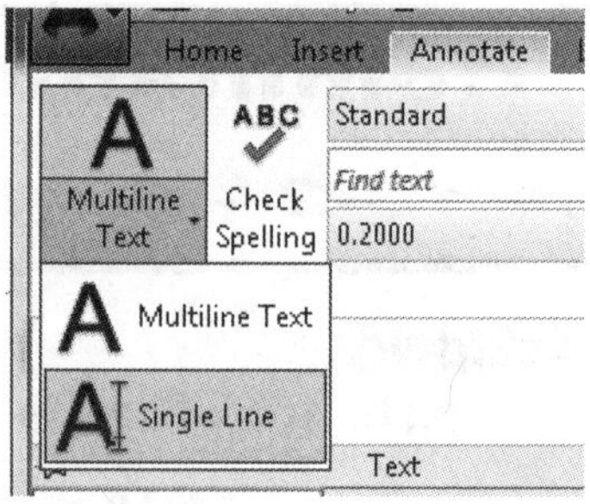

8. Press <ESC> to exit the command.

9. Invoke the ‘Single Line Text’ command.

10. Type **J** for Justify and press <ENTER>.

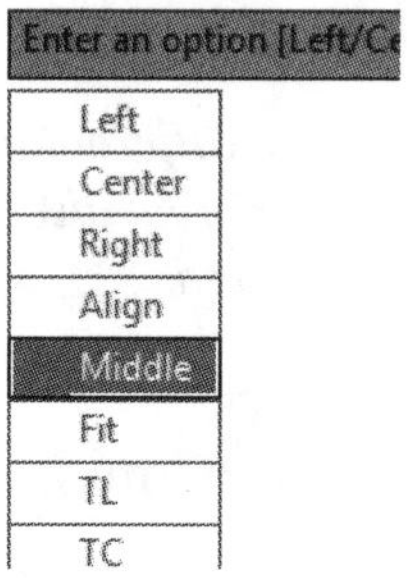

11. LMB on **Middle**.

12. With the Node OSNAP enabled, pick the node to be used for the middle text.

Specify height <0.5000>:

13. Press <ENTER>.

Specify rotation angle of text <0>:

14. Press <ENTER>.

Enter text:

15. Type **middle** and press <ENTER>.

16. Press <ESC> to exit the command.

17. Repeat the Single Line Text command with the RMB (dt, dtext, text or <ENTER>).

18. Type **J** for Justify and press <ENTER>.

19. Select **Center** or type 'C' for Center and press <ENTER>.

Specify center point of text:

20. Pick the center point with the LMB.

Specify height <0.5000>:

21. Press <ENTER>.

Specify rotation angle of text <0>:

22. Press <ENTER>.

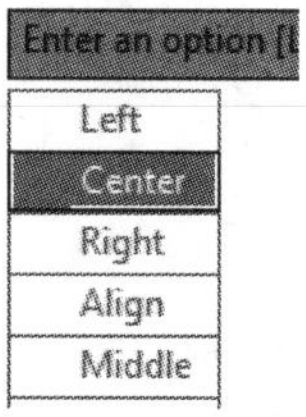

Enter text:

23. Type **center** and press <ENTER>.

24. Press <ESC> to exit the command.

25. Repeat the Single Line Text command with the RMB (dt, dtext, text or <ENTER>).

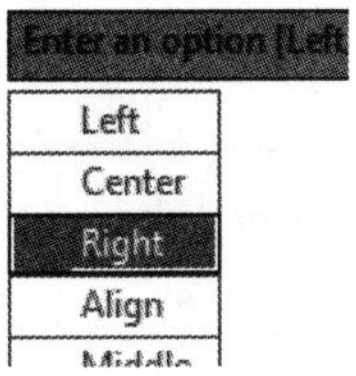

26. Type **J** for Justify and press <ENTER>.

27. Select **Right** and press <ENTER>.

Specify right end point of text:
28. Pick the right end point with the LMB.

Specify height <0.5000>:
29. Press <ENTER>.

Specify rotation angle of text <0>:
30. Press <ENTER>.

Enter text:
31. Type **right** and press <ENTER>.

32. Press <ESC> to exit the command.

33. Repeat the Single Line Text command with the RMB (dt, dtext, text or <ENTER>).

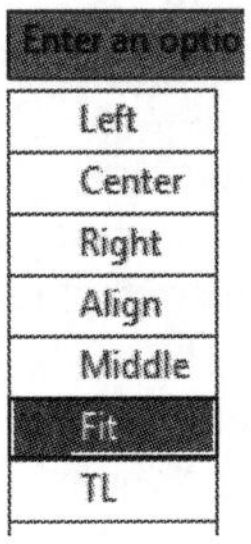

34. Type **J** for Justify and press <ENTER>.

35. Select **Fit** or type **F** for Fit and press <ENTER>.

Specify first endpoint of text baseline:
36. Pick the first point with the LMB.

Specify second endpoint of text baseline:
37. Pick the second point with the LMB.

Specify height <0.5000>:
38. Press <ENTER>.

Enter text:
39. Type **fit** and press <ENTER>.

40. Press <ESC> to exit the command.

Tips & Tricks

- *Remember to press <ESC> to exit a command.*

Multiline Text

Command Locator

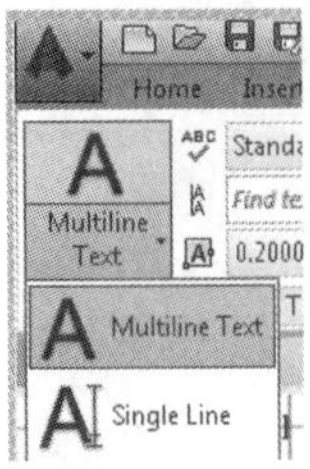

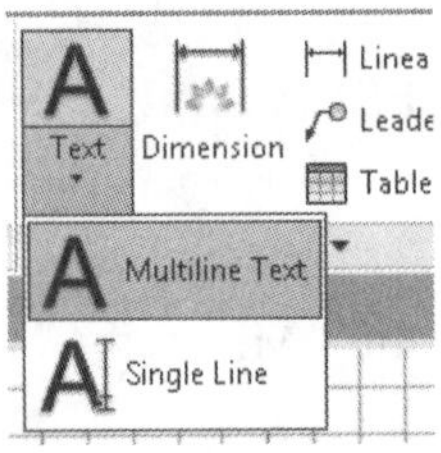

Toolbar Menu	**Draw, Text**
Pull Down Menu	**Draw→Text→Multiline Text**
Home or Annotation Ribbon	**Annotation Panel/Multiline Text**
Command	**Mtext**
Alias	**T**
RMB Shortcut Menu	**Multiline Text Editor**
Dialog Box	**Multiline Text Editor**

Command Overview

Create paragraphs of text with the Multiline Text command. Define the area where the Multiline text should appear in the drawing by picking the opposite corners of the *text box* in the drawing window. Type the text in the Multiline Text Editor dialog box. Multiline Text can be moved, rotated, scaled, copied or changed after it has been placed in the drawing. Use the grips to adjust the paragraph width. When typing in the text editor, the spacebar will create a space, and the <ENTER> key will act as a carriage return and bring the cursor to the next line. The cursor may be place between letters by picking once (LMB). A double click will select an entire word and a triple click will select the entire sentence. The <ENTER> button on the mouse (RMB) when placed within the Multiline Text Editor dialog box will invoke a shortcut menu with options to Cut, Copy, and Paste selected text. To resize the Multiline Text Editor, select a corner of the window with the LMB and drag. The Editor contains four tabs: Character, Properties, Line Spacing, and Find/Replace. Begin the Multiline text command, specify the first corner, then the opposite corner of the window. Type text in the Multiline Text Editor, use the available options, then select OK to place the text in the drawing. The Edit Text command will open the same Text Editor dialog box with the selected text for editing.

Multiline Text Editor Contextual Ribbon

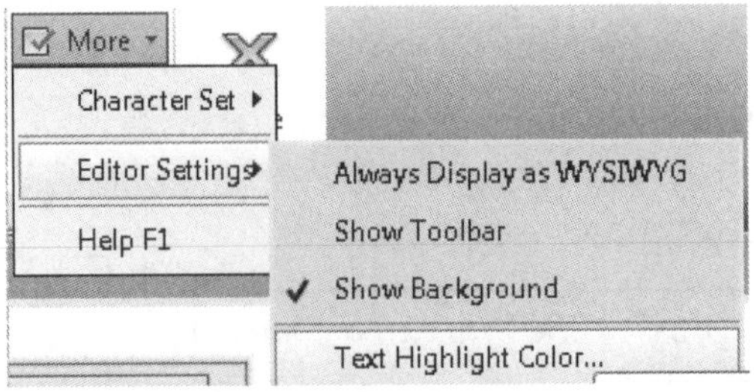

If you select the ***More*** *button at the far right of the MTEXT dialog, you can control the appearance of the MTEXT dialog box.*

Multiline Text Editor Option	Overview
Font	Change the font of selected words with this option. This option should be used when changing only a few selected words. If a global font change is preferred, use the Text Style command.
Font height	Change the height of selected words.
Bold	Make selected text Bold, when applicable to the font.
Italics	Make selected text *Italic,* when applicable to the font.
Underline	Underlines selected text.
Undo	This option will undo the last step in the dialog box.
Redo	This option will undo the last undo.
Stack	This option will stack selected words or text when separated by a forward slash.
Color	This option will make selected text a different color. Select a color from the list. Color changes to selected text will override color changes applied to the layer or the object.

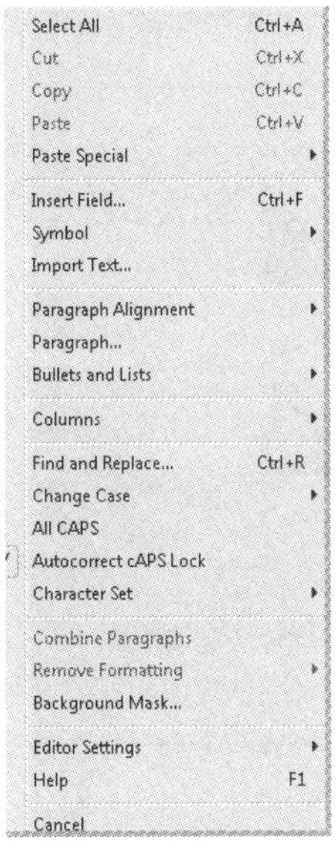

MTEXT Options Shortcut Menu

If you RMB click in the MTEXT window, you have several more options available to you, including placing Indents and Tabs, insert symbols, insert fields, and modify the text.

General Procedures

1. Invoke the Multiline Text command by typing T or selecting the icon from the draw toolbar.
2. Specify Text area by picking the first corner, then the opposite corner in the drawing Window.
3. Type the Multiline Text Editor dialog box.
4. Select OK to exit.

Tips & Tricks

- In the Multiline Text editor, single click (LMB) to insert words or letters. Double click to highlight the entire word. Triple click to select the entire sentence.
- Pressing the <ENTER> button on the mouse (RMB), with the cursor in the text box, will bring up the cursor menu with the Windows Edit options.
- Type text using the space bar (and not <ENTER>) to allow sentences to wrap.
- After exiting the multiline text dialog box, use grips to adjust the width of the Multiline Text.
- Documents to be imported into the text editor should be saved in Text (.txt) or Rich Text Format (.rtf).
- Exploding Multiline text will make single lines of text.

Command Exercise

Exercise 10-3 – Multiline Text

Drawing Name: **mtext1.dwg**
Estimated Time to Completion: 5 Minutes

Scope

Use the Multiline text command to create the text as indicated.

Multiline Text Exercise

Solution

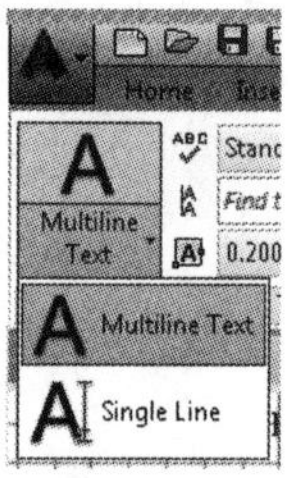

1. Invoke the Multiline Text command (mt or mtext).

Specify first corner:

2. Use the Node Object Snap to select the upper left point.

Tips & Tricks

- *The text is wrapped automatically to fit into the specified window. Use the grips to adjust the paragraph width.*

Specify opposite corner or [Height/Justify/Line spacing/ Rotation/Style/Width]:

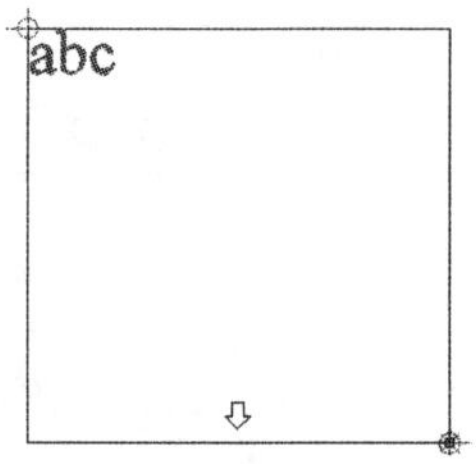

3. Use the Node Object Snap to select the lower right point.
4. Type the text as shown on the left side of the screen.
5. Use your mouse and click and drag with the LMB to highlight the last two words **text editor**.
6. Press the **U** (Underline) button on the ribbon to underline the text.

7. Press **X Close Text Editor** on the Ribbon to close the dialog.

Command Exercise

Exercise 10-4 – Formatting Multiline Text

Drawing Name: **mtext2.dwg**
Estimated Time to Completion: 5 Minutes

Scope

Use the Multiline text command to create and format the text as indicated.

You can stack
words and numbers
$\frac{1}{2}$ and change the
font and color of
individual words.

Multiline Text Exercise

Solution

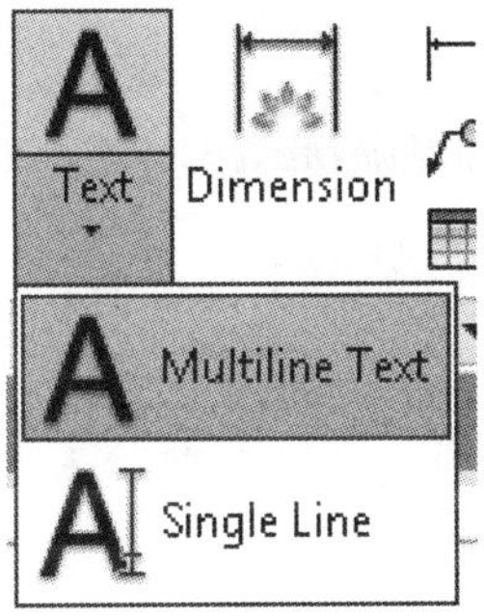

1. Invoke the Multiline Text command (mt or mtext).

Specify first corner:

2. Use the Node Object Snap to select the upper left point.

Specify opposite corner or [Height/Justify/Line spacing/ Rotation/Style/Width]:

3. Use the Node Object Snap to select the lower right point.

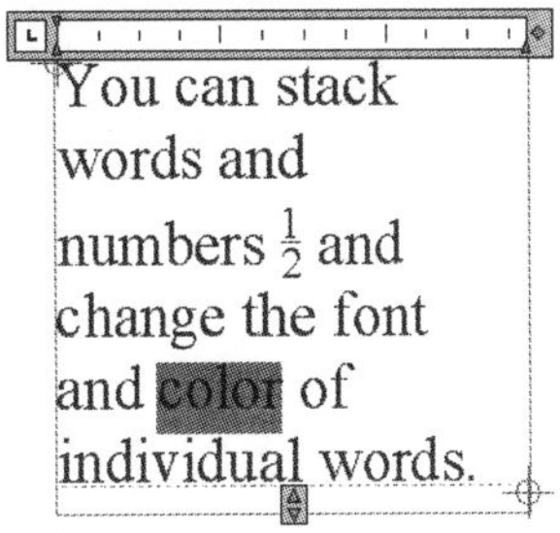

4. Type the text as shown on the left side of the screen.

5. Highlight the word **color**.

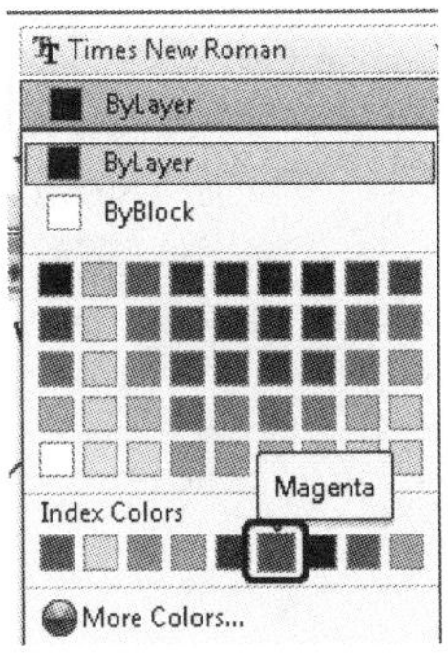

6. Select the desired color for the selected text from the drop-down list located on the Ribbon.

7. Highlight the word **font**.

8. Select the desired color for the selected text from the drop-down list located on the Ribbon.

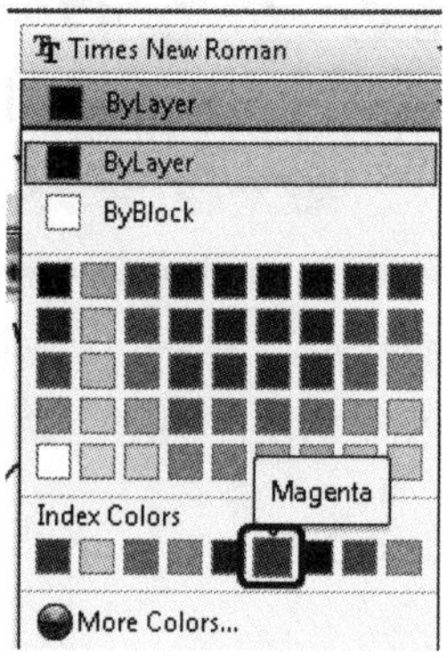

9. While the word **font** is still highlighted adjust the font style for the selected text by using the drop-down list box. Set it to the **scripts** font.

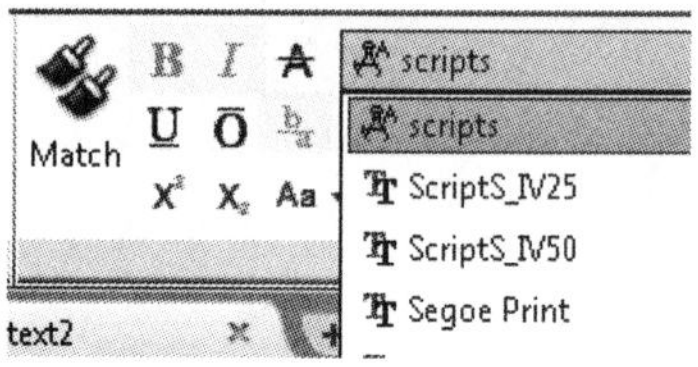

Note that the text will preview as you mouse over different font styles.

10. Left click outside the text edit window to exit the Text Edit mode.

Tips & Tricks

- To edit MText, double left click on the text or select the text, right click and select Mtext Edit.

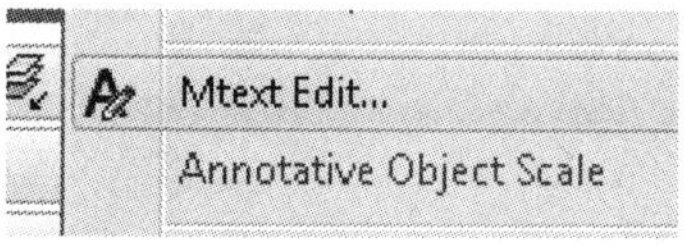

Text Style

Command Locator

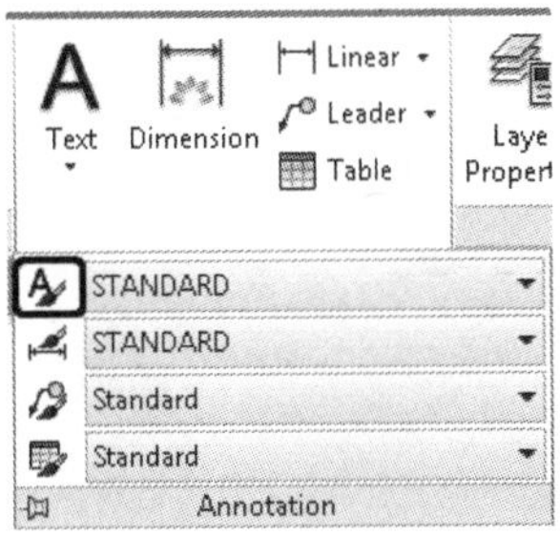

Ribbon	**Annotation pull-down**
Toolbar Menu	**Styles, Text**
Pull Down Menu	**Format / Text Style…**
Command	**Style**
Alias	**ST**
Dialog Box	**Text Style**

Command Overview

In addition to the Standard Text Style, additional styles can be created. Text will be typed in the current text style and may be changed from one style to another. Applying a different font to a Text Style will globally change the font of any text in the drawing that has been typed in that style. AutoCAD supports most Windows fonts including TrueType fonts. Text Styles may be deleted or Purged only if there is no text in the drawing referencing that style, or it is not the current style.

Text Style Option	Overview
Style Name	The current style will be at the top of the list of Text Style in the drawing. The default style is Standard with the txt.shx font.
New	Select this button to make a new Text Style. The default name will be style1, however it may be renamed.
Rename…	Select this button to rename a selected Text Style.
Delete	Select this option to delete a selected Text Style. There cannot be text in the drawing using that Style.
Font	Select a Font from the Font Name list. The default font for the Standard style is txt.shx. AutoCAD supports most Windows fonts including TrueType fonts.
Font Style	Font style options will be displayed according to the Font selected. Some fonts do not have Font style options.
Font Size	When the Text Style height is 0.0, the user will always be prompted for a text height when using the DTEXT command. Text style height can be pre-set; however, it is always possible to change the height of text in the drawing. When Annotative is enabled, the text will automatically be scaled depending on the annotative scale. Instead of creating text styles for different text heights, you can use annotative scale to control the size of the text.
Effects	These are hardly used options that include Upside down, Backwards, and Vertical. A Width factor of 1.0 is a normal width. Greater than 1 is a wider letter, and less than 1 is a narrower letter. Oblique Angle creates a slant letter.
Set Current	Select this button to apply changes to the Text Style before exiting the dialog box.

General Procedures

Making changes to the Standard Text Style:

1. Invoke the Text Style command.
2. Select a different Font from the drop down list.
3. Select Apply, then Close the dialog box.

Creating a New Text Style:

1. Invoke the Text Style command.
2. Select "New" and type a name for that style (or accept the default name).
3. Select a Font from the drop down list. Optional: Type the Height for the new text style.
4. Select Apply, then Close the dialog box.

- Use this dialog box to make a Text Style current.
- Changes applied to a Text Style will globally affect any text in the drawing referencing that style.
- Avoid having an excessive number of Text Styles. Some common text styles might be made for notes, dimensions, and the Title Block.
- Refer to the following Text Height Chart for large format drawings. For instance, if the drawing area is 12 x 9, a text height of .2 might be good. However, if the drawing area is 120 x 90, a text height of 2 would be more appropriate (.2 x 10).
- You can use PURGE to eliminate any unused text styles from your drawing.
- You can import text styles from one drawing to another using the Design Center.
- You can store text styles in your template for easier access.

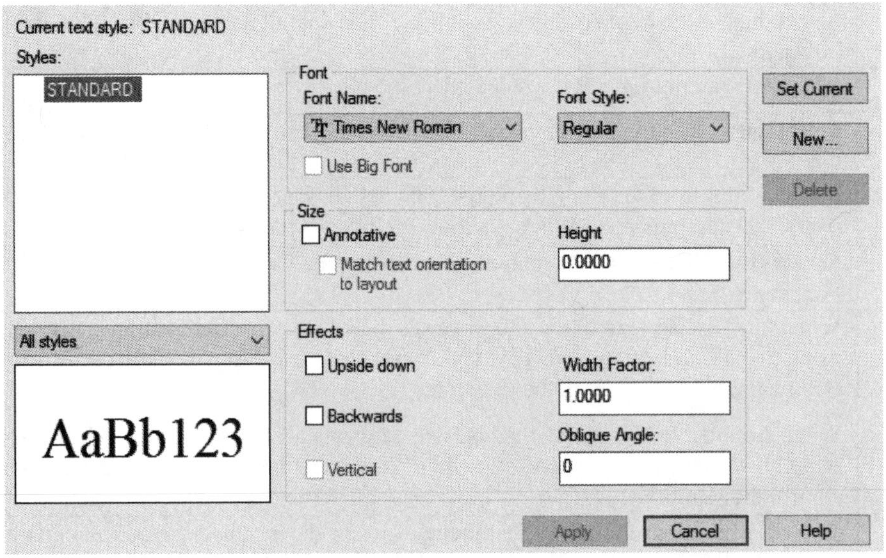

Text Style Dialog Box

Command Exercise

Exercise 10-5 – Creating Text Styles

Drawing Name: **style1.dwg**
Estimated Time to Completion: 10 Minutes

Scope

Create a text style called TEXT1 and apply a text height of 0.4 and the font called Arial to that style. Type the text as indicated in the new style.

Create several
Text Styles for
your prototype
drawing.

Text Styles Exercise

Solution

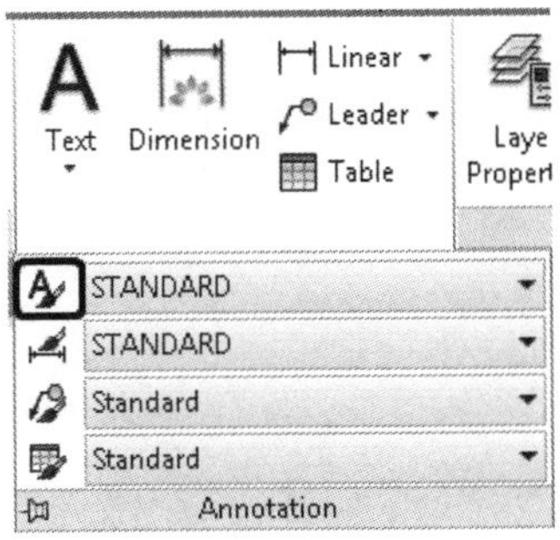

1. From the Home ribbon, select the Text Style tool on the Annotation pull-down.

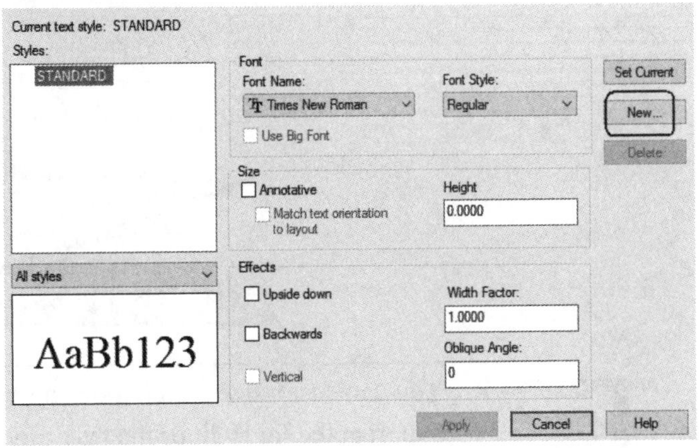

2. Press the **New** button in the Text Styles dialog box.

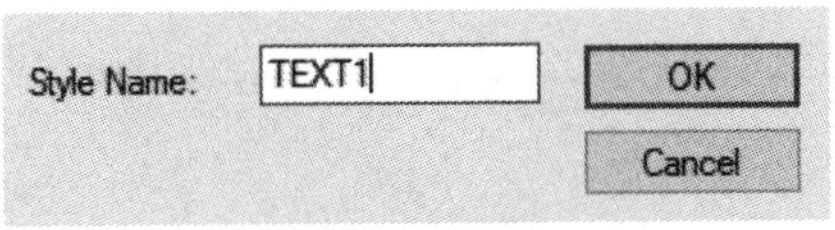

3. In the New Text Style dialog box, enter **TEXT1** for the name of the new text style and press **OK**.

4. Fill in the remaining information in the Text Style dialog box as shown.
   Set the Font Name to **Arial**.
   Set the Font Style to **Regular**.
   Set the Height to **0.4**.

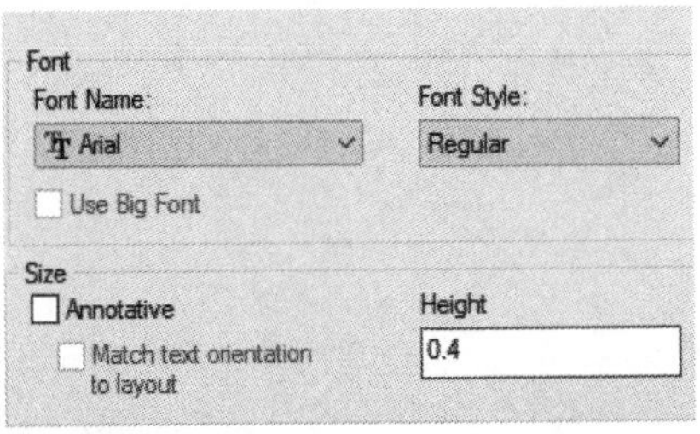

5. Press the **Apply** button first and then the **Close** button to apply the changes to TEXT1 and then close the dialog box.

6. Invoke the Multiline Text command (mt or mtext).

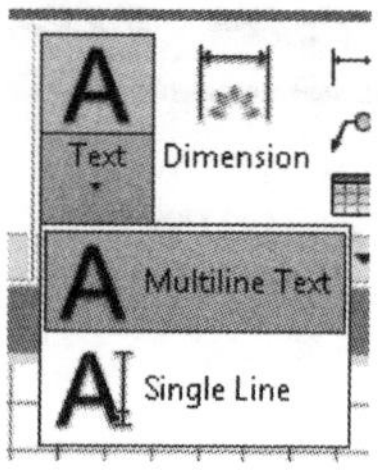

Specify first corner:
Notice that the current style is TEXT1.

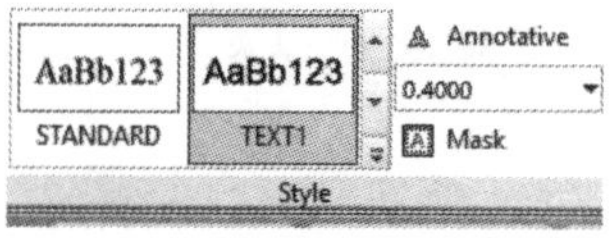

7. Pick the upper left corner of the multiline text window with the LMB.

Specify opposite corner or [Height/Justify/Line spacing/ Rotation/Style/Width]:

8. Pick the lower right corner of the multiline text window.

9. Type the desired text into the Multiline Text Editor and press 'Close Text Editor' to exit.

Note that the text style you just created is the current text style.

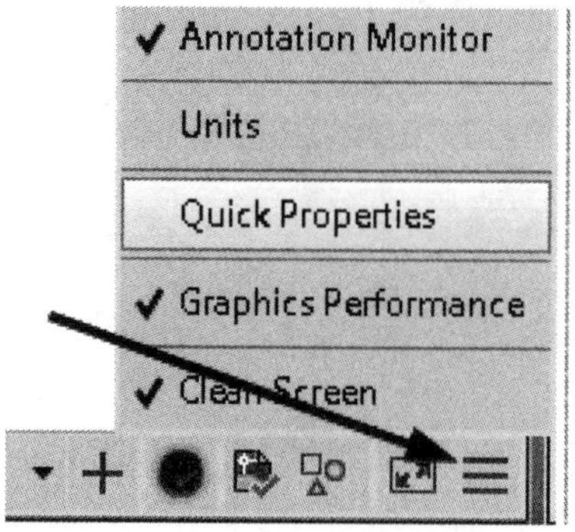

Tips & Tricks

- You can customize which tools appear on the task tray by using the Customize button at the far right of the task tray.

Command Exercise

Exercise 10-6 – Purging Text Styles

Drawing Name: **style2.dwg**
Estimated Time to Completion: 5 Minutes

Scope

Use the Purge command to delete the text style called TEXT2, or delete it from the dialog box.

Solution

1. From the Home ribbon, select the Text Style tool on the Annotation pull-down.

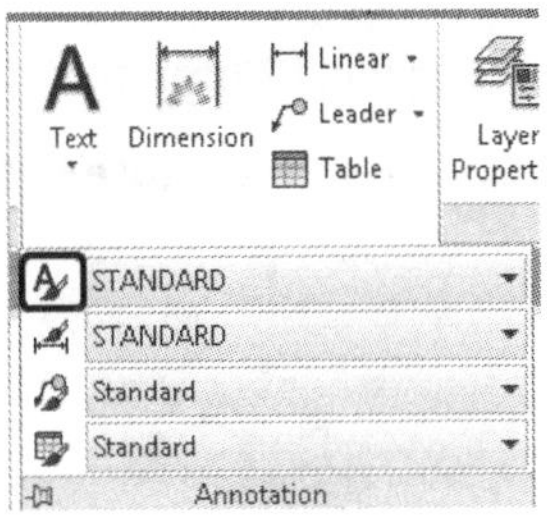

2. Highlight the **Standard** text style and press the **Set Current** button to make it current.

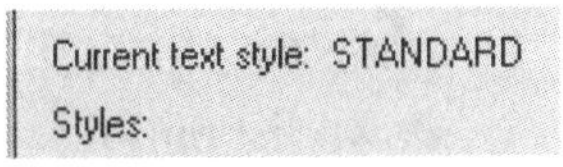

3. Press **Close** to close the Text Style dialog box.

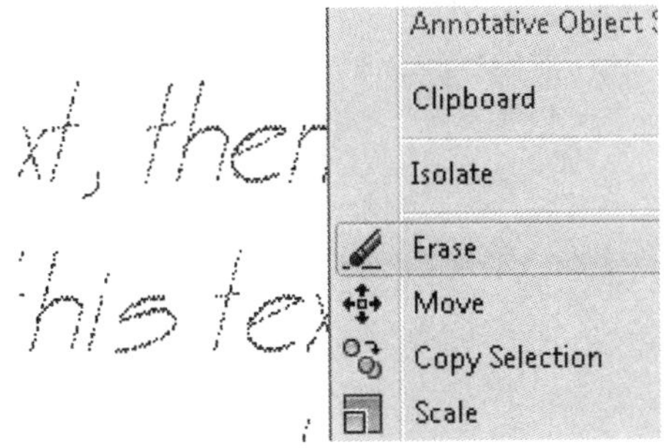

4. Select the text.
5. RMB and select **Erase**.

Invoke the Purge command.

6. From the File ribbon panel, select **Drawing Utilities→Purge**.

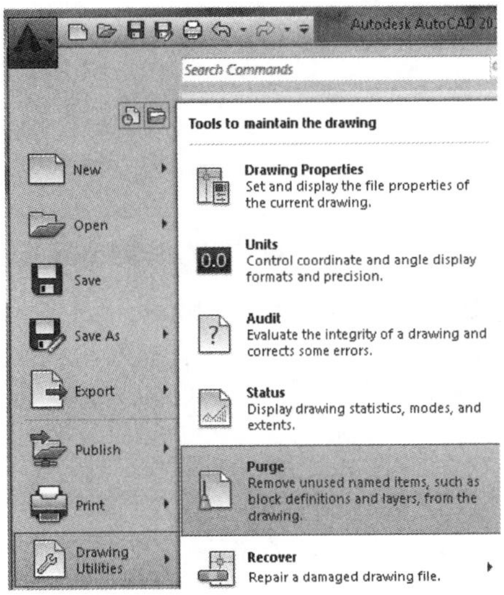

7. Expand the Text Styles category. Highlight **TEXT2**.

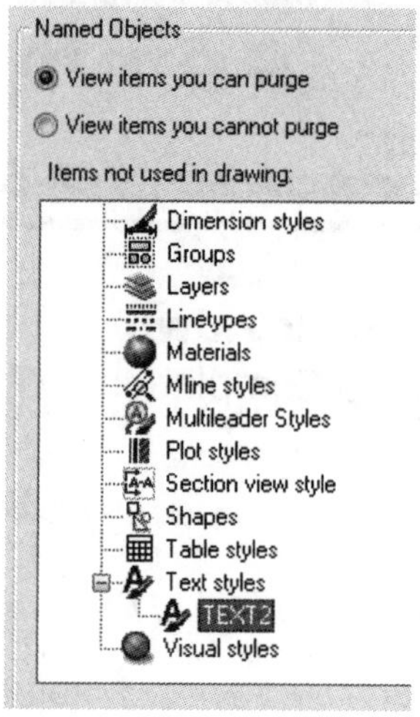

8. Select the **Purge** button.

A dialog will pop up to verify that you want to purge the text style.

9. Select **Purge this item**.
10. Press the **Close** button.

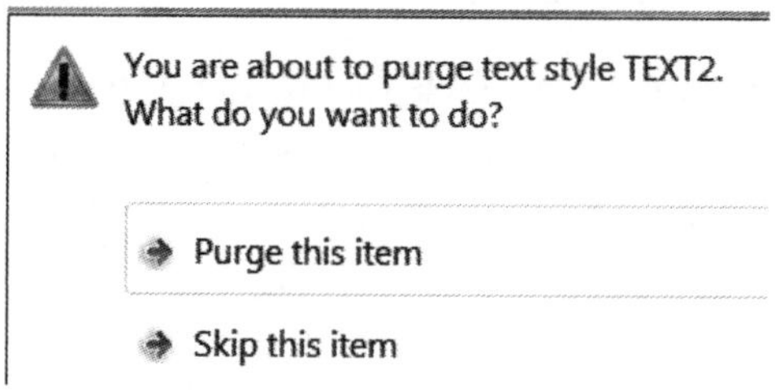

11. From the Home ribbon, select the Text Style drop-down list pull-down.

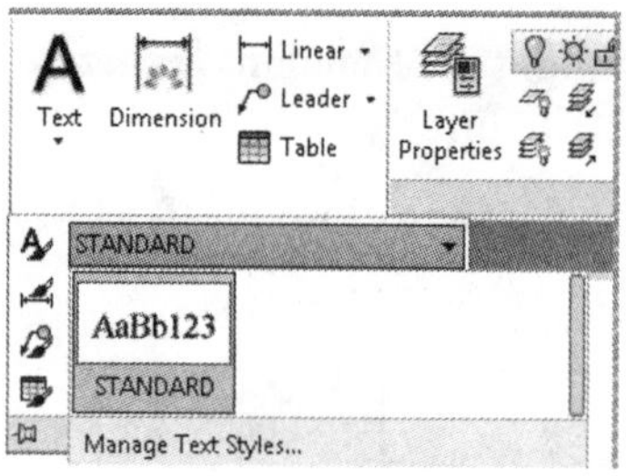

The TEXT2 text style is no longer available.

Tips & Tricks

- *You can only purge text styles that are not in use.*
- *The Styles toolbar can be used to quickly switch from one text style to another.*

Edit Text

Command Locator

Toolbar Menu	**Text→Edit Text**
Pull Down Menu	**Modify→Text...**
Command	**Ddedit**
Alias	**ED**
RMB Shortcut Menu	**Text Window**
Dialog Box	**Edit Text (when Single Line text is selected)** **Multiline Text Editor (when Multiline text is selected)**
	Double left click on the text object to edit

Command Overview

Use the Edit Text command to change the contents of Text in the drawing. For Single Line text, this will display the single line Text Editor. Text may also be edited using the Properties command. This contains additional options to change the text properties.

General Procedures

1. Invoke the Edit Text command (ED). Select the text to edit.
2. Make corrections to the text by typing over the highlighted text, or place the cursor between letters or words and type.
3. Select OK to exit.

Tips & Tricks

- Place the cursor in the text area and press the RMB to Copy, Cut, Paste, or Delete selected text.
- The Edit Text command works with dimension text, Multiline Text, and Single Line Text.
- To exit the Edit Text mode, simply left click outside the text edit box.

Command Exercise

Exercise 10-7 – Edit Text

Drawing Name: **etext1.dwg**
Estimated Time to Completion: 5 Minutes

Scope

Edit the Single Line and Multiline Text using the Edit Text (DDEDIT) command. Edit the text on the right to be like the text on the left.

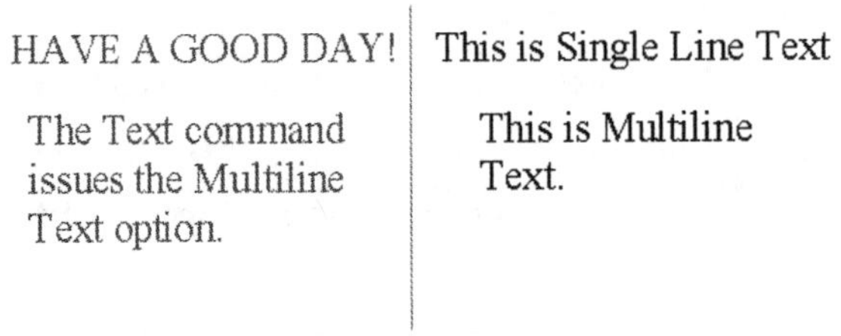
HAVE A GOOD DAY!
The Text command issues the Multiline Text option.
This is Single Line Text
This is Multiline Text.

Exit Text Exercise

Solution

Select an annotation object or [Undo]:

1. Double left click to edit the "This is Single Line Text."
   In the Edit Text dialog box, type over the existing text.

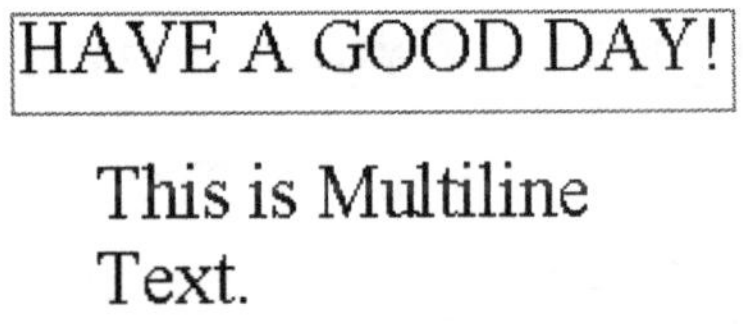
HAVE A GOOD DAY!
This is Multiline Text.

2. Type **HAVE A GOOD DAY!** and press <ENTER>.

3. LMB click on the multiline text to activate the edit box.

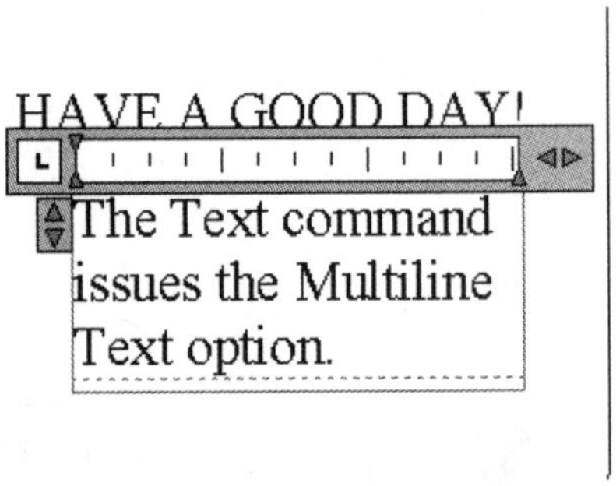
HAVE A GOOD DAY!
The Text command issues the Multiline Text option.

4. Modify the text and press LMB outside the text edit box to exit.

5. Press <ESC> or right click and select <ENTER> to exit the command.

Command Exercise

Exercise 10-8 – Edit Text Properties

Drawing Name: **etext2.dwg**
Estimated Time to Completion: 10 Minutes

Scope

Edit the Single Line and Multiline text using the Quick Properties tool.

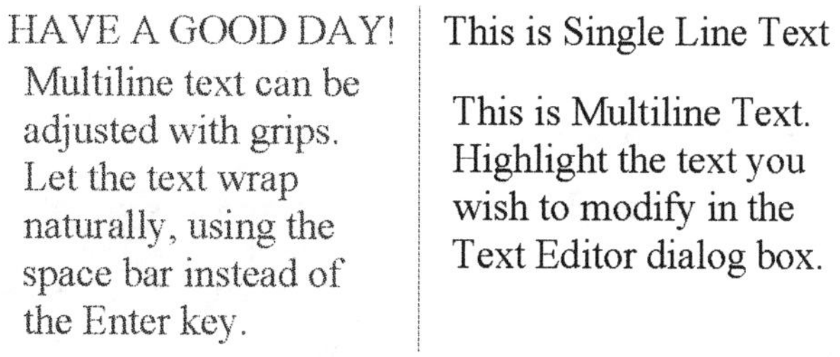
HAVE A GOOD DAY!
Multiline text can be adjusted with grips. Let the text wrap naturally, using the space bar instead of the Enter key.
This is Single Line Text
This is Multiline Text. Highlight the text you wish to modify in the Text Editor dialog box.

Text Quick Properties Exercise

Solution

1. Enable **Quick Properties**.

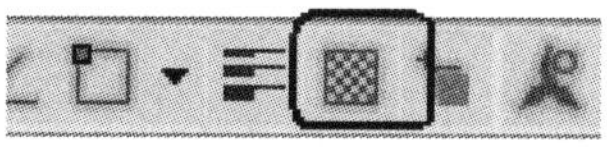

The tool is enabled if it is highlighted in blue.
If you don't see the tool, enable it using the Customize tool on the task bar.

2. Use the LMB to select the single line of text located on the right side of the drawing.

3. In the Quick Properties dialog box, highlight the existing text and change it to **HAVE A GOOD DAY!**

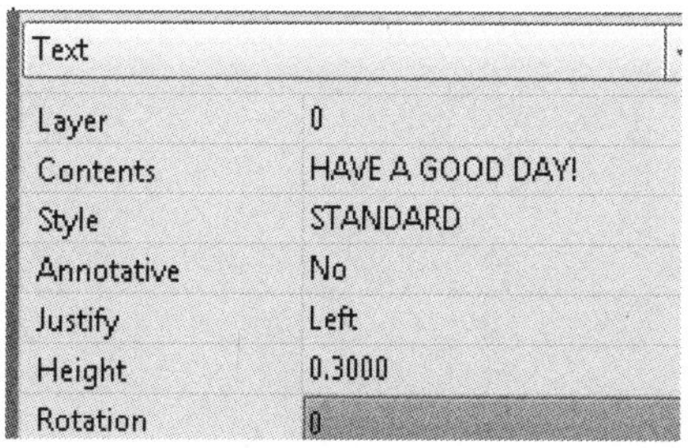
Text
Layer
0
Contents
HAVE A GOOD DAY!
Style
STANDARD
Annotative
No
Justify
Left
Height
0.3000
Rotation
0

4. Adjust the Height to **0.3** in the Quick Properties dialog.

5. Press the <ESC> button to release the selection.

Notice how the text changes.

6. Use the LMB to pick the Multiline Text.

7. Notice the changes in the Quick Properties dialog box.

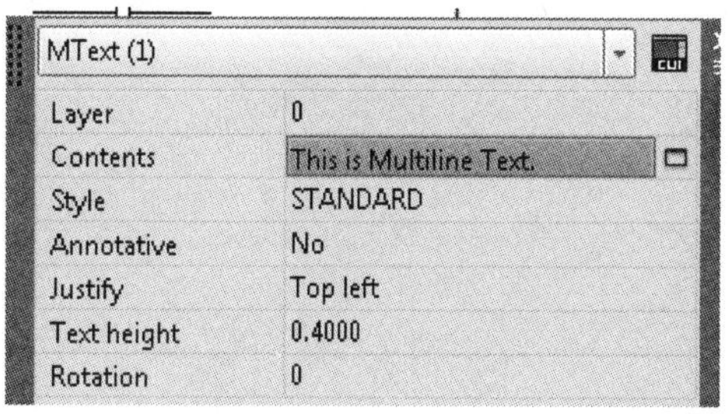
MText (1)
Layer
0
Contents
This is Multiline Text.
Style
STANDARD
Annotative
No
Justify
Top left
Text height
0.4000
Rotation
0

8. Pick the  Button next to the Contents of the text.

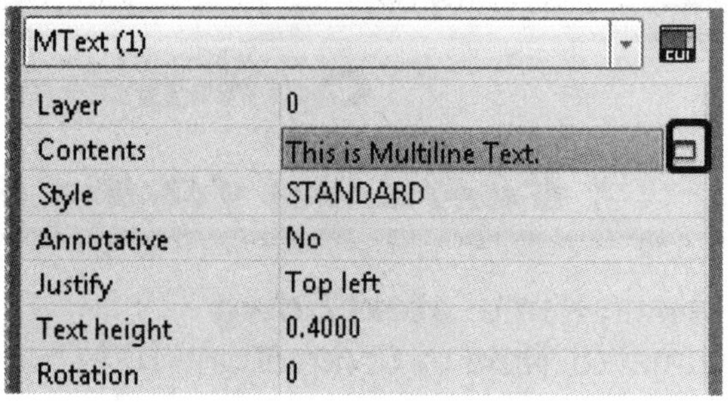

This will activate the Multiline Text Editor.

You will only see the button if you left click in the Contents field.

This is the same as double left clicking on the text.

9. Highlight the existing text, type in the new text and press **Close Text Editor**.

10. Back in the Quick Properties dialog box, change the height to **0.3000**.

11. Press the <ESC> button to release the selection.

Notice how the text changes.

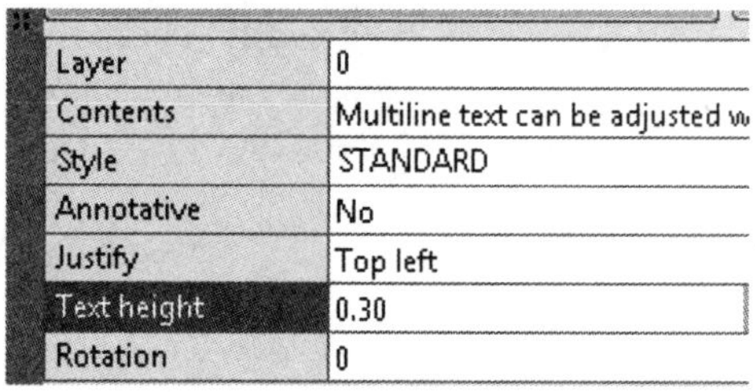

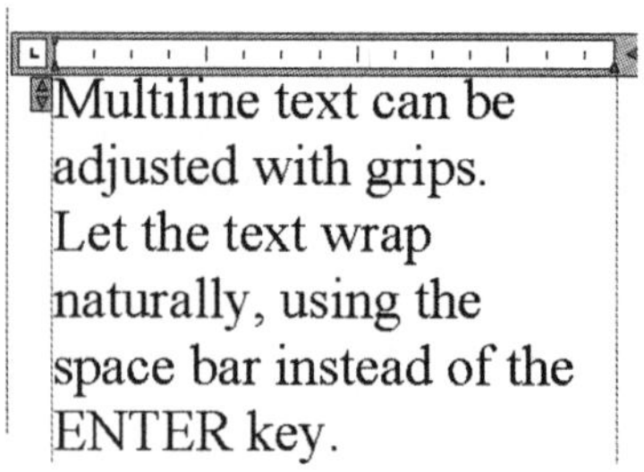

Command Exercise

Exercise 10-9 – Edit Text with Grips

Drawing Name: **etext3.dwg**
Estimated Time to Completion: 5 Minutes

Scope

Using grips, move and stretch the multiline text paragraph into the box.

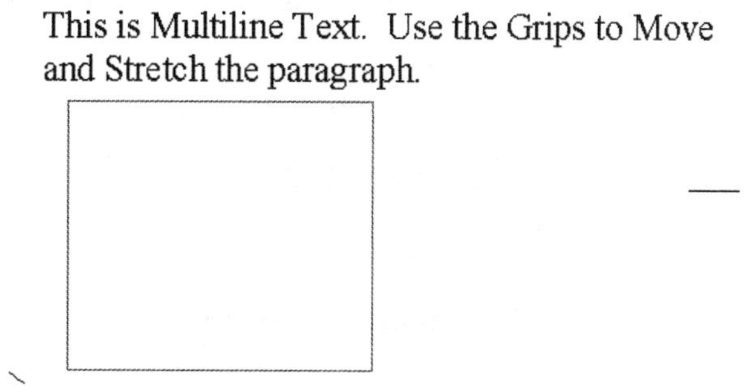
This is Multiline Text. Use the Grips to Move
and Stretch the paragraph.

Text Grips Exercise

Solution

1. Make sure the command line is clear.
2. Enable OSNAPs.
3. Select the black multiline text.

Notice how the grip points appear.

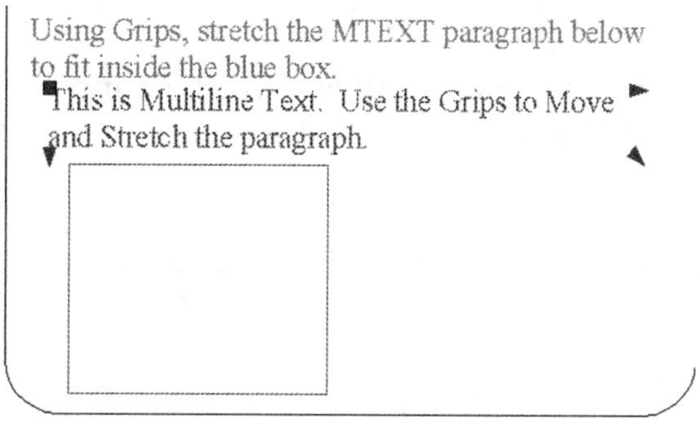
Using Grips, stretch the MTEXT paragraph below
to fit inside the blue box.
This is Multiline Text. Use the Grips to Move
and Stretch the paragraph.

Specify stretch point or [Base point/Copy/Undo/ eXit]:

4. Click the upper left grip point on the text; it will turn red. Move to the upper left endpoint of the box and click again. The text will move down to the box.

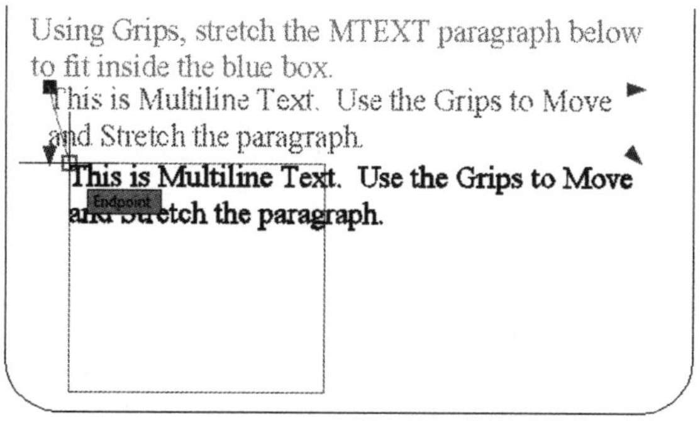
Using Grips, stretch the MTEXT paragraph below
to fit inside the blue box.
This is Multiline Text. Use the Grips to Move
and Stretch the paragraph.
This is Multiline Text. Use the Grips to Move
Endpoint
tch the paragraph.

Specify stretch point or [Base point/ Copy/Undo/eXit]:

5. Click the lower right grip point on the text. Move to the lower right corner of the box and click again.

The text will stretch itself to fit inside the box.

6. Press <ESC> to release the selected text.

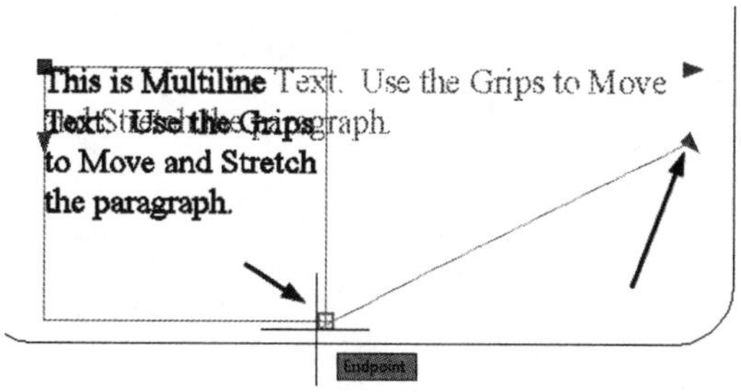
This is Multiline Text. Use the Grips to Move
to Move and Stretch
the paragraph.
Endpoint

Command Exercise

Exercise 10-10 – Edit Text Properties

Drawing Name: **etext4.dwg**
Estimated Time to Completion: 5 Minutes

Scope

Change the Style of the text to TEXT2 using the Quick Properties dialog.

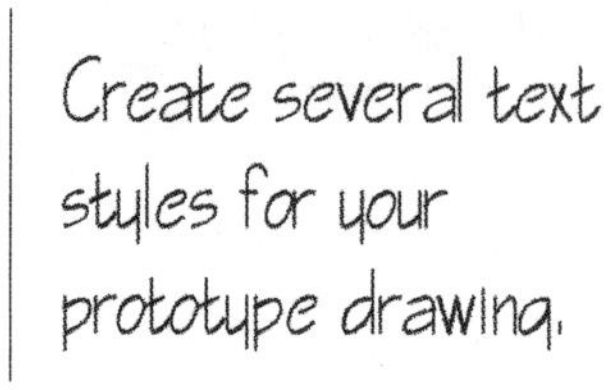
Create several text
styles for your
prototype drawing.

Text Properties Exercise

Solution

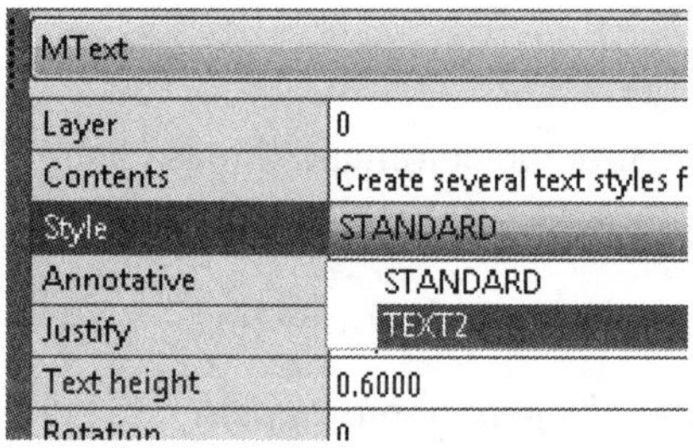
MText
Layer
0
Contents
Create several text styles f
Style
STANDARD
Annotative
STANDARD
Justify
TEXT2
Text height
0.6000

1. Select the text with the LMB to activate the grips. The Quick Properties dialog will appear.

2. In the Properties dialog box change the Style to **TEXT2**.

3. Press <**ESC**> to release the selection.

Find and Replace

Command Locator

Pull Down Menu	**Edit→Find**
Command	**Find**
RMB Shortcut Menu	**Text Windows in the dialog box**
Dialog Box	**Find and Replace**
Annotate Ribbon	**Text panel**

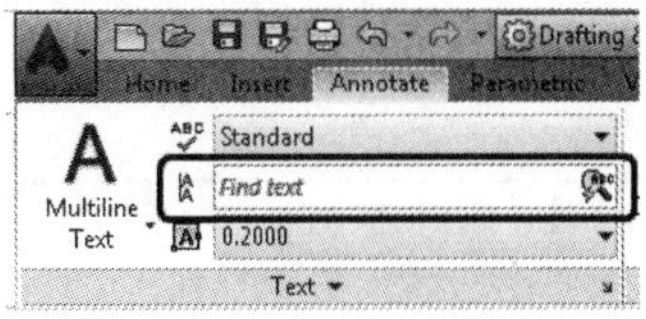

Command Overview

The Find and Replace command provides text search with the options to perform a global search or to search selected text. Type in the Text string to find, and type the replacement text.

General Procedures

1. Invoke the Find and Replace command.
2. Type the text string to Find, and type the replacement text.
3. Select the Find button, then select "Replace All."

Tips & Tricks

- Using this command with selected text is the same as using options in the Find/ Replace tab of the Multiline Text dialog box.
- Use the Window option located in the upper right corner to limit the find and replace operation to a specific section of a drawing.

Spell Check

Command Locator

Annotate Ribbon	
Text Toolbar	**Spell Check**
Pull Down Menu	**Tools→Spelling**
Command	**Spell**
Alias	**SP**
RMB Shortcut Menu	**Text Window of the dialog box**
Dialog Box	**Check Spelling**

Command Overview

Check for spelling errors. Select one line of text or all the text in the drawing. Add words to build a custom dictionary.

Spell Check Option	Overview
Current word	The misspelled word will appear in this area.
Suggestions	Spell check will provide a list of suggested words.
Ignore / Ignore All	Ignore will keep the misspelled word or words as they are.
Change / Change All	This option will substitute the misspelled word or words for a suggested word.
Add	Build a custom dictionary with the Add option.
Lookup	This option will look up more words based on the highlighted suggestion.
Change Dictionary	There are several language dictionaries available with Spell Check, including the custom dictionary.
Context	The sentence context of the misspelled word will appear in this area.

General Procedures

1. Invoke the Spell command. Select the text to check.
2. Select a suggestion from the list if the current word is incorrect.
3. Select Change, then select OK.

Tips & Tricks

- Building a custom dictionary is useful when abbreviations or technical terms are used frequently in the drawing.

Command Exercise

Exercise 10-11 – Spell Check

Drawing Name: **spell1.dwg**
Estimated Time to Completion: 5 Minutes

Scope

Correct the spelling in the text provided.

Solution

1. From the Annotate ribbon, select **Check Spelling**.

2. In the Where to check: drop-down, select **Selected objects**.

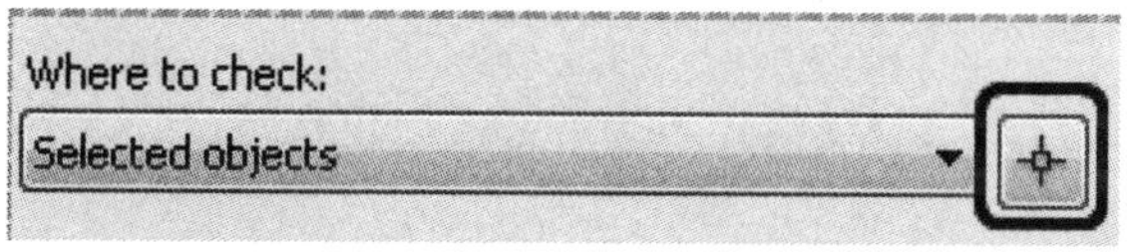

3. Press the Select tool to activate the selection mode.

Select objects:

4. Use the LMB to pick the text to check and press <ENTER> or type **ALL** to check the spelling for the entire drawing.

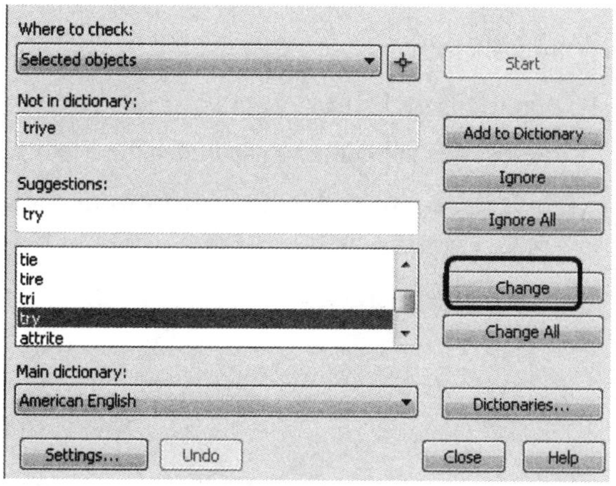

5. Press **Start**.

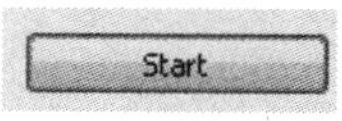

6. Locate the correct spelling under Suggestions and press **Change**.

The spell checker will advance to the next misspelled word.

7. Change that one as well.

8. Press 'OK' when notified that Spell Check is complete to finish the command.

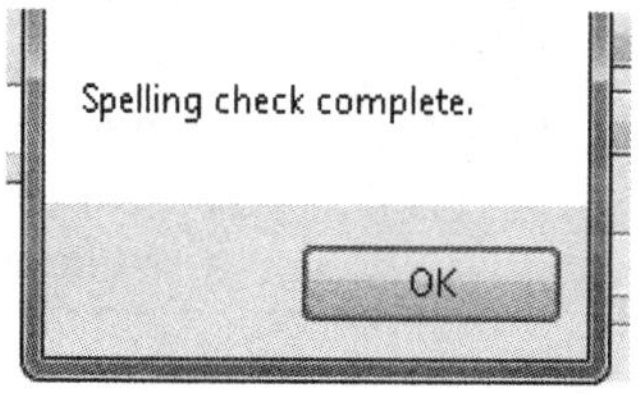

9. Close the Spell Check dialog.

Fields

Command Locator

Insert Ribbon	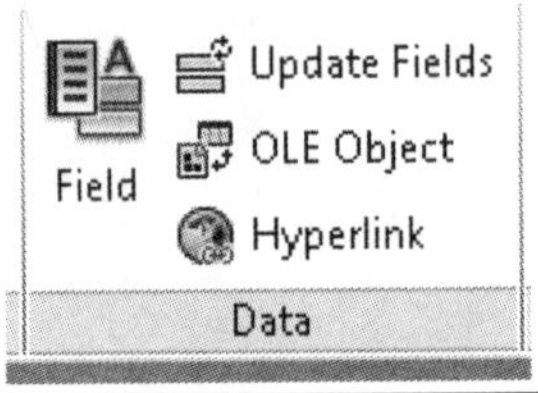
Pull Down Menu	**Insert→Field**
Command	**Field**
Alias	**Ctl+F**

Command Overview

Fields can be used in MTEXT or attribute definitions. You can use fields to display the area of a polygon or for title block information. Fields are also used in sheet sets. You can access the command by right clicking in the MTEXT window and selecting *Insert Field.*

There are several system variables that control how fields work. FIELDDISPLAY allows you to turn off the gray box under any defined fields. The gray box is not printed even when it is visible. FIELDEVAL sets how fields are updated upon saving the drawing, plotting the drawing, or on Regen. FIELDUPDATE is used to update fields manually.

When you insert the field, there are two options available: Text Height and Justification.

General Procedures

Inserting a Field:

1. Go to Insert, Field.
2. Select the field data to use under the Field Category list.
3. Select the format (Upper Case/Lower Case/Sentence Case/Title Case) to be used for the field.
4. Press OK to close the dialog.
5. Select the insertion point for the field.

Tips & Tricks

- The insertion point of the field is the upper left corner of the text.
- The Date field can only be updated using the UPDATEFIELD command.
- Spell check does not work on the values stored in fields.
- Fields are linked but not attached to objects. This means you can move the object and the field will not move with it. To have the field move with an assigned object, use **Group**.

Command Exercise

Exercise 10-12 – Adding Fields to Objects

Drawing Name: **fields2.dwg**
Estimated Time to Completion: 15 Minutes

Scope

Adding Fields to an object.

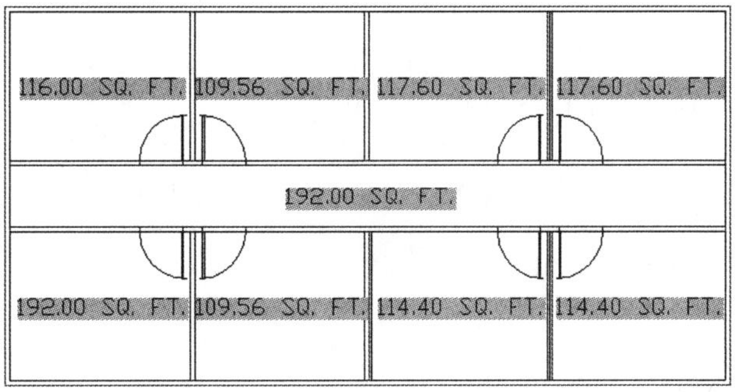

Fields Exercise

Solution

1. Activate the Insert Ribbon.

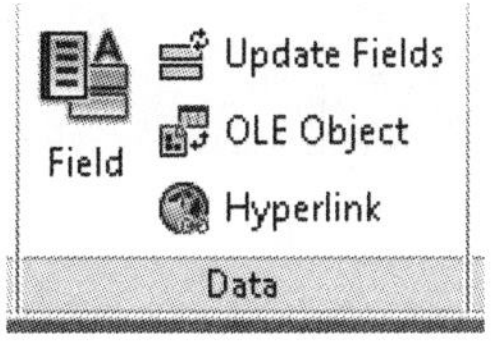

2. Select the Field tool.

3. Under the Field Category, select **Objects**.

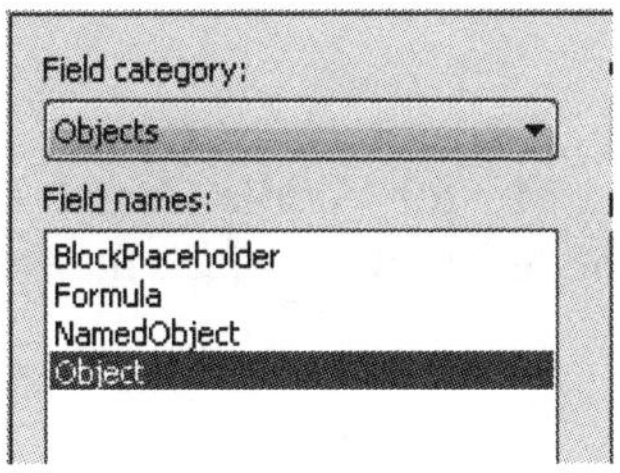

4. Highlight **Object** under Field names.

5. Select the **Select Object** tool.

6. Select the first rectangle in the upper left corner.

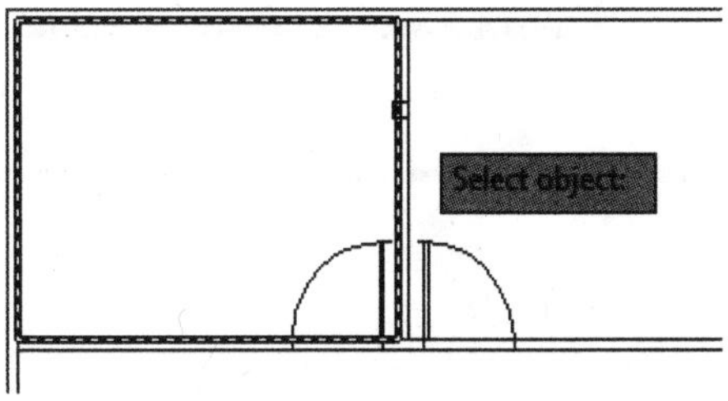

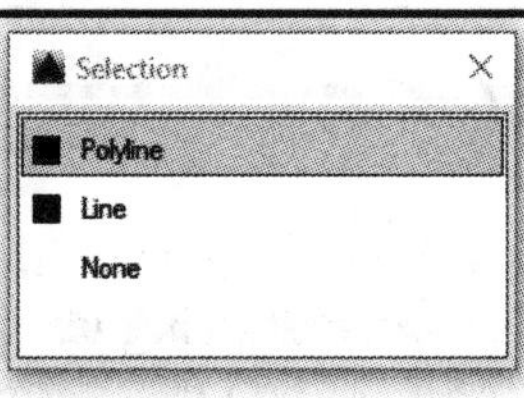

A selection box should appear to allow you to choose the Polyline.

A rectangle is considered a polyline.

> *Make sure you select the rectangle and not a line or the object properties will not display properly.*

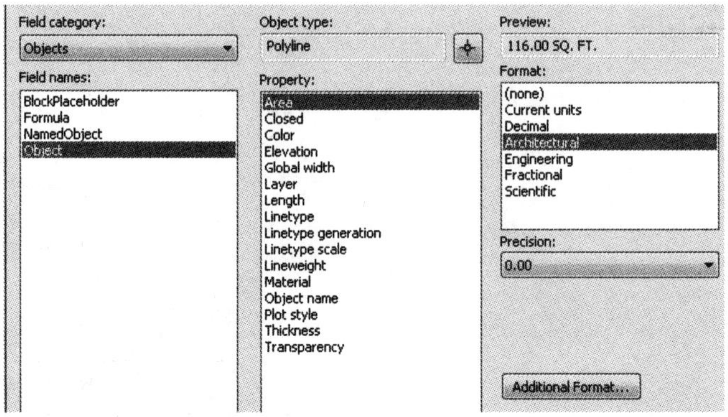

7. Highlight **Area** under Property.

8. Select **Architectural** under Format.

9. Set the Precision to two decimal places.

10. Press **OK**.

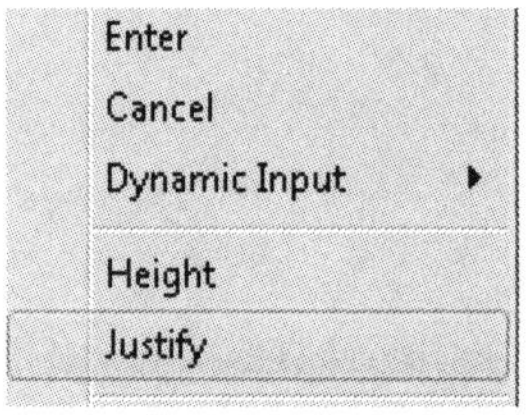

11. RMB and select **Justify**.

12. Select **MC** for Middle Center.

13. With Justification set to MC for Middle Center, use the Geometric Center of the rectangle to place the field.

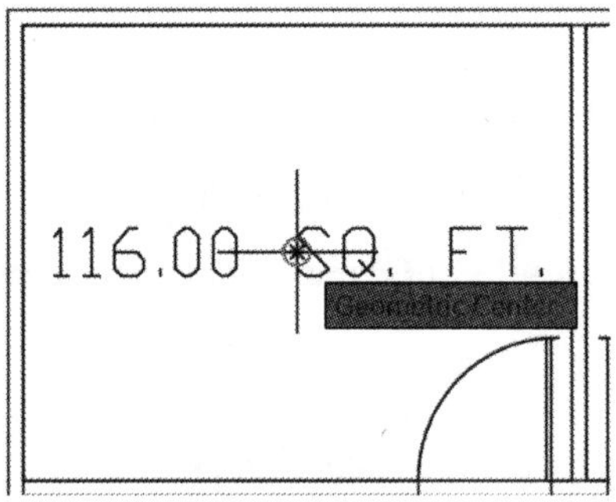

***Extra:** Repeat for the other rooms in the layout.*

Tables

Tabulated Drawings: Many companies use tabulated drawings for their designs. A tabulated drawing is used when the basic design is the same, but the dimensions change depending on the part number. Tables can be used in these drawings.

Command Locator

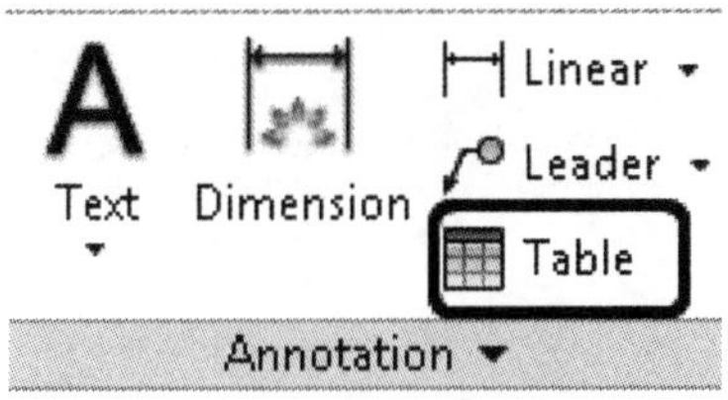

Home Ribbon	**Annotation/Table**
Toolbar Menu	**Draw→Table**
Pull Down Menu	**Draw→Table**
Command	**table**
Alias	**tb**

Command Overview

Tables can be defined with a specific number of columns and rows. You can save table styles to be re-used in other drawings.

General Procedures

Inserting a Table:

1. Go to Draw, Table.
2. Select the number of columns, the column size, and the number of rows.
3. Press OK to close the dialog.
4. Select the insertion point for the table.

Tips & Tricks

- Tables can be exported to Excel or a text file.
- It is helpful to create text styles for the font styles to be applied to cells. Simply select the cell(s) and assign the desired text style.
- Columns can be combined to create headers.
- Borders can be turned off and on to create more elaborate tables.
- Cells can be colored to provide shading.

Command Exercise

Exercise 10-13 – Adding a Table

Drawing Name: **table1.dwg**
Estimated Time to Completion: 30 Minutes

Scope

Adding a table to a drawing.

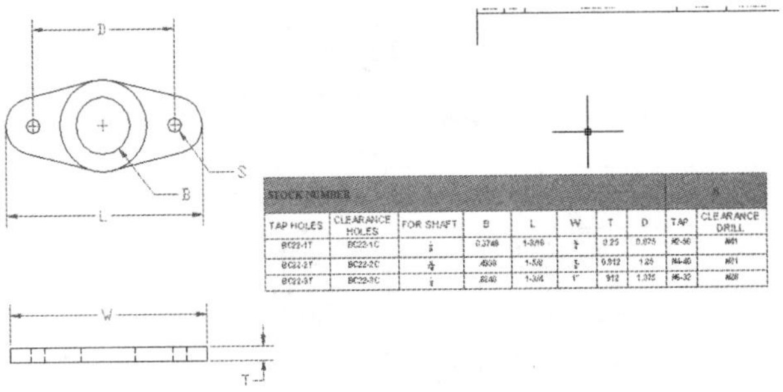

Table Exercise

Solution

1. Activate the **Plan** layout by selecting it.

2. Select the **Table** tool from the Home ribbon.

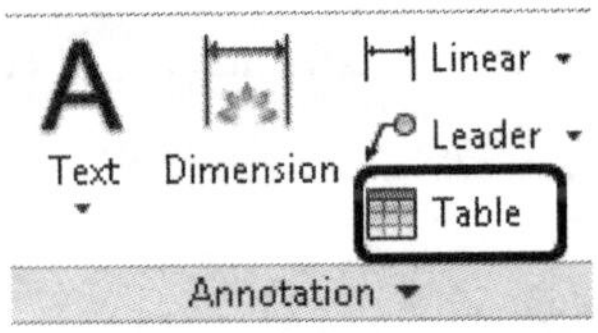

3. Set the Columns to **10**.
4. Set the Column width to **0.75**.
5. Set the Data Rows to **5**.
6. Set the Row Height to **1**.
7. Press **OK**.

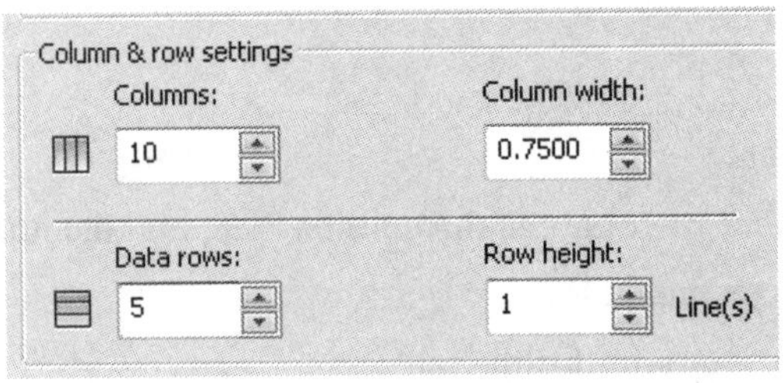

8. Place the table on the right side of the drawing.

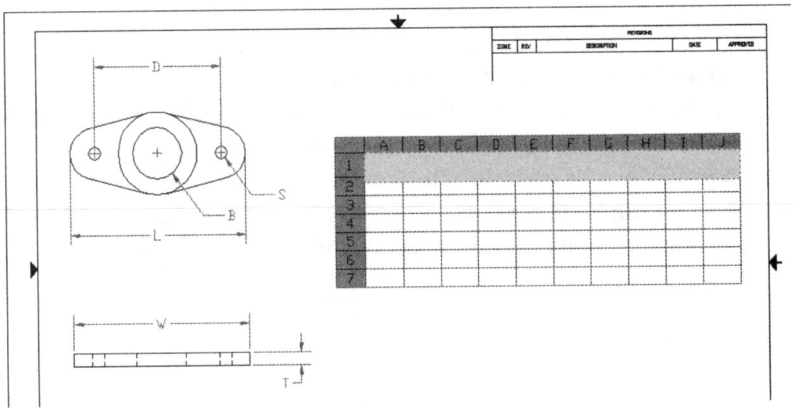

9. Enter **Stock Number** on the first row.

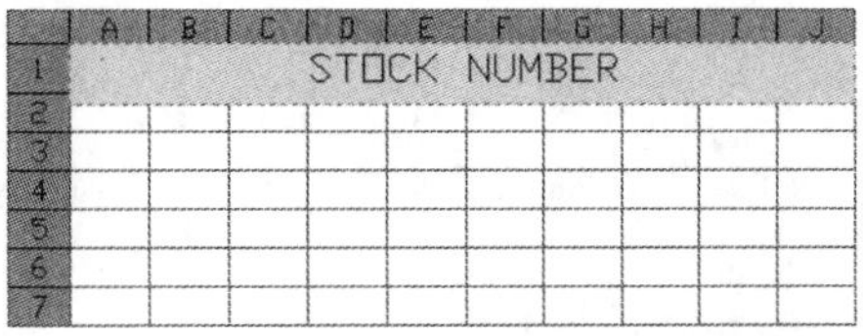

On the Ribbon:

10. Apply **Main Header** as the text style for the top row.
11. Set the Text Size to 0.100.
12. Press **OK**.

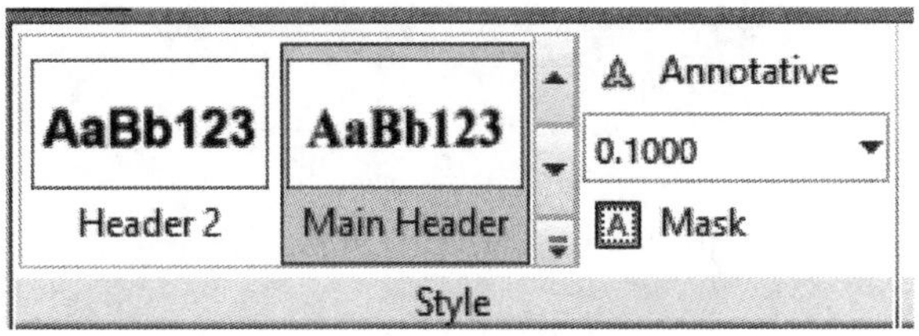

13. Fill in the cells for the second row. Use the <TAB> key to move to the next column. The cell is activated for data entry when it is shaded.

STOCK NUMBER									
TAP HOLES	CLEARANCE HOLES	FOR SHAFT	B	L	W	T	D	TAP	CLEARANCE DRILL

14. Use crossing to select the first column, rows 2 through 7. You can also hold down the <SHIFT> key and select each cell. Use grips to widen the column.

15. Adjust the width of the other columns as needed using grips.

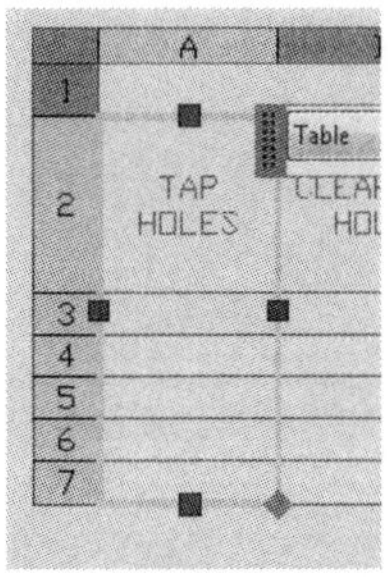

16. Fill in the third row. Adjust the column widths as needed.

STOCK NUMBER									
TAP HOLES	CLEARANCE HOLES	FOR SHAFT	B	L	W	T	D	TAP	CLEARANCE DRILL
BC22-1T	BC22-1C	$\frac{1}{8}$	0.3748	1-3/16	$\frac{3}{4}$	0.25	0.875	#2-56	#41

17. Fill out the table as shown.

STOCK NUMBER									
TAP HOLES	CLEARANCE HOLES	FOR SHAFT	B	L	W	T	D	TAP	CLEARANCE DRILL
BC22-1T	BC22-1C	$\frac{1}{8}$	0.3748	1-3/16	$\frac{3}{4}$	0.25	0.875	#2-56	#41
BC22-2T	BC22-2C	$\frac{3}{16}$	.4998	1-5/8	$\frac{7}{8}$	0.312	1.25	#4-40	#31
BC22-3T	BC22-3C	$\frac{1}{4}$	.6248	1-3/4	1"	.312	1.375	#6-32	#26

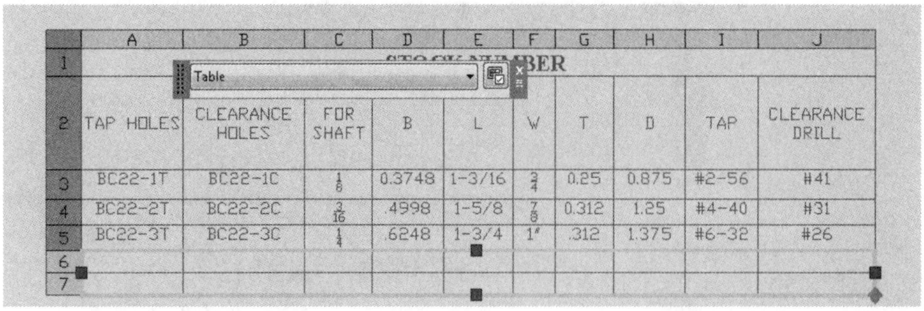

18. Hold down the <SHIFT> key and select the cells in the last two rows by picking the two rows.

19. Select **Delete Rows** from the Table ribbon.

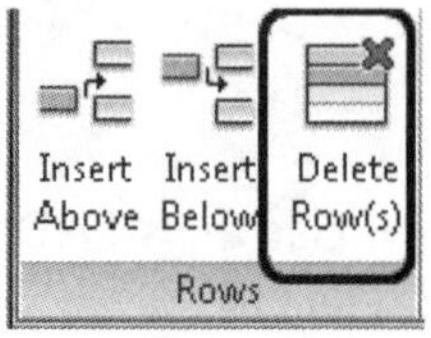

20. Select the cells in the second row.

21. On the ribbon, set the Style to Header
OR
RMB and select **Cell Style→ Header**.

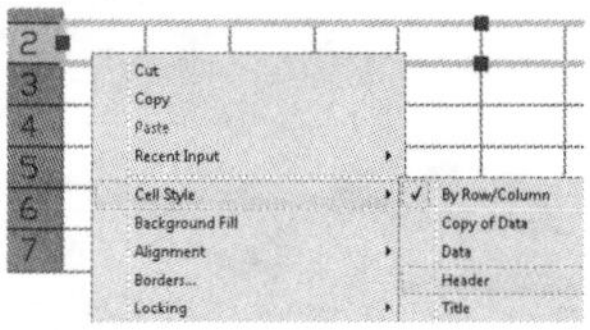

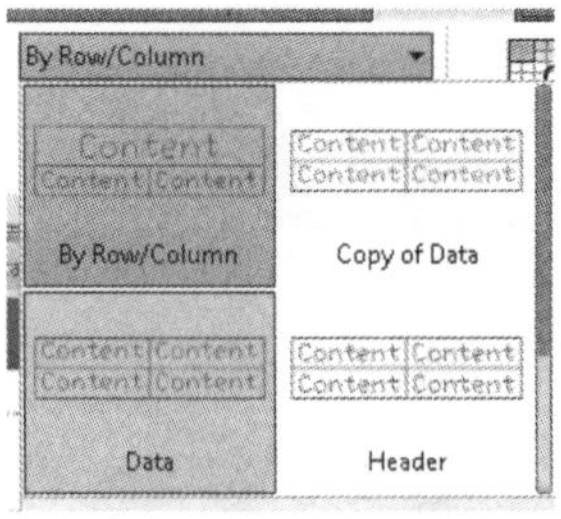

22. For the rows 3 to 5:
Set the Cell style to **Data**.

23. Select the top row.

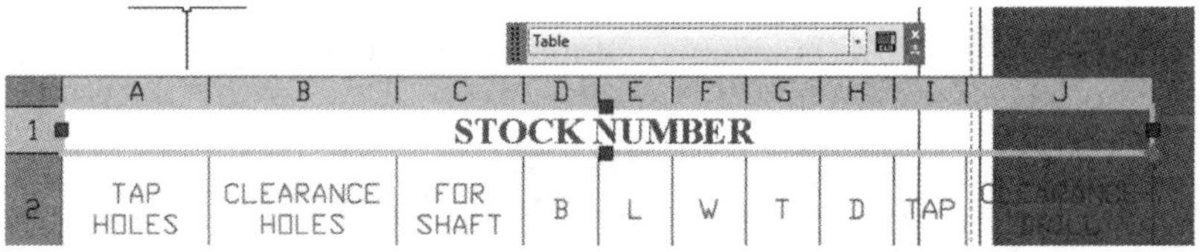

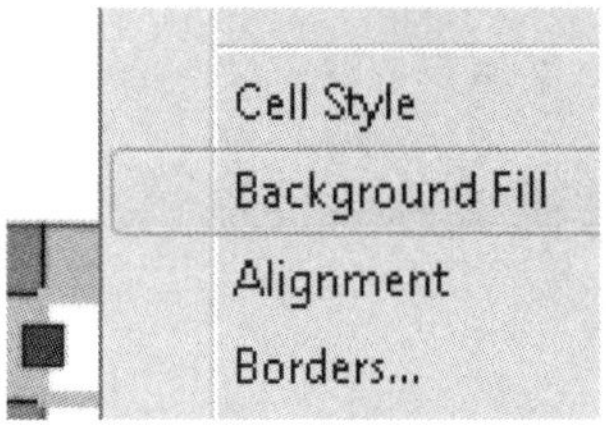

24. Right click and select **Background Fill.**
25. Set the Background fill to **Cyan.**
26. Press **OK** then press <ESC> to release the selection.

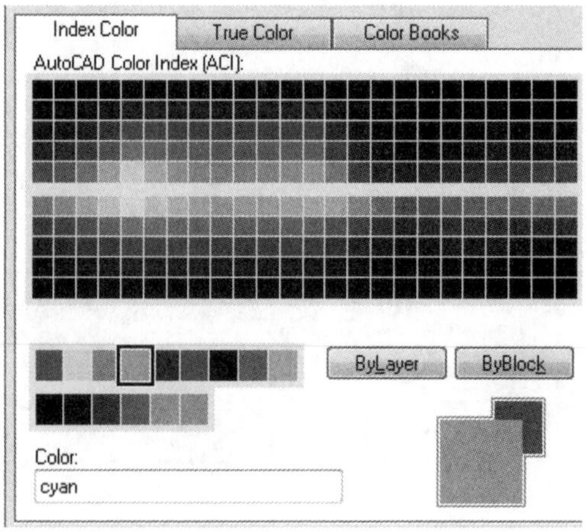

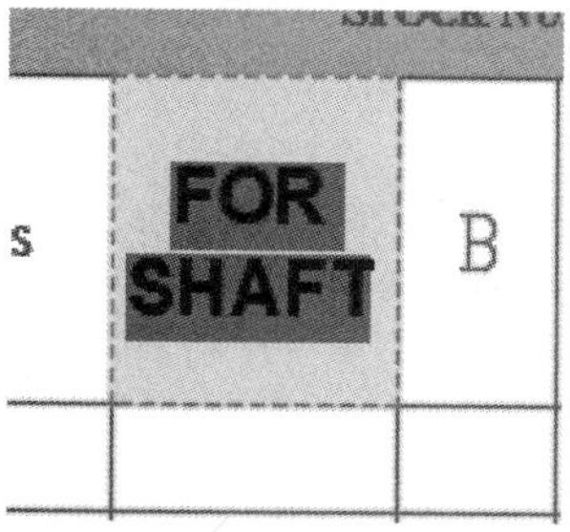

27. Highlight the text in each cell of the second row.

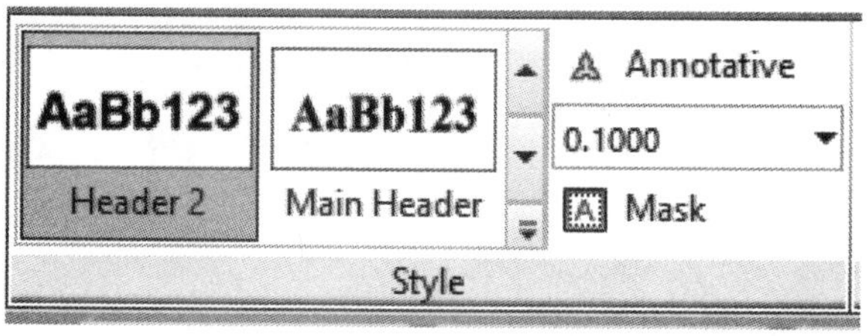

28. Set the Text Style to Header 2.

29. Set the Text Size to 0.100.

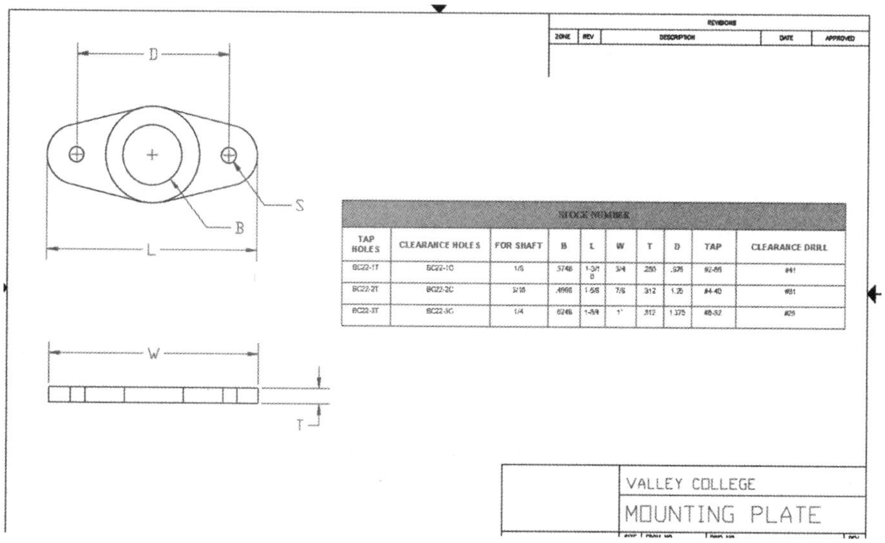

30. Adjust the location and size of the table so it fits onto the drawing properly.

> *To change the colors used to indicate the cells and rows when a table is activated, select the table. Right click and select Table Indicator color. Select the desired color and press OK.*

Command Exercise

Exercise 10-14 – Exporting a Table

Drawing Name: **table2.dwg**
Estimated Time to Completion: 15 Minutes

Scope

Exporting a table to EXCEL.

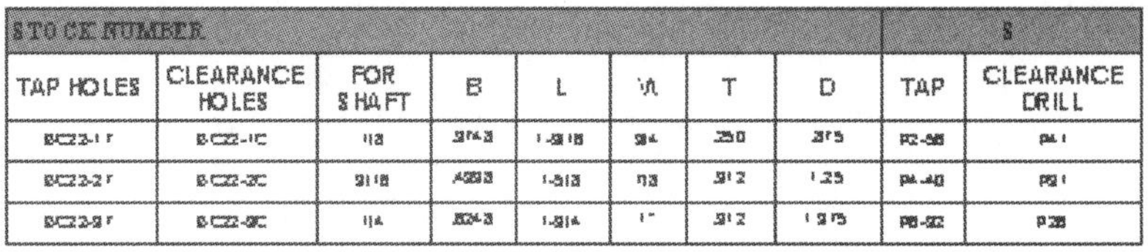

STOCK NUMBER								S	
TAP HOLES	CLEARANCE HOLES	FOR SHAFT	B	L	W	T	D	TAP	CLEARANCE DRILL
[illegible]	[illegible]	[illegible]	[illegible]	[illegible]	[illegible]	.250	[illegible]	[illegible]	[illegible]
[illegible]	[illegible]	[illegible]	[illegible]	[illegible]	[illegible]	.312	1.25	[illegible]	[illegible]
[illegible]	[illegible]	[illegible]	[illegible]	[illegible]	[illegible]	.312	[illegible]	[illegible]	[illegible]

Exporting a Table Exercise

Solution

1. Select the table in the drawing.
2. Right click and select **Export**.

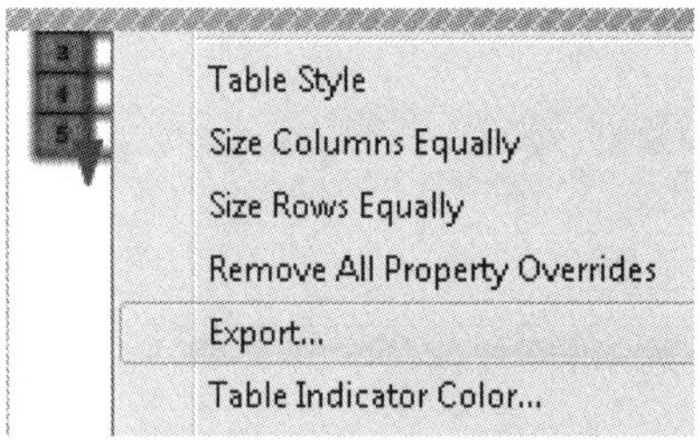

3. Browse to the folder where you want to save the file.
4. Press **Save**.
5. Launch EXCEL.
6. Select **Open**.
7. Set the Files of type to Text Files.
8. Highlight the *table1.csv* file.
9. Press **Open**.

10. You will have to format the columns to get the table to look proper.

> *You can only import text from a txt or rtf file. To import a Word file, save as txt or rtf.*

> *To open a csv file in Excel, you need to set the Files of Type to 'Text files' or you won't be able to see the file listed.*

Command Exercise

Exercise 10-15 – Adding Blocks and Symbols to a Table

Drawing Name: **table3.dwg**
Estimated Time to Completion: 15 Minutes

Scope

Adding blocks and symbols to a table.

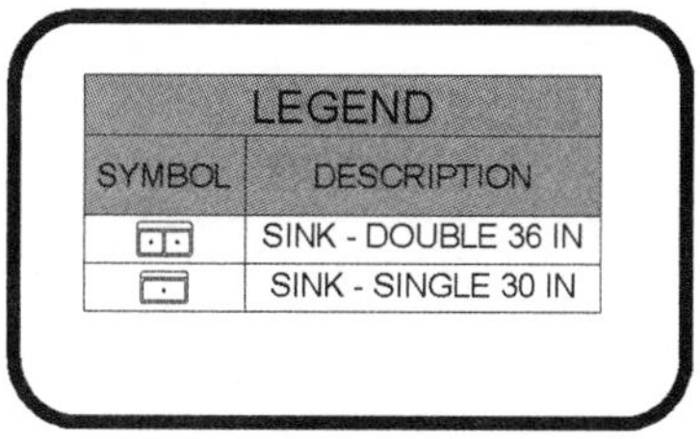

Adding blocks to a Table Exercise

Solution

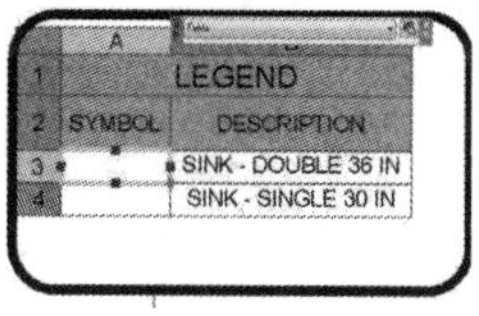

1. Select the 3A cell.

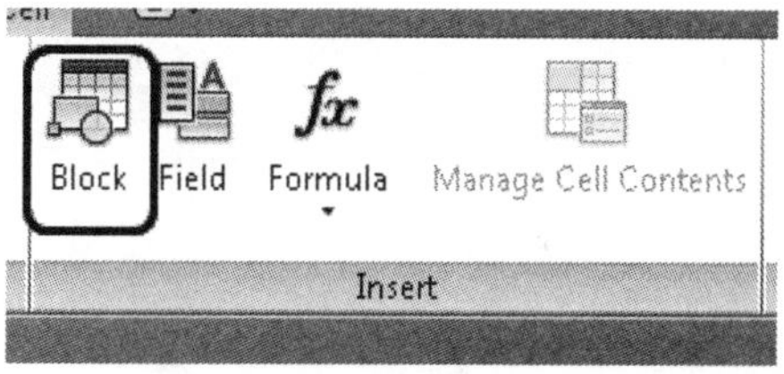

2. Select the **Insert Block** tool from the Table ribbon.

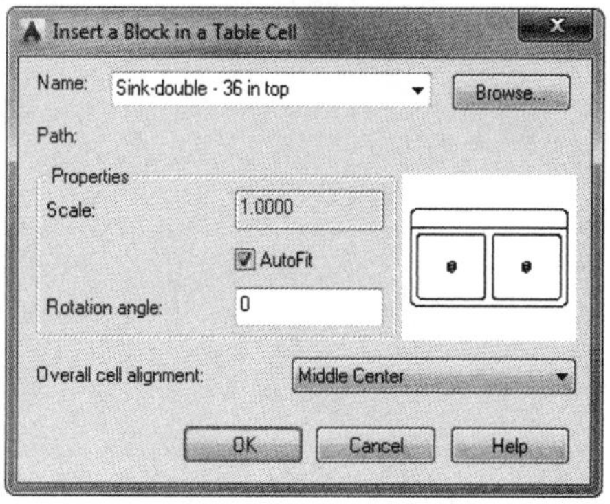

3. Select the **Sink-double-36 in top** from the drop-down.

These blocks are pre-loaded in the drawing.
If you need to locate a block, use the Browse button.

4. Enable **Autofit** to scale the block to the cell size.

5. Set the **Overall cell alignment** to **Middle Center**.

6. Press **OK**.

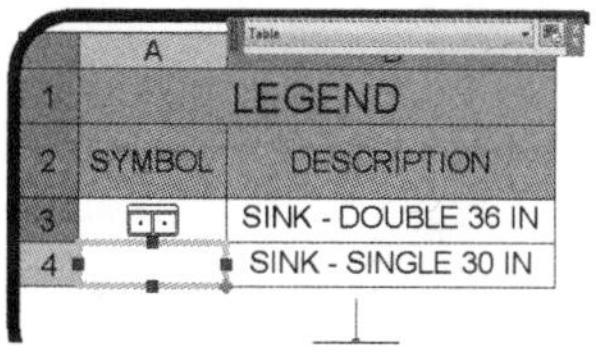

7. Select the 4A cell.

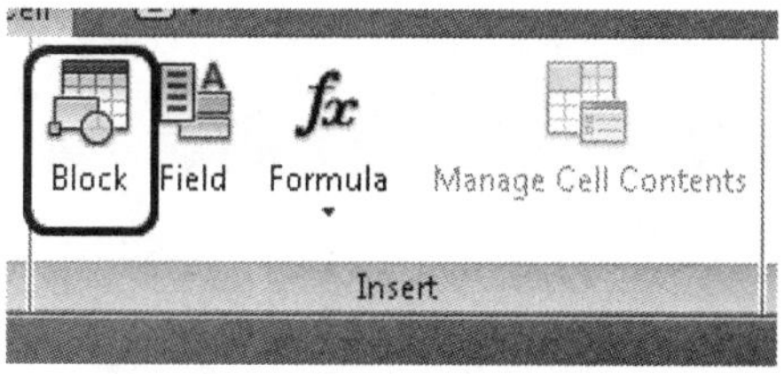

8. Select the **Insert Block** tool from the Table ribbon.

9. Select the **Sink-single-30 in top** from the drop-down.

These blocks are pre-loaded in the drawing.

If you need to locate a block use the Browse button.

10. Enable **Autofit** to scale the block to the cell size.
11. Set the **Overall cell alignment** to **Middle Center**.
12. Press **OK**.

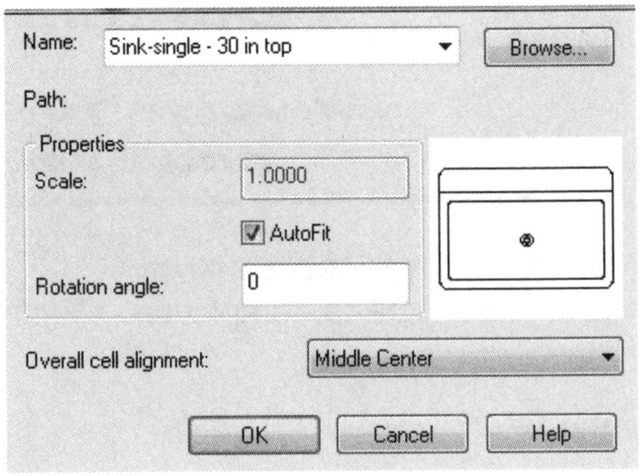

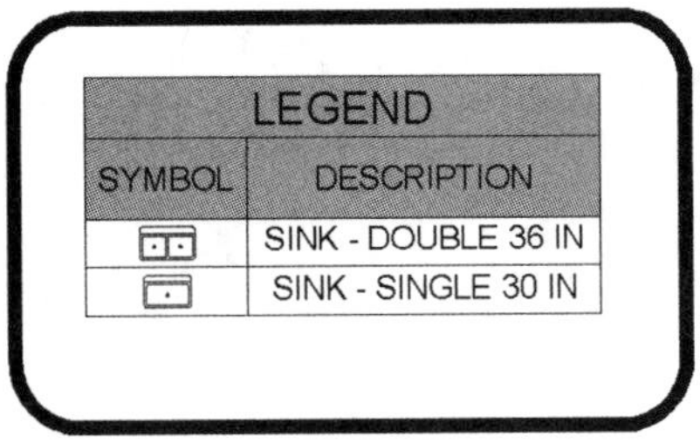

The legend is completed.

Review Questions

1. To change the justification of text in the MTEXT dialog, select here.

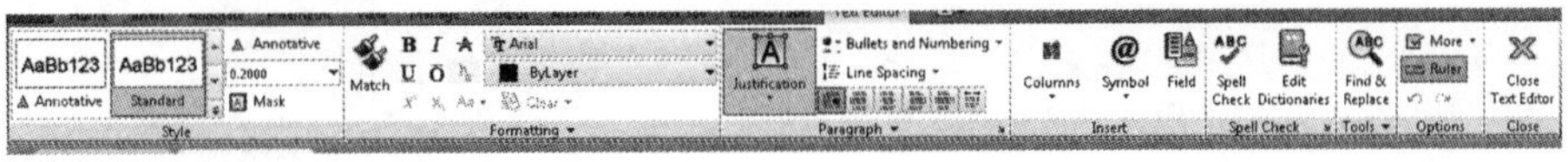

2. To eliminate unused text styles in a drawing, use:
   - ❑ Erase
   - ❑ Purge
   - ❑ Delete
   - ❑ Eliminate

3. **T F** If a text height is specified in the text style, the user will not be prompted for the text height.

4. **T F** Spell check can be used on fields.

5. **T F** Fields can be applied to objects.

6. In order to import a text file into MTEXT, the file should be this format:
   - ❑ Txt or rtf
   - ❑ Doc or csv
   - ❑ Xls or csv
   - ❑ Txt or doc

7. Data exported from a table will be in this format:
   - ❑ Xls
   - ❑ Csv
   - ❑ Txt
   - ❑ Dwg

8. **T F** You can control the text style inside of tables.

9. **T F** You cannot add or delete columns or rows from a table once it has been placed.

10. **T F** You can control the appearance of the MTEXT dialog.

Review Answers

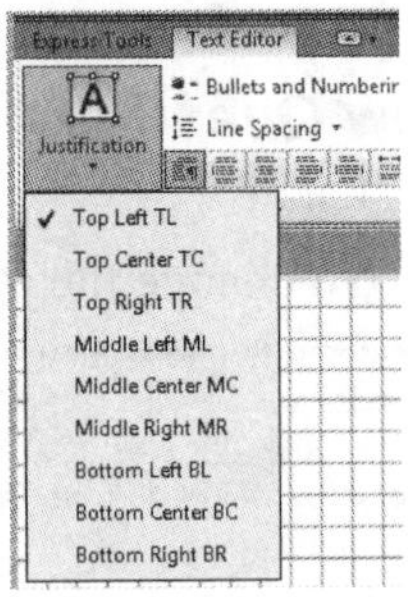

1. To change the justification of text in the MTEXT dialog, select here.

2. To eliminate unused text styles in a drawing, use:

   Purge

3. **T F** If a text height is specified in the text style, the user will not be prompted for the text height.

   True

4. **T F** Spell check can be used on fields.

   False

5. **T F** Fields can be applied to objects.

   True

6. In order to import a text file into MTEXT, the file should be this format:

   Txt or rtf

7. Data exported from a table will be in this format:

   Csv

8. **T F** You can control the text style inside of tables.

   True

9. **T F** You cannot add or delete columns or rows from a table once it has been placed.

   False

10. **T F** You can control the appearance of the MTEXT dialog.

    True

Lesson 11.0 – Title Blocks and Templates

Estimated Class Time: 4 Hours

Objectives

Students will learn how to create Title blocks and templates using drawing tools, fields, and attributes.

- **Templates**
  Templates are used as the starting point for a drawing and can store layers, linetypes, text styles and dimension styles.
- **Title Blocks**
  Titleblocks are used to track a drawing's name, part number, revision level, and other important information.
- **Fields**
  Fields are linked to drawing properties
- **Attributes**
  Attributes store data and are easily edited.
- **The Define Attribute Command**

One of the options when you create a drawing is to use a template. Many companies set up and use templates to ensure their drafters comply with their internal standards. Templates are great because you only need to set up your layers, title blocks, and dimension styles once.

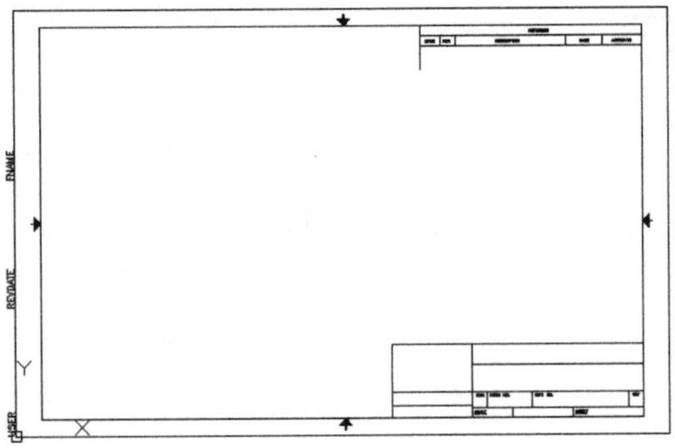

Technical drawings require a title block and a border.

You will notice that there are four arrows on the border, one on each side. The arrows are a leftover from the days when technical drawings were done on vellum. Drafters would create drawings using multiple sheets. Each sheet would act as a layer. The arrows were used to line up the views so that the overlays would match.

Most companies have a title block template that contains their company name and logo, as well as company address and contact information. As drafters, you need to know how to create and modify title blocks in case the company information changes and how to insert title blocks for use in your drawings.

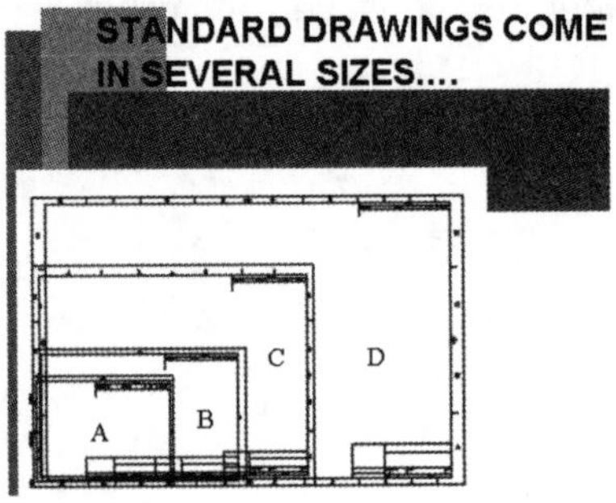

Each title block size is double the previous size...

A SIZE:	8-1/2 X 11
B SIZE:	11 X 17
C SIZE:	17 X 22
D SIZE:	22 X 34

In AutoCAD, all models and views are drawn 1:1. That way we can compare parts to make sure they fit together. In order to plot, we scale the title block and then scale the plot.

AutoCAD comes with standard title block templates. They are located in the Templates subdirectory under *Users\<User Name>\AppData\ Local\Autodesk\ AutoCAD 2017\R21.0\enu \Template.*

If you are using Windows 7 or Windows 8, the templates are stored under *Users/<user name>/AppData/ Local/ Autodesk/AutoCAD 2017/R20.1/enu/Template.*

Many companies will place their templates on the network so all users can access the same templates. In order to make this work properly, set the Options so that the templates folder is pointed to the correct path.

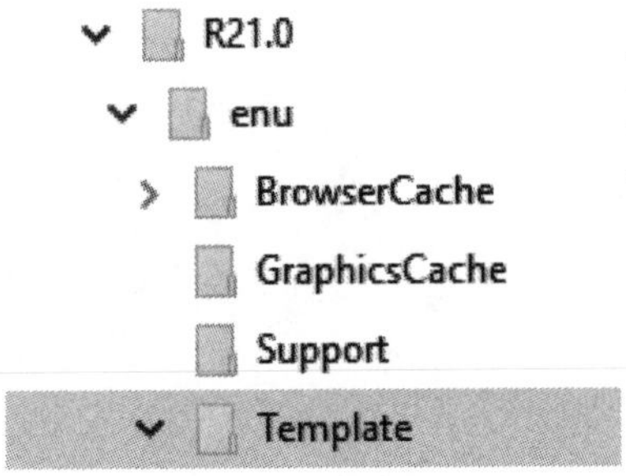

By adding attributes and fields to a title block, we can easily modify the text values and we can later learn how to export the attribute values to create a database for our parts drawings.

Define Attribute

Command Locator

Insert Ribbon	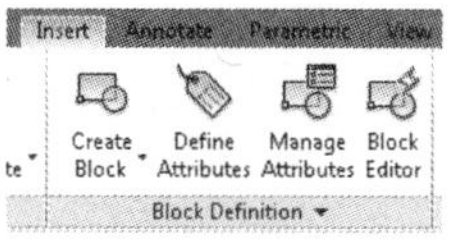
Pull Down Menu	**Draw/Block/Define Attributes**
Command	**ATTDEF**

Command Overview

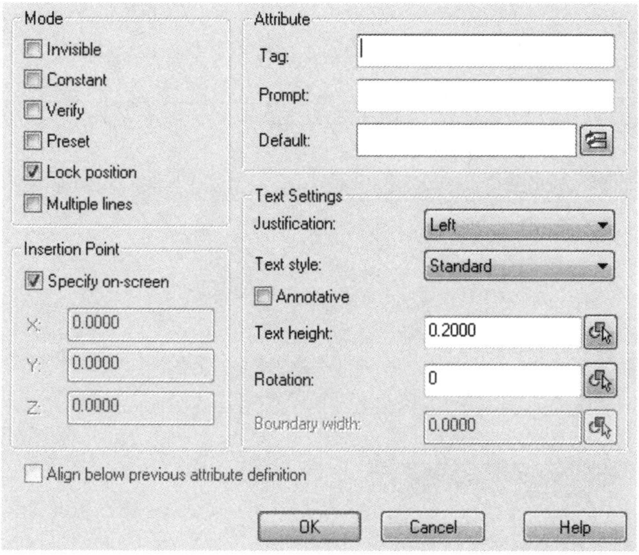

The Define Attribute dialog allows fields to be used as attributes. Field data is set up in the File Properties dialog. Once you enter the data in this dialog, the fields will automatically update in any corresponding locations.

There are four modes of Attribute definitions:

- Invisible
- Constant
- Verify
- Preset

Invisible attributes are used to store information in a drawing that is not seen in normal mode. Some companies will create a set of invisible attributes that list the layer standards. Drafters then turn the attribute display on so they can see the layer standards and turn them off when they are ready to plot their drawings. Other companies use invisible attributes to store cost information for parts. They don't want the customer to see how much the material costs, but they need the information to estimate project costs.

Constant attributes are used when the value does not change, such as company name, but the information is needed for extraction to a database.

Verify mode prompts the user with a Yes/No after they enter the attribute value to give them a chance to recheck their entry.

Preset sets the attribute to its default value when you insert a block containing a preset attribute.

Lock Position fixes the position of the attribute so it cannot be moved.

Multiple lines allows you to create an attribute using the MTEXT editor. You can use the editor to determine the width of your paragraph.

Tips & Tricks

- *To control the display of attributes use the command ATTDISP. Normal is normal/ default viewing mode. ON allows you to see invisible and visible attributes. OFF makes all attributes invisible.*

Command Exercise

Exercise 11-1 – Define Attribute

Drawing Name: **ANSI B title block.dwg**
Estimated Time to Completion: 70 Minutes

Scope

Add attributes and fields to a title block.

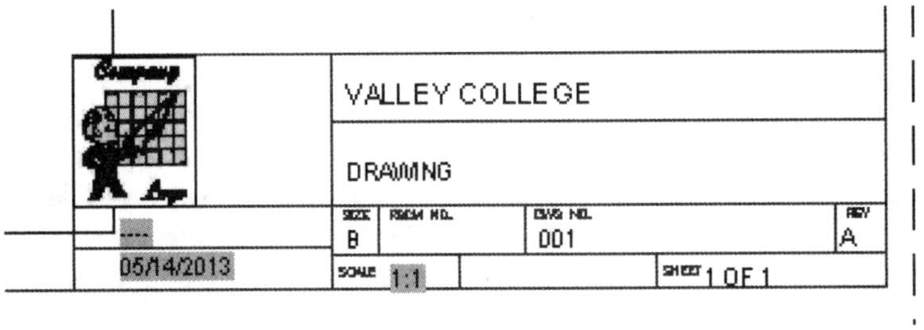

Define Attribute Exercise

Solution

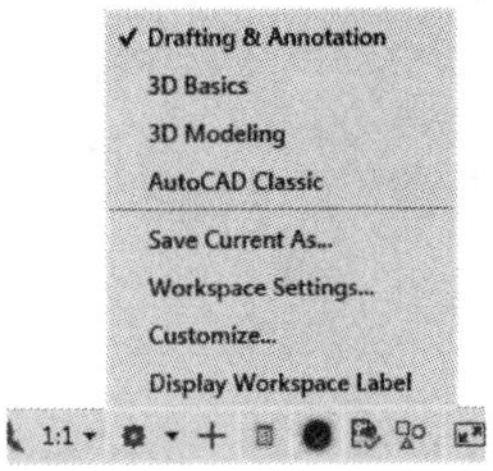

1. Verify that the active workspace is **Drafting & Annotation**.

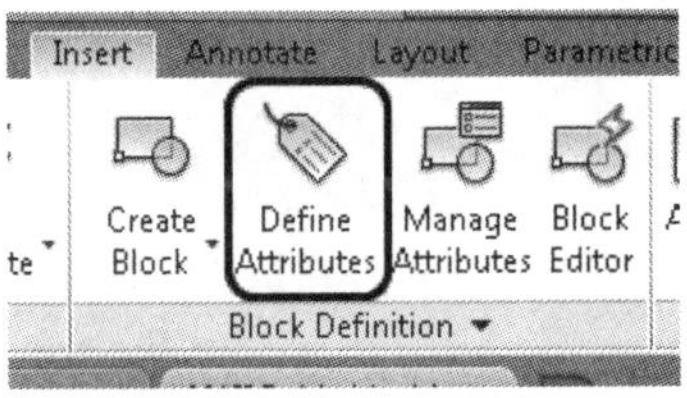

2. Activate the **Insert** tab on the ribbon.
3. Select the **Define Attributes** tool.

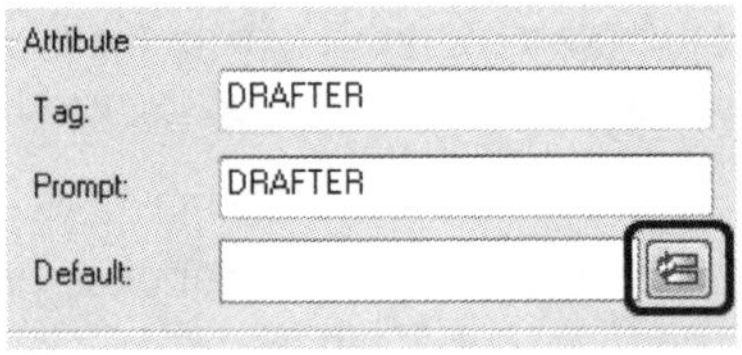

4. Enter **DRAFTER** in the Tag field.
5. Enter **DRAFTER** in the Prompt field.
6. Then select the **Insert Field** button.

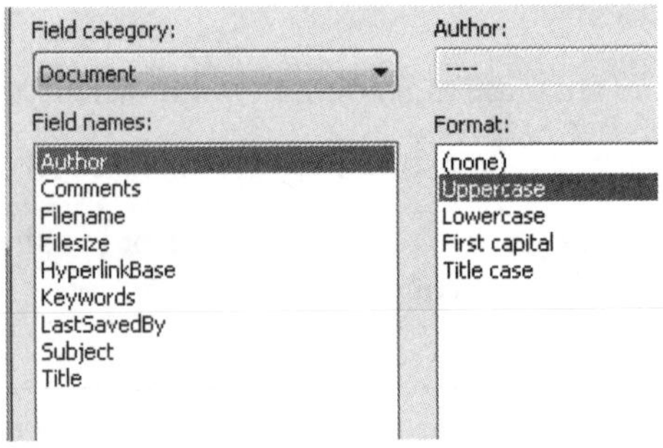

7. In the Field category, select **Document**.
8. Highlight **Author** in the Field Names window.
9. Highlight **Uppercase** in the Format window.
10. Press **OK**.

11. Under Insertion Point:

    Set X to **9.5**.

    Set Y to **0. 75**.

    Set Z to **0**.

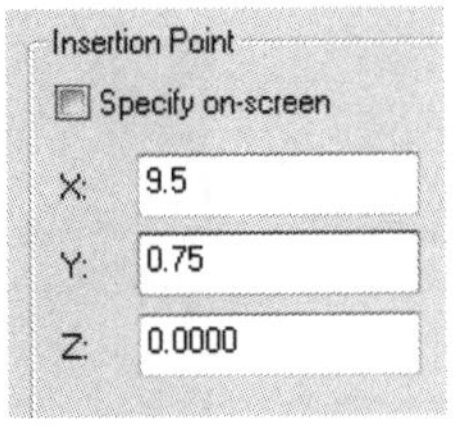

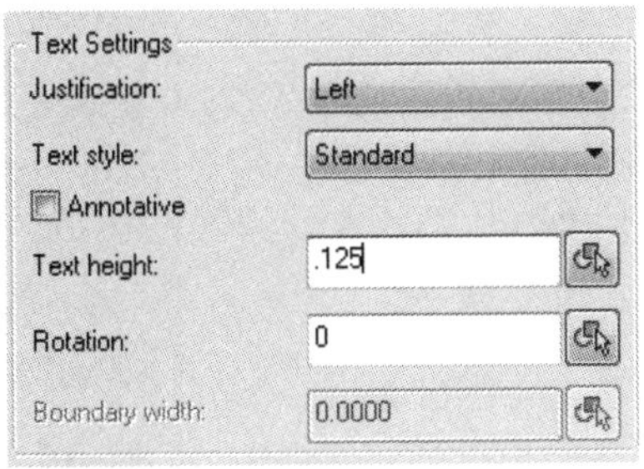

12. Under Text Options:

    Set the Height to **.125**.

13. Press **OK**.

The field appears in the title block.

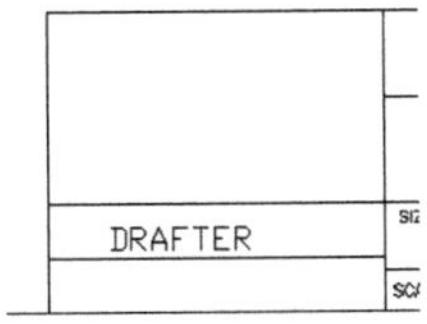

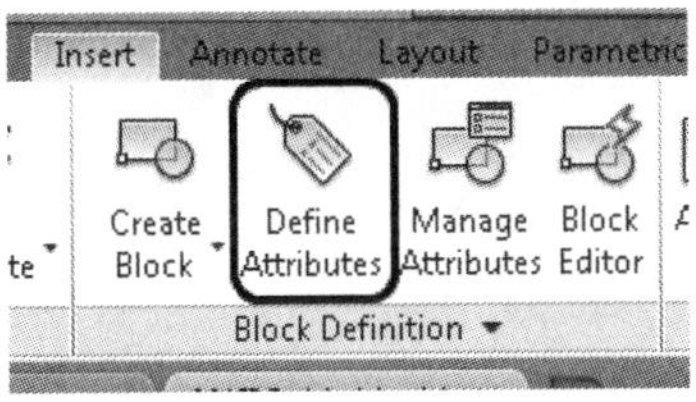

14. Select the **Define Attributes** tool.

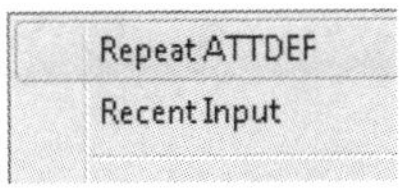

*You can also right click and select **Repeat ATTDEF** from the shortcut menu.*

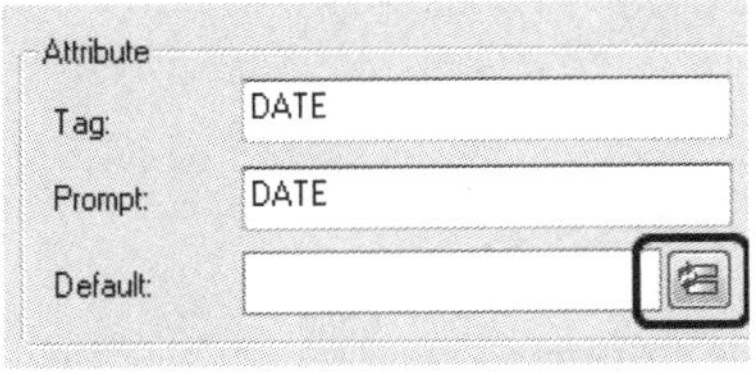

15. Enter **DATE** in the Tag field.
16. Enter **DATE** in the Prompt field.
17. Then select the **Insert Field** button.
18. In the Field category, select **Date & Time**.

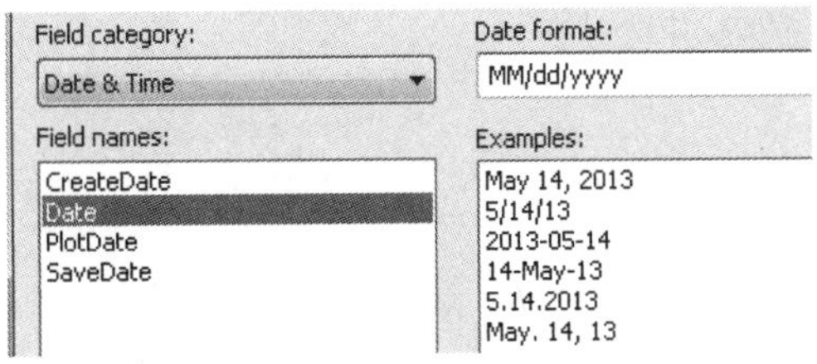

19. Highlight **CreateDate** in the Field Names window.
20. Type **MM/dd/yyyy** in the Date format field.
21. Press **OK**.

22. Under Insertion Point:

    Set X to **9.5**.

    Set Y to **0.5**.

    Set Z to **0**.

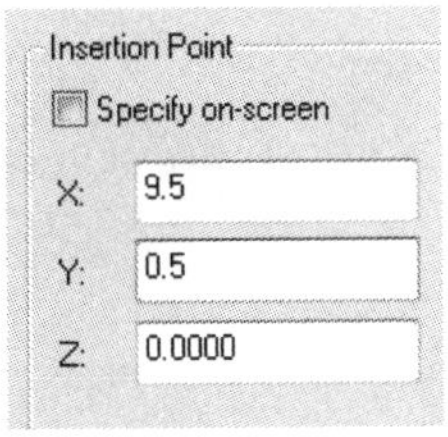

23. Under Text Options:

    Set the Height to **.125**.

24. Press **OK**.

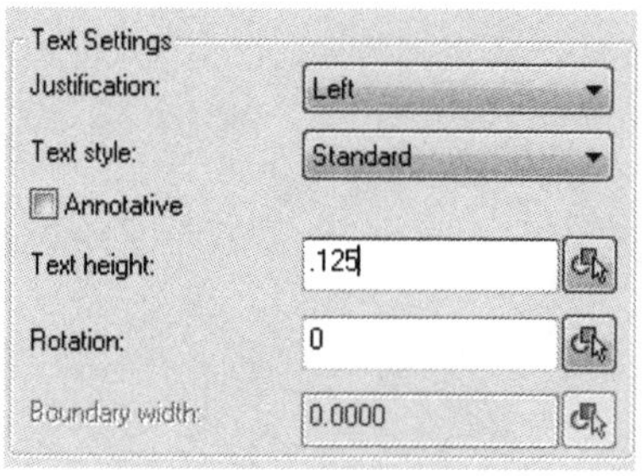

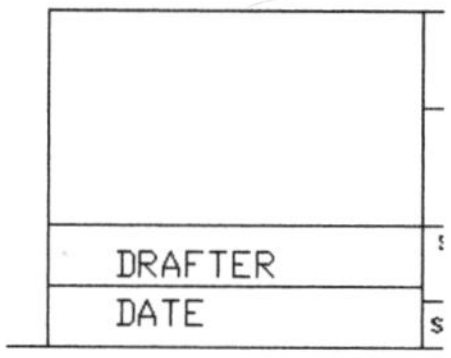

The field appears in the title block.

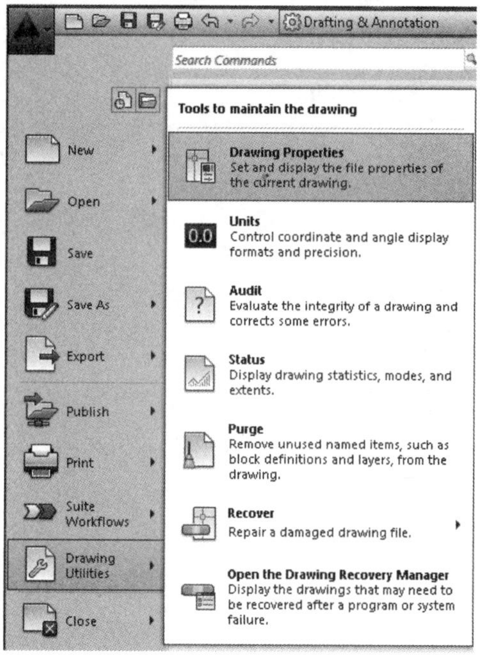

25. Go to **File→Drawing Utilities→ Drawing Properties**.

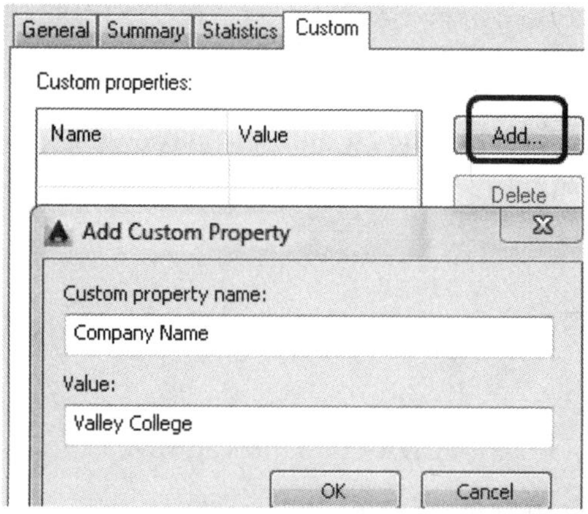

26. Select the **Custom** tab.

27. Press the **Add** button.

28. Type **Company Name** in the Custom property name field.

29. Type your school or company name in the Value field.

30. Press **OK** twice.

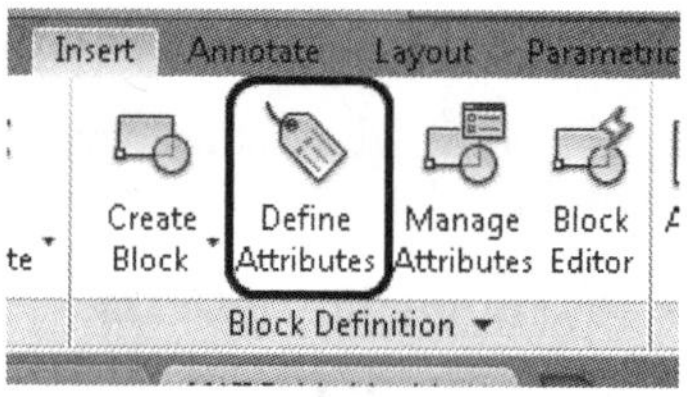

31. Select the **Define Attributes** tool.

*You can also right click and select **Recent Input →ATTDEF** from the shortcut menu.*

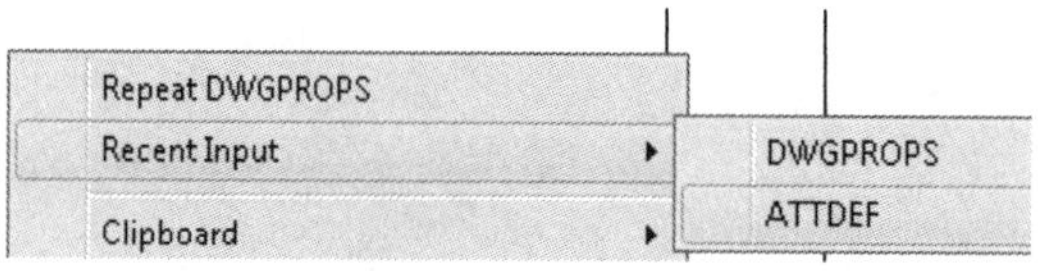

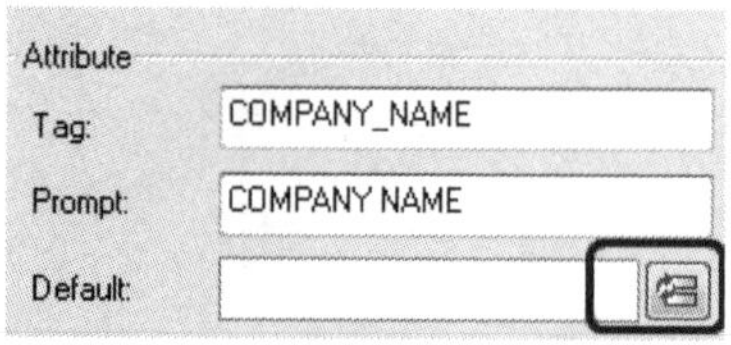

32. Enter **COMPANY_NAME** in the Tag field.

33. Enter **COMPANY NAME** in the Prompt field.

Note that the Tag field does not allow spaces.

34. Then select the **Insert Field** button.

35. In the Field category, select **Document**.
36. Highlight **Company Name** in the Field Names window.
37. Highlight **Uppercase** in the format field.
38. Press **OK**.

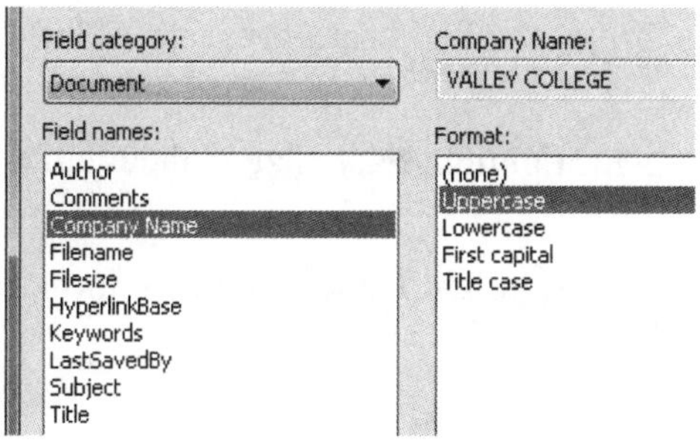

Tips & Tricks

- *Address, phone, and other data may also be defined as custom properties.*
- *Right click and use Recent Input to access your most recent commands. Simply select the command you want to use from the list.*
- *Custom Properties must be defined before they are available as fields.*

39. Under Insertion Point:

    Set X to **11.25**.

    Set Y to **1.75**.

    Set Z to **0**.

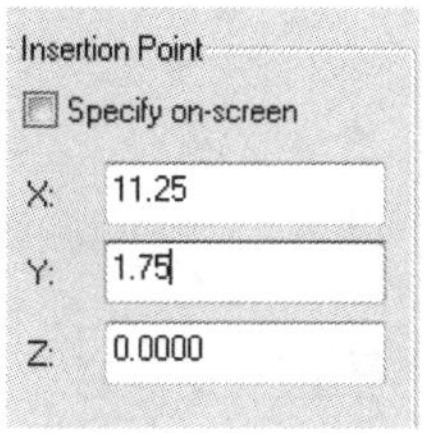

40. Under Text Options:

    Set the Height to **.1575**.

41. Press **OK**.

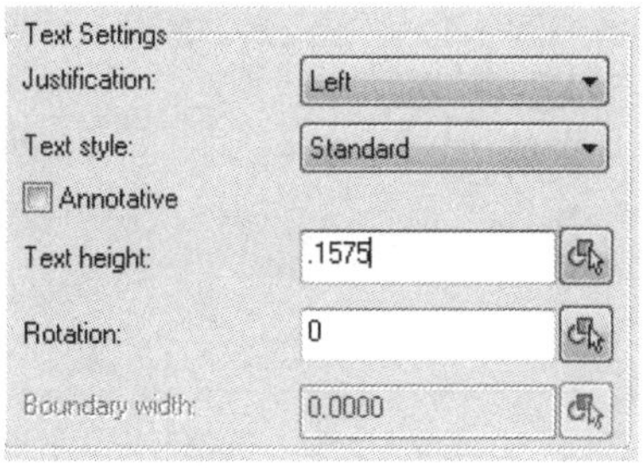

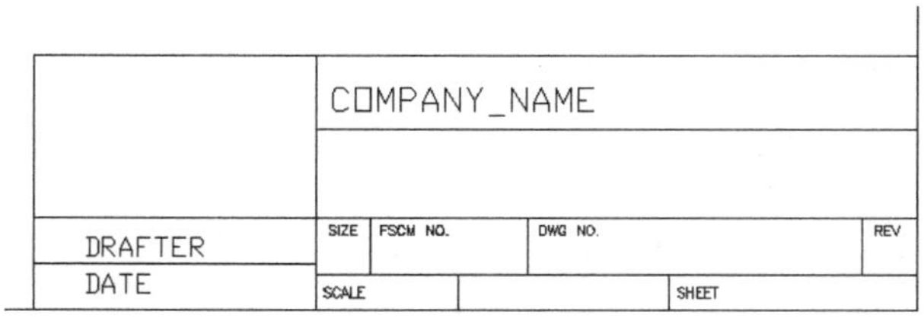

The field appears in the title block.

42. Select the **Define Attributes** tool.

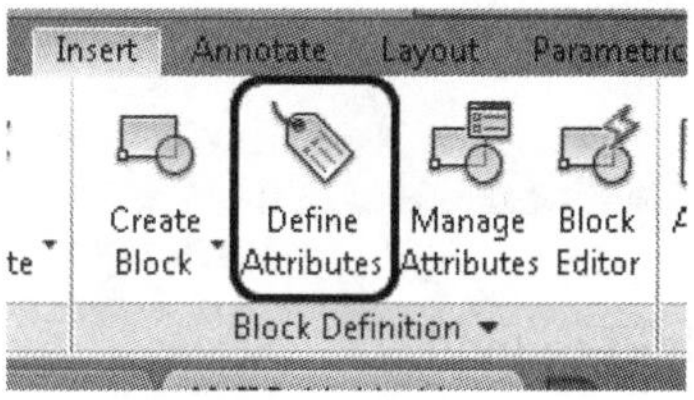

43. Enter **DWG_SIZE** in the Tag field.
44. Enter **DWG SIZE** in the Prompt field.

45. Then select the **Insert Field** button.

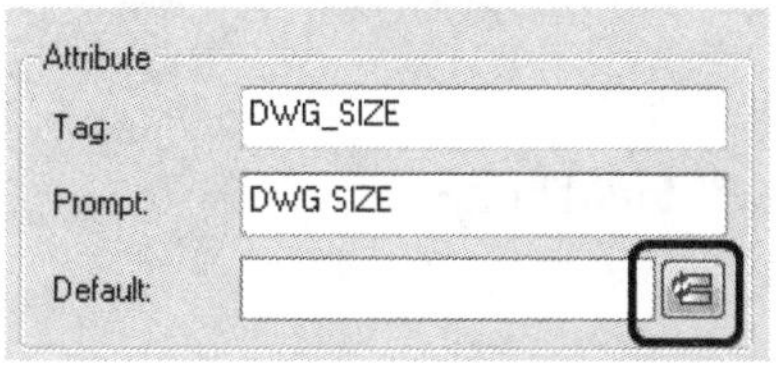

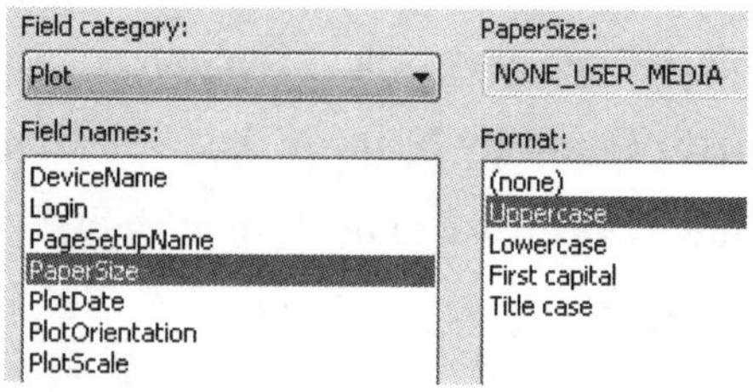

46. In the Field category, select **Plot**.

47. Highlight **PaperSize** in the Field Names window.

48. Highlight **Uppercase** in the format field.

49. Press **OK**.

By using a field for the paper size, the paper size will adjust based on the layout size used...you can change the paper size and the field will automatically update.

50. Under Insertion Point:

    Set X to **11.3**.

    Set Y to **0.695**.

    Set Z to **0**.

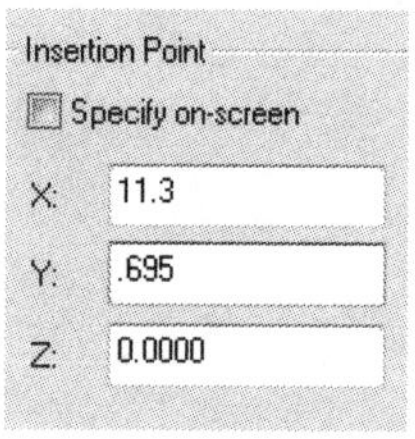

51. Under Text Options:

    Set the Justification to **Center**.

    Set the Height to **.125**.

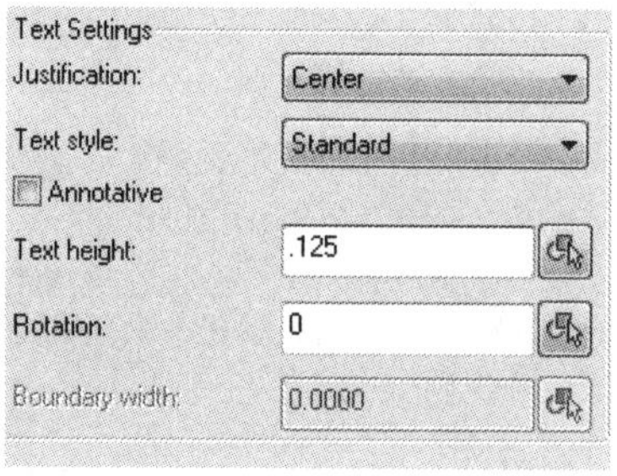

52. Press **OK**.

The field appears in the title block.

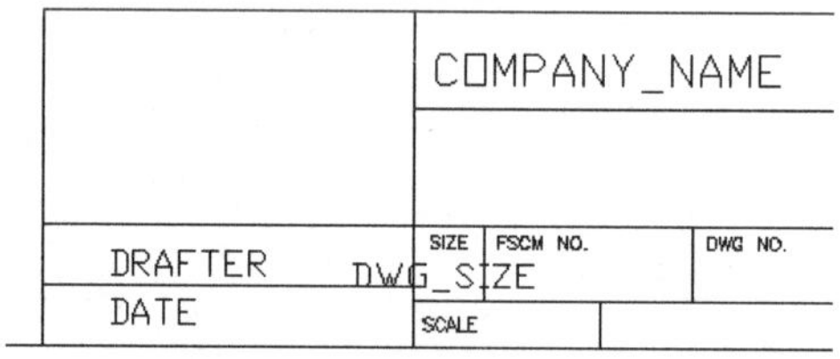

Don't worry about the field going outside the box as it will only be one character.

53. Select the **Define Attributes** tool.

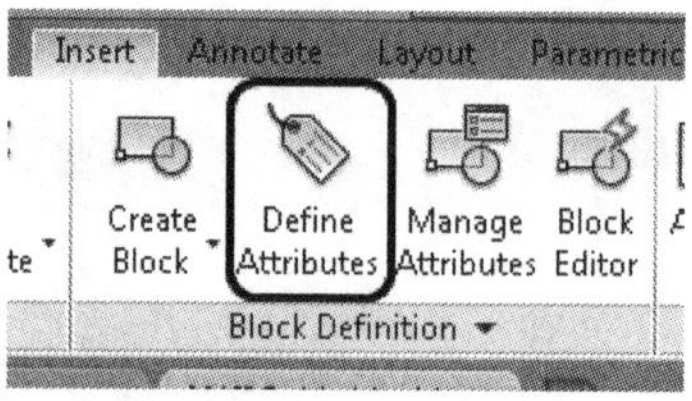

54. Enter **REVISION** in the Tag field.

55. Enter **REVISION** in the Prompt field.

56. Then select the **Insert Field** button.

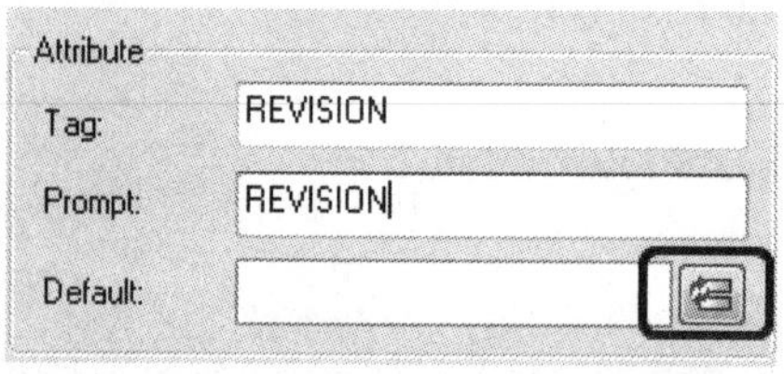

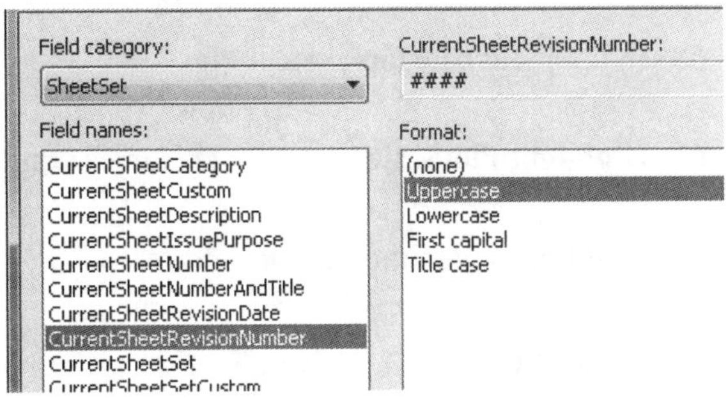

57. In the Field category, select **SheetSet**.

58. Highlight **CurrentSheetRevisionNumber** in the Field Names window.

59. Highlight **Uppercase** in the format field.

60. Press **OK**.

By using a field for the sheetset, you can have multiple layouts in a drawing and use the revision on that specific layout for the revision number.

61. Under Insertion Point:

    Set X to **15.1**.

    Set Y to **0.695**.

    Set Z to **0**.

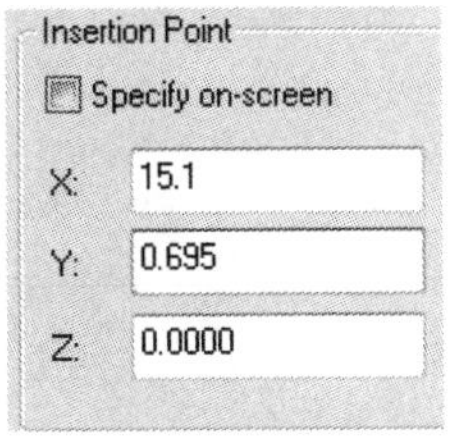

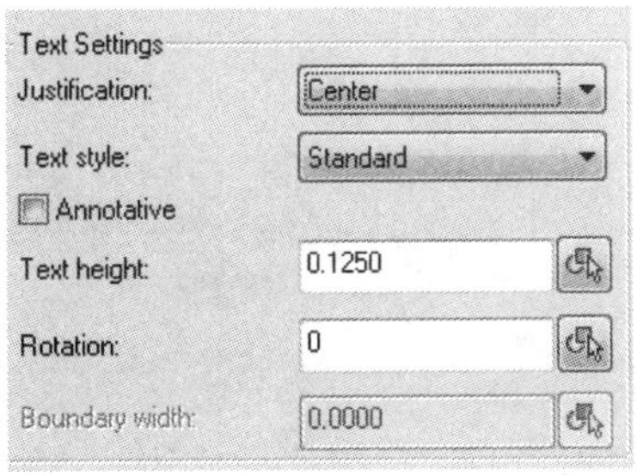

62. Under Text Options:

    Set the Justification to **Center**.
    Set the Height to **.125**.

63. Press **OK**.

The field appears in the title block.

Don't worry about the field going outside the box as it will only be one to three characters.

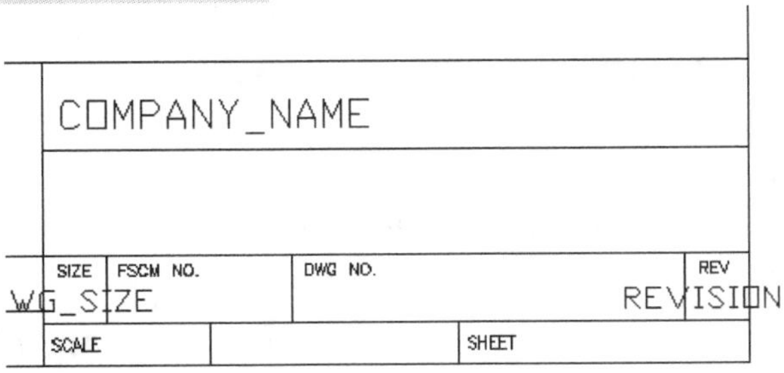

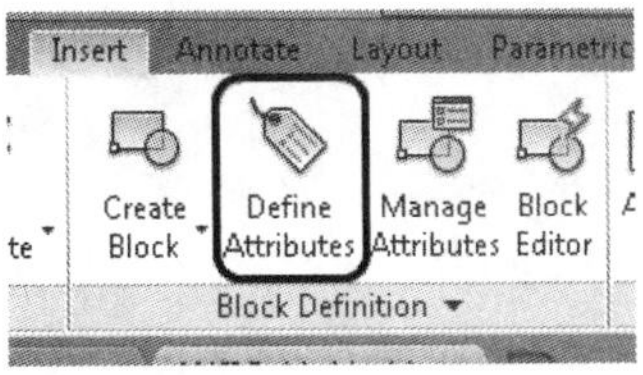

64. Select the **Define Attributes** tool.

65. Enter **DWG_SCALE** in the Tag field.

66. Enter **DWG SCALE** in the Prompt field.

67. Then select the **Insert Field** button.

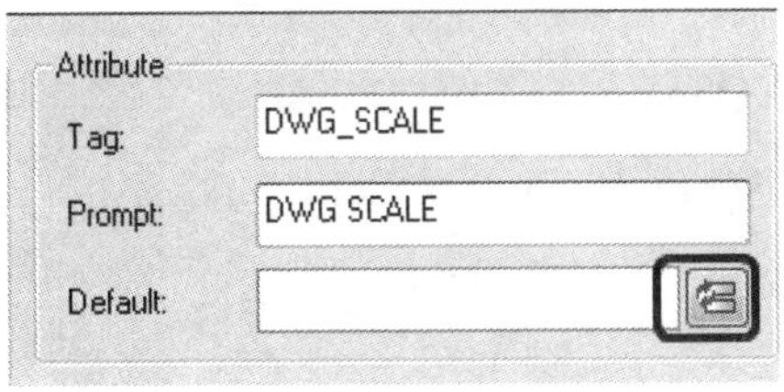

68. In the Field category, select **Plot**.

69. Highlight **PlotScale** in the Field Names window.

70. Highlight **1:#** in the format field.

71. Press **OK**.

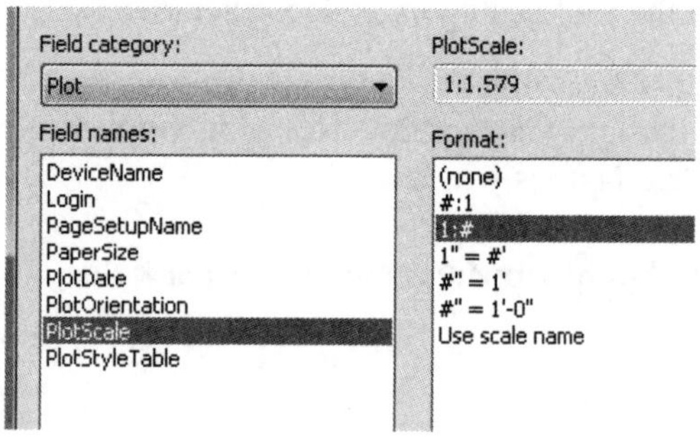

By using a field for the plot scale, you can have multiple layouts in a drawing and use the plot scale on that specific layout.

72. Under Insertion Point:

    Set X to **11.6**.

    Set Y to **0.40**.

    Set Z to **0**.

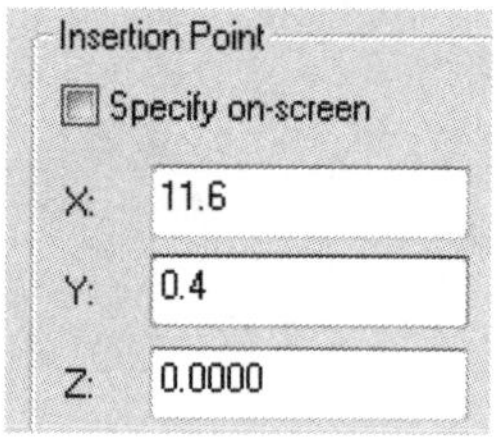

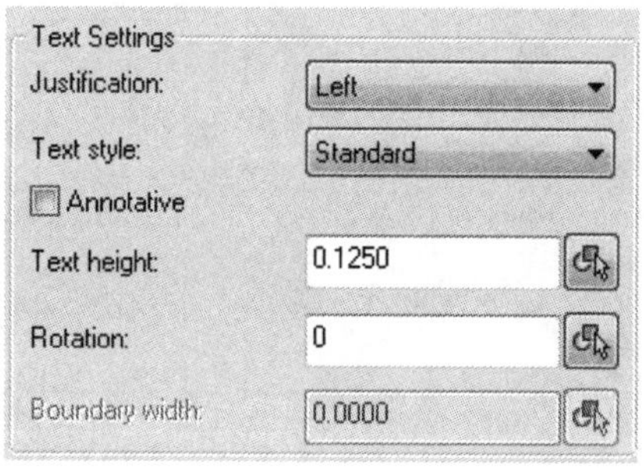

73. Under Text Options:

    Set the Justification to **Left**.

    Set the Height to **.125**.

74. Press **OK**.

The field appears in the title block.

Don't worry about the field going outside the box as it will only be a few characters.

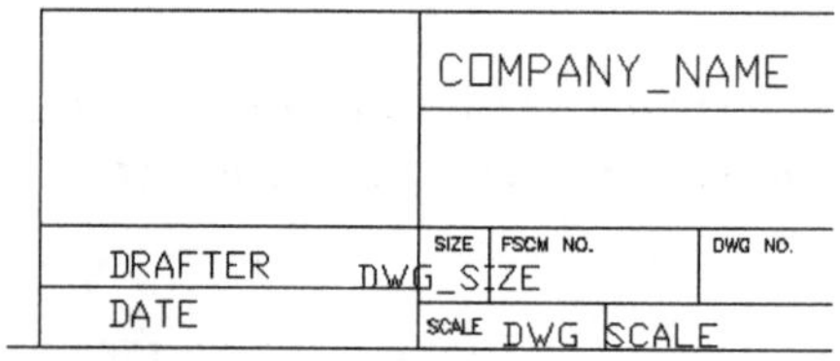

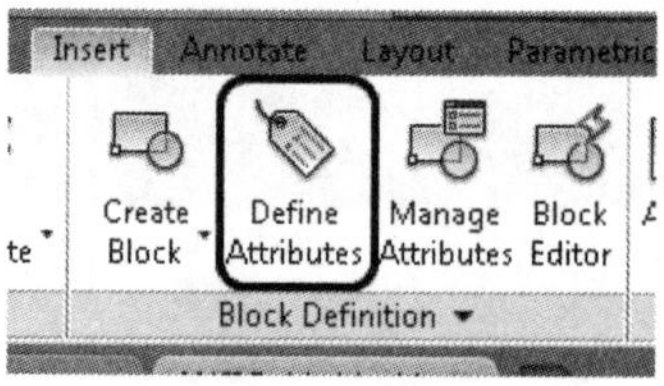

75. Select the **Define Attributes** tool.

76. Enter **SHEETNO** in the Tag field.

77. Enter **SHEET NO** in the Prompt field.

78. Enter **1 OF 1** in the Default field.

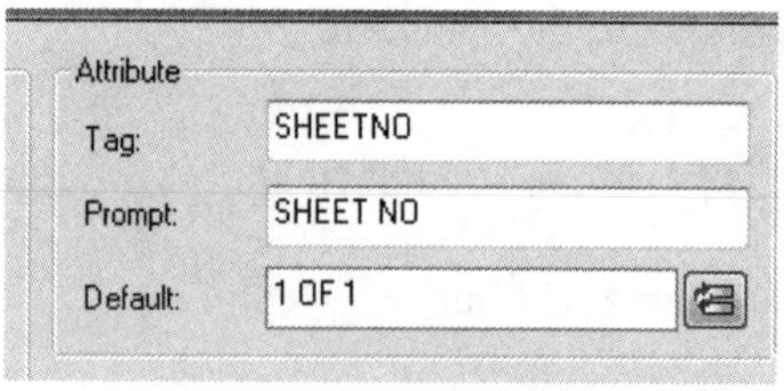

79. Under Insertion Point:

    Set X to **14**.

    Set Y to **0.40**.

    Set Z to **0**.

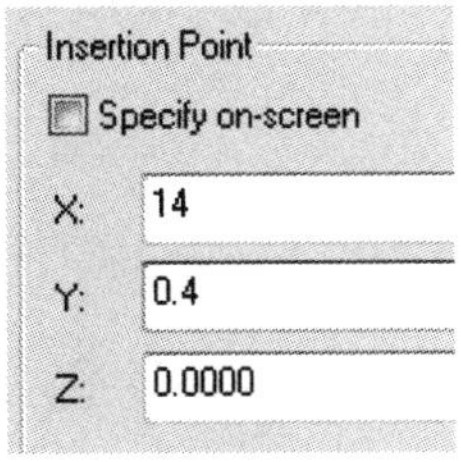

80. Under Text Options:

    Set the Justification to **Left**.

    Set the Height to **.125**.

81. Press **OK**.

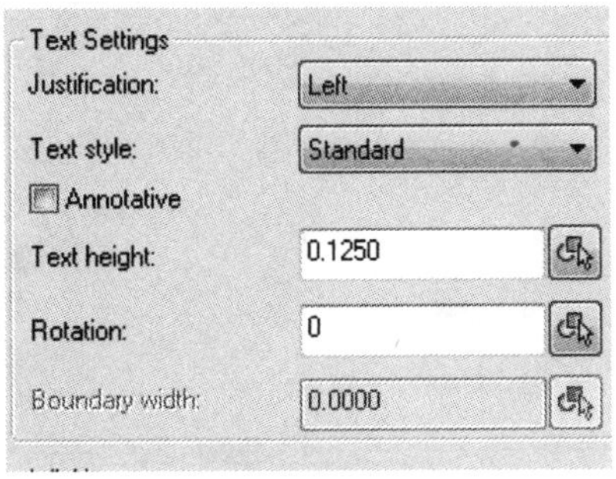

The field appears in the title block.

Don't worry about the field going outside the box as it will only be a few characters.

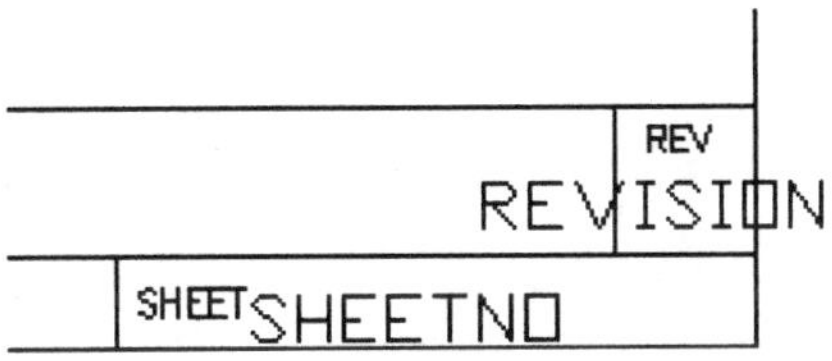

82. Select the **Define Attributes** tool.

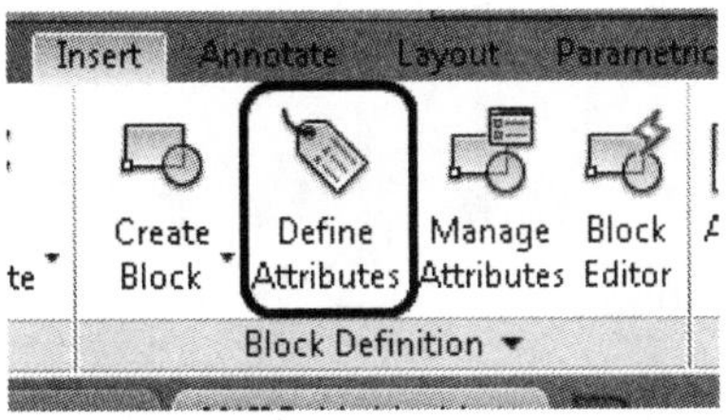

83. Enter **DWG_NO** in the Tag field.
84. Enter **DWG NO** in the Prompt field.
85. Then select the **Insert Field** button.
86. In the Field category, select **Document**.

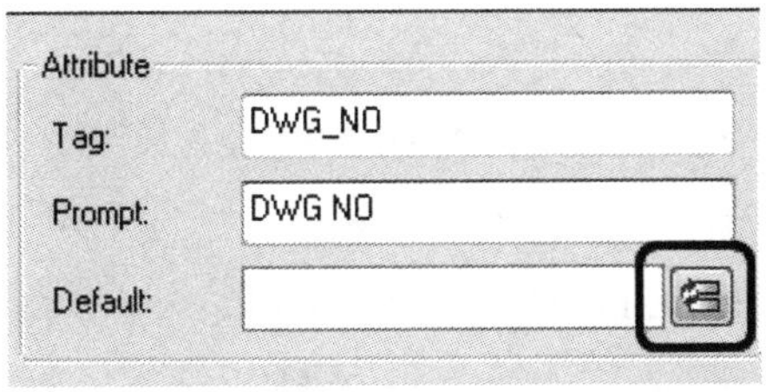

87. Highlight **Filename** in the Field Names window.
88. Highlight **Uppercase** in the format field.
89. Enable **Filename only**.
90. Disable **Display file extension**.

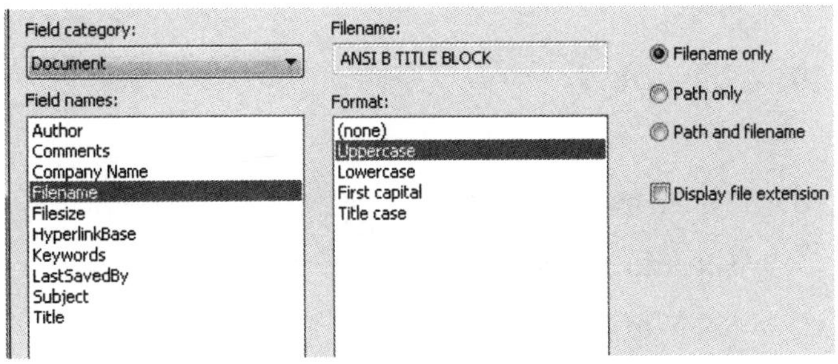

This removes the .dwg from the file name.

91. Press **OK**.

92. Under Insertion Point:

    Set X to **12.75**.

    Set Y to **0.695**.

    Set Z to **0**.

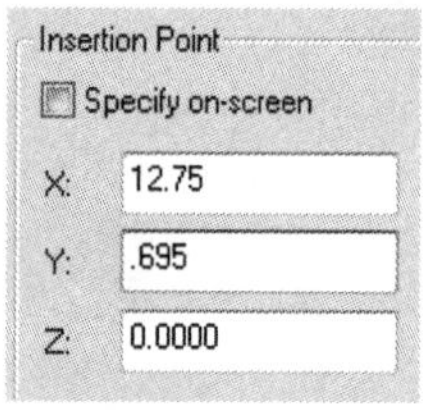

93. Under Text Options:

    Set the Justification to **Left**.

    Set the Height to **.125**.

94. Press **OK**.

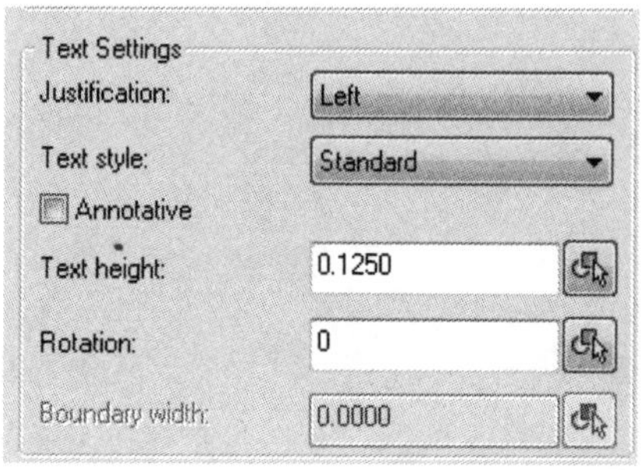

The field appears in the title block.

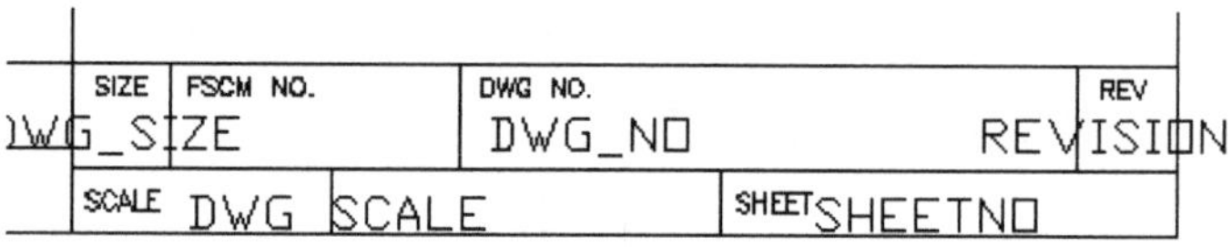

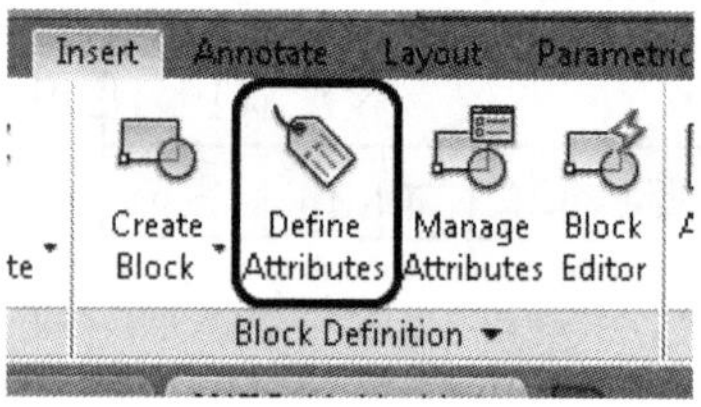

95. Select the **Define Attributes** tool.

96. Enter **TITLE** in the Tag field.

97. Enter **TITLE** in the Prompt field.

98. Then select the **Insert Field** button.

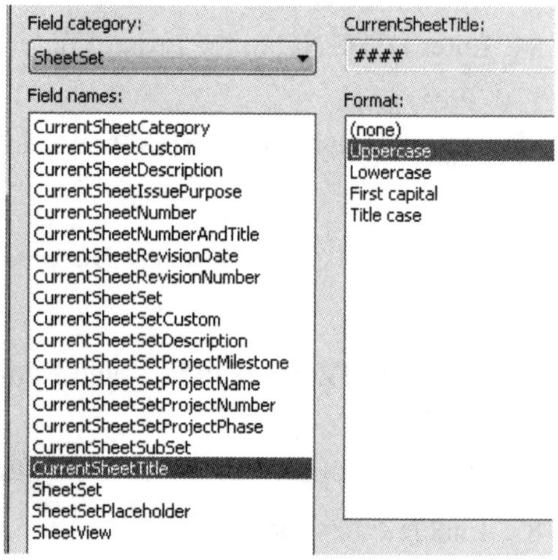

99. In the Field category, select **SheetSet**.

100. Highlight **CurrentSheetTitle** in the Field Names window.

101. Highlight **Uppercase** in the format field.

102. Press **OK**.

103. Under Insertion Point:

     Set X to **11.25**.

     Set Y to **1.2**.

     Set Z to **0**.

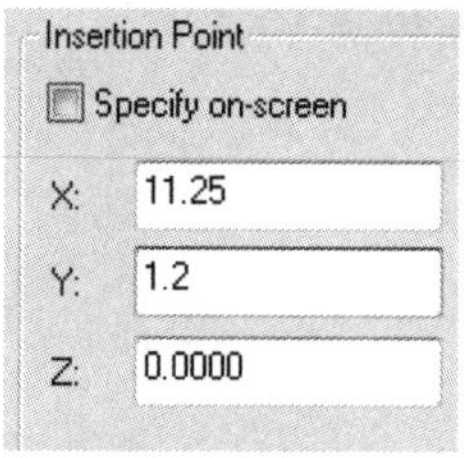

104. Under Text Options:

Set the Justification to **Left**.
Set the Height to **.25**.

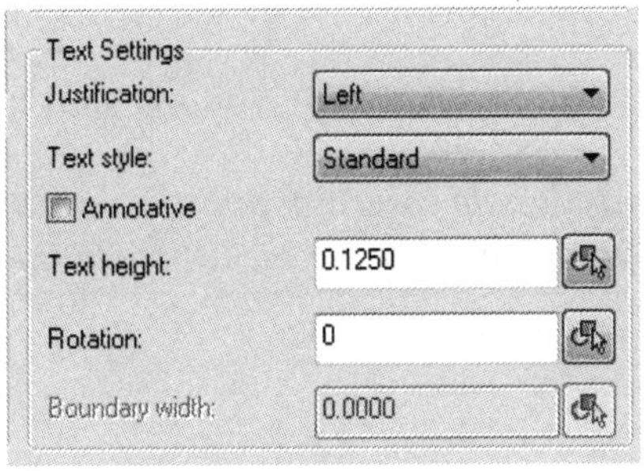

The title block should appear as shown.

You'll notice that some of the attributes don't fit properly in the title block. This is OK. The values will fit just fine.

You can adjust the position of any of the attributes using the MOVE tool.

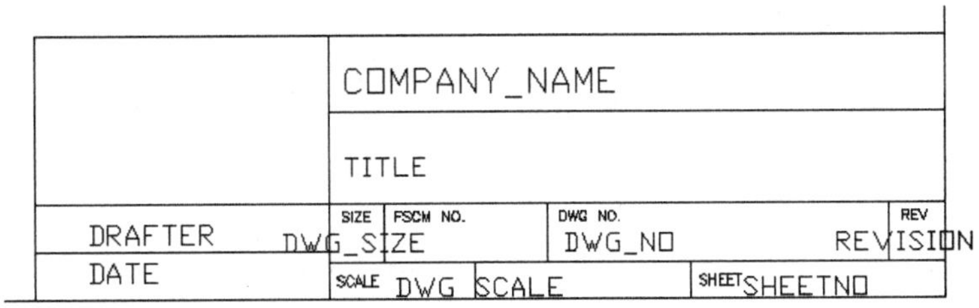

105. Erase the pre-defined attributes in the title block located on the left vertical side.

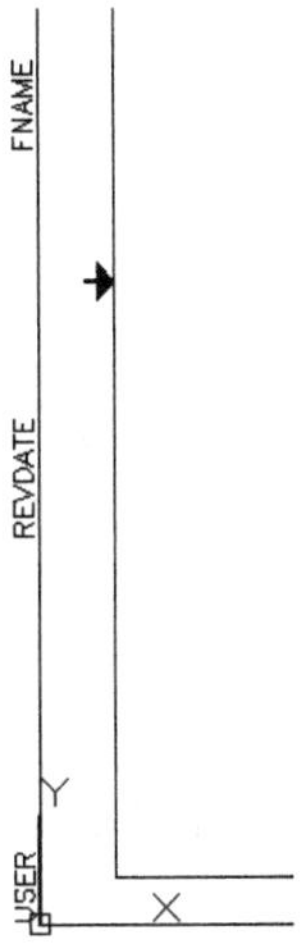

106. Select the **Field** tool from the Insert ribbon.

107. In the Field category, select **Plot**.

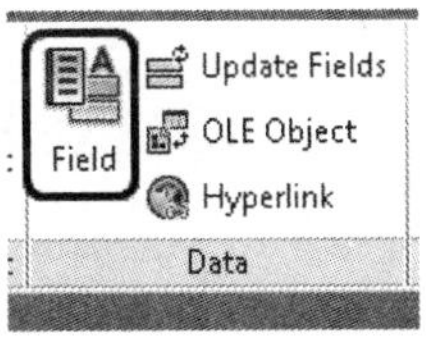

108. Highlight **PlotDate** in the Field Names window.

109. Highlight **M/dd/yyy h:mm tt** in the format field.

110. Press **OK**.

111. Place the field above the lower left corner of the title block.

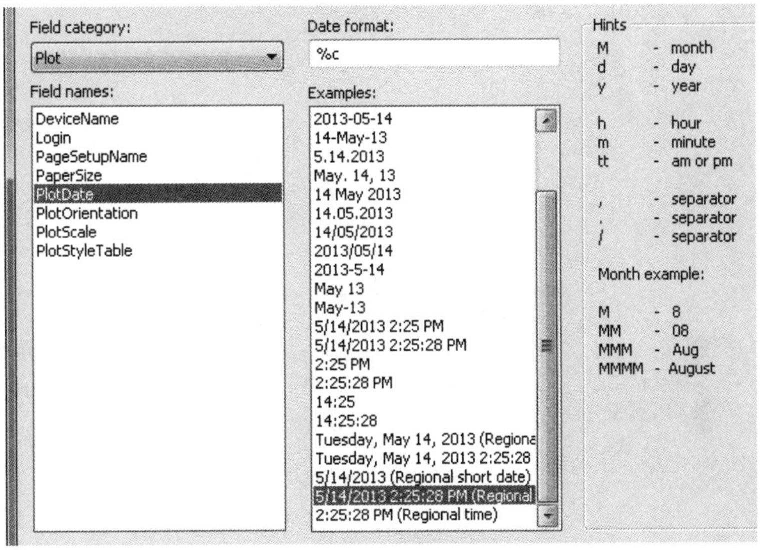

112. Rotate the field so that it is vertical.

This will act as a plot stamp for the sheet when it is plotted.

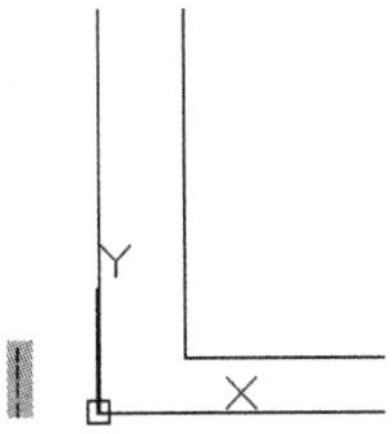

- *The default insertion point for any block is 0,0,0.*
- *If you forget to assign an insertion point, your attribute will be placed at 0,0,0. You can use the move tool to relocate the attribute into the title block.*

Adding a Logo

Many companies like to see their logo in the title block. AutoCAD allows you to insert graphics into drawings. Any image file (gif, jpg, bmp, etc.) can be inserted.

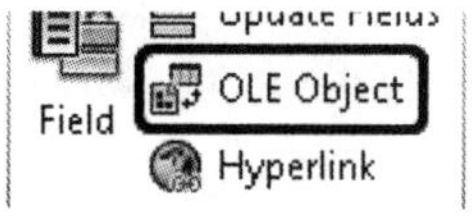

113. On the Insert ribbon, select **OLE Object** on the Data panel.

114. Enable **Create from File**.

115. Use the **Browse** button to locate the image file.

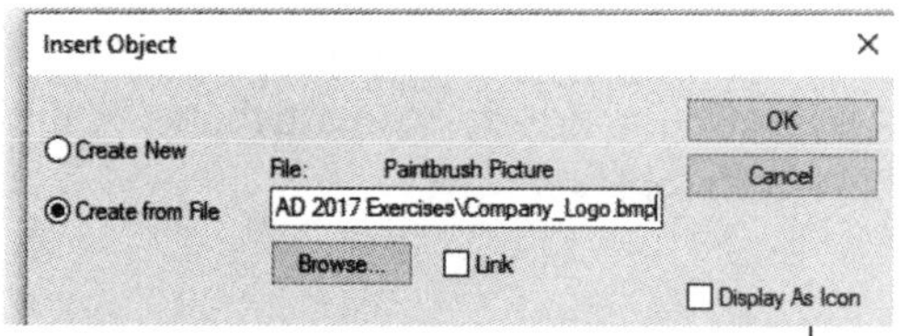

Use the image file provided in the textbook downloads or use an image of your choice.

116. Press **OK**.

117. Position the graphic as shown.

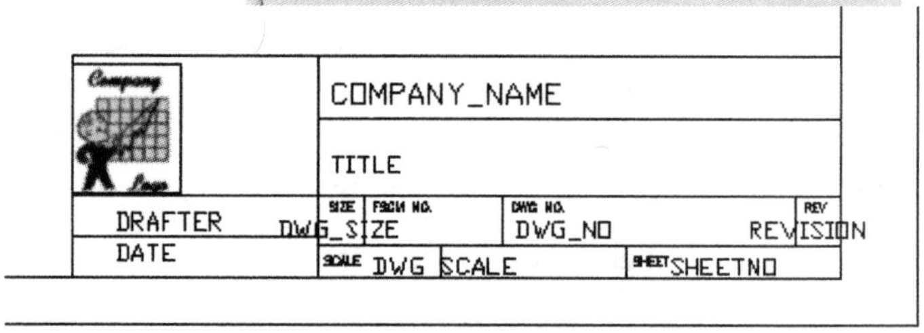

You can use the grips on the image to move and stretch the image file.

118. Save the file as '*Custom-B.dwg*'.

- *It is a good idea to save any custom blocks, toolbars, etc. in a separate directory away from AutoCAD. That way you can easily back up your custom work to use on another workstation and if you need to reinstall AutoCAD for any reason, you will not lose your work.*
- *Use a BMP image file to embed it into an AutoCAD file. Otherwise, it is just a link or reference.*
- *Think of an attribute as a box and the value as the item stored in the box. The attribute name is the name of the box and acts as a pointer to what's inside. Many students confuse the attribute name with the value.*

Command Exercise

Exercise 11-2 – Inserting a Title Block

Drawing Name: **new drawing**
Estimated Time to Completion: 15 Minutes

Scope

Insert the Custom-B title block into a drawing layout.

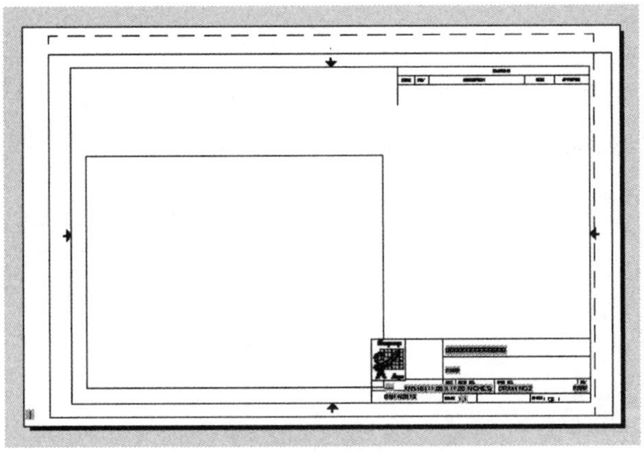

Insert Title Block Exercise

Solution

1. Start a new drawing using the acad.dwt.
2. Select the **Layout 1** tab.

3. Activate the **Insert** ribbon.
4. Select **Insert** from the Block panel.

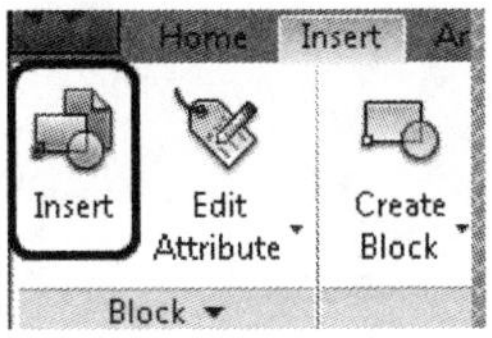

5. Browse for the Custom B title block created in Exercise 11-1. Press **Open**.
6. Disable the Insertion point, the scale, and rotation options.
7. Press **OK**.

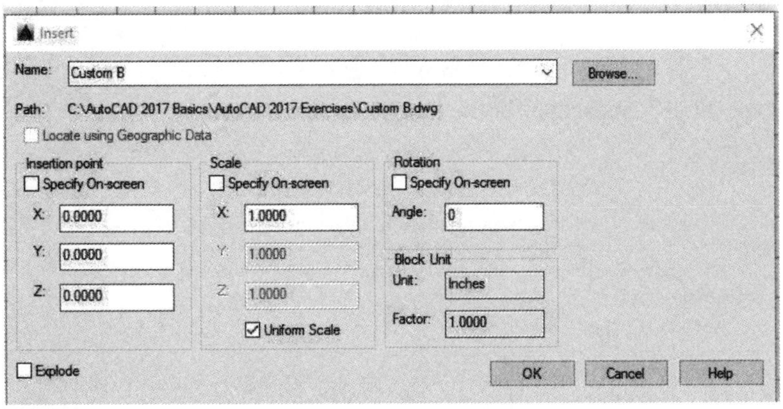

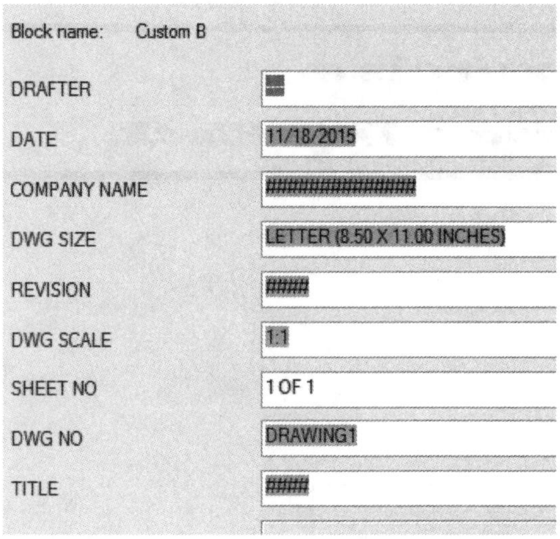

The Edit Attributes dialog will appear.

Any attributes which are controlled by field properties are shaded. Non-shaded fields can be modified.

8. Press **OK.**

The title block is too large for the sheet.

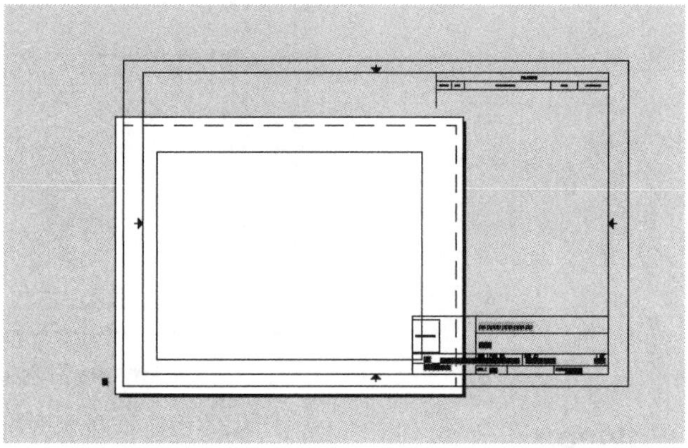

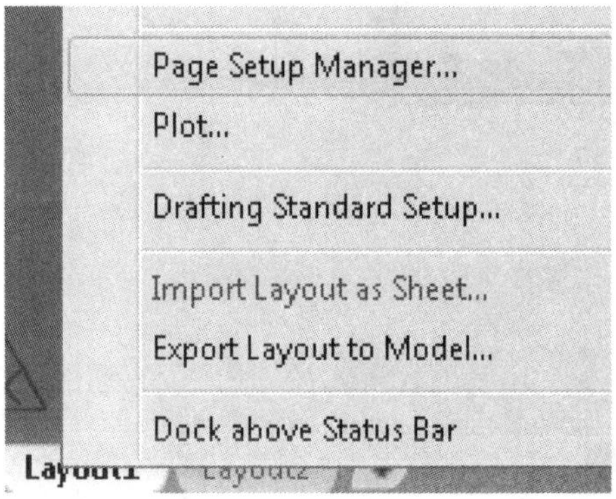

9. Right click on the layout tab.
10. Select **Page Setup Manager.**

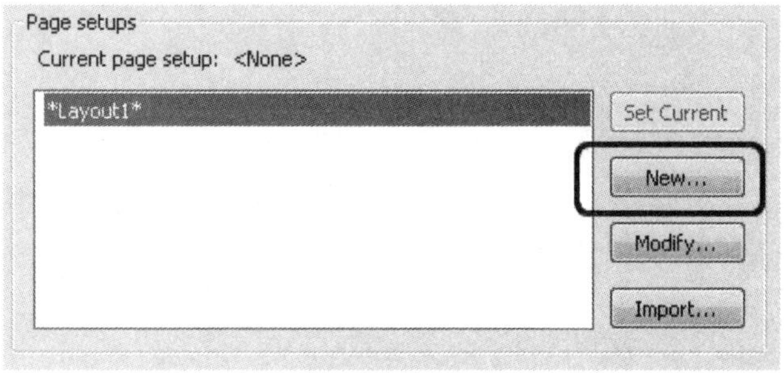

11. Select **New**.

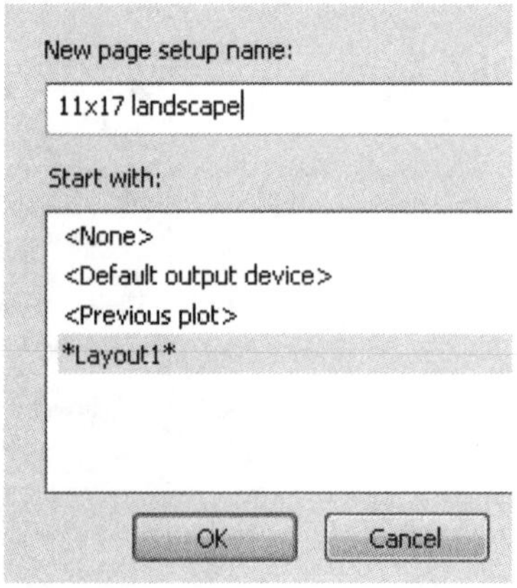

12. Type **11x17 landscape** for the new page setup name.
13. Press **OK.**

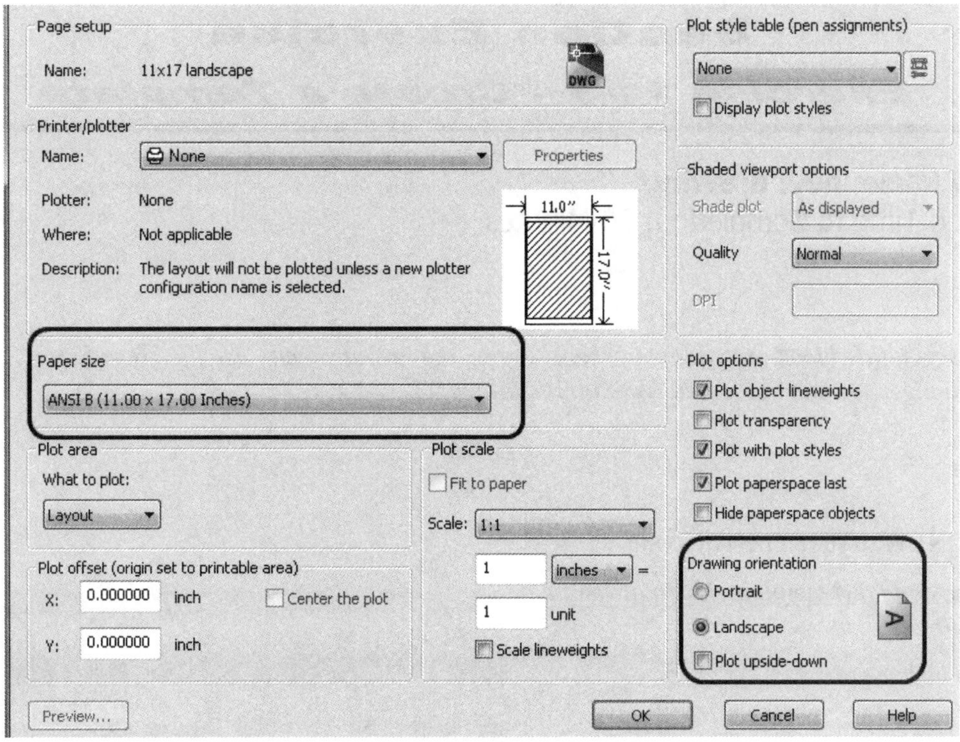

14. Set the Paper size to **ANSI B (11.00 X 17.00 Inches)**.
15. Set the Drawing orientation to **Landscape**.
16. Press **OK**.

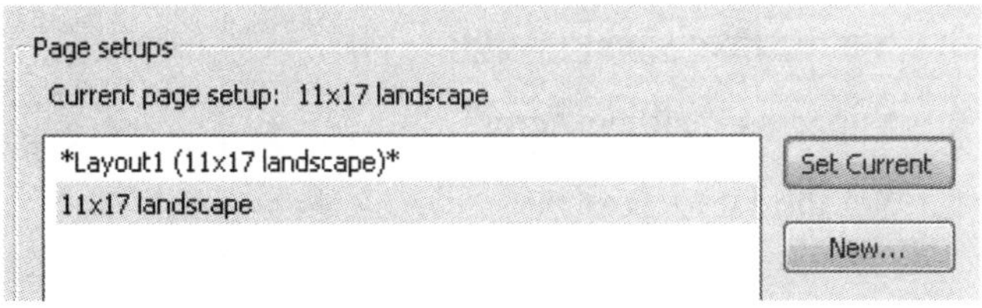

17. Highlight the **11x17 landscape** page setup.
18. Press **Set Current**.
19. Press **Close**.

The title block now fits on the sheet.

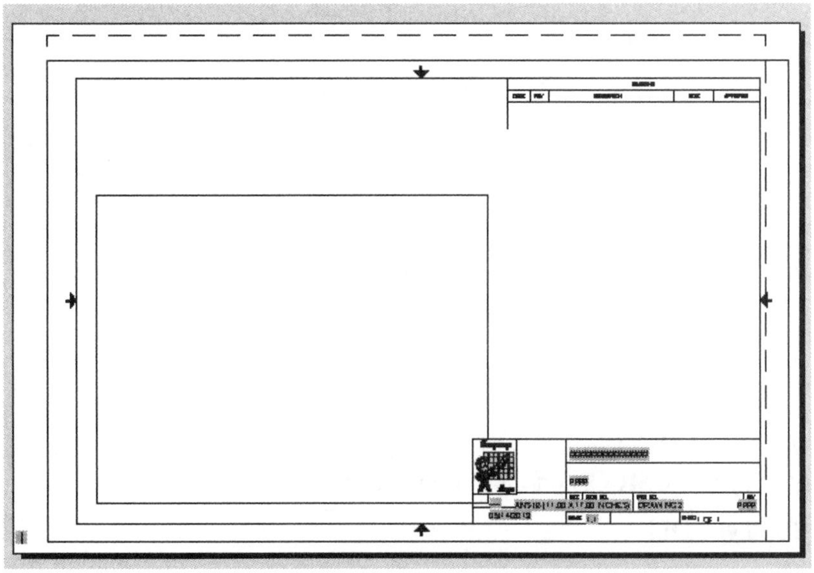

Section Exercise

Exercise 11-3 – Create a Template

Drawing Name: **new drawing**
Estimated Time to Completion: 30 Minutes

Scope

Insert a title block onto a layout sheet. Set up the layout sheet. Use the Sheet Set Manager to control the field data on the title block.

Solution

1. Start **QNEW** to start a new drawing.

Use the acad.dwt template, if you have not set a default template.

2. Set up your layers:

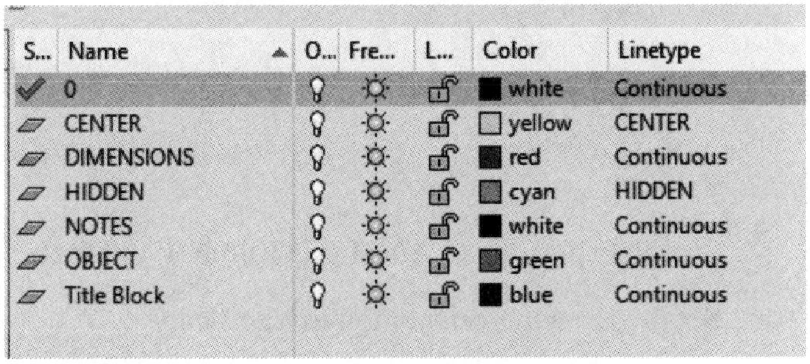

Set up your dimension style:

3. Set the Precision to **0.000**.
4. Suppress Leading Zeros.
5. Set the Fit to **Text**.

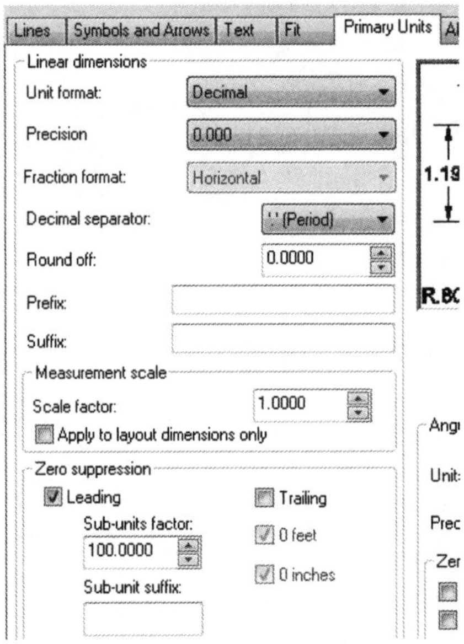

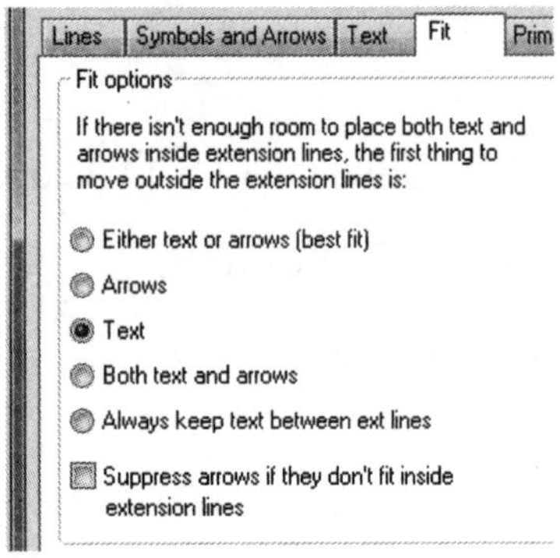

Set the limits.

6. Type **LIMITS** on the command line.
7. Set the lower left corner to 0,0.
8. Set the upper right corner to 34, 22.

Turn the UCSICON off.

9. Type **UCSICON** on the command line.
10. Type **OFF**.

11. Activate **Layout 1**.

12. Right click on the Layout tab and select **Page Setup Manager** from the shortcut menu.

13. Select **New**.

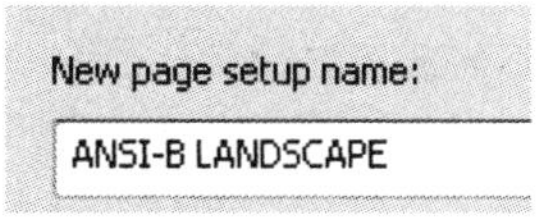

14. Type **ANSI-B LANDSCAPE** for the new setup name.

15. Set the Printer/plotter to **DWG to PDF.pc3**.

16. Set the Paper Size to **ANSI B (11 x 17.00 Inches)**.

17. Set the Plot style table to **Grayscale.ctb**.

18. Press **OK**.

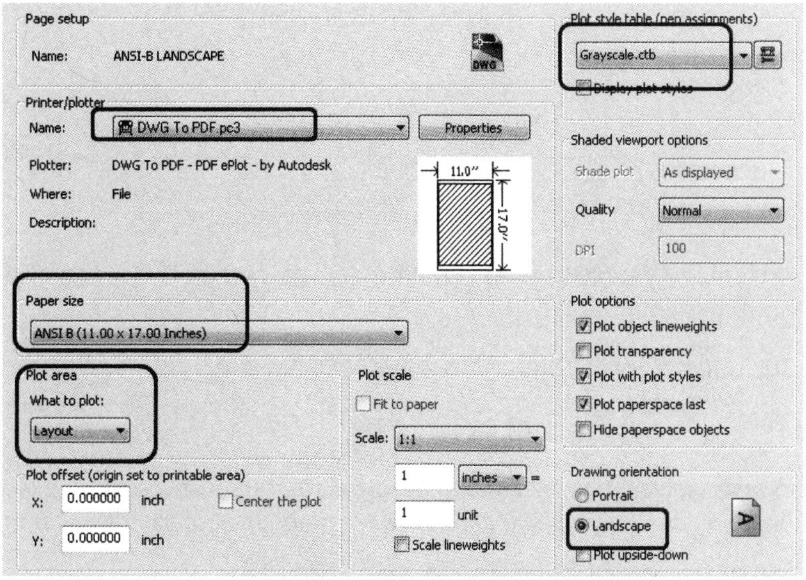

19. Highlight the **ANSI-B LANDSCAPE** page setup.

20. Press **Set Current**.

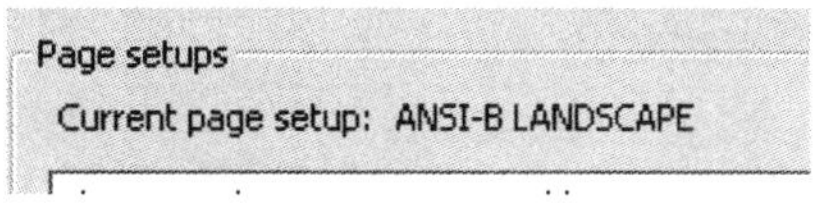

Note that it shows the current page setup.

Verify that the page setup details are correct.

21. Press **Close**.

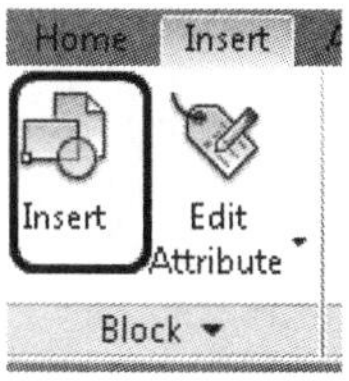

22. Select **Insert Block**.

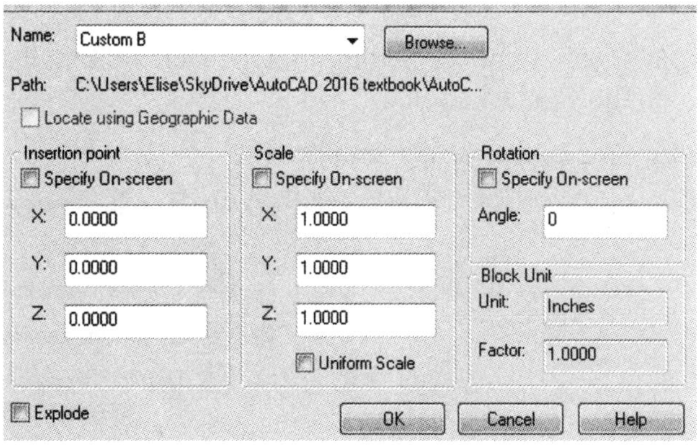

23. Locate the *custom-B* title block.

24. Enable **Specify On-Screen**.

25. Press **OK**.

26. Press <ENTER> to insert the title block at 0,0.

27. Adjust the position of the title block as needed.

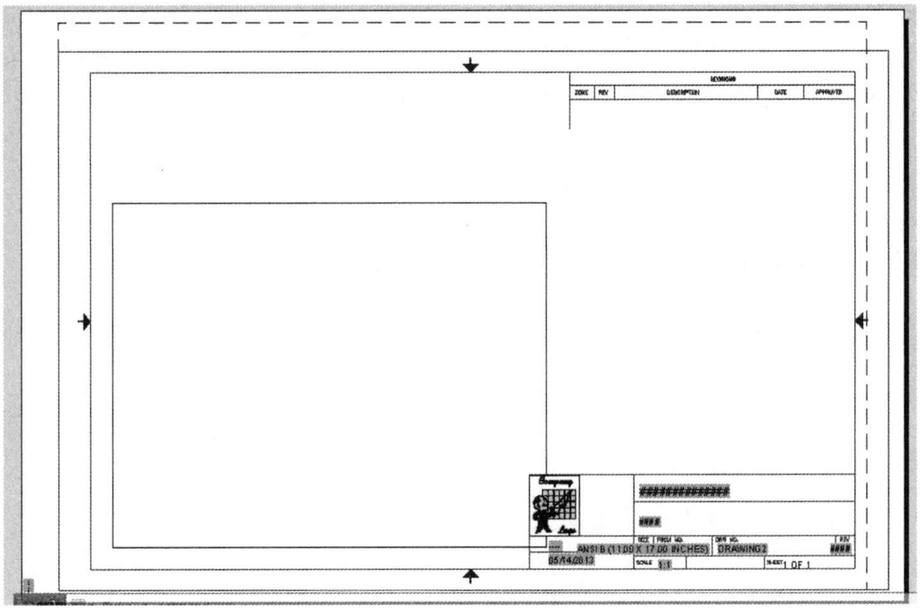

28. Go to **File→Save Drawing As**.
29. Call your template *standard.*
30. Under Files of Type, select *AutoCAD Drawing Template (*.dwt).*

Store your template in a directory away from AutoCAD – NOT in the Templates subdirectory. That way you can back up and copy your template to a different work station as needed.

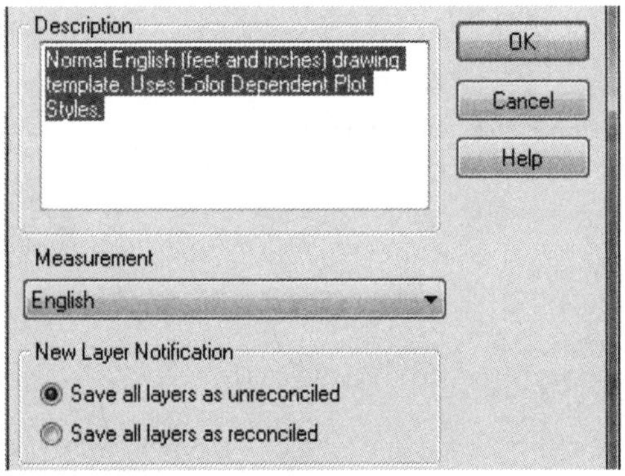

31. Enter a description for your template.
32. Press **OK**.
33. Right click in the AutoCAD drawing window and select **Options**.

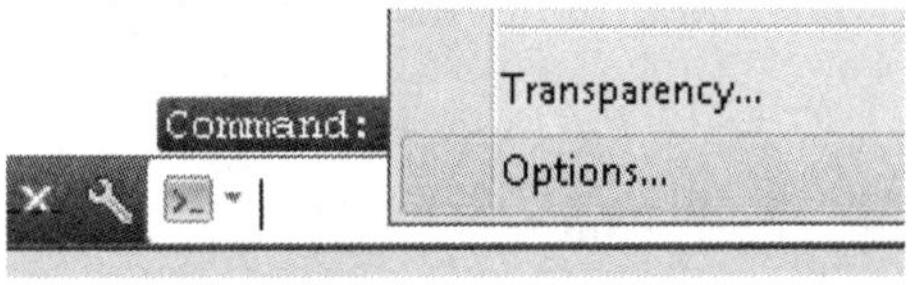

34. Select the File tab.
35. Under Template Settings, set the Default Template File Name for QNEW to use the standard.dwt file you just created.
36. Save and close the template file.

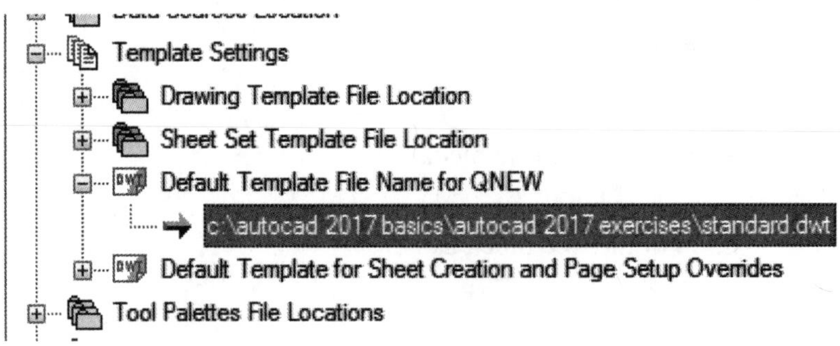

Section Exercise

Exercise 11-4 – Use a Template

Drawing Name: **new drawing**
Estimated Time to Completion: 30 Minutes

Scope

Test the new template file.

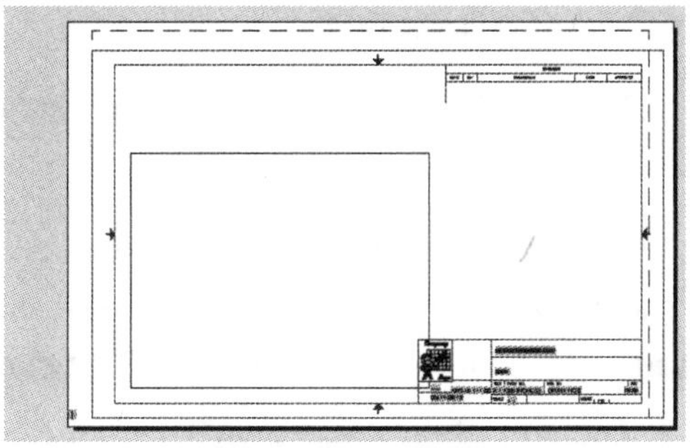

Test Template Exercise

Solution

1. Start **QNEW** to start a new drawing.

Use the standard.dwt template created in Exercise 11-3.

Note your layers are already set up.

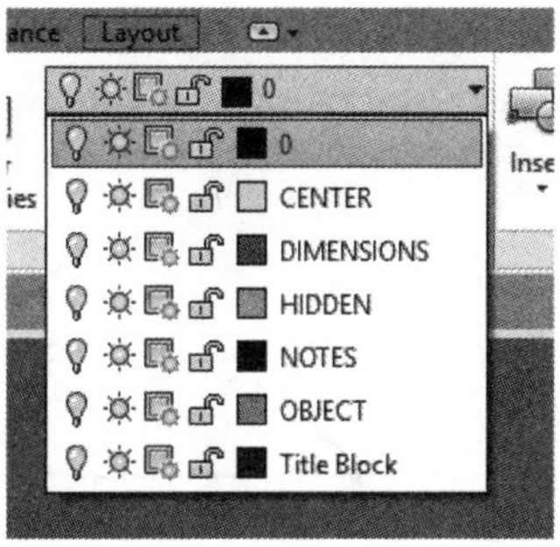

2. Activate **Layout 1**.

Note the layout has the title block ready to go.

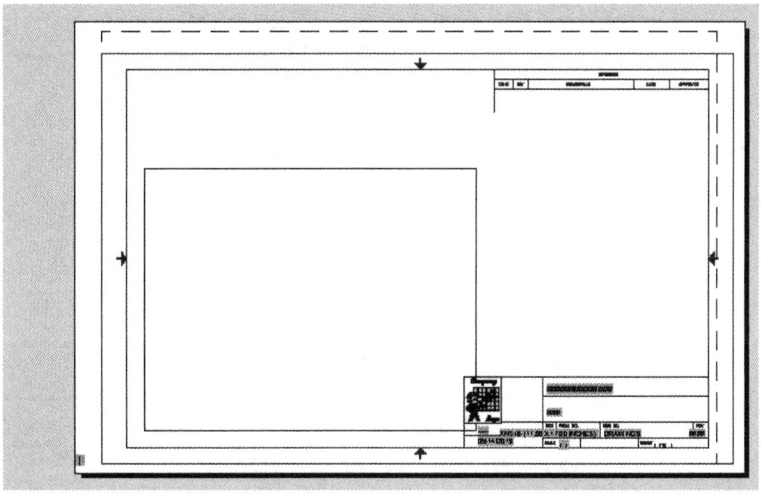

A Word about Blocks

Blocks are useful and boost productivity. Blocks allow you to re-use objects. There are two types of blocks—local and global. Local blocks are created 'on the fly' and used inside a single drawing. A global block is a separate drawing—like the title block template—which can be inserted into another drawing. Local blocks are created using the Create Block tool. Global blocks are created using the Write Block tool.

Blocks can be edited and modified. However, if you edit a block, it is only modified in the existing drawing—it does not update the external drawing file.

You can explode a block—which basically 'unblocks ' the object and restores it back to the basic elements. Blocks can include text, fields, and attributes.

There are a great number of blocks available for use and download on the internet, in the Design Center, and in the Autodesk resource area. Before you create common objects from scratch, like doors, windows, furniture, plants, etc. do a search for blocks. You may be surprised what you find.

Many companies consider their block libraries proprietary. They have spent time and money creating the blocks they use in their drawings and they don't want competitors using their blocks. To avoid this, many companies will type EXPLODE ALL before they send out a drawing to ensure any blocks cannot be used or they will only send drawings out in pdf format to protect their intellectual property.

As you work in industry and start using blocks, you may start collecting your own favorite blocks to use in your career.

If you think you will use an object or drawing more than once, chances are you have a potential block.

Create Block

Command Locator

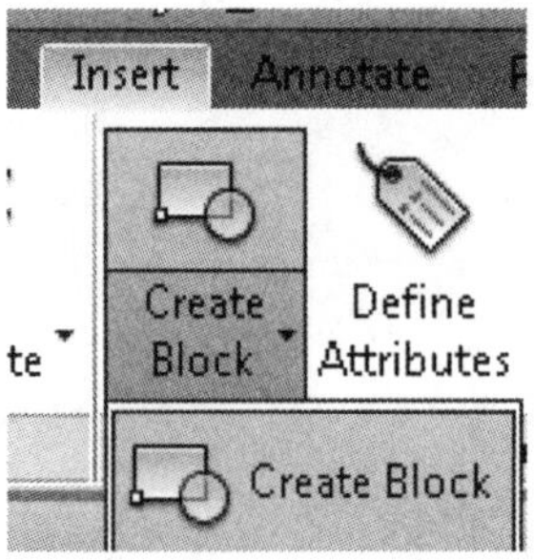

Command	**Block**
Alias	**B**
Insert Ribbon	**Create Block**

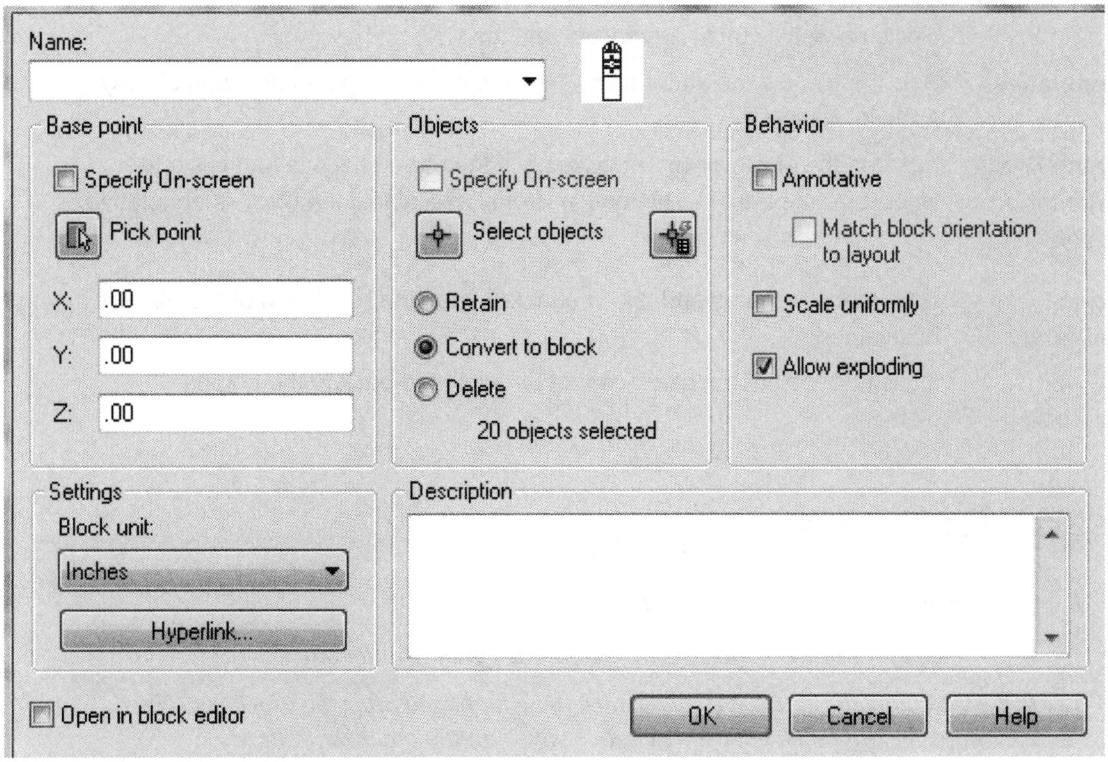

Name Assigns a name to the block.

Base point Assigns an insertion point for the block. If no point is selected, then the block is automatically defined in relation to the 0,0,0 position

Block unit Specifies unit of measurement:

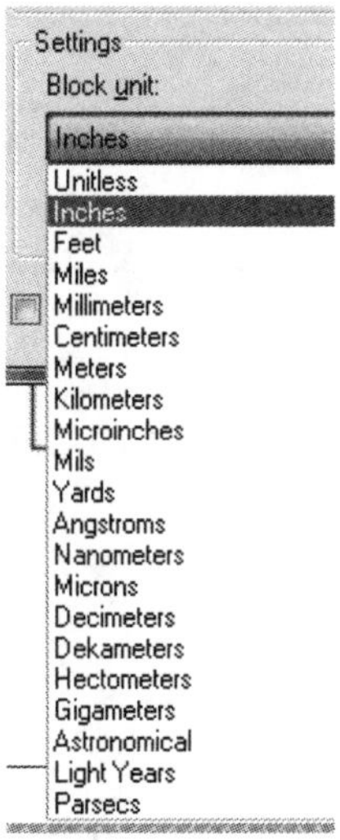

Hyperlink Adds a hyperlink to a part. This may be used to link a block to a vendor website, so users can purchase the item.

Objects Allows the user to select which elements are used to define the block.

Retain/ Convert to Block/Delete Retain keeps the selected elements as they are. Convert to block converts the selected elements to the block definition. Delete erases the selected elements, but the block definition is saved.

Open in Block Editor	Opens the block editor once the OK button is pushed. The Block Editor allows the user to add constraints, controls to flip, rotate or stretch the block, as well as other advanced settings.
Annotative	Sets the block to be annotative—which means the block will automatically scale in viewports.
Match Block Orientation to Layout	Ensures the block will orient correctly if the paperspace layout is set to landscape or portrait. This option is only available if the block is annotative.
Scale uniformly	If the block is scaled and this is enabled, then the resolution of the block is maintained.
Allow Exploding	If this is disabled, the block cannot be exploded back to the original elements.

General Procedures

1. *Select the objects desired for a block.*
2. *Select the point to be used for the insertion/base point for the block.*
3. *Determine how the existing elements are to be managed after the block is created (retain as individual elements, delete or convert to the block definition).*
4. *Determine how the block should react in paper space—Annotative or non-annotative.*
5. *Set the block units. By default the block will use the existing or current unit settings.*
6. *Press OK.*

Write Block

Command Locator

Command	**Wblock**
Alias	**W**
Insert Ribbon	**Write Block**

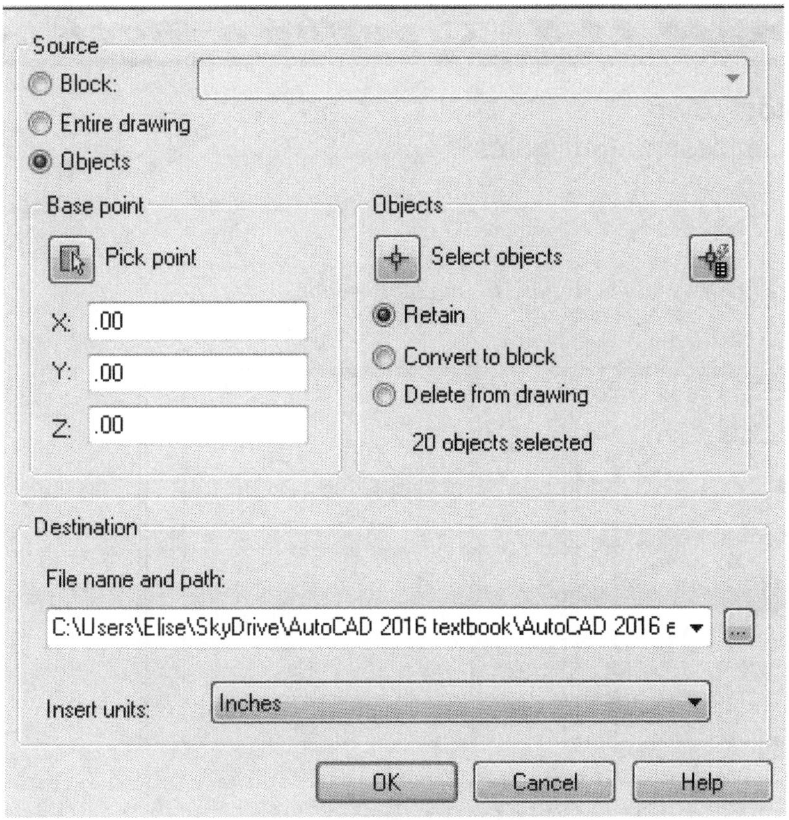

File Name and path	Browse to the folder where you want to store your block and enter in the desired name.
Base point	Assigns an insertion point for the block. If no point is selected, then the block is automatically defined in relation to the 0,0,0 position.
Insert units	Specifies unit to be used when block is inserted
Objects	Allows the user to select which elements are used to define the block.
Retain/ Convert to Block/Delete	Retain keeps the selected elements as they are. Convert to block converts the selected elements to the block definition. Delete erases the selected elements, but the block definition is saved.

General Procedures

1. *Select the objects desired for a block.*
2. *Select the point to be used for the insertion/base point for the block.*
3. *Determine how the existing elements are to be managed after the block is created (retain as individual elements, delete or convert to the block definition).*
4. *Set the block units. By default the block will use the existing or current unit settings.*
5. *Browse to the location where the block file should be saved and name the block.*
6. *Press OK.*

Command Exercise

Exercise 11-5 – Creating a Block

Drawing Name: **mblock.dwg**
Estimated Time to Completion: 45 Minutes

Scope

Create some blocks and use them to furnish an empty room.

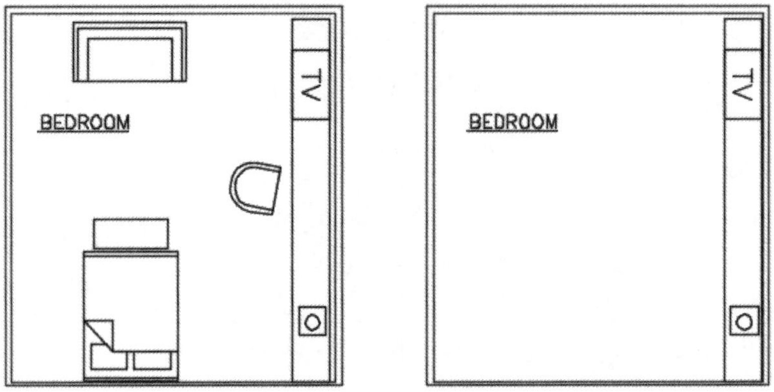

Create and Write Block Exercise

Solution

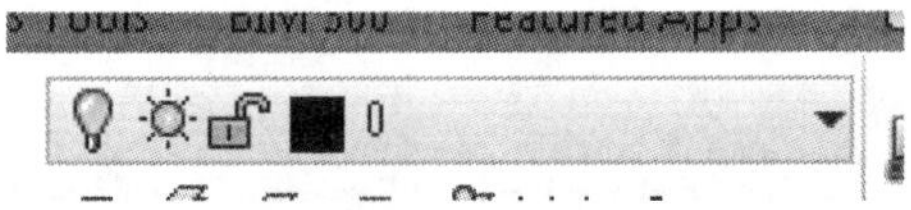

1. Verify that the current layer is set to **0.**
2. Window about the bed to select all the lines that define the bed object.
3. On the Insert ribbon on the Block Definition panel, select **Create Block**.

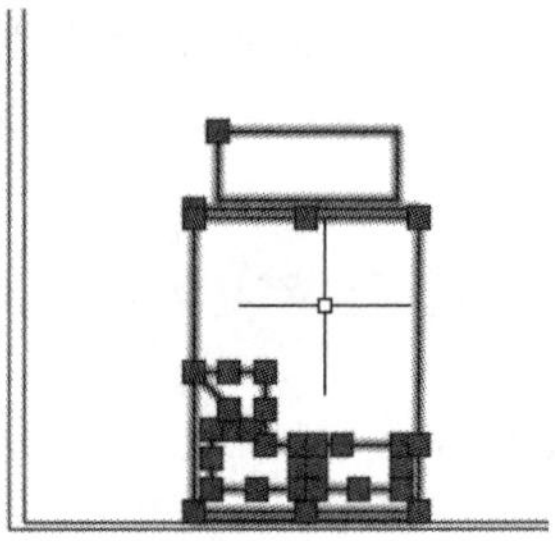

On the Home ribbon on the Block panel, select **Create.**

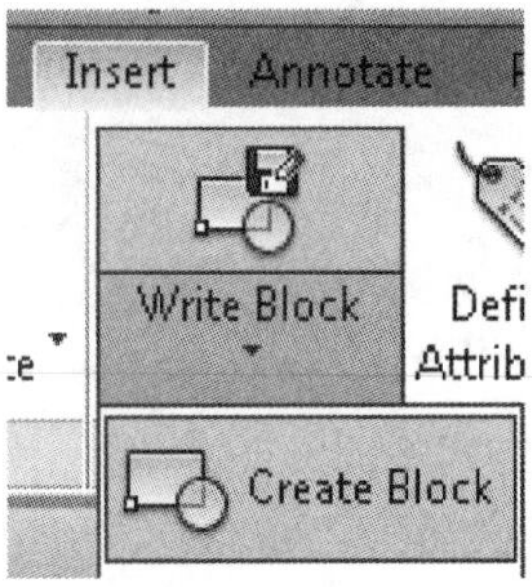

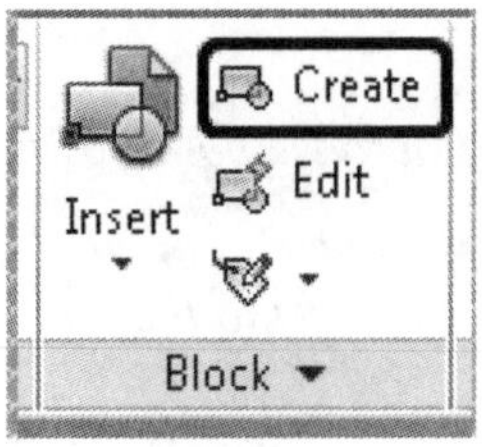

4. Type **queenbed** in the Name field.
5. Select the pick point icon to set the Base point.
6. Select bottom midpoint of the bed (by the pillows or head of the bed) as the Base point.
7. Type **queen bed** in the description.
8. Disable **Annotative.**

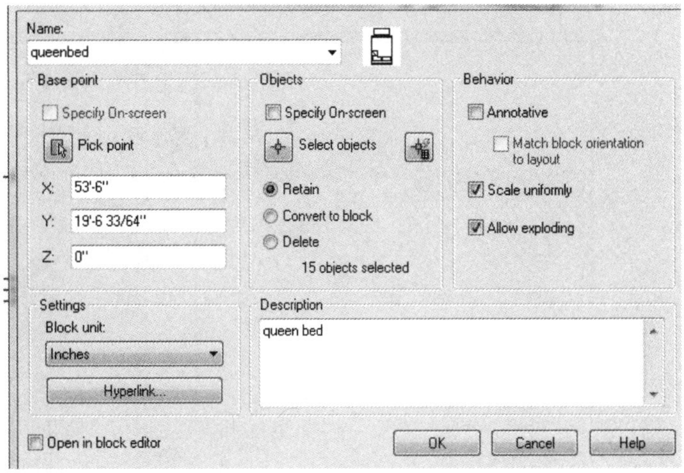

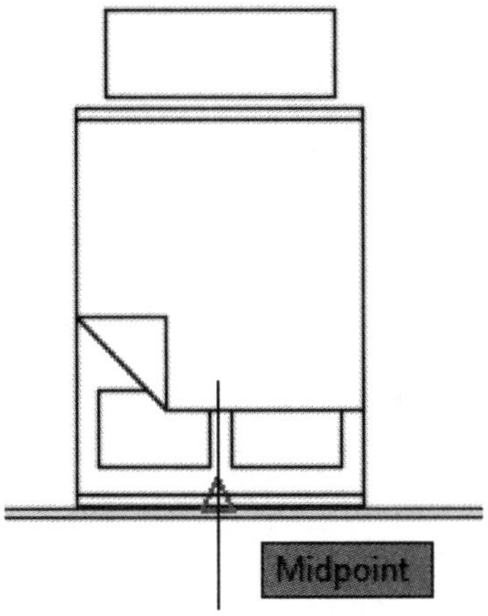

9. Enable **Allow Exploding**.
10. Enable **Retain**.
11. Enable **Scale uniformly.**
12. Uncheck **Open in block editor.**
13. Press **OK.**

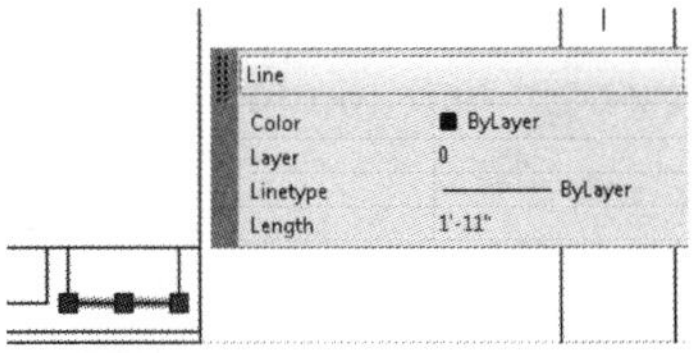

14. Select one of the lines that is part of the pillow.

Note that the elements are still individual elements since you used the Retain option when creating the block. Notice that the element is on Layer 0.

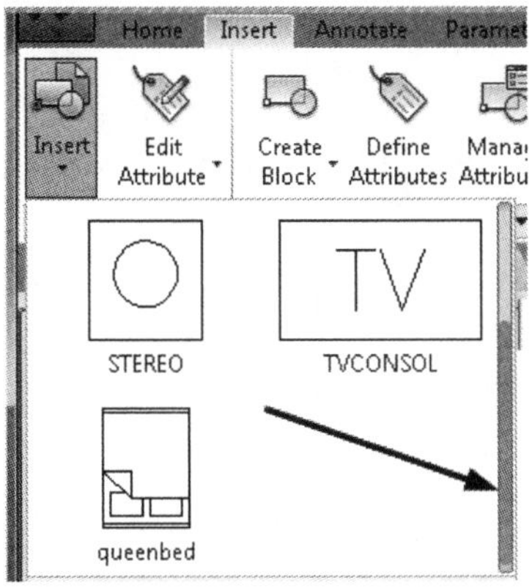

15. On the Insert ribbon: Select the scroll bar under the Insert tool. Note that all the local blocks in the drawing are listed.

You can also use the Insert tool on the Block panel on the Home ribbon.

Select the **queenbed** block you created.

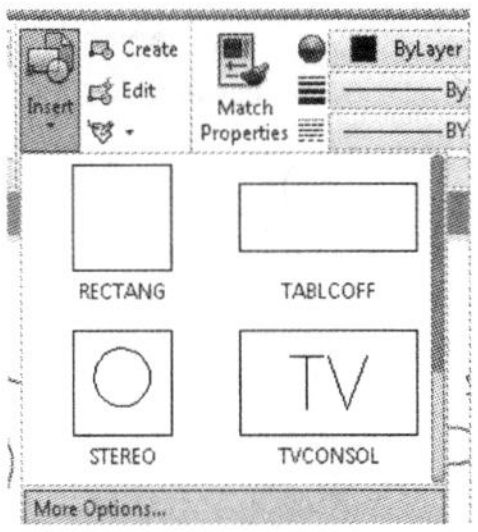

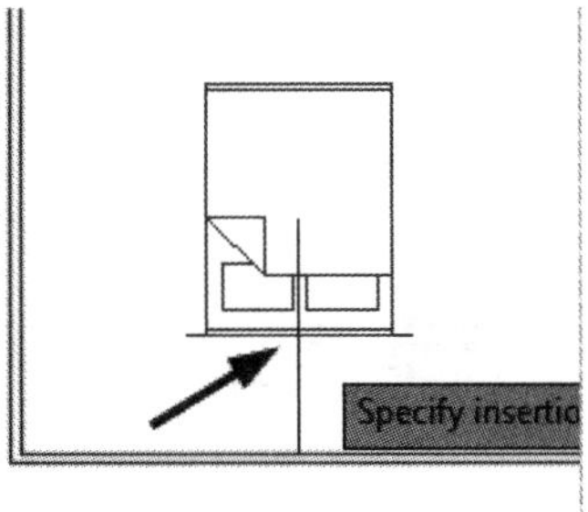

16. Notice that the cursor is located at the selected base point (the midpoint of the block) as you drag the block into the drawing.

If you did not select a base point, the insertion point is automatically set to 0,0,0.

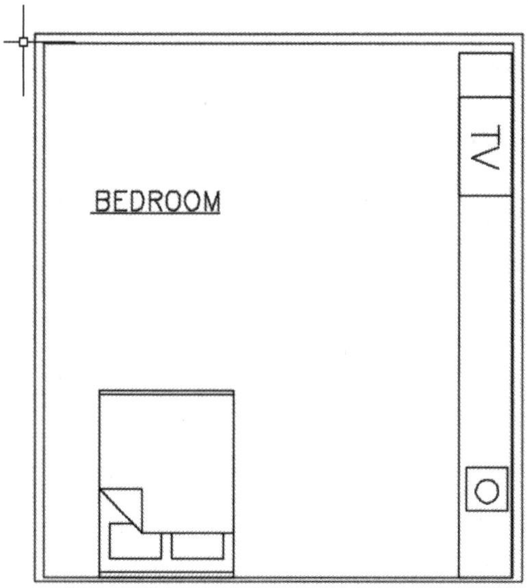

17. Place the bed in the empty bedroom on the right using the NEA Osnap to place it along the bottom wall.

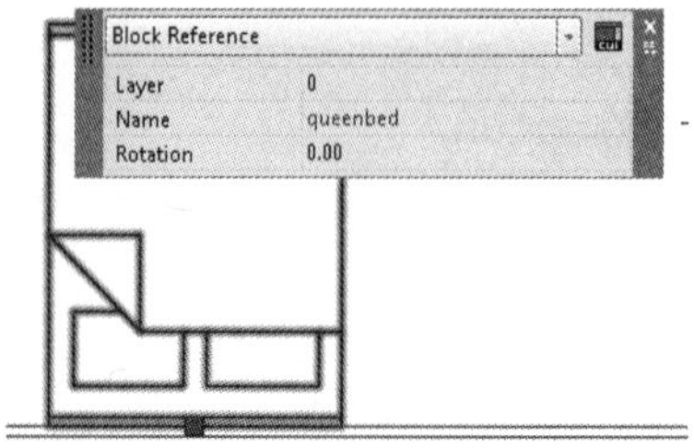

18. Select the block that was placed.

On the Quick Properties palette, you should see the Name and the Layer set to 0.

Blocks that are created on Layer 0 will adopt the properties of the current layer when placed.

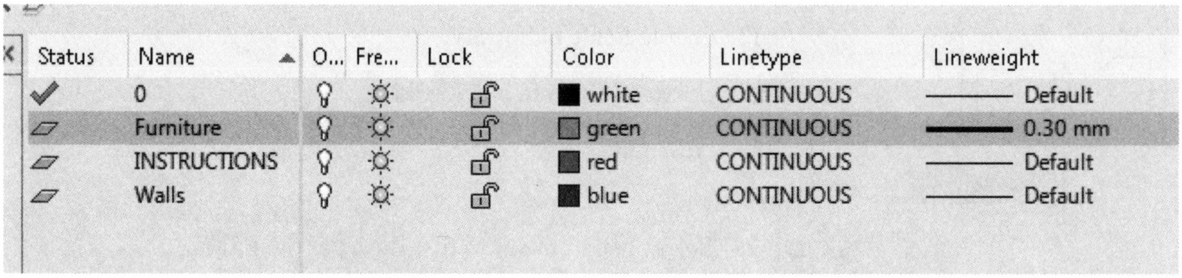

Status	Name	O...	Fre...	Lock	Color	Linetype	Lineweight
✔	0				white	CONTINUOUS	Default
	Furniture				green	CONTINUOUS	0.30 mm
	INSTRUCTIONS				red	CONTINUOUS	Default
	Walls				blue	CONTINUOUS	Default

19. Create a new layer called **Furniture.** Set the Color to **Green** and the Lineweight to **0.30 mm**.

20. Set the Current Layer to **Furniture**.

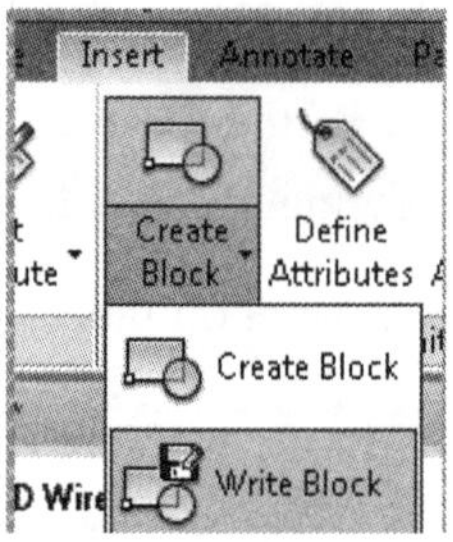

21. Select **Write Block** from the Insert ribbon.

22. Select the Pick point icon under Base point.

23. Select the top midpoint (rear of the sofa) for the sofa's Base point.

24. Select the Select objects icon under Objects.

25. Window around the entire sofa to select it. Press ENTER.

26 Browse to your work folder and save the block as **mysofa.dwg**.

27. Press **OK**.

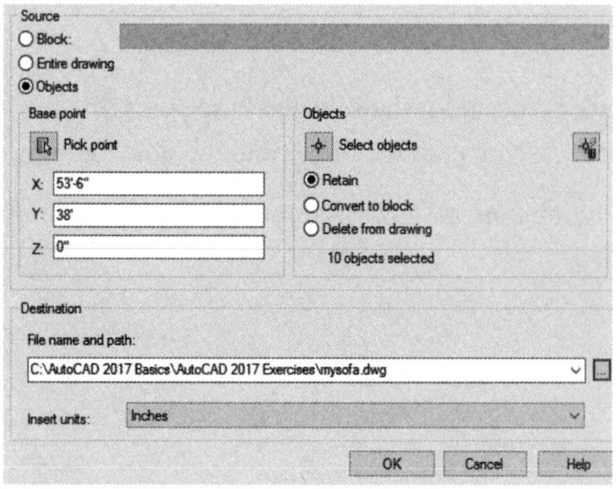

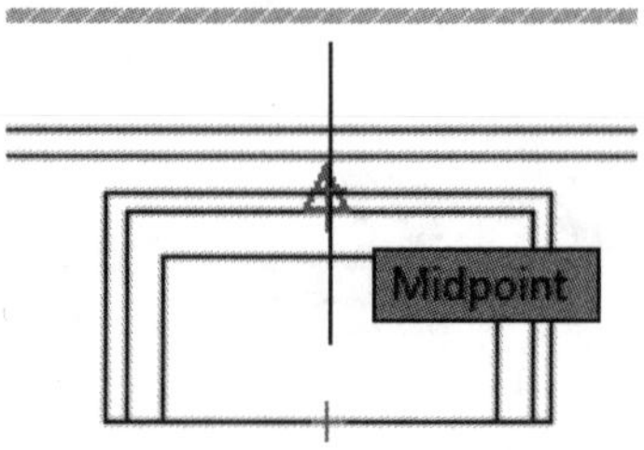

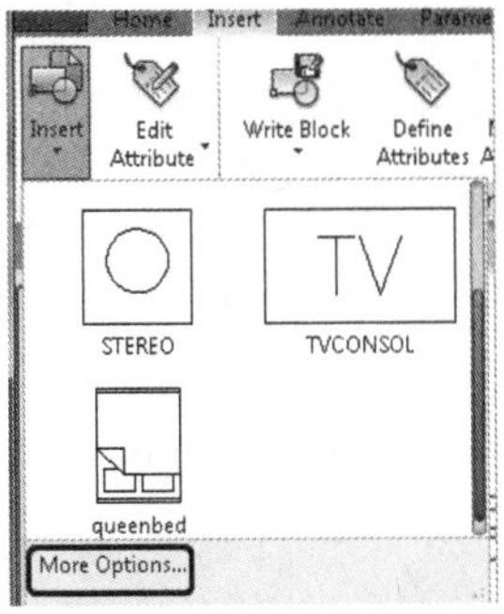

28. Go to the Insert tool.

When you scroll down, you won't see the mysofa block. That is because you created a global block, not a local block. The block is stored externally so it can be inserted into any drawing.

29. Press **More Options**.

30. Select the **Browse** button.
31. Locate the *mysofa* file and press **Open.**

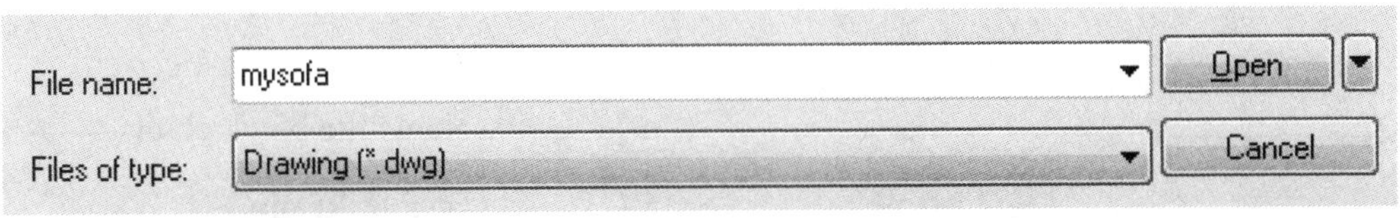

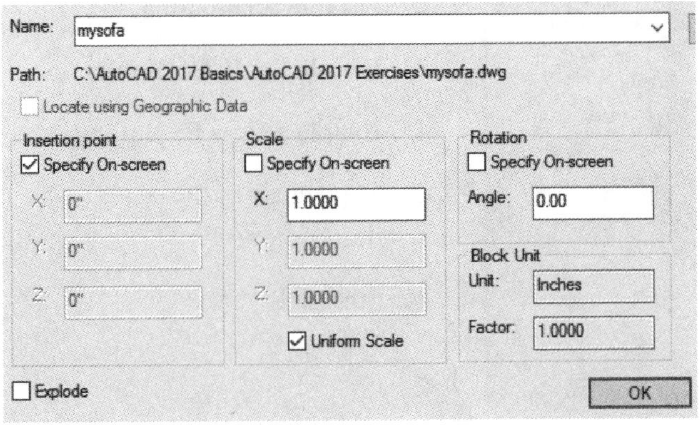

32. Enable **Specify On-screen** for the insertion point.
33. Press **OK**.

If you see this dialog, press OK.

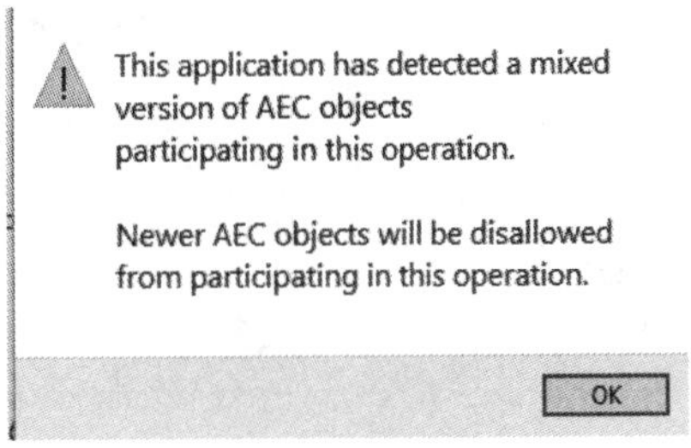

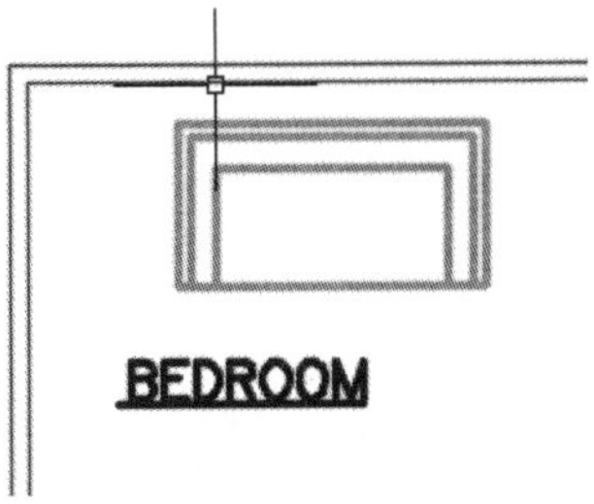

34. Place the sofa block in a similar location as the room on the left.
35. Select the sofa block to inspect the Quick Properties.

Note that the sofa is placed on the layer Furniture—the current layer.

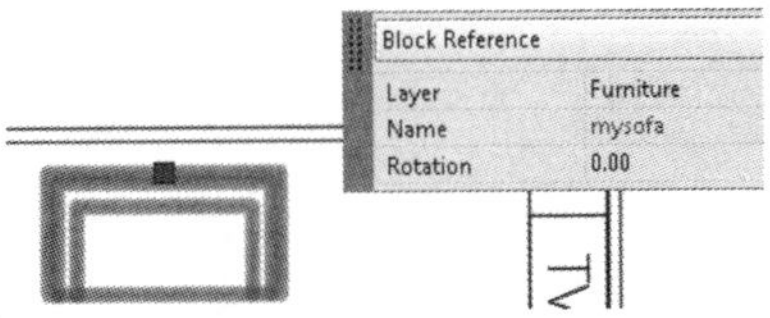

Press ESC to release the selection.

36. Select the chair located in the room on the left by windowing around it.
37. Place it on the Furniture layer using the Quick Properties dialog.

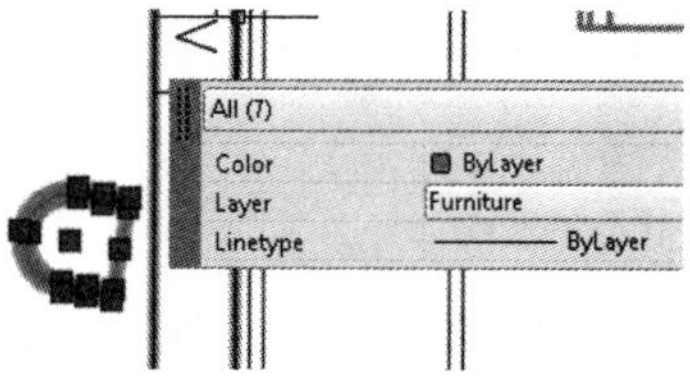

38. With the chair selected, select **Create Block** from the Insert ribbon.

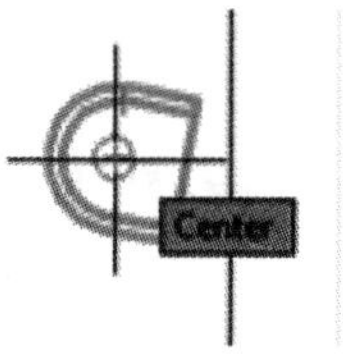

39. Use the center point of the arc as the Base Point for the block.

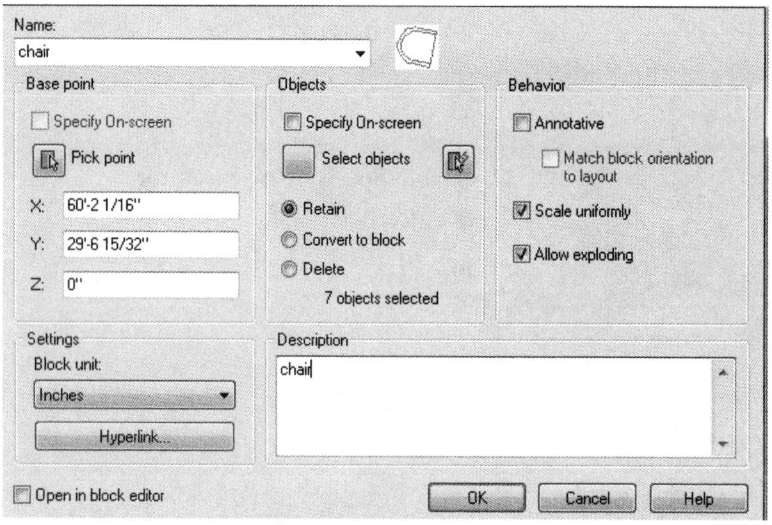

40. Name the block **chair**.
41. Enable **Retain.**
42. Disable **Annotative.**
43. Enable **Scale Uniformly.**
44. Enable **Allow Exploding**.
45. Type **chair** as the description.
46. Press **OK**.

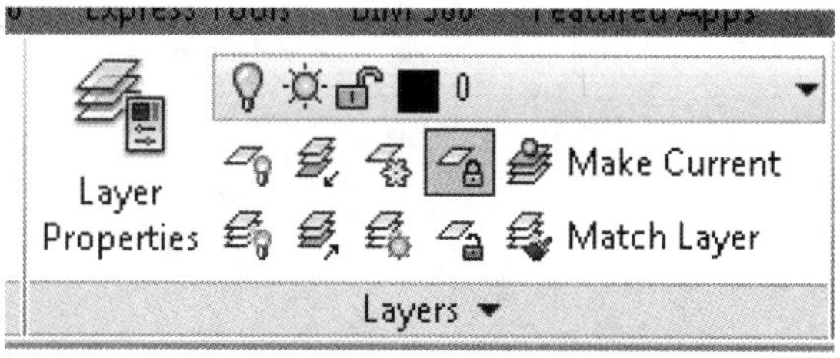

47. On the Home ribbon, set the Current Layer to **0.**

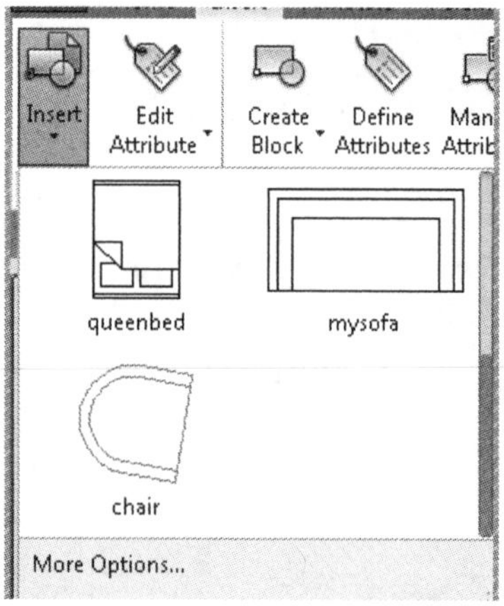

48. Activate the Insert ribbon.
49. Select **Insert.**
50. Scroll down to see the chair block.

Note we see the chair because it was defined as a local block.

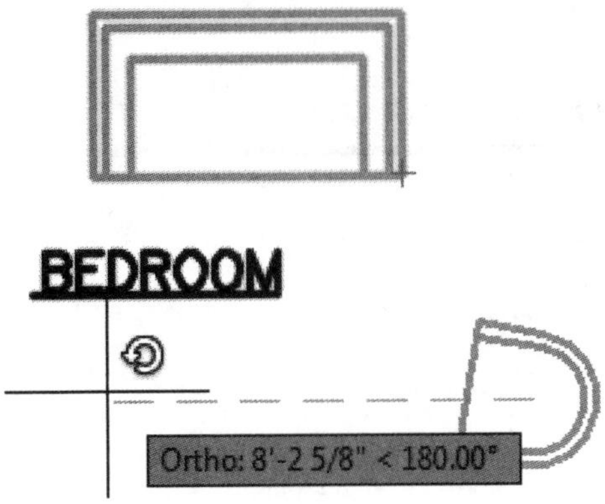
BEDROOM
Ortho: 8'-2 5/8" < 180.00°

51. The chair block appears at the end of the cursor.
52. Place the chair in the room on the right.

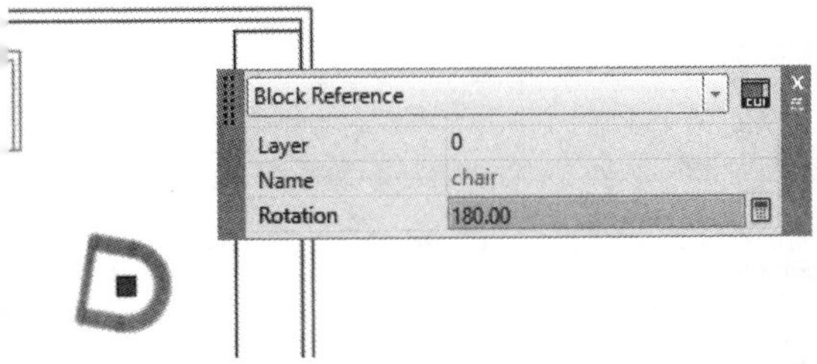
Block Reference
Layer 0
Name chair
Rotation 180.00

53. Select the chair and check the Quick Properties.

Notice that the chair is located on the current layer—0, but retains the properties of the furniture layer.

54. Change the Rotation to 180.00°.
55. Press ESC to release the selection.

- *Blocks created on layer 0 will adopt the properties of the layer where they are placed.*
- *Blocks created on layers other than 0 will retain the properties of their birth layer.*
- *Blocks can be stored internally in a drawing file or externally as a separate file.*

Command Exercise

Exercise 11-6 – Modifying a Block

Drawing Name: **blockedit.dwg**
Estimated Time to Completion: 30 Minutes

Scope

Modify a block and verify that it was done correctly.

Modify a Block Exercise

Solution

1. Select the middle Triple-dormer block.

The selection filter dialog can help you select the block.

2. Right click and select **Edit Block In-place**.

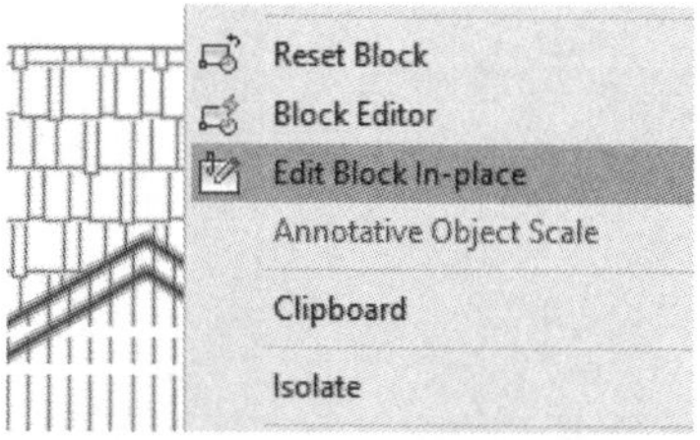

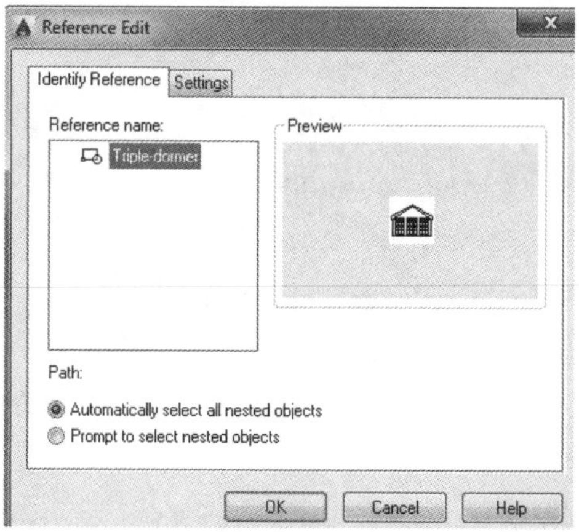

3. Enable 'Automatically select all nested objects'.
4. Press OK.

5. Select the left and right windows.

You can select each individual line or window around each area. Be careful to only select the windows!

Right click and select **Erase.**

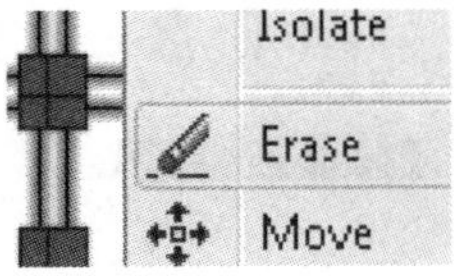
Isolate
Erase
Move

Save Changes
Discard Changes

6. On the ribbon, select **Save Changes.**

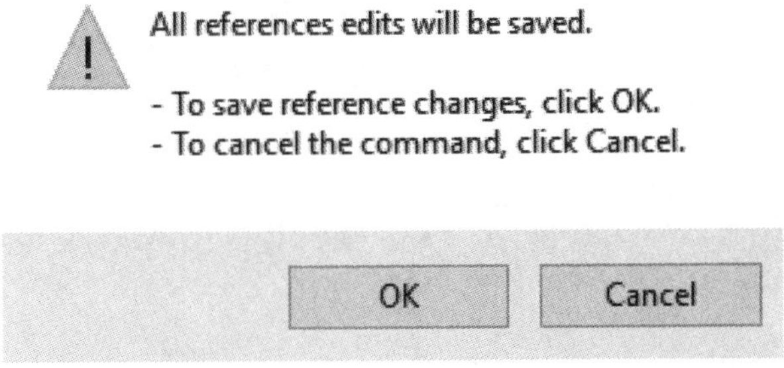
All references edits will be saved.
- To save reference changes, click OK.
- To cancel the command, click Cancel.
OK
Cancel

7. Press **OK.**
8. Select the hatch inside the dormer.

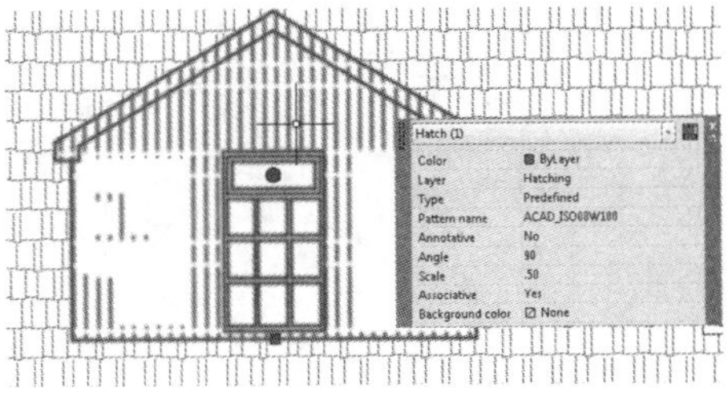

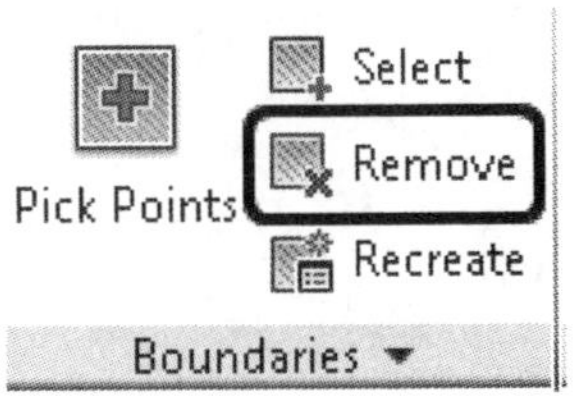
Select
Pick Points
Remove
Recreate
Boundaries

9. Select **Remove** to delete the boundaries created by the deleted windows.

10. Select the lines and rectangles for the two deleted windows.
11. Press **ENTER.**

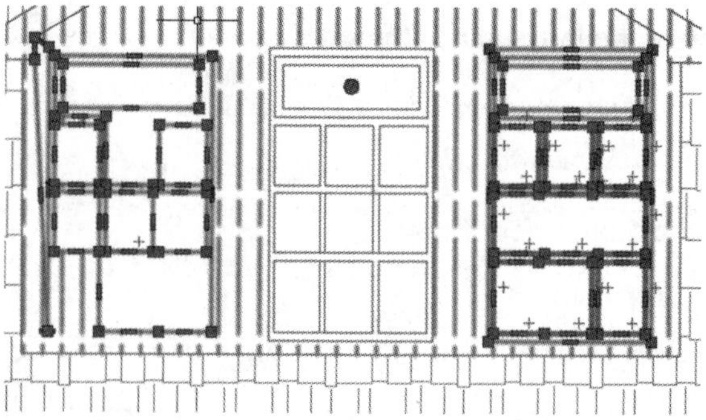

12. Select **Close Hatch Editor** from the ribbon.

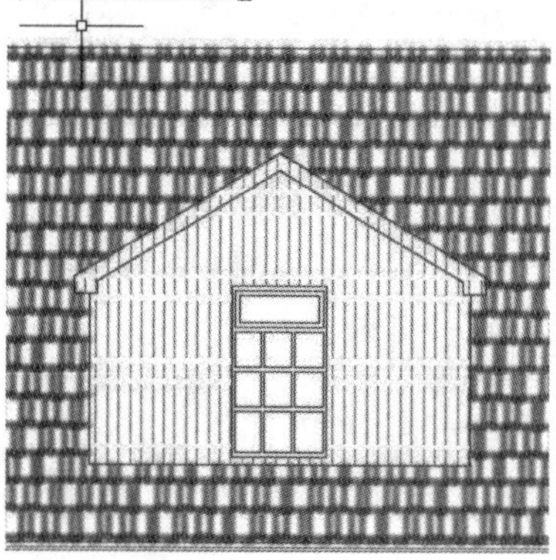

13. The hatch regenerates to fill the dormer.

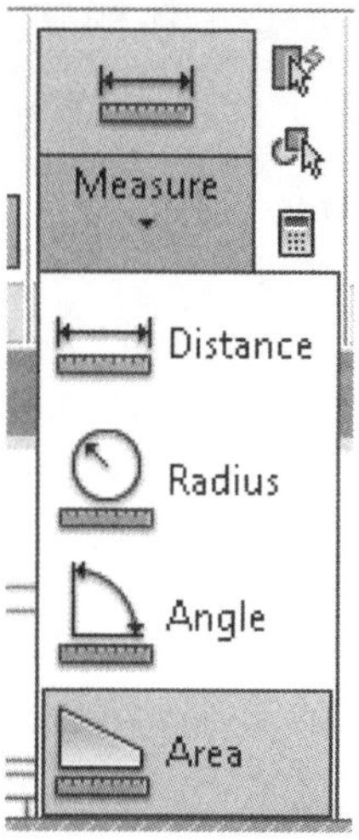

To determine the area of the hatch:

Type **area** or select **Area** from the Home ribbon.

Right click and select **Add Area.**

Trace around the inside of the dormer by selecting vertex points. Right click and select ENTER.

Right click and select **Subtract Area.**

Trace around the outside of the window.

Right click and select **ENTER.**

The area will be displayed.

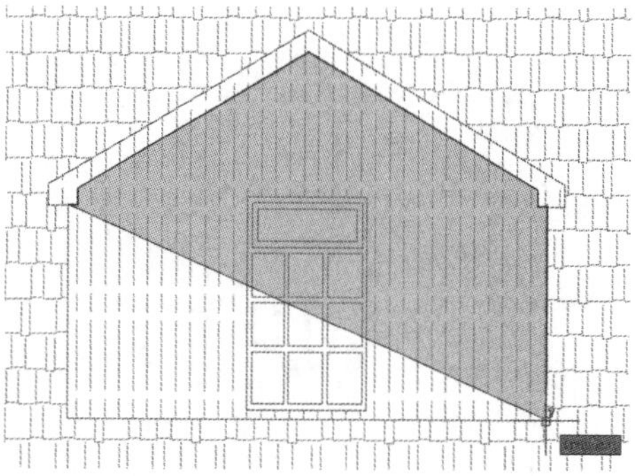

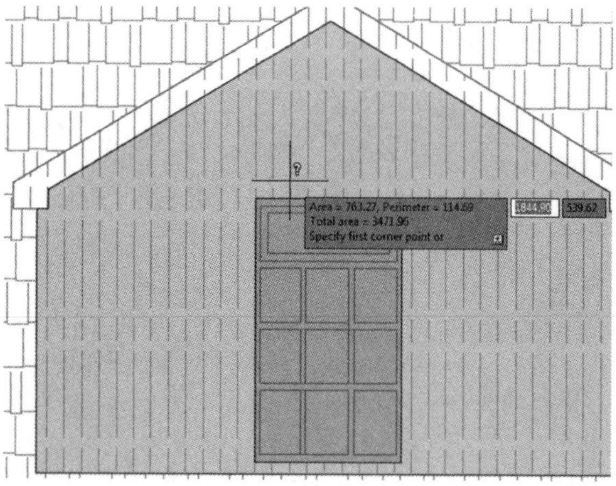

As you select points you will see an overlay to indicate the area selected.

Command Exercise

Exercise 11-7 – PDF Import

Drawing Name: **pdfimport.dwg, office plan.pdf**
Estimated Time to Completion: 10 Minutes

Scope

AutoCAD 2017 allows users to import PDFs and convert them to AutoCAD drawings. In order for the PDF to convert properly, it must contain vector graphics. If the PDF contains renderings or shading, it is not a vector PDF. It is a raster PDF and would need to be vectorized prior to import.

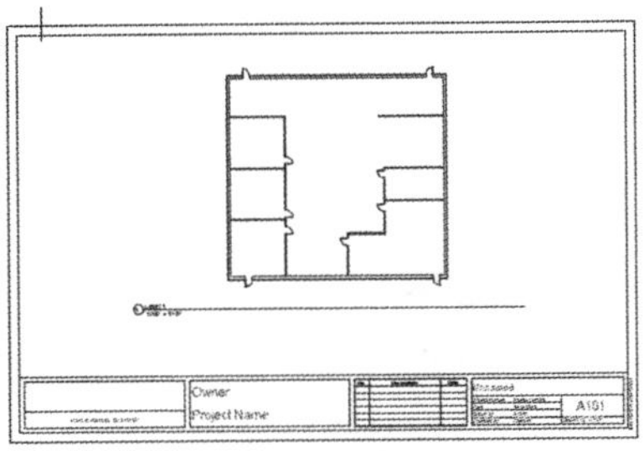

Import PDF Exercise

Solution

1. Verify that the Model tab is enabled.

2. Select Import on the Insert ribbon.

3. Set Files of type to PDF.

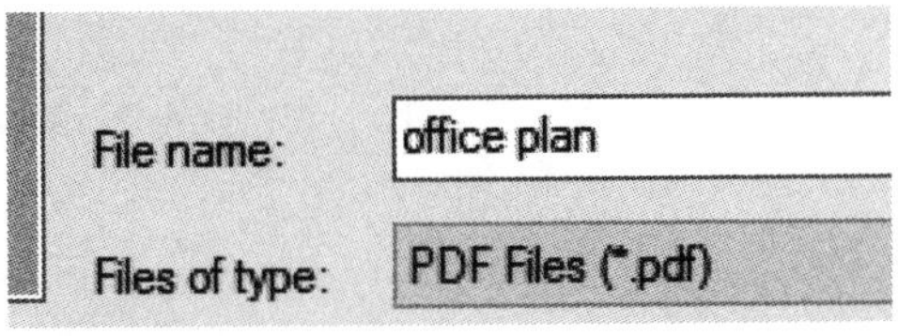

4. Browse to your exercise folder. Select *office plan.*
5. Press Open.

Tips & Tricks

➢ *Use the Layer Translator to move PDF layers to the preferred AutoCAD layers.*

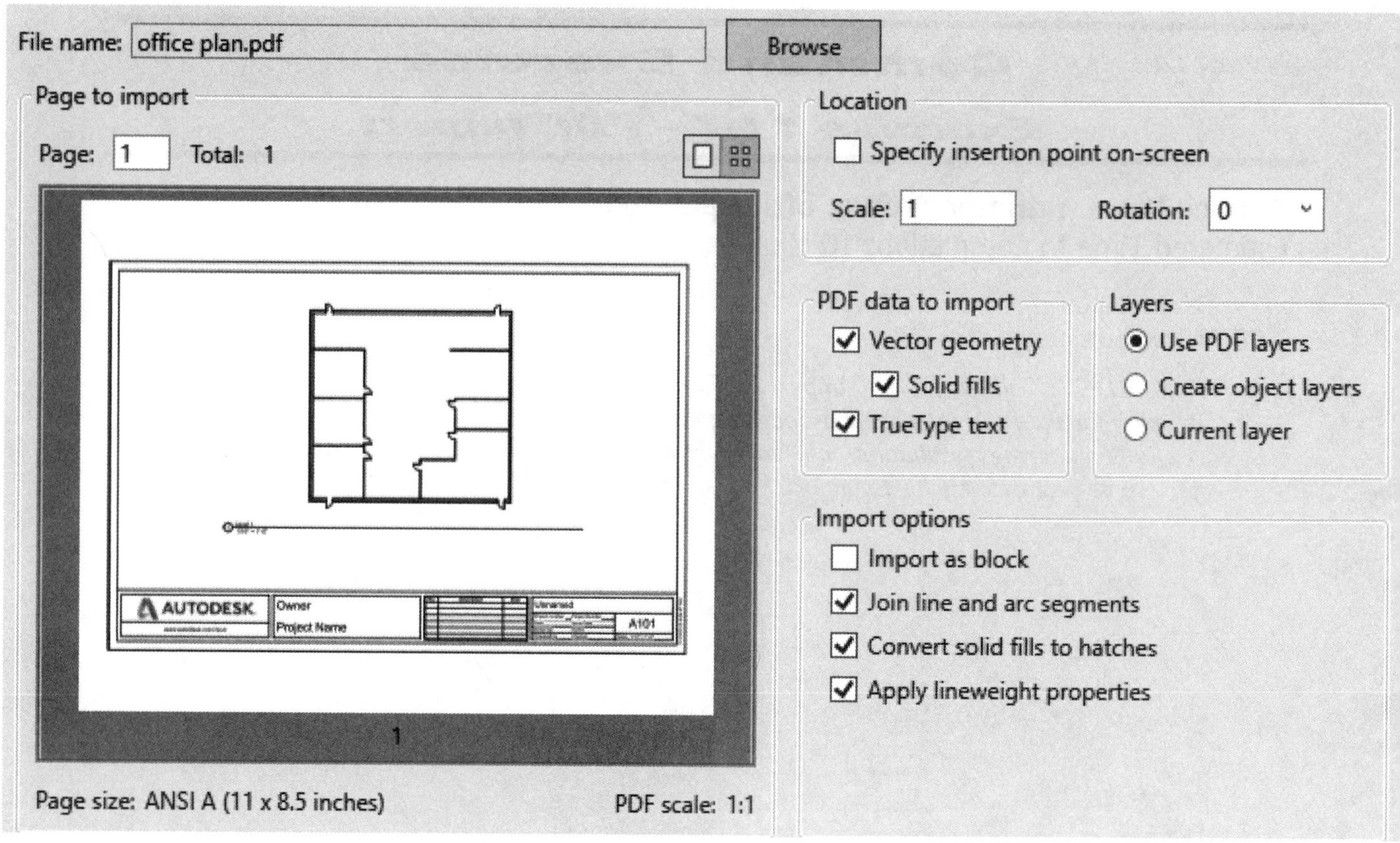

6. There is only a single page in this pdf. It is previewed.

7. Under Location: Uncheck Specify insertion point on screen. *This will automatically insert the PDF at the origin (0,0).*

8. Under PDF data to import:

Enable Vector geometry.

Enable Solid fills.

Enable TrueType font.

9. Under Layers:

Enable Use PDF Layers.

This will use any PDF layers that have been assigned. If PDF layers exist, they will be listed with a prefix of PDF_. If there are no PDF layers, the Create object layers option will automatically be used. The layers created will be called PDF_Geometry, PDF_Solid Fills, and PDF_Text.

10. Press OK.

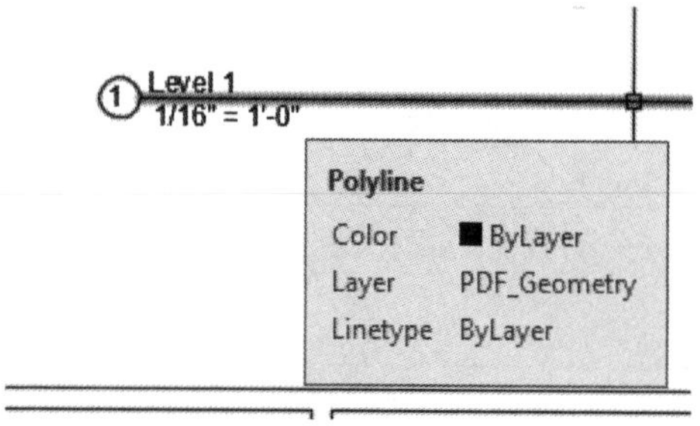

11. If you mouse over any of the geometry, a dialog will display indicating that it has been imported as an AutoCAD element and the layer it has been placed on.

Review Questions

1. **T F** If you insert a titleblock into a drawing and then modify the external titleblock drawing, it will automatically update in the drawing(s) where it was inserted.

2. You have a local block with multiple insertions in a drawing. You need to modify the block. You explode one of the block insertions and make the change. You then use BMAKE and select the modified former block. You assign the original block name to the modified block. What happens to the other block insertions in the drawing?

   - ❑ They remain unchanged.
   - ❑ They are deleted.
   - ❑ They update to the new block definition.
   - ❑ They become unnamed blocks.

3. **T F** If you do not assign an insertion point to a block, it will by default use the center of the object selected.

4. An insertion point for a block can be defined by:

   - ❑ Entering an X, Y, and Z value in the Block Definition dialog box.
   - ❑ Entering an X, Y, and Z value in the Block Definition dialog box.
   - ❑ Enabling the Align Below Previous Attribute.
   - ❑ All of the above.

5. **T F** Blocks can have names up to 255 characters long and include spaces.

6. **T F** When defining a block, you can determine the units or if it will be Unitless. For example, if a block were defined with units of inches and then inserted into a drawing whose base units were millimeters, it would automatically scale by a factor of 25.4.

7. Attributes are created using the _________ command.

   - ❑ ATTREQ
   - ❑ ATTDIA
   - ❑ ATTDISP
   - ❑ ATTDEF

8. You create a title block drawing with attribute definitions. Next you wblock it and try to insert it into a separate drawing. You then get this error message:

   - ❑ Block is Redefined
   - ❑ Block references itself
   - ❑ Memory overload
   - ❑ Fatal error – computer will now reformat your hard drive

Review Answers

1. **T F** If you insert a titleblock into a drawing and then modify the external titleblock drawing, it will automatically update in the drawing(s) where it was inserted.

   True

2. You have a local block with multiple insertions in a drawing. You need to modify the block. You explode one of the block insertions and make the change. You then use BMAKE and select the modified former block. You assign the original block name to the modified block. What happens to the other block insertions in the drawing?

   They update to the new block definition.

3. **T F** If you do not assign an insertion point to a block, it will by default use the center of the object selected.

   False

4. An insertion point for a block can be defined by:

   All of the above

5. **T F** Blocks can have names up to 255 characters long and include spaces.

   True

6. **T F** When defining a block, you can determine the units or if it will be Unitless. For example, if a block were defined with units of inches and then inserted into a drawing whose base units were millimeters, it would automatically scale by a factor of 25.4.

   True

7. Attributes are created using the _________ command.

   ATTDEF

8. You create a title block drawing with attribute definitions. Next you wblock it and try to insert it into a separate drawing. You then get this error message:

   Block references itself

Lesson 12.0 – Viewports and Layouts

Estimated Class Time: 2.5 Hours

Objectives

This section will cover how to create a drawing Layout from a Model and how to plot a drawing. The general idea is to create the drawing in the Model space window and plot the drawing from the paper space Layout window. Drawings may also be plotted in Model space. There are advantages and disadvantages to using the Model or Layout mode to plot a drawing.

Model Space is the environment in which you create your two–dimensional drawing, or your three–dimensional model. Paper Space (Layout) is the environment where you set up your drawing or model to plot. Although you can plot your drawing in Paper Space or in Model Space, there are certain advantages to setting up your drawing to plot in Paper Space. In Paper Space, you can create multiple views at multiple scales of the same model or drawing. You can also freeze layers in selected paper space view ports. There are a few tricks to working with Paper Space such as controlling line type scales and dimensioning.

Sheets Sets are used to plot multiple drawings. They are an easy way to organize drawing packages for plotting and editing.

Section Objectives:

- **Drawing Layout**
  Create a drawing layout from the drawing Model.
- **Drawing Layout Viewports**
  Insert a title block in the paper space Layout and create drawing views.
- **Adding Viewports**
- **Converting Existing Dimensions to Annotative**
- **Using Annotative Scales**
- **Controlling Viewport Properties**
- **Nonrectangular Viewports**
- **Using the Layout Wizard**
- **Controlling visibility of layers in viewports**
- **Plotting and Output**
- **Layout Settings**
- **Sheet Sets**
- **Sheet List Tables**

Command Exercise

Exercise 12-1 – Adding Layout Ribbon

Drawing Name: **new**
Estimated Time to Completion: 5 Minutes

Scope

Add the Layout Ribbon to the Drafting & Annotation Workspace.

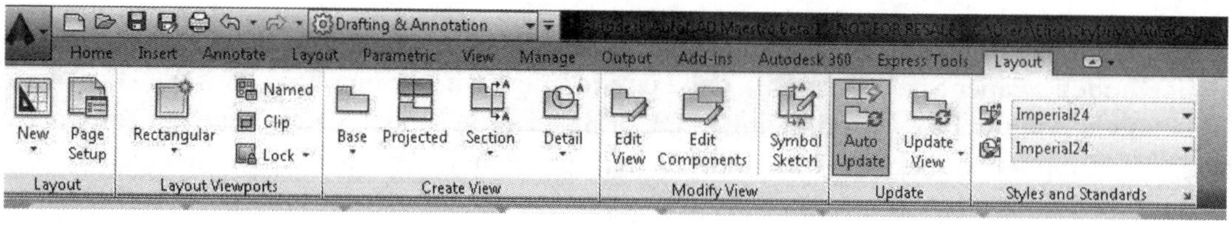

The Layout Ribbon

Solution

1. Type **CUI** on the command line.

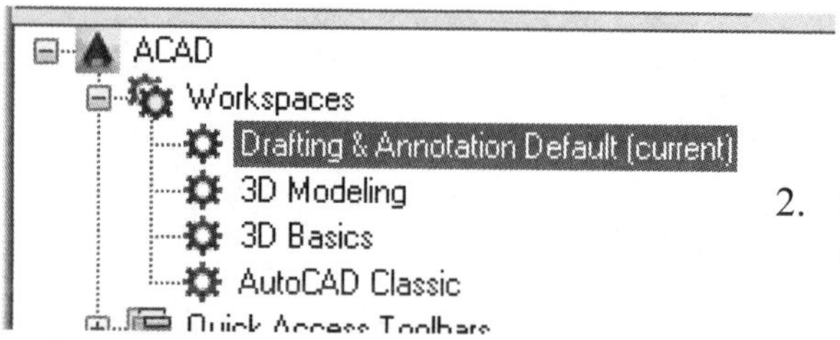

2. Highlight the **Drafting & Annotation Default** workspace in the left panel.

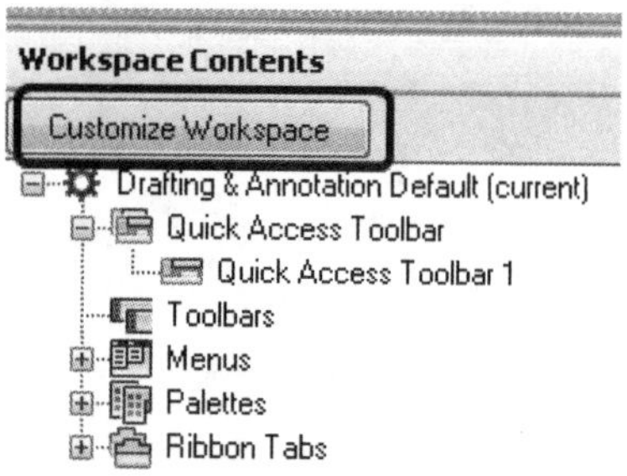

3. Press the **Customize Workspace** button on the right panel.

4. Expand the Ribbon Tabs list on the left panel. Scroll down until you find the Layout tab. Place a check next to the Layout tab.

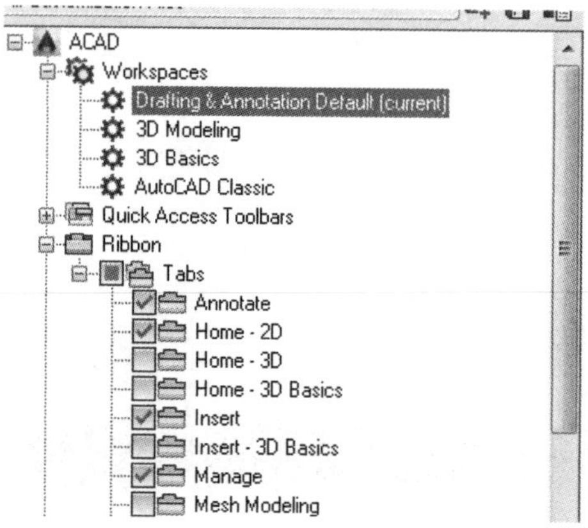

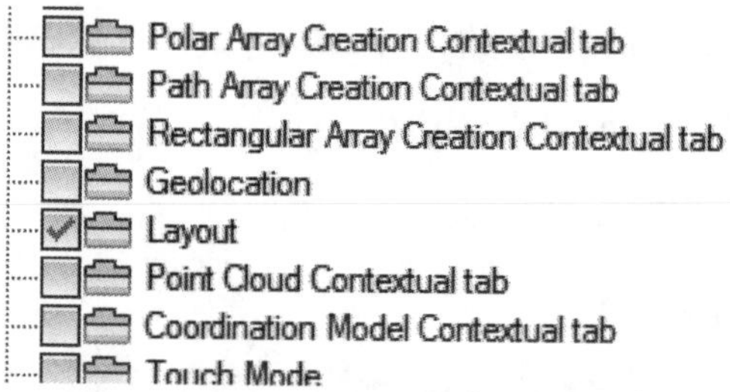

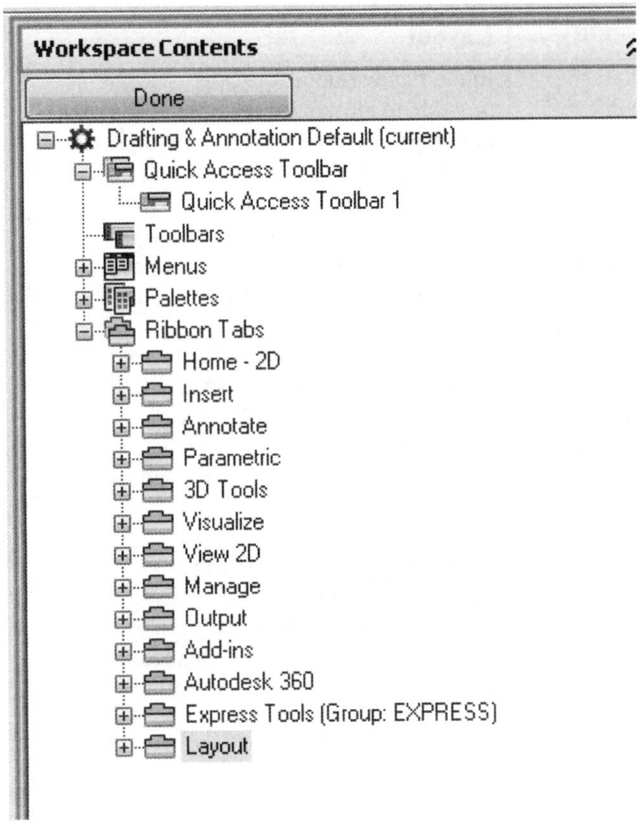

In the right panel, you should see the Layout tab added to the list of Ribbon Tabs.

You can drag and drop it to a different position.

5. Drag and drop the Layout tab below the Annotate tab.

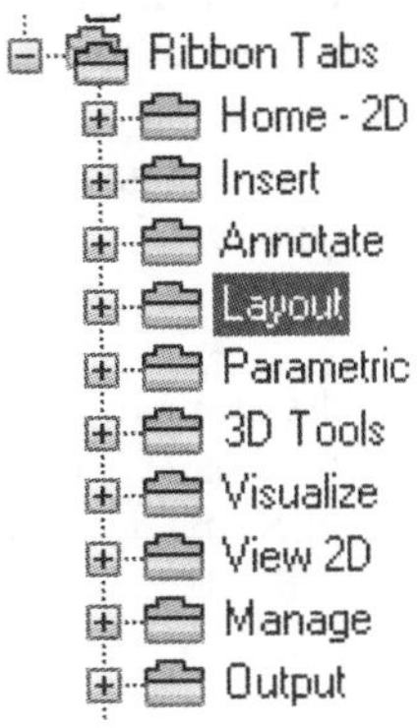

6. Press **Apply**. You should see the Layout tab appear on the ribbon.
7. Press **OK**.

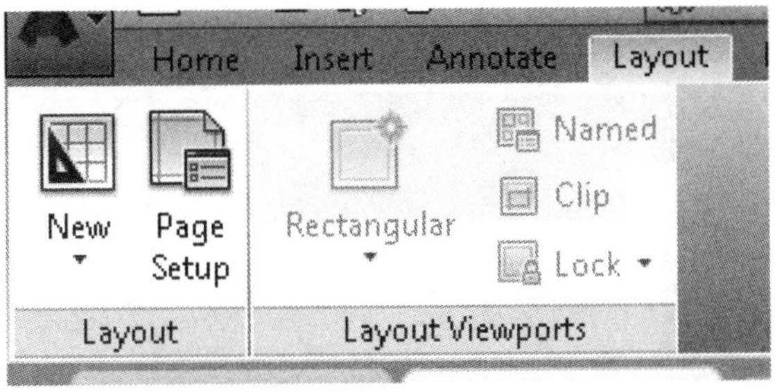

If you don't see it, try switching to a different workspace and then switch back.

Option	Model	Layout
Drawing views	In model space, only one view of the drawing may be printed at a time.	In the Layout mode, or paper space, it is possible to plot multiple views of the same drawing. These views can show different parts of the drawing, and views can be zoomed at different scales.
Drawing Layers	In model space, layers are either visible or not since there is only one view port.	In the Layout mode, Layers can be frozen in one view port, but not in the other.
Plot Scale	In model space, the drawing must be plotted to scale. It is therefore important that the drawing limits and title block reflect the drawing scale. Text, Dimension Styles and LTSCALE (linetype scale) must also reflect the plot scale.	Drawings views placed in the Layout Mode must be zoomed to scale (X/XP). Dimensions, notes and the title block are placed in the Layout at a scale of 1. The drawing Layout is plotted at a scale of 1.
Drawing Revisions	In model space, the drawing must be revised in each instance the image is copied in the drawing (for instance if a detail was shown at a scale of 1:1 and 1:10).	In the drawing Layout, each view represents a single drawing. Therefore, if a change is made to the drawing in Model space, the changes will automatically be reflected in the Layout view ports.

Drawing Layout

Command Locator

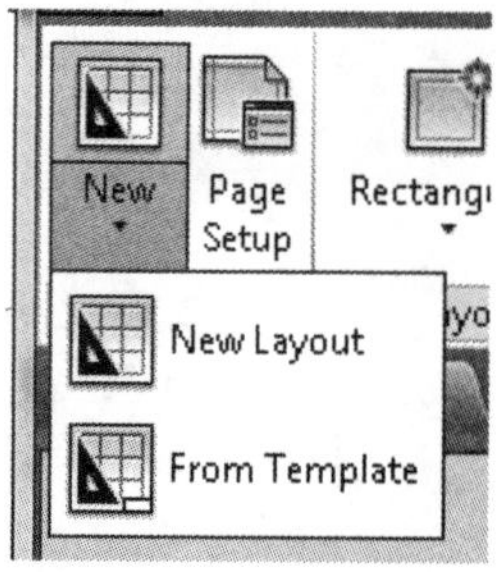

Layout Ribbon	**Layout Panel/New Layout**
Toolbar Menu	**Layouts / New Layout** and **Layouts / Layout from Template**
Pull Down Menu	**Insert / Layout /** *(select option)*
Command	**Layout**
Dialog Box	**Page Setup Layout**

Command Overview

The first time the Layout tab is selected, the user will be presented with the Page Setup Layout dialog box. Plot settings for the drawing layout can be chosen here, or specified later by invoking the Plot command. If the default settings of the Page Setup Layer dialog box are accepted (press OK), the Layout will display a single view of the drawing. The dashed line in the drawing layout will represent the plot area of the paper.

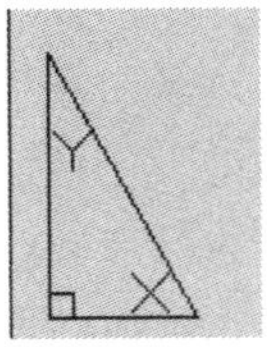

The icon in the lower left corner indicates that the user is viewing the drawing Layout or *paper space*. When the Zoom command is used in the PAPER space mode, the entire drawing layout is affected. When the Zoom command is used with the viewports in the MODEL space mode *(see next section)*, only the active viewport will be zoomed. The Title block should be inserted in the Layout PAPER space mode. The Title block should always be slightly smaller than the paper size, because the plot area will always be less than the paper size, as indicated by the dashed rectangle.

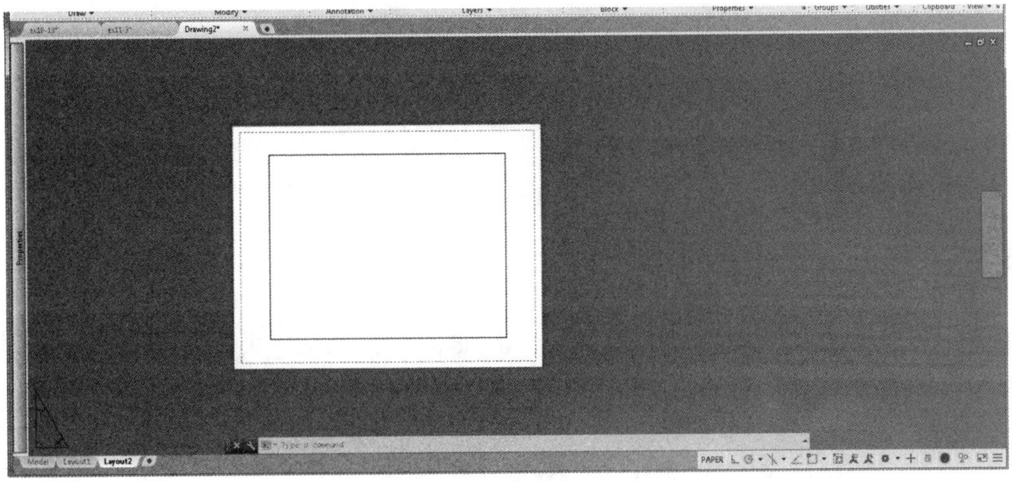

Drawing Layout, Paper Space

General Procedures

1. Create the drawing in Model space mode.
2. Select the Layout tab in the Drawing Window.
3. Select OK to accept the Page Setup Layout defaults.
4. Use the Block Insert command to insert a Title Block.

Tips & Tricks

- The Layout Page Setup can be changed by invoking the Plot command or the Page Setup command.
- Select the Model tab in the drawing window to return to Model space.
- The Title Block insertion point is typically 0,0. The scale factors should be 1 and the rotation angle should be 0.
- Place the viewport on a layer that is set not to plot and you will never have to worry about the viewport border being visible in your plots.
- Create as many layouts as needed to show all the views of the drawing necessary.
- You may name the layout using up to 255 characters; however, only the first 32 characters will show on the name tab.
- You can move your layouts so that they are in a desired order to make it easier to navigate through a drawing set.

Command Exercise

Exercise 12-2 – Creating a New Layout

Drawing Name: **nlayout1.dwg**
Estimated Time to Completion: 5 Minutes

Scope

Create a new layout in the drawing called 'Plan'.

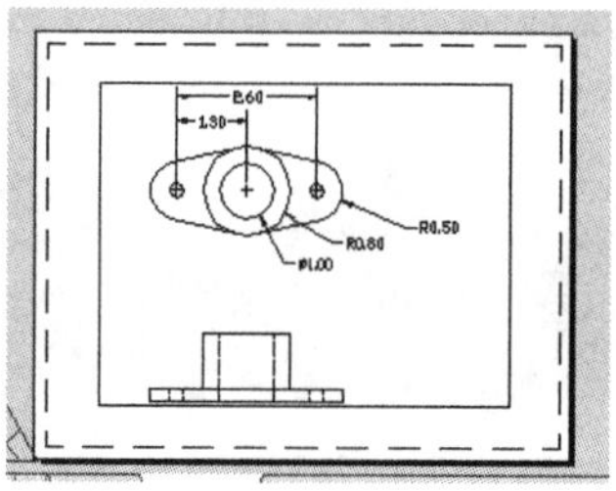

New Layout Exercise

Solution

1. Left click on the + tab next to Layout1 to add a layout.

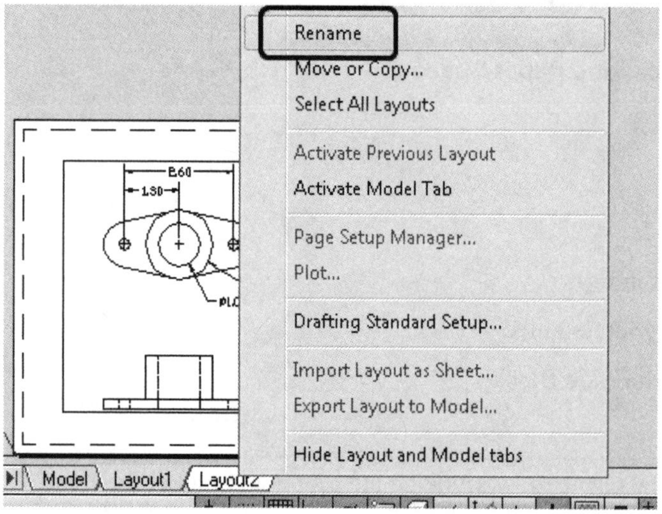

2. RMB on the new layout tab.
3. Select **Rename**.
4. Type **Plan** to change the layout name.

5. Click on the new **Plan** tab.

6. Click on the viewport border to activate its grips.

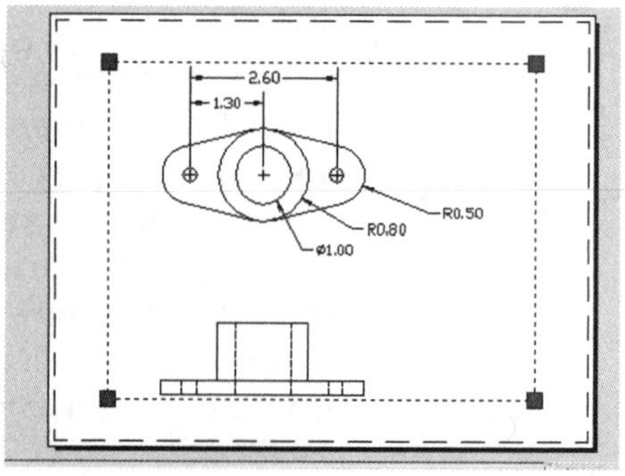

Specify stretch point or [Base point/ Copy/Undo/eXit]:

7. Stretch the border as shown in the following figure to show only the plan (top) view of the drawing.
8. Press <ESC> to release the grips.

You should only see the top view.

9. Close without saving.

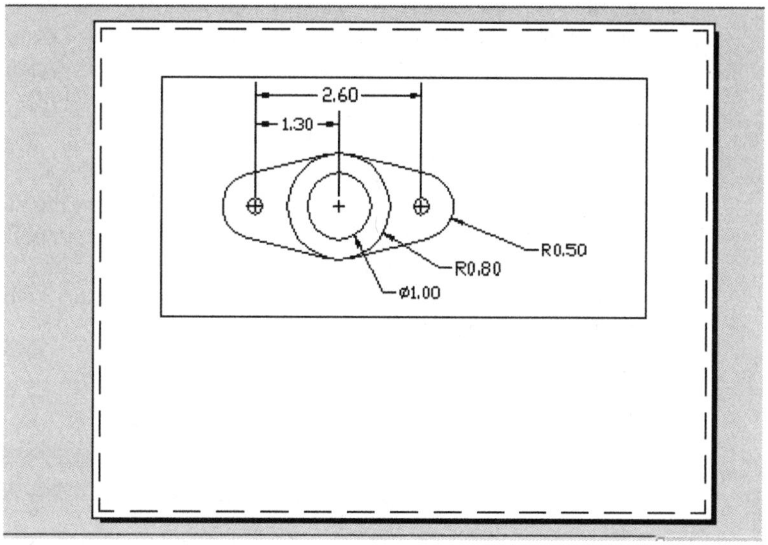

Viewports

Command Locator

Layout Ribbon	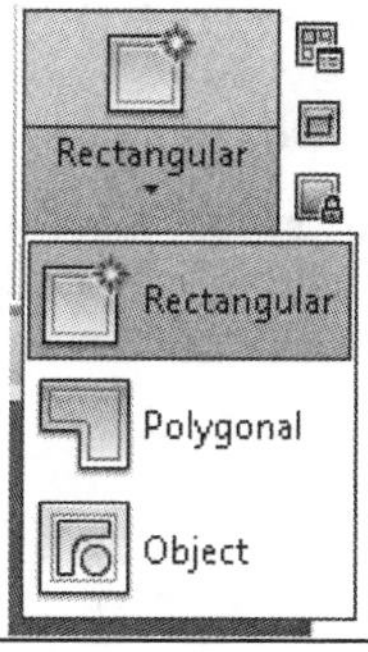
Toolbar Menu	**Viewports**
Pull Down Menu	**View→Viewports** / *(select option)*
Command	**viewports**
Alias	**vports**
RMB Shortcut Menu	**Viewports** *(when New viewports is selected)*

Command Overview

Unlike tiled viewports in the Model space drawing window, viewports in the Layout window can be rectangular or irregular polygon shapes. They can be moved, resized, rotated, and copied using the grip options or the regular Modify commands, and they can be *clipped*. They can even overlap other viewports. For this reason, they are sometimes referred to as *floating* viewports. When the drawing is zoomed in the PAPER space mode, the entire Layout is zoomed.

When the Layout viewports are switched from the PAPER space mode to the MODEL space mode from the Status Bar, only the active viewport will be zoomed. Select the viewport to zoom and Zoom All first. Repeat the zoom command by pressing <ENTER> or by typing Z. Type the scale factor, followed by XP (for *times paper space*). For example, 1xp would be a scale of 1:1, and 1/2xp would be a scale of 1:2. When all of the viewports have been properly zoomed, switch back to the PAPER space mode by selecting the word MODEL in the Status Bar.

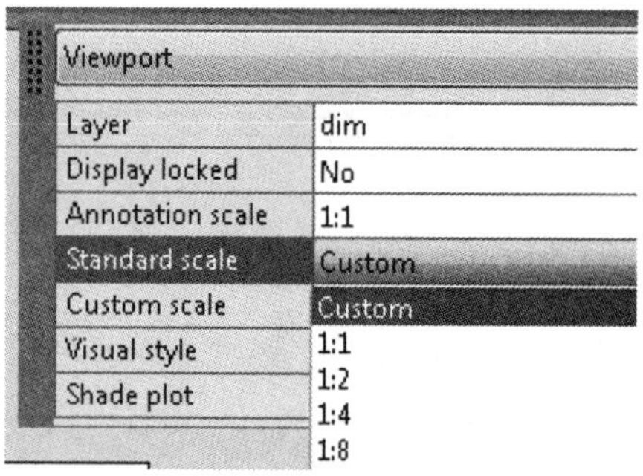

Applying a Viewport Scale

You may also use the Viewport Standard Scale Control. This is a drop-down list of the available scales and is much easier to use than setting the zoom factor correctly. To use this, just select the border of the viewport to scale, then select the scale from the Quick Properties dialog.

The general rule is to create the drawing in the Model space window, and set up the drawing to plot from the Layout tab. Use either the PAPER or MODEL mode to adjust the viewport size and views. Then switch back to PAPER to plot the drawing.

General Procedures

1. Create the drawing in Model space (the Model tab should be selected).
2. Select the Layout tab in the Drawing Window. Select OK to accept the Page Setup Layout defaults.
3. Use grips to re-size the viewport. Use the Viewports command options to create additional views.
4. Select PAPER in the Status Bar. This will switch the viewport mode to floating MODEL space. Select a viewport and Zoom the drawing view to scale.
5. Select MODEL in the Status Bar to switch the viewport mode back to PAPER space. Add notes, dimensions, etc. and plot the drawing.

Command Exercise

Exercise 12-3 – Adding a Viewport

Drawing Name: **nlayout2dwg**
Estimated Time to Completion: 15 Minutes

Scope

Create a new viewport. Add a scale to the scale list. Set the viewport scale. Lock the viewport display.

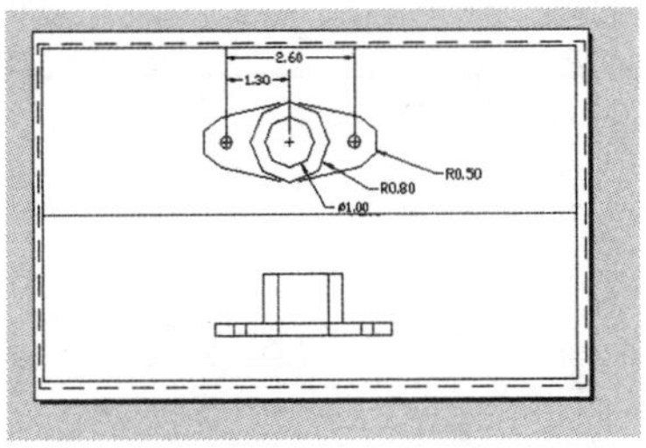

New Viewport Exercise

Solution

1. Select the Layout 1 tab.

There should not be a viewport on it.
You should see only a blank sheet of paper.

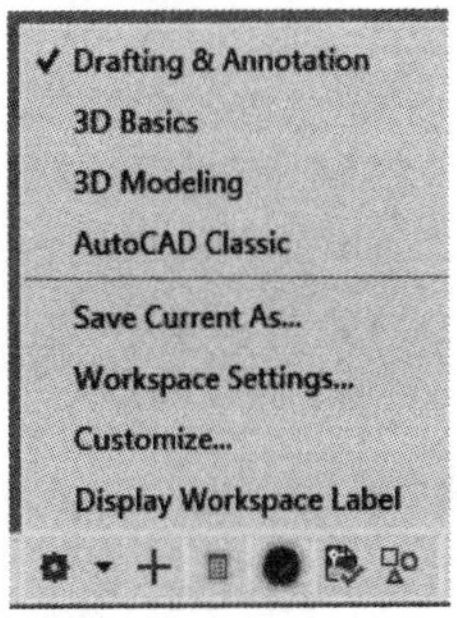

2. Set your workspace to **Drafting & Annotation**.

3. Verify that Quick Properties is **enabled**.

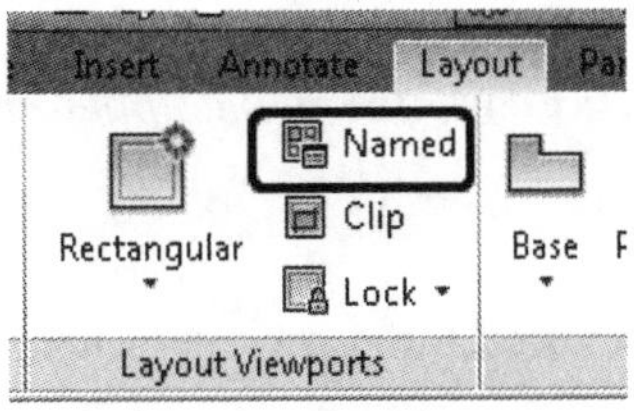

4. Select the **Named** viewport tool on the Layout ribbon
   OR
   Type **VPORTS** anywhere in the display window.

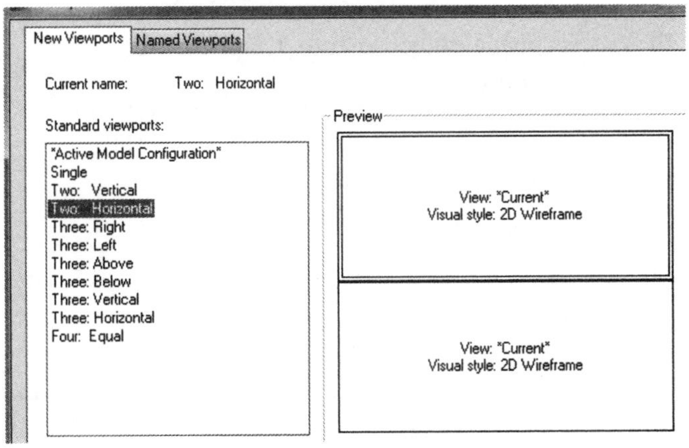

5. Select the **New Viewports** tab.

6. Select the **Two:Horizontal** option.

7. Press **OK**.

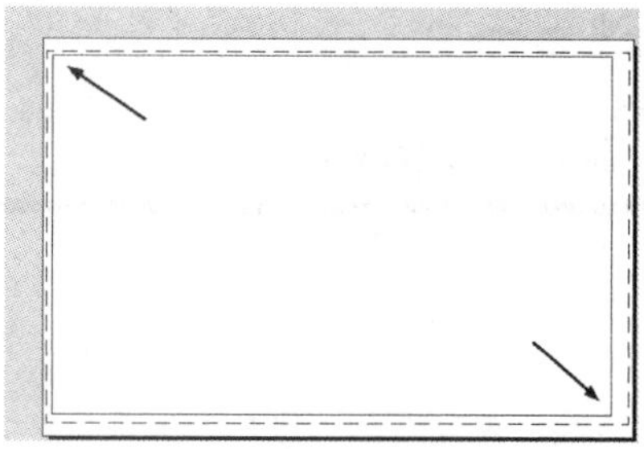

8. Select two points (similar to drawing a rectangle).

The active viewport's border will appear bold.

9. Double click LMB inside the lower viewport to activate MODEL space.

You also will see a ViewCube in the upper right corner and the View Controls and Visual Style Controls in the upper left.

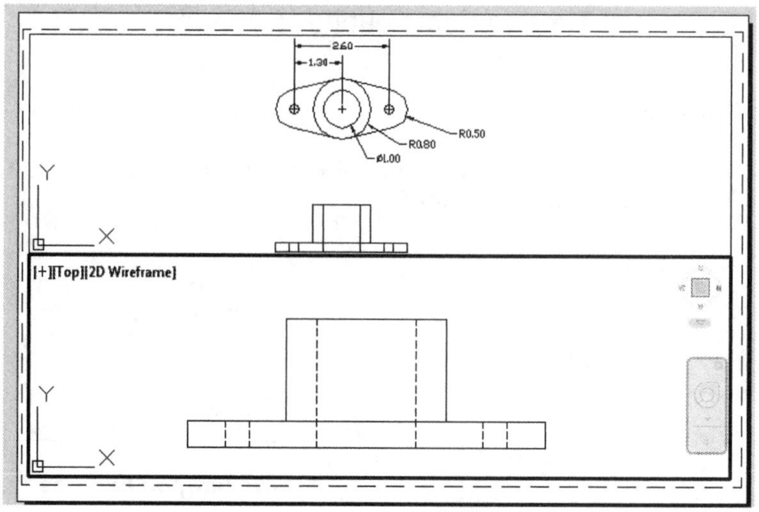

10. Use **Zoom Window** to zoom into the front view of the model.

11. Click outside of the paper to deactivate the viewport.

12. Select the top viewport border so it highlights.

The scale of the viewport is displayed on the Status Bar.

13. Left click on the viewport scale indicator.

A list of available scales is displayed.

14. Select the 3:1 scale.

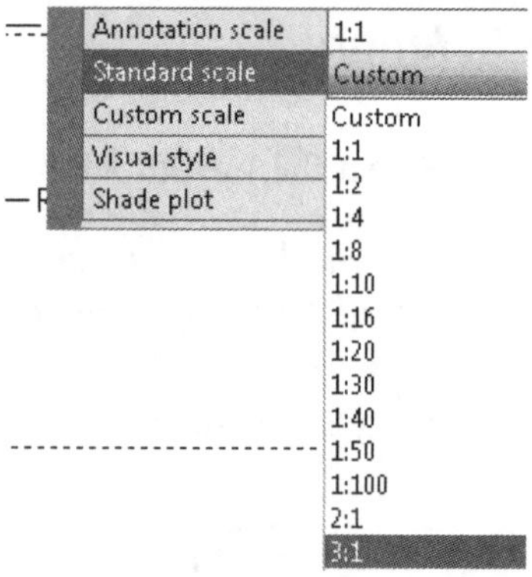

15. Double click LMB inside the top viewport to activate MODEL space.

The active viewport's border will appear bold.

You also will see a ViewCube in the upper right corner and the View Controls and Visual Style Controls in the upper left.

16. Use **Pan** to position the top view of the model.

17. Click outside of the paper to deactivate the viewport.

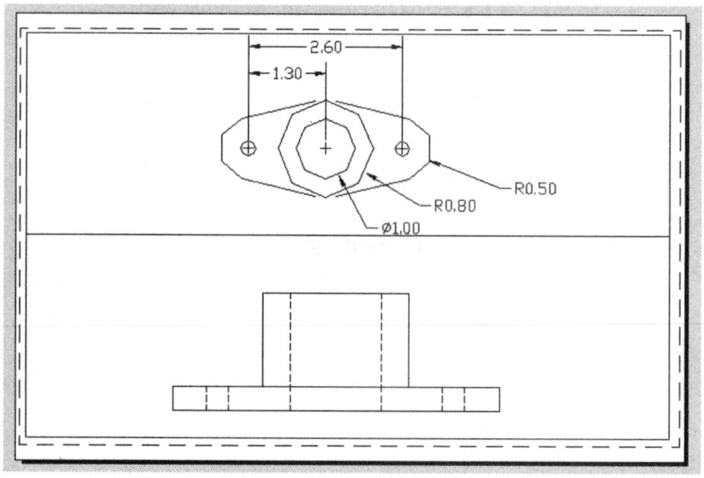

18. Select the bottom viewport border so it highlights.

The scale of the viewport is displayed on the Status Bar.

19. Left click on the viewport scale indicator.

A list of available scales is displayed.

20. Select the 3:1 scale.

21. Line up the top and bottom views.

22. Adjust the sizes of the viewports as needed using grips.

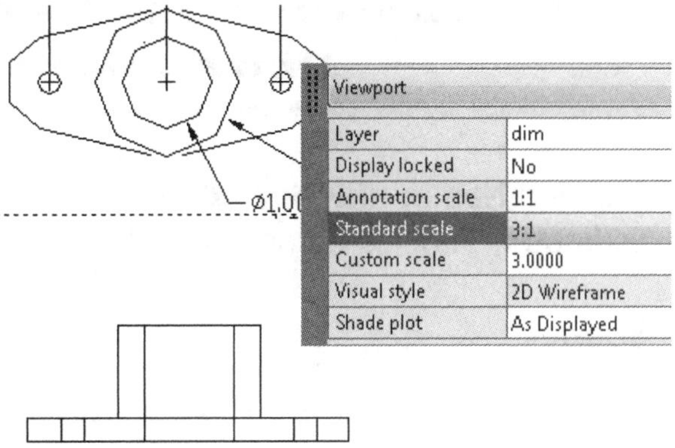

23. Select the top viewport border so it highlights.

24. In the Quick Properties dialog, set Display Locked to **Yes**.

25. Repeat for the bottom viewport.

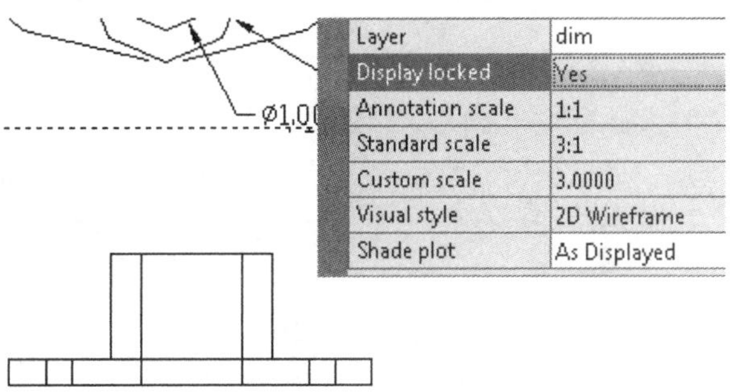

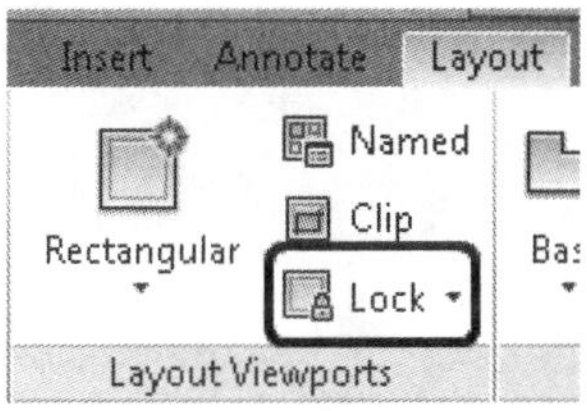

You can also lock a viewport by selecting the LOCK tool on the ribbon.

26. Double click LMB inside the lower viewport to activate MODEL space.

27. Select **Zoom Extents**.

Note that your display changed, but the view in the viewport did not. That is because you locked the viewport display. It is a good idea to lock your viewport display once you have set up your view to ensure that it does not accidentally get changed as you move about your drawing.

Tips & Tricks

- Annotative Scale allows the user to automatically set the scale for dimensions and notes to match the scale of viewports and layouts. You can reset the Annotative Scale on the fly as needed.
- If you elect to use this feature, set up your layouts and viewports before you add any dimensions or text. That way you know what scale you will be using for your views.
- Once you have determined the scale assigned to each viewport, you can set your annotation scale so that it matches and your annotations will automatically scale accordingly.
- You can set the visibility of annotations so only those objects set to the active annotation scale are visible using the Annotation Visibility tool in the Status Bar tray.

Command Exercise

Exercise 12-4 – Converting Existing Dimensions to Annotative

Drawing Name: **nlayout3.dwg**
Estimated Time to Completion: 20 Minutes

Scope

Change existing dimensions to annotative, so that they can use Annotative Scale.

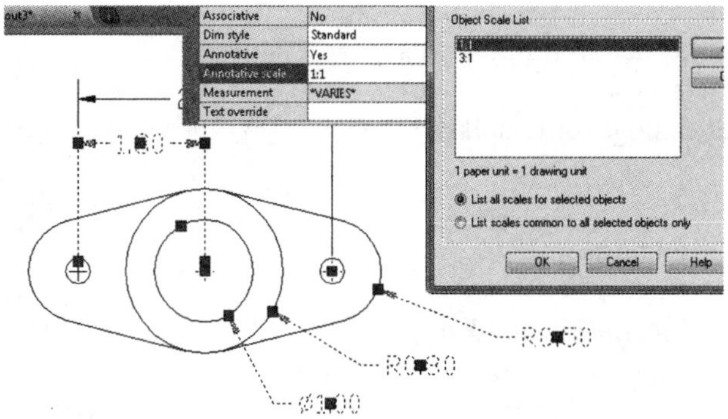

Annotative Dimensions Exercise

Solution

1. Verify that the Model tab is active.

2. Verify that Quick Properties is **enabled.**

3. Select the **2.60** dimension so it is highlighted.

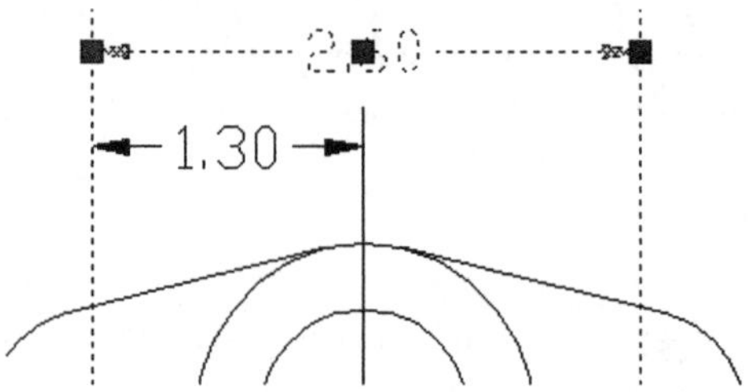

In the Quick Properties dialog:
4. Set Annotative to **Yes**.

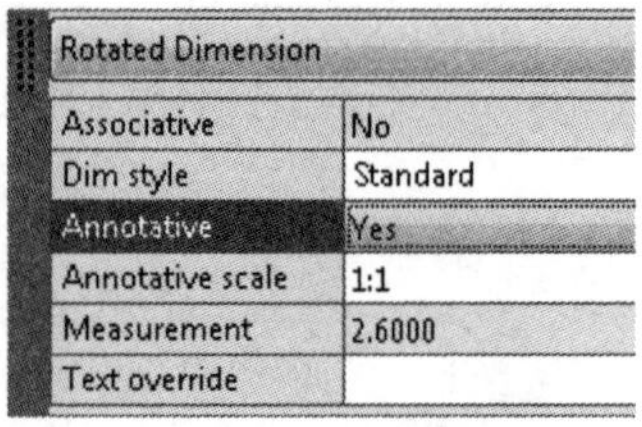

The Annotative scale field appears.

5. Select the **...** button.

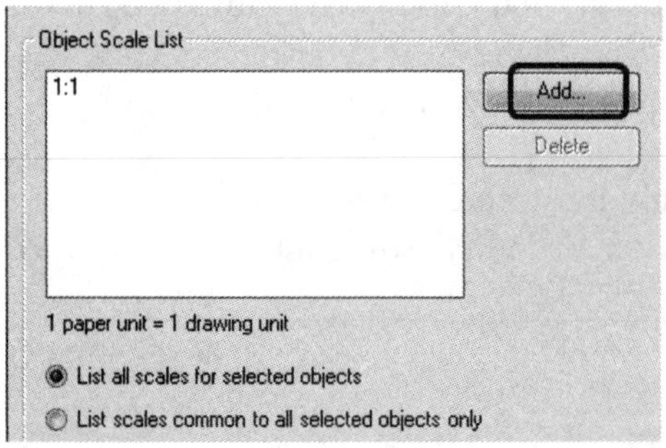

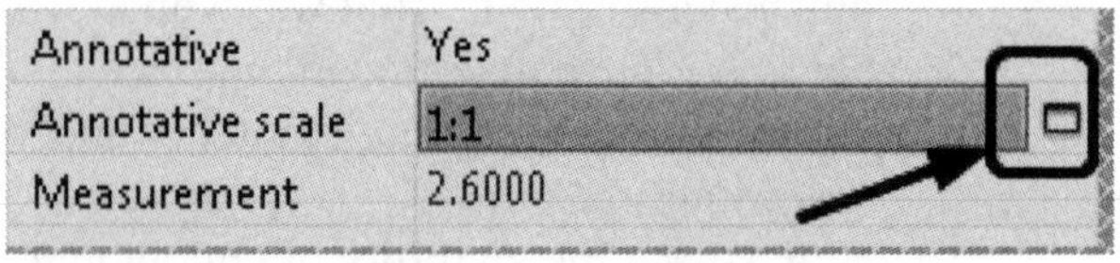

6. Select the **Add** button.

The 3:1 scale does not exist in the list.

7. Press **Cancel** to exit the Annotation Object Scale dialog.
8. Press **ESC** to release the selected dimension.
9. Type **scalelistedit** on the command line.

If you type SC in the display window, AUTOCOMPLETE will provide you with a list of commands that start with SCA.

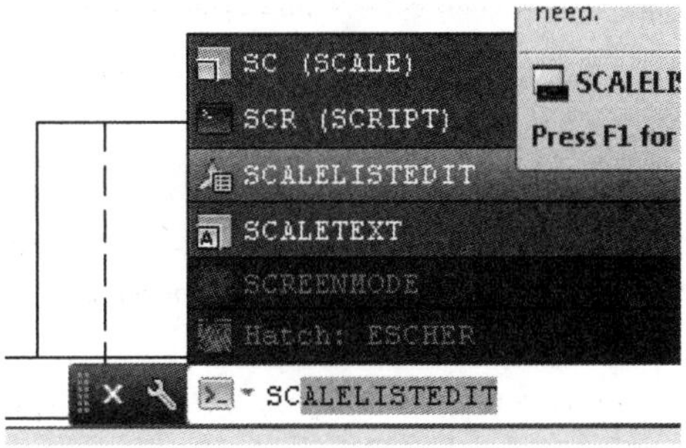

If you press the <TAB> key, AutoCAD will advance your cursor down the list of available commands.

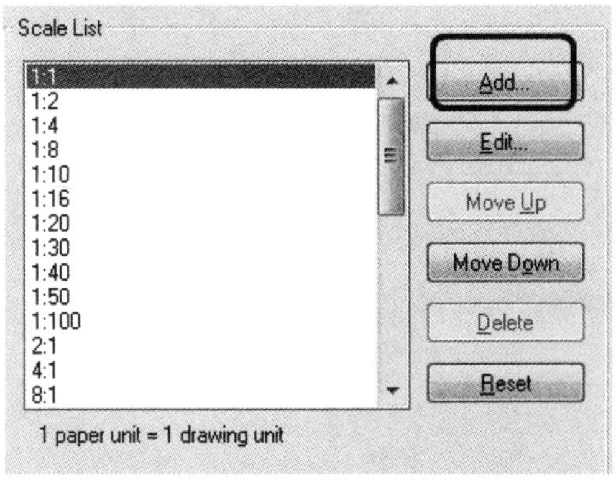

The list of available scales is shown.

10. Press the **Add** button.
11. Type **3:1** in the first field.

    Set the paper units to **3**.
    Set the drawing units to **1**.

12. Press **OK**.

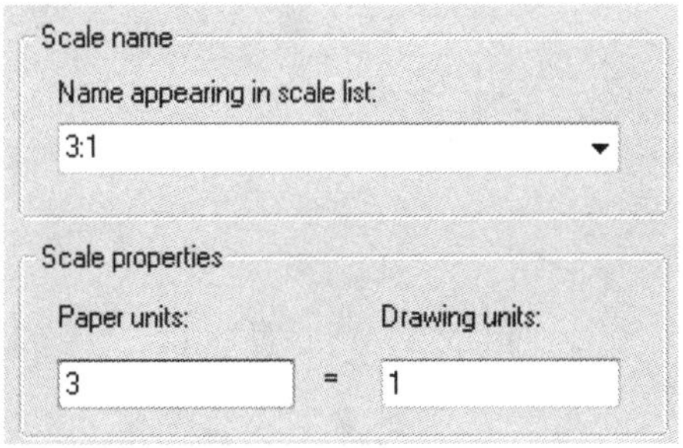

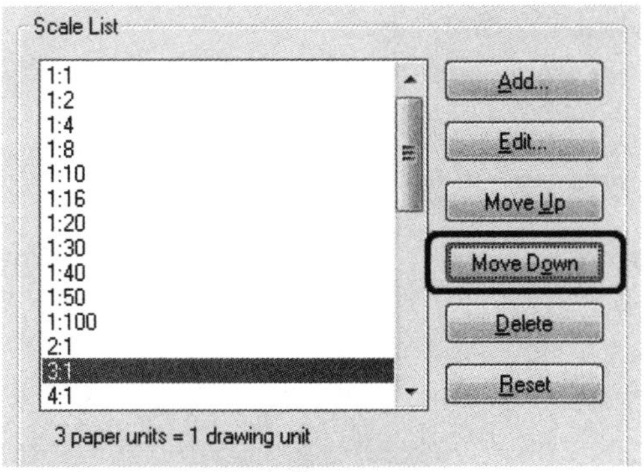

13. Use the **Move Down** button to position the 3:1 scale between the 2:1 and 4:1 scales.
14. Press **OK**.

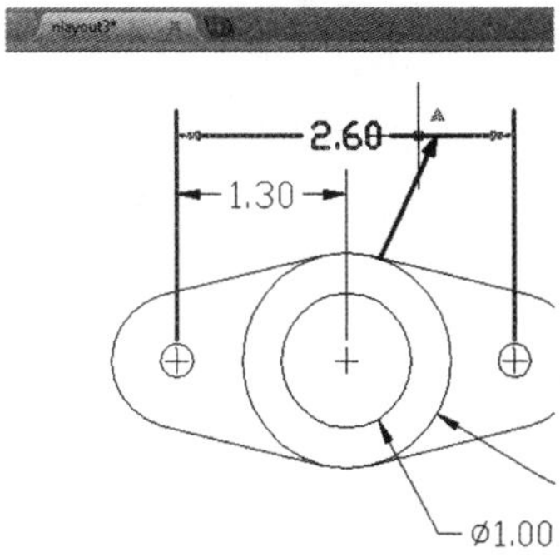

Note when you mouse over the 2.60 dimension, a small icon now appears indicating that it is an annotative dimension.

15. Select the 2.60 dimension so it is highlighted.

The Annotative scale field appears.

16. Select the **...** button.

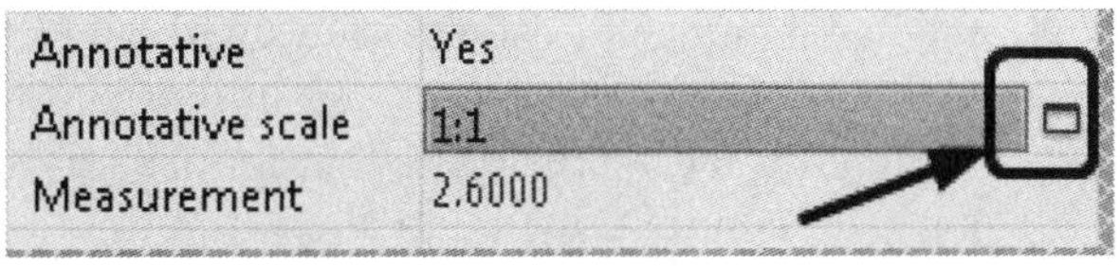

17. Select the **Add** button.

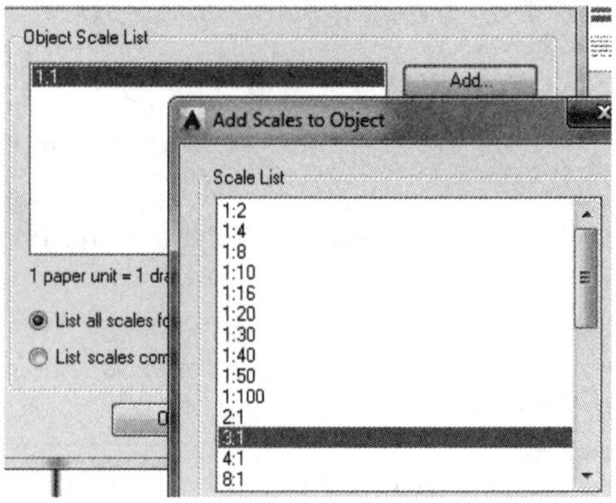

*The **3:1** scale is now included in the list.*

18. Select the 3:1 scale and press **OK**.

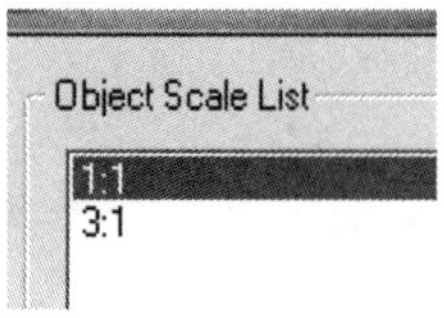

The 3:1 scale is now available as an annotative scale.

19. Press **OK**.

20. Set the remaining dimensions to Annotative and assign the 3:1 scale to them. You can select all the dimensions as a group and set them Annotative and add the 3:1 scale.

You do not have to select each one individually.

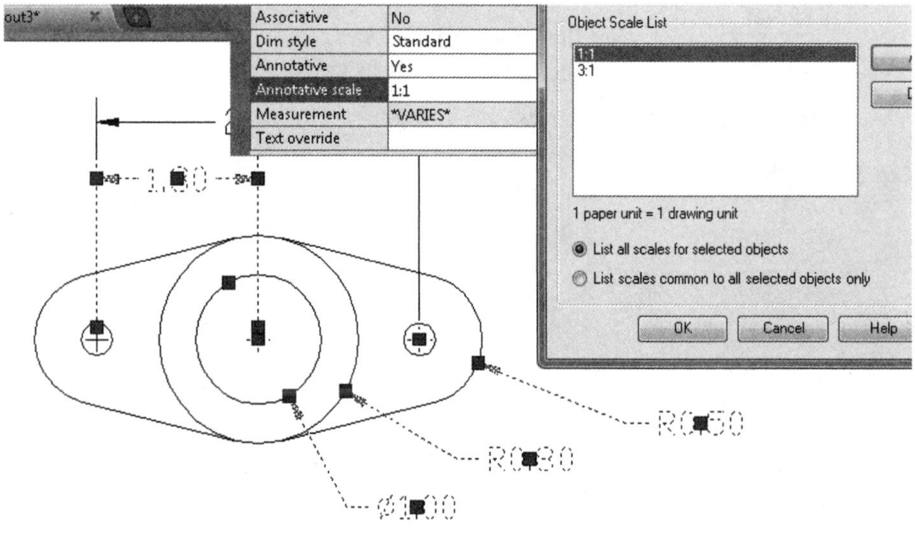

Note when you mouse over the dimensions, the Annotative icon now shows that more than one Annotative scale is available.

The number of clouds indicate the number of scales available.

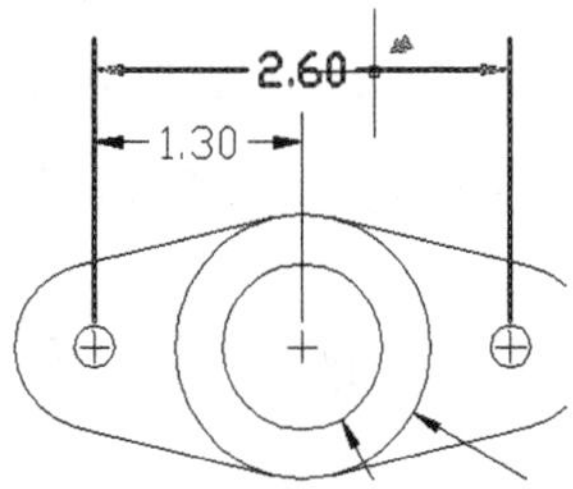

- Make modifications to the drawing any time in the Model tab. Select Layout to switch back to the drawing Layout.
- Avoid placing one floating viewport inside another, as it may be difficult to select a floating model space viewport.
- After the drawing view is properly scaled in the floating MODEL space viewport, use the Pan command to adjust views without changing the scale.
- You can insert several drawings into model space using the INSERT or XREF command. Then create a layout for each drawing. Using this method, you can set up a master control drawing to allow you to view a complete drawing package.

Command Exercise

Exercise 12-5 – Using Annotative Scales

Drawing Name: **nlayout4.dwg**
Estimated Time to Completion: 5 Minutes

Scope

Change the annotative scale used by a viewport.

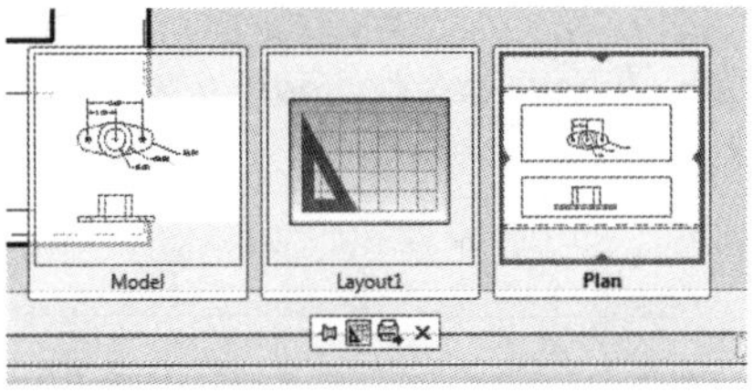

Change Annotative Scale Exercise

Solution

1. Verify that the **Plan** tab is active.

2. Select the top viewport so it is highlighted.

The Status Bar updates to show the VP Scale (viewport scale) and whether an Annotation Scale is applied.

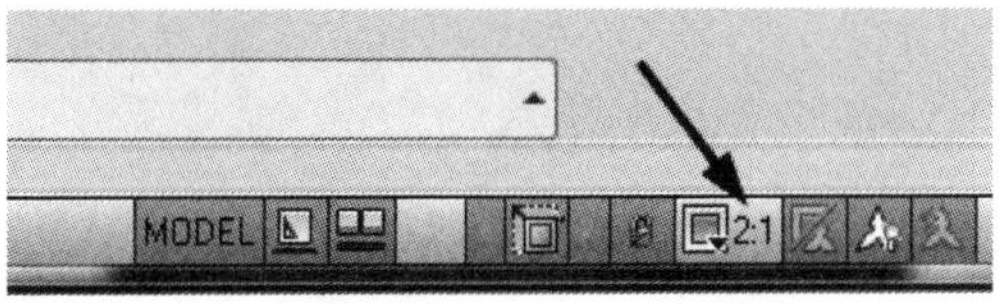

With the top viewport selected:

In the Quick Properties dialog:

3. Set Display Locked to **No**.
4. Left click on the down arrow next to the Annotation Scale and you will see the list of scales available.
5. Select **3:1**.

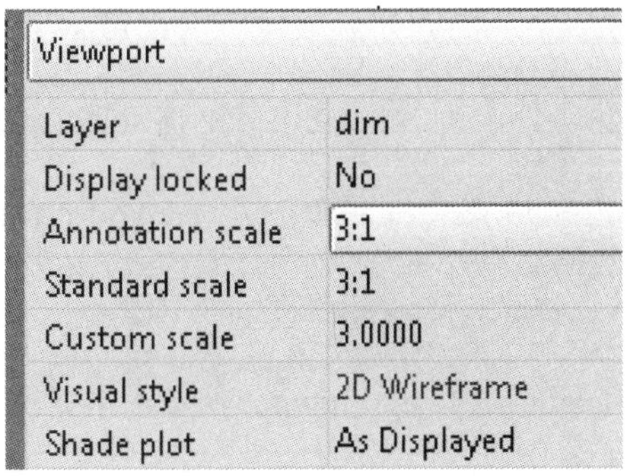

Note how the dimensions change size.

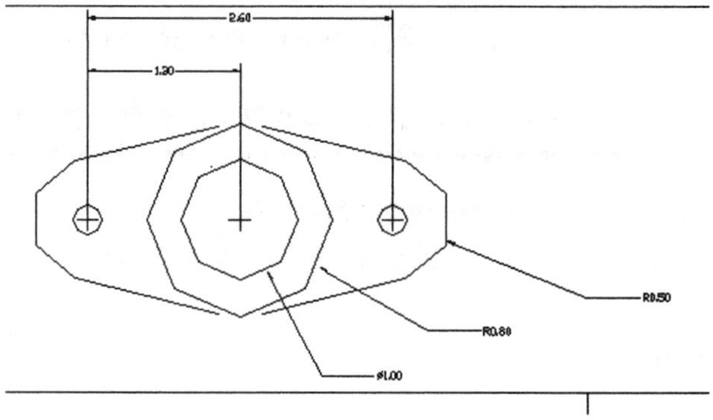

6. Select the Model tab.

Note that the actual size of the dimensions has not changed.

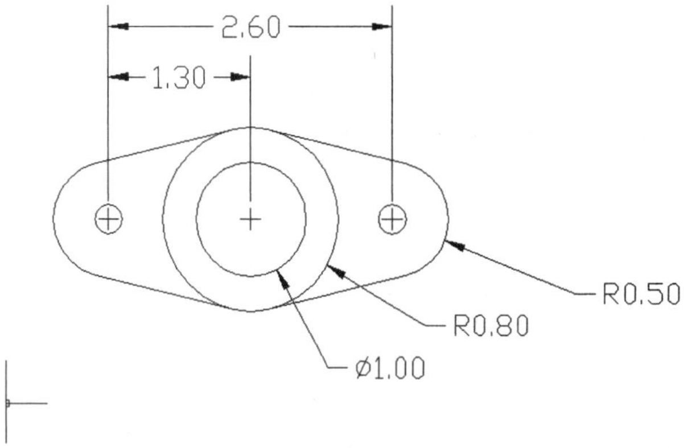

Tips & Tricks

➢ To display the active workspace on the status bar, enable **Display Workspace Label.**

Command Exercise

Exercise 12-6 – Rotating a Viewport

Drawing Name: **rviewport.dwg**
Estimated Time to Completion: 5 Minutes

Scope

Rotate a viewport.

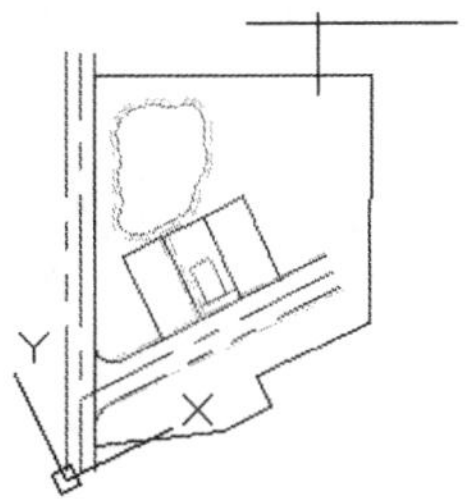

Rotate Viewport Exercise

Solution

1. Verify that the **Layout1** tab is active.

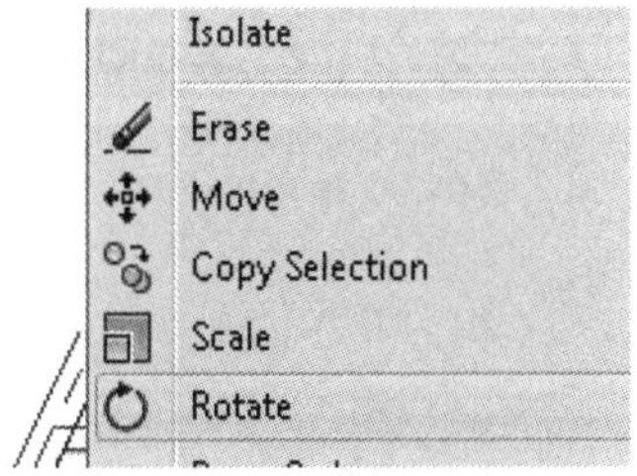

2. Select the viewport.
3. RMB and select **Rotate**.
4. Select the lower left corner of the viewport as the basepoint.
5. Type **26** for the rotation angle.

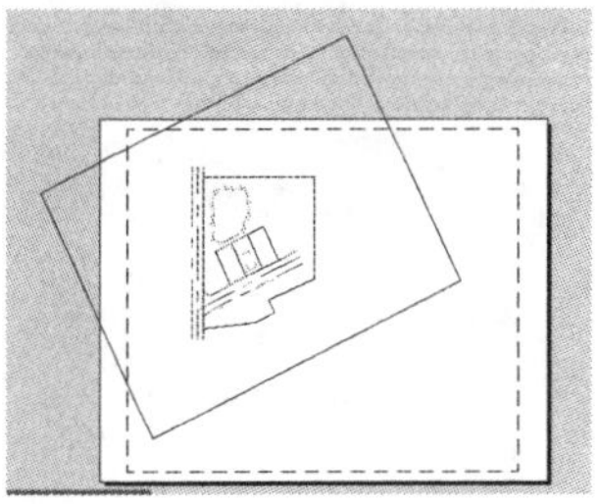

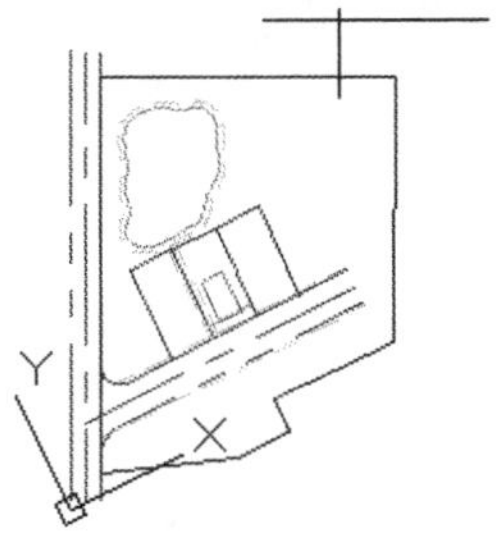

The viewport is rotated.

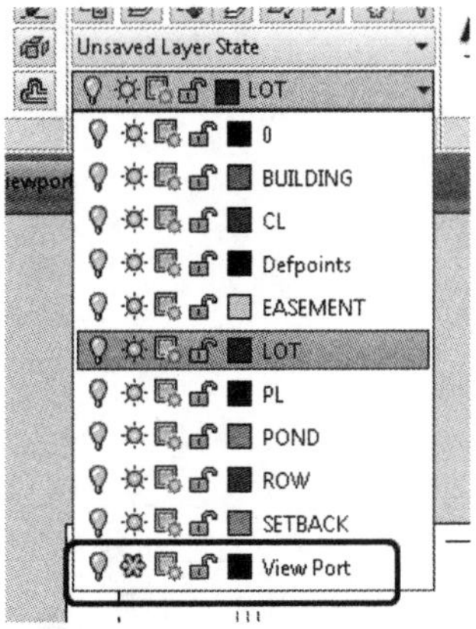

6. Freeze the viewport layer.
7. Select the **MODEL** tab.

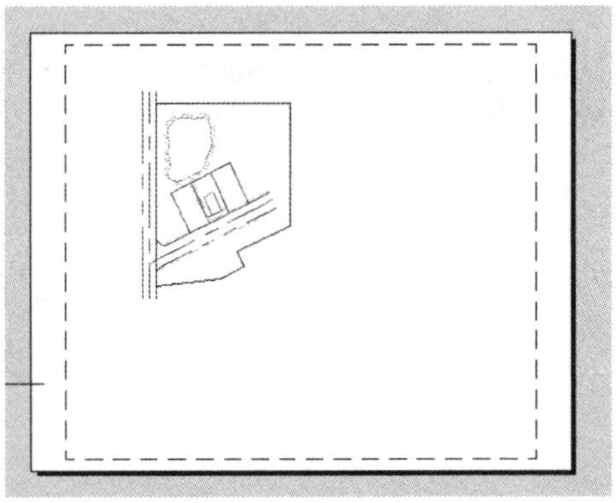

Your rotated view should look like this.

Notice the objects have not rotated in the model tab.

Command Exercise

Exercise 12-7 – Controlling Viewport Properties

Drawing Name: **paper2.dwg**
Estimated Time to Completion: 5 Minutes

Scope

Make the floating viewport window frame invisible. Use the Properties Command to set the viewport frame on the VP layer. Freeze the VP layer. Fill in the information in the title block.

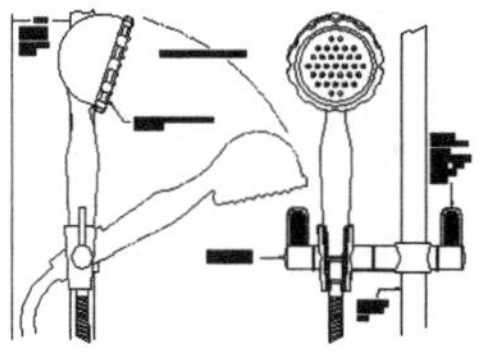

Drawing Layouts Exercise

Solution

1. Select the Layout1 tab at the bottom left corner of the drawing window.

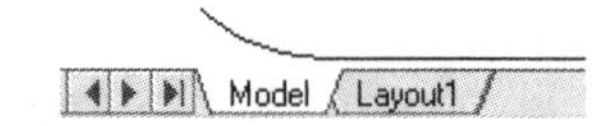

2. Set your workspace to **Drafting & Annotation**.

Verify that Paper space is set at the Status line.

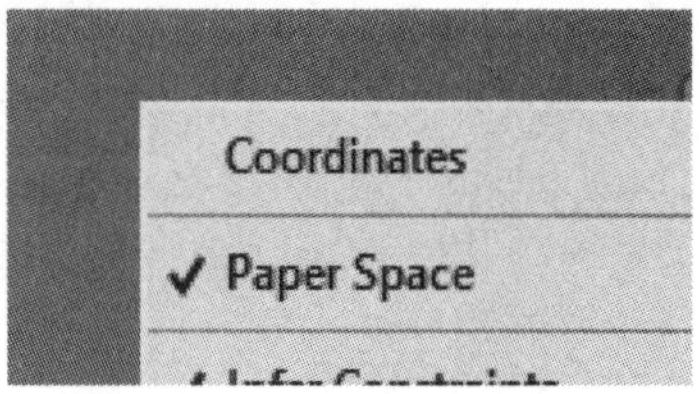

If you don't see the PAPER/MODEL toggle on the status bar, right click on the status bar and enable it.

3. Select the border of the single viewport with the LMB and change the layer to **VP** in the Quick Properties dialog.

   Notice that the single viewport window frame changes color. It is now on the VP layer.

4. Deselect the viewport by pressing **<ESC>**.

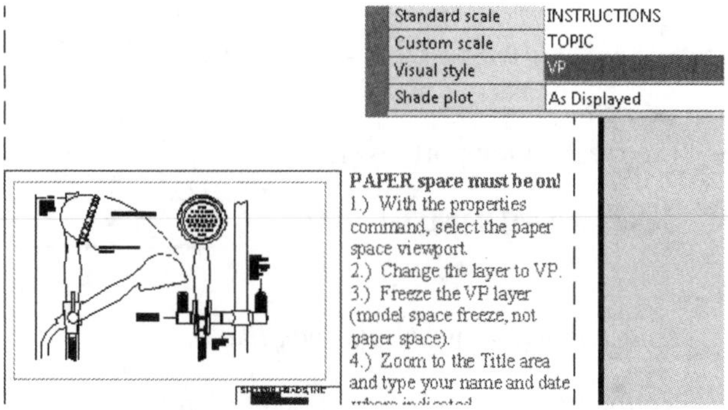

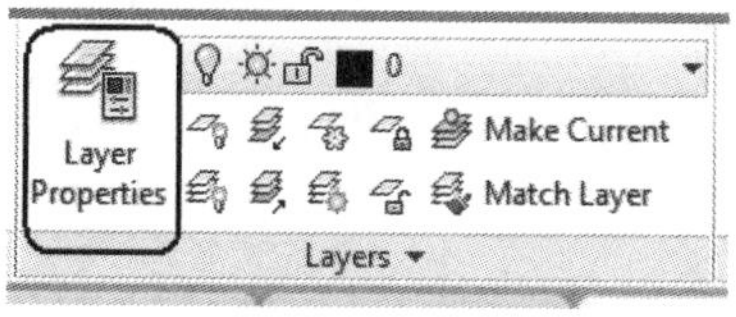

5. Activate the **Home** ribbon.
6. Select the **Layer Properties** tool.

7. Set the VP layer to **No Plot**.

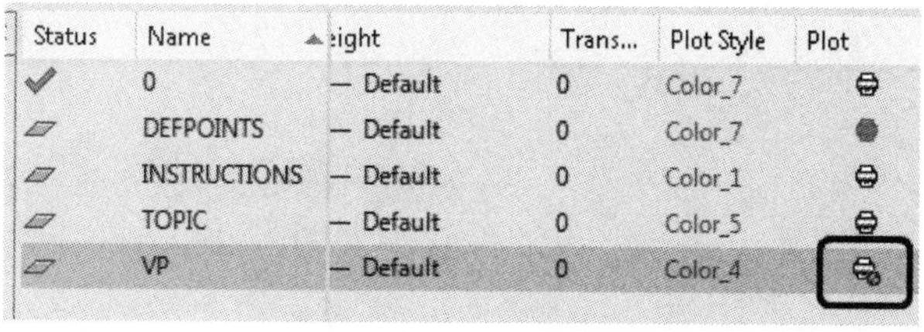

> ➢ When a layer is set to **No Plot**, it can remain visible but won't be printed.

8. Close the Layer Properties Manager.

9. Activate the **Output** ribbon.
10. Select **Preview**.

The Plot preview shows that the Viewport border is not visible.

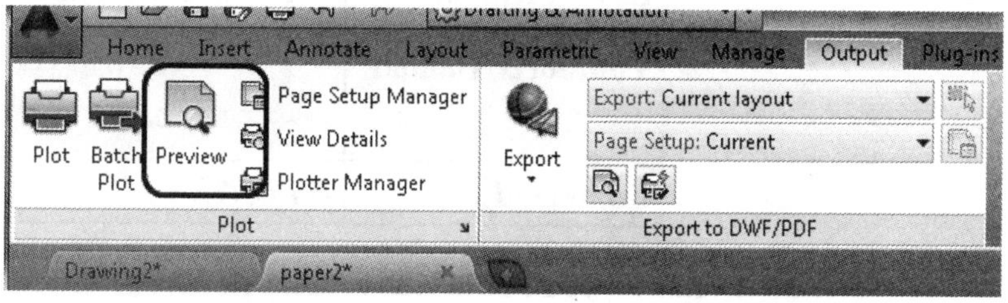

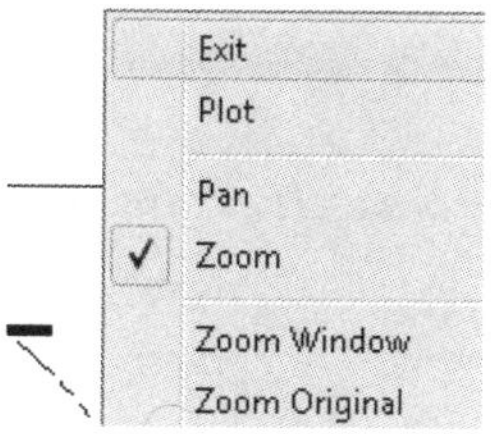

11. Right click and select **Exit** to exit the preview mode.

> ➢ *The white area in the layout indicates the actual piece of paper. The paper size is controlled in the Page Setup dialog box.*

Nonrectangular Viewport

Command Locator

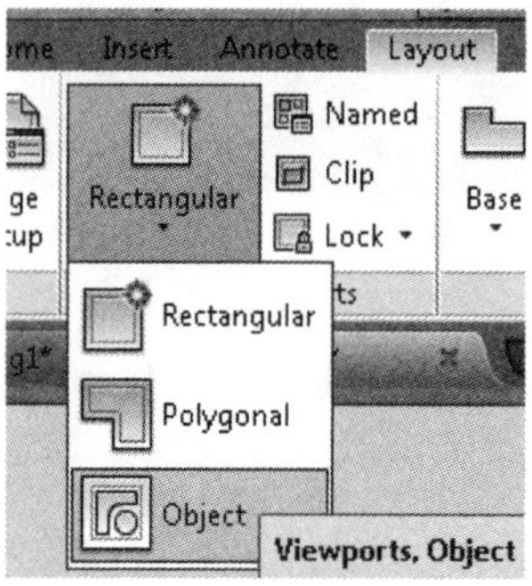

Layout Ribbon	*Layout Viewports/Polygonal or Object*
Viewports Toolbar	
Command	*-VPORTS*

Command Overview

Non-rectangular viewports can be used to create a cropped view of a very specific area. They also can be used to create a more interesting and visually appealing lay-out.

General Procedures

1. Select the Polygonal Viewport tool.
2. Select points to define the polygonal shape.
3. Close the shape and the polygonal viewport will be created and placed.

Command Exercise

Exercise 12-8 – Nonrectangular Viewport

Drawing Name: **nrview1.dwg**
Estimated Time to Completion: 10 Minutes

Scope

Create a viewport by drawing a hexagon. Then use the object option to create a viewport out of the star shape already in the drawing.

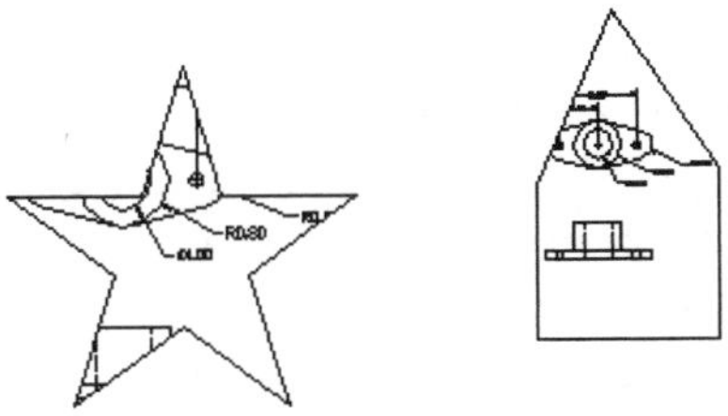

Nonrectangular Viewport Exercise

Solution

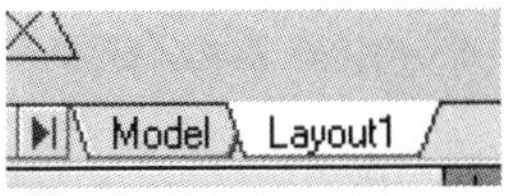

1. Select the Layout1 tab at the bottom left corner of the drawing window.

2. Set your workspace to **Drafting & Annotation**.

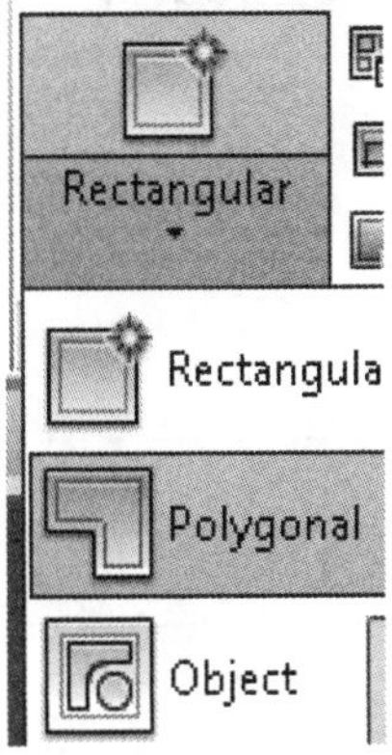

3. Invoke the **Polygonal Viewport** command, and from the Layout ribbon, select **Polygonal**.

Specify start point:

4. Draw a closed hexagon shape; do not worry about it being a perfect hexagon.

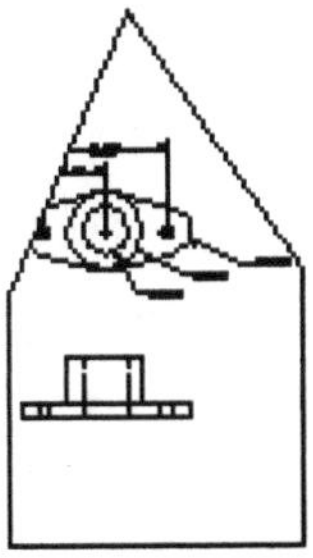

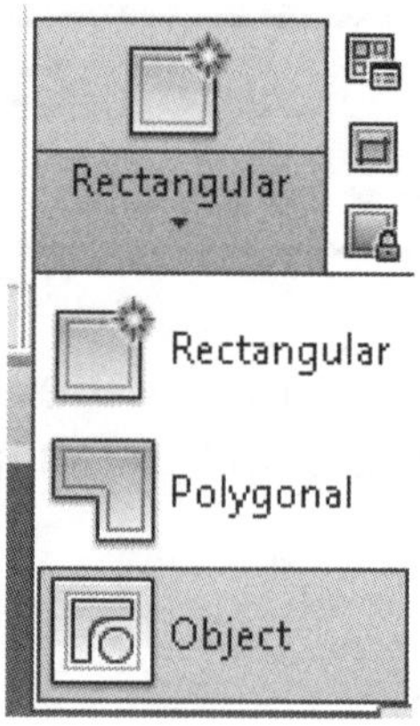
Rectangular
Rectangular
Polygonal
Object

5. Select the **Object** tool on the Layout ribbon.

   This is located as a drop-down under the Polygonal tool.

Select object to clip viewport:

6. Select the star shape.

Extra: *Activate each viewport and get the view to look proper.*

- *To use the **From Object** viewport tool, simply sketch out the desired viewport shape using lines, arcs, and circles. The object must be a closed polygonal shape with no gaps, openings, or intersecting lines.*

Page Setup

Command Locator

Output Ribbon	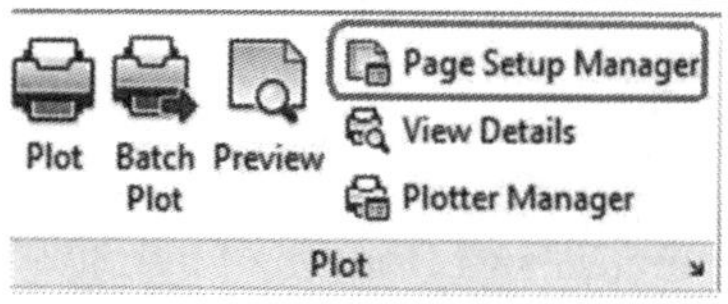Page Setup Manager View Details Plotter Manager Plot Batch Plot Preview Plot
Toolbar Menu	**Layouts→Page Setup**
Pull Down Menu	**File→Page Setup…**
Command	**pagesetup**
RMB Shortcut Menu	**Right-click on the tab of the current layout/Page Setup…**
Dialog Box	**Page Setup**

Command Overview

The Page Setup command is a mixture of the old plot dialog box from earlier releases of AutoCAD and most windows print setup dialog boxes. In this dialog box, you can set up the layout and plotter settings for the current layout. This command is run automatically every time you select a layout tab that has not yet been set up. It is typically run whenever you create a new layout, unless this setting has been turned off by unchecking the 'Display when creating a new layout' checkbox at the bottom of the dialog box. The page setup is saved with its layout, so each layout in a drawing can have a different page setup.

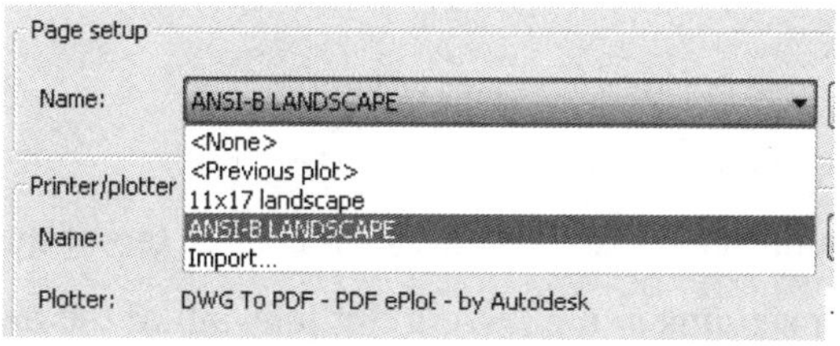

You may edit the name of the layout in the Layout name field. The Page setup name is a drop-down list of available named page setups from which you can select a setup to apply to the current layout. If the setup you want is not in the available list, but is in a different drawing, or if you want to add a named setup, press the 'Add' button. This will open the User Defined Page Setups dialog box.

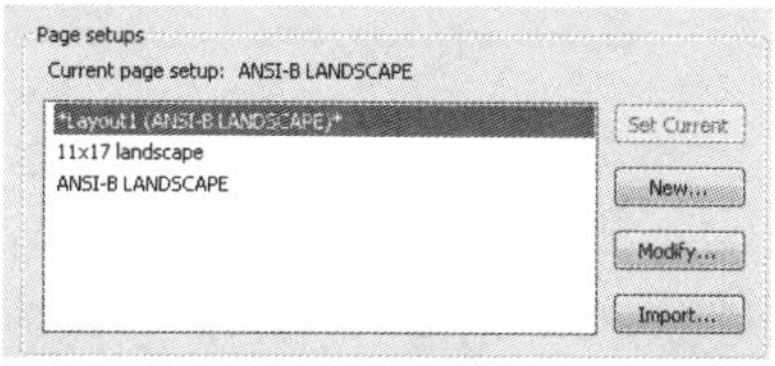

To create a named page setup from the current settings, type in the name in the top field and press 'OK'. To rename an existing setup, click on the name of the setup to highlight it, press 'Rename' and type in a new name. To delete an existing setup, click on the name of the setup to highlight it and press 'Delete'. To import a setup from another file, press 'Import'. Select the file with the setup in the Select File dialog box and select the setup from the dialog box that opens.

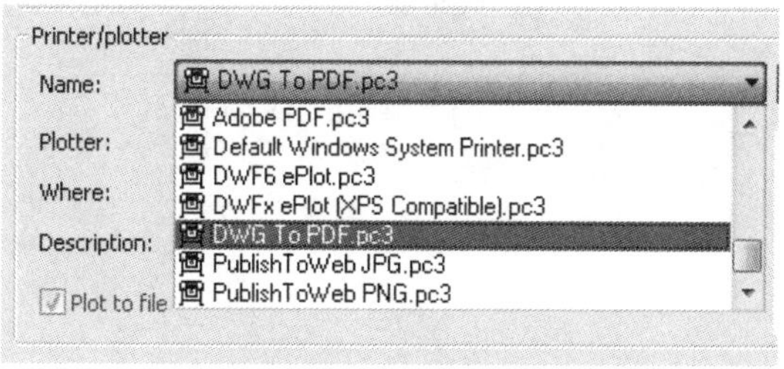

The Plot Device tab of the dialog box allows you to select the plotter to use for the layout, its properties and a plot style table. There is a drop-down list of currently available printer/plotters. You must make sure to set up your printer/plotter in Windows before selecting it here. The 'Properties…' button opens the Plotter Configuration Editor dialog box.

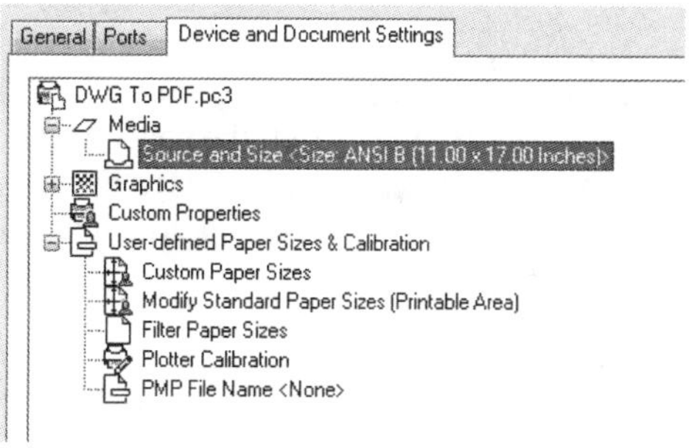

The Properties button for the selected printer brings up the Plotter Configuration dialog box. The General tab displays general information about the drivers for the selected printer/plotter. The Ports tab allows you to set which port to print to including the ability to print to a file or to a spool. The Device and Document Settings tab has many settings for the media to use, graphic quality, etc. Click on the setting to adjust and the bottom of the dialog box shows available settings to adjust.

Back in the Plot Device tab of the Page Setup dialog box, you may also select a plot style table to use for the layout. A plot style adjusts the color, lineweight, linetype, fill style, and other settings for plotted output. They are covered in more detail later in this section.

General Procedures

1. Invoke the Page Setup command.
2. Set the plotter configuration and style in the Plot Device tab of the dialog box.
3. Set the rest of the plot settings in the Layout Settings tab of the dialog box.
4. Press 'OK'.

Layout Wizard

Command Locator

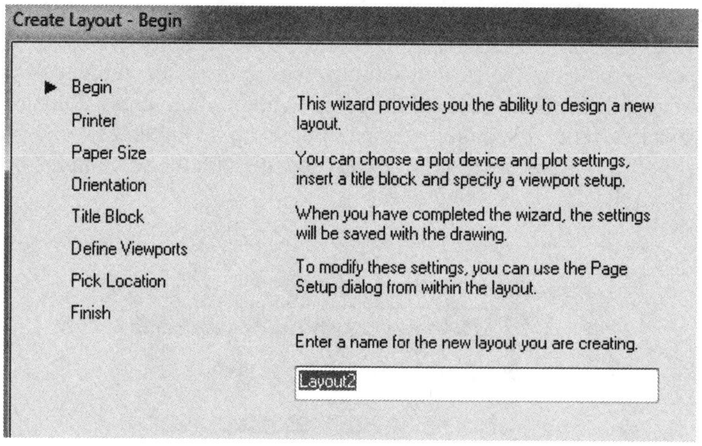

Command	**layoutwizard**
Dialog Box	**Create Layout**

Command Overview

The Layout Wizard quickly steps through all of the settings to create a layout from the beginning. The wizard prompts you for the plotter to associate with the layout, the paper size to use, orientation of the paper, title block to insert and viewports to create. This is all done in a step by step dialog box. Once all of the prompts are responded to, the command creates the layout according to your settings.

General Procedures

1. Type 'layoutwizard' on the command line.
2. Type in the name of the new layout in the Create Layout – Begin dialog box and press 'Next>'.
3. Select a plotter/printer from the list in the Create Layout – Printer dialog box and press 'Next>'.
4. Select a paper size and the drawing units in the Create Layout – Paper Size dialog box and press 'Next>'.
5. Select the orientation in the Create Layout – Orientation dialog box and press 'Next>'.
6. Select a title block and type of insertion in the Create Layout – Title Block dialog box and press 'Next>'.
7. Select the viewport setup and scale in the Create Layout – Define Viewports dialog box and press 'Next>'.
8. Set the location of the viewport(s) in the Create Layout – Pick Location dialog box and press 'Next>'.
9. Press 'Finish'.

Tips & Tricks

- Use the Layout from Wizard command to create a layout using a step by step interface that is simple to follow.
- The templates linked to the Layout Wizard Dialog are located using the Files Options setting for templates. If you do not see any templates files in the dialog, reset the path for the templates on the Files tab in the Options dialog.

Command Exercise

Exercise 12-9 – Layout Wizard

Drawing Name: **wlayout.dwg**
Estimated Time to Completion: 10 Minutes

Scope

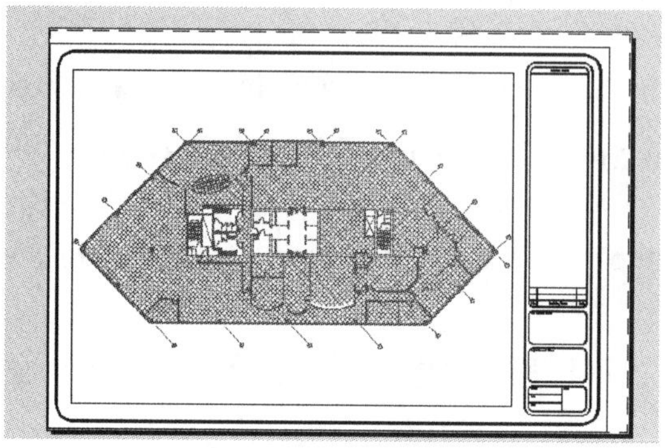

Layout Wizard Exercise

Solution

1. Type **LAYOUTWIZARD** at the command prompt.

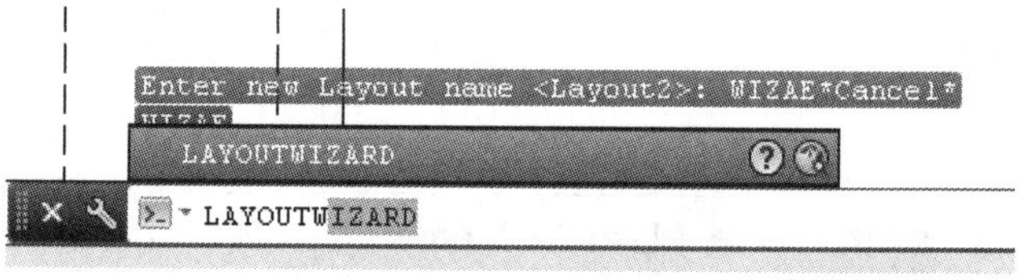
Enter new Layout name <Layout2>: WIZAE*Cancel*
LAYOUTWIZARD
LAYOUTWIZARD

2. In the Create Layout – Begin dialog box, type in **Wizard** and press **Next**.

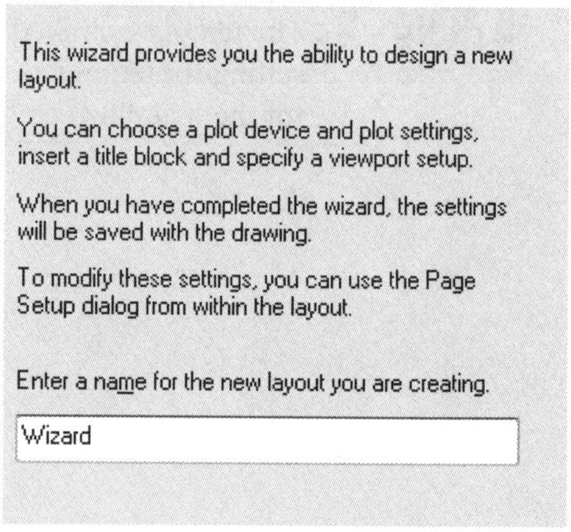
This wizard provides you the ability to design a new layout.
You can choose a plot device and plot settings, insert a title block and specify a viewport setup.
When you have completed the wizard, the settings will be saved with the drawing.
To modify these settings, you can use the Page Setup dialog from within the layout.
Enter a name for the new layout you are creating.
Wizard

3. In the Select a configured plotter, select **AutoCAD PDF (General Documenation).pc3** and press **Next>**.

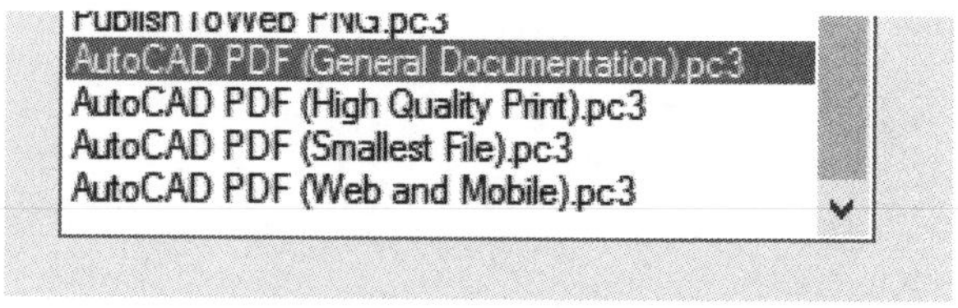
AutoCAD PDF (General Documentation).pc3
AutoCAD PDF (High Quality Print).pc3
AutoCAD PDF (Smallest File).pc3
AutoCAD PDF (Web and Mobile).pc3

Your plotter list will look different than mine unless you have the same printers I have in my office.

4. In the Create Layout – Paper Size dialog box, select **ARCH D (24 x 36 in)** from the drop–down list and Inches for units and press **Next>**.

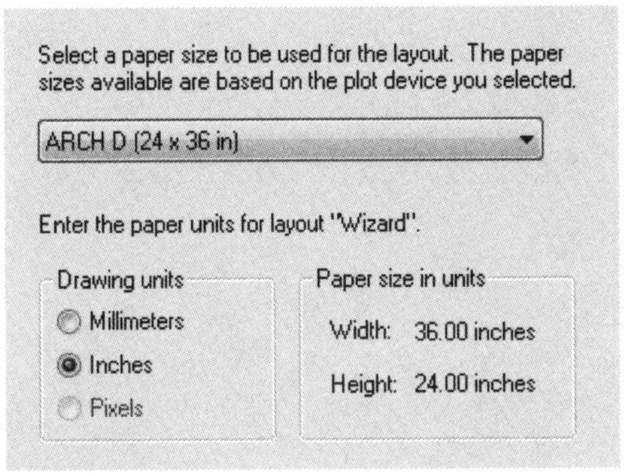

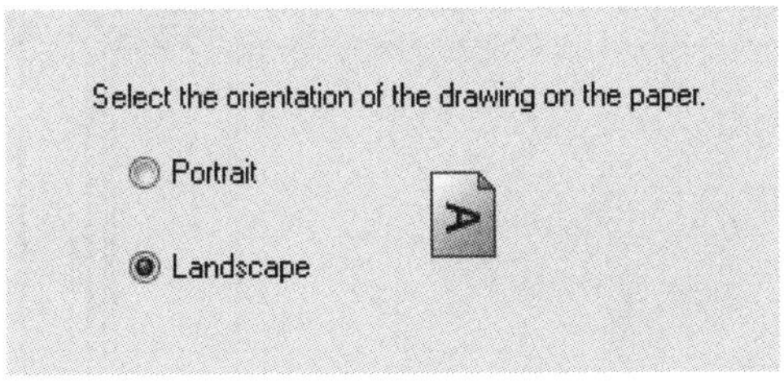

5. In the Create Layout – Orientation dialog box, select '**Landscape**' and press **Next>**.

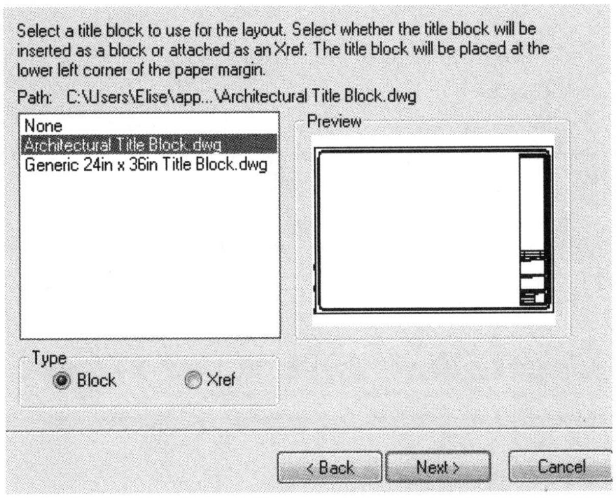

6. In the Create Layout – Title Block dialog box, select ***Architectural Title Block.dwg*** from the list.

7. Select **Block** for the type and press **Next>**.

You will not see the list of title blocks unless you have set the Drawing Template path properly on the Files tab in the Option Dialog. If you want to use a custom title block set the path to the file in the Options Dialog.

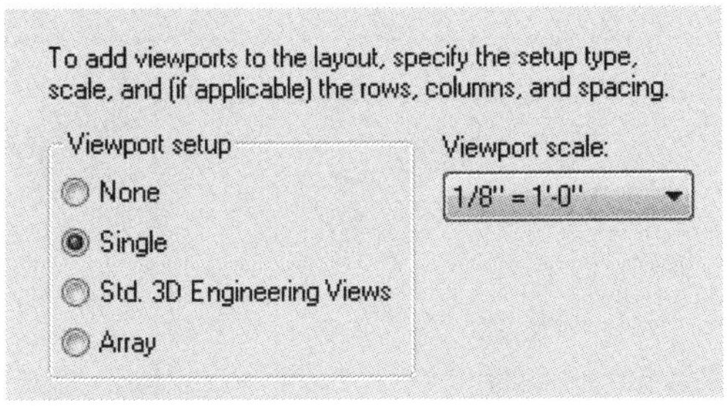

8. In the Create Layout – Define Viewports dialog box, select a **Single** Viewport Setup.

9. Select **1/8″= 1′-0″** from the scale drop–down list and press **Next>**.

10. In the Create Layout – Pick Location dialog box, press **Select location <**.

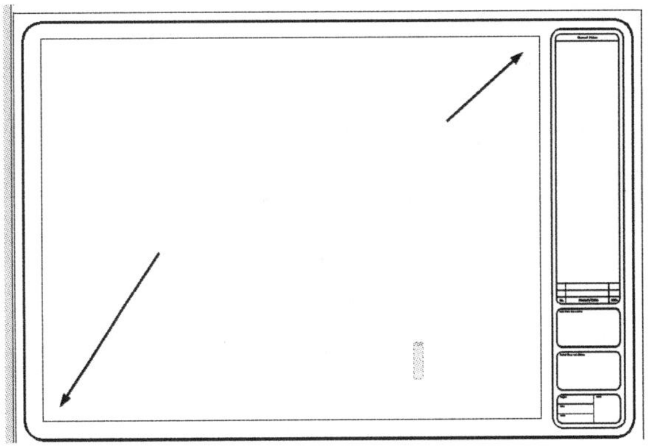

11. *Specify first corner:*
    Select a corner of the viewport to create just inside the title block.

12. *Specify opposite corner:*
    Select the opposite corner of the viewport to create.

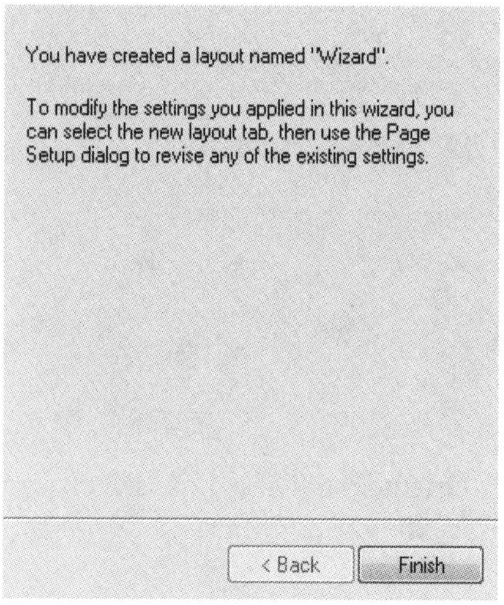
You have created a layout named "Wizard".
To modify the settings you applied in this wizard, you can select the new layout tab, then use the Page Setup dialog to revise any of the existing settings.
< Back
Finish

Note that the name of the layout is Wizard.

13. In the Create Layout Finish dialog box, press **Finish**.

14. Double click in the viewport to activate.

15. Zoom Extents to see the model layout.

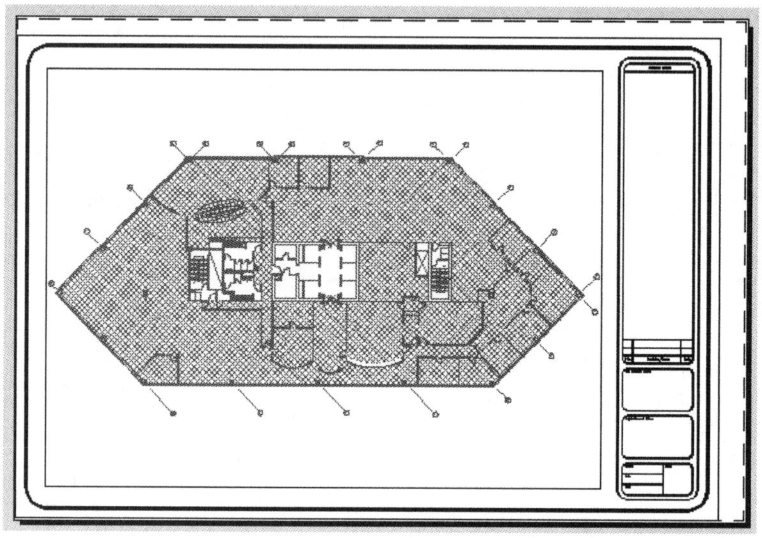

Controlling Layers per Viewport

Command Locator

Home ribbon	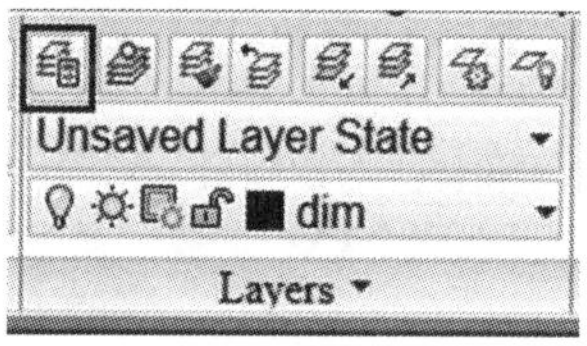Unsaved Layer State dim Layers
Pull Down Menu	**Format →Layer…**
Command	**Layer**
Alias	**La**
Dialog Box	**Layer Properties Manager**

Command Overview

With TILE mode off and MODEL Space on, layers can be frozen in selected viewports. The Layer Control Dialog has two columns: 'Active VP Freeze' and 'New VP Freeze'.

Options:

Active VP Freeze – This will freeze a selected layer in the active viewport.
New VP Freeze – This will freeze a selected layer in any new viewport created.

General Procedures

Freezing Layers in Active Viewport Only:

1. Select a floating model space viewport (TILE should be OFF, MODEL should be ON in the Status Bar).
2. Select the layer from the Layers Dialog Box and select Active VP Freeze.
3. Select OK.

Freezing Layers in New Viewports Only:

1. Invoke the Layer command.
2. Select the layer from the Layers Dialog Box and select New VP Freeze.
3. Select OK.

Command Exercise

Exercise 12-10 – Controlling Layers per Viewport

Drawing Name: **pslayer1.dwg**
Estimated Time to Completion: 5 Minutes

Scope

Switch to Paper Space and freeze (in paper space) the layers in the selected viewports, as indicated in the drawing. Freeze (in model space) the layers VP, which contain the paper space viewport borders and Notes.

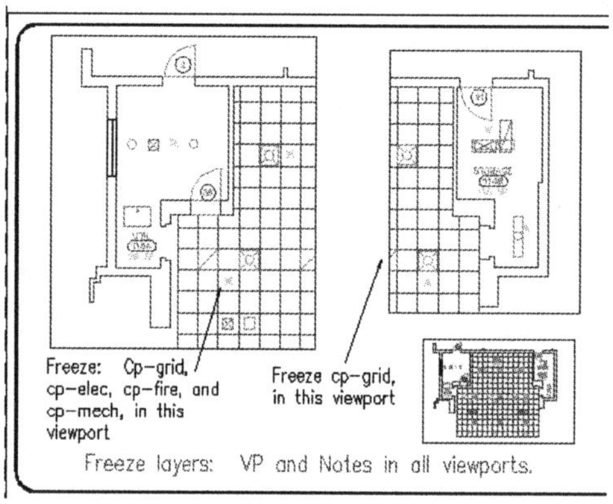
Freeze: Cp-grid, cp-elec, cp-fire, and cp-mech, in this viewport
Freeze cp-grid, in this viewport
Freeze layers: VP and Notes in all viewports.

Viewport Layers Exercise

Solution

1. Switch to Layout 1 by clicking on its tab at the bottom of the drawing window.

Model
Layout1

2. Activate the upper left viewport by double clicking within the viewport area.

3. Activate the Home ribbon.

4. Select the Layers **CP–GRID**, **CP–FIRE**, **CP–ELEC**, and **CP–MECH** in the Layer drop-down and enable the Freeze in Current Viewport option.

Simply left click on the Freeze in Current Viewport icon to enable.

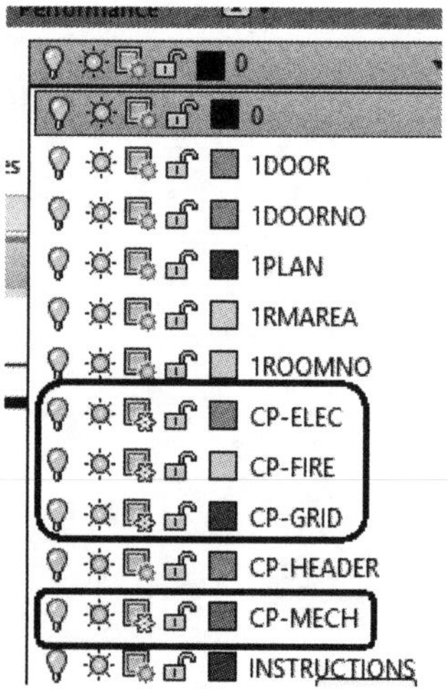
0
0
1DOOR
1DOORNO
1PLAN
1RMAREA
1ROOMNO
CP-ELEC
CP-FIRE
CP-GRID
CP-HEADER
CP-MECH
INSTRUCTIONS

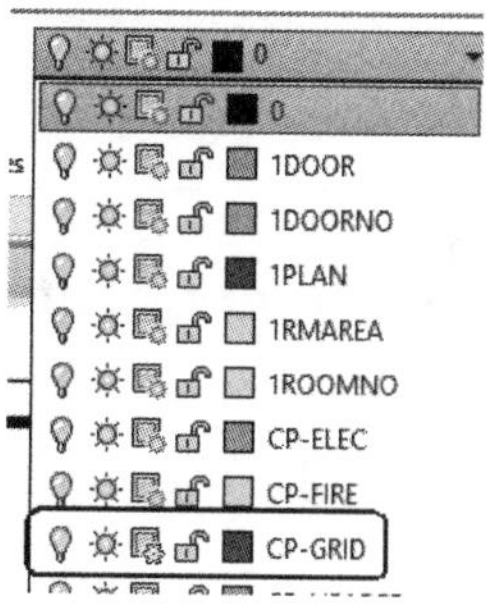

5. Activate the upper right viewport by clicking within its border.

6. Using the Layer drop-down list freeze the layer CP–GRID in that viewport.

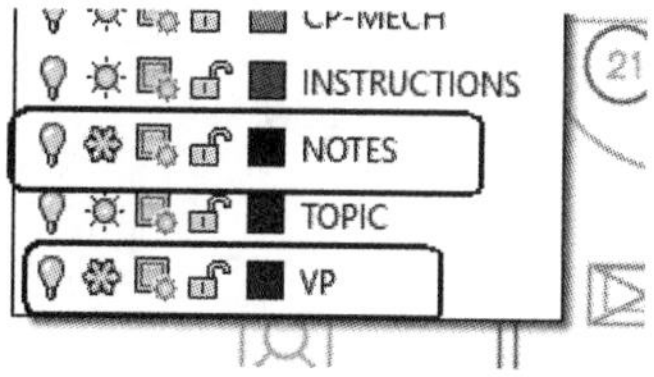

7. Freeze the layers named **VP** and **Notes** in all view ports by selecting the Layer Control drop down list and choosing the **Freeze in ALL viewports** icon for both layers.

Compare the three viewports.

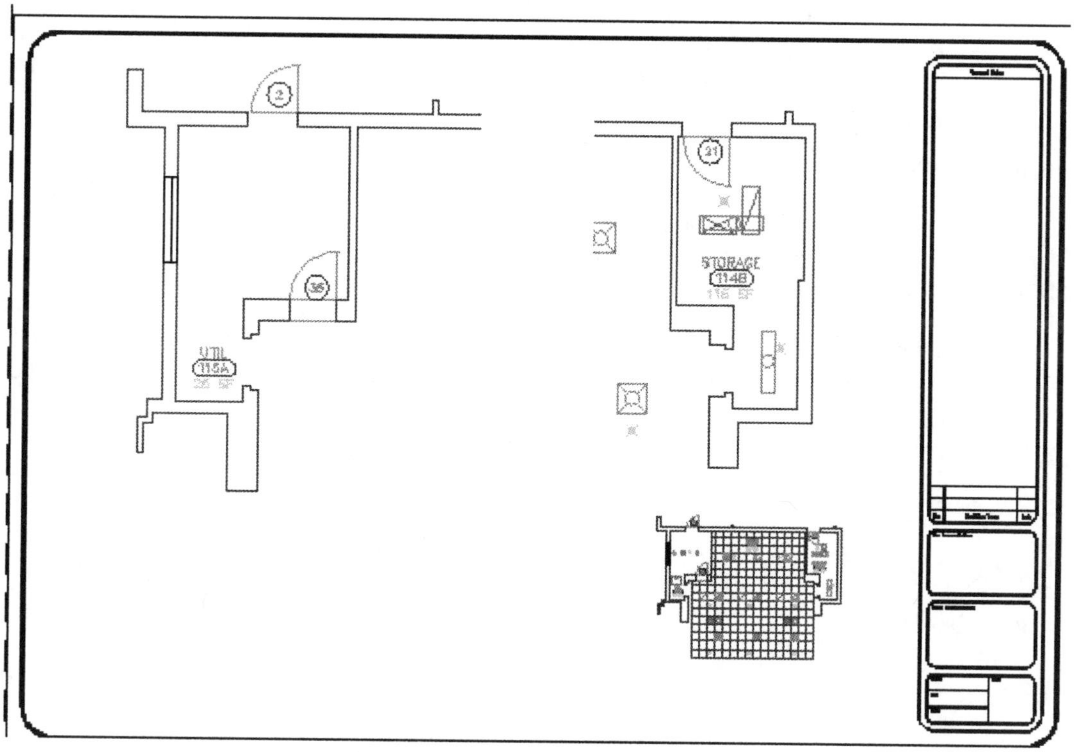

Plot

Command Locator

Output Ribbon	
Toolbar Menu	**Standard** 
Pull Down Menu	**File →Plot**
Command	**Plot**
Alias	**Ctrl+P**
Dialog Box	**Plot**

Command Overview

Drawings may be plotted from the Model tab or the Layout tab. For 2-dimensional drawings, the user may opt to plot either way, though there are certain advantages to plotting from the Layout tab, such as including multiple views of the same drawing. For 3-dimensional drawing, it is necessary to use the Layout tab to print multiple views, such as a top, front and side view, of the 3-D Model on a single page. The Plot command will bring up the Page Setup dialog box. This dialog box includes the Plot Device tab and the Plot Settings tab. Basic options will be covered in this Tutorial. In addition to the plot command is the Preview Plot command, which previews a plot according to the latest plot settings.

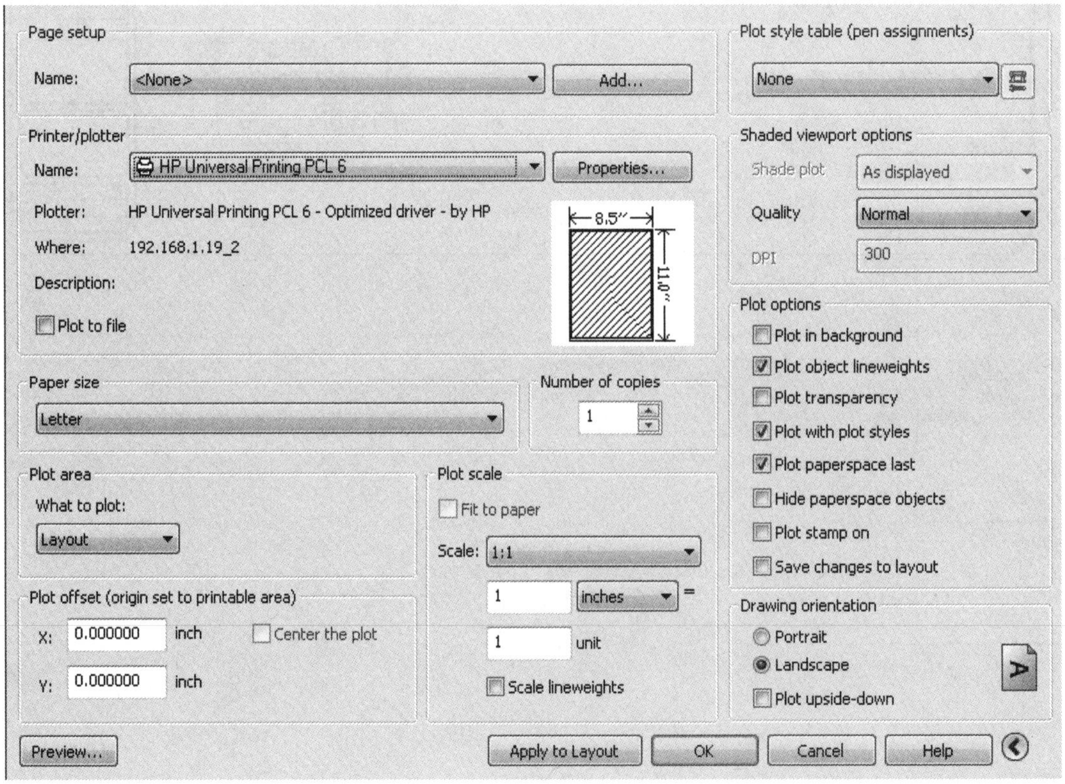

Plot Dialog Box

Plot Option	Overview	Typical Options to Choose
Plotter Configuration	Select a Plotting device from the drop down list if the desired plotter does not appear at the top of this list. Select the Properties button to make changes to the Plotter Settings.	Use the default Plotter. Select a different plotter from the drop down list.
Plot Style Table **(pen assignments)**	This section allows the user to assign color numbers to pen numbers and set how objects are plotted.	Use the default setting (none)
What to Plot	Allows the user to plot all of the Layout tabs or only the Current tab. Multiple copies can be specified.	Current tab Selected tab All Layout tabs Any number of copies
Plot to File	This section allows the user to create a plot file (.plt) instead of an actual plot. Plot files contain the drawing information with all of the Plot command settings and can be plotted later.	None (leave blank)
Paper size and paper units	The available paper sizes will depend on the plotting device. The printable area will always be less than the paper size because the rollers on the printer need to feed the paper through the machine. The printable area also depends on the printing device. Choose inches or mm, depending on the drawing units.	Select the paper size from the drop down list.
Drawing orientation	Choose Portrait, Landscape, or Plot upside-down. It is usually necessary to Preview the drawing first, to know which drawing orientation is correct.	Do a Full Preview first, then select Portrait or Landscape as required.
Plot area	The options in this area pertain to the part of the drawing that gets plotted: the drawing Limits, the drawing Extents, the current Display, or choose Window to make a window around the part of the drawing to plot.	Plot Limits *or* Select Window and make a window around the drawing area to plot.
Plot scale	This area controls the Plot scale. It is very easy at first to select "Scale to Fit"; however, eventually the user should learn how to plot to a specified scale.	Select or type a Plot Scale
Plot offset	The default start point for the plot area is 0,0. To change this, type another coordinate or select "Center the plot" (as best as possible).	(Either setting)
Plot options	The miscellaneous options in this section include to Plot with the lineweights that were set in the Layers dialog box, and plot using a pre-set plot style (Hide plot is for 3D drawings.	Plot with lineweights
Full Preview	Select this button for a full Plot preview. Press the RMB (to exit) to preview and return to the Plot dialog box. If there is something wrong with the preview, make adjustments in the Plot dialog box, and Preview again.	Select this option
Partial Preview	This is usually a quicker plot preview, especially if the drawing is large. The paper size, the printable area, the area that will contain the plot and warnings for errors will be listed.	

General Procedures

Plot a drawing:

1. Invoke the Plot command.
2. Select the Plotter and Paper size.
3. Select the Plot area. Select or type the Plot scale.
4. Select "Full Preview." Right-click in the preview page and Exit to continue. Make any necessary adjustment to the Plot settings. Then press OK to plot.

Set up a Drawing to Plot the Layout tab:

1. Create the drawing in the Model tab.
2. Select the Layout tab in the Drawing Window. Select OK to accept the Page Setup Layout defaults.
3. Insert a Title Block where the insertion point is 0,0, the x and y scale factors are 0, and the rotation angle is 0.
4. Use grips to re-size the existing viewport, or use the Viewports command options to create additional viewports.
5. Select PAPER in the Status Bar. This will switch the viewport mode to floating MODEL space. Select a viewport and Zoom the drawing view to scale.
6. Select MODEL in the Status Bar to switch the viewport mode back to PAPER space. Add notes, dimensions, etc. and plot the drawing.

Set up a Drawing to Plot the Model tab:

1. Start a New drawing. Set the Drawing Units, and the drawing limits (according to the Drawing Limits / Scale Chart). Zoom All.
2. Insert a Title Block where the insertion point is 0,0, the x and y scale factors are equal to the Plot scale, and the rotation angle is 0.
3. Create the drawing in designated drawing area, then plot the drawing.

Tips & Tricks

- When selecting Plot Extents, be careful that there is not any geometry that may have gotten thrown out into space by accident. This is one reason why it is good to periodically Zoom All, or Zoom Extents to erase errors such as this.
- To add a plotter, open the Plotter Manager from the File pull-down menu. Select "Add a Plotter Wizard."
- Plot settings are saved on the computer and do not automatically go with the drawing. PC2 and PCP files save the plot settings. These are files separate from the drawing file. Plot settings can be saved and used with other drawings. The Batch Plot Utility command contains options that utilize PCP and PC2 files.

Plot Style Table Editor

Command Locator

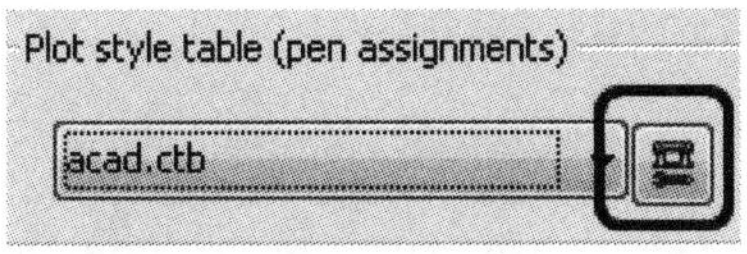

Plot Dialog	Upper right corner
Pull Down Menu	**File / Plot Style Manager…**
Command	**stylesmanager**
Dialog Box	**Plot Style Table Editor**

Command Overview

The Plot Style Table Editor allows you to edit the plot styles found in a plot style table. Color–dependent plot style tables must have 255 plot styles mapped to 255 colors so you cannot add or delete plot styles in this type of table. However, a named plot style table can have any number of plot styles and the editor will allow you to add and delete styles from this type of table.

The dialog box has three tabs. The first, General, gives general information about the table file. The second and third tabs contain the editable information about the plot styles in two formats, tabular and form. Select the tab of the format you prefer working with; both give the same information.

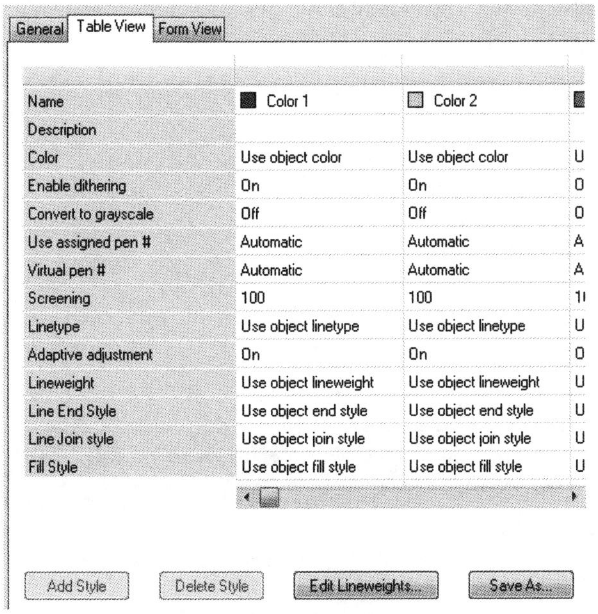

Plot Style Table Editor Dialog Box
Table View

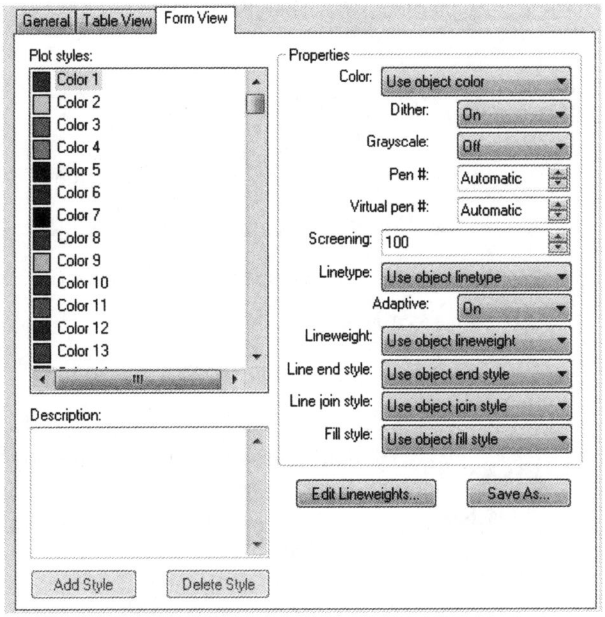

Plot Style Table Editor Dialog Box
Form View

Each plot style has a description and twelve properties.

Color sets the color the object will be plotted with regardless of the color the object was drawn with. The default setting is 'Use object color'.

Dither turns on or off dithering. This is the process of plotting lines as a series of dots in an attempt to create more colors in the plotted output.

Grayscale will convert the color of the object to grayscale.

Pen number sets the number of the pen to use for this style; available numbers are 1 – 32. If you have set the color to 'Use object color' or are using a color–dependent plot style table, you cannot change this setting from 'Automatic' which causes AutoCAD to use the pen with the closest color to that of the Color setting.

Virtual pen is used for non–pen plotters that are set up with virtual pens. Virtual pens can be programmed into many plotters to set up the pen's width, fill pattern, end style and color. If a virtual pen is selected, the other settings for the plot style will be ignored. If the plotter used is a pen plotter or does not have virtual pens set up, this setting is ignored.

Screening sets the intensity of the color to use as a percentage. Setting this to 0 will use no ink and therefore change the color to white, while 100 will set the color to full intensity.

Linetype allows you to set the linetype to use for the style. The default linetype is 'Use object linetype'.

Adaptive adjustment sets the linetype scale of the object to complete the linetype pattern without ending it in the middle. If your drawing looks correct, turn this off; if linetype scaling is not as important as making sure the linetypes show up correctly, turn this on.

Lineweight sets the lineweight of the objects. The default setting is 'Use object lineweight'.

Line end style sets the end style of your lines. The styles available are Butt, Square, Round and Diamond. The default setting is 'Use object end style'.

Line join style sets the style of the joints of lines. The styles available are Miter, Bevel, Round and Diamond. The default setting is 'Use object join style'.

Fill style sets the fill style for the objects. Styles available are Solid, Checkerboard, Crosshatch, Diamonds, Horizontal Bars, Slant Left, Slant Right, Square Dots and Vertical Bar. The default setting is 'Use object fill style'.

General Procedures

1. Invoke the Plot Style Manager command.
2. In the Plot Styles window, double click on the file to edit.
3. Set the desired settings in the dialog box.
4. Press 'Save & Close'.

Tips & Tricks

- Another way to get to the Plot Styles window is to double click on the Autodesk Plot Style Manager in the Windows Control Panel.

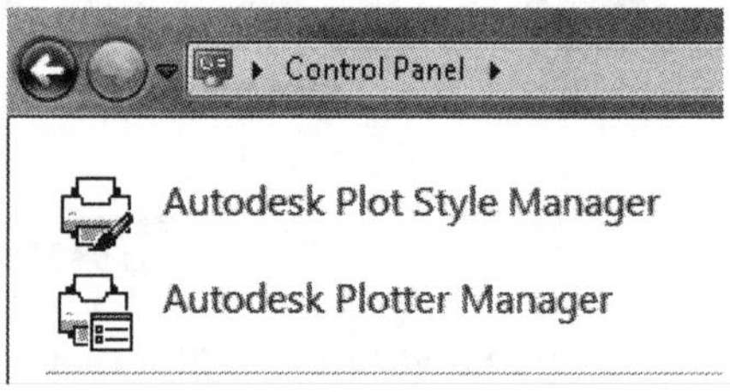

Section Exercise

Exercise 12-11 – Layout Setup

Drawing Name: **Lesson 12 aec.dwg**
Estimated Time to Completion: 10 Minutes

Scope

Select the Layout1 tab to create a new Page Setup. Select a Plotter and establish Layout Settings for plotting a D-size drawing. Then create Viewports, both rectangular and non-rectangular.

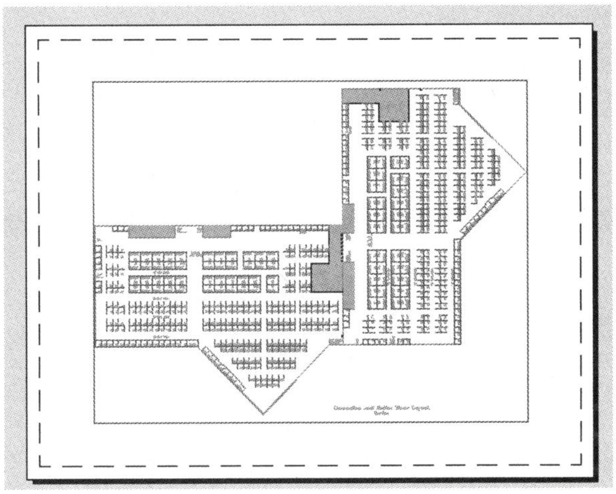

AEC Plotting and Output Exercise

Hints

1. Select the Layout1 tab and set the page settings.
2. Set the scale of the viewport created and then perform a polygonal clip on the existing viewport.
3. Create a rectangular viewport.
4. Insert the title block (there is a block pre-loaded in the drawing called Title).

Extra: *Perform a Plot Preview to see what color the yellow entities will be when you plot.*

Sheet Sets

Command Locator

View ribbon	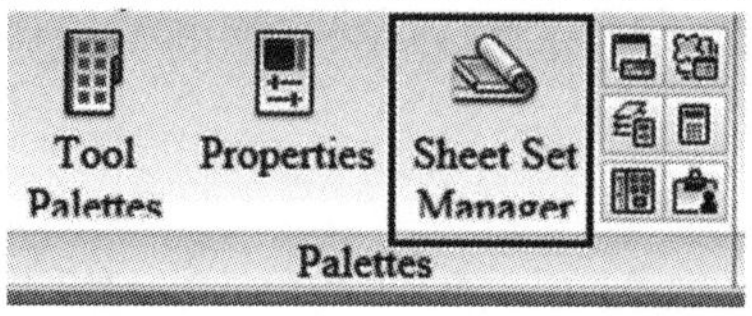Tool Palettes Properties Sheet Set Manager Palettes
Command	**Sheetset**
Alias	**SSM**
Keyboard Shortcut	**Ctl+4**

Command Overview

The Sheet Set Manager: Most users don't just create one drawing and send it off. Instead, they create documentation or drawing packages. These are mini-booklets of drawings that detail a mechanical assembly or building project. The problem many designers have is managing these documentation packages: making sure that the correct revision drawing is included in each package, that there are no missing drawings, etc.

The Sheet Set Manager allows you to manage your documentation package by creating a sheet set list, printing and publishing your sheets, adding and deleting sheets as needed. You can also create different versions of the same sheet set to send to different sub-contractors.

General Procedures

1. Create drawings as usual. These are the resource drawings.
2. Create named views in model space. These are listed in the View List tab.
3. Invoke the Sheet Set Manager command.
4. Create the sheet set.
5. Assign a template to be used.
6. Create a table of contents for the entire sheet set.
7. Plot or publish the sheet set or a sub-set of the sheet set.

Tips & Tricks

- You can create different styles for your sheet set tables.
- You can use existing drawings to create your sheet sets or start with a new project.
- Once you have placed the sheet set table, you can update it if any of your sheets are modified.
- You can use the Sheet Set Manager to open and close drawings within the sheet set.
- You have to have at least one drawing open in order to launch the Sheet Set Manager.

Command Exercise

Exercise 12-12 – Create a New Sheet Set

Drawing Name: **8th floor.dwg**
Estimated Time to Completion: 15 Minutes

Scope

Create a new sheet set from an existing set of drawings.

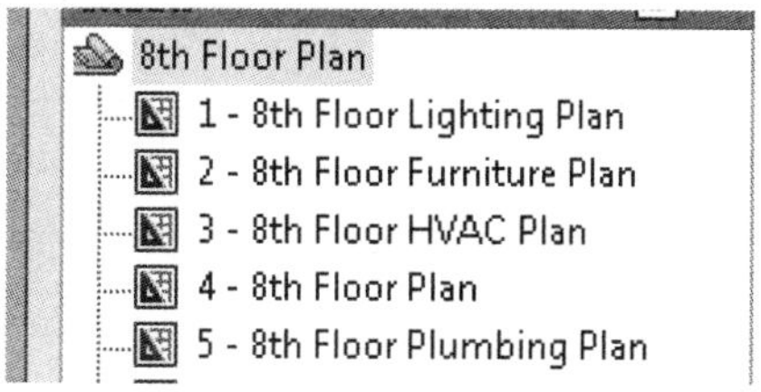

Sheet Set Manager Exercise

Solution

Invoke the Sheet Set Manager.

1. Type **SSM**.

2. Go to **New Sheet Set…**

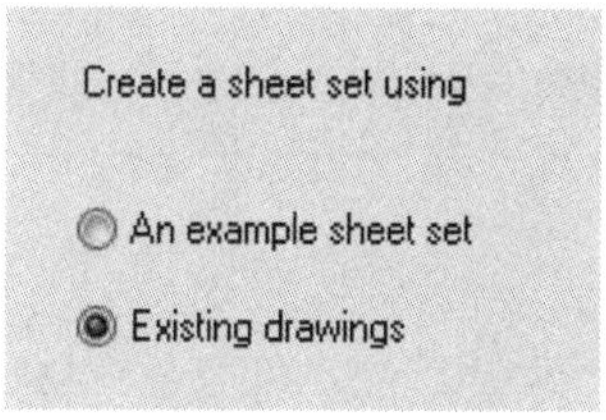

3. Enable **Existing drawings**.
4. Press **Next**.

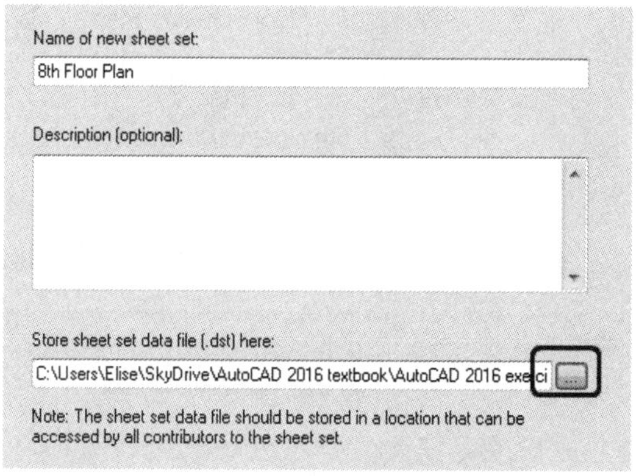

5. Enter **8th Floor Plan** in the Name of new sheet set field.
6. Browse to a location to store the sheet set data file.

The data file keeps track of what drawings and views are included in each sheet set.

7. Press the **Sheet Set Properties** button.

8. Select the ... button next to Sheet creation template.

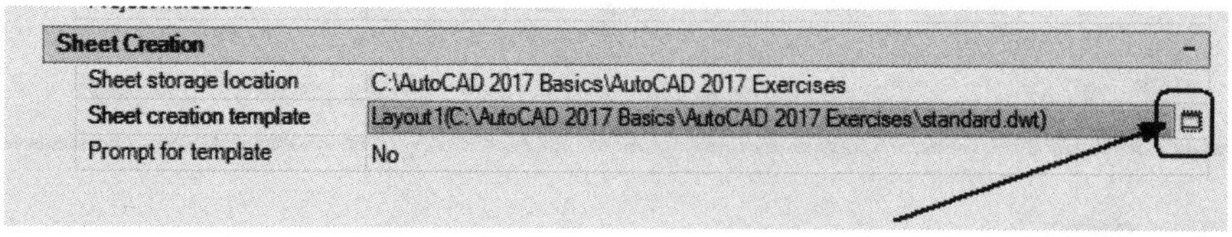

9. Set the Sheet creation template to the *standard.dwt* template file created earlier.

10. Press **OK**.

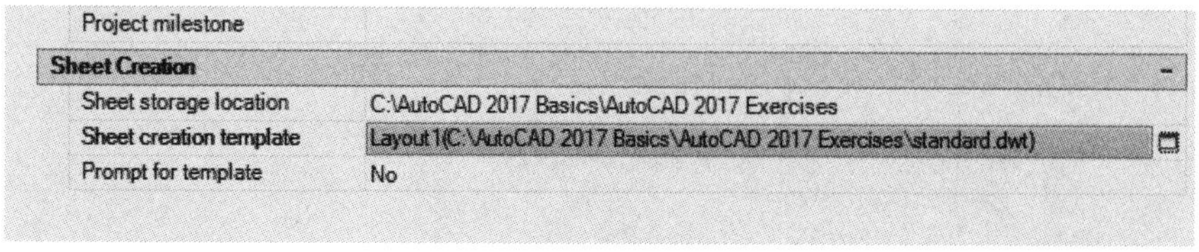

11. Select **Next**.

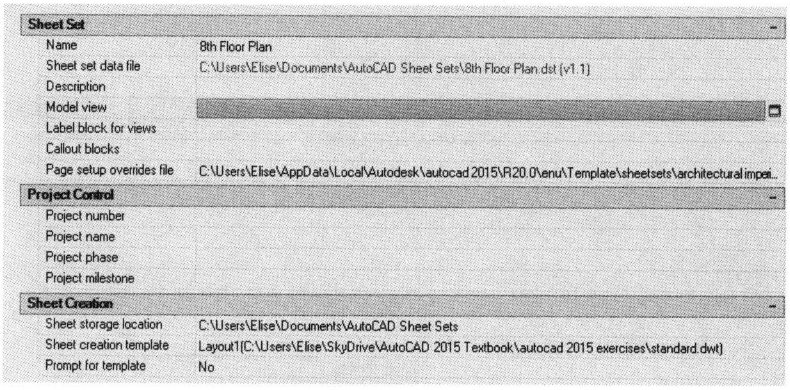

12. Select the **Browse** button.

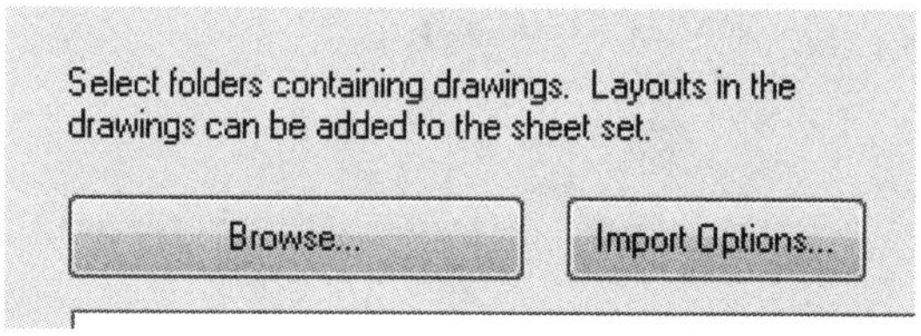

13. Select the folder containing the exercise files.

14. Press **OK**.

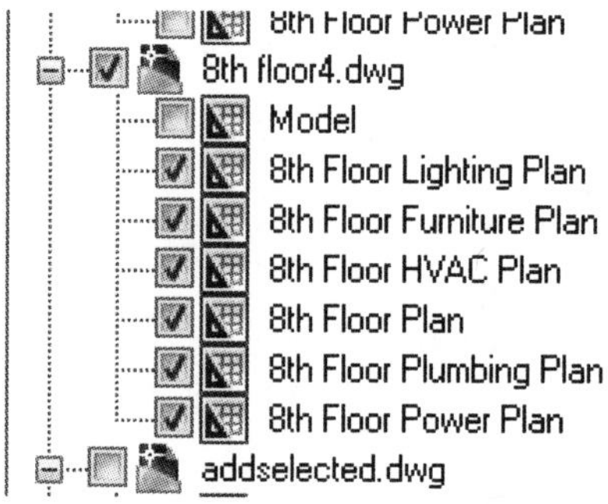

15. Locate the 8th floor drawings.

16. Uncheck all the files except for the *8th floor4.dwg* file. Note that all the xrefs linked to the 8th floor4.dwg file are listed.

17. To clear all the selected files, simply uncheck the top folder. Then select only the *8th floor4.dwg* file.

18. Press **Next**.

You can preview the sheet set that is being created.

Notice how the sheet titles are prefixed with the file name.

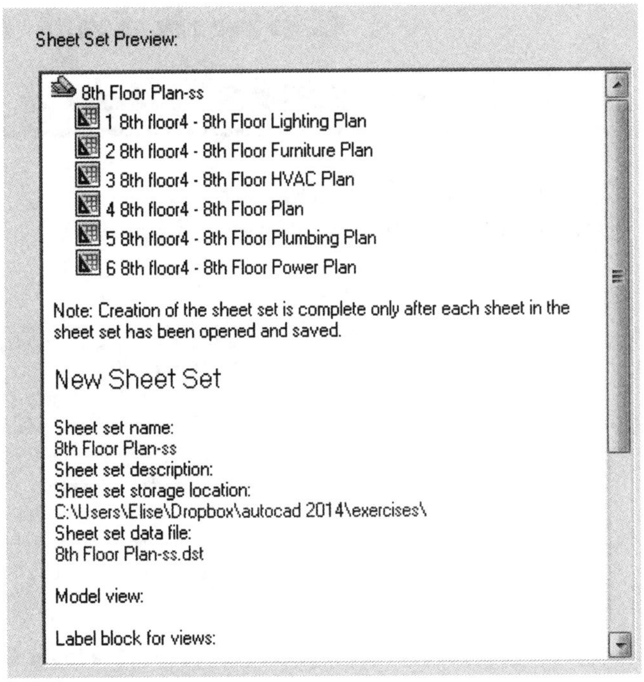

19. Press **Back**.

20. Press the **Import Options**.

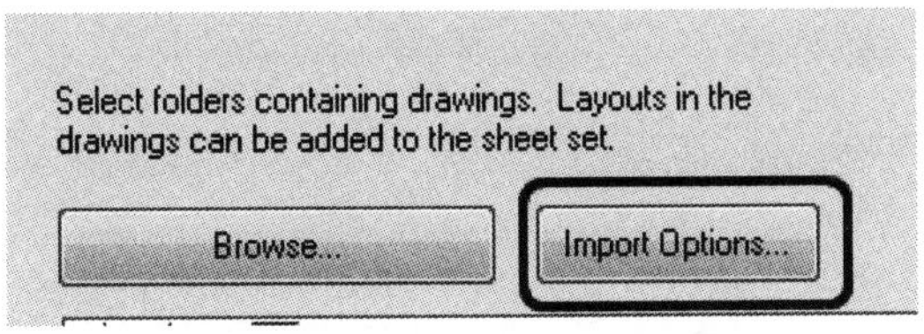

21. Disable the **Prefix sheet titles with file name** option.

22. Press **OK**.

23. Press **Next**.

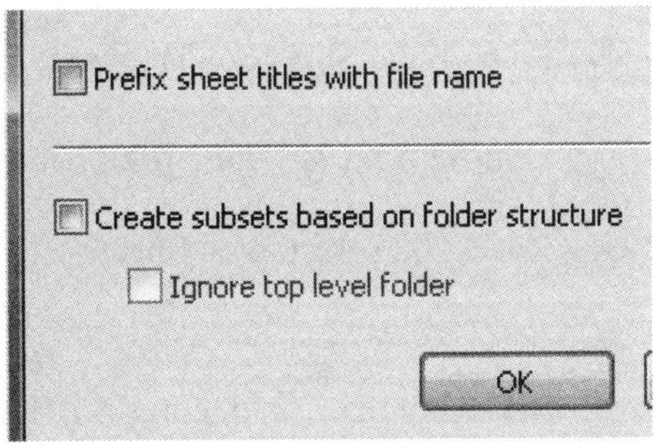

The preview now displays with the layout names only.

24. Press **Finish**.

The sheets are listed in the Sheet Set Manager.

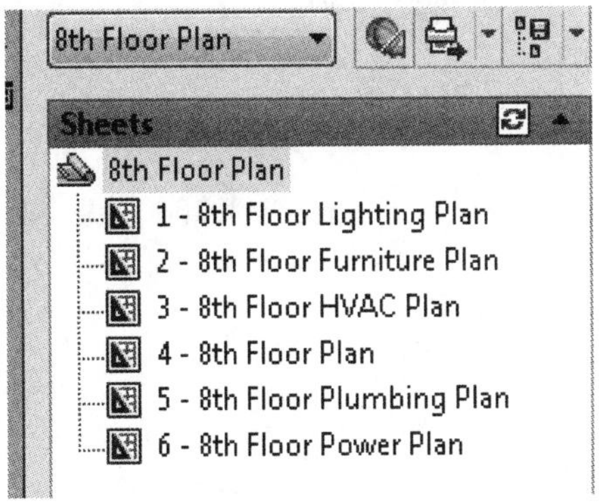

Tips & Tricks

- To access shortcut menus needed for sheet list table operations, the *Shortcut menus in drawing area* option must be enabled in the Options dialog box, User Preferences tab.

Command Exercise

Exercise 12-13 – Add a Sheet to a Sheet Set

Drawing Name: **8th floor 2.dwg**
Estimated Time to Completion: 5 Minutes

Scope

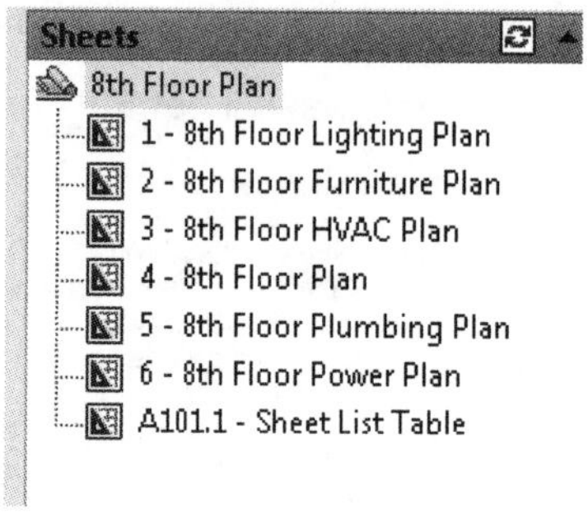

Sheet Set Manager Exercise

Solution

1. Launch the Sheet Set Manager.
2. Highlight the 8th **floor plan** header on the Sheets tab.
3. RMB and select **New Sheet**.

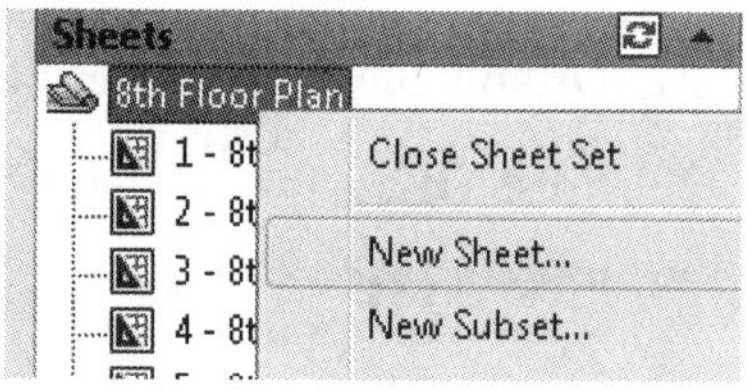

4. In the Number field, enter **A101.1**.
5. In the Sheet title field, enter **Sheet List Table**.
6. Press **OK**.

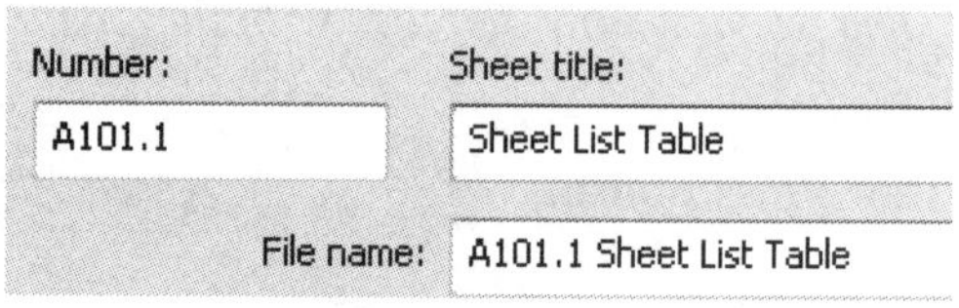

7. The new sheet is listed in the Sheet Set Manager.

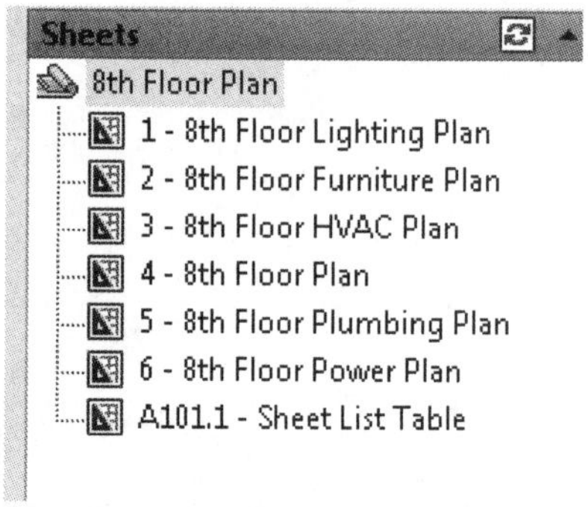

Command Exercise

Exercise 12-14 – Copy Text Styles Using Design Center

Drawing Name: **8th floor 5.dwg**
Estimated Time to Completion: 5 Minutes

Scope

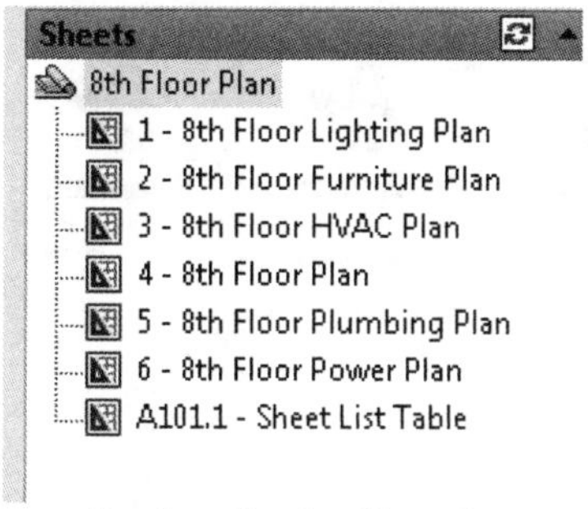

Design Center Exercise

Solution

1. Launch the Sheet Set Manager.
2. Open the 8th floor 5.dwg.
3. Highlight the Sheet List Table in the SSM.

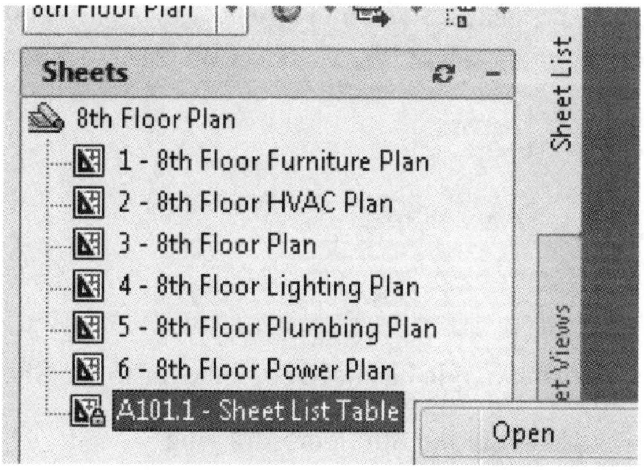

4. RMB and select Open.

You should have both files open—the 8th floor5 and the Sheet List Table.

5. Type **DC** on the command line to launch the Design Center.

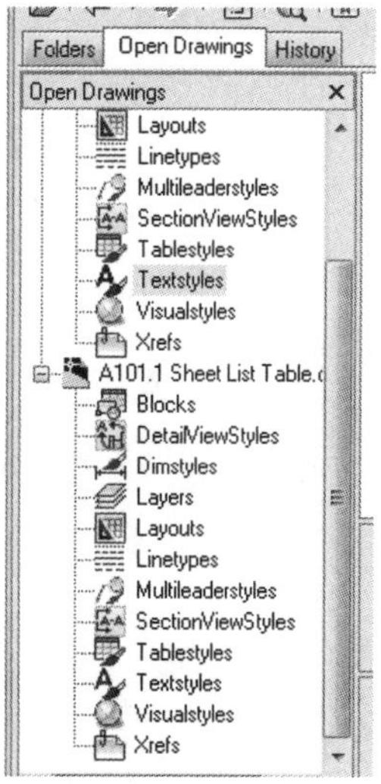

6. Select the Open Drawings tab on the Design Center.
7. Highlight the Textstyles in the 8th floor5 drawing. A list of available textstyles will display.

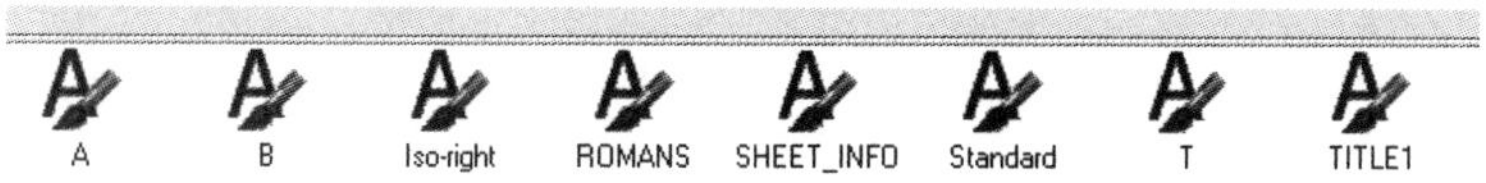

8. Highlight the TITLE1 textstyle in the Design Center.
9. Activate the tab for the Sheet List Table.
10. Drag and drop the text style onto the drawing.

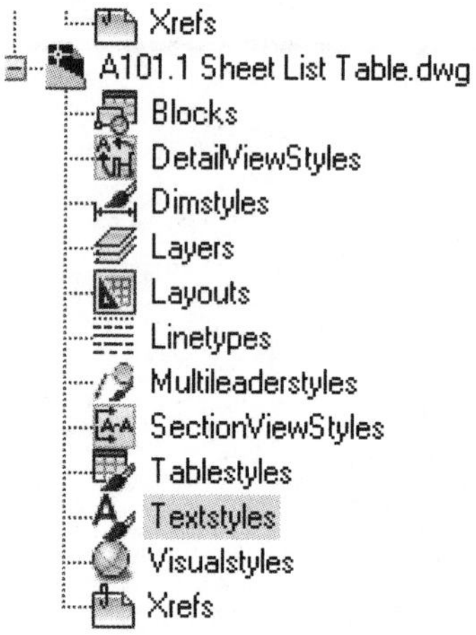

11. Highlight the Textstyles folder under the Sheet List Table drawing.

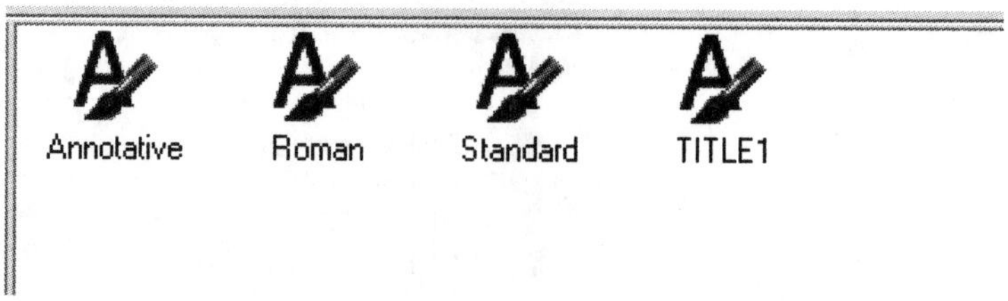

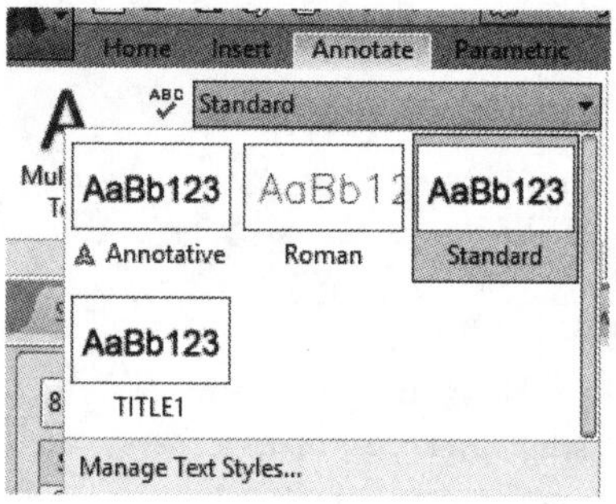

You can also verify that the text style has been copied over by opening the drawing and going to the Annotate ribbon. The text style should be listed in the Text Panel.

The textstyle has been copied over to the Sheet List Table drawing.

12. Close the 8th floor5 drawing.
13. Close the Design Center.

Command Exercise

Exercise 12-15 – Creating a Sheet List Table

Drawing Name: **8th floor5.dwg**
Estimated Time to Completion: 15 Minutes

Scope

Creating a Sheet List Table.
Add the table to a sheet.
Modify the table.

Some students might opt to continue working in the file from the previous exercise. If you do that, some text styles and other information will not be available.

Sheet List Table
Sheet Title
8th Floor Furniture Plan
8th Floor HVAC Plan
8th Floor Lighting Plan
8th Floor Plan
8th Floor Plumbing Plan
8th Floor Power Plan

Sheet List Table

Solution

1. Launch the SSM if it is not already launched using Ctrl+4.

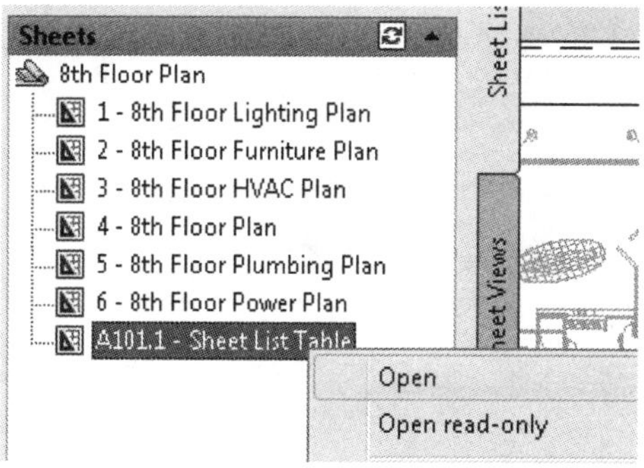

2. Activate the **Sheet List Table** layout.

   Highlight the Sheet List Table in the sheet set manager. RMB and select **Open**.

3. Highlight the **Sheet List Table** in the SSM.
4. RMB and select **Insert Sheet List Table**.

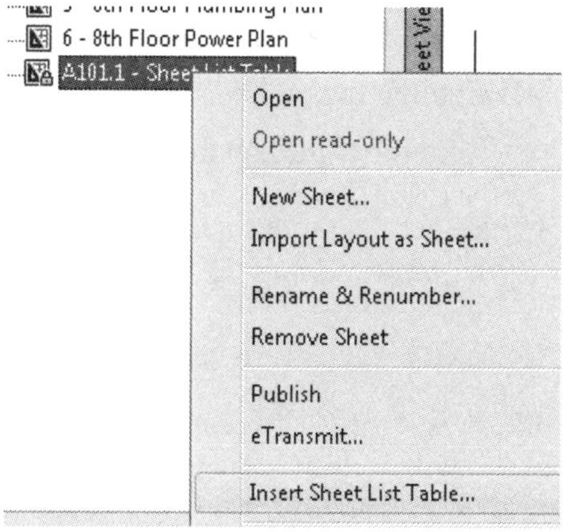

You must be in PaperSpace mode for this option to be available.

Check the status bar to see if the drawing is in PAPER space mode.

By default the sheet number, sheet title, and drawing title are displayed on the table.

If 'Show Subheader' is enabled, then the table will be organized by sub-categories.

5. From the list, highlight Sheet Number and click **Remove** to remove it from the list.
6. Click **OK**.

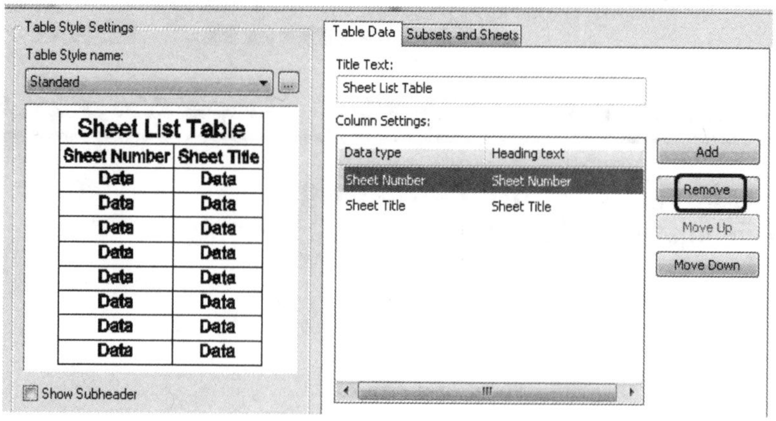

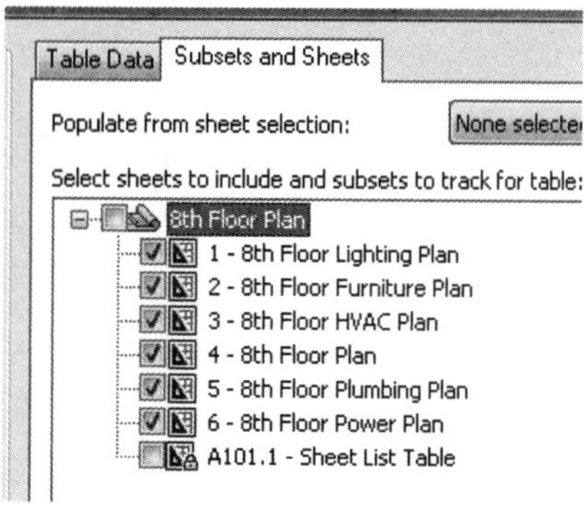

7. Select the Subsets and Sheets tab.
8. Place a check next to all the sheets EXCEPT for the Sheet List Table.
9. Press **OK**.

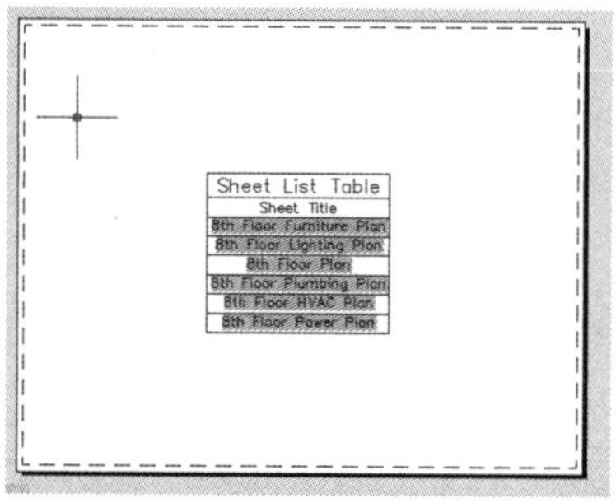

10. Place the table on the sheet.

11. Move the 8th Floor Lighting Plan below the 8th Floor HVAC Plan on the Sheet Set Manager by dragging and dropping it into place.

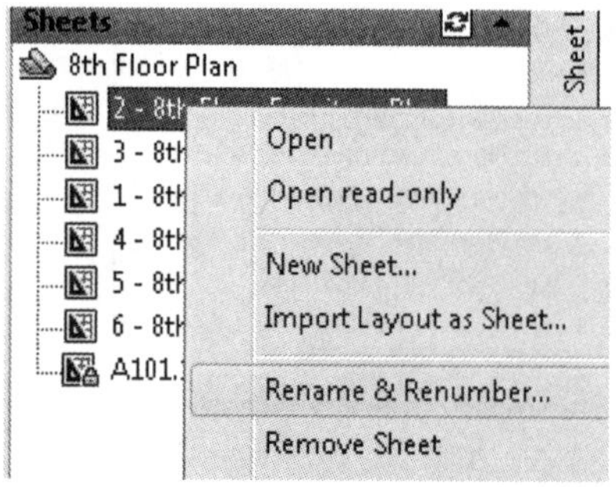

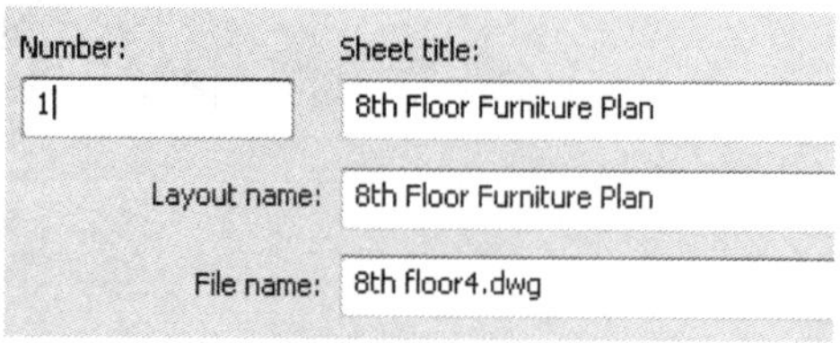

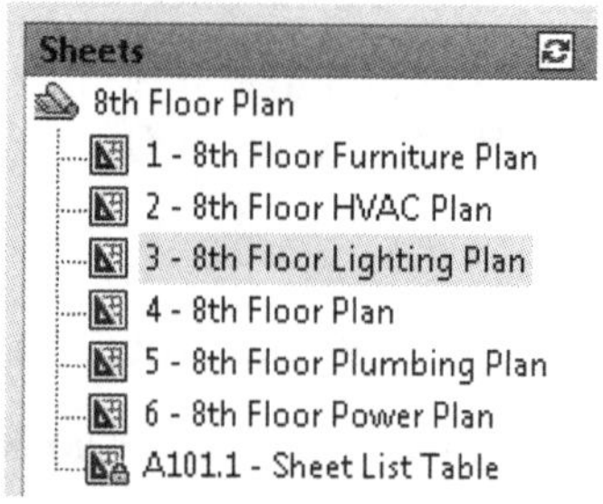

12. Right click on the reorganized sheets.
13. Select **Rename and Renumber**.
14. Change the number to the new order position.
    Renumber the top three sheets.

15. Select the table so it highlights.
    Window around the table to select it.

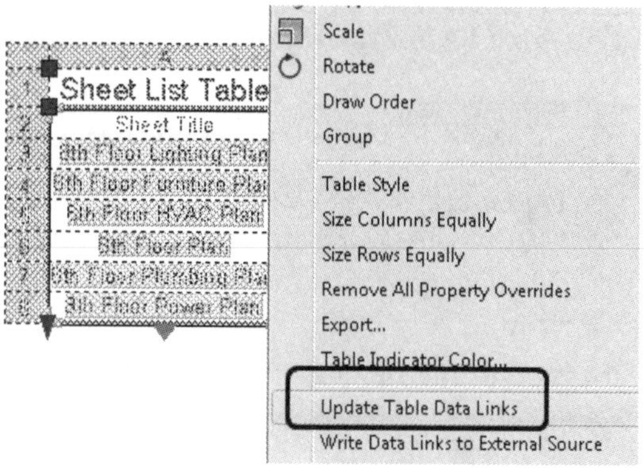

16. RMB and select **Update Table Data Links**.
17. Press <ESC> to release the selection.

The table updates.

18. Activate the **Annotate** ribbon.

19. Launch the Table Style dialog.

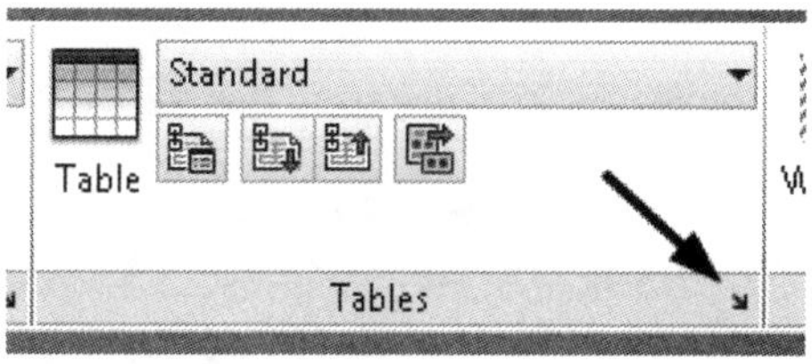

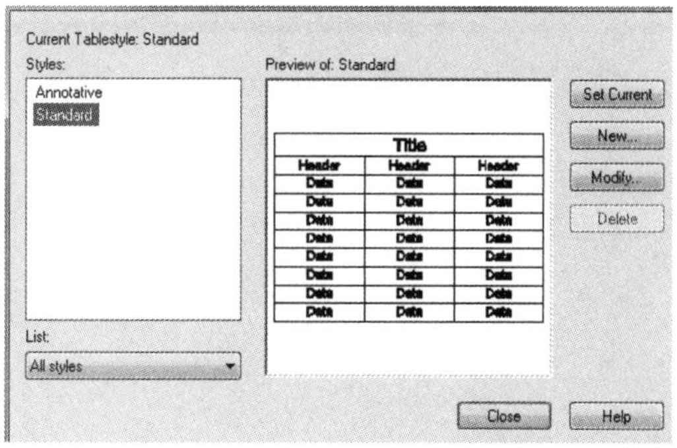

20. Press **Modify**.

21. Select the table to start from button at the top of the dialog.

22. Then, select the Sheet List Table that is placed in the drawing.

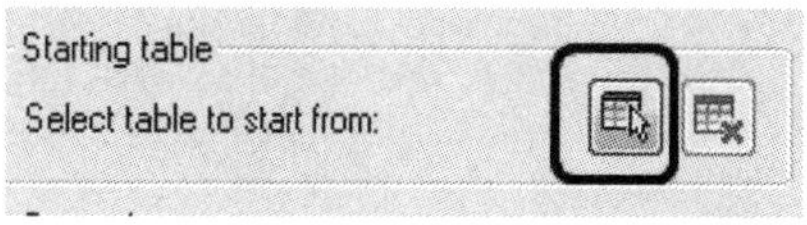

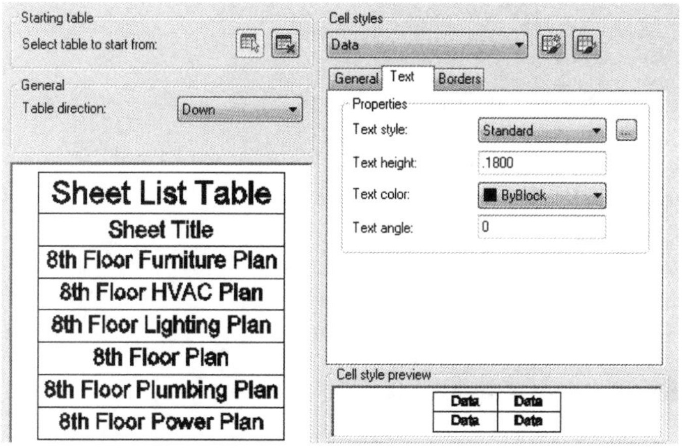

A preview of the selected table will appear in the preview window.

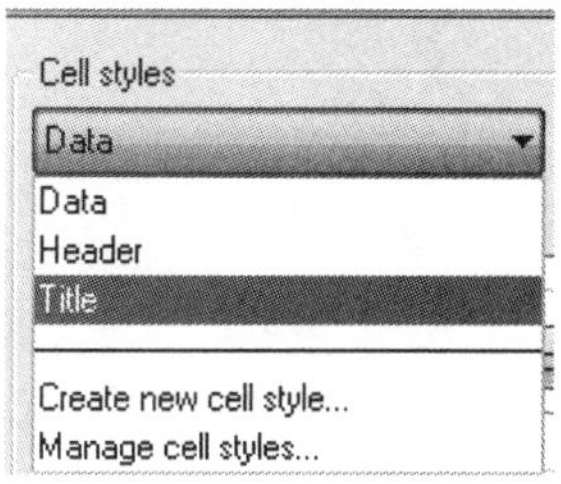

23. Select **Title** under Cell Styles.

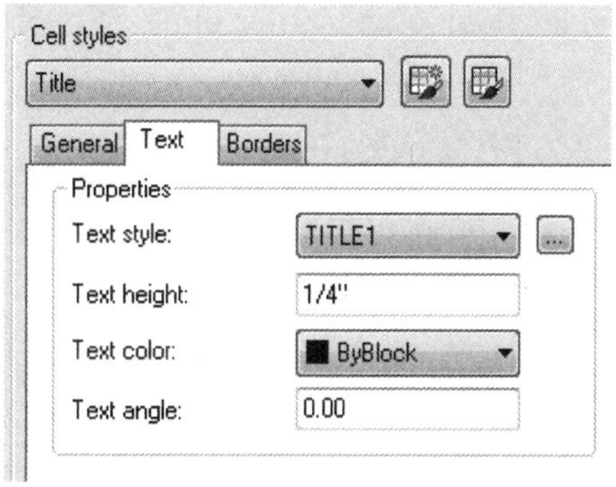

24. Set the Text Style to **TITLE1**.

25. Set the Text height to **1/4"**.

26. Press **OK** and **CLOSE** to close the dialog.

27. Highlight the second row.

Two icons will appear when the row is selected.
The lock indicates the data is locked and cannot be modified.
The rings indicate that the data is linked to the Sheet Set Manager.

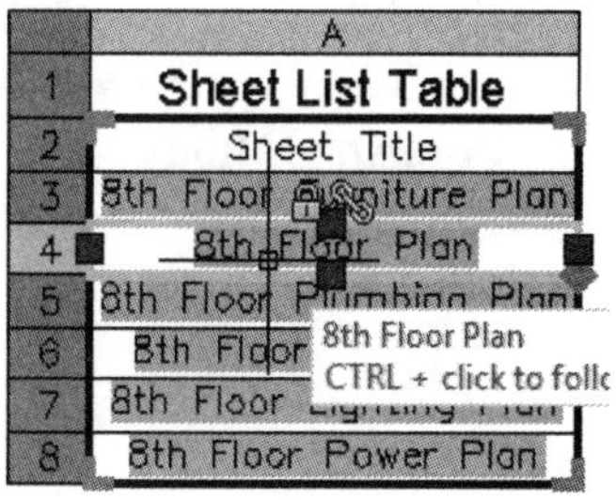

Command Exercise

Exercise 12-16 – Publishing a Sheet Set

Drawing Name: **pdf1.dwg**
Estimated Time to Completion: 10 Minutes

Scope

Plot a sheet set to PDF.

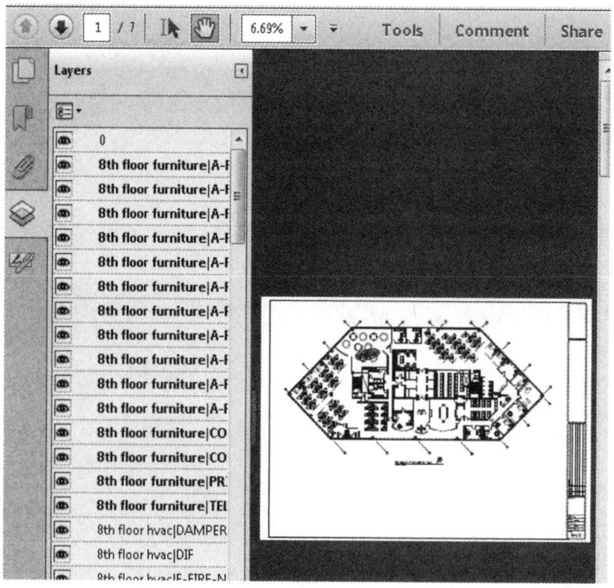

Publishing a Sheet Set Exercise

Solution

1. Highlight the **8th floor plan** header on the Sheets tab.

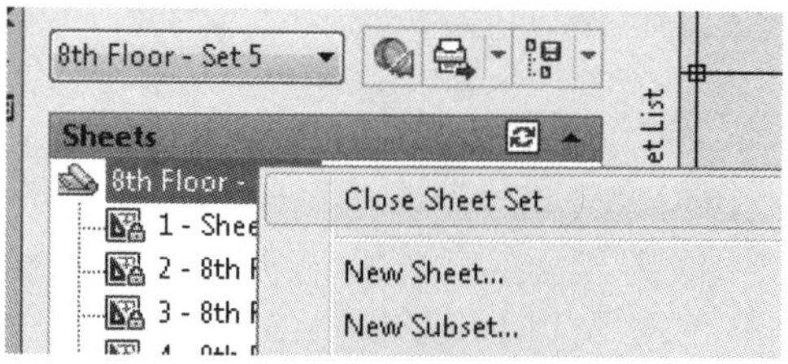

2. RMB and select **Close Sheet Set**.
3. Go to **Recent…8th floor plan.dst** to re-open the sheet set.

   The sheet set is now listed.

4. Highlight the sheet set header.
5. RMB and select **Publish→Sheet Set PDF Publish Options**.

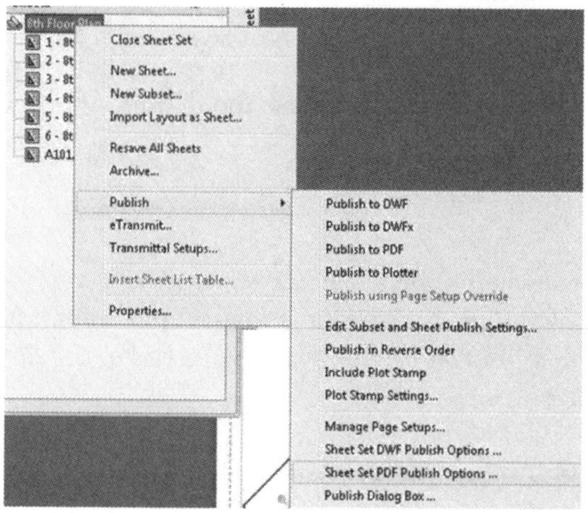

6. Locate the folder where you wish to store the pdf file you will be creating.

7. Enable **Multi-sheet file**.

8. Enable **Prompt for name**.

   Note that you can include the Layer information so users can turn layers on and off in the viewer.

9. Press **OK**.

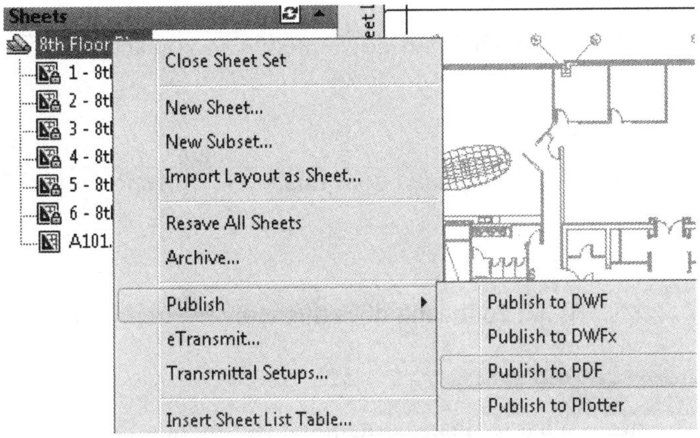

10. Highlight the sheet set header.

11. RMB and select **Publish→Publish to PDF**.

12. The **Select PDF file** dialog will open to the folder specified.

13. Press **Select**.

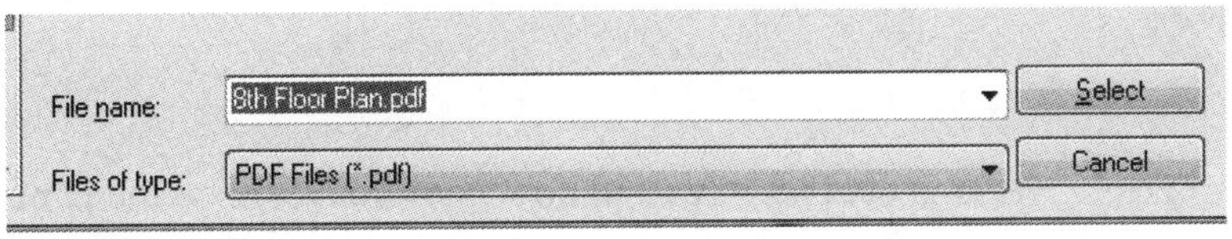

14. Press **Close**.

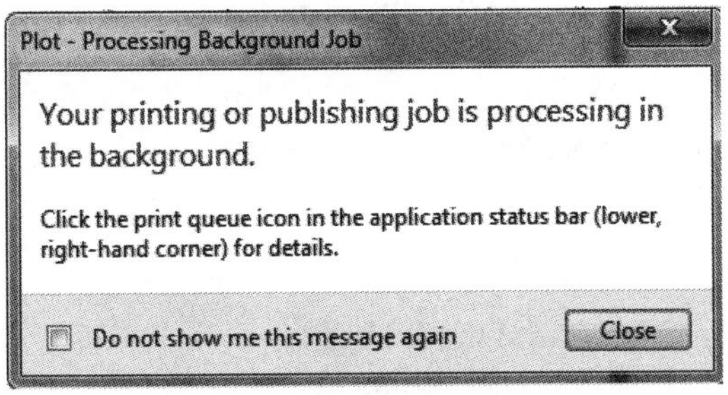

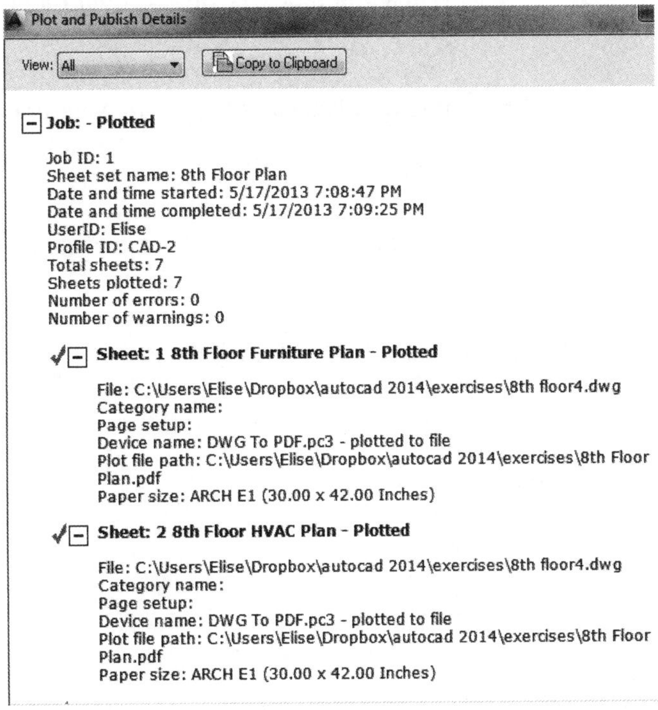

15. When the plot job is complete, you can read a report of any problems.

Review Questions

1. What does this icon represent?

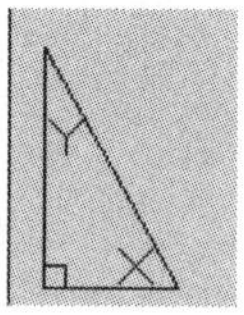

2. **T F** You should create your drawing in Model Space but you can plot your drawing from either the Layout tab (paper space) or the Model tab (model space).

3. From what pull-down menu can you access the Floating Viewports command?

4. What command does this icon  represent and in what toolbar is it located?

5. What command does this icon  represent and where is it located?

6. What toolbars contain the commands for creating drawing Layouts and Viewports?

7. What is the Plot Area and how does this relate to the paper size?

8. **T F** When you plot your drawing in Paper Space, your plot scale is 1=1.

9. What are some advantages to plotting your drawing in Paper Space?

10. With the Model tab selected, what happens when you select the model button 

?

11. With the Layout tab selected, the PAPER button switches to MODEL. What is the difference?

Review Answers

1. What does this icon represent?

   Paper Space

2. **T F** You should create your drawing in Model Space but you can plot your drawing from either the Layout tab (paper space) or the Model tab (model space).

   True

3. From what pull-down menu can you access the Floating Viewports command?

   View

4. What command does this icon  represent and in what toolbar is it located?

   Plot, Standard

5. What command does this icon  represent and where is it located?

   Plot Preview

6. What toolbars contain the commands for creating drawing Layouts and Viewports?

   Viewports

7. What is the Plot Area and how does this relate to the paper size?

   The Plot Area is the sheet size.

8. **T F** When you plot your drawing in Paper Space, your plot scale is 1=1.

   False...sometimes, but not always.

9. What are some advantages to plotting your drawing in Paper Space?

   You are able to plan how your drawing will look when it is plotted.

10. With the Model tab selected, what happens when you select the model button 

?

    You are in Model Space.

11. With the Layout tab selected, the PAPER button switches to MODEL. What is the difference?

    The Model Space is activated for a viewport or a viewport is made active.

Notes:

About the Author

Elise Moss has worked for the past thirty years as a mechanical designer in Silicon Valley, primarily creating sheet metal designs. She has written articles for Autodesk's *Toplines* magazine, AUGI's PaperSpace, DigitalCAD.com and Tenlinks.com. She is President of Moss Designs, creating custom applications and designs for corporate clients. She has taught CAD classes at DeAnza College, Silicon Valley College, SFSU, and for Autodesk resellers. She is currently teaching CAD at Laney College in Oakland. Autodesk has named her as a Faculty of Distinction for the curriculum she has developed for Autodesk products. She holds a baccalaureate degree in Mechanical Engineering from San Jose State.

She is married with three sons. Her older son, Benjamin, is an electrical engineer. Her middle son, Daniel, works with AutoCAD Architecture in the construction industry. His designs have been featured in architectural journals. Her youngest son, Isaiah, is now a high school graduate and starting college. Her husband, Ari, has a distinguished career in software development.

Elise is a third generation engineer. Her father, Robert Moss, was a metallurgical engineer in the aerospace industry. Her grandfather, Solomon Kupperman, was a civil engineer for the City of Chicago.

She can be contacted via email at elise_moss@mossdesigns.com.

More information about the author and her work can be found on her website at www.mossdesigns.com.

<u>Other books by Elise Moss</u>

AutoCAD Architecture 2017 Fundamentals
Autodesk Revit Architecture 2017 Basics